# ARSENAL OF DEMOCRACY II

D0521630

## AMERICAN MILITARY POWER IN THE 1980s AND THE ORIGINS OF THE NEW COLD WAR

With a Survey of American
Weapons and Arms Exports

BY TOM GERVASI

DESIGNED BY NEIL SHAKERY

GROVE PRESS, INC./ NEW YORK

First Evergreen Edition 1981
First Printing 1981
ISBN: 0-394-17662-6
Library of Congress Catalog Card Number: 80-993

Library of Congress Cataloging in Publication Data
Gervasi, Tom.
   Arsenal of Democracy II.
   Bibliography.
   Includes index.
   1. Munitions—United States.   2. Weapons systems.   3. United States—
Military policy.   I. Title. HD9483.U52G47   1980   382 ′.456234′0973
80-993   ISBN 0-394-17662-6 (pbk.)

Manufactured in the United States of America

GROVE PRESS, INC., 196 West Houston Street, New York, N.Y. 10014

# CONTENTS

# AUTHOR'S NOTE

The preparation of this book would have
been impossible without a great deal of assistance.
The degree of cooperation extended by many
has been unprecedented. One consequence of this is
that the identities of a few must remain undisclosed.
All of the others are acknowledged at the back
of the book. I am deeply grateful both to those
whose names are printed there and those whose
names are not, for all of their help.
No one but me is responsible for any errors in the book.

The book is dedicated to Amy and Stephen.
May theirs be a more peaceful world
than the world reflected in these pages.

# THE PRICE OF DEFENSE

*Arsenal of Democracy* appeared in 1978, three years before the present volume. Since that time, a world already encumbered with incalculable risks has spent its greatest effort to become a more dangerous place. With an investment in war 2,500 times that of its stake in peace, it has met with appalling success. By the end of 1978, the human race had tested nuclear weapons a total of 1,165 times, and was in a position to inflict upon itself a measure of destruction equivalent to the explosion of one million Hiroshima bombs. The world military budget in 1978 was $400 billion. It rose to $425 billion the following year, and to $470 billion the year after that. It has reached $540 billion today. This means that right now we are spending money to prepare for war at the rate of more than $1 million per minute. Richard Barnet of the Institute for Policy Studies estimates that four hours of such spending could eradicate malaria from the earth.

Today we can explode the equivalent of one and a half million Hiroshima bombs. In just three years we have increased the destructive power of our nuclear arsenals by 50 percent. This has happened despite the agreement by 114 nations to sign the Treaty on Nonproliferation of Nuclear Weapons in July of 1968. Of the 153 nations in the world today, among those that have not signed the Treaty are India, which tested a nuclear device in 1974, and Israel and South Africa, which have probably tested them too. Also among the nonsignatories are Pakistan, Argentina, Brazil, Taiwan, South Korea, Libya and Iraq. All of these nations are expected to have nuclear weapons within the next 15 years, more than doubling the number known to have them today—and thereby, according to most specialists in arms control, doubling the likelihood of nuclear war.

The nations that already have nuclear weapons are those that have increased the stockpile. Third World leaders call this "vertical" proliferation, and they regard it as no less dangerous than the "horizontal" spread of nuclear weapons to nations that did not have them before.

The United States alone plans production of more than 18,500 additional nuclear warheads in the next decade, implementing programs already approved. These include the supply of warheads for 3,418 Air-Launched and 650 Ground-Launched Cruise Missiles, for 500 Lance, 72 Pershing IA and 108 Pershing II Missiles, for 3,000 rounds of 155mm and 203mm artillery projectiles, and for 1,000 new B-83 nuclear gravity bombs. Many of these warheads will be improved versions of those that already equip the 7,000 tactical nuclear weapons we now deploy in Europe, and will be sent there as replacements. The Pershing IIs and 464 of the Ground-Launched Cruise Missiles, however, will augment that force. W-85 air-burst and W-86 earth-penetrator nuclear warheads are now in development for the Pershing II.

In addition, 4,224 warheads with explosive yields of 80 kilotons each will be needed for the 528 Trident I C-4 Missiles to be deployed on our *Ohio* class Trident submarines, along with 768 more for the 96 Trident I Missiles that will complete a retrofit in progress on 12 of our *Lafayette* class Poseidon submarines. 900 Mk 12A warheads with yields of 335 kilotons each will be used for a retrofit now underway on 300 of our 550 Minuteman III Missiles, and between 2,000 and 2,400 of the Mk 12A will be required for the 200 MX Missiles now planned.

In time, our 19 remaining Poseidon submarines may be refitted for the Trident Missile, and the Trident I Missile itself may be replaced with the Trident II D-5 Cleardeck, each of which will deploy 10 Mk 12A warheads, so that for this retrofit another 7,600 Mk 12As will then have to be produced.

Nuclear warheads are currently assembled at only seven locations in the United States, including Miamisburg, Ohio, Rocky Flats, Colorado, the Bendix plant in Kansas City and the Pantex plant in Amarillo, Texas. At other locations, such as the Getty Oil Company's Nuclear Fuel Services plant in Erwin, Tennessee, nuclear fuel materials are processed for military use. The Department of Energy, responsible for nuclear warhead production, will spend $94 million this year on its Weapons Complex Restoration Initiative, a program to improve and expand these facilities to other locations as well. For the first time in 15 years, we will increase production of weapons-grade plutonium and tritium, resuming operation of two more reactors at Barnwell, South Dakota, where three other reactors already produce bomb-grade materials. In 1981 we will spend $3.7 billion on the production and assembly of nuclear warheads.

Nor does all of this include the cornucopia of conventional, or nonnuclear, munitions we have furnished to the stockpile. Ruth Leger Sivard, a former chief of the economics division of the United States Arms Control and Disarmament Agency, tells us that in sheer tonnage there is more explosive material on earth today than there is food.

Today more than a quarter of all the world's scientists, and more than half of those trained in physics and engineering, work exclusively on military projects, funded by more than $30 billion a year. What has the cost of that been to our productivity, the quality of our lives, our level of health care, the repair of our cities? More than 1,600 military satellites now orbit above us. Each will eventually disintegrate and probably be replaced. Skylab and Cosmos 954 have shown these exchanges are not so safe as once they were presumed to be. We have sent 278 nuclear submarines to sea. Yet fewer than 250 commercial power reactors now operate throughout the world. This means that today more nuclear power is actually being generated within the depths of our oceans than on land. What are the implications of all this for our environment?

## The American Military Budget

The United States defense budget has grown from $116.5 billion in 1978 to total appropriations of $171.2 billion in 1981. A budget for this year of $137.5 billion had been submitted originally to Congress early in 1980, but in subsequent months that body of our elected representatives, inspired by the testimony of Pentagon officials and selected information provided by the most powerful lobby groups in the world, added $33.7 billion to it by making cuts elsewhere in the nation's budget. These included reductions of $1.75 billion in federal aid to cities, and $1.35 billion for transportation. It marked the first time in ten years that Congress had raised the military budget over the White House request.

Before it left office the Carter administration requested a further supplemental authority for $6.3 billion in the 1981 defense budget, and simultaneously proposed cuts of $683 million for health care and $980 million for child nutrition subsidies and welfare. The Reagan administration then sought $7.4 billion more for defense this year, raising the 1981 military budget to $178.2 billion in appropriations and $193.5 billion in total obligational authority. It has sought an additional $30.5 billion for defense in 1982, raising the budget that year to a total of $222.8 billion.

America's military budget now represents more than 20 percent of all federal spending and over five percent of the country's gross national product. Much more is planned. General David C. Jones, Chairman of the Joint Chiefs of Staff, wanted to see military spending rise to the point where it would occupy 28 percent of the federal budget, equal to seven percent of our GNP. The Reagan administration plans to raise military outlays to 32 percent of the budget by 1984. President Carter had earlier projected increases for the next five years, raising the defense allocation to $225 billion by 1985. President Reagan will almost reach that level of spending next year. According to projections by the Office of Management and Budget, through 1986 the new administration plans to add a total of $169.5 billion to the increases already planned by its predecessor.

To help accomplish this, and in a declared attempt to raise productivity and lower inflation, cuts totalling $44.4 billion have been proposed in social programs, including reductions in outlays for Medicaid, unemployment insurance, food stamps, minimum social security benefits, and federal aid to education and mass transit. At the same time, the ceiling on our national debt has been raised by $50 billion, further mortgaging America's future. President Reagan's supply-side economists expect that a simultaneous tax cut and deregulation of industry, together with speeded depreciation of capital equipment, will encourage new investment, raising productivity and so reducing inflation.

Yet little expanded investment is likely to occur. While the cuts in social programs were designed in part to reduce the federal deficit, the tax cuts and increases in defense spending will enlarge it by $18 billion. The deficit will grow to a record $45 billion by 1982. Consequently, interest rates will not drop, and new investment capital will continue to be scarce.

Nor are the deregulated corporations under any obligation to take the money they will save and invest it in expanded production. Business has always preferred to maximize profits on old investments as long as possible. That is why defense contractors have refused conversion to civilian production. Rather than undertake costly changes in tooling and dies to manufacture tractors instead of tanks, they have preferred to continue making tanks whether or not tanks were any longer needed. That is why the vast influx of added funds now planned for defense will not produce an expansion of industrial capacity so quickly as it will raise the price of equipment already in production. That is why the newly decontrolled oil companies, after having predictably raised their prices, are now increasing their investments for profit rather than stepping up research into alternate energy sources.

We have always regarded as sacrosanct the right to stress profit over productivity. That is why productivity is low. There is no longer any control over this trend today, because in most sectors of our economy a free market, responsive to the laws of supply and demand, no longer exists. Today large corporate conglomerates simply set prices, free of competitive restraint. The financial community is sufficiently aware of this to recognize the poor prospects for investment under the Reagan program. That is why the Dow Jones Industrial Average dropped by 13.7 points the day after it was announced.

The Reagan program will only add to inflation. The cuts in social programs will cost the public more than cuts in taxes will return. Those hardest hit by these cuts will have to contend, at the same time, with a new wave of inflation. Nevertheless, having spent over $1 trillion on defense in the past ten years, the United States now plans to spend another $1 trillion in only the next four, and $1 trillion more in the three years after that. This will match the estimated $3 trillion spent by the rest of the world on defense in the past quarter century.

## Defense Spending and Inflation

We are told that a major reason for these startling increases in defense spending is inflation itself. Not true. The Carter administration called in 1979 for an increase in the military budget of three percent after adjustments to take account of inflation, and got it. It called in 1980 for an increase of 5.4 percent after inflation, and got it. The nation has increased its real military spending for four years in a row. Next year, our spending will outstrip inflation by 9 percent. By the same token, world military expenditures increased by 21 percent last year, outpacing inflation for the eighth year in a row.

In driving up the costs of military equipment each year, a factor far more important than inflation is the guarantee of payment in most military contracts for cost overruns. In 1977 alone, an additional $17.4 billion was taken from the taxpayer and given to industry for overruns on military programs, including $1.6 billion in the Navy's F-18 Hornet fighter program, and $1.2 billion for Trident submarine construction. These added costs must be apportioned to the fixed number of weapon systems procured, increasing the unit cost of each by an amount far greater than inflation.

Increased defense spending, on the other hand, ranks with the better-publicized cost of energy as one of the major causes of inflation. Freedom from cost constraints allows defense manufacturers to bid up the prices of raw materials without fear of penalty, and this affects prices in every other industry. The drain of technological skills from the civilian sector makes civilian production inefficient, and the resulting higher costs are passed on to the consumer. American manufactured goods no longer favorably compete in quality with foreign products. Consequently imports are raised and exports lowered in just the manner we have witnessed in the past decade, with a serious adverse impact on our balance of trade. The resulting decline of the dollar means we must pay more for imports in our own currency than in foreign currencies, and thus we contribute to rising costs at the base of the system.

While presumably serving to protect our national security, weapons perform no useful service to the economy. They are capital-intensive totems, sitting in their silos, aircraft hangars and vast armoured vehicle parks year after year, never—one fervently hopes—to carry out their intended tasks. Wages earned by the labor force that produced them have in the meanwhile accumulated buying power, but the defense industry has not created a corresponding supply of goods and services to absorb all this money. The resulting intensified demand for existing products drives up prices again.

This is not to suggest that we need no military equipment. However, it does suggest that it is now crucial for us to determine how much we really need, and how much we can afford without destroying the very system it is meant to defend.

It is absurd to look for the answers from those who are asking for the weapons. Yet this is frequently what we do. We have made military people our foremost military experts. Can we really expect them to tell us that on second thought they don't need half of what they have requested? Why should they be careful about spending our tax dollars? It is equally absurd to look for the answers from those who make the weapons. These are the people who receive our tax dollars. Nor can we look for the answers from those who plead on their behalf, from the ostensibly neutral ground of academic think tanks, foundations and political action committees. These people are the beneficiaries of former, present or future relationships with the defense industry.

Nor can we necessarily look for the answers in higher places. Fear, pride and outright greed continue to rule the conduct of most of those who might restrain this spending and redirect the use of our resources. Fear can be summoned up to justify decisions motivated by greed. The fear we instill in others we may begin to believe ourselves. Thus the myth of a threat from abroad is born. Pride can mask fear. Sometimes these emotions cannot be sorted out. Does Ronald Reagan really want to shoot from the hip? Not even he may know. The rest of us can only hope never to find out.

Meanwhile the arms race has moved into a higher gear. The human and social costs of diverting irretrievable resources to defense have already been staggering. The increased pace of such activity may now quickly lead to conditions worse than the conflicts it is presumably designed to avoid.

Not that we fail simultaneously to increase the risk of conflict. Historically, defense expenditures have only aggravated existing tensions. That is why we have

had disarmament conferences, arms limitation agreements, arms control agencies and, recently, a policy in our own country that attempted to reduce arms exports. All of these efforts are an acknowledgment that arms promote conflict more often than they deter it.

Opinions on this matter still vary. Russell Warren Howe, the author of the book *Weapons*, a study of the international arms trade, suggests that "the arms race curiously perpetuates a form of peace." It is a curious form of peace, when you consider that since the end of World War II more than 25 million people have died in over 150 armed conflicts of one scale or another, from revolutions and *coups d'etat* to resistance movements and outright declarations of war. That figure exceeds the total of Soviet dead, civilian and military, throughout World War II. This year alone, 37 major or minor conflicts involving more than eight million people in uniform are being fought on every continent except Australia.

Nuclear war between the superpowers remains less likely than those planning for it would have us believe, but they have certainly succeeded, whatever else it is they think they are doing, in multiplying its risks.

### American Arms Exports

This curious peace throughout the world is fueled by an arms trade that supplies a growing number of countries with what they imagine—or what they are told—they need. Like every other measure of defense spending, this trade has grown too, from $28 billion at the end of 1978 to more than $40 billion today. In 1978 the world's underdeveloped countries imported $20 billion in arms, with a devastating effect on their aggregate debt. Since 1977, the Arab nations have ordered and received arms worth a total of $35 billion—which is equal to the entire United Nations budget for 70 years.

Most of the wars that are fought are fought on the soil of poorer nations with arms supplied by the richer nations. The United States, the world's leading supplier

three years ago, continues to export more than half of the global trade. The Shah of Iran purchased more than $20 billion in American arms, nearly half of which was delivered before he was relieved of his Peacock Throne. In the past eight years the Pentagon, our principal but by no means sole channel for arms transfers, sold $79 billion in military equipment and services abroad.

Total exports of arms from this country have risen from $17.2 billion in 1978 to an anticipated $20.3 billion today. The government acknowledges rather less than these amounts, recording only $13.6 billion in 1978 and estimating $15.6 billion for 1980. Its figures will later be adjusted, as those for previous years have been. The official total of 1976 exports, for example, was revised upward from $9.9 billion to $16.5 billion.

Still missing from all of the official figures, however, is a growing volume of commercial sales of arms or equipment suitable for military use, licensed by the Departments of Commerce and State. Most of these, when broken up into individual orders that do no exceed limitations of value prescribed by current law, escape Congressional review, and are free to violate such policy objectives as arms embargos voted by Congress against specific countries. Even more of them are not included at all in official yearly reports of total sales volume, though in fact their true volume is often more than double the volume reported.

While the foregoing figures include funds for military grant aid administered by the Pentagon, they do not include substantial amounts administered by other agencies. It is not generally known that in 1978 $2.2 billion in funds administered by the Agency for International Development were used to provide military equipment and services for countries abroad. These funds are variously identified as "Economic Support Funds" (ESF) or, as they are known in the Pentagon, "Security Support Assistance."

Funds allocated to AID for this purpose in 1980 totalled $1.9 billion, while an additional $21 million in funds for peacekeeping organizations (PKO) was administered that year by the State Department. In all, more than $22 billion in military equipment and services, or in funds for their purchase and maintenance, was transferred abroad last year under various United States government programs.

It was in the context of this variety of

3

programs, and in admission that the United States should not be "the world's leading supplier of weapons of war," that President Carter announced a policy of arms restraint in 1977. He promised a reduction in the volume of Foreign Military Sales in 1978 from their 1977 goal. He also said his administration would "henceforth view arms transfers as an exceptional foreign policy implement."

The reduction, even in the single category of exports the President chose, proved impossible to make. Only by deliberately increasing the volume of 1977 sales with an even less restrictive approval of arms requests that year, by exempting Australia, New Zealand, Japan and every NATO country from inclusion in the following year's total of sales—though not from the 1977 total with which they would be compared, and by the intervention of a *deus ex machina*: a Pentagon bookkeeping error which further raised the 1977 total of sales by $1.4 billion, was the President able to save face and claim a theoretical reduction. Sales to the President's non-exempt group of countries in 1978 totalled $9.5 billion. If one compares apples with apples, however, Foreign Military Sales to *all* countries still rose from $11.3 billion in 1977, the bookkeeping windfall included, to $13.4 billion in 1978.

The President had only begun to realize he was up against one of the most powerful sectors of our economy. Hand in hand with the economic forces behind our arms exports are the diplomatic temptations. American arms are a preferred currency. It seems we often view them as the only bargaining chips we have. Far from being an exceptional implement of policy, arms transfers have instead become the rule, committing the American taxpayer to record amounts in military credits and grant aid to foreign countries whose compliance we seek in support of what our government perceives as its foreign policy goals.

### Base Rights and Military Aid

In 1979 we reached new agreements with Portugal for continued use of our air base in the Azores in return for $140 million in military aid, and with the Phillippines for use through 1983 of Clark Air Force Base and the naval facility at Subic Bay in return for $500 million in military and economic aid. To these two countries and to Spain, where we also have air and naval bases, an additional $105 million

has been requested for aid under the Military Assistance Program (MAP) in 1981. Spain this year will also receive $120 million in Foreign Military Sales credits, $2 million in International Military Education and Training (IMET) funds, and $7 million in Economic Support Funds, as required under the 1976 Spanish-American Treaty of Friendship and Cooperation. Spain anticipates full entry into NATO this year.

Having earlier planned the withdrawal of United States forces from South Korea, and settled on a $2.2 billion package of military aid to that country to strengthen its defenses in their absence, the Carter administration met with stern warnings from their commander-in-chief, Lieutenant General John K. Singlaub. President Carter promptly relieved him of his command, and then followed his advice, announcing the decision to keep the troops there. President Reagan then vigorously reaffirmed this decision, vowing not to reduce our military presence in Korea. Meanwhile much of the aid, disembodied from its original intent, continued to flow.

Having agreed at the Guadeloupe Conference in 1979 to share in a $3.2 billion package of military aid for Turkey from several industrial nations, we last year approved an additional $450 million of our own in military and economic aid to that country, in exchange for the reopening of twelve United States bases on Turkish soil out of 29 that had been closed in retaliation for our 1975 arms embargo. The embargo, in turn, had been imposed by Congress in response to Turkey's unauthorized use of American weapons in the 1974 invasion of Cyprus.

We are now operating air bases at Incirlik and Adana, a radar intelligence station at Sinop on the Black Sea, a seismic station near Ankara, a communications terminal at Izmir, and additional facilities at Pirinclik and at Karamursel on the Sea of Marmara. These we regard as partial compensation for the loss of radar intelligence stations at Beshahr on the Caspian Sea, at Kabkan, Klarabad, the sites known as Takman I and II, and other locations in Iran. We abandoned all of

those during the growing civil unrest through the winter of 1978 and 1979, and removed some of the more sensitive equipment they contained to Dubai.

Claiming we were temporarily unable, after the loss of these posts, to monitor Soviet missile test sites at Tyuratum and the Baikonur space center near Leninsk, we became concerned that we would not be able to ensure Soviet compliance with the testing provisions of SALT II. Yet our Senate showed little urgency in ratifying that Treaty, and President Carter, who initially made much of its signing, appeared in subsequent months to withdraw his support for it. So perhaps our capability for monitoring Soviet test activities was not so adversely affected as the public was told. This would not be suprising in view of the many other means of surveillance at our disposal. Perhaps the loss of our Iranian listening posts was simply dramatized as another example of America's loss of power—which a new administration, yet to be elected, would help to regain, and another reason to bolster the contention of Reagan supporters that SALT II should be "renegotiated."

In any case, it is now doubtful whether the Soviets would any longer honor SALT II. Since the Treaty was signed, France has announced it would develop and test a neutron bomb. In this country, Defense Secretary Casper Weinberger announced he would recommend production of our own "enhanced radiation weapon." When our European allies balked anew at this, and the city of Nagasaki, which ought to be credited with a certain expertise in such matters, urged the whole world to reconsider deployment of any kind of neutron bomb, Secretary of State Alexander Haig, in the classic tradition of confirmation and denial, gave reassurances that our decision was not yet firm. Two additional promises of a change in the balance of power, one false and one real, had also been made in the summer of 1980, when the Carter administration announced an apparent shift in nuclear strategy, aiming for a first strike capability against the USSR which we claimed we did not have before, and announced our decision to sell to Mrs. Thatcher's government 100 Trident I Missiles.

Following the sale of these missiles we will probably also supply Great Britain with nuclear materials for the assembly of the total of 800 to 1,000 warheads it is often forgotten this number of missiles of that type will carry. It will mark the first time in history that we have exported weapons-grade nuclear materials abroad. That is quite a different step from the sale of 38 tons of uranium to India for its Tarapur power plant, shipments of which Congress has asked both the Carter and Reagan administrations to suspend.

Responding to intensifed warnings that Turkey was becoming a weak link in NATO, Congress forgot about Cyprus and voted an end to the Turkish arms embargo in the summer of 1978. It hadn't mattered anyway. In 1977, while the embargo was presumably in force, we supplied Turkey with $175 million in military aid. The following year, we sold Turkey 40 F-4 Phantom fighter aircraft for $400 million, and the President asked that the embargo be ''relaxed'' so we could give Turkey $175 million in Foreign Military Sales credits toward this purchase, and deliver some of the aircraft. Throughout the entire period, Turkey had in any case purchased American equipment through the NATO Maintenance and Supply Agency. Meanwhile, the Cyprus problem remains unresolved, the Turkish opium problem may resurface, and we still have not obtained permission from Turkey to fly U-2 reconnaissance flights out of Incirlik.

This final difficulty could be due to the fact that the Turkish government has exercised its sovereignty in making agreements with other countries beside our own, and that it feels foreign activities on its soil as provocative as U-2 flights could strain such relationships. For example, in June of 1979 it signed an agreement with the Soviet Union for $8 billion in economic assistance, involving construction in Turkey of more than 20 projects including a nuclear plant with a guaranteed uranium fuel supply for 20 years.

In any case, we have continued to fly our reconnaissance missions from the Indian Ocean base of Diego Garcia, which has undergone costly expansion and improvement, as well as from Qena in Egypt. This new ally has also permitted us use of the Red Sea naval base of Ras Benas, and of Cairo West Air Base, where last year a squadron of 12 United States F-4 Phantom aircraft conducted joint exercises. A light infantry force of 1,400 United States combat troops also conducted exercises in Egypt last year, and similar exercises have been carried out in Oman and Liberia.

Landing strips at Egyptian air bases are now being strengthened and extended to permit use by our long-range B-52 bombers, which already use Diego Garcia. These bombers belong to our Strategic Air Command. They carry nuclear weapons, unlike the Soviet Tu-22M ''Backfire'' bombers, which we claim have a strategic role but which in fact are assigned to defense of the Warsaw Pact and to naval patrol duties.

In September of 1980 we opened negotiations with Australia to allow our B-52s to use its facilities at Darwin after extended flights across the Indian Ocean. These aircraft presently must stage at Guam. When the discussions were announced, the Soviet Union promptly warned Australia that it might now be targeted with nuclear weapons. Australia responded that it was sure it had already been targeted. The negotiations are under review by the Reagan administration, but will certainly be pressed forward.

In return for a commitment to Greece of $700 million in military and economic aid over the next 4 years, we have requested continued use of the naval base at Suda Bay, air bases at Herakleion and Hellenikon, and communications and intelligence intercept stations at Nea Makri, Kato Souli, Mount Pateras, Mount Ehedri and Levkas Island in the Ionian Sea. These facilities have become a political liability for the current government, which faces elections this year. The Panhellenic Socialist Movement, which may come to power, has vowed to shut down the bases. It could not do so, however, if Greece, which left NATO in 1974 to protest the Turkish invasion of Cyprus, were to rejoin that organization as it now plans.

The difficulty has been that every NATO member has veto power over the reentry of Greece. One member is Turkey, which has looked forward to an expanded role in NATO, with responsibility for areas of the Aegean previously controlled by Greece. The Greek government warned that it would have to shut down the bases, along with five NATO early-warning sites in northern Greece and a NATO missile-firing range at Namfi, if Turkey exercised

its veto or the decision was postponed much longer. After a coup in Steptember of 1980, a new government was formed in Turkey. It may come as no surprise if this new regime declines its veto and Greece reenters NATO well before election time.

Having promised to reduce our military presence abroad, we last year expanded it, adding three more nations to the 42 that already harbored the vast network of our military bases overseas. We agreed to supply $53 million in military aid to Kenya, in return for use of a naval base at Mombasa, and $100 million to Oman in return for use of the airfield on Masirah Island and port facilities at Qabus and Raysut, while we set aside $200 million more to improve those facilities. We also agreed to provide $45 million in military aid to Somalia, together with an additional $111 million in refugee and development aid over the next two years, in return for use of the naval base of Berbera on the Gulf of Aden, and of the airfield at Mogadishu, whose 15,000 foot runway can also accomodate the B-52.

In August of 1980 we obtained Somalia's word that it would no longer press its claim to the Ogaden region of neighboring Ethiopia, a claim whose validity almost every other African nation denies. At the same time we promised Kenya, which refused our use of the port of Mombasa without such an assurance, that we would not supply ''offensive'' weapons to Somalia. Ethiopia, which now looks to the Soviet Union for military support, has threatened to invade Somalia if we supply it with any arms at all. The House Foreign Operations Subcommittee on Africa held up shipment of the arms until it could be assured Somalia had withdrawn its troops from the Ogaden. ''Verified assurance'' of this was given by the State Department in January of 1981. At that time, however, three battalions of Somali regular forces were still in position there, only 150 miles from Berbera.

Our new alliance with Somalia thus risks our involvement in a proxy war with the Soviet Union, which may increase both its aid to Ethiopia and its own presence there. It is a dangerous situation. In our determination to establish bases along the Indian Ocean, for possible use in the event of a new emergency in that part of the world, we overlook the likelihood that in Somalia we are causing that emergency to occur. We are driven, however, by the momentum of our preparations to deal with contingencies that may develop before we are ready to introduce our recently inaugurated Rapid Deployment Force.

### The Rapid Deployment Force
The Rapid Deployment Force, which would free us from dependence on local states in the Persian Gulf or other areas of the world, and which in fact presumes America's growing need to operate in a largely hostile environment, was officially established in March of 1980 as a new organizational entity under the command of Marine Lieutenant General Paul X. Kelley, with headquarters at MacDill Air Force Base In Florida. The Reagan administration now contemplates moving its headquarters to Brussels and placing it under regular Army command in the NATO structure. To achieve its objectives, the Pentagon asked last year for $81 million to develop the CX, a new long-range cargo aircraft to supplement and eventually replace the fleet of C-5A Galaxys we now use. Approximately 50 CX aircraft are planned. Another $300 million was also requested for initial investment in a series of fifteen high-speed L-7 cargo ships, which could reach the Persian Gulf in 15 days and wait there, pre-positioned as floating bases, with supplies sufficient to support combat operations for several tactical air squadrons and a full brigade of men for two weeks.

The Pentagon has announced that Rapid Deployment Force preparations and programs will cost a total of $10 billion. The Congressional Budget Office estimates a rather higher cost, from $23 billion to $33 billion. The latter range of figures seems more on the mark. The force of CX cargo aircraft, now expected to cost $180 million each, will by itself total $9 billion. Each L-7 cargo ship is expected to cost $280 million, so that the fifteen planned will cost a total of $4.2 billion. In addition, each cargo ship will carry approximately $500 million worth of tanks, heavy artillery pieces, ammunition and other equipment. $7.5 billion of such equipment must therefore be purchased to properly stock the entire fleet of these new floating arsenals. Thus an expenditure of more than $20 billion, or twice the Pentagon estimate, has already been planned.

Varying in composition and size according to the mission at hand, the Rapid Deployment Force will initially draw on

several divisions including the Army's 82nd Airborne, 101st Airborne and 24th Mechanized Infantry Divisions, and on the 7th Marine Amphibious Brigade, a new force of 12,000 men. General Kelley or his successor may select for his task only a few hundred Special Forces troops, or he may build a full corps comprising several divisions, together with tactical air wings and naval carrier forces. His ground fighting units alone could swell to a force of 200,000 men, and that is about what the Pentagon thinks it might need in a "worst case" scenario.

### The Threat to the Oilfields
The "worst case," of course, is a Soviet invasion of the Persian oilfields. These oilfields have been a focus of strategic interest since the turn of the century. It was one of Field-Marshal Rommel's primary missions to seal them from Allied access during World War II. Now we are told the Soviet Union is after them. Indeed, the Soviet invasion of Afghanistan in December of 1979, and the new threat this allegedly posed to the oilfields in Iran, were given as the primary reason for creation of the Rapid Deployment Force.

If the Soviet Union poses a threat to these oilfields, the threat is not a new one, and it is not from Afghanistan. Look at a map. The point on the Afghan border nearest Abadan and the heart of Iran's oilfields is still 800 miles away. In support of a Soviet airdrop, ground columns, whether moving from Herat through Meshed in the north or from Kandahar through Zahedan in the south, would have to cover a distance of more than 1,100 miles on Iranian soil, reaching Isfahan and crossing the Zagros mountains before descending to Abadan.

If instead Soviet air invasion forces came from the north, crossing the Iranian border with Soviet Azerbaijan at Nakhichevan, they would fly only 600 miles in Iranian airspace to the same destination. Supporting ground columns would move directly south through Tabriz on major highways, for a distance of only 840 miles. Massing in their own territory, they would be better equipped and sup-

plied, and possibly less immediately observable. The Soviets have shared a order with Iran ever since Azerbaijan became a Soviet Republic. For the better part of half a century, therefore, the Soviet Union has been within closer striking distance to the Iranian oilfields than it is from Afghanistan. Chairman of the Joint Chiefs of Staff General Jones has publicly acknowledged this, adding that even if the Soviets chose to blockade oil shipments rather than seize the oil itself, and consequently struck not at Abadan but at Bandar Abbas on the Straights of Hormuz—a point which is more than 100 miles closer to the Afghan border—road conditions and other geographical factors would forbid the more direct route, and the invasion would still come from Azerbaijan. Yet in all this time they have not invaded.

Nevertheless, largely on account of this contingency, a minimum of $20 billion will be taken from the taxpayer to create a new force that presumably will deal with it in some way—though how it would deal with an actual Soviet invasion of Iran, should that ever occur, and how it could deal with it any better than forces which already exist, are matters very much open to question.

### The Afghan Intervention
If oil was not the reason for invading Afghanistan, then why did the Soviets invade? To understand this, we must first appreciate how the Soviets see themselves. We ought to begin with history, with the invasion of Russia by Japan in the east and then, years later, the invasion from Germany in the west. The latter event resulted in terrible losses, which the Soviet gerontocracy in power remembers firsthand and wants never to see repeated. We ought to consider the Soviet view that it is now hemmed in on the west by NATO and on the east by China, a country once part of the international Communist conspiracy but now, Kremlin leaders observe, an ally of the United States, having established formal ties with us in December of 1978 and exchanged embassies in March of 1979.

In September of 1980, a delegation of 22 American scientists and military experts headed by William J. Perry, under secretary of Defense for Research and Engineering, visited China for a two-week study of her military needs. Dr. Perry said that it was "one of a series of exchanges designed to broaden contact between the defense establishments of the two countries.'' While the United States government maintained it would not sell weapons to China, it did not say it would prevent American companies from negotiating directly for portions of China's 1981 military budget of $13.l billion. The Soviets observed that they had already been doing so.

We have already approved more than 20 licenses for the sale of military equipment to the People's Republic, and another 400 for the sale of technology with military application. Western Geophysical has sold the Chinese a high-speed computer more advanced than any equipment ever approved for sale to the USSR. The Bell Division of Textron is completing negotiations to build a helicopter factory in Harbin. China, in turn, has agreed to sell the United States large supplies of titanium, vanadium and tantalum, materials scarce in the West and critical for defense manufacturing. China has become a military ally of the United States. There has been no comparable shift in the balance of power since the formation of NATO. The Soviets, faced with all this, may feel a good deal more on the defensive than we realize.

The Soviet leaders observe within their own borders an increasing ethnic separatism, along with the growth of a Moslem population that may outnumber Russians themselves by the end of this century. They have had to decentralize power within the Soviet Union itself, yielding greater administrative autonomy to each of the 15 Republics. If the labor crisis in Poland persists, and they feel compelled to take stronger steps to preserve Soviet hegemony, military action of the kind they once undertook in Hungary and Czechoslovakia will be their very last resort, for with those costly lessons of the past behind them they cannot be unaware today of the loss of prestige and political favor this would precipitate throughout the world.

The Soviet Union probably looks at the Iranian revolution less as a defeat for the West than another warning of the rise of Islam on its own southern flank. Since the time of Czar Nicholas II it has regarded Afghanistan as an area of key strategic importance because it adjoined that flank. It has tried for decades to maintain stability in Afghanistan by supporting regimes friendly to Soviet interests and by exert-

ing its influence to make them more so. It has observed increasing Western intervention in Afghanistan, dating back to United States support of Mohammed Daud in 1973, all of which was designed to make these regimes *less* friendly to Soviet interests.

Indeed, Birch Bayh, Chairman of the Senate Select Committee on Intelligence, reported that our CIA had been supplying arms to the rebels in Afghanistan, in violation of the Hughes-Ryan amendment that prohibited such covert action, well before the Soviets intervened there. At the same time, President Carter was pressing Congress to ratify a new CIA charter which would legally free that agency to do what it was already doing.

Intervention of this kind can lead to destabilization. It makes the Soviets feel the way some Americans felt when they were told the Castro revolution in Cuba could not have succeeded without Soviet help. Destabilization is an attempt to change the balance of power. It is feared that other nations, and possibly one's own electorate, might consider this dishonorable, and therefore it is kept covert. It was noteworthy, then, that six weeks after the Soviet invasion we publicly announced we had undertaken a covert operation to supply arms to the Afghan ''freedom fighters,'' as though no one in Afghanistan could have been fighting for freedom until the Soviets got there.

An open announcement of covert action is something of a contradiction in terms. In an attempt to resolve it, we made a second announcement five months later. This time we said that if we admitted we were supplying arms, the Soviets would use this to support their claims that they were protecting Afghanistan from outside interference. Silence from the start on our part would have cast more doubt on these claims, had they been of any real concern to us. But outside interference is perfectly acceptable when it is aid to a people newly oppressed by a superpower bent on world domination.

All that concerned us, then, was to establish that our assistance did not begin until after the Soviet intervention. Our

announcement of a ''covert'' operation was an attempt to do this. If Senator Bayh's revelation of earlier covert operations could be made to appear mistaken, and somehow confused with a new operation only just begun, then the period of our earlier activities could be more plausibly denied. Those activities, after all, took place before the Soviet intervention, and probably helped to precipitate the events that led to it. The whole episode lent more legitimacy to Soviet claims than the Soviet leaders deserved.

Whatever the degree of our involvement, it should be clear that Soviet forces moved into Afghanistan not to prepare for a strike at the Persian Gulf but to preserve security on their southern border. The timing was significant in other respects. Four months before the invasion, American ratification of SALT II was again postponed when Henry Kissinger called for ''linkage'' of its approval to higher defense spending. This encouraged conservative forces to reopen the debate on the magnitude of the Soviet threat.

President Carter, who until then had been urging immediate approval of SALT II, suddenly found a more dramatic reason of his own to delay it, thus stealing away the initiative from his political opponents. In September a squadron of eighteen new Soviet MiG-23 aircraft was reported in Cuba. 2,600 Soviet troops were also discovered there, allegedly for the first time, though it turned out they had been there for 17 years. Before proceeding with SALT II the President now insisted on Soviet assurances that their aircraft were not equipped with nuclear weapons and their troops not disposed as a ''combat brigade.'' Andrei Gromyko duly gave these assurances to Secretary Vance, but SALT II remained shelved as the President rode with the new political tide, and as the defense community, fortified by Soviet armoured divisions crossing the Afghan border and a small contingent of American hostages in Teheran, moved to educate the public—and a very responsive press—on the need for an even stronger military establishment.

Meanwhile, to demonstrate firm resolve in response to the new dangers unveiled in Cuba, the President established a Caribbean Joint Task Force Headquarters at Key West Naval Air Station, Florida, and placed Rear Admiral Thomas Replogle in command of its staff of 60 officers. He also ordered 1,600 Marines to take part in well-publicized maneuvers at our naval base at Guantanamo Bay, which the Cuban government continues to allow us to operate on its soil, collecting a rent of $4,000 a year.

The only American base in a Communist country, Guantanamo has more symbolic than strategic value. We have occupied it since 1898, reinforcing our claim to it with passage of the Platt Amendment after the Spanish-American War. Further complicating its status, a Cuban Constituent Assembly accepted the Platt Amendment, in return for political independence, by a margin of one vote in 1901. When the Platt Amendment was abolished in 1934, the base was leased by the United States for an ''indefinite period.'' Fidel Castro has limited that period to 100 years, dating not from 1934 but from 1898. Since the attempted invasion at the Bay of Pigs in 1961, the Castro government has avoided implying acceptance of our terms of lease, placing our uncashed rental checks in a Swiss safety deposit box.

It may be important, also, to note that Soviet forces appeared at Kabul airport just 46 days after Brezhnev, having earlier withdrawn 20,000 troops and 1,000 tanks from East Germany, asked NATO to reconsider its planned deployment of 108 Pershing II and 464 Ground-Launched Cruise Missiles in Western Europe, and was turned down. It is seldom mentioned that these missiles will double NATO's nuclear capability, already far superior to that of the Warsaw Pact, while the much-publicized Soviet deployment of mobile medium-range SS-20 missiles does not achieve an equivalent increase in capability for the Pact, let alone a parity in theatre nuclear strength. Something had reached the breaking point in the Kremlin.

Most probably, the Soviet Union has now embroiled itself in its own Vietnam. It has no more right to be in Afghanistan than the United States had to be in Southeast Asia. Its war in Afghanistan promises to be as long and as costly, though no one in the Pentagon regrets that. In political and diplomatic terms, the Soviets have lost favor throughout the world. The Western Nations, especially the United States, have made enormous capital from this blunder.

Afghanistan has led to the embargo of 17 million metric tons of wheat to the Soviet Union, and to the draft registration of four million young Americans who are needed not nearly so much as the pilots,

missile control officers, mechanics and radar technicians we have spent hundreds of millions of dollars to train but have lost to civilian industry. Afghanistan has led to our boycott of the Moscow Olympics, in which our athletes, if they had to play any role at all in the new Cold War, might have played a more effective one as participants.

Our military manpower problems are real, but they are not the problems usually presented to the public. We are told that six of the ten Army combat divisions in the United States are not combat-ready. In peacetime—a condition we presumably still enjoy—that is hardly unusual. Last year Army Chief of Staff General Edward C. Meyer ordered 6,000 sergeants in Europe and 900 in South Korea reassigned to the United States to help put these divisions in shape. We are left with the impression that this seriously impairs the strength of our front-line units abroad.

In fact, the return of these noncommissioned officers has left our authorized strength in both theaters at 100 percent, down from 102 percent in Europe and 103 percent in Korea.

We are told that the draft is needed because we have a shortage of manpower. In fact, all services except the Marine Corps exceeded their recruiting goals in the first nine months of 1980. We are told that the draft would raise the proportion of raw recruits with high school degrees. In fact, that proportion stands today at 84 percent in the Army, as compared with 57 percent when the draft ended in January of 1973.

We have a shortage of *qualified* manpower, which a draft would do nothing to cure. Higher salaries for the rank and file would keep qualified personnel from leaving the military services. Funds to achieve these higher salary levels could be obtained not only by eliminating redundant weapons procurement programs, but also by a reform that is long overdue of the military retirement pay system. $12 billion has been allocated for retirement pay in 1980. The sum is expected to increase to $20.2 billion in 1985. A high proportion of its recipients, known as ''double

dippers,'' have left the military at the midpoint of their working lives for much more lucrative positions in civilian industry, and simultaneously receive retirement benefits from their new employers.

However unwarranted, then, the dramatic gestures of the Olympic boycott and the draft registration were an attempt at resolute action in the face of what was made to seem a new level of threat. By affecting millions of American families in a mildy adverse way, they implied that the adversity we felt was the result of what the Soviets did in Afghanistan, and thus they lent validity to the notion that the threat was genuine. But was it?

President Carter called the Afghan intervention the ''gravest threat'' to world peace since 1945. Presidential security advisor Zbigniew Brzezinski called it a watershed event, pointing out that it was the first time Soviet troops had been used beyond Soviet or Warsaw Pact borders. Even those who conceded that the event posed no new threat to our oil supplies still insisted that it represented a major shift in the global balance of power.

If the Soviets remain in Afghanistan they will share a border with Pakistan. This is a local strategic novelty that excites the domino theorists, who apparently believe any Communist nation is bound to have more influence upon its neighbor than its neighbor can have in return. Aside from that, it is difficult to see how this Soviet intervention accomplishes any more of a change in the global balance of power than did the United States interventions in Panama in 1903, in Nicaragua in 1911, in Haiti in 1915, in Mexico in 1914 and 1916, in Guatemala in 1954, or in the Dominican Republic in 1903, 1916 and 1965.

Each of these episodes in Latin America was presented as an attempt to prevent change. In each case, force was used to overcome a government grown hostile, or to thwart some external power, real or imagined, that seemed to threaten the status quo. In rather more instances than Mr. Brzezinski could cite on behalf of the Soviet Union, we made the watershed decision to send troops beyond our own borders. In most cases, the result of our action was locally devastating, yet barely felt throughout the rest of the world. We moved, in our hemisphere, to assure ourselves of stability on our southern border. How, in its own hemisphere, does the recent Soviet action differ?

It will escape no one's attention that

each of our own interventions was as much a violation of another nation's sovereignty as we rightly claim the Soviet action to be. In order more effectively to protest the transgressions of another nation, however, we have learned to overlook our own. The moral outrage we are then free to express enriches the public sense of our opponent's treachery, presenting a more urgent need than may actually exist to protect ourselves from it. In this sort of atmosphere, requests for higher defense outlays meet with a more sympathetic ear.

Toward that end, much example was made of Afghanistan. The creation of the Rapid Deployment Force was presented as a direct response to the Soviet invasion. In fact, planning for it dates back to a presidential directive (PD 18) in August of 1977, more than two years before the Afghan intervention, and a year and a half before the Shah's departure from Iran began a series of crises between that country and our own.

These plans were not publicly announced, however, until later events made it more propitious to do so. The seizure of the American hostages at the embassy in Teheran in November of 1979, and the Soviet intervention in Afghanistan the following month, had brought the American public through its winter of discontent. We were frustrated with our inability to protect our embassies, and fearful of our inability to protect the oil on which we were told we relied. Administration officials appealed to these feelings as they announced their plans for an expansion of American military power and requested the funds to support it. Yet this vast expansion was already well under way when the events of that difficult winter took place.

### America's Power Projection Capabilities

We have, of course, had rapid deployment forces for some time. They are called the Marine Corps. They celebrated their 200th anniversary six years ago. They are a force of 189,000 men, complete with its own tank battalions, artillery regiments, tactical air wings, and a new fleet of helicopter carriers and landing ships. The only Soviet forces with a comparable capability are the Soviet Naval Infantry, numbering just 12,000 men.

Our Marines were rapidly deployed to Hawaii in 1893 to assist in the overthrow of the native government of those islands, to Peking in 1900 to join an interna-

tional force protecting diplomatic personnel—in an age when this was still possible—from the Boxer rebellion, to Lebanon at that country's request in 1958 to restore internal order, and on most of the occasions already cited to various points in the Caribbean and Central America.

The Rapid Deployment Force, then, is simply an expansion and refinement of a capability we have had for more than a century. Its aim is to bring a larger force to an area of conflict more quickly than current capabilities are said to allow, and to sustain that force in combat for a longer period of time.

It would now take us about ten days to airlift a light infantry brigade of 4,000 men to the Persian Gulf, bringing with them just enough equipment and supplies to fight for five days. To airlift a divisional force of 13,000 men to the same location, and to transport its heavy equipment—which would include 300 tanks—would currently require three weeks. The Pentagon claims its Rapid Deployment Force will be able, by 1985, to airlift 16,500 men to the Persian Gulf with all of their heavy equipment in only five days, and to sustain them for 30 days of combat operations. This will achieve for us a capability, to which many Pentagon planners have long aspired, to fight a conventional "war and a half," usually depicted as a full-scale war on the NATO battlefield with a simultaneous major confrontation somewhere in the Middle East, Africa or Asia.

The Rapid Deployment Force commander claims he could right now drop a battalion of paratroopers—possibly 800 men—into a Persian Gulf state in just 48 hours, "if someone allows us to move." There's the rub. Congress would have to allow it. This takes time. If a president chose to act unilaterally, in the interests of national security, the War Powers resolution would severely limit his authority. This resolution, adopted in 1973 in an attempt to avoid the recurrence of such episodes as Nixon's foray into Cambodia, forbids a president to send our armed forces anywhere abroad, except in response to an attack upon the United States, its territories, or its armed forces.

Yet the frequency with which we refer to states in the Persian Gulf as soil on which we might freely trespass suggests we will have no more scruples about doing so today than we have had in the past. In our minds today, there is a sense of greater urgency. This probably did not begin with Afghanistan, or even with the revolution in Iran. It probably began with our defeat in Vietnam in 1975.

### America's Waning Power in the World

Many Americans regarded Vietnam as a profound lesson. It demonstrated that social change could not be arrested by force, that we could no longer be assured of success in imposing our will on another nation, that military power was no longer a decisive implement of foreign policy. Other Americans, however, were humiliated. Their only reaction was that the world's greatest military power lacked sufficient power, and sufficient freedom to use it. Their only prescription has been to increase both. It is this latter group which helped to bring the current administration into office.

Along with a fear of our waning military might, and the conviction that this explained all our adversities in the world, there developed a fear of growing Soviet might, and of our inability to contain it. If we could not contain it, we might still slow the Soviets down, we believed, and make it costly for them to expand their sphere of influence. This we did by arming some people to fight a little longer, though we knew they could not win, and though it was frequently doubtful whether they deserved to.

This, as former CIA Angola Task Force chief John Stockwell points out in his book *In Search of Enemies*, was the only goal of Henry Kissinger's policy of American intervention in Angola, a policy we began to implement just months after we fled Saigon in 1975. Such policies persist. Continuing support for the Afghan rebels will never enable them to overcome the Soviet Army. The most it will do is prolong the fighting and so deny the Soviets an easier victory. James A. Nathan, associate professor of political science at the University of Delaware, recently wrote in *The New York Times* that "to intensify Afghan suffering in the hope of making the Soviet Union pay a price verges on a kind of racism."

Aside from the cynicism of encouraging bloodshed for no reason other than spite, or for what Professor Nathan calls "larger diplomatic purposes," we have frequently also demonstrated some ignorance, as we involved ourselves in distant conflicts, about what was really taking place, and some confusion about what our purpose ought to be.

Generally, as in Vietnam and Angola, what was taking place was not an instance of Soviet expansionism but a civil war, the final stage of an internal revolution not precipitated by the Soviet hand. Unfortunately, we tend to see most revolutions as a threat. That is because a socialist regime is frequently the first option of a people throwing off the yoke of imperialism, and we are bound to the view that socialist nations are unstable, less friendly to us, and more friendly to the Soviet Union.

History regularly contradicts this view. It has only been true as a self-fulfilling prophesy. The hostility we feel from many Third World countries is provoked by our own distrust. There is no reason for this. We could tomorrow restore trade with Cuba, forget the United Fruit Company's loss of what it claims to be its bananas, and end Cuba's dependence on the Soviet Union.

We could today condemn the violent and repressive policies of President Duarte of El Salvador, enjoin the Organization of American States to enforce an embargo on all shipments of arms to that country, negotiate an armistice between the government and guerilla forces, and press for free elections supervised by the United Nations. This would preempt Soviet involvement, precisely as it has done in Zimbabwe. Instead, on very slim evidence, we have laboriously constructed a case of "Soviet-bloc" support for the guerillas that is reminiscent of our State Department's White Paper on Vietnam—all in order to justify our support of a military regime whose brutality has been condemned by almost every Central American state. This fateful choice may involve us in a new Vietnam, at which point the Soviets, who are quite as adept as we at playing the role of guardian angel to the oppressed, may truly become involved.

Once again, we will have lost potential new friends. Once again we will have backed the wrong side, polarizing popular sentiment against us and in favor of the Soviets. If our attempts to bolster the Duarte regime succeed, we will lose political favor throughout the world community precisely as the Soviets have lost it over Afghanistan. If we do not succeed, it will

all be taken as one more sign of America's decline in power—when in fact it will merely reflect the continuing deterioration of our political judgment and moral principle.

At the same time, we are told that the Soviet Union has expanded its influence throughout the world. On the contrary, over the past decade the Soviets have suffered several losses, and many of their losses have been our gains. They have lost Egypt, the Sudan, Somalia, Guinea, Indonesia, and most important of all, China. In his book *World Power Trends*, which rates the influence of nations by an aggregate of economic, geographic, demographic and military factors, former CIA analyst Ray Cline traces this loss of Soviet power, attributing to the Soviet Union and Warsaw Pact countries a combined share today of 20 percent of the world's power, as compared with 70 percent for the United States, the Western nations and China.

The idea that a nation can do whatever it likes with its power has always been an illusion. The idea that American power is dangerously declining while Soviet power grows is a myth, the frustrated response of those who can no longer make the illusion work their way.

### The Crisis in Iran
That few of our adversities abroad can be plausibly laid to the Soviet Union does not mean that we have had none. As the revolution unfolded in Iran, we suffered a series of shocks. The first of these was a sense of having been taking by surprise, as though we had been unable to predict events in advance. President Carter complained of an "intelligence failure."

This was less of a failure to gain access to the pertinent facts than a failure to evaluate them sensibly. Because we had placed the Shah on his throne, and had done so largely by covert means, we were more than normally committed to the success of his regime, and more inclined than usual to disregard its flaws. While the rest of a horrified world learned of the havoc the Shah had wrought upon his people, and it daily became more evident what the consequences would be, we

could not acknowledge that he might ever lose control. A belief in having done the right thing makes it difficult to learn that it was the wrong thing.

This form of bias reflects a potential weakness in the link between every nation's intelligence and policy-making establishments. Leaders are too often told what it is presumed they want to hear. In this case our intelligence product—the finished reports for the President and his advisors—continued to minimize the growing risks to the Shah's regime, leaving us unprepared for his final overthrow. That was our failure—though it isn't clear what we might have done had we been any better prepared.

In the end, the intelligence community turned all of this to advantage, graciously acknowledging its failure of analysis in order to argue for strengthened capabilities of a kind very different from those that had been in question—paving the way for the resurgence of covert action policies that had been so roundly condemned, only a few years earlier, during Congressional investigations of intelligence abuses. These abuses now became lost arts, to be revived.

Our next shock was the seizure of the hostages. This, too, could have been avoided. It was odd that we did not remove all our diplomatic personnel from Teheran at the same time we removed the ambassador himself. The danger was clear, and it had been stated. It was odd that we allowed the Shah into this country when the availabilty in Switzerland of equally competent treatment for his condition made his visit here unnecessary.

It was odd that President Carter allowed himself to be persuaded into accepting the Shah by men like Henry Kissinger and David Rockefeller, whose previous support for the Pahlevi dynasty placed them on the defensive, and who did not care how much trouble they caused in order to reassert the rightness of their view. Once the hostages were taken, it was odd how effective Richard Nixon's ethic that "you don't welch on a friend" proved to be, as though betrayal of the Shah's trust in a man like Nixon outweighed the Shah's betrayal of the trust of his own people.

The taking of hostages, being a recognized act of aggression, entitled us to a measure of moral outrage, which we used to eclipse Iran's claims that we owed an apology for our infamous role in its affairs. Had there been no hostages, on the other hand, these claims would have captured the world's attention only briefly. By portraying the demands for the Shah's return as an attempt at extortion, we were able to make our own refusal to forfeit him seem a defense of our honor, in which cause we enlisted concurrence even from the hostages themselves.

In fact, to have given up the Shah would have implied his guilt and our complicity, yielding the point that we had not behaved honorably in the past. Most of our policy-makers viewed this as an unwarranted humiliation, and were determined above all to concede no such thing—which is how the Shah became more important to us than our own citizens in Teheran.

Yet a promise that we would not again interfere in Iran's affairs was one of the conditions for the hostages's release. The condition was met. Another condition was the return of Iranian assets frozen in American banks when the hostages were taken. When this condition, too, was met, there were outraged cries that the money was ransom, and ought not be paid. The fact that the money belonged to Iran was wholly overlooked.

The whole episode was taken as proof that America had lost the ability to command respect in the world, even though history demonstrates that revolutionaries are seldom swayed by respect for anything. We could only regain this ability, we were told, by expanding our military strength. Military strength might ensure a degree of respect if somehow it can be brought to bear. But it has not been demonstrated how any military capability of a kind we now profess to lack could either have prevented the seizure of the hostages or affected events afterwards without possibly involving us in a major war.

The hostages might have been returned well before 444 days had finally elapsed. Months earlier, President Carter might have taken the rare opportunity to make the apology the whole world knew we owed. He might have recognized the legitimacy of Iranian claims without condoning the action of the Iranian militants. He might have condemned the Shah's regime for what it was, deplored the role of previous American administrations in supporting him, and affirmed a new commitment to the primacy of respect for those human rights which the Iranian people had so categorically been denied.

This could have been done when the Shah was still alive. It probably would have led to a negotiated exchange of the hostages and the Shah. Certainly, it would have gained more respect for the United States throughout the world than we can ever earn through the further deployment of military power. Because it would have cleared the air of false posturing and lies, it would have helped finally to expiate this nation's guilt for the role it has played in the past, so that we might break from the mold of imperialism, with its childish belief that we are uniquely immune from guilt, and so move on to a more sophisticated and civilized stage of political life.

Senator Edward Kennedy saw that this could be done, and before last year's elections he said so. He was accused of political opportunism, and of failure to rally to the President's support in that time of crisis. There was a good deal more opportunism in this response to him than in anything the Senator said or did.

Unfortunately, the men in and out of government who were the original architects of our policy toward the Shah succeeded in making President Carter feel their support was crucial to his political survival. Unfortunately, too, Carter valued his survival more than an opportunity to make a profound contribution to American political growth. So the crisis continued, daily reported on the front page of every major newspaper until the rescue attempt in April of 1980, after which coverage of our efforts to release the hostages almost ceased for the next three months, only to resume toward the end of the summer as elections loomed, and Carter decided to make their release the final act of his presidency. It is probable that their release only came when it did because the Khomeini regime had realized nothing more could be gained by holding them any longer. Nor did the Carter administration, in working out the final negotiations, ever concede America's original responsibility for bringing about this crisis by having placed the Shah on the throne.

### The Hostage Rescue Attempt
The rescue attempt seemed a case of tragic bad luck. Much capital was quickly made of our poor capability for carrying out any military mission effectively, so that again the public was reminded of an urgent need to expand our military resources, as though more resources might defeat fate. However, what appears to have happened in the desert at Dasht-e-Kavir could as easily have happened to the Israelis at Entebbe. Theirs was a mission much simpler than ours, but its risks were still sufficient to have made the outcome wholly unpredictable. This merely defines the conditions for which special operations are planned. The failure of our mission, in itself, need raise no doubts about our skills in such operations.

The report of Admiral James L. Holloway's Special Operations Review Group concluded the mission would have been better organized had it been placed in the hands of an established military command rather than a newly created one, and that an excessive concern with security hampered planning. It judged, however, that three additional RH-53D helicopters could have been used, along with a C-130 Pathfinder aircraft to help them all find their way, with no compromise to security. The report does concede that at the time the mission was planned, the limit of eight helicopters used may have seemed "the best compromise between operations security and equipment redundancy."

What is odd is that five separate equipment failures were reported in three of the helicopters, even though the Review Group found that maintenance aboard the carrier *Nimitz* was "excellent." It is odd that our meteorologists claimed to have known nothing about dust storms and claimed they could not easily be detected by weather instruments, that a helicopter pilot selected for this mission was reported to have suffered from vertigo—a condition that ought to have barred him from entering any aircraft at any time, that we were told no mission abort was ever rehearsed, and that in every rehearsal sandscreens were used for the helicopters—though the mission itself was reportedly flown without them.

It is also odd that we claimed we were unable to destroy aircraft left behind which carried classified documents and equipment. If such material really was left behind, then it was odd that we chose to announce that fact to the world, unless the material we left behind was disinformation. A public statement neither improves the impression that false information is real nor increases the suspicion that real information is false. All of these reports certainly raise doubts about our planning, but they also strain credibility. It may be some time before we know what really happened.

Most odd, however, was that we undertook the mission at all. The Pentagon had estimated in advance that the Special Forces D Detachment commanded by Colonel Beckwith might suffer as many as 30 dead, and the hostages 15, before they made their escape. If those were the risks, it appears that we had planned for the kind of pyrrhic triumph we achieved in April of 1975, when we suffered 91 casualties, including 41 dead, to rescue, along with America's honor, 38 crewmen of the *S.S. Mayaguez* who appeared on the verge of being released anyway.

Of course, the rescue attempt did suggest, at a time when certain doubts had developed, that we cared as much for the hostages as we did for the Shah, and that the President was doing everything he could to gain their release. It also helped to raise world sympathy on behalf of the United States, and against the Khomeini regime.

Most of our policy-makers, however, do not worry much about world sympathy. They do not even operate on the moral plane—a fact in which they take some pride as hard-headed realists. They recognize that political leverage is gained from exploiting moral issues in the court of public opinion. If they tell us America has been wronged, and that it is time to make America strong again, that is because they know that money will flow into the Pentagon coffers, and that anger and fear will turn the tide of opinion against critics of interventionism, freeing us to do what they genuinely believe must be done.

To these men, the crisis of Iran was not related to some hostages about whose fate they suspected little might be done, or to our role in Iran's history, which most of them would repeat tomorrow if given the chance. To them, the crisis was simply the loss of a regime on which we depended heavily for a decade to protect what they saw as vital interests in the Persian Gulf.

### The Power Vacuum in the Persian Gulf

This special dependency on the Shah dates back to the violent terrorism that flared against the British in Aden in 1967, culminating in Great Britain's decision to withdraw most of its forces from the Persian Gulf by 1971. In 1969, in response

to that decision, a United States National Security Decision Memorandum (NSDM-92) determined that we could not take over the British role without incurring the same risks, and without meeting opposition at home from critics of intervention who were then quite powerful. It was preferable, therefore, that we form a cooperative alliance with the Shah to ensure regional stability. In return for the vast supply of American arms which began to flow into Iran early in 1970 as a result of this policy, and the extravagant costs of which were to wreak havoc with Iran's economy, the Shah took his role of regional policeman seriously indeed—using his troops, for example, to help Oman's Sultan Qabus Sa'id overcome the leftist Popular Front uprising in Dhofar.

It was the Shah, we are told, who kept the Soviets out of the Persian Gulf, and whose departure leaves a power vacuum we must now fill by taking up a direct role ourselves. The need for this is all the more urgent because the threat is alleged to have grown. The Soviets, the CIA tells us, face a decline in oil production in the 1980s and are more desperate than ever for new supplies.

Among those who dispute this apprehension is Marshall Goldman, a professor of economics at Wellesley and a specialist on Soviet resources, who reported in *The New York Times* that contrary to any sign of a future decline in Soviet oil production, the USSR has actually improved productivity through more efficient production technology, and has also adopted strong oil conservation measures whose purpose is necessarily to mitigate dependence on any external source of supply.

In any case, for the Soviets the costs of intervention in the Persian Gulf would probably far exceed the gains. While that is equally true for the United States, our Rapid Deployment Force has nonetheless been presented as the means of meeting this new threat.

Aside from the doubtful reality of the threat, the feasibility of countering it in this way bears examination. In this scenario, our planners conceive of the Rapid Deployment Force as a tripwire, deployed

rapidly enough to arrive at some point in the Persian Gulf before Soviet forces can get there, thus placing responsibility fully upon them for the commencement of hostilities. This is supposed to give them pause from engaging us in combat, as though they had lost the game.

It seems more probable that if the Soviets invaded, they already would have accepted responsibility for engaging us in combat, whether or not we arrived before them. If we arrived first, we could not be sure this would deter them any more than if they arrived first, they could be sure that would deter us. Unable to rule out the possibility of combat, regardless of timing, they would be fully prepared for a fight, and a fight would ensue. Neither side could pause. The rules of the game get broken.

In fact, the only rule in combat is that the force threatened with defeat breaks the rules. The further implication of this is that once hostilities have begun between the two superpowers, there is no assured way of controlling their escalation. This is why a confrontation of any kind between them in the Persian Gulf, the Horn of Africa or anywhere else, is a contingency both nations must avoid.

If the tripwire strategy is bankrupt, and a Soviet invasion of the Persian Gulf too dangerous and too far-fetched for other reasons, that doesn't diminish the likelihood of any of several other contingencies in an area of the world that has always been fraught with economic, political and religious conflict. War could break out between a pair of neighboring Persian Gulf states. A political upheaval in any one of them could threaten its future relations with the West. It would be difficult, for example, to predict the consequences of a fundamentalist Islamic uprising against the ruling Wahhabi conservatives in Saudi Arabia.

### The Yemen Crisis

Such contingencies seem bound to provoke American action, and the credible threat of such action, our government believes, helps to prevent their occurrence. When war broke out between the two Yemens in February of 1979, President Carter ordered the carrier *USS Constellation* and three other vessels from Subic Bay to the Indian Ocean for a traditional show of the flag. On March 9 he invoked, for the first time in history, an emergency provision of the Arms Export Control Act to circumvent, on grounds of a threat to our national security, the requirement for Congressional approval of the immediate sale and delivery to North Yemen of 12 F-5E fighter aircraft, two C-130 Hercules transport aircraft, 64 M-60A1 tanks, 50 M-113 armoured personnel carriers and 72 M-167 Vulcan antiaircraft guns, all worth a total of $383 million.

Arthur Schlesinger, Jr., writing in *The New York Times*, wondered against whom this equipment might be used in the future, just as many Americans continue to wonder how the immense arsenal of American equipment in Iran might be used.

What was less clear to the public was that on March 2, a week before this emergency decision was made, North and South Yemen had already signed a ceasefire agreement negotiated by the Arab League. What was not known at all was that the arms we insisted on sending anyway were part of a larger request submitted by North Yemen on February 12, including additional antiaircraft guns, howitzers and antitank missiles—the whole shipment valued at $540 million, all of which was to be paid by the Saudi Arabians, who had earlier supplied North Yemen with 50 M-113s of their own. What has only recently emerged, in the testimony before a House Military Affairs subcommittee of John J. Ruszkiewics, former military attache to North Yemen, is that this equipment was not intended for the defense of Yemen but simply to keep its president in power.

The *Constellation* appeared in the Indian Ocean on March 16, well after the ceasefire. Nevertheless, a recent issue of *Forbes* magazine, arguing for a stronger Navy, commented that when the task force appeared and the arms were delivered to North Yemen, ''the Soviet surrogates got the point. They backed off.'' Since they had backed off before any of this happened, *Forbes* possibly meant that we were now assured of North Yemen's allegiance.

Yet that is no more clear than it ever has been in the case of any other recipient of American arms, or of anyone else to whom we have shown the flag. In June of 1979, as if to confirm Mr. Schlesinger's doubts, North Yemen signed an agreement with the Soviet Union for delivery of no less than 500 T-55 tanks, 40 Mig-21 and 22 Su-22 aircraft, 65 SAM-6 mobile antiaircraft missiles and 18 ZSU-23 self-propelled antiaircraft guns from Soviet and Warsaw Pact stocks. If arms are of

any influence at all, then which power has the stronger influence in North Yemen is anyone's guess.

On our part, the episode appears to have been a whimsical domestic political gesture, as if to show that we could act quickly and decisively. But what quick and decisive action can we really take? How can we actually implement our policy of taking up a direct role in the Persian Gulf? If we introduce our Rapid Deployment Force, that will presumably be in an attempt to secure our oil supplies and the route of oil to the West. But is that a feasible mission?

We would be faced with the gargantuan task of preserving intact and simultaneously operating 700 oil wells and 150 processing plants connected by more than 7,000 miles of pipeline over an area, most of it desert, larger than all of Western Europe. To accomplish this would require an American civil and military presence larger than that committed at its peak to Southeast Asia, at a cost far beyond the value of the oil we consume from this part of the world, and also well above the expected investment required to develop alternate energy supplies.

That, of course, doesn't mean we would flinch from such a task. We would more likely welcome it as a salve to the recent frustrations of our policy objectives abroad. In view of our record, it is difficult not to assume that we now anticipate, and are possibly attempting to bring about, political changes in the Persian Gulf that would justify establishing an American presence there *before* any conflict breaks out to threaten our oil supplies. All we need, as our more intrepid planners certainly realize, is a new Ngo Dinh Diem, or to take the latest Soviet example, a new Babrak Karmal, followed by the inevitable request for American assistance.

### The Role of the Oil Conglomerates

If we are willing to risk so much, at such a staggering cost, when our actual consumption of Persian Gulf oil is lower than that of Japan or of Western Europe, and when the safer, less costly—and less bloody—option exists of developing alter-

nate energy sources, that is only because our oil conglomerates do not plan to surrender the substantial profits they make from supplying this oil. They also foresee less profit from alternate sources of energy, in which they have not made a comparable investment.

In 1970, a President's Cabinet group studying oil imports found that the United States and Canadian oil fields could produce 92 percent of our 1980 consumption without rationing, even if we were wholly cut off not only from Middle Eastern but from South American supplies as well. Yet the Arab embargo of Middle Eastern oil in 1973 was held responsible for the continuing spiral of higher prices of gasoline and heating fuel that has afflicted this country since, bringing about almost insupportably high housing and transportation costs to millions of Americans—when in fact the flow of oil to the West was not reduced at all. It was our own government which cooperated with this deception in the hope that higher prices would cause conservation of a resource it knew was finite—though it has not dared risk much interference in the sanctity of private enterprise in order properly to regulate its supply.

These alleged shortages, comprising probably the greatest fraud ever perpetrated upon the American public, did little to improve conservation, but have achieved record profits for the oil companies, including a 56 percent increase in Exxon's 1979 profits, totalling $4.3 billion out of gross earnings for that firm of $84.4 billion—a figure that is itself slightly higher than the entire gross national product of Sweden.

It was only in May of 1979 that the Department of Energy, identifying 109 cases of possible fraud including price manipulation and false resales of crude oil supplies, accused seven leading oil importers of overcharging consumers by $1.7 billion since 1974. Representative John Conyers, chairman of the House Judiciary Subcommittee on Energy and Power, announced that our government was ''sitting on top of the largest criminal conspiracy in America, that is costing the American public billions of dollars.'' Meanwhile, Rawleigh Warner, Jr., chairman of Mobil, increased his salary by 27 percent last year to $1.187 million.

Though the major oil companies have made use of enormous advertising budgets to inform the public that they are reinvesting their profits in research and development and the search for alternate energy sources, they have in fact been increasing their control over the existing energy market by investing in other established energy concerns. Mobil recently purchased General Crude for $782 million. Exxon purchased Reliance Electric for $1.1 billion. They have also been investing in businesses not related to energy at all. Senator Howard Metzenbaum has listed 21 such proposed acquisitions in 1980 worth a total of $2.6 billion, including Gulf's proposal to purchase Ringling Brothers Circus.

While 98 percent of Federal land in the United States, much of which may contain large oil reserves, remains unexplored because it would yield a lower margin of profit, Mobil spent just $86 million, or 7 percent of its $1.2 billion in 1979 profits after taxes, in research and development.

What is needed is a reform of the oil industry, on a scale to match the reforms which decentralized the utility industry in 1928. Instead, the attitude of the government is best expressed by the Ford administration's Interior Secretary Rogers B. Morton, who at a White House briefing in 1974 told a group of oil industry managers: ''Our mission is to serve you, not to regulate you.'' Rather than jeopardize their interests, we will remain committed to Persian Gulf oil.

Among the risks of this wholly avoidable dependency is a variety of economic threats. However much the oil producers of the Gulf depend on us, in turn, for technology and as a market, they can afford to withdraw from that market if political factors seem to warrant economic action against us. In order to influence United States policies in the Middle East, for example, a Gulf state could threaten to raise its prices to an intolerable level, or to reduce its output, or fully to boycott American oil importers.

Saudi Arabia is powerful enough that it could threaten to ruin the dollar by accepting payment only in other currencies. It could threaten to create financial chaos in the West by withdrawing its vast deposits from American banks, or by selling its extensive holdings in American Treasury bills. This capacity, together with our determination to replace Iran with Saudi Arabia as our new military proxy in the Persian Gulf, lies at the heart of our willingness to accede to the Saudi demand that we sell them advanced AIM-9L Sidewinder air munitions, FAST Pack

conformal fuel pallets, bomb ejector racks, seven KC-135 tanker aircraft and five E-3C AWACS command and surveillance aircraft to support the force of F-15 fighter aircraft they purchased earlier, even though we promised Israel that we would never allow the Saudis this additional equipment in view of the added threat it would pose to Israel's security. It is also at the heart of our inability to extract from the Saudis, in return for this new sale, a commitment to the support of the Treaty of Peace between Egypt and Israel, and thus to the promotion of stability in the Middle East for which all this equipment is presumably designed. Our continued dependency on Saudi good will, on which our oil conglomerates insist, has even brought about our betrayal of our best ally in the Middle East.

### The Price of Peace in the Middle East

The single issue that has most stirred Arab feeling against America, that continues to deny us stable relations with the oil producing countries, and that adversely affects our relations with the entire Third World, is the question of a Palestinian homeland. Despite the Camp David Accords, the Framework for peace and the ratification, in April of 1979, of a Peace Treaty between Egypt and Israel, the solution for the Palestinians seems no closer at hand. Since that time, an adversary attitude has developed again, each party encouraging the other's intransigence, ''each allowing the other,'' in the words of Egypt's Foreign Minister Boutros Ghali, ''to escape responsibilities.''

Israel has now claimed all of Jerusalem as its capital, and will not move its settlements from the West bank of the Jordan. The Palestinians are represented only by terrorist organizations. Israel will not deal with terrorists, and so cannot deal with the Palestinians. The Begin administration, worried that Israel will cease to become a Jewish state, has unwittingly moved it closer to becoming a racist one. The Arab nations will not even accept the principle of Israel's right to exist.

The American administration, quick to condemn Arab obstinacy, hesitates to censure Israeli excesses for fear of losing

the Jewish vote—though many American Jews have made it clear they no longer condone the Begin administration's extremist policies. The Soviets have been excluded entirely from participation in the Palestinian talks, with the result that they would prefer to encourage instablility in the Middle East than see a purely Western solution. Much of the Middle Eastern arms race might otherwise have been avoided.

Paradoxically, in an attempt to seal the fragile peace that exists, we have raised this arms race to a new level. Over the next five years, the American taxpayer will fund a Treaty commitment to Egypt and Israel of $5 billion in military and economic aid, which must be added to prior commitments, continuing for the forseeable future, of $1.8 billion annually to both countries. That means that within the next five years the total United States contribution to this imperfect effort at peace will probably exceed $14 billion, making it the largest single aid program this country has undertaken since the Marshall Plan that followed World War II.

Under our Military Assistance Plan of grant aid, Egypt received $750 million in 1978, while Israel received $300 million, together with an additional $800 million in cash loans—$500 million of which was exempt from repayment, following a custom with Israel that will probably continue for many years. Of the $5 billion Treaty allotment of aid, Egypt will recieve $2 billion—$1.5 billion in cash loans and Foreign Military Sales credits, and $500 million in grant aid. Israel's $3 billion under the Treaty allotment comprises $2.2 billion in cash loans, and $800 million in military grant aid to be used to build two new airbases in the Negev, replacing some of the bases Israel lost on withdrawing from the Sinai.

For Egypt, these sums will purchase 35 F-4 Phantom fighter aircraft that have already been delivered, 1,350 M-113A2 armoured personnel carriers, 300 M-60A3 tanks, 43 M-88A1 armoured recovery vehicles, 12 mobile Triad batteries of Improved HAWK antiaircraft missiles, Maverick, Sidewinder and Sparrow aircraft munitions, and at a later date, 40 F-16 fighter aircraft, four destroyers, a submarine and 12 Sea Spectre naval patrol boats.

As part of a series of sales of aircraft to the Middle East—linked by President Carter in 1978 to the controversial sale, for which he knew he could not otherwise gain approval from Congress, of 60 advanced F-15 Eagle fighter interceptor aircraft to Saudi Arabia—Egypt had also expected to take delivery of 42 F-5E and 8 F-5F Tiger II aircraft, the $590 million bill for which Saudi Arabia had agreed to pay, together with the costs of munitions, spares and support that would have brought the total to $730 million. However, after President Sadat's peace initiatives later that year, Saudi Arabia withdrew from this commitment, and the aircraft have not been delivered.

The aid to Israel will in part purchase 200 M-60A3 tanks, 800 M-113A2 armoured personnel cariers, 200 M-109 155mm self-propelled howitzers, 200 M-107 175mm self-propelled guns, Maverick and Sidewinder aircraft munitions, and 55 F-16 fighter aircraft that had originally been in production toward fulfillment of an Iranian order for 160 aircraft of this type—an order subsequently cancelled by the Khomeini government. Another 75 F-16s from this production run will later be purchased for Israel's *Heyl Ha' Avir*, which will also soon begin receiving 25 additional F-15 Eagle fighter interceptor aircraft, eventually raising its total inventory of the Eagle to 65. That is only the beginning of what Israel wants. It has also requested permission to co-produce the F-16, as well as our Navy's new F-18 Hornet fighter aircraft. Former defense minister Ezer Weizman's plan for Israel's defense, known as Matmon C, sought a total of $10 billion in arms from the United States through 1985. "A billion dollars," Mr. Weizman observed, "simply isn't what it used to be."

### The American Arsenal in Iran

The diversion to Israel of F-16 aircraft originally intended for Iran is but one example of our prompt action to find new recipients for arms ordered by the Shah but cancelled by his successor. Seven Boeing E-3A AWACS command and surveillance aircraft, sold to Iran in 1978 for $1.2 billion, will be delivered instead to NATO, which plans to deploy 18 of them to augment its battlefield control system.

When Iran cancelled its contract, valued at $1.6 billion, for four *Spruance* class destroyers under construction by Litton, President Carter obtained approval from Congress in February of 1979 for a supplemental defense budget appropriation of $765 million to purchase two of the vessels for our own Navy. *Spruance* class destroyers built to our Navy's specifications that year were valued at $543

million each, so that at first this additional purchase seemed an economical means of expanding our destroyer fleet. But it was afterward learned that the cost of modifications required to upgrade these ships to Navy standards would exceed the amount saved.

Nevertheless, had measures such as these not quickly been taken to find new buyers at home and abroad for weapons already in production for Iran, that country's cancellation of nearly $10 billion in American arms would have presented a serious setback for our defense industry. The industry's fears of reduced profitability were also relieved by a sharp increase in the sales of other weapons to Jordan, to North Yemen and the Sudan, and to Saudi Arabia—which not only paid for most of the arms acquired by these other Arab states but has also, since Iran announced its cancellations, purchased $2.2 billion in American arms of its own, and requested $1.5 billion more. In the wake of Iran's withdrawal from the arms market, the Saudis have also assumed preeminence as America's foremost arms client, having accumulated a total of $22.2 billion in purchases of military equipment and services from the United States since 1974.

Yet the single most important measure to offset the loss of arms sales to Iran, contributing a sum by itself equal to more than half of that loss, remains the massive increase in military grant aid allotted to Egypt and Israel as signatories of the Middle Eastern Treaty of Peace. Because grant aid is appropriated from Federal revenues to pay full market value to manufacturers for arms to be transferred abroad, the American taxpayer has once again played a pivotal role in the rescue of a defense industry that would have suffered heavy losses, not only in jobs but in profits, from Iran's change of government.

Of the awesome stock of American equipment delivered to Iran before the Shah's demise, much has fallen into disrepair, lacking not only replacement parts which we generally refused to send, but also the maintenance help once provided by 45,000 American military and civilian technicians whom we have long since withdrawn.

In best condition, at the outset of Iran's war with Iraq, were Iranian F-4D and F-4E Phantom fighter-bombers, F-5E and F-5F Tiger II fighter interceptors, and C-130E and C-130H Hercules transport aircraft. Iran's force of several hundred Boeing, Bell and Sikorsky helicopers, on the other hand, was only 31 percent operational at the start of that war. Of its main battle tanks of American manufacture, approximately 72 percent were operational.

Over $550 million in spare parts for much of this equipment was blocked from shipment to Iran after the seizure of the hostages, and while some of that material still awaits clearance at McGuire Air Force Base in New Jersey, most of it has been returned to military supply depots. Because it was already paid for, it is included among the Iranian assets to be returned under the terms of the hostage agreement. Secretary of State Alexander Haig, however, has vowed that no military equipment will be shipped to Iran from this country. No matter. The Khomeini regime doesn't want most of it. For the cost of whatever is not shipped, Iran will have to be reimbursed.

The most controversial of Iran's weapons are the 80 advanced F-14A Tomcat fighter interceptors ordered by the Shah in 1974 for $1.9 billion. Of these, 56 are now stationed at Isfahan and 21 at Shiraz, while two others crashed in training and a third is undergoing repairs in the United States. These are the aircraft fitted with the highly classified Hughes AN/AWG-9 fire control radar, which the Iranians claim to have removed and safeguarded. Damage assessments conducted by our intelligence agencies, with the participation of British intelligence, conclude that by now secrets of the radar's technology should be considered compromised. As a result, several changes have been made in the radar's circuitry on our own aircraft of this type, as well as in the command and homing circuitry of the Phoenix missiles it guides, to defeat such countermeasures as may have been developed. The costs of these changes, and therefore the costs of having relinquished control over such technology through the original sale of the F-14 to Iran, have so far run in excess of $285 million.

Iran has offered to sell these aircraft back to us for a reasonable price, substantially lower than their original purchase price. This might have given our Navy the opportunity to purchase a large number of front-line interceptors, which it claims it desperately needs, at a significant saving. But industry representatives persuaded the Pentagon that the offer should be rejected, because the purchase would lower the Navy's future F-14 procurement on which the manufacturer had already planned—albeit at a higher price—and the loss of such sales would lower the manufacturer's anticipated revenues, affecting future profitability. Clearly, sacrifices in the name of national defense are not being made by all Americans.

The past three years, then, have seen not ony a substantial increase in the volume of our arms sales abroad, but also a major expansion of our foreign military aid—adding heavily to the taxpayer's burden, while the effects of both these programs on our policy aims abroad remain heavily in doubt. Seldom is the allegiance of a foreign nation assured. Rarely can we rest in the certainty that we have preserved the peace. Despite the fact that our expenditure over the past decade of over $1 trillion on military power has wholly failed to improve our ability to control world events, we are going ahead and devoting a growing proportion of our defense budget to the projection of more American power abroad, from the acquisition of additional military bases to the creation of new mobility forces, all designed to meet contingencies that may be neither a threat to us nor even likely to occur.

**American Military Power Overseas**
Yet an even larger portion of our military budget goes toward support of American military forces that have already been established throughout the world. Just one of our military services, the Air Force, this year maintains 2,813 airbases and other installations worldwide, supporting three air wings in Asia and another eight in Europe. Our 1980 budget for the operation and maintenance of all forces was $43.4 billion. This supported, among other units, the 39,000 members of the Second Infantry Division in Korea, elements of the 25th Infantry Division in Hawaii, 14,000 military personnel in the Philippines, a brigade of infantry each in Alaska, Panama and the city of Berlin, and our entire Seventh Army in Europe, which includes the 1st and 3rd Armoured and 3rd and 8th Mechanized Infantry Divisions together with three additional brigades and two armoured cavalry regiments.

To garrison 46,000 members of the Third Marine Division and one Marine Air Wing in Okinawa costs the taxpayer $1 billion a year. That is equivalent to Japan's entire 1980 defense budget, which represents a much smaller percentage of gross national product than does our own. This exercise of restraint is a key factor in Japan's much higher rate of productivity. Indeed, since the end of World War II, the rapid economic recovery and impressive commercial success of both West Germany and Japan has been due in no small part to the restrictions the Allies imposed on their postwar activities. These restrictions, incidentally, are now being relaxed. That is because today we trust these former enemies more than we trust the Soviet Union, a nation we have never fought, even though they have shown as great a propensity as have the Soviets for occupying territories not their own.

The major reason for our rapid increase in defense spending in the past few years, and for the further increases planned in the next five, is to strengthen those forces, both conventional and strategic, designed to meet what we perceive as the key threat to world peace: the Soviet Union's growing power to wage war. This year we will spend $51.9 billion for the improvement and expansion of general purpose forces and another $10.9 billion for strategic forces. Procurement of new weapons and equipment will rise from $35.8 billion in 1980 to $44.2 billion in 1981. These sums are required, we are told, to catch up with Soviet expenditures, which promise otherwise to give the Soviets a dangerous lead upsetting the balance of power.

**The Soviet Threat**
That final formulation, the pivotal argument in all appeals for added military funds, involves a number of questionable assumptions. Are the Soviets really spending more than we are? Does the nation that spends more get more? Does the military superiority of one necessarily pose a threat to the other? Has there ever really been a balance of power? Is there likely to be one? Does it matter whether such a balance exists, if there are suffi-

cient forces, in any case, to deter aggression? Does each superpower possess a credible deterrent? If evidence in the answers to these questions contradicts what our military establishment tells us, why is our military establishment saying what it says?

"Since 1970," President Reagan announced in February of 1981, "the Soviet Union has invested $300 billion more in its military forces than we have." What is startling about this statement is that there is no way for the President or anyone else to be sure it is true. It was based on an estimate from the CIA that had been released only days before. The agency claimed that over the last decade the Soviet Union had spent 40 percent more than the United States on defense activities.

This was an odd claim, in light of another estimate released by the CIA only a year before, when it reported that for the past decade Soviet defense spending had been running about 30 percent higher than in the United States. Are we to believe that in one year the Soviet Union increased its margin of investment over ours by an additional 10 percent? Apparently not, because at the same time the agency gave its new estimate, it stated that since 1976 American investment had grown faster than estimated Soviet investment.

This discrepancy can only be explained as the result of another of the CIA's revised estimates. Each time these estimates have been revised, the agency has lost a further degree of credibility in presenting them. The most serious loss of credibility occured in December of 1976, when a significant revision gave rise to the official conclusion that the Soviet Union was engaged in a massive arms buildup.

Actually, there were two CIA estimates that year, one made by the agency's regular analysts and the other by a special panel of academics and former defense officials known as Team B. The regular analysts concluded that industry in the USSR was far less efficient than they had previously supposed, and that the ruble's purchasing power was weaker than they had allowed. Consequently, they decided, for many years defense had been absorbing not 5 or 6 percent of that country's gross national product, as they had estimated before, but between 11 and 13 percent. This did not affect their estimate of the *amount* of defense equipment produced each year in the Soviet Union, but merely its value as a proportion of Soviet GNP.

Team B interpreted this reassessment to mean that the Soviets had just doubled their rate of expenditure, and had begun to produce twice as much military equipment as in previous years. It meant nothing of the kind. Nevertheless, Team B's conclusion was adopted as the official CIA estimate by its director, who was then George Bush.

It was Bush who had called in Team B, among whose members were Richard Pipes of Harvard University and William R. Van Cleave of the University of Southern California, both of whom later became Reagan advisors. Also on Team B were Paul Nitze, former deputy Secretary of Defense and delegate to the SALT talks, who today heads The Committee on the Present Danger, and Lieutenant General Daniel O. Graham, former director of the Defense Intelligence Agency and a member today of the American Security Council. Mr. Nitze's Committee and General Graham's Council are both private organizations dedicated to informing the public about the Soviet threat. The latter group includes two former chairmen of the Joint Chiefs of Staff, no fewer than 2,544 retired admirals and generals, and such luminaries as James Angleton, former Chief of Counterintelligence for the CIA, and Dr. Edward Teller, the man who helped invent the bomb which helped create the problem he and his fellow Council members now presumably address.

In January of 1980 the CIA reported that the Soviet Union would spend an estimated equivalent of $165 billion on defense in the following year, a figure that was bound to be compared with our own 1980 budget of $139.3 billion for defense. While less dramatic than the agency's estimates for the previous decade, this figure still suggests a Soviet spending margin of 18 percent over ours, and gives seeming cause for alarm.

These estimates begin, of course, with a list of what the Soviets have added to their arsenal in a given year, together with a tally of the number of personnel, in their armed forces. We would then expect to learn what is spent for all of this in rubles, and next have that converted into dollars, whose buying power is familiar to us. This process risks distortions. The official exchange rates do not adequately relate the purchasing power of the ruble in the USSR to that of the dollar in the

United States. But at least we would know how many rubles were being spent, and what they were paying for.

This information is certainly available. The CIA knows perfectly well how many rubles Soviet procurement agencies are charged for each tank, and how many of each kind of tank are produced in a given year, as well as what the average Soviet soldier is paid. Rather than offer these figures, the agency offers instead an estimate of what it would cost in dollars to purchase the same number of comparable weapons at current American prices charged by American industry, and to pay the same number of personnel by American pay standards.

We must look to the Swedish International Peace Research Institute (SIPRI) in Stockholm, and to the International Institute for Strategic Studies (IISS) in London, for more accurate assessments of the Soviet Union's expenditures on defense. Both institutions note that the Soviet government gives the figure of 17.1 billion rubles for the Soviet military budget in 1980. At the official exchange rate of $1.60, that is equivalent to $27.4 billion, less than 17 percent of the "comparable dollar estimate" offered by the CIA.

Both institutions agree that actual Soviet expenditures in 1980 were higher than $27.4 billion, but also agree that this figure is less misleading than the figure offered by the CIA. IISS, which will not make an estimate of its own, notes that "estimating how much it would cost to produce and man the equivalent of the Soviet defence effort in the USA tends to overstate the Soviet defence effort."

SIPRI goes further. Even though it gives the ruble maximum purchasing power, converting rubles into dollars at a higher rate of exchange, and so raising their dollar equivalent, its figures still show American military expenditures exceeding those in the Soviet Union by a wide margin every year for the past decade. In 1977, SIPRI says, our spending exceeded that in the USSR by 44 percent. If the SIPRI figures are adjusted to the official exchange rate, our margin of spending in that year increased to 93 percent. By the same token, we outspent

the Soviets in 1979 by 67 percent, and in 1980 by 80 percent.

The CIA's method of estimating Soviet expenditures achieves its inflated proportions in several ways. The method assumes, first of all, that price is related to value in the same way in both economies. It is no more simple to determine true value in a forced production economy than in a free enterprise one, though we strongly suspect there is underpricing in the former, and we already know there is overpricing in the latter. This means that the Soviets will generally pay less than we would have to pay for the same equipment. The inflated estimate offers us only the options of ignoring that likelihood, or of accepting it and thereby gaining the impression that the Soviet military purchases more equipment than it actually does.

The method next assumes that the same equipment is involved, utilizing materials of equal value in both economies. There is seldom any comparable equipment at all. In the *Bulletin of the Atomic Scientists*, the economist Franklyn Holzman pointed out that nations adjust their patterns of production to make use of their most abundant resources rather than scarce ones, and to draw on technical capabilities already developed rather than emphasizing more advanced and more costly technology. It costs the Soviets more rubles to purchase microchips and printed circuitry than it would cost us if we used the same rubles in the United States. It costs us more dollars to purchase titanium than it would cost the Soviets if they used our dollars in the Soviet Union. The result is equipment employing different materials, and different proportions of the same materials, which have different values to the nations that produced them.

Most of our military equipment is more sophisticated, employing much higher technology than characterizes the mass of Soviet equipment. This is partly the result of our quest for superior quality and, precisely because of its higher cost, partly the choice of American industry. However, the more sophisticated Soviet weapons require an even greater effort from Soviet industry than they would from American industry. Former Defense Secretary Harold Brown has noted that "the Soviets probably have to invest more resources than we do to achieve a comparable military result."

So it is important to know precisely

what equipment the CIA is talking about. If the comparison leaves us with a lower total expenditure, that may only mean that the Soviets are producing fewer high technology weapons, and that we are defeating them in quality. If the comparison leaves us with a higher expenditure, it could still mean the Soviets were producing more low technology weapons, and defeating us in mass.

Further serious distortion takes place in the assumption that Soviet military salaries have been brought up to a level comparable with ours, so that the Soviet Army, more than double ours in size, appears to consume twice as much of a comparable dollar expenditure. In fact, Soviet soldiers are paid 40 percent less than the average wages of Soviet civilians, who in turn are paid 60 percent less than the average wages of American workers. In 1975, according to the Department of the Army's *Handbook on Soviet Ground Forces* (FM 30-40), a Soviet soldier was paid only $5.00 a month as a private. That figure has risen today to four rubles, the equivalent of $6.40 at the official rate of exchange. American base pay, however, is now $500 per month. To assign the Soviet soldier an equivalent pay, as the CIA does, is therefore both deliberately and flagrantly misleading.

The margin of error produced by this particular distortion increases each time we raise our military pay, and simultaneously pretend that Soviet forces have received an equivalent raise. The larger number of Soviet military personnel gives the total Soviet defense expenditure what is made to seem a proportionately larger increase over ours. John O'Grady of the Center for Defense Information notes that "under this statistical construct the faster we run the further behind we get."

In reality, despite the greater number of personnel on the Soviet military payroll, that payroll in comparable costs is but a fraction of our own.

Nor is the CIA's estimate compared with the same aggregate of our own activities which the agency admits are included in its Soviet figure. To make a proper comparison with its estimated Soviet expenditure of $165 billion in 1980, we would have to add to our own 1980 defense budget of $139.3 billion another $4.7 billion for the military exploration of space, $2.8 billion for civil defense, $2 billion for the manufacture of warheads budgeted to the Department of Energy, and $20.5 billion for the Veterans Admin-

istration. This brings the total of comparable spending in the United States to $169.3 billion, rather higher than even the CIA's inflated figure for the USSR.

Despite the distortions in the CIA estimates, which SIPRI says are "wholly misleading for virtually any purpose," and despite the availability of more accurate comparisons, most of the American public, the press and even Congress accepts the CIA figures without questioning their legitimacy or the purpose behind them. The purpose is not obscure. Stephen Johnson of the University of Oregon reminds us that within days after the Carter administration first took office on the promise that it would support detente, the CIA's estimate of Soviet defense expenditures was revised upward by more than 25 percent. SIPRI notes that the "clear bias in propositions about Soviet military expenditures" has been "central to presentation of the threat," and calls the result "a successful propaganda exercise," chiefly responsible for large increases in spending by the North Atlantic Treaty Organization.

Indeed, a more relevant comparison than that between ourselves and the Soviet Union, and one less clouded by estimates from the CIA, is that between the level of spending by NATO countries and spending by the countries of the Warsaw Pact. This comparison, available from SIPRI, the IISS and the Center of Defense Information in Washington, indicates that NATO spending exceeded the estimated spending of the Warsaw Pact each year through the 1970s, ending in 1979 with a total of $212 billion in NATO expenditures against an estimated total of $175 billion for the Warsaw Pact. Former Secretary of Defense Harold Brown estimates that in the past decade NATO outspent the Warsaw Pact by $318 billion.

## The Military Balance in Europe

If comparisons of spending cannot be persuasive once public opinion is properly informed, comparisons may be made of manpower and equipment. These, however, must be highly selective in order to magnify the threat. We are told, for example, that the Soviet Navy is stronger than

ours in all parts of the world. In the Indian Ocean, it is said, the Soviets have 21 ships while we have only 17. We are not told that this comparison includes all Soviet vessels but only our surface combatants, that 16 of the Soviets vessels are support ships, leaving them only 5 surface combatants to our 17, and that our support ships in the area, an additional 15 vessels, raise our actual total of ships there to 32. Nor are we told that there is a total of 54 NATO ships in the Indian Ocean, including 14 French and 8 British vessels. In addition to our naval base at Diego Garcia, and to our newly arranged access to the ports of Mombasa, Berbera, Ras Benas, Qabus, and Raysut, the Reagan administration is now negotiating for the use of Karachi as a naval base, in return for more than $1 billion in military aid to Pakistan over the next two years.

Nonetheless, it is pointed out, the Soviet Navy has 1,764 ships while the US Navy has only 462. Of the Soviet vessels, 1,045 are mine warfare, patrol or auxiliary types, but the USSR still has 269 major surface combatants against our 178. This does not take into account that Soviet surface combatants are for the most part confined to single salvos from antiship missiles, while each of ours is a floating munitions depot capable of sustained fire from guns and missile launchers for several hours. Nor does it consider that our ships employ much higher technology in fire control, missile guidance, radar, antiaircraft, antimissile defense and antisubmarine warfare systems.

There is no mention of the fact that the Soviet Navy has 50 nuclear attack submarines, while we have 75, or that the Soviets have 870 naval combat aircraft while we have 1,820, 1,100 of which are deployed on aircraft carriers—of which we have 13 while the USSR has two. Most important of all, the pleas for a stronger Navy overlook the fact that the Soviets must maintain fleets in the Black Sea, the Baltic and Barents Seas and the Sea of Japan, where they may easily be denied access to the open oceans, as recent NATO exercises have shown. Because many Soviet surface combatants are consequently stationed outside the NATO area, NATO holds the preponderance of naval force, with 485 surface combatants on station against the Warsaw Pact's 195. This gives NATO a two-to-one advantage in tonnage alone, aside from the technological superiority and incomparable lethality of these vessels.

Our Navy already has 109 more ships under construction, and 60 of these will have joined our fleet by 1985.

If the Soviet naval threat vanishes, there is still the vast armada of Soviet aircraft, giving the Warsaw Pact a numerical superiority of 5,745 aircraft against the commonly-cited figure for NATO of 3,300. However, this NATO figure does not include the U.S. Navy's entire strength of 1,100 carrier-borne aircraft, 400 French combat aircraft, and an additional 100 dual-purpose NATO aircraft capable of a combat role. Almost all of these would be committed to any outbreak of hostilities in Western Europe, raising the actual NATO complement of aircraft to 4,900. An additional 807 Tornado multi-role combat aircraft now being added to the British, Italian and West German Air Forces brings NATO air strength very close to numerical parity.

NATO planners know this, of course. They also know that most of the Soviet Union's aircraft are committed to an air defense role, and that of its 16 tactical air armies the USSR has committed just four, comprising 1,700 aircraft, to the Warsaw Pact. They know that among these are only 530 of the 1,750 MiG-23s so far produced. They know that most of the remaining aircraft, including almost all of those deployed by other nations of the Warsaw Pact, were built in the 1950s and 1960s, including large numbers of MiG-17s and MiG-21s. Czechoslovakia has just twelve MiG-23s, and Bulgaria two.

Therefore, NATO planners know that the major proportion of Warsaw Pact aircraft cannot perform competitively against ours. NATO has a higher proportion of multi-purpose aircraft, and almost all its aircraft have far more advanced navigation, flight control, weapons delivery and electronic countermeasures systems. Of highly advanced aircraft, only 300 MiG-27Ds and 250 MiG-25s have been produced to date, as compared with 600 U.S. Air Force F-15s and 350 U.S. Navy F-14s already in service.

Manpower comparisons are another means of raising fear of the Soviet threat. It is usually pointed out that of its 3,650,000 uniformed personnel, the Soviet Union has 1,825,000 in its Army, while the U.S. Army musters only 774,000. However, 800,000 Soviet soldiers, including six armoured and 40 motor rifle divisions, together with 25 percent of Soviet tactical air strength, have been

assigned to the defense of a border with China that is 5,813 miles long. This new adversary in the east musters 4,445,000 in its military services, including 3,600,000 in the Chinese Army.

Just 600,000 Soviet Army troops are committed to the Warsaw Pact, and 25 percent of these, according to NATO Commander-in-Chief General Bernard W. Rogers, "are there to maintain the reliability of Pact forces," including four guard divisions in Hungary and five in Czechoslovakia. Since 1967 the USSR has added 25 divisions to its Chinese border, bringing its total strength there to 46 divisions, while in the same period it has added only 4 divisions to the Warsaw Pact, which now includes just 30 Soviet divisions.

Today there are 64 active NATO divisions pitted against 68 in the Warsaw Pact, which seems to suggest that the Pact has an edge in manpower. The reverse is true. NATO has a standing force of 2,800,000 compared with the Pact's 2,600,000. What if there were full mobilization? The addition of all available reserve strengths would give NATO a force of 5,184,500 compared with the Pact's 4,800,000—thus increasing the edge. Nor does this include 326,800 troops in the French Army.

Only in Central Europe did the Warsaw Pact have a superiority of roughly 23,000, with forces of 805,000 facing 782,000 NATO troops. It was precisely because of this, and very much in the spirit of detente, that Brezhnev unilaterally withdrew 20,000 troops and 1,000 tanks from East Germany late in 1979. Brezhnev had hoped that in turn we would reconsider our planned deployment of Pershing II and Cruise Missiles in Western Europe. We did not. There is now almost a perfect parity of forces in Central Europe, though available French forces would give the West a total strength in this region of 1,062,000.

Manpower comparisons of United States and Soviet forces usually are made only between army strengths, since by ourselves we exceed the Soviet Union in every other major category, with 555,000 in our Air Force compared with 475,000 in theirs, 528,000 in our Navy compared

with 433,000 in theirs, and 189,000 in our Marine Corps compared with 12,000 in their Naval Infantry.

The most impressive comparison used for winning hearts and minds, and for opening the public purse, involves the unquestioned Soviet lead in numbers of tanks. It is offered that the Warsaw Pact has 27,200 tanks compared with only 11,800 for NATO and France. This gives the Pact what seems so decisive a lead that you begin to wonder why, in the past few years, we have agreed to provide 1,015 advanced M-60A3 and 771 M-48A5 tanks to various countries in the Middle East and Asia, and why the British planned to provide Iran with 800 Chieftain tanks, when all this equipment would have gone some distance toward mending what we are told is a critical shortage.

Apparently it has been more important to lower the unit procurement costs of these weapons by raising their production runs to fill additional requirements abroad—requirements that do not arise on their own so much as they are solicited by us for this very purpose. It will be argued that some of these requirements meet legitimate security needs, though that is said of every weapons sale. Either these needs were greater than the alleged threat to NATO, or NATO's primary concern has been costs. If costs are such a preoccupation, then either our economic system is not competitive with the Soviet system, or the defense of Western Europe is not so much in jeopardy after all.

Former Defense Secretary Harold Brown knows that superior numbers of certain types of equipment are no assurance of a superior military capability. "Measures of assessment," he recently testified, "in which, for example, Soviet and American tank inventories are compared, are rarely illuminating about the expected outcome of a battle." He knows this because he also knows that NATO now deploys 193,000 antitank weapons, most of them precision-guided missiles, while the Warsaw Pact can muster 68,000 such weapons, few of them comparable in lethality. Dr. William Perry, under secretary of Defense for Research and Engineering, confirms that the United States has "a substantial lead" in precision-guided weapons, which he considers to be "the most significant application of technology to modern warfare."

Among the missiles in our antitank arsenal are the AGM-65 Maverick series of air-to-ground munitions with electro-optical, laser or infrared guidance, and the Army's M-47 Dragon and MGM-71 TOW. The TOW is mounted on a variety of vehicles from jeeps to armoured personnel carriers, and is the standard armament for the AH-IQ and AH-IS Cobra and Hughes AH-64 attack helicopters. Congressmen who have learned how well the TOW performs are warned that the armour on the Soviet T-72 tank is too tough to be penetrated by the TOW warhead. What they are not told is that every TOW missile in the NATO inventory has been equipped with an improved TOW-2 warhead that penetrates up to twice the thickness of that armour.

The capability of the TOW is matched by that of most of our other antitank missiles, as well as by the Copperhead laser-guided 155mm artillery projectile, the Walleye television-guided bomb, the GAU-8/A 30mm multibarreled antitank cannon mounted on the A-10 Thunderbolt close air support aircraft, and the Mk 118 antitank fragmentation bomb that is used in our new Rockeye cluster munitions, producing fragments that cut through armour at speeds of up to 4,000 feet per second. "The technology balance," Dr Perry allows, "is shifting in favor of the antitank systems." He adds that NATO leads in the lethality of tanks, artillery and rocket launchers, as well as in the quantity and quality of antitank missiles and combat aircraft."

Nevertheless, the larger number of Warsaw Pact tanks continues to be intoned as proof of Soviet might and the military decline of the West, despite the fact that this threat is more than offset by the larger number and superior quality of our antitank systems, despite the fact that by every other measure of comparison NATO holds the lead, and despite the immense advantages, consistently ignored by alarmists, of the *defensive* role we would presumably play in the event of combat—a role that does not even require the superiority we already have.

Much of NATO's equipment, we are warned, is not standardized. It was never intended to be. The advantages of this "lack" of standardization are never publicized. The Soviets, for example, must attempt to develop effective countermeasures to the radar, fire control and homing mechanisms that guide no fewer than 103 missiles now deployed by NATO and French ground, air and naval forces. Such advantages more than offset the logistical problems of handling so many

different kinds of equipment. Indeed, the complexities of logistics arise less from the variety of equipment NATO deploys than from the number of separate military commands responsible to its several member governments. This condition equally burdens the Warsaw Pact.

What, then, has the crisis been all about? If the Soviet superiority in conventional weaponry does not exist, why have certain facts and figures been selected to make it look as though it did? If confronted with this, military planners will admit that NATO has a clear advantage, and that they are exaggerating the Soviet threat. But they will say they are perfectly justified in doing so, because it is the only way to mobilize public support for increased defense spending. We must recall Senator Arthur Vandenberg's advice to President Truman that if we wanted to expand military preparedness we would have to "scare the hell out of the country."

But if we hold the lead in military power, why do we have to increase it? In order to avoid losing it, the argument runs. Losing the lead will lose a measure of the security we have already invested so much to achieve. The Soviets, after all, will continue their attempts to catch up with us. We must anticipate these developments in advance, and make further gains of our own in order to keep the lead we have. If the cost of this effort places a greater strain on our economy than may be absolutely required, is it not more responsible to err on the side of caution? This is the classic justification for the arms race. The nation that has fallen behind feels morally bound to catch up. The nation that has moved ahead fears it may soon be challenged. Each sees itself acting solely in defense. Each sees the other as the only possible aggressor. We childishly assume the world is safer if we hold the lead in military power, while obviously in the Soviet view the reverse seems true. In the name of responsibility, we overlook the increasing likelihood that we may go bankrupt in order to defend the bank.

A much higher degree of security, at a far lower cost, could be achieved through what specialists on arms control call parity, a genuine balance of military power

in which neither side can claim a decisive advantage. The elimination of sudden and significant military advantages is the key to attaining this balance. Yet neither side will give up its efforts to achieve such advantages. If there has ever been a balance between the United States and the Soviet Union, neither country admits having been aware of it. The inability to extend trust probably precludes recognition of it.

Whether the many perceptions of an imbalance have been imagined or real, each nation has anticipated the other's attempt to offset one imbalance by creating a new imbalance of its own. Each prefers to retain an advantage than let it slip away for the sake of parity. This is why an arms limitation discussion frequently becomes a comedy of cross purposes. Consequently, there will probably never be a balance of most kinds of military power. There will probably only be a higher level of potential destruction, further complicating perceptions, and raising the risks of miscalculation. The sense that this was an inevitable trend led Lord Mountbatten to warn that "it is a dangerous misconception to believe that by increasing the total uncertainty one increases one's own certainty." President Reagan's new determination to achieve "military superiority" over the Soviet Union will do nothing to increase our certainty. We have always had superiority and we have it now. Continued commitment to this goal is more than deterrence requires. It only prolongs our commitment to an excess of military power, to unrestrained growth in the defense sector of our economy, and to an outmoded imperialism in foreign policy that attempts to justify both. It will only make the world a still more dangerous place.

### Tactical Nuclear Weapons

For the past three decades, the total uncertainty in Europe has increased, with a steady buildup of military power in the East and in the West, including our introduction in 1954 of what we called tactical nuclear weapons. These, of course, stood as a powerful deterrent to any Soviet military action. They also introduced the risk that conventional warfare on the NATO battlefield might escalate into a nuclear exchange.

For many years we minimized this risk, insisting that the Soviets look upon our nuclear weapons as battlefield systems, to be used only against military targets in the combat theater. The Soviets, however, did not accept this prescribed view. They took note of the fact that many of these weapons, especially those carried by aircraft with ranges of up to 1,200 miles, were well within reach of major cities deep in the Soviet heartland, and they never forgot it. What we regarded as a deterrent they saw as a threat. Barely able, at first, to participate in a nuclear exchange, they built their forces until they had managed, three years after us, to introduce their own tactical nuclear weapons with the Warsaw Pact.

By 1957, then, both superpowers had deployed a tactical nuclear deterrent in the European theater, and had also developed much stronger strategic forces that might be unleashed in the event of its use. The risks of nuclear escalation had grown.

In a recent reversal of our original policy, we now acknowledge these risks, and claim that on account of them battlefield commanders may hesitate to use tactical nuclear weapons, preferring to accept defeat at the hands of conventional forces than take the responsibility for initiating what could become an unlimited nuclear exchange.

This faith in humanitarian instinct is an unusual doctrine for us to profess. But it is enough to destroy the credibility of the tactical nuclear deterrent that has been the cornerstone of our NATO policy for the past 26 years. We are told that our NATO allies, too, worry that we may not use these weapons, even though they rely on them for their defense, and that in the face of a presumed Soviet advance we may simply withdraw, since it would not be our own soil we were defending.

Yet many Europeans, because the fighting would take place on their soil, are probably not concerned that we may fail to use such weapons. Probably they are concerned that we will be perfectly willing to use them. By doing so we would not, after all, be risking the immediate destruction of our own cities, or the extermination of our own civilian population. That is why the Greeks recently were so angered at the revelation that ever since 1959 secret agreements between the Greek and American governments have given us exclusive control over nuclear weapons we placed in that country, contrary to public agreements which seemed to commit us to joint control. That is why the Turks, Spaniards and Portuguese will be

angered, too, if similar agreements are found to exist governing the use of our nuclear weapons in their homelands.

When our original policy held that the Soviets would be checked by the presence of tactical nuclear weapons, it was more difficult to persuade the public that we needed a larger conventional force at the same time. But when we recently announced that such weapons probably never would be used and had therefore lost their deterrent value, the public was encouraged to suppose that we would now have to be able to fight a NATO war without them. It followed as an imperative that we needed sufficient conventional forces to win such a war. In this way, the alleged abandonment of tactical nuclear weapons was linked to the need for increased defense spending to achieve the massive buildup in conventional forces now proposed by the Reagan administration.

In fact, our NATO allies and we have never relied on tactical nuclear weapons as our sole deterrent, because we have always had more than sufficient conventional strength to prevail in the event of a Warsaw Pact assault. Unfortunately, this does not eliminate the risk that tactical nuclear weapons may be used. In the first place, they will continue to be available. For contrary to the suggestion implicit in our new doctrine, we have not abandoned them.

Today in Europe we and our NATO allies deploy more than 7,000 tactical nuclear weapon systems of American manufacture. These include 180 Pershing IA Missiles with a range of 450 miles. 72 of the Pershing 1As are in the West German Army, which also deploys 91 Honest John Missiles. Of the 90 Lance Missiles in Europe, 54 are deployed by West Germany, Belgium, the Netherlands, Italy, and Great Britain. Also in Europe are 3,800 rounds of 155mm and 203mm artillery projectiles with nuclear warheads for use, respectively, by the 215 M-109 and 300 M-110 self-propelled howitzers allocated to our Seventh Army's battalion and divisional artillery units. In addition, we deploy 400 Hound Dog air-launched missiles, a precursor of the Cruise Missile with a range of 800 miles, and 2,500

B-61 and B-72 nuclear gravity bombs for delivery by the 390 U.S. Air Force F-4 and F-III aircraft and 100 U.S. Navy F-4, A-6 and A-7 aircraft that have been assigned NATO theater nuclear targets. The 807 Tornado multirole aircraft now entering service with our European allies will also ''be employed in the nuclear strike role,'' according to General David C. Jones, Chairman of the Joint Chiefs of Staff. Finally, 400 warheads have been allocated to NATO theater targets from our Poseidon submarine fleet.

Once again, we have achieved an overwhelming preponderance of power. The Soviet Union, which must also contend with the strategic nuclear forces of China, Great Britain and France, disposng between them an additional 700 to 1,000 warheads, has allocated 2,586 warheads to the Warsaw Pact theater. Its major tactical nuclear weapons are the SS-4 and SS-5 missiles, and the SS-20, a new version of the SS-5 with three warheads instead of one, which began entering service in 1976. To date, about 120 SS-20s have been produced, and half are deployed with the Warsaw Pact. Of the 80 Tu-22M Backfire bombers produced to date, 50 are allocated not to strategic targets in the United States, as is frequently claimed, but to theater nuclear targets in Europe.

Even if the current disparity in tactical nuclear power did not exist, and the Soviets did not withdraw their 590 SS-4s and SS-5s as planned, at the current rate of production of 50 SS-20s per year it would take them another 33 years before they could balance the additional 5,000 tactical warheads we will have in Europe, with or without SALT II, by 1985. At the current production rate of 30 Backfire aircraft per year, it would take them 25 years before they could balance the force of 807 Tornado aircraft that will all be in NATO service by 1986.

Now, far from planning the withdrawal of any of our tactical nuclear weapons from Europe, we plan to deploy an additional force of 108 Pershing II and 464 Ground-Launched Cruise Missiles (GLCMs) in Europe. These are said to be needed to counter the presence of the new Soviet SS-20, whose initial appearance allegedly sent NATO into shock because its accuracy and range enabled the Soviets—for the first time, we were told—to strike at major European cities well behind the NATO front line. In fact, Soviet SS-4 and SS-5 missiles have been able to strike at European cities for the past 20 years.

We claim that our new missiles are needed to reassure our European allies of our commitment to their defense. Our European allies are not at all reassured. Every one of them bitterly resisted accepting these weapons. That is because they realize that if such weapons are used, they are going to be used on European soil, well within the retaliatory range of Soviet theater nuclear weapons, new and old.

The Pershing II was exempted from SALT II because we claimed it had a range of only 400 miles and therefore should not be classified as a strategic weapon. It has a range of 1,200 miles. The GLCM has a range of 2,500 miles. General David C. Jones acknowledges that the Pershing II and Cruise missile force will "pose a credible threat to the Soviet Union."

Once the true ranges of these missiles had been revealed, we were told they were needed to remind the Soviets that they could not attack Europe without risking a nuclear attack on their homeland. Yet they have faced this same risk for 26 years. If the power of our previous theater nuclear arsenal has not discouraged them from continuing their alleged buildup, why will additional new weapons discourage them now?

We were next told that the real purpose of the new weapons was "psychological." Surely, Soviet military analysts are expected to provide an accurate assessment of the physical threat, not a psychological response. It was said that these weapons would improve Soviet "perceptions" of our deterrent power. Will Soviet perceptions be influenced by whatever we do and say? If so, having appealed to Congress for higher defense spending, should we now expect immediate Soviet action against us to take advantage of the military vulnerability we claim to suffer? Fortunately, the Soviets do not believe this claim. Neither should anyone else.

The decision to deploy Pershing II and Cruise missiles, a decision not taken by NATO without considerable urging by the United States, is the latest round of excessive reaction in the arms race. Our new missiles will do nothing to improve the defense of the West, but they are going to be deployed all the same. Their very presence will be a commitment to their use. Neither we nor the Soviets intend to begin using tactical nuclear

weapons the moment hostilities begin. What neither we nor they can predict, however, is what will happen after the fighting has progressed to the point where one side believes it is threatened with defeat. We cannot be sure that a stalemate will occur. That is the danger point. The addition of more redundant tactical nuclear power in Europe only further raises the risks of such escalation.

If we can be made to believe our conventional forces are weak, then this notion certainly justifies the need for increased defense spending to strengthen them. But it also requires us to uphold the doctrine that a conventional war can be fought and won without eliciting an available nuclear response. This requires a selective understanding of human nature. Battlefield commanders will naturally hesitate to use nuclear weapons. No one wants to begin what may be the end of the world. But commanders are also trained to win, to use all the resources at hand, and to regard defeat not as a personal loss but as the shame of a nation, the downfall of a way of life. Better dead then red, the slogan of the 1950s ran.

Once the use of nuclear weapons has begun, it is even less clear what the response will be. Is "first use" the only sin? After one force has sustained the first nuclear stirke, will its commander feel no less compunction about responding in kind? Will he find any comfort in knowing that he did not personally start the holocaust about to ensue? As he feels the first pulse of heat from the fireball that he knows will melt his eyes from their sockets, will he stop to think about the future of mankind, and stay his hand from the button that assures instant revenge?

Because it is intended to raise public support for increased preparedness, and also to suggest to the Soviets that we are already prepared, *The Third World War*, an account by several NATO generals of a possible NATO war, makes a nuclear exchange feasible, portraying the destruction of the cities of Birmingham and Minsk. But it is only able to offer the political collapse of the Soviet System as the reason why the exchange stops there. Nuclear war will seem a good deal less

feasible if you remember the vision Albert Einstein had of it when he said: "I can tell you what the Fourth World War will be fought with— bows and arrows."

If we insist that we may be sure of our own commanders, that the West will never initiate a nuclear war, that is still not quite sufficient to eliminate risk. What about the Soviets? What about a different scenario from the one always given of an overwhelming Soviet armoured assault successfully breaking through Western defenses? What about the far more likely possibility that our greater numbers, our superior readiness and training, and our actual preponderance of superior equipment have brought the Soviets to the point of imminent defeat, and they must consider retreat or surrender? Can we be sure that they will not then respond with nuclear weapons? Do we believe that the Soviets want above all else not to initiate their use, and would prefer to let us destroy their armies and do what we will to their peoples as punishment for their iniquities? The decisions they make are beyond our control.

As in the Persian Gulf or any other areas of the world where Soviet and American forces might join in battle, the only rule of combat on the NATO battlefield is that the force threatened with defeat may break the rules. It is impossible to predict what the outcome of such a confrontation may be. Both sides know that the risk of escalation is too great. The only prudent response to this risk is not to presume escalation can be controlled but to avoid war. Consequently, the nuclear deterrent in Europe has worked very well. So long as rational men are in command, it is unlikely there will ever be any kind of war between NATO and the Warsaw Pact.

But it is not impossible. The one caution to this reassuring conclusion arises from the schizophrenic atmosphere in which military leaders continue urgently to plan for a confrontation they know bears unacceptable risks and therefore cannot be undertaken in the first place. The planning denies this. The need for preparedness requires a firm commitment to a course of action that reasonable men can only regard as suicidal. In order to make this experience tolerable, we may suspend reason. In order to persuade our potential enemy that we are willing to go to war, we must demonstrate conviction. If we become convinced of our willingness, then we have become willing. At this point we are no longer rational men. At this point war cannot be ruled out.

### The Strategic Balance of Power

The strategic balance between the two superpowers is no more comforting. From the beginning, the United States has led the strategic arms race, each time using a "gap" of alleged Soviet gains to justify taking the next step in the escalation of nuclear power. We detonated our first atomic bombs in August of 1945, but it was not until August of 1949, four years later, that the Soviets detonated the first of theirs. In 1948 we began talking of a "bomber gap," warning that the Soviets had deployed an overwhelming force of long-range bombers capable of launching a surprise attack. Billions of dollars were spent to produce the B-52s of our Strategic Air Command, which first entered service in 1955. Even by that time, however, the Soviets had no strategic bombers at all.

Nevertheless, the bomber scare was still with us the following year, when President Eisenhower broke off arms limitation talks he himself had initiated with the Soviet Union, claiming that any agreement at that time would leave the Soviets with a "clear strategic lead." What made him change his mind? 1956 was an election year, and his challenger, Adlai Stevenson, had supported the arms talks. Ending them made Stevenson seem ignorant of the true threat, and defeated him.

In August of 1957 the Soviets tested their first ballistic missile, and two months later they used it to launch the first Sputnik satellite into orbit. Our leadership responded as if in deep shock. We claimed this missile could reach targets in the United States. In fact, it could reach no farther than Western Europe. The Gaither Committee warned that by 1959 the Soviets would be able to launch 100 intercontinental ballistic missiles (ICBMs) at the United States. In fact they had produced only 35 ICBMs by 1960. However, since at that time we had built only 18 ICBMs, this created what seemed a genuine "missile gap."

John F. Kennedy made much of this presumed gap in his 1960 election campaign against Richard Nixon, charging that the Republicans had "allowed the nation to fall hostage" to Soviet missiles. This prompted President Eisenhower, before he left office, to restore funds he had earlier cut from the budget for the B-70

bomber. In 1961, the newly inaugurated President Kennedy announced he had been relieved to discover that the missile gap did not exist, and that the United States was well ahead of the USSR in strategic strength.

The gap had never existed because, within months after the launching of Sputnik in 1957, and before the Soviets had any ICBMs at all, we deployed 105 Jupiter intermediate range ballistic missiles (IRBMs) in Turkey and Italy. These were easily able to reach targets in the Soviet Union, long before the Soviets could hope to reach targets in the United States. Even by 1960, when the Soviets briefly had twice as many ICBMs, only four of their liquid-fueled missiles were operational at Plesetsk. Our force of IRBMs assured that we still had three times as many missiles, all of them operational, targeted on Soviet cities.

The Jupiter missiles remained in Western Europe until the Cuban missile crisis of 1962, which Kennedy was able to end only by secretly agreeing to remove them provided Khrushchev would remove the fewer than 40 Soviet missiles in Cuba, most of which had ranges of less than 250 miles and could barely reach Miami from San Cristobal. Our 105 IRBMs no longer mattered to us anyway, because by that time we had built 156 ICBMs while the Soviets had only 64.

In 1960 the Soviets placed in the ocean their first submarine equipped with submarine-launched ballistic missiles (SLBMs). Again, these SLBMs had a range of only 350 miles. We quickly announced an "SLBM gap," even though we had in the same year launched our first Polaris submarines, whose missiles had a range of 1,200 miles. It was not until 1968 that the Soviets launched a submarine whose SLBMs had a comparable range, but by that time our Polaris A-3 missiles were deployed, with a range of 2,500 miles. It was also in 1968 that we tested the first Multiple Independently Targetable Reentry Vehicle (MIRV), which allowed several nuclear warheads to be placed on a single missile. The Soviets did not test MIRVs until 1973. All the same, we had announced a "MIRV gap," requiring that we bend every effort to catch up with the nonexistent Soviet lead,

so that by 1970 we were deploying our first MIRVed missiles, while the Soviets did not deploy theirs until 1975.

The first SALT agreement, in 1972, limited the number of Americans ICBMs to 1,054, and the number of American SLBMs to 656, while the Soviets were allowed 1,618 ICBMs and 740 SLBMs. Were our leaders compromising our security by allowing the Soviets greater numbers? No. These different quantities were quite acceptable to us, because by that time we had accumulated enormous advantages over the USSR, including three times as many nuclear warheads on our MIRVed missiles, and a bomber force of more than 400 aircraft, as compared with only 140 Soviet strategic bombers. Even today, our Strategic Air Command keeps a force of 348 bombers on active duty, while the Soviets have a total of just 156.

SALT I, however, did not limit improvements in the precision, reliability and explosive yield of those weapons already permitted, nor did it prevent other qualitative improvements, such as the development of the Cruise Missile and the neutron bomb. Consequently, qualitative improvement was the direction nuclear weapons technology would take in the future.

SALT II would limit all strategic delivery systems on both sides, including ICBMs, SLBMs, and long-range bombers, to an initial total of 2,400 and a final total of 2,250 by 1981. Within this total other limitations would also be specified, including the number of bombers that may be armed with cruise missiles, the number of cruise missiles each bomber may carry, and the number of ICBMs and SLBMs that may be MIRVed. Yet there is no limit to the number of warheads that may be placed on each MIRVed missile, or to the size or character of their explosive yield, or to refinements that may be made in their accuracy. These available goals, consequently, set the direction nuclear weapons technology will continue to take even if SALT II is revived and adopted.

We are now warned that the Soviets have 2,504 delivery systems of all types, including bombers and missiles, while the United States deploys a total of only 2,057. They have 950 SLBMs to our 656, and 1,398 ICBMs to our 1,053. There is much talk of the greater size and "throw-weight" of Soviet ICBMs, and of their greater yield in explosive force. The strategic nuclear weapons presently deployed by the Soviets can provide them with a combined total explosive yield of 7,672 megatons, compared with only 5,444 megatons available to United States strategic forces.

What is overlooked is that the Soviets have deliberately raised the explosive yield of their weapons in order to compensate for their inferior accuracy, as well as for the much lower number of warheads they have been able to deploy on each of their MIRVed missiles. The Modification 2 conversion of the Soviet SS-18 ICBM, first deployed in 1977, can carry no more than 8 warheads. As long ago as 1970 we deployed the Poseidon C-3 SLBM, which carries up to 14 warheads. This leads to the most telling fact of all, though it is rarely told: our larger strategic bomber force and our superior MIRV capability now make available a total of 11,893 deliverable strategic warheads for United States forces, while the Soviets can have a maximum of no more than 7,004. This even assumes that all but 74 of the 308 Soviet SS-18 ICBMs now operational have undergone conversion to Modification 2, when in fact the true number of MIRVed SS-18s is probably much smaller. Therefore, each time with a devastation equivalent to the largest of Soviet warheads, the United States can strike almost twice as many targets.

The more accurate the missile, the lower the explosive force it requires to destroy even a hardened target. By 1985 we will have 13,766 warheads, and the power of these devices is so unimportant, compared with their precision, that the combined explosive yield of this larger number of warheads in 1985 will actually drop from 5,444 megatons to only 4,908 megatons.

While the accuracy of Soviet missiles has improved, so has ours, and the precision of ours has long been superior. The Mark 12A warhead now being retrofitted on our Minuteman III missile will reduce the weapon's theoretical margin of error in striking the center of its target from 350 meters to less than 200 meters. The MX missile, if it is ever built, may carry more than the ten warheads usually reported. It may carry from 12 to 15 Mark 12A warheads, or as many as 20 Mark 500 MARV (Maneuverable Reentry Vehicle) warheads. The Mark 500 is generally thought to have poor accuracy, because it was designed primarily to penetrate air defenses by evasive maneuvering. But it may be equipped with terminal guidance

that will enable it to strike within 100 meters of its target center.

Such accuracy, and such numbers, are not required to present the Soviets with an effective deterrent. An effective deterrent is simply a force that remains immune from preemptive strike, and is sufficient to inflict unacceptable damage on the Soviet Union. It has been our ostensible policy since 1950 that all we needed was to maintain such a deterrent force. Secretary of Defense Robert McNamara estimated that a force of 100 nuclear weapons with explosive yields of no more than 50 kilotons each would suffice as a deterrent, because it would be capable of destroying 25 percent of the Soviet population, or 65 million people, and 50 percent of Soviet industrial capacity.

Robert Aldridge, an aeronautical engineer who worked on the design of several of our nuclear weapon systems, adds that "allowing for repairs and maintenance, misfires and Soviet defenses, 400 warheads would constitute a more-than-adequate deterrence capability." Yet more than that number remain safely out of reach of Soviet attack in only two of the 31 Poseidon submarines we now deploy. Each Poseidon submarine carries 16 missiles, and each Poseidon missile may carry 14 warheads. The whole Poseidon fleet, 25 of whose boats today carry the Poseidon C-3 SLBM and 6 the Trident C-4 SLBM, may right now dispose 6,368 warheads. An additional 10 Polaris submarines dispose another 480 warheads. By 1985 we will have six Trident submarines patrolling the oceans as well. Each of these will carry 24 MIRVed SLBMs, and each SLBM may eventually carry 10 warheads, so that by then 1,440 more nuclear warheads will have been added to our strategic arsenal at sea.

If 400 warheads should suffice, why have we built 11,493 more? Why do we plan to build another 18,500 by 1990? Including our 22,000 tactical nuclear weapons, we now have an arsenal of almost 32,000 nuclear devices of all types, and are committed to production that will raise this total to 52,500 by the end of the decade. Is all of this to persuade the Soviets that we mean business? If they do not believe we mean business with the

excess of destructive power now in our possession, will an even greater excess make any difference?

We need to improve our arsenal, we are told, because our existing deterrent force is no longer invulnerable, and therefore lacks credibility. We are told that the accuracy of Soviet missiles, while far short of the pinpoint precision of ours, has improved sufficiently to threaten us with a first strike on our own strategic forces, preempting their use as a deterrent and leaving us unable to respond to further attack. The Soviets, it is said, are moving toward this first strike capability by redirecting their missiles from industrial and population centers to military targets.

We are told that our land-based missiles, even in their hardened silos, are now vulnerable to a first strike. In light of the accident that occured at a Titan II silo in Damascus, Arkansas in September of 1980, there is reason to question how effectively these silos have been hardened, and to wonder whether they have not always been vulnerable to far less accurate nuclear strikes ever since the missiles they are meant to protect were first deployed 17 years ago. When the missile's rather unstable hydrazine fuel came into contact with its oxidant and ignited, the explosion of these nonnuclear materials blew off the silo's 750-ton reinforced concrete door, leaving a 250-foot crater. The blast that occurred, compared with the nuclear explosion the door was supposed to withstand, was like that of a punctured balloon to the detonation of a hand grenade.

In an attempt to make our land-based missiles less vulnerable, the mobile MX system has been proposed, each of whose missiles would move between a series of sheltered positions to escape detection and targeting. Regrettably, if such a system is built, it will also complicate procedures for verifying that the number of MX missiles deployed does not exceed the total allowed by whatever SALT agreement may prevail. Nor is it explained why a new strategic missile system that may cost $60 billion before it is operational, and that was originally presented as a purely defensive system, requires the extraordinary accuracy the MX warheads would possess, far exceeding what would suffice for the deterrent purpose it is alleged to have.

We are told that because our force of B-52 strategic bombers is now 20 years old, it would suffer heavy losses from

Soviet air defenses in any attempted attack on the USSR. That, it seems, is why the B-1 penetrating bomber was originally proposed. Nor is the B-1 dead. While President Carter vetoed its production in favor of the Cruise Missile, Congress has every year appropriated funds for its continued development, including $375 million last year, and the Reagan administration this year announced plans to revive either an updated version of the B-1 design or a stretched version of the FB-111 to serve as our new strategic penetrating bomber in the 1990s.

Meanwhile, having already spent more than $1 million per aircraft to upgrade the electronic countermeasures capabilities of 296 of our B-52G and B-52H bombers, and another $359 million to fit these aircraft with rotary launchers for the AGM-69A Short Range Attack Missile (SRAM), we will this year spend $597 million more to further modernize the B-52 fleet. Shortly, each of our 151 B-52Gs will be fitted with launchers to carry the AGM-68A Air-Launched Cruise Missile (ALCM), the very weapon President Carter favored over the B-1, and whose range of 1,200 miles on its own power gives it a stand-off capability, allowing the B-52s to operate at the perimeter of Soviet air defenses, and precluding the need for a new bomber to penetrate them. Eventually 1,200 ALCMs will be deployed. Initial operating cabability is expected for the first squadron of B-52Gs, equipped with 300 ALCMs, at Griffis Air Force Base, New York, in 1982.

Those who claim that our bombers and land-based missile forces are vulnerable to a first strike overlook the fact that they must first be struck before they are lost. It would take Soviet ICBMs 30 minutes to arrive on target in the United States after they were launched, and it would take Soviet SLBMs a minimum of 15 minutes. This time cannot effectively be reduced. Hyper-velocity boosting techniques are being developed, but not for this purpose. Instead, they are designed to lift the missile in a higher trajectory above the atmosphere, where navigational errors due to the force of gravity will be minimized. Depressed trajectories have shortened the distance, and hence the time, from launch point to target, but a law of diminishing returns is here at work. We have already flattened the trajectories of our ballistic missiles as far as possible, while still retaining sufficient ability to predict their behavior. Any further attempt

to depress a trajectory, or to reduce a missile's flight time by increasing its speed, would make it impossible to predict its accuracy in striking its target. This would render it useless for military purposes.

As it is, our assessment of missile accuracy is largely theoretical, based in part on empirical data extrapolated from tests, but mostly on mathematical calculations. Hyper-velocity boosting techniques may improve the likelihood that a missile will conform to those calculations, but will also increase, rather than reduce, its time to target, because they will greatly increase the distance it must travel.

Within 20 seconds after a missile had departed from any launch point in the world, one of our satellite surveillance systems would have detected and reported it. Within five minutes, the network of our early-warning systems would have checked and coordinated this information not only to verify that the warning was not in error, but also to identify the target. This would confirm whether the strike was aimed at our own strategic forces.

Let us assume that Soviet SLBMs, the missiles that could arrive most quickly, would be launched simultaneously at our long-range bombers, the targets that would take the most time to become airborne in order to avoid destruction. If the first bomber at each airfield took five minutes to become airborne and another was airborne every 30 seconds thereafter, we would have a minimum of 200 of our bombers in the air before even the first Soviet SLBM struck. In fact, Strategic Air Command readiness alert exercises have placed bombers in the air rather more quickly than this. The Global Shield exercises held in February of 1981 removed 400 aircraft from 70 bases in less than 10 minutes. If the SLBM launch were anything but simultaneous, more bombers would survive. Nor would our aircraft yet be irrevocably committed to specific targets in the Soviet Union, or to any retaliatory strike at all.

As for our ICBMs, all of which could be launched simultaneously in less than five minutes, the military axiom goes that ''it's better to use them than to lose

them.'' They could all be held until just before the first Soviet missiles arrived, giving us the maximum time in which to assess the character of the Soviet attack and decide which targets to strike in response.

Thus, the notion that the Soviets might attempt a first strike in the hope of destroying part of our retaliatory force is seriously in error. Our early-warning systems make it impossible to do so, just as Soviet early-warning systems make it impossible for us. As long as these systems are in place, they serve as an effective deterrent to such temptations.

Aside from our satellite surveillance systems, we deploy in our early-warning network the Space Detection and Tracking System (SPADATS) comprising the U.S. Air Force 496L Spacetrack and the U.S. Navy SPASUR, the Ballistic Missile Early Warning System (BMEWS) in Alaska, Greenland and Great Britain, the Distant Early Warning (DEW) Line, the Pinetree Line in Central Canada, the 474N SLBM detection and warning net now being replaced by the phased-array radars of the FPS-115 Pave Paws system, the Perimeter Acquisition Radar Attack Characterization System (PARCS), the Cobra Dane radar in the Aleutians, the Back-up Interceptor Control (BUIC) system, and the Semi-Automatic Ground Environment (SAGE) and Manual Control Centre (MCC) stations which, together with Air National Guard and Federal Aviation Administration ground radar stations, are being replaced by the Joint Surveillance System (JSS). The entire network comprises more than 200 stations and control centers throughout North America and scattered across the world.

Too great a reliance on this network, built up over the past three decades at a cost of several billion dollars, is said to lead inevitably to a ''Launch-on-Warning'' strategy, a dangerous policy that places strategic forces on a hair-trigger alert, creating an atmosphere in which mistakes are more easily made. It leads to nothing of the kind. There is no question that mistakes can be made, and that both men and machines are capable of making them. That is why it is dangerous to have nuclear weapons at all. There is no question that if we were all on a hair-trigger alert, disastrous mistakes could be made. A nation might launch some of its weapons before it had confirmed it was under attack. But no one is on such a hair-trigger alert. There is no need. There is time to confirm that an attack is under way, time even to discover what kind of attack it is and what targets it is directed against. A government which has nothing to lose, and a great deal to gain, would obviously take this time. That is why there is no such thing as a "Launch-on-Warning" strategy.

The recent computer errors at North American Air Defense Command (NORAD) headquarters in Cheyenne Mountain were taken as evidence of how close to a hair-trigger response we are, and of how easily dangerous mistakes can be made. In fact, they demonstrate just the reverse. Twice in June of 1980, failure of a micro-chip in an integrated circuit caused a Data General NOVA computer at NORAD to feed false satellite and radar early warning information, indicating the launch of Sovi-et ICBMs at the United States, into the World Wide Military Command and Con-trol System (WWMCCS) of 35 computers at 27 sites around the world, including the Military Command Center in the Penta-gon and Strategic Air Command at Omaha. Our 1,054 ICBMs were placed on red alert, and our Poseidon and Polaris sub-marine fleets on yellow alert. One hun-dred B-52 bombers were prepared for takeoff, along with the President's modi-fied Boeing 747 Airborne National Com-mand Post at Andrews Air Force Base.

WWMCCS was installed in 1971 at a cost of $1 billion. However, it is only part of a much larger $15 billion network of electronic information systems, none of the rest of which confirmed the NORAD alert. With this series of independent radar and satellite verification systems, it took officers at the Pentagon just three minutes to determine the NORAD warning was false, both times. The incidents were similar to one in November of 1979, when a mechanical error sent wargame information into WWMCCS warning of an attack from a single Soviet submarine in the northeast Pacific.

After the mishaps in June, General David C. Jones said he hoped they would remind the Soviets how rapidly we were able to determine we had false informa-tion. The message seemed to be that we still had plenty of time to avoid losses from a preemptive first strike. But since the Soviets already know this, and since these errors occur rather more frequently than the public hears about them, it is more likely that the failures in June were well advertised to remind the public that nuclear dangers exist, but might subside

a little if there is strong support for the new nuclear weapon systems coming up for debate in Congress. More specifically, it was possibly a message to Congress that $140 million requested for mainte-nance and modfication of WWMCCS, refused on the advice of the General Accounting Office, might be well spent, and ought to be reinstated in the budget.

Our long-range bomber force and our land-based force of ICBMs are but two legs of what the United States calls its Strategic Triad. Continuing attempts to persuade us of the vulnerability of either or both of them, despite clear evidence to the contrary, are made irrelevant in any case by the perfect invulnerability of the third: our fleet of strategic ballistic missile submarines, whose submerged locations are impossible for the Soviets to detect, and whose SLBMs right now may dis-pose a total of 6,848 warheads—enough, all by themselves, to obliterate the whole of the Soviet Union four times over.

It is said, however, that improvements in antisubmarine warfare technology may some day overcome current obstacles, making a first strike at our submarines possible. In fact, most obstacles will never be overcome. Active radar and laser detection systems based on satel-lites will never be able to detect more than surface wakes or submarines in shallow water. Thermal imaging with infrared sen-sors will never be able to distinguish the radiation of a submarine from any of the millions of schools of fish or warm cur-rent shifts in the ocean. Magnetic anomaly systems deployed on aircraft will never detect targets deeply submerged. The Soviet Union does not control the shore-lines along the world's deep ocean ba-sins, and so will never be able to deploy an effective network of passive acoustic devices comparable to our own vast Sound Surveillance System (SOSUS). Active sonar, such as that on the new *Alpha* class of Soviet hunter-killer submarine, will always have the disadvantage of giv-ing away its own location. It would take the Soviets another 30 years to build a sufficient fleet of these merely to track our own boats. Even then, the threat is only theoretical. Targets must not only be detected but fixed.

Soviet acoustic technology is so far behind ours that ten years ago a U.S. Navy submarine penetrated the hydro-phone barrier at Murmansk, entered the harbor, and there placed sensors on the Soviet sensors so that we could listen to what they were hearing. Even if their technology were to improve, the Soviets would still lack the highly sophisticated mainframe computers comparable to our ILLIAC-4 to perform parallel processing of signals. Without this capability, now completely lacking in the Soviet Union, they would never be able to analyze what-ever acoustic information they were able to collect.

Even if all these obstacles were one day overcome, the mobility of our sub-marines will always make it impossible for the Soviets to target them with suffi-cient accuracy and speed for a guaran-teed preemptive strike. In addition, the risks of attempting such a strike will always remain forbidding. If a strike by the Soviets missed only one submarine, the destruction of more than 100 Soviet cities would follow. The rational mind can only view this as an unacceptable level of damage, and therefore to risk it is to incur an unacceptable level of risk.

Most of these considerations are not made known to the general public, but they are known to the experts. The scien-tist and weapons analyst Kevin Lewis has observed: "From an operational military point of view there is no validity to asser-tions that the U.S. retaliatory capability is eroding. Moreover, it is extremely unlike-ly that the situation will change in the foreseeable future."

### The Counterforce Doctrine
But the public is told that if the Soviets have achieved greater accuracy in the delivery of nuclear weapons, this gives them the capability for a first strike whether or not they intend to use it. Since we cannot know their intetions, it is argued, we must prepare for the possibility that they will use it, and move toward that same capability ourselves.

It is a favorite ploy of alarmists to direct our attentions either to capability or intent, depending on which of the two best furthers their cause for alarm. If we attribute to the Soviets a desire as great as ours to avoid a nuclear war that may end in mutual destruction, we begin to doubt their intent to initiate such a war. The alarmists then concentrate on capabil-ities, suggesting that these speak for themselves and that we can never be sure of intent. They purposefully overlook the defensive reasons for the development of certain Soviet military capabilities, while insisting that all of our own capabilities were developed solely for defense. If, on the other hand, the Soviets lag behind us in some area of capability, and fail thereby to pose a credible danger, the alarmists switch horses and become quite sure of Soviet intent, pointing out that ever since 1917 the Soviets have been bent on world domination—even though they know perfectly well that such a goal is no longer possible and real.

Nuclear strategists call the modern first strike capability a counterforce. Possession of a counterforce, they say, enables a nation to fight an extended nuclear war limited to military targets, in an attempt to destroy command centers and deterrent forces that might otherwise be used against industrial and population centers. The counterfroce doctrine is even presented as humane. Civilian populations are supposed to be spared.

Yet it is obvious that many critical military targets are located in major cities or adjacent to them. It is also obvious that, once the military targets are gone, we cannot be sure if the force threatened with defeat will any longer abide by some prior understanding and hesitate at that point to retaliate against civilian populations. Indeed, in the event of such an exchange between ourselves and the Soviet Union, should we succeed in eliminating Soviet leadership as our counterforce strategy now directs, we would simultaneously eliminate the small assurance we might have had that the war would remain orderly and limited. It is impossible to predict how those who would then take charge of surviving strategic forces in the USSR might wish to dispose of them.

This is so obvious that the counterforce doctrine was officially rejected by the United States government in the 1960s. We were told its risks were so great that to embrace them was simply irresponsible, and that the very concept of fighting a limited war brought total war closer because it made a nuclear confrontation seem feasible to survive, when in fact survival was impossible to predict. We were also reminded that the invulnerability of our deterrent force was sufficient to preserve our national security, and made further development of offensive nuclear weapons redundant.

Yet the counterforce doctrine is the very concept embodied in Presidential Directive 59, announced in August of 1980. The reason given for its adoption is the alleged Soviet deployment of a counterforce, as though we now faced a ''counterforce gap.'' Since the greater accuracy of our own missiles gave us a counterforce capability long before the Soviets had one, and since the greater number of our missiles permitted us to begin aiming hundreds of them at Soviet military targets as long ago as 1964, eleven years before the Soviets had even begun to plan such targeting refinements, this gap is no more real than the gaps which preceded it.

Military targets have been part of our Single Integrated Operating Plan (SIOP), which directs the deployment of our strategic weapons, for 16 years. SIOP 5-D, the version of that plan which currently prevails, has been active for the past 26 months and has required no modifications since the announcement of PD 59.

Soon after the new doctrine was announced, it was possible for the administration to admit what it had refused to concede in two previous years of discussion about the proposed MX missile: that the MX had been designed not only to escape a first strike but also with the required precision to make one.

The most difficult counterforce targets, of course, are superhardened ICBM silos. Randy Forsberg of the Institute for Defense and Disarmament Studies in Massachusetts notes that the only warheads believed sufficiently accurate to be credited with a 90 percent probability of destroying such targets are the Mark 12A now being fitted on our Minutemen III Missile and the Soviet SS-18 Modification 2 warhead. Until such time as the MX is built, such weapons will continue to be scarce. Approximately 75 SS-18 and 100 Mark 12A warheads are currently deployed. There is now speculation, all of it eminently reasonable, that if the Soviets feel their military targets are threatened, this would make nuclear war more likely. Indeed it could. But the Soviets began worrying whether we intended one day to use our first strike capability as long ago as 1955, when our Strategic Air Command first received the B-52 bombers whose only

mission was to threaten or carry out such a strike. They began worrying about our counterforce capability as long ago as 1974, when our missiles first gained sufficient accuracy to warrant concern. That should explain any Soviet attempts to develop more accurate weapons of their own. They felt forced to do so, just as we now claim we are.

If, with strategic forces already mobile in the seas, we develop the MX to make our land-based missiles mobile too, the Soviets are likely to respond by developing an MX of their own. This would further complicate verification problems. It would also complete a new round in the arms race that could leave us further behind than we claimed we were when we began it.

The public announcement of PD 59 was certainly timed for political reasons. It helped to preempt discussion of whether new weapon systems like the MX were really needed. It helped to enhance Congressional approval of such systems. It also helped to rebut Republican charges that the Carter administration had failed to provide an adequate defense. Even so, the decision to make the counterforce doctrine known is no less significant. It reveals how our planners are thinking, and indicates that our government now believes it needs and can obtain public support for this strategic posture.

While the public mood has been steered toward a greater militarism, the risks of the counterforce strategy may grow more obvious with time. For it does not make the world a safer place. It makes it more dangerous. The Soviets have certainly realized that the only defense against a possible first strike is a first strike of their own. The temptation to preempt a preemptive strike raises the risk that one nation or another may actually try it. Indeed, if one nation believes that the other, in accordance with the new doctrine, is going to retaliate first against only military targets, and that its cities will therefore remain unharmed after the first exchange, the deterrent effect of a risk to its cities collapses, *encouraging* the temptation to make a first strike.

After the announcement of PD 59 there emerged a preliminary consensus of opinion that the new doctrine afforded the United States an alternative to what Ronald Reagan called the options of ''defeat or surrender'' and what the Carter administration at the same time told the nation was a choice between ''suicide and surrender." This view acknowledges that the Soviets now have the ability to inflict unacceptable damage on us. That much is certainly true—unless we begin to believe that such damage is acceptable after all, and that a nuclear war can be "won." But our counterforce argument then goes on to suggest that the Soviets do not face the same threat from us, and that therefore they have different options. They do not have different options. They face precisely the same threat. They will go on facing it, whether or not it is they who attempt a first strike.

Former Defense Secretary Brown described our options differently, when he supported the counterforce doctrine by saying it would protect us from "the stark choice of either making no effective response or totally destroying the Soviet Union." This concedes that we have the capacity to do just that. Since we have that capacity, the Soviets cannot be sure we are bound to prefer Secretary Brown's other option of making no response. It is on this understanding that the theory of deterrence continues, quite effectively, to rest.

Nevertheless, the consensus for a counterforce now prevails. Its proponents suggest that the Soviet Union will achieve a counterforce capability before the United States, when in fact the United States has made much greater progress toward that goal, and when the matter is academic, as neither nation is likely ever to achieve it. They suggest that the two superpowers can simultaneously possess a first strike capability, though by definition that capability exists only when there can be *no* retaliation from the nation first struck.

Counterforce doctrine proposes that a surprise attack by one nation will leave it with such overwhelming strength that the nation first struck will sue for peace rather than risk further devastation. It therefore recommends that we build the mobile MX missile, which would be immune to attack. Yet the strategic forces of both superpowers, apart from some of their long-range bombers, are already immune to attack—their submarine fleets more mobile now than the MX ever could be, their land-based missiles in readiness for launch before enemy missiles can strike.

Were these land-based missile forces vulnerable to each other, it ought to be kept in mind, as well, that 70 percent of Soviet strategic strength is allocated to ICBMs, while only 25 percent of ours is

so deployed. A first strike on the Soviet ICBM force would leave that nation 1,535 warheads with which to retaliate, whereas a first strike on ours would leave us 8,921. Just 10 percent of our surviving arsenal would suffice to destroy every military target in the USSR, every Soviet city, 60 percent of Soviet industry and 90 million Soviet people.

Counterforce doctrine formalizes its thinking with such terms as "Limited Nuclear Options." It talks of a "countervailing strategy" to "contain" a nuclear war, of retaining the "flexibility" to employ strategic force "selectively," in order to respond in a "timely and controlled" manner to "intermediate levels of aggression," so that we might retaliate against "any or all components of Soviet power," providing "extra rungs on the ladder of escalation" to address "the full spectrum of Soviet threats." How the top rung on the ladder of escalation may be avoided is not explained. The idea that both nations can fight a prolonged and limited war is simply said to be more "realistic" than the prospect that each nation may finally unleash all it has to inflict unacceptable damage on the other. The doctrine fails to explain how the risk of that possibility can be realistically ruled out. Those who are more "realistic" are the ones who remain aware of the danger of escalation. Those who deny this danger, and believe that escalation can be controlled, are the ones who have ceased to live with reality.

Counterforce doctrine also talks of "Regional Nuclear Options," reviving the threat of "tactical" nuclear retaliation against conventional forms of agression that otherwise cannot be deterred. General Richard Ellis of our Strategic Air Command recently testified that because of a shift in the strategic balance, "deterrence can no longer be neatly divided into subgroups, such as conventional and nuclear. It must be viewed as an interrelated single entity." The general did not have in mind the NATO battlefield, where in fact we enjoy superiority in conventional military power, but areas of the world like the Persian Gulf, where conventional power may not suffice to protect our interests, and where our general lack of power leaves events beyond our control.

This is a throwback to the policy of John Foster Dulles, who could threaten "massive retaliation" in those years before the Soviet Union had developed the capacity to respond in kind. A brutally effective policy then, it is a very dangerous one today. While we retain an enormous lead despite this shift in the strategic balance, the introduction of tactical nuclear weapons in any area of the world would nonetheless risk escalation today just as much as would a direct "limited" exchange between the superpowers. Events in the Persian Gulf, meanwhile, will probably remain beyond our control.

Counterforce doctrine also asks us to accept that the Soviets have long considered it possible to survive and win a nuclear war, and have "never accepted" the theory of deterrence, though it gives little supporting evidence that this is how the Soviets have ever thought. Indeed, the only evidence of such a view, which is therefore constantly cited by the alarmists as proof of true Soviet intent, is Soviet Marshal Vassili Sokolovsky's book, which states that the USSR is fully prepared to fight and win such a war. The book, however, was written in the early 1960s, when the Soviets had so little retaliatory power that any attempt on their part to engage in nuclear war would have been suicidal. The book was a desperate attempt to build Soviet morale.

While it concedes that after a first exchange the Soviets might sacrifice the lives of million of their citizens, counterforce doctrine presupposes that this would not deter them. It warns that they would still have more missiles with which to completely destroy us—the very outcome this more "flexible" and "realistic" doctrine is supposed to avoid—while at the same time it overlooks the fact that we, too, would have more missiles with which to respond in kind.

Attempts have also been made to discredit the theory of deterrence, which is based on the recognition that there is a risk of mutual assured destruction (MAD). One description of the MAD theory has called it "Strangelovian," as though, by the meaning implicit in this acronym, there were madness in recognizing such a risk. There is a good deal more madness in failing to recognize it.

While PD 59 has been presented as a major shift in American strategic thinking, adoption of the counterforce doctrine was not, in fact, President Carter's decision. Some preparatory work was made by his administration to concede this, with the suggestion that PD 59 evolved from concepts first developed by the State Department's Leon Sloss in 1978, and a later suggestion that it really began in 1976 with a National Security Decision Memorandum (NSDM 242) composed by the Ford administration.

The sad truth is that the counterforce doctrine has been our unofficial policy since 1974. The public reasons given for its adoption are very different from the real ones. In truth, the counterforce doctrine is an attempt to return to the era of unchallenged nuclear supremacy we enjoyed from the end of World War II to 1967. During that period, because we were the only nation with a sufficient number of nuclear weapons, we possessed a genuine first strike capability, and could threaten to wreak massive nuclear destruction upon any country in the world, including the Soviet Union, without fear of retaliation.

It was an era in which nuclear weapons had far greater diplomatic than military value, and when the mere threat of their use almost always gave us our way in the world. Consequently, most presidents frequently made such threats. While it is publicly known that we threatened the use of nuclear weapons to force the Chinese to withdraw from encircled Marine Corps units at the Chosin Reservoir in Korea in 1953, and again threatened their use during the Berlin crisis in 1961 and the Cuban missile crisis in 1962, it is not generally known that we also threatened their use to enforce acceptance of our terms of peace at Panmunjon, Korea, in 1953, and to end the Chinese blockade of the offshore islands of Quemoy and Matsu, occupied by Nationalist Chinese forces, in 1968. These threats were secretly made to the government of the People's Republic of China, and they were kept from the American public.

Nor is it generally known that we offered tactical nuclear weapons to the French for use in defending Dienbienphu in 1954, or that we planned their use in 1967 at the Mu Gia pass in Laos to obliterate the Ho Chi Minh Trail, and in 1968 for the defense of encircled Marine Corps units at Khe Sanh. Nor is it well known that President Nixon secretly threatened the Hanoi regime that he would use nuclear weapons to escalate the war if it did not accept his peace terms in 1969—terms it did not accept only because the North Vietnamese knew that Nixon faced massive opposition to the war at home.

Counterforce doctrine promises to return to this posture of unrestrained belligerence. If we could achieve a new first strike capability, we would be able, once again, to further our interests anywhere we wished in the world, reinforcing our conventional defense of any ally, and supporting our intervention in any region we pleased, with the threat of decisive superiority at every possible level of nuclear escalation should we be opposed. This ability to move through the world with impunity is what the Reagan administration seeks to restore.

Sadder still is the fact that the development of nuclear weapons might have stopped in 1966, at the point when we became assured we could always preserve an effective deterrent force. It did not stop. Though deterrence no longer required it, we continued to improve the accuracy of our weapons, simply because there was no other direction in which continued development could go. Once sufficient accuracy for a counterforce weapon became technically feasible, we foresaw the possibility of a new first strike capability, and this in turn gave birth to the vision of a new American empire ruled by nuclear coercion as before. We adopted the counterforce doctrine based on that capability. Counterforce doctrine merely ratifies what technology has wrought, and upholds what imperialism aspires to.

The hope of achieving this new level of supremacy is an illusion. We lost our first strike capability in 1967, when the Soviets achieved a level of strategic power sufficient to inflict unacceptable damage upon us, thereby ushering in a new era of mutual deterrence. Their effort to narrow our margin of superiority, and thus ensure themselves an effective deterrent, was undertaken out of sheer terror, and while the economic burden of that effort has certainly never surpassed our own, it has been almost as severe. The Soviets are no longer willing to live with the threat we have imposed on the rest of the world since 1945. Their deterrent force certainly cannot match ours, but it remains sufficient—just as ours would have been had we saved hundreds of billions of dollars and stopped producing nuclear weapons a decade ago. If we continue to develop new weapons, and continue to plan for a counterforce, threatening their deterrent capability, the Soviets are not going to stand still. Far from shifting the balance of power in their favor, they have stabilized that balance between us. If we now attempt to destabilize it, they will bend every effort to keep pace with us, in order at the very least to preserve an effective deterrent. There is no reason to think they will fail.

Therefore, our counterforce plan can never be assured of success. The staggering costs of attempting it may exceed our capacity. Aside from these facts, a program to achieve global military supremacy, so that we might have our way in the world regardless of whether we deserve it, is not only morally repugnant but reckless. Its risks are as great as those we undertook each time we threatened the use of nuclear weapons in the past. The costs of miscalculation are so immense, the potential for human suffering so vast, that such a policy could not possibly gain the public support a democracy is supposed to require. That is why so many of our previous threats to use nuclear weapons were kept secret from the public, and that is why the real purpose of our counterforce doctrine has been kept out of public discussion now, and why it has been justified instead by a series of calculated exaggerations of Soviet capability and distortions of Soviet intent.

All this has made the world a much more dangerous place than it needed to be. The deterrent to nuclear war is now no longer an assured retaliatory strike. On the other hand, neither can the counterforce doctrine assure that a retaliatory strike may not still occur. Indeed, it raises the risks that it will. A first strike may not eliminate all of an opponent's retaliatory forces. Civilian populations may still become targets. PD 59 even acknowledges this when it calls for a reserve force of missiles in a prolonged nuclear exchange. Unacceptable losses may be incurred after all. Thus, risk itself has become the only remaining deterrent.

While this state of affairs is far from desirable, and much worse than it used to be, it still seems possible to manage. Risk ought to be a sufficient deterrent.

Yet counterforce doctrine attempts to deny risk. It suggest that a series of wholly unpredictable events can be kept under control. So far as it concedes any risk, its view is that the opponent is the only party willing to undertake it, just as the opponent is always the only aggressor. Therefore we tell ourselves that the Soviets are willing to risk losses in order to win a nuclear war with us. They, in the meanwhile, are telling themselves the reverse. Not only does fighting such a war then become conceivable. It seems to become necessary.

The result of this is the kind of thinking expressed by Nigel Calder in his book *Nuclear Nightmares*. "Winning a nuclear war," he writes, "is the second worst thing in the world, but it is not quite as bad as losing it." On the contrary, for all we know it may be much, much worse. The survivors may envy the dead.

The attitude that it is possible to win such a war means there is no longer supposed to be any such thing as an unacceptable level of losses. Any level of losses is acceptable, so long as we win. Once we are willing to believe that, we are willing to go to nuclear war. That is the danger.

Why have we placed ourselves so close to the edge of survival? Why have we continued to develop a technology we did not need, and which subjects the mind to such pressures of doubt, fear, pride and greed that they threaten to overthrow reason?

Sadly, the only reason why we continued this work was because it was there. The specialized laboratories, scientific skills and production facilities had all been developed. An enormous investment had already been made to bring these resources together. The jobs—sometimes the careers—of physicists, aeronautical and mechanical engineers depended on moving forward. More important, banks and corporate shareholders depended on moving forward. They looked to industry managers to see that their investments would produce the anticipated returns. The vision of expanded investments in a world whose resources we one day controlled through nuclear supremacy further encouraged this work.

The work was sought and provided. Project proposals were drawn up, concept definition studies assigned. Contracts for research, development, testing, evaluation and production engineering followed. The momentum of this work has been such that in 1981 the taxpayer will provide industry with $17 billion for research and development on behalf of strategic and tactical weapon systems.

## The Return of the ABM

These projects include the continuing development of anti-ballistic missile (ABM) systems, on which research has never ceased despite our 1972 treaty with the Soviet Union limiting their deployment to no more than 100 missiles at no more than two separate sites. Our first strategic air defense missiles were the Nike-Zeus and Nike-Hercules systems, the latter of which reached its peak deployment of 134 batteries in 1963. We began to withdraw these from service in the late 1960s, anticipating deployment of the new Sentinel system at 14 sites throughout the country. While no longer operational within the continental United States, Nike-Hercules is still deployed with many of our allies abroad.

Designed to intercept and destroy approaching enemy ballistic missiles both above and below the atmosphere, Sentinel was intended to defend both American cities and strategic forces. Due to its high anticipated cost of $6.6 billion, as well as its dubious effectiveness, the Sentinel proposal met with such heavy criticism that it was withdrawn. It was quickly replaced, however, by the plan for a new Safeguard system—which turned out to be essentially the same as Sentinel, though its missiles were to be based at only 12 sites. One Safeguard complex, deploying high-altitude Spartan missiles with warheads in the megaton range, and terminal intercept Sprint missiles with warheads in the kiloton range, was completed at Grand Forks, North Dakota in 1974, at a cost of $5.4 billion. Because the treaty with the USSR prevented the full Safeguard system from being built, no further sites were completed, and the 100 missiles finally deployed at Grand Forks were allocated to the defense of our Minuteman ICBM force.

It had already been shown that an attacking missile force, by deploying a greater number of multiple warheads and additional decoys, could defeat the Safeguard system at a fraction of the cost of enlarging the system itself. Because the only complex built proved costly to maintain, Congress reconsidered these earlier views and voted to shut down the site at Grand Forks in 1975.

Each year since that time, however, we have continued to spend more than $250 million on further ABM research. $266 million is allocated for this purpose in 1981. Now that we have publicly conceded our counterforce strategy, whose goal of gaining a decisive edge is fully compatible with the ABM concept, expanded research on ABM systems may soon be funded. Currently, a high-altitude intercept missile with a conventional warhead is planned, at a cost to completion of $10 billion by 1990. A high-speed low-altitude missile with a nuclear warhead, to intercept incoming missiles after they have reentered the atmosphere, could also be made operational by 1986. The concept behind these programs is identical to that which guided design of the Spartan and Sprint before them. While missile propulsion and guidance technologies have made enormous strides in the five years since Safeguard was deactivated, the countermeasures these new missiles would have to defeat in the next decade seem far more prodigious than those which rendered the Safeguard system useless.

## Lasers and Particle Beams

An ABM system so effective that it promises to obsolesce ballistic missiles, thereby dangerously destabilizing the balance of power unless both we and the Soviets perfect and deploy it simultaneously, may result from the use of directed-energy weapons. A laser beam propagates its energy at the speed of 200,000 miles per second, so that an attacking missile, ten miles away and moving at twice the speed of sound, could be identified, struck and destroyed before it could move one inch. Computer-steered mirrors could direct such a weapon to one target after another in fractions of a second. Our first prototype laser weapon was built by Hughes Aircraft and TRW for the Defense Advanced Research Projects Agency (DARPA) and the US Navy. It has been fired repeatedly at flights of missiles launched simultaneously and moving at speeds between 450 and 780 miles per hour, on one occasion detroying four out of four, on another, eleven out of eleven.

A more compact weapon, a 15,000 watt carbon dioxide laser built by United

Technologies, has been mounted in an experimental US Air Force NKC-135 aircraft, and is undergoing tests at Kirtland Air Force Base. In the past ten years, over $2.4 billion has been spent on developing laser weapons, $1.3 billion of it by DARPA and the military services, and the other $1.I billion in independent research by universities and the leading defense manufacturers. Another $1.3 billion will be spent by the military in the next five years, including $210 million in 1981. An additional $1 billion may be spent by industry in further lethality demonstrations, which could lead to an operational laser weapon by 1985.

Because it is a form of light, however, laser energy can only propagate itself in clear air. Haze and clouds render it useless. Smokescreens have already been used to defeat laser-guided munitions systems. A particle beam, on the other hand, does not depend on translucent air for its effectiveness. A stream of subatomic particles accelerated at very high speeds, it works precisely like a lightning bolt, and will travel through anything. We have already spent $145 million in particle beam research, including $90 million in 1980 and $110 million in 1981, and we are going to spend much more.

Due to assertions by General George Keegan, the former head of Air Force Intelligence, that the Soviets have 350 laboratories and more than 2,000 scientists engaged in research on particle beam weapons, and that they are building prototype weapons at Semipalatinsk and at Azgir in Kazakhstan, a Nuclear Intelligence Panel was convened to examine his findings. The Panel's report, in turn, gave rise to formation of a particle-beam technology study group of 53 physicists and engineers under the direction of Dr. Ruth Davis, undersecretary of defense for research and advanced technology. This group has quietly but urgently recommended an immediate increase in funding for particle beam weapon research, and there is evidence that we have begun engineering for the production of a prototype beam weapon of our own, which will cost an additional $750 million over the next six years.

### The War in Space
Since laser and particle beam weapons can be mounted in satellites, and since they would be far more effective in orbit above the atmosphere, where interference to laser propagation would be eliminated

and reaction time to a hostile missile launch greatly increased, designs for their use have taken strategic war into space. A 1967 treaty prohibits the use of nuclear weapons in space, but mentions no other weapons.

Lasers of relatively low power would suffice to blind the infrared sensors on many early warning satellites. When one of our MIDAS satellites over the Indian Ocean was blinded in October of 1975, and two US Air Force satellites over the Soviet Union were blinded the following month—one of them for more than four hours—they may well have been the targets of illumination by Soviet lasers.

Because both we and the Soviets increasingly depend on satellites for military communications, navigation and early warning functions, we have become more aware of their vulnerability to attack, with the result that we have developed more plans both to defend them and to attack them. Satellites are now also a primary means of policing the SALT agreement, and while that agreement prohibits interference with "technical means of verification," whether or not this applies to satellites is a matter, as lawyers invariably say, "of interpretation."

Interference with early warning systems is potentially so serious that we now regard confirmed evidence of it as evidence of preparation for a first strike. Since such systems themselves provide some of this confirmation, development of the capability to interfere with them, from ground-based lasers to orbiting killer satellites, is a dangerous step, bringing us closer than almost any other military action to the "hair-trigger" atmosphere of doubt and confusion that can precipitate a nuclear war.

If one superpower takes a dangerous step, so must the other. In 1967 we built two antisatellite bases armed with nuclear missiles at Kwajalein Atoll and Johnston Island in the Pacific. Because they proved, when discovered, to be particularly provocative, we shut them down in 1975. By that time, however, the Soviets had begun to develop hunter-killer satellites. To date they have conducted tests of such weapons 16 times. As a result, we have continued research of our own, and have

budgeted $125 million for antisatellite programs in 1981.

A variety of new antisatellite weapons is under development, from space mines, planted in orbit to explode on command when they come within striking distance of a hostile satellite, to the Vought Corporation's Miniature Homing Vehicle, a weapon weighing only four lbs that would be carried above 100,000 feet by an F-15 aircraft, and there launched to home on its target by use of an onboard computer and infrared sensor.

Many defensive strategies are contemplated, including the use of "silent spares," orbiting satellites that remain inactive, and become operational only on command, to replace others that have been destroyed. Current defensive satellite programs include the improvement of sensor systems with optical filters to guard against laser blinding, the hardening of solar panels, and the development of small nuclear power plants such as that used by the Soviet Cosmos 954, to eliminate the need for solar panels entirely. Antijamming equipment and improved encryption devices have also been developed to resist electronic interference with communications relay satellites—which now carry more than 70 percent of United States overseas military communications. The ground terminals that relay all our data from satellites are vulnerable as well. Consequently, mobile terminals are being developed.

All told, in the last 20 years we have spent more than $50 billion on military space projects, from the fractional orbiting bomb—whose lower orbit reduces early warning reaction time by half—to manned military stations in space. In 1981 we will spend $4.2 billion on such programs.

### Chemical and Biological Warfare
As General Keegan warned of Soviet progress with particle beams, so does our nation warn of similar Soviet progress in chemical and biological warfare, though there is a good deal less evidence of it. Whenever we are about to proceed with programs for weapons prohibited by international treaty, or generally regarded to be inhumane—though you would think that by definition all weapons are, it seems that our style is to point first to the Soviet Union, even if no one can see what we are pointing at.

Thus we announced in 1978 that people were dying in Novosibirsk as a result of an accident at the germ warfare laboratory there, though we provided no evidence to support this allegation. In March of 1980 we circulated reports from the previous four months of a serious outbreak of anthrax in Sverdlovsk, again claiming it was the result of an accident at that city's bacteriological warfare laboratory. The Soviets said it was the result of infected meat supplies. Neutral evidence from the International Red Cross appears to confirm that the type of anthrax suffered was gastric—the wrong kind to result from release of a bacteriological agent, which would have caused pulmonary anthrax.

Nonetheless, these claims helped gain support in Congress for the $20.4 million budgeted in 1981 for research and development in biological warfare.

It took the United States 50 years to ratify the Geneva Protocol of June 1975 prohibiting the use of chemical weapons. Even so, we have stockpiled 150,000 tons of chemical agents, including 100,000 tons of GB, the form of nerve gas known as Sarin, with which we have filled three million 105mm and 155mm artillery shells and a variety of mines and air munitions. Best known of the air munitions is the Mk 116 Mod O Weteye, a 750 lb bomb filled with GB. 901 of these were produced but only 888 exist today, due to a controversial series of leaks.

Less publicized than the Weteye leaks are the 854 others that have occurred in the past ten years at the Rocky Mountain and Pine Bluffs Arsenals, the Dugway Proving Grounds, the Lexington, Umatilla and Pueblo Depot Activities, and the Anniston and Tooele Army Depots, as well as at two installations abroad. Due to this deterioration, whose risks to the environment are greater than those to the military balance, it is estimated that the entire stockpile will not be "militarily usable" after 1990.

After 6,400 sheep died from nerve gas at Skull Valley, Utah, 27 miles from its point of release at Dugway in 1968, a ban on further production of chemical weapons was announced the following year. None of the 259 contracts for further production, however, were cancelled.

After this moratorium of eleven years, we are now prepared to move more openly. Two years ago we announced that Soviet-made Egyptian and Syrian armoured vehicles captured by the Israelis after the Yom Kippur War of 1973 were found to be equipped with rubber seals,

air filters and decontamination equipment. We said this indicated the Soviets were in a high state of readiness for war with chemical weapons, and fully prepared to use them. Of course, this might only have indicated the Soviets knew *we* were ready to use them.

In January of 1980, after the Soviet invasion of Afghanistan, the American intelligence community told the news media that it had evidence from five separate sources that the Soviets had used a form of nerve gas known as Soman at Faizabad and Jalalabad. No casualty figures were available. In April, Professor Perry Robinson of the University of Sussex told the *New Statesman* that "how Afghans unacquainted with chemical weapons had managed to identify Soman is a mystery," because "even a trained chemist would need a laboratory to know." He added that all the reports cirulating appeared to be based on the testimony of one defecting Afghan officer, who had heard the stories himself at second hand.

There is little doubt that if any real evidence of death from nerve gas had existed, we would have found it, had the bodies autopsied by an international panel of recognized medical authorities, and dragged the whole issue before the World Court. This has not happened.

Nevertheless, these reports were followed by William Safire's column in *The New York Times*, in which he said the Soviets were using the TMS-65 truck in Afghanistan. This truck, he pointed out, is used to wash down military vehicles exposed to chemical agents, and its presence there proved that the Soviets "can and will use poison gas in counterinsurgency." The TMS-65 truck is in fact standard equipment for every Soviet Army division, and is also used to clear snow from airfield runways.

Our 1980 budget for chemical warfare included $60 million for production of protective equipment and training in its use. It may be worth noting that American and NATO troops are equipped with a light protective suit, weighing four lbs, which may be worn at temperatures up to 78 degrees for 24 hours, while the Warsaw Pact is equipped with a heavier

rubberized suit that cannot be worn for more than four hours or at temperatures above 60 degrees.

$5 million was also in the 1980 budget for continued development of a new generation of binary nerve gas weapons, which had first been proposed by the Chemical Corps as long ago as 1954. In 1981 we will spend $4.2 million for maintenance of the existing chemical stockpile, $3.15 million to begin construction of a new plant at the Pine Bluffs Arsenal to manufacture binary weapons, and $19 million for equipment for that plant. Production is planned of both 155mm and 203mm artillery shells filled with Binary GB, as well as a new series of air munitions called Bigeye and filled with VX, a more persistent form of nerve gas that keeps target areas contaminated for up to one week. It will take $30 million to complete the Pine Bluffs facility by 1982. The new chemical weapons program on which we have embarked is anticipated to cost $4 billion, including $1.6 billion for the manufacture of the new binary weapons and $2.4 billion to decontaminate and destroy the existing stockpile.

**Stealth Aircraft**
At the frontiers of military research and development, the program that has most stirred the public imagination, as well as political trouble, has been the one referred to as the "stealth aircraft" in August of 1980 by Defense Secretary Brown, who called it "virtually invisible to radar."
In fact for some time many different types of aircraft have been somewhat less than fully visible to radar for a variety of reasons. Yet the Secretary's announcement seemed to indicate that the United States had made significant progress in one of the appropriate areas of technology, or in successfully combining several technological capabilities at once.

Coming in an election year, the announcement was subject to accusations of political gain, even though such accusations are themselves an attempt at political gain. The Republican camp charged that the disclosure had helped the Soviets to determine where best to concentrate their energies in discovering and developing the same technology, as well as in developing countermeasures against it.

The Soviets cannot ignore the possibility that this announcement may have been made in part to misdirect their energies. Nor would they have failed to be aware already of the various means of reducing an aircraft's radar "signature," and heavily engaged in determining the potentials and limitations of technology toward that end.

Nevertheless, the Republicans claimed the announcement was an attempt to show that defense policy was already in excellent hands, and an irresponsible act because it had compromised national security in disclosing what should have been kept a secret. Henry Kissinger said: "We never leaked it. When I was in office it was considered that this was one of the most sensitive secrets we had." President Carter pointed out shortly afterward that the project had not even been classified when Kissinger was in office, and that he had classified it himself in 1977.

On balance, it appears more likely that progress with this technology, long reported in the technical journals to which all intelligence services in the world subscribe, had reached the point where expenditures for it could no longer be kept classified in the budget. Secretary Brown claimed its costs had grown "one hundred times as large" as they had been when he took office. His announcement could have been a sophisticated move to persuade Congress to appropriate much larger funds than it normally would for a classified project. The project will remain classified, and no one will know how the money will be spent.

"Stealth" technology itself is simple to understand, though the procedures required to put its principles into practice are highly complex. Size and design are important. The smaller an object, the smaller the total area it disposes for contact by radar waves, and the fewer the returning radar signals. The smoother an object's design, the fewer the areas it offers to full contact by radar waves, only portions of which strike these surfaces, and do so obliquely, so that the returning signals are weaker. The best design for this purpose eliminates sharp angles and protuberances, and favors curved surfaces over flat ones. All of this was known as long ago as World War II.

A small object like the Northrop Chukar II target drone, designed to be highly visible to radar, has a boxlike shape and sharp intersecting edges at its wing roots. It often appears on the radar screen as a much larger aircraft. Conversely, a large object like the Lockheed SR-71 Blackbird reconnaissance aircraft, with its slim fuselage and very narrow frontal exposure, has no flat surfaces at all. It was designed

to offer a minimum radar signature, and it succeeds. The fastest aircraft in the world, it is also our original "stealth" aircraft, and has often been seen by the naked eye on approach before it can even be found on a radar screen.

The SR-71 is also coated with a thick black paint that absorbs heat, including the energy of radar waves, further diffusing their impulses and weakening returning signals. Built 17 years ago, however, this aircraft is constructed almost entirely of titanium for optimum strength. Technology has since provided even stronger materials, from boron-epoxy compounds and high-strength ceramics to resins and graphite fibers in a carbon matrix. These materials, more and more frequently used today in aircraft construction, absorb a great deal of energy, reflecting less radar energy back to its source of transmission. Plastic polymer coatings also absorb radar energy, further weakening the signals that return.

This technology is combined, of course, with engine baffles to reduce noise, infrared plume suppressors to reduce the detectable radiation of engine exhaust heat, and electronic countermeasures systems that either jam a broad spectrum of radar frequencies or analyse the specific frequency being used, compute a false flight path for the aircraft, and emit signals at the appropriate frequency and bearing but at a higher signal strength, so that the genuine returning signals are drowned and the hostile radar deceived.

The most sophisticated technique of all, and the one most recently perfected, is that of destructive interference, which reflects part of a radar wave from the aircraft's surface coating and part from the material beneath it in such a way that the two sets of reflected waves will be out of phase. When this happens, the two sets of waves cancel each other out, and no signal returns at all.

The problem has been that a given coating applied to a surface material could only combine with it to defeat one specific band of radar frequencies. While these materials might be prepared to conform to those bands most frequently used by air defense radars we may be planning to penetrate, a sophisticated air

defense system employs a variety of radar frequencies, and it is standard procedure to change a radar's frequency while it is in use.

This problem has been overcome by developing plastic and resin coating materials laced with electrical filaments which heat them and cause them to expand. Controlled by a computer that is part of the aircraft's electronic countermeasures power management system, the filaments automatically heat and expand the coating to a predetermined setting which ensures that the radar waves used at any given time to detect the aircraft, and whose frequency has already been analyzed by the aircraft's radar receiver, will be out of phase. Such coating materials have been applied to wing and other leading edges of several test aircraft with effective results against a significant number of commonly used military radar bands.

## The Defense Establishment

Apart from the occasional advance of this kind, in which technology has a substantial military impact, the bulk of the projects pursued in our research and development programs is rather less practical, frequently redundant, and soon abandoned. Pentagon files bulge with the records of projects begun and cancelled—usually at an enormous cost to the taxpayer. Far from developing in the arcane atmosphere of think tanks, most of these projects are based on proposals from industry. Some are approved and completed whether or not they are needed.

One of the great myths of our system, often propounded by the same people who complain that there is too much government interference, too little laissez faire, is that the development and production of weapons depend solely on requirements set by the government, and defined as a military need.

Yet the B-1 bomber is not a military need, according to the former president who vetoed it. The F-18 Hornet fighter aircraft is not a military need, according to the military service that will soon begin deploying it. The Navy has repeatedly tried to drop the F-18 program, but it cannot. The Congressmen who speak for the corporations producing this aircraft won't let it. This program may cost the taxpayer more than $26 billion before the planned procurement of 800 F-18 aircraft is completed. Three different heavy-lift helicopters were not a military need, nor were two different airborne warning systems, the Boeing E-3A AWACS and the Grumman E-2C Hawkeye. Much of this duplication of effort was achieved because industry wanted the work. $40.5 billion will be spent on weapons procurement in 1981.

It is difficult to control a sector of our economy that absorbs more than $55 billion in military contracting each year. As it is, the defense industry produces more weapons than our military services need. This is partly a result of the continued growth of those firms engaged in their manufacture. They have no alternate economic model to follow. Like all other business firms, they plan increases in revenues and profits each year, whether or not there is any comparable expansion of genuine need for their product.

To justify their growth, our defense manufacturers exaggerate the need for weapons by exaggerating the threat they are meant to counter. Thus, the defense manufacturing community is the first to raise fears of growing Soviet military power. But it is not the last. The military establishment, in turn, supports this view of the threat.

This is partly because the military is charged with our nation's security, and would prefer to err on the side of caution, neglecting the possibility that too much caution may be more harmful to our security than too little. It also prefers not to question an industry that may provide a future career after military retirement, and which more and more frequently does so. Finally, aware of the credibility problem these tendencies create in the eyes of Congress, it feels it must exaggerate the threat to unlock military funds.

In step with economic expediency, our foreign policy establishment adjusts to the military-industrial view by turning the magnified threat into official doctrine.

The result is a war economy whose output we cannot absorb. This situation is aggravated by the high costs American industry charges for modern weapons. The costs of many weapons have outstripped the available funds to procure them. In many cases, procurement of a sufficient number of weapons for our own needs requires that we support their expanded production in order to lower their unit costs. Thus, industry finds itself looking abroad for markets to absorb the balance of production. Inevitably, those markets are found. That is why America

will probably continue to be the world's largest arms supplier.

The costs of some weapons, indeed, are so high that you wonder if this industry will be able to continue turning out the quantities we require without first bringing our economy to its knees. You wonder if the corporate system is the wrong one to rely on for such vital needs, and whether a good deal more government regulation and less laissez faire are not in order to ensure our survival. Billions of dollars in cost overruns, as a first step, could be saved.

But the problem goes deeper than that. While the defense industry continues to grow, working on more different weapons than we ever asked for—though producing too few of those we need and at too high a price—it grows only by the sober degrees mandated by corporate accountants. It is careful to operate close to capacity, limiting excess overhead, keeping employment to a minimum, maximizing profits. This is considered virtuous by those who do not closely examine the relationship between corporate overhead and corporate earnings, as well as by those who do not define any social responsibility for one of the major institutions created by Western society.

What this means in the defense industry, however, is that if we suddenly needed to acquire a great many more weapons, as the Reagan administration now claims we do, and appropriated the additional funds to procure them, industry would not expand its capacitiy to produce them so quickly as it would raise the prices for those weapons it was already able to provide. This presents a potentially serious conflict of interest between our economic system and the genuine needs of national security.

It is rather like the unhappy result of Medicare. The sudden introduction of an enormous increase in funds to purchase medical services was met by no corresponding increase in the medical work force. This drove up the costs of services charged by the medical establishment well beyond the ability of most people to pay for them, while it only slightly increased the availability of those services.

Thousands of people in genuine need of medical care continued without it.

A recent article in *Forbes* magazine, arguing for a "citizen army"—which is to say the draft—and for large-scale military production, recognizes that our weapons cost too much, and that they also have high failure rates and are difficult to maintain. These problems are all the result, it believes, of too great an emphasis on high technology.

The article reminds us that the Soviets update and improve their weapons by an evolutionary process of sequential modifications, while we strive for revolution, designing new weapons from the ground up. Demonstrating that "programs lag when technology dictates the product line," it outlines the military and economic disadvantages of "staying on the drawing board when you can get on the learning curve."

Citing a recent internal memorandum from former Defense Secretary Brown which questions whether we have made the right choice in emphasizing quality over quantity, *Forbes* answers that it has been the wrong choice, and recalls that in World War II the Germans, who led the world in technology, made the same mistake. President Roosevelt promised that we would "bury them in sheer numbers of equipment," and we did. *Forbes* recommends that we therefore return to producing greater quantities of "workmanlike but workaday" equipment.

Aside from the fact that simpler equipment has nearly as high a rate of failure, that in numbers we do not lag behind the Soviets nearly so much as the article suggests, and that higher technology has more than offset those imbalances that do exist, what this article chiefly overlooks is that without a fundamental change in government control over the entire industrial complex, we could not produce greater numbers of weapons even if we needed to. Industry has made the choice for higher technology, because it has been more profitable.

It seems paradoxical that a sector of our economy so privileged as the defense industry could be so inefficient and produce such waste. But there is a simple reason for this. While the military services, the government and the taxpayer all experience it as waste, the defense manufacturers do not. They experience it as profit. They may be inefficient at making weapons, but not at making profit. The purpose of a corporation, after all, is to make profit, whatever else it makes or fails to make.

In fact, military appropriations are the single most concentrated source of profit for American corporations. Military contracts are preferred above all others, because they provide several unique advantages in meeting corporate goals. Production is for the most part based on outside capital, invested by the government rather than by the corporation itself. Production is remarkably free of risk, because military contracts will guarantee payment for cost overruns that have been as high as 800 percent, and which no other purchaser would tolerate. The industry is relatively free from competition—one of the few normally stabilizing factors that tend to inhibit higher prices in those other sectors of the economy not already controlled by monopolies of their own. Finally, there is a continuing demand for new product, because the pace of military technology ensures that the greater portion of what has already been produced will become obsolete.

As a result, American defense contractors, according to the General Accounting Office, have averaged profits—after taxes—of 56 percent over the past decade.

This industry claims it is also supporting a large labor force. If it did, its margin of profit would not be so high. If the labor force expanded according to need and to the funds supplied, the industry would certainly be more productive and more efficient. But it does not expand in this way. Indeed, the more specialized an industry becomes, the more capital-intensive. The defense industry has a *decreasing* requirement for labor.

Because some weapons are needed while others are not, and because the genuine needs may or may not be recognized, the defense labor force is wholly dependent on the random results of these varying perceptions, and of the procurement decisions to which they lead in Washington. It is further dependent because it is too poorly oriented to cost efficiency and too highly specialized for immediate applications in the civilian sector without costly restraining. Consequently, while many workers may still be swayed to patriotism by the propaganda of the new cold war, labor tends not to seek defense work.

Organized labor, in light of this instabili-

ty, has been calling for conversion to civilian production now for over ten years, and has supported most legislation before Congress to provide for it, including the Defense Economic Adjustment Act (S.2279-HR 10648) sponsored by Senators McGovern and Mathias, and the 1975 Transfer Amendment to Congressional budgeting procedure.

How important, then, is the defense industry in providing employment? Not very. A Chase Econometrics Associates study in 1975 compared the proposal to spend $17 billion over the next nine years on the Rockwell B-1 bomber with two alternate programs: a $17 billion tax cut and a $17 billion housing program. It found that if the money were returned to the public in the form of a tax cut, by 1980 induced consumption spending would have created 30,000 more jobs than Rockwell would have offered, and that the housing program would have created 70,000 more jobs. A study by the Public Interest Research Group concluded that for every billion dollars spent by the government, the defense industry created fewer jobs than any other program except that of the National Aeronautics and Space Administration.

## The Real War

Defense manufacturers, in any case, are not concerned with providing jobs, whatever they may say. Their industry is the most buoyant sector of our economy, and they reap its rewards even as unemployment rises. High unemployment is no more a threat to them than it is to any other major industry. In fact, they view it as beneficial. It raises the efficiency of the surviving worker force, and weakens its union bargaining power, holding wages down. It encourages government to relax costly regulations protecting worker health and safety, as well as those protecting the environment.

If unemployment reaches a crisis point in our society, threatening a general recession, this is dangerous only for small businesses. Large corporations continue to benefit. Business taxes are lowered, the press becomes more tolerant of abuses,

consumer complaints are ignored, criticism is silenced, and the public in general is depoliticized. Everyone falls into line. Meanwhile, investors continue to increase their share of income while the proceeds to labor are proportionately reduced.

The growth of income in one group has a proportionate effect on the income of another, as economists know, because the total income produced by a society is finite. If more income goes to one group, less of the total remains to divide among the rest. Because it is an axiom of corporate growth that income must increase, each year more income is distributed to corporate investors, and less remains for those who cannot invest. The body of investors and property owners in our society is not increasing commensurately with the growth of corporate income. In fact, it is rapidly decreasing, and therefore the gap between income groups is widening at the same pace.

Today, less than two percent of the American people earn over $50,000 a year, while more than 75 percent earn less than $20,000. Eventually 60 percent of all our income, or $1.2 trillion a year, will be in the hands of eight percent of the people, leaving $800 billion for the remaining 92 percent.

Income, of course, has never been equally distributed in our society, which proudly guards the right of all citizens to engage in free enterprise in order to increase it. But while all of us have the right, few have the means, regardless of the contribution they may be willing and able to make to society, and the number of those who do have the means continues to shrink. As this economic inequality grows, it will endanger our national security far more than any alleged Soviet threat.

The business community itself is not unaware of this. *Business Week* now refers to the growth of a "two-tiered society." *Fortune* magazine predicts "a profound change in income distribution, with explosive political consequences."

Inflation will bring us to this point sooner. Its effects, we are told, strike everyone. But they do not strike equally. To the large corporations with earnings to reinvest, inflation is simply part of our system. We have had it for more than 100 years. Our oil conglomerates, which by themselves represent nearly 25 percent of the value of all stocks traded today, are not affected by inflation. Property owners with sufficient income to absorb the shocks of inflation do not make sacrifices. The majority does.

Yet the Soviet threat, the need to arm up, to protect America's might, save her honor, and make the world safe for democracy—all are appeals which claim the right to tax more money from a majority whose real income, already insubstantial, has been further reduced by inflation. These appeals are really only a means of requiring those who can least afford it to further subsidize corporate growth. We are asking them to commit a slow, steady form of suicide.

Meanwhile our economy veers toward recession. This does not affect large corporations, which simply substitute investments and markets abroad for their original domestic counterparts. At home, social security and unemployment insurance are cut back, while the government attempts to solve the crisis by raising the money supply. This does not enable us to purchase more goods. It just raises the prices of goods already available.

Sixteen million people in the United States now survive on public assistance of one kind or another. The members of *Business Week's* upper tier are often those who first complain of the high costs of public welfare. The burden of welfare would not be so great, and the need for it less, if income were distributed more evenly. A redistribution of income, beginning with a complete restructuring of our tax system, would be one major step toward solving this problem. Another would be the establishment of controls to discourage wasteful growth in our defense manufacturing sector, and the return of its surplus earnings to the taxpayer. Another would be the creation of a military budget based upon genuine rather than counterfeit needs for the protection of this nation's security.

Hand in hand with such a budget, we must take other steps to provide for our security. We need an immediate ratifica-

tion of SALT II, with or without agreement on verification procedures. We need a ban on all further nuclear weapons tests. We need a declaration from every nation in the world, but most especially from the United States and the Soviet Union, that it will not be the first to use nuclear weapons. We need to remove all nuclear weapons, including "tactical" types, from Europe. We need an international agreement prohibiting the introduction of nuclear weapons in the Middle East or in any other areas of the world presently free of them. We need a ban on the introduction of all weapons in space.

Possibly, with these measures, we may avoid the holocaust. The abolition of war is no longer an ethical question of curbing man's instinctive aggression. Nuclear war removes this question from the moral arena. It is now simply a question of survival. Rear Admiral Gene R. LaRocque recently wrote: "Nuclear war is not a means by which the forces of good vanquish the forces of evil. In a nuclear war both good and evil perish."

The current mood in our nation raises little hope that measures like these will be taken. Instead, in the midst of the worst economic crisis we have suffered in many years, we have planned the largest single increase in military spending in American peacetime history.

What we are witnessing, in this call to arms, is one more attempt to hold on to what we have. We have been the beneficiaries of an unprecedented luxury which probably will not be seen again. The historical period in which we happened to live is coming to an end. Western society has comprised only one quarter of the world's population, but it has been the owner of three quarters of its product. The United States holds only five percent of the world's population, but it has lived off 30 percent of its resources.

Resources are the key. Many will allow that war with the Soviet Union is unlikely to occur, though they may prefer to remain ignorant of its risks. They say that the real war is economic, and they have named it "the war called peace." They say that this war is not only with the Soviet Union but the whole world. In any part of the world, they will concede, we are less concerned over whether a regional peace can be maintained than over whether we can protect our access to its

resources. That is what really determines our foreign policy goals. We are engaged in a resource war, they will say, and now they see our options shrinking, our control diminishing, the American empire vanishing.

Wars will most probably continue to occur. Throughout the world, new crises will develop. In order to survive them, and in order to play a responsible role in world affairs, we must first solve a far more serious crisis at home. Our current mood of militarism is an attempt to take our frustrations abroad. Throwing more money at the military will not make it do what no longer can be done by military power, and only aggravates the real crisis. Observers say that the nation's moods are cyclical. Given the nature of the cycle on which we are now embarked, we will be fortunate if we complete it.

Therefore more than luck is needed to see us through. What is needed is the participation of masses of people in this country and throughout the world in a protracted and determined effort to protest the uses of being made of their income and their resources, and of the risks being played with their lives. Governments exist to serve the people. They must be responsive to the will of the people. The people have the power to assert that will. In this country, that power is embodied in our Constitution. Let it never be forgotten that in 1969 hundreds of thousands of people in this country demonstrated to assert their will, and their will was done. They forced our government to withdraw from Vietnam. The Nixon administration did everything it could to prevent them from learning how effective their protest was, because it feared the power that knowledge would confer. Let that power be understood now. The American people did it. They can do it again.

New York
May 1981

# ARSENAL II

## A SURVEY OF AMERICAN WEAPONS AND ARMS SALES

Much of the material in this section was first published in *Arsenal of Democracy* in 1978. Most of the entries have been revised or updated to accomodate developments that have taken place, or facts that have come to light, since that time. For some corrections the author is indebted to several individuals whose names appear in the Acknowledgments.

Since 1978, there has been a record number of new sales of almost every weapon produced in the United States— and therefore almost every weapon in this book. Due to limitations of space, it has not been possible to place this information in the individual entries for each weapon system. Consequently, full details of these sales will be found at the back of the book in the *Registry of Major American Arms Transfers Since 1978*. Similarly, new prices will be found in the *Current Unit Procurement Prices* section at the back of the book.

The introductory section, *America's Role in the Arms Trade*, deals for the most part with the many means by which arms are transferred abroad from this country, and examines the laws governing such transactions. It also examines our arms export policy, citing several examples of its risks. One of these examples was our decision to provide, over the course of several years, almost $20 billion in highly advanced weapons to Iran, a country still ruled by the Shah when *Arsenal I* appeared. In retrospect its warnings about Iran seem appropriately prophetic. In fact, most observers at the time offered similar warnings. Because this episode has some historical value as an example of a policy that may be repeated, it has been retained here.

Following the fall of the Shah, and the decision of a new regime to cancel more than $8.7 billion in contracts for American military equipment and services, we quickly found new markets for most of the arms the Khomeini government chose to decline. The key buyers to emerge for this surplus were the American taxpayer, who will underwrite the costs of more than $14 billion in military and economic aid to Egypt and Israel over the next five years, and Saudi Arabia, which has now replaced Iran as our largest arms client, and upon which nation we lavish all the weapons it desires because we hope it will also replace Iran as our new military proxy in the Persian Gulf, filling a power vacuum we presume to exist in the wake of the Shah's demise, and promoting peace and stability throughout the region.

Regrettably, Saudi Arabia seems no more capable than the Shah of performing such a role, and a good deal less willing to do so. Its attitude toward Israel promises that it may take the initiative in undoing the very peace our massive program of aid to Egypt and Israel is designed to secure.

Since *Arsenal I* was published, our sales of arms have continued to be used primarily to enhance the profitability of those corporations which produce them, to achieve economies of scale in procurement for our military services, and to recycle petrodollars we would not have to spend if we more vigorously pursued a program of energy independence. To justify its acceleration of these sales activities, the Reagan administration has now recycled the Soviet threat, removing the last vestiges of restraint imposed more in spirit than in fact by the administration before it. Under Secretary of States James L. Buckley announced in May of 1981 that sales of our weapons abroad would ''complement and supplement our own defense efforts'' in ''facing up to the realities of Soviet aggrandizement.''

However, our own defense presumably comes first, and our attempts to persuade the American people that we need more weapons to match the Soviets tank for tank and ship for ship may fall on deaf ears once the people are better informed. How, for example, will the public be able to continue believing we suffer the dangerous weakness in tank strength it is told exists, once it learns that over the past decade we have been perfectly willing to increase this ostensible weakness by selling more than 8,800 tanks and self-propelled guns to other nations instead of keeping them for ourselves, or that our Navy really needs more warships when in the same period we have opted to supply more than 300 such vessels to navies abroad?

Arms sales have continued to bear the same liabilities as before. Frequently, arms are more of an economic burden to their new owners than a military gain. Frequently, they are used for purposes other than those we intended. The likelihood improves that some of them may one day be used against us. This was precisely the prospect facing our hostage rescue attempt in Iran. Frequently, arms sales aggravate regional tensions rather than promoting stability. Our sales of advanced F-15 and E-3C AWACS aircraft to the Saudis may endanger Israel's security more than they improve Saudi Arabia's.

Not only do other nations frequently find themselves unable to operate and maintain many of the weapons we sell, but sometimes our military services cannot provide the technical and training assistance needed to ease their absorption without unduly straining our own limited resources. Sales of highly sophisticated equipment to unstable regimes may also compromise our own military security by placing advanced technology in unfriendly hands, thus neutralizing the technological edge we invested so much to achieve.

Frequently, too, our sales of arms have introduced a higher level of technology to a new region, destabilizing its prior balance of power and guaranteeing a new regional arms race. Our announcement in June of 1981 that we would sell advanced F-16 aircraft to Venezuela, when only a few months earlier we were unwilling to offer Mexico anything more modern than the F-5, certainly opens up a lucrative market for our defense manufacturers, as neighboring nations strive to attain the same level of military capability. But it is also a level of capability previous administrations worked hard to avoid introducing in Latin America. That work has now gone in vain. Our decision to supply the same F-16 aircraft to Pakistan, announced shortly after the Venezuelan sale, will have a comparable effect in Southern Asia.

Similarly, both Taiwan and the People's Republic of China will soon begin to purchase new American arms, though neither nation recognizes the other's right to have them. How the Reagan administration plans to resolve this dilemma remains a mystery. Most likely, it has no plans at all. But it seems certain that higher levels of military technology will be introduced into this part of the world as well.

The gravest consequence of our deep-ening military alliance with the People's Republic may be its effect in deepening Soviet insecurities. As the Soviets feel more threatened by growing Chinese military capabilities, they may abandon the reluctance they have hitherto shown to take military measures in Poland in order to preserve the stability of their western flank.

Having already initiated a new strategic arms race between the superpowers, the Reagan administration, through its controversial decisions to sell advanced weapons to nations in the Middle East, Asia and Latin America, has launched a series of regional arms races as well. It has shown such zeal in pursuing these policies that it probably does not even want to absolve itself of the responsibility it must surely take for accelerating the onset of a new Cold War. Even so, the decline of detente and the pattern of conflicting goals and troublesome consequences of our arms sales policies were already well established trends by the time Reagan arrived in office.

# AMERICA'S ROLE IN THE ARMS TRADE

In the past decade the United States, always a major producer and supplier of arms, has taken the lead in an increasingly competitive market and become the world's foremost merchant of military hardware. This country is now responsible for more than half of the $22 billion in weapons currently traded each year. Our closest competitor, the Soviet Union, can account for only about 24 percent of that total. France and Britain follow, with arms exports of $1.9 billion and $1.4 billion respectively.

## The Policy of Deterrence

Several factors have contributed to the American ascendancy in the arms trade. The ambivalence of our foreign policy has played an important role. Over the past twenty years, as we developed a posture of detente with the Soviet sphere, we began to reduce force levels abroad, withdrawing some American troops and closing some military bases. At the same time, we increased arms exports and military aid to the very countries we had quit. For while we hoped to reduce international tensions, and to encourage reciprocation from the Soviet Union, we also wished to ensure the security of those areas of the world no longer directly protected by the American presence.

The assumptions behind this policy have been outlined by Deputy Secretary of Defense Charles Duncan in his testimony to Congress of 24 March 1977:

*We believe that when countries know that they are capable of defending themselves, they will be more likely to feel secure enough to hazard a negotiated peace, less likely to take preemptive military measures, and less likely to require direct U.S. assistance.*

This reflects two of the basic convictions held by those in our country who make or deploy arms. They believe that arms are a deterrent, needed not to make war but to preserve the peace. They also believe that arms can be an equivalent to our own combat troops as a deterrent force, eliminating the need for direct American support.

The influx of arms that consequently follows American force reductions abroad demonstrates that, while we had first hoped to diminish the level of tension between certain nations, what ultimately concerns us more is to ensure that those who confront our allies in our absence will remain as cautious as they ever were. The weapons we export are meant to sustain a sufficient level of tension to guarantee such caution. The new level of tension may equal or even surpass the old, and thus the results may at times contradict our original intent.

These attitudes continue to prevail, and promise in the near future to account for a sizeable increase in our arms exports, despite recent expressions of hope to reduce them. In the wake, for example, of the planned withdrawal of 33,000 American troops of the Second Infantry Division and other units from South Korea, a sale of more than $8 billion in arms to that country has been proposed, including missiles, destroyers, helicopters, field artillery, and 240 jet fighter aircraft, 90 of them new-generation F-16s, together with technical assistance in establishing domestic tank production facilities. The first $1.8 billion worth of these weapons and services has been proposed for transfer next year.

Certain other objectives, too, are accomplished by substituting American weapons for American military personnel. We increase the flexibility of our power by disengaging combat troops for redeployment wherever else they may be deemed needed, and the weapons that replace them serve as further extensions of that power. Our weapons have in effect become a new form of colonialism, expanding our influence, we believe, in perfect accord with the Nixon-Kissinger doctrine of enlisting other nations, whenever possible, to do our fighting for us. As we implement this doctrine, we also find new markets for our weapons industry.

It is difficult to know whether or not the need on the part of our weapons makers to find a wider market has sometimes influenced presidents and generals to choose this option of policy. It is not difficult to see that the policy itself is unreliable. We cannot be sure that another country will fight the war we wanted fought, or that if it does it will fight on the side we had anticipated, using the weapons we supplied against the adversary we had foreseen. The political alignments of countries change, and history has shown that while arms may play a considerable role in the course of those changes the nature of their role is unpredictable.

Weapons have little diplomatic influence. To their suppliers they have been of dubious value in ensuring the allegiance of the countries that receive them. When M-47 and M-48 Patton tanks were supplied to Pakistan, she used them in 1965 to go to war with India, facing M-4 Sherman tanks also directly supplied by the United States. The transfer of these weapons did so little to establish Pakistan's reliability as a long-term ally that President Carter's recent reluctance to supply that country with 110 A-7 Corsair II attack aircraft, a $770 million sale, appears at the time this is written to be the only sale he has successfully blocked.

**M-48 Tank**

More than one war has been fought with American weapons on both sides. The M-48 tanks we supplied to the Jordanian and Israeli armies did not deter the one country from using them against the other in 1967. Far from deterring conflict, weapons frequently promote it, making it more feasible than in their absence, and escalating the threat of a wider war in direct proportion to their sophistication and lethality.

It is clear that most of the time we mean to use weapons only as a deterrent. Few really want a war, though there are also some who do. There may have been times when weapons have succeeded in their deterrent role. That is difficult to ascertain. Unfortunately, there is more than ample evidence that they have also regularly failed. A policy that may only work part of the time is a poor risk.

### Recession and the Oil Crisis

In the early 1970s an increase well above previous levels in the flow of American arms exports was generated by a recession in this country's economy that happened to coincide with a 400 percent rise in the price of oil imposed by Middle-Eastern producers. The end of the war in Vietnam, and our resulting decline in productivity, occurred at the same time as the permanent end of an inexpensive supply of one of the world's major energy resources. The arms and aerospace industries in particular had grown to a point where the domestic market could no longer sustain them. They began to look for new markets. What more natural way to pay for the oil, to redress our balance of payments, to keep the production lines open and recycle the petrodollar back into our own economy than by selling arms? Consequently, we began subsidizing an arms

race in the Middle East.

During the 1960s the Foreign Military Sales agreements signed by the United States government and administered by the Department of Defense averaged $1.5 billion yearly. Commercial exports of arms, licensed by the Department of State's Office of Munitions Control, averaged an additional $200 million per year in the same period. By 1972, arms exports under the Foreign Military Sales (FMS) program had jumped to $3.2 billion, and in 1973 they reached $5.7 billion. They nearly doubled the following year, rising to $10.6 billion, while commercial exports climbed to $502 million in 1974 and $580 million in 1975. Middle-Eastern markets in 1975 accounted for $5.2 billion in American arms sales.

During these years of expanded arms deliveries to the Middle East three countries alone, Saudi Arabia, Iran and Israel, accounted for 52 percent of all United States Military exports.

Israel's share of these exports was largely due to the war she fought with Egypt and Syria in 1973 and 1974. During those two years we responded to her needs with close to $1.2 billion in arms, including 400 M-60 tanks, 200 M-48 tanks, 35 F-4E Phantom jet fighter-bombers, eight CH-47 transport helicop-

**M-163 Self-Propelled Vulcan Air Defense System**

ters, a number of M-113A1 armoured personnel carriers, and a variety of anti-tank, surface-to-air and anti-radiation missiles. A further $980 million in arms, the balance authorized under the Emergency Security Assistance Act of 26

**DD-963 USS Spruance Destroyer**

December 1973, was delivered to replenish her inventory after hostilities ceased.

However, the bulk of our arms exports in the 1970s has gone to the Arab oil-producing countries. In the same two years that we delivered $2.18 billion in arms to Israel, we delivered $3.7 billion to Iran, a country not at war. According to a recent United States Treasury Department study, Saudi Arabia, the United Arab Emirates and Kuwait now account for 28.3 percent of all our arms exports.

From 1974 through 1976, we signed agreements to sell M-48 tanks to Morocco, C-130 Hercules transport aircraft to Morocco, Egypt and the Sudan, A-4M Skyhawk aircraft to Kuwait, TOW anti-tank missiles to Lebanon and Oman, HAWK antiaircraft missiles, Vulcan 20mm antiaircraft cannon and F-104A Starfighter aircraft to Jordan, and HAWK missiles and Maverick television-guided air-to-surface missiles to Saudi Arabia. In 1976 the Saudis alone spent $2.5 billion on military equipment, most of it supplied by the United States.

But our largest customer by far was Iran. After President Nixon's visit to the Shah in 1972, at which time he promised to supply Iran with anything it wished from our arsenal, the Shah's government signed agreements to purchase 105 Northrop F-5E Tiger II aircraft, 36 F-4E Phantom fighter-bomber aircraft, 293 UH-1B Iroquois transport helicopters, 80 of the Navy's new F-14A Tomcat fighter aircraft, 160 F-16 air superiority aircraft (in a contract worth $2.4 billion), 202 AH-1J Cobra attack helicopters, 65 of them equipped with

TOW anti-tank missile launchers, six KC-135 tanker aircraft, three Tang Class submarines, six Spruance Class destroyers that will carry more modern weapons and electronic equipment aboard than we plan to fit on our own destroyers of the same class, and a $500 million communications intelligence system known as Ibex. In 1976, Iran spent $10.4 billion on arms.

In addition, the Shah asked for 250 F-18L aircraft, the land-based version of a new Navy carrier fighter, and seven Boeing E-3A AWACS (Airborne Warning and Control System) radar surveillance and battlefield control aircraft. He even expressed interest in purchasing the SR-71A strategic reconnaissance aircraft and the B-1 strategic bomber—on which research and development continues despite the Carter decision to cancel its procurement for our own Air Force.

The Saudis, too, have a long shopping list, including 110 Northrop F-5E and F-5F aircraft, 60 of our Air Force's new F-15 Eagle fighter interceptors, 2000 AIM-9L Sidewinder air-to-air missiles, 1800 TOW anti-tank missiles, and 1000 laser-guided bombs. They would also like to increase their inventories of HAWK antiaircraft and Maverick air-to-surface missiles. All of these proposals have been under consideration by Con-

gress, the Pentagon and the Department of State.

The 650 Maverick missiles and 30 F-5E aircraft that the Saudis already possess combine to form the most sophisticated anti-tank system now in existence. What threat do they meet? The Saudis explain that they must be prepared for tank attacks along their border with Iraq. Intelligence analysts think that threat to be unlikely, but agree that in the event of a new outbreak of war between Israel and any bordering Arab country, those F-5Es and Maverick missiles will probably find their way to the Arab confrontation state.

As though to confirm this probability, Saudi Arabia has undertaken to build along her border with Jordan three of the largest fighter-bomber air bases in the Middle East. These should be completed within the next six months.

Thus, while weapons may not always perform their deterrent or defensive role, it seems they are capable of finding other roles to play. They appear to have a life of their own. As few of the weapons

**A-4C Skyhawk Attack Aircraft**

sold to Saudi Arabia, Iran or other Middle-Eastern countries are required for defensive purposes, we must understand why they have been purchased. In the first place, attempts are made to sell them. In the second, there may be other than clear military reasons why they are desired. Indeed, there may even be other than rational motives for their appeal.

## Sales Efforts and the Arms Race

It has always been the task of a salesman to create a need when his market fails to perceive one. Along with a number of independent arms brokers, the sales representatives of all the major arms manufacturers in our country roam the world. Their value to the companies they serve lies in the contacts they have made, and these they do all they can to develop. They bribe handsomely. The enormity of a weapons sale makes exhorbitant fees and commissions perfectly tolerable to pay, and far too tempting to resist. In 1971 Lockheed sold 14 C-130 Hercules transport aircraft to Italy for $60 million, after a $2 million investment in commissions and fees.

These salesmen entertain lavishly, print extravagant brochures and display materials, and exhibit their wares at a variety of general and highly specialized international gatherings, from the Paris Air Show to the symposia of the Society of Photo-Optical Instrumentation Engineers.

They also work closely with the members of our Military Assistance Advisory Groups (MAAG) and the military attaches of our embassies abroad, who in turn arrange introductions for them to the key procurement officers in each country's military establishment. Needless to say, it is a short step from embassy garden parties to private meetings where the salesmen recommend their products, and are quick to show how these are superior to competing weapons systems and why their prospective client needs them.

A recent report on arms control, based on a Presidential Review Memorandum prepared by the National Security Council and released to Congress by the Carter administration*, recognizes the significant difference this kind of activity makes, and acknowledges the permissive and even supportive role that our government has frequently played:

*More stringent controls on private industry and some revisions in internal United States government procedures could result in further reduction or elimination of those factors which some view as providing the incentive to stimulate foreign government interest in purchasing United States defense articles and services. Commercial firms are most successful in promoting sales where United States government guidance is permissive or susceptible to foreign or domestic political pressures.*

As part of a new arms control policy announced by the President on 19 May 1977, anticipated arms sales are now to be discussed with appropriate officials in

our government, and approved by them before a sales representative approaches a foreign government.

However, like most of the other provisions of the new policy, this is an impossible restriction to enforce. The meetings are in fact still held, the needs discussed, the new weapon systems described, even demonstrated, and the bribes paid. Only recently, the Grumman Corporation planned to pay $28 million in fees and commissions to its agents for completing the sale of 80 new F-14A Tomcat fighter aircraft to Iran, and paid $6 million of this amount before the Iranian government objected.

Formal arms requests from foreign governments are sent, as they always have been, through their official purchas-

**F-14A Tomcat of the Imperial Iranian Air Force**

ing missions in this country, through MAAG and other United States military channels or through the American manufacturer to the Pentagon, where their impact on our industrial capacity and force readiness is analyzed to ensure that they do not conflict with the priority needs of our own military services. From there certain requests are sent to the Department of State and, if sufficiently large or sensitive, to Congress for Approval. The President now reviews some of the larger arms sales.

In an economy move the United States has decided to terminate MAAG units in Argentina, Bolivia, Brazil, Colombia, Ethiopia, Iran, Japan, Kuwait, Liberia, Morocco, Pakistan, Saudi Arabia, Taiwan, Venezuela and Zaire. Since this list includes some of our largest arms clients, we clearly do not feel the lack of MAAG personnel will jeopardize future arms sales. Presumably, the security requirements of those countries on the list will be well met by an established contingent of sales representatives from the private sector who function effectively on their own, whether or not they abide by the rules.

In any case, should official security

assistance be required by any of these countries, both House and Senate have approved permission for United States military teams of as many as six people to continue to be stationed in any American embassy abroad.

Why does the market respond to sales efforts with needless purchases of arms? The answer to that question goes to the roots of the human psyche. Weapons promise death. They are the ultimate symbols of power. They are salves to our feelings of vulnerability, goads to our instincts for domination. Through them we are believed, respected, approached with caution, frightening when we choose to be. Most of all we are real. With weapons in hand we must be acknowledged when otherwise we might have been ignored.

Modern weapons fascinate us by their sheer precision and ingenuity. The dazzling complexities of the latest generations of American missiles, aircraft and automatic gun systems may very well represent the highest achievements of modern technological skill. As we continue to develop and improve these systems, toughening them, increasing their speed, their accuracy and destructive power, making them ever more impervious to radar and infra-red detection, more resistant to defenses and counter measures, it is as though we had tried to conquer all the possibilities of error by man or machine, to encompass all the vagaries of chance, to dissect the mechanics of fate, to be God.

As a commodity, weapons may be unique. No other material wares play at once upon so many depths of human instinct. Few other commodities, with the possible exception of narcotics, have such a high intrinsic value as to make the application of bribes an economical means of increasing their distribution. No other commodity can expand its market by the simple device of selective sales. All the salesman need do is sell the latest weapon to one country and wait for its neighbor to respond with jealousy or fear. That is how arms races are born. Generations of weapons quickly obsolesce their predecessors, and that is how arms races are continued. What we have not learned is how they are ended.

*Report to Congress on Arms Transfer Policy, 1977. PRM 12, National Security Council, 1977.

### The Changing NATO Market

The momentum of our industrial expansion, towards limits of growth not fully understood or even accepted by the credo of free enterprise, has caused our arms manufacturers to find other markets in addition to the Middle East. The NATO countries have been an important market, and exports to this bloc have been encouraged by the priorities of our foreign policy. However, FMS exports to NATO have dropped from $3.149 billion in 1975 to $1.096 billion in 1976.

This is partly due to the growing number of co-production agreements which, in an attempt to standardize NATO equipment and munitions, have begun to replace a share of our former arms exports. The Dutch firm of Fokker and Belgium's Fairey/SABCA will each assemble 174 of the new F-16 fighters for European deliveries. Northrop's F-5A and F-5E aircraft have been licensed for production in Canada, Spain and The Netherlands. Oto-Melara in Italy produces M-113 armoured personnel carriers under license from FMC Corporation, as well as General Motors Corporation's M-109A1 self-propelled 155mm howitzer. Lockheed's F-104 Starfighter aircraft have been licensed for production in Italy, West Germany, Belgium and The Netherlands. Italy's firm of Agusta makes Bell helicopters.

Aside from affording these countries increased political and military self-sufficiency, co-production agreements expand their available labor force, increase its level of technological skill, and most important of all, reduce the balance of payments each country must meet. More than half of the 65 major co-production agreements signed from 1957 to 1976 have been with NATO countries. (Major American weapons systems co-produced in other countries now include TOW and Maverick missiles as well as helicopters in Iran, helicopters, HAWK and NIKE missiles and F-4 Phantom aircraft in Japan, helicopters and F-5E aircraft in Taiwan, and ammunition and M-16 rifles in South Korea).

But the reduction in exports to NATO is due in the main to competition from growing indigenous arms industries in the NATO countries themselves, which not only now supply the major proportion of equipment for their own armed services, but have also begun for the first time to supply weapons systems to

**Euromissile's ROLAND Air Defense System**

United States armed forces, inluding the Hawker-Siddeley Harrier fighter-bomber, 102 ot which have been procured by our Marine Corps, and Euromissile's Roland II surface-to-air point defense missile, co-produced by Germany's Messerschmitt-Bölkow-Blohm and France's Aerospatiale, and recently adopted by the U.S. Army for licensed production in this country by Boeing and Hughes Aircraft.

### Arms to the Third World

We have had to look elsewhere to expand our weapons sales, and one of the most controversial of our markets has been the Third World. American arms exports to the developing non-oil producing countries in 1976 totaled $2.3 billion. According to the State Department's Arms Control and Disarmament Agency, between 1971 and 1975 we supplied to these countries 3,560 tanks and self-propelled guns, 5,240 armoured cars and armoured personnel carriers, 63 major naval surface combatants, 22 submarines, 593 supersonic combat aircraft, 460 helicopters, and a total of 10,035 missiles of a variety of types*.

Many of these sales have been financed by United States government guaranteed loans, and the credit terms are liberal. This encourages developing nations to buy weapons they may not need. It also increases their heavy bur-

*World Military Expenditures and Arms Transfers, 1966-1976, United States Arms Control and Disarmament Agency

den of debt. In 1964, the developing countries were already paying out an aggregate of $4 billion in foreign exchange for debt services. This nullified the effects of the economic aid they were simultaneously receiving.

According to the Agency for International Development, the last ten years have seen an increase of 90 percent in military expenditures by developing countries, while developed countries have increased their military expenditure by an average of approximately 23 percent.

By 1972 the aggregate debt of the world's developing countries had grown

**A Harrier V/STOL Aircraft of Britain's RAF**

to $90 billion, and in the past five years that figure has doubled. It is an intolerable situation which several factors have combined to produce, among them the rising price of oil and the reduction of exports to fully industralized nations whose purchasing power was cut by recession. But the sales of arms, supported by liberal bank credit, have played a major part.

Developing nations used to complain that if we refused to sell them arms we were keeping them defenseless, and dependent upon us for protection. Now they argue that by selling them arms we keep them equally dependent upon us, because we keep them poor. They are right. It has been argued that they don't have to buy. Neither, it should be countered, do we have to sell.

But of course, we believe that we must sell. We believe this because we believe the arms are needed. We believe they are needed because we are making them.

### The Growth of the Defense Establishment

In all probability, some weapons of some kinds will always be needed. An industrial force of some finite size will always be required to provide them. A nation, regrettably, must arm itself in order to maintain a credible warfighting capability. This should be done in response to only the most objective assessment of the threat which may confront it. The problem lies, always, in forming and sustaining an objective view of the threat.

As our policy makers expand their sphere of interest, the nature of the threat in their eyes grows more complex and comprehensive. The arms industry, meanwhile, grows at its own steady and seemingly irreversible pace, encouraging a magnified view of the threat in order to justify its growth, and receiving in turn the support of a military bureaucracy which must retain full confidence in its ability to rely on our industrial capacities in time of need. To curb or interfere with industry is the last thing it would do.

This attitude is well reflected in a recent statement from the Department of Defense on the impact of arms export controls on our military capabilities:

*Currently, readiness in terms of industrial preparedness is enhanced by maintaining an active production base, through foreign military sales, for defense materiel where domestic orders are insufficient to support continued production.\**

In effect, we are maintaining a war economy whose output we cannot absorb.

The relationship of mutual support between government and industry breeds serious distortions in their shared perception of our need for arms. It is an inevitable result of the continued growth of the military-industrial complex, that entity about which President Eisenhower, leaving office eighteen years ago, warned us in his parting comments to the nation. It has all grown much as he feared it might. Aside from the 2.1 million uniformed personnel and 850,000 reservists who currently make up our armed forces, and the additional one million civilians who work for the Department of Defense, 35,000 of them in the Pentagon itself, there are today more than 1,100 major American corporations employing a total of more than 700,000 workers, and engaged almost exclusively in the research, design, development, testing, evaluation and production of weapons.

This complex web of government agencies, private organizations, think

\*DOD/Impact of Arms Transfer Restraint on our Military Posture, 1977

tanks, business firms, bureaucracies and lobby groups has spun about itself so many threads of mutual affirmation, shared assumptions about the national interest, common policies on parity, deterrence and readiness, and underlying philosophies of human behavior as to weave an almost impenetrable fabric of doctrine to validate its vested interests.

Thus, in addition to the belief that arms can function solely as a deterrent, that regardless of the historical record arms may be relied upon to control rather than to breed aggression, it is also held that the United States has a global responsibility, that to protect its interests it must protect the interests of a large number of other nations, that these nations are its allies and that it is entirely up to the United States whether they remain so, that military assistance is the primary means to ensure their continued allegiance, that the demand for arms grows purely out of rational need, that the makers of arms cannot and do not stimulate that demand but are merely supplying an existing market, that if we do not supply that market someone else will, that the only way to ensure industrial stability is to expand productive capacity, that corporations therefore have a continuing obligation to do so, that we cannot sit idly by and watch the Soviets expand their sphere of influence by supplying arms, that we must compete with them for influence everywhere in the world, that there is no other form of economic competition so effective as arms exports, and that the threat of Soviet expansion is, as one key National Security Council memorandum (NSC-68) termed it, "limitless."

While every one of these ideas can and should be challenged, they serve to justify the continued rise in arms production, and so far have enabled the military-industrial community to go about its business effectively shielded from most attempts at economic reform or political reevaluation. It finds reliable support in Congress, most of the members of whose oversight committees on armed services and foreign affairs regard themselves more as extensions of the defense community than its critics, and can be counted on to reflect its in-

terests, or the compatible interests of their own constituencies, before they consider the views of the taxpayer and general public.

Indeed, Congress will often provide more support than the Pentagon desires. When the Navy recently attempted to cancel its F-18 fighter development program, even so outspoken a Senator on arms control as Edward M. Kennedy of Massachusetts fought, and with his

**F-18L Cobra Fighter Aircraft**

colleagues from that state succeeded, in keeping the project alive so that the Lynn, Massachusetts assembly line for the F-18's General Electric F404 engine would remain open, and the threatened jobs secured.

An interesting result of this is that the Vought Corporation, whose assembly line for its A-7 Corsair II attack aircraft was threatened with closure due to cancellation of the sale of 110 of these aircraft to Pakistan, has suggested to the

**A-7E Corsair II Attack Aircraft**

Navy that it replace the current A-7 engine with two of the GE F404 engines made in Massachusetts, and that the Navy substitute the A-7 for the proposed F-18, thus making everyone happy.

Congress did recently oppose the sale of seven Boeing E-3A AWACS surveillance aircraft to Iran. The sale was consequently delayed, though not cancelled. For once, there was no counter pressure to push the sale through on behalf of the large Boeing constituency.

That is probably because the Boeing Company, which has developed the new cruise missile, is in the midst of expansion to prepare for the missile's engineering and production, as a result of President Carter's decision at the end of June to proceed with the missile and cancel Air Force procurement of the B-1 strategic bomber—a decision, incidentally, for higher military technology and not for economic reform. Boeing has all the work it can handle.

Congressional opposition to the AWACS sale was based not upon the realization that Iran could do very well without the aircraft but on the fear that in Iranian hands, so close to the Soviet border, the AWACS risked a compromise of security, jeopardizing our exclusive control of the very advanced and highly classified technology in the aircraft's computer, radar and cryptographic equipment. Some of this equipment, however, would not be installed on the Iranian version of the AWACS. The rest of it, an Air Force major told me, would be safe. "We do not," he said, "regard the transfer of equipment as a transfer of technology. We may give equipment to another country and teach them how to operate it. But they could never learn how to manufacture it."

One wonders if this confident attitude is encouraged by the fact that there would be other advantages to the sale. The value of the Iranian contract for seven of these aircraft is $1.23 billion, or $175.7 million per aircraft. That is a very high unit cost when compared with our Air Force procurement cost, and the reason for this is that the contract includes the costs of spare parts, training and technical services, and a good share of the original AWACS research and development costs. The Iranians know this and are happy to assist Boeing in paying that share of its development costs. They have the money and they want the aircraft. The result would be to reduce the sum of research and development costs currently apportioned to each unit in our own Air Force procurement program for the E-3A AWACS.

Air Force procurement costs for the AWACS have risen from $65.6 million per aircraft at the program's inception to $80.9 million per aircraft in Fiscal Year 1978. The current unit share of research, development, testing, evaluation and spares brings the total unit program costs of the AWACS in 1978 to $126.3 million. The Air Force will purchase three of these aircraft in 1978, and has estimated the unit procurement cost, without adding costs of research and development, to go as high as $95.8 million before the program is completed. The available funding will now procure only 25 aircraft, though the Air Force had originally wanted 34. They would still like to have them. If the Iranian sale goes through, lowering the unit costs to the Air Force, then they will get them.

The danger of placing technology in the wrong hands is also minimized in Iran, with whom we obviously enjoy a

**F-5E for the Saudi Air Force,**

very special relationship. Aside from the fact that the version of the AWACS proposed for the Iranian sale would have a reduced load of computer and radar equipment aboard, scaled down mostly to better suit less sophisticated Iranian requirements, the remaining equipment would be operated and kept under the supervision of American technicians. There are 30,000 Americans in Iran now, and more are on the way. We seem intent, as we step up our assistance to this country, on keeping an eye on her activities and keeping close control over the technology we have provided her.

A more serious compromise of technology could be the transfer that has been proposed of 60 F-15 Eagle fighter interceptors to Saudi Arabia. In comparison with Iran the Saudis have poor security. As they further fund and cooperate with Egyptian and Syrian programs in the Middle East, it would grow progressively more difficult for them to protect the F-15 technology from reaching the Soviet Union.

It should be noted that in the case of

the F-15 two Senators, Hubert H. Humphrey and Clifford P. Case, did object to its proposed sale to Saudi Arabia, not only because it contradicted President Carter's stated policy on limiting arms sales abroad, nor simply because it would tend to destabilize the military balance in the Middle East, but also because the Saudis are not yet ready to handle it. The Saudi Air Force is still in the midst of a three-year training program to fly a much simpler aircraft, the F-5.

Despite these many objections the Air Force sees the F-15 sale as it sees the AWACS sale. It is a step to increase production and reduce unit costs. One source was quoted as saying, "The F-15 has a cost problem and, to a degree, it makes sense to amortize the overrun with a big sale to the Saudis."

The arms makers, meanwhile, with such a combination of interests supporting them, turn to the more practical benefits of this cooperation. Termination contracts are signed ensuring the manufacturer that, in addition to recouping his original investment, he will also receive from the government a generous portion of his planned income from a project in the event it is cancelled. Thus, a contract with the Vought Corporation for Fiscal Year 1977 procurement specified the production of 360 non-nuclear Lance surface-to-surface battlefield support missiles and warheads for a total of $77.5 million, and when it was decided to terminate the non-nuclear Lance program procurement was reduced to 180 missiles. The total amount to be paid for this smaller order is $74.5 million. Acknowledging that half as many missiles were to be bought for almost an equivalent sum, the Pentagon explained that the "associated costs" were for "missiles, termination of non-nuclear Lance, and training."

Little training can be involved in a program that has reached completion. The escalating factor is the "termination" cost. It raises the cost per missile from $215 thousand to $413 thousand. But it ensures a minimum total loss to the manufacturer.

At the same time as they negotiate generous contract guarantees, the weapons makers also recruit valuable personnel. In the arms business retired military officers are highly prized for their contacts in the military services, their knowledge of the procurement process, and their potential influence on procurement decisions. Increasingly, they have been drawn from the military into the defense corporations where, along with their civilian salaries, they frequently collect retirement pay from the United States government—a practice known as "double dipping."

An investigation of the flow of former military personnel to the private sector was made by the House Armed Services Committee in 1959. It found that 1,426 retired military officers were employed among 72 of our leading arms manufacturers. 251 of them were former generals or admirals, and both Lockheed Aircraft and General Dynamics each employed 27 former generals or admirals at the time. Ten years later Senator William Proxmire conducted a similar investigation. By that time, 2,072 officers who had retired at the rank of colonel or above were employed among the country's 100 leading defense contractors, and over half of that number were employed by only ten of these firms. Since 1969, an additional 1,785 transfers have taken place, 1,406 of them from the Defense Department or the military services to private industry, and 379 from private industry to the Department of Defense.

In the Office of Defense Research and Engineering alone, the Fitzhugh Commission found that of 101 employees who had served as director, deputy director or a member of its management group since 1958, 31 had taken jobs with defense contractors, 16 of them with the same firms that employed them before they joined the Department of Defense. A recent transfer from this office was Malcolm R. Currie, its director before the Carter administration. Mr. Currie now works for Hughes Aircraft.

All of this leads to a variety of potential conflicts of interest. It means that procurement decisions worth millions of dollars may be made by men who formerly worked in the defense industry, and who might well tend to favor their former employers, or by men who look forward to a second career in industry, and who do not want to jeopardize their prospects for such employment by questioning cost overruns or production failures too closely, or by enforcing too stringently the terms of a contract with a potential future employer.

This deteriorates the normal relationship between buyer and seller, in which the seller must meet the criteria of quality and prompt delivery, absorbing unanticipated costs, and in which the buyer tries to ensure quality and the lowest possible cost. The consequent abandonment of normal controls can lead to such extravagant waste that a section of the United States Criminal Code has for many years prohibited retired military officers for the rest of their lives from selling anything to the Department of Defense. However, the regulations specify no penalties, and have never once been enforced. New legislation has just been approved by the Senate to amend the Defense Production Act to prohibit a defense contractor from employing any former procurement officer if that officer dealt with the contractor in his official capacity. But the prohibition would only last for two years after an officer's retirement, and if it became law there is no guarantee that, for even this period, it would be enforced.

Procurement officers have themselves occasionally criticized the wastefulness and irresponsibility that stem from this lack of controls. Usually, they have been effectively silenced with demotions or new assignments well out of the public eye. The unwritten policy is simply to preserve the financial health of the major defense contractors, regardless of the cost to the nation and taxpayer.

To this end, the Defense Department has made considerable commitments. During the Korean War it was granted the authority to declare a state of emergency and by this means give financial assistance, without Congressional approval, to any manufacturer whose productivity it declared was essential to national security. That authority has never been rescinded, and the Defense Department has since that time invoked it more than 3,000 times to negotiate contract adjustments or to provide emergency loans to industry. It has also twice purchased all of the stock of companies in financial trouble.

What is important to understand, and what is all the more frightening, is that most of the members of this vast and intricate establishment are decent people, who believe wholeheartedly in what they are doing. They see no conflict of interest. They have no intention of abusing the prerogatives of their office, or of compromising professional standards of conduct, and most of them never will. They are dedicated, competent, frequently brilliant at what they do.

**Arms Transfer Agreements to Third World by Suppliers, 1972-1976** ($ in billions)

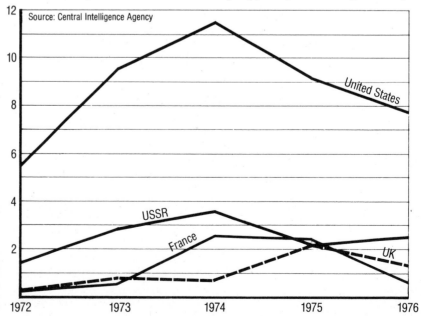

They want to continue doing it. So far as they have thought about the issues involved in their work, the very nature of it invariably gives them a sense that they are in public service, that they have our most vital interests at heart. Even though they are engaged in the production of weapons, or in their procurement and deployment, the majority of them abhor violence and do not want to see any part of the world at war.

Like most of the rest of the world today, these people are also fully absorbed in what they do. This fixation upon work promotes, as it always has, the stability of a large sector of our economy, chiefly by imposing a narrowness of vision. In the military services there are requirements to be met, orders to follow, deadlines and schedules, levels of operational readiness to maintain for men and equipment. In industry, the top executives are concerned with the balance sheet and the bottom line, with profitability and the report to the shareholder. The managers are intent on improving efficiency and productivity. The designers and engineers are engrossed in the intricacies of technology, and in the endless demands of development and refinement. All are carried away by momentum and the need for steady work.

Consequently, as in most other fields of institutional endeavor, the implications of arms production and procurement go largely unappreciated by its practitioners, its real effects insufficiently examined, and hence their chosen beliefs and rationales for their work remain unchallenged.

There are, of course, some people in the defense establishment who do nothing but think. They are paid to do it. Precisely because of that, however, it is difficult for them to challenge the convictions of their employers. They cannot be concerned with questioning the basic tenets of our foreign policy, or with finding ways to halt the growth of arms production or to extricate ourselves from the grip of industrial momentum. They are never asked to question such things. They are committed to different tasks of

analysis, tasks set by managers who do not have the time to think for themselves, and who are certainly unaware that the only questions to which they seek answers presuppose the continuity of a status quo. It must all go on. Perhaps as a consequence of this, most of the thinkers, when faced with questions that do challenge the status quo, appear fatalistic in their approach to what we have wrought.

Among the professors in the research institutes, the contingency planners in the Pentagon, the military analysts and futurists throughout the defense community, those who foresee the risks arising from a growing proliferation of arms, even those who foresee the possibility of a major war, are sanguine. They seem to believe that the human race will survive a holocaust, and most of them seem coldly unconcerned with the question of who the survivors will be. Their attitude, in which they seem to take pride, as though having accomplished true objectivity at great personal expense, appears to be a new application of Darwinian selectivity. They reason, for example, that if the Soviets win a war with the West, they are the fittest and should survive. Might, it would appear, still makes right, after all our years of descent from *homo erectus*.

## The Cost of Weapons
A final major reason for the rise in American arms exports is the sharp rise in the costs of weapons themselves. This rise in costs has far outstripped the available procurement funds, despite a steady increase in the size of our defense budget. In order to acquire a sufficient

**E-3A AWACS Aircraft**

quantity of a given weapon system to meet prescribed force levels, we must do all we can to increase its production run, so that each unit, as in the case of the Boeing AWACS, absorbs a smaller amount of the basic investment in research and development. More and more regularly, the size of the production run required sufficiently to reduce this cost far exceeds the needs of our

own armed services. Hence, we increasingly look abroad for markets to absorb the balance of production. In order to arm ourselves, we must arm the world.

The high priority we assign to weapons procurement also dampens the normal desire to impose proper regulatory controls on industry contracts. Generous guarantees and cost overruns are therefore the rule, and are rarely challenged. This is one factor in the growth of the cost of weapons. As it has gone largely unchecked, it is difficult to measure the role this factor plays.

## Inflation
Inflation is a large factor, too, and its contribution is simpler to determine. The 1966 United States defense budget of $64.7 billion was worth $76.04 billion in 1970 dollars, and is worth $138 billion in 1977 dollars. As the 1978 defense budget authorizes appropriations of $118.5 billion with only $105.9 billion in expenditures, such figures are sometimes used to suggest that this country has reduced the growth of its total defense outlay.

In 1966, however, we were engaged in a war in Vietnam, and the high levels of defense procurement at that time represent an exception to the normal pattern of growth. This can be seen by comparing our defense budgets before, during and after the Vietnamese war in constant 1970 dollars. By that standard, defense expenditures sharply rose by more than $12 billion from $63.75 billion in 1965 to $76.04 billion in 1966, and dropped from $72.09 billion in 1972 to $68.58 billion in 1973. The rather milder drop of $3.5 billion indicates that the normal pattern of growth was continuing after the war, rather than being reduced.

The high procurement levels of the Vietnamese war contributed to a boom in the arms and aerospace industries. As we have seen, far from reducing production and adjusting to a smaller market after the war, these industries continued to expand, and had to look abroad to maintain their growth.

By and large they have succeeded. Aerospace industry sales alone reached

$30.1 billion in 1976, with exports totalling a record high of $8.4 billion in 1977. This, of course, includes deliveries of some civilian aircraft, engines, parts and spares, along with the bulk of military equipment. But to determine the total volume of weapons and supporting military equipment currently produced in this country, one need only add the total of exports to total domestic procurement.

**The Volume of Arms Production**
The $105.9 billion in authorized defense expenditures for Fiscal Year 1978 represents 20 percent of the total Federal budget for that year of $503.45 billion. Of this $105.9 billion 34 percent, or $36 billion, has been authorized for weapons procurement. Figures for arms exports in 1977 and 1978 can only be estimated, but the figures for 1976, which have just become available, are as follows: $8.66 billion under the Pentagon's Foreign Military Sales (FMS) program, $1.1 billion in licensed commercial sales, and an additional $210 million in grant aid, for a total in exports of $9.97 billion. Most observers agree that, while these export levels may increase at a slower rate than was anticipated before the Carter administration, they certainly will not drop. This means, then, that at even a fairly conservative estimate the total volume of arms production in this country, to meet both domestic and foreign sales, has reached a level of approximately $46 billion. This, of course, is based on official figures. We shall later see that the true volume of production is rather higher.

Of this $46 billion, 21 percent in 1976 was exported—a much higher share than was reached during the 1960s. In effect, through exports and co-production agreements our military services are maintaining an increase in the rate of weapons procurement, and the industry that serves them, supported by a wider market, helps to maintain that increase by sustaining its own growth.

To understand how much destructive power we are actually adding each year to the arsenals of the world, we must examine the composition of our military exports. General Howard M. Fish, until recently director of the Defense Security Assistance Agency, told me that only about 40 percent of the materials exported under the Pentagon's FMS program comprised weapons and combat

equipment. The balance of 60 percent is made up of supporting equipment, including radios and other electronic items, vehicle parts and spares, medical supplies, uniforms, technical manuals and countless other articles. This, he indicated, has been a fairly constant ratio in past years.

This might suggest that 60 percent of our military exports are really quite harmless. In truth, all of our exports are equally important in providing a foreign country with some sort of combat capability. A sale of weapons might expand or modernize that country's arsenal, but sales of spares and support equipment are vital in keeping its weapons systems operational. The Presidential report to Congress on arms control acknowledges this:

*To deny sales of weapons and ammunition is to deny an increase in combat capability and possibly cause a gradual diminution of current capability through obsolescense; to deny spare parts or supporting equipment is to cause a rapid decrease of current capability.*

We must also understand the composition of worldwide military expenditure. Some reporters have cited $300 billion as the world's current annual expenditure on arms. In fact, the most generous estimate of an annual expenditure on weapons themselves, excluding the costs of manpower, training, military construction and supporting equipment, is approximately $180 billion worldwide. In view of the size of our own industry, our knowledge of other major arms industries, and intelligence estimates of the size and composition of Soviet and Eastern European industries, that figure seems about right. It is still impressive enough, equal to half a billion dollars a day.

However, if one adds the costs of manpower, training, military construction and literally tens of thousands of items of supporting equipment, the world's total annual military expenditure well exceeds $400 billion.

What inflation and the lack of regula-

tory controls have recently combined to do is to raise, over a period of four or five years, the original estimated cost of a number of weapons systems by as much as 50 percent. The Budget Guidance Manual of the Department of Defense defines the dollar value of a weapon system in the year of its development estimate as the base-year dollar value. The base-year dollar unit procurement cost of the Air Force's new F-15 Eagle fighter interceptor was $12.962 million, based on the purchase of 108 aircraft. The Air Force plans a total procurement of 729 aircraft in the

**F-15 Eagle Aircraft**

F-15 program. For the Fiscal Year 1978 budget, the purchase of 78 additional F-15s has been estimated to cost $17.948 million per aircraft. This estimate is in what the Manual calls then-year dollars, reflecting price levels for materials and labor at the time expenditures are actually made, and including an estimate of inflation. These figures are for the procurement of identical aircraft, equipped with the same avionics, electronic warfare and weapons systems, and the very sophisticated Hughes AN/APG-63 radar.

**The Cost of Advanced Technology**
Finally, the overall costs of weapons have been multiplied by the requirements they must meet in order to be effective and survive on the modern battlefield, and by the costs of the increasingly complex technology that provides them with these capabilities.

Advances in metallurgy and the chemistry of high explosives, refinements in ballistics and aerodynamics, developments in optics and laser technology with numerous applications in missile guidance, sighting, ranging and night vision systems—all these have been achieved only at an enormous cost in materials and man-hours for research and engineering. The RDT&E budget (Research, Development, Testing and Evaluation) for all three military services in 1977 was $10.942 billion, and will be $11.899 billion in 1978. These costs add to the final prices of the weapons they improve, as do the manufacturing costs of the new components they engender.

Military applications in the fields of electronics and data processing thrive, and are among the most costly. Computers, display terminals, optical scanners, data link and telemetry systems have automated the modern battlefield, eliminating human error in the calculation of angles of fire, rates of speed and the directional bearing of targets. Improvements in radio transmission have increased the power, range, flexibility and security of communications systems. Applications of scanning and acquisition radars have revolutionized fire control systems for missiles and automatic guns. In avionics, ground mapping radars are employed to navigate an aircraft, night or day, at any altitude, in any weather, by matching its course with known contours of the terrain over which it flies. Inertial guidance systems now keep naval vessels on course. Acoustic and infra-red sensors, and magnetic anomaly detectors, are used for the location and identification of targets. Missiles are guided by passive and active radar, infra-red heat seeking, television and electro-optical homing systems.

The receivers, pulsers, mixers, processors, analyzers and jammers of electronic warfare, including counter measures and electronic intelligence equipment, accounted for sales of approximately $500 million in 1975, and

**USAF B-52G of Strategic Air Command**

are estimated to reach a total of more than $2 billion in sales in 1977.

One program to add what the Air Force calls Phase VI ECM (electronic counter measures) suites to 296 of the B-52G and B-52H long-range bomber

aircraft in our Strategic Air Command will cost approximately $1 million per plane. It includes such equipment as the AN/APS-105, a radar homing and warning receiver which alerts the crew to the range, bearing and type of enemy radar searching for the aircraft and which indicates whether or not the radar is locked onto its target, six additional radar warning receivers, the AN/ALQ-127, a tail pulse doppler radar warning receiver and jammer, the AN/ALQ-59, which jams enemy radio and VHF (very high frequency) data link transmissions, chaff dispensers to mislead oncoming enemy missiles, the AN/ALE-20 flare dispenser to confuse infra-red heat seeking missiles, the AN/ALQ-77 noise jammer, which confuses enemy radar by filling its returning signals with what the operators call dirt, three additional radar spot jammers for specific bands of radar frequencies, a barrage jammer to interfere with radar over a broad spectrum of

**AN/ALQ-131 ECM Jamming Pod under wing of F-16 Fighter**

frequencies, and the AN/ALQ-122 false target generator, a type of deception jammer which imitates the characteristics of returning enemy radar signals and, like a ventriloquist, beams back signals indicating a false position for the aircraft, using such a high output of power that the genuine returning signals are lost.

The Air Force has spent $25 million to date developing the Westinghouse AN/ALQ-131 modular tactical jamming pod, which can be externally mounted on the F-4, A-7, A-10, F-15 or F-111 aircraft. Independently powered by its own ram air turbine engine, the pod will provide what is called dual mode jamming, employing both noise and deception techniques, over five bands of radar frequencies. According to the colonel in charge of development at Wright-Patterson Air Force Base, two prototypes have thus far been built and are undergoing evaluation. The pods are fourteen feet long by a foot wide, and weigh 831 lbs. each. The heart of their system, a Loral Electronic Systems re-

ceiver and processor, weighs just 30 lbs. These prototype components are literally worth several times their weight in gold.

The Air Force expects the first production units of the AN/ALQ-131 pod to cost $340 thousand each. Subsequent runs, in quantities of two or three hundred, may reduce the cost to $285 thousand per pod.

Naturally, technology is under development to defeat the effects of these electronic counter measures systems. Such technology is producing what specialists call electronic counter counter measures equipment. Electronic warfare has become a new battlefield for the expansion of the arms race.

Avionic equipment, including navigational, flight control and landing systems, accounts also for a steadily growing proportion of the costs of aircraft and missiles. Missile guidance, now averaged at about 44 percent of the total missile cost, will increase to approximately 53 percent of that cost by 1981. In the case of aircraft, avionic equipment currently accounts for an average of 30 percent of total cost. A $10 billion industry this year, avionic equipment is anticipated to attain sales of more than $11 billion in 1978.

### Sales Procedures

The export of arms from this country is regulated by a variety of Federal laws, including the Mutual Security Act of 1954 as amended, the Foreign Assistance Act of 1961 as amended, the International Security Assistance and Arms Export Control Act of 1976, which amends and largely replaces the earlier Foreign Military Sales act, and the International Traffic in Arms Regulations (ITAR) which constitute Parts 121 through 128 of Title 22, the United States Code.

This body of law currently permits the flow of arms and other military equipment from the United States to a foreign government or other purchaser through one of four basic procedures. There may be a private transaction, in which a manufacturer or independent broker in this country sells arms to a foreign business firm or individual. There may be a commercial transaction, in which the manufacturer or broker sells arms to a foreign government. Both of these forms of sale are licensed by the State Department's Office of Munitions Control.

There may be a United States government sale to a foreign government, falling under the auspices of the Pentagon's Foreign Military Sales program, and administered by the Defense Security Assistance Agency (DSAA). In these cases—which comprise, as we have seen, the bulk of our arms exports—the DSAA acts in effect as a purchasing agent for the recipient government, arranging for the supply of materials either directly from the American manufacturer or from existing United States military stocks, including at times some equipment classed as excess defense articles. While the Department of State is usually aware of these sales in advance, Section 212 of the Arms Export Control Act waives the requirement that they be licensed.

Finally, arms and other equipment may be exported as grant aid under our Military Assistance Program, which is also administered by the DSAA.

## Private and Commercial Sales

The International Traffic in Arms Regulations include the United States Munitions List, a series of definitions of those items of equipment and materials under export control. The definitions are sufficiently broad to cover almost every conceivable item that might have military application, including the machinery with which it can be made. It excludes only such articles as shotguns with barrels over 18 inches long, or firearms that clearly have value solely as antiques or for sporting use.

Section 215 of the Arms Export Control Act selects from this Munitions List a further category of specific items it calls "major defense equipment." Such equipment is defined as any item having a non-recurring research and development cost of more than $50 million, or a total production cost of more than $200 million. The export of these items is meant to be under more stringent control, and while there are currently only 188 of them listed as major defense equipment, among them are many of the newest aircraft, missiles, vehicles and munitions in active inventory with our armed services.

Manufacturers or private individuals

wishing to export arms from this country must first be registered with the Office of Munitions Control. They must next apply to that office for an export license, valid for a period of one year, for each separate shipment of arms. The license application, form DSP-5, requires detailed information describing the equipment involved in the sale, the quantity of each item included, the total contract price, the name and address of the recipient, and the proposed date of shipment.

There are certain restrictions. Commercial sales of major defense equipment to countries outside of NATO will not be granted a license if they total $25 million or more. Such sales can only be made through the Pentagon's Foreign Military Sales program. However, if the recipient country is a member of NATO, then a commercial sale of major defense equipment in any amount may be licensed. Additionally, if the sale includes no major defense equipment, then it may be licensed for any amount, to any country, whether or not that country is a member of NATO.

A commercial sale that totals $25 million or more is subject to prior Congressional review before a license may be issued. This holds true regardless of the equipment being sold or its destination. In addition, the Arms Export Control Act of 1976 amended the law to require that a sale of major defense equipment to a country outside of NATO totalling $7 million or more would also be subject to Congressional review. Congress, in these cases, must be given thirty days of time in which to review such applications before a license may be issued.

All of this would appear to restrict the proliferation of more sophisticated weapons, or of large numbers of any sort of weapon, and these rights of Congressional review are often cited as an example of our firm control over the flow of arms, and of our desire to adhere to President Carter's stated intent to curb the introduction of higher levels of military technology to certain areas of the world, as well as to reduce the flow of arms all over the world.

However, the review process is seldom exercised for commercial licenses. Nor, in those cases when an application actually has been sent to Congress, is there any record of a veto.

Certainly there is little, under these regulations, that Congress is permitted to see. Rarely is major defense equipment included in commercial sales. That material is generally in high demand by our own armed services, who are sensibly given priority deliveries, and as we have seen, the sales of extra production runs of such equipment are almost exclusively handled if not actually planned well in advance of production by the Department of Defense or the military services themselves.

In addition, there are seldom sales of sufficient size to come under review. The 1976 total of $1.1 billion in commercial sales, recently reported to Congress by the Office of Munitions Control, has to be apportioned among the 16,111 licenses granted that year. It is clear that few single sales totalling $7 million, let alone $25 million, could have been among so many licenses. In any case, if a sale does total an amount sufficient to require Congressional review, there is absolutely nothing to stop a manufacturer or broker from breaking it up into smaller shipments, each requiring a separate license and each totalling less than the amount which would bring it under review.

In cases involving Congressional review an additional form, DSP-83, must accompany the license application. DSP-83 is a certificate of end use. It represents that the recipient of the shipment is also the party intending to use the arms, or if this is not the case it identifies the final user, who in turn agrees that those arms will not be transferred, in future, to any other party. The end use certificate is thus meant to provide our government with a means of controlling the disposition of all arms commercially sold, and of keeping track of their whereabouts.

In order to enforce this policy, military personnel in our embassies abroad are enjoined to monitor major arms shipments. They are asked to make sure that arms we have sold arrive at their point of destination and remain in the hands of the government that purchased them. They are also asked, from time to time, to trace how certain shipments of American arms we did not knowingly sell have ended up, as they frequently have, in foreign inventories.

Violations are to be reported to the Office of Munitions Control. They are regarded as a serious matter. Individuals convicted of willful misrepresentation of facts on form DSP-83 may be subject to a fine of $100 thousand and imprisonment for two years. Governments found in violation may be subject to trade restraints of the withdrawal of grant aid. "There is a presumption but not a requirement," according to one source in the current administration, "that all security assistance for serious violators will be terminated or suspended."

But violations do in fact occur. Foreign governments frequently act in the role of middleman between buyer and seller, often without the seller's knowledge. Iran has sold patrol boats from the United States to the Sudan. Israel has sold Mystere jet aircraft newly equipped with American engines to Honduras. Libya has sold Northrop F-5 aircraft to Turkey.

**PBR River Patrol Boat of USN**

All of these sales were without prior United States government knowledge or consent.

A typical example of this practice occured in 1966, when the West German government was approached by the German firm of Merex A.G., acting as broker for the government of Iran, with a request for some of the North American F-86 Sabre jet aircraft then in the Luftwaffe inventory. The West Germans had originally purchased 225 Sabres from Canada, where they were under licensed production. Finally they agreed to sell 90 of the aircraft to Iran for $75 thousand each.

**A Canadair CL-13B Sabre VI
of the West German Bundesluftwaffe**

Officials in Washington learned of the sale and were at first puzzled, knowing the Iranians had no use for the aircraft themselves.

It happened, in this case, that the merchandise was quickly located. War had erupted between India and Pakistan, and reports soon confirmed that large numbers of F-86 Sabres were in combat over the battlefields, carrying Pakistani Air Force markings. Pressure was brought to bear on Teheran, and the Iranians agreed to repurchase the aircraft and to keep them. All but six were returned. The price that Pakistan paid to Iran is still not known. But some idea of that price can be gained from the price that Iran paid to take the aircraft back: $111 thousand each.

As one of this country's most prominent arms brokers told me, "There are countries that will sell you arms with no questions asked. Their commission is built into the price."

In most cases, of course, when a shipment of arms fails to appear in the country listed on the certificate of end use, it is more difficult to discover whence it has been diverted. If an identical weapon has been sold in quantity by the United States to more than one foreign country, and it then begins to appear in a third country with which we have had no dealings, it is frequently impossible to learn which of its original recipients now has less of that item in its inventory.

The Presidential report to Congress concedes that this problem is growing:

*With the quantity of arms of United States origin increasing around the world and old inventories being replaced, it becomes harder to monitor foreign compliance either through military contacts or intelligence sources and the risk of unauthorized transfers increases substantially.*

It also concedes that foreign governments may not always care about how we respond to their violations:

*In periods of tension or conflict, a recipient with a large volume of equipment might perceive its own political interests as more important than any undertaking with the United States government regarding arms transfers, and proceed to supply equipment of United States origin to a neighbor in need—contrary to United States wishes.*

In short, many violations of the policy of end use go undiscovered. When they are discovered it is after the fact, and little effective action can be taken. Foreign governments know this. They and the private arms brokers continue to act as purchasing agents for confidential buyers, and they usually do so with impunity.

In addition to this, many violations also go unreported, for those who discover them often feel there exist extenuating circumstances which make a report inappropriate. This is primarily due to the many conflicting interpretations of policy which our government tolerates in its midst, and to the many available ways of safely asserting dissenting opinion, even though it be in violation of procedure and at the expense of justice.

For example, a country may be found to have violated the end use agreement and, without our knowledge or consent, transferred weapons purchased from us to South Africa—a country toward which we maintain an arms embargo. But the people who find the violation might feel that our policy is wrong, that South Africa ought not be subject to an arms embargo and is, instead, entitled to the military assistance we mean to deny it. In such a case, these people are inclined to look the other way.

Helpless to learn of unreported violations of the end use agreement, helpless to prevent undiscovered ones, and with little effective action at its disposal once a violation has been established, the Office of Munitions Control has no way of enforcing the end use policy. A policy that cannot be enforced is redundant.

A similar situation prevails with regard to licensing agreements for the production of American weapons abroad. The agreements include guarantees that weapons produced under license from a United States manufacturer will not be sold to other countries without our government's knowledge and consent. In addition, Congressional approval is required to produce major defense equipment in countries outside of NATO. Such controls are meant to extend even to the use of American components in weapons primarily of foreign manufacture.

Thus it is that Israel has had to seek permission, and has thus far been refused it, to sell to Ecuador 24 of its Kfir jet fighter-bomber aircraft, which have a greater range and greater speeds than the F-5E Tiger II aircraft the United States had originally tried to sell to that country. The Kfir is equipped with the General Electric J-79 jet engine, an item on our major defense equipment list.

It would be difficult to hide the presence of Kfir aircraft in Ecuador. But there are numerous cases where the request for permission to sell an item might well be the only indication we would ever have of its intended transfer.

More serious is the fact that foreign production is a step removed from domestic production, and by that degree further weakens the extent of our control over the weapons produced. A licensed foreign manufacturer might sell its weapons of American design to an approved buyer, who might then turn around and sell them to a third country we wholeheartedly disfavor. The foreign manufacturer rightly disclaims responsibility for their end use. Nothing can be done. Here again, violations frequently occur that are never brought to light or go ignored.

In addition to submitting certain license applications for prior Congressional approval, the Office of Munitions Control also estimates the value of licensed sales for each forthcoming year, and sends quarterly and yearly reports to the Speaker of the House and the Senate Foreign Relations Committee showing the number and value of licenses approved to date.

In 1976, the Office of Munitions Control received 20,403 applications for licenses to export unclassified items on the Munitions List. This was an increase of two percent over the previous year. Of these applications, it disapproved only 238, and returned 2,354 more for resubmission due to clerical error or incomplete information. As we have seen, the report to Congress of licenses approved showed a total value of $1.1 billion in 1976.

The information is incomplete. The value of the licenses listed in the report is indeed $1.1 billion, but their number is far fewer than the 17,811 licenses given approval that year. This is because Section 211 of the Arms Export Control Act provides that when commercial licenses involve major defense equipment, only licenses for $1 million or more of such equipment need be reported. Licenses for smaller sales of major defense equipment are thus left out of the report.

The major defense equipment list includes some of the weapons most in demand around the world. While we know that large quantities of such equipment are usually sold directly to governments through the Pentagon's Foreign Military Sales program, there is nothing to stop smaller sales from being handled commercially by manufacturers or private agents.

Many items on the major defense equipment list, such as bombs and artillery ammunition, rocket launchers and anti-tank weapons, and even the M-16A1 5.56mm rifle, can be sold in large quantities without exceeding $1 million in a single sale. An M-48 or M-60 tank, or three or four artillery pieces or armoured personnel carriers, can also be sold in this way. And often, that is just how they are sold.

In the same way as a commercial seller, in order to avoid Congressional review, can break up his shipments to

**M-60 Tank**

amount to single sales of less than $25 million in defense articles, or less than $7 million in major defense equipment to countries outside of NATO, so can he break up smaller shipments of major defense equipment in lots of less than $1 million, and avoid their being reported at all.

The report to Congress is seriously limited in a further respect. It includes only licenses for unclassified items on the Munitions List. There are also classified items. They are classified usually because they involve high technology, and they are therefore expensive. Sales of these items are not reported.

License applications for the export of classified items are made on a different form, DSP-85. In 1976, in addition to the 20,403 applications it processed for the licensed export of unclassified defense articles, the Office of Munitions Control received 706 applications on form DSP-85. This represented an increase of 14 percent over DSP-85 applications in the previous year, which had already shown an increase of 14 percent over the year before that. Exports of classified military equipment are clearly rising. The amounts involved in these sales are unknown.

What we do know is that the total value of all the applications received in 1976 was $3.5 billion. This includes license applications for classified as well as unclassified items, applications rejected as well as all of those approved, and licenses for the many unreported sales as well as those reported to Congress.

A conservative estimate is that the sales reported by the Office of Munitions Control, together with unreported sales of classified items and unreported sales of less than $1 million each in major defense equipment, brought the total sales of arms and related equipment licensed through that office in 1976 to a minimum of $2.5 billion—not the $1.1 billion reported to Congress. This figure is probably a fair yearly average.

### The Role of the Pentagon
The Pentagon's Defense Security Assistance Agency (DSAA) administers the

**E-2 Hawkeye Airborne Early Warning Aircraft**

Foreign Military Sales program, through which weapons and other military articles are sold directly to foreign governments by agreement with our government. General Howard Fish, the former director of DSAA, estimates that 90 percent of these sales are now in cash. The equipment sold may be supplied directly from the manufacturer or from current stocks owned by one of our military service departments. In either case, the contract is with the supplier, and the United States government acts only in the formal role of purchasing agent.

General Fish is careful to point this out. "There are no contracts between governments," he told me, "simply agreements to procure."

The Pentagon is understandably sensitive to claims by manufacturers that it has interfered with open market competition by persuading foreign governments, from time to time, to purchase certain weapons instead of others. Grumman Aerospace Corporation, for example, believes that its E-2C Hawkeye early warning aircraft remains the most appropriate choice for NATO needs in creating an airborne radar defense system. But Grumman has never been allowed to exhibit the E-2C to NATO defense ministers because the Pentagon, for some time, has wanted NATO to adopt the Boeing E-3A AWACS. So far, NATO has agreed only in principle to the AWACS purchase.

At a cost of $32 million per aircraft, the E-2C Hawkeye would also be a good deal less expensive than the Boeing AWACS even though the Pentagon, as an inducement to acceptance, was offering the AWACS to NATO at a cost of approximately $69 million per aircraft—considerably lower than its current Air Force unit procurement cost of $80.9 million. NATO would purchase from 16 to 18 of the aircraft.

The final NATO decision on the AWACS is still pending at this time. For several months the West German gov-

**Chrysler XM-1 Main Battle Tank Prototype**

ernment held it up, showing reluctance to accept the Pentagon's proposal until the United States agreed to standardization of major components of the new German Leopard II and American XM-1 tanks under development, including use of a common 120mm cannon, common motors, track assemblies and fire control systems. Great Britain then set back the AWACS sales effort by deciding to wait no further and proceed with development of its own radar defense system based on eleven specially equipped Hawker-Siddeley Nimrod long-range reconnaissance aircraft.

But in truth, because it relies on industry to furnish what it needs, the military establishment is fully committed to furthering the interests of our arms and aerospace manufacturers. There is sometimes a passionate chauvinism. Commenting on the likelihood of full standardization of the new West German and American tanks, the late General Creighton Abrams said that a German tank would be adopted by the United States "over my dead body."

And yet, while Pentagon officials try as far as possible to enhance rather than obstruct the opportunities for individual corporations to compete for sales, they do have a variety of concerns, some of them sensible, some less so, which make the choice of weapons sold abroad an inevitable area for strong policy control. These interests range, as we have seen, from the occasional fear of escalating warmaking capabilities in one corner of the world to the determination that they remain balanced in another; from the need to work towards NATO standardization to the urgent requirement for weapons of high technology that we cannot afford on our own.

Without denying that the Pentagon holds enormous influence over the entire arms sales process, or that it uses that influence whenever it is needed, and without addressing the fact that the Pentagon's Foreign Military Sales program, since its inception, has tripled the size of the industry it assists, General Fish underlines the government's *laissez faire* role as purchasing agent. "We do not want to make a profit," he assured me. "We will procure, and the purchaser will pay the costs."

One would never have assumed that the Pentagon was out for profit, though it is clear enough that others are. Neither does the Pentagon lose any money. Since the days of Robert McNamara's term as Secretary of Defense, Pentagon department heads and agency directors have been applying the principles of accounting procedure they first learned from him. Today the Department of De-

53

fense realizes savings in a variety of ways. The foreign government purchasing arms through the Pentagon does pay the costs. An administrative fee of two percent of the total procurement value of a contract is now charged for the time spent by DSAA and the military services in processing each sale. This, together with a proportionate amount of non-recurring costs of research and development, is added to the final price of each contract signed between a foreign government and its American supplier.

DSAA estimates that an average of $30 million in administrative fees will be returned from FMS sales processed, delivered and billed each year. The only awkward aspect of this is that the personnel assigned to DSAA and the military service departments to process FMS agreements all draw regular pay. Their salaries are included in defense budget appropriations. The administrative fees which, thus, twice remunerate them for the hours of time they spend on FMS sales are regarded, it seems, as a commission of just the sort a purchasing agent might be expected to earn.

### The Military Assistance Program

These fees are sometimes described as reimbursing the DSAA account for administrative costs. It is sometimes suggested that they replace proportionate amounts of money appropriated yearly from Congress for the Military Assistance Program (MAP), a plan of grant aid to selected countries which is also administered by DSAA. One might conclude, then, that an average of $30 million yearly in appropriated grant aid funds is saved and reimbursed to the Treasury.

Not so. The surplus funds in fact remain at the disposition of the Department of Defense, which uses them not to replace appropriated MAP funds but to add to those funds, increasing the total annual MAP expenditure. Thus, a total of $228.9 million has been appropriated for grant aid in Fiscal Year 1978 to Jordan, Turkey, Greece, Portugal, Indonesia, Spain, Thailand and the Philippines. An additional $54.6 million in accumulated reimbursements and recoupments from prior years is being added to the appropriated amount, to implement a total program of $283.5 million that year.

This increases by $54.6 million the total value, with related costs, of

weapons and military equipment this country will export abroad in 1978. A similar practice has been followed in previous years.

The MAP funds are used in another way. They are not spent on contracts with manufacturers for new equipment, but are transferred to the receivables accounts of our military service departments for the purchase and rehabilitation of surplus equipment from our own inventories. This is equipment for which the services already paid, perhaps years ago, with funds appropriated in the defense budgets for those years.

The sales value of a surplus item, known as an excess defense article, is defined as either the cost of restoring it to suitable condition for export and use, or its current market value, whichever is greater. The current market value is almost always greater than the cost for repair and rehabilitation, which is seldom required. But an obsolete item can also have a very low market value when compared with its original purchase cost. As surplus the venerable jeep, for example, has a sales value to the Pentagon of $653. Its original acquisition cost was much higher. The current acquisition cost of a new M151A2 jeep to the army is $7,693, to the Marine Corps $8,540. For each jeep purchased by MAP, however, just $653 is charged to the MAP account by the service department—in this case either the Army or the Marine Corps.

The shipping costs of MAP equipment must also be added, and are paid from the MAP account. Thus, $5.4 million of the total of $283.5 million in the 1978 MAP program will pay for supply operations to deliver previously granted materials to Korea, Ethiopia, Bolivia, the Dominican Republic, El Salvador, Guatemala, Honduras and Panama.

Every time an item's market value exceeds its repair cost and its pro-rated shipping cost—which is almost all the time—the service department makes a profit. While the services regard this money as only a token reimbursement for the loss of a surplus item often never used, and whose original acquisition cost was much higher, it is in fact

surplus money, over and above what is appropriated in the defense budget each year, and it can be used in any way the service department wishes.

MAP expenditures in 1976 totalled $210 million. But this figure does not include the original acquisitions costs of the excess defense articles purchased by MAP at their market value and exported that year. It has been standard operating procedure to subtract these costs from the MAP purchase prices, so that greater amounts of equipment could be procured at the lower prices represented by market value. The original purchase price, however, was once paid. It should be included as part of the total value of the equipment. These costs for articles exported under MAP in 1976 totalled $63 million. Thus the total value of military exports under MAP in 1976 was $273 million, not the $210 million represented by appropriations. Equivalent amounts in original acquisitions costs must be added each year to the MAP program costs to obtain an accurate idea of the true value of MAP exports.

While the Department of Defense regards the uncharged acquisitions costs of those excess defense articles transferred under MAP in 1976 as a loss in value of $63 million, that loss is more than compensated for by the major portion of $210 million in 1976 MAP funds spent neither on costs for repairs nor on costs of delivery, and which represents an unbudgeted gain in income to the

**M-109 Self-Propelled 155mm Howitzer produced in Italy under FMC License**

military service departments.

In this way, MAP funds are appropriated yearly to buy a second time what has already been bought before, the current total value of which is obscured by deletion from the account of original acquisition costs. Rather than reducing the size of its yearly MAP appropriations, and so passing on to the Federal budget the advantage gained in having purchased surplus equipment at a time when its total value was much lower, the Department of Defense exploits this advantage itself by appropriating sufficient MAP funds to cover the market value of this equipment as well as its repair and shipping costs, and pays the excess to its own service departments.

This creates a sizable fund not accounted for in the defense budget, and thus not subject to the normal restrictions on its use. No one knows how this money is used. A very low estimate of the funds recoverable from MAP appropriations is an average of $100 million each year.

For wholly unrelated reasons, funds for the Military Assistance Program are diminishing each year, following a policy to give away less and sell more. This was a trend which began in the early 1960s under Secretary McNamara. In 1953, when the major portion of our arms exports was still in the form of grant aid, we gave away $1.96 billion in arms under MAP, and sold only $230 million. By 1968 grant aid under MAP had been reduced to $466 million, while sales had risen to $1.5 billion. The trend continues. Excess defense articles are now also sold under the Foreign Military Sales program. Fewer surplus items remain in inventory, and it is preferable for a variety of reasons to sell new equipment. Today when countries are too poor to purchase what we or they believe they need, we encourage them to take arms from us on credit, under a rapidly expanding program of financed sales.

### Cumulative American Arms Exports
Under the authority of the Mutual Security Act of 1954, the Foreign Assistance Act of 1961 and subsequent legislation, the Military Assistance Program has provided over the past three decades $32 billion in grant aid to approximately 80 allied and friendly nations. A special Military Assistance Service Funded (MASF) program of grant aid to Korea, Laos, Thailand, the Philippines and Vietnam provided an additional $22.7 billion

in arms and related equipment in support of American military operations in Southeast Asia from 1966 through 1975. Thus, a cumulative total to date of $54.7 billion in military equipment has been given away by the United States under the MAP and MASF programs.

Of the $14.8 billion in arms and equipment granted to Vietnam under MASF, more than $5 billion worth of materiel was left in that country in the American withdrawal. This equipment included 100 A-1H and A-1E Skyraider attack aircraft, 39 A-37A and 155 A-37B

**UH-1B Helicopter fires rocket in Vietnam**

Dragonfly jet attack aircraft, 51 F-5A and 22 F-5E jet fighter aircraft, 90 M-551 Sheridan light tanks, 170 M-60A1 and M-60A2 main battle tanks, 340 M-48A3 tanks, 80 M-107 self-propelled 175mm guns, 1,250 105mm and 155mm howitzers, an IBM military computer, over 1,780 M-113 armoured personnel carriers, over 400 V-150 Commando armoured cars, 196 UH-1B armed transport helicopters, 168 UH-1N helicopters, 66 AH-1G HueyCobra attack helicopters —30 of these in mint condition, unassembled and crated in their original packing grease, 15,000 M60E2 7.62mm machine guns, 791,000 M-16 rifles, more than a million other light weapons, including rifles, pistols, mortars, grenade and rocket launchers and recoilless rifles, more than two hundred transport and utility aircraft, nearly 50,000 trucks, 130,000 tons of ammunition and over 940 landing craft, patrol craft, riverine warfare and other naval vessels. The Vietnamese are now attempting to sell some of this equipment on the open market.

In addition to our $54.7 billion in

military grant aid, we have sold another $56.9 billion under the Foreign Military Sales program. In short, since 1950 the United States has sold or given away a total of $111.6 billion in arms and military equipment.

### Foreign Military Sales
The Pentagon's Foreign Military Sales program accounted for 98 percent of the estimated arms export orders received in this country in 1976, and for 87 percent of arms export deliveries completed in that year. In recent years the FMS program has accounted for an average of 43 percent of worldwide arms transfers. The total volume of FMS orders in 1976 was $8.66 billion. General Fish anticipates that sales will remain at this level in the immediate future, and estimates $8.8 billion in FMS orders in 1978. Of the average of 8,000 FMS agreements processed each year by his DSAA office, from 10 to 20 percent are for sales to the NATO countries, Japan, Australia and New Zealand. The bulk of orders, as we have seen, goes to the Middle East, averaging from 50 to 60 percent of total sales.

United States military sales to the Middle East, together with sales to East Asia, Africa and the American Republics, totalled $6.16 billion in agreements and $3.12 billion in deliveries in 1976. According to the Central Intelligence Agency, Soviet arms deliveries to the same four regions in 1976 were worth the equivalent of $2.19 billion.

On receipt of a formal request from a foreign government, DSAA asks the appropriate military departments to check priorities and ensure that the arms requested are available, and that their sale will not interfere with the needs of our own services. Deputy Secretary of Defense Charles Duncan describes how this is presently done:

*The Defense Department has developed a system for reviewing on a quarterly basis the projected availability of some 63 weapons systems that are in high demand by our own forces and those of friendly and allied nations. This management tool provides us with the means of insuring that foreign countries receive the earliest production available without interfering with the programmed needs of the U.S. forces.*

Identifying major weapons systems and reviewing their availability on a quarterly basis may not, however, suffice to ensure that our own needs will be met.

**M16A1 Rifle**

According to the General Accounting Office, there have been several occasions when foreign arms sales have weakened our military capabilities precisely by delaying our scheduled acquisition of certain weapons in order to transfer existing supplies of those weapons to foreign buyers.

In a recent report the GAO pointed out that while most FMS agreements committed us to making available spares and other key components on a continuing basis for the future support of weapons sold, production limitations and competing demands for those components were not taken into account in the Pentagon's planning. The GAO reports that continuing United States requirements for the supply of 45 percent of such support materials have not even been established, and that these materials could not now be supplied to fulfill the terms of existing FMS agreements without adversely affecting United States readiness.

A likely example of this is the latest proposed FMS agreement with Iran, recently approved by President Carter and soon to be reviewed by Congress. The agreement would sell equipment and services worth a total of $1.1 billion, $800 million of which comprises training and supply support for weapons already sold to Iran in previous agreements. It would also bring to $3.98 billion the current total of FMS sales to Iran in 1977, and to $10.23 billion the total of pending orders to that country through 1982. Aside from $250 million to build and operate helicopter maintenance centers, $167 million for a training center for helicopter pilots and mechanics, and $183.7 million to train Iranian personnel to operate HAWK antiaircraft missile systems, the agreement includes $139 million for a helicopter logistics system and $57 million for continuing supplies of spare parts in logistic support of Iran's 202 AH-1J Cobra attack helicopters. The supply of these helicopter parts and spares may disrupt logistic support of our own helicopter forces. No one in the Pentagon knows whether or not that is the case, because no one has checked.

Approximately 100 countries are now considered eligible to make purchases under the Foreign Military Sales program. A country becomes legally eligible for FMS purchases after the President determines that sales to that country will serve world peace and strengthen the security of the United States. No such determination has ever been required, however, for commercial transactions.

FMS sales must in theory have prior approval by the Department of State. Much is made of this requirement to suggest that the proper checks and balances exist in the sales review process. But in fact the State Department several years ago divided the list of countries eligible for FMS sales into two groups, A and B, granting the Department of Defense unconditional authority to approve all sales to countries in Group A without prior State Department review. Group A

**AH-1J Cobra Helicopter of the Imperial Iranian Air Force**

countries include Australia, New Zealand, Japan, 11 of the 15 countries belonging to NATO (excluding Iceland, Portugal, Turkey and Greece) and all the remaining developed countries in Western Europe—for example Sweden and Switzerland—with the exception only of Spain. No sales to these countries are ever reviewed by the State Department.

Group B comprises the remaining 75 countries in the world eligible for FMS sales. Prior State Department approval is required for sales to these countries —but only if a sale involves the transfer of major defense equipment. If it does not, then there is no requirement that the State Department review it at all.

In the Pentagon, the military departments report to the Office of the Secretary of Defense in those cases where they have been able to ascertain that foreign requests for arms might conflict with United States requirements. The Secretary of Defense has the authority to determine military priorities. In the meanwhile, such requests as remain

subject to State Department approval are being reviewed in the light of political priorities. If a particular request meets Defense Department approval but the Department of State views it with disfavor, the Department of State does not have the right to veto. Conflicts between the two departments are resolved in the National Security Council.

The next stage in the FMS procedure is to establish a contract price and probable delivery date for the equipment requested. One of five FMS case officers in the DSAA office supervises the collection of this information in response to each approved request, referring to the appropriate military service department for the types of equipment involved. Production schedules and current inventories are checked, and estimates are made of training, support and maintenance needs. Frequently a team of American officers visits the recipient country to assess its ability to assimilate, service, repair and operate the weapons it desires. Will construction be required to house large weapons systems or their maintenance equipment? How much training will be required?

Estimates of the costs of contracts to provide these services are included in an estimate of the full price for the agreement. An administrative fee, as we have seen, is added. If the request involves aircraft, vehicles, self-contained weapons systems, missiles or communications equipment, then a surcharge is added representing a portion of each item's original research and development costs.

Based on the composition of FMS orders in 1976, 49.7 percent of the equipment ordered in that year fell into those categories eligible for a research and development surcharge. These surcharges in 1976 comprised 4.5 percent of the export value of that equipment, and in recent years the Pentagon's recoupment of research and development costs through these surcharges has averaged a saving, in constant 1975 dollars, of $191.7 million per year.

When the total contract price for a request has been established and delivery dates have been estimated, this information is incorporated into a draft of a letter of offer and availability, our government's formal response to an approved arms request.

Before these letters are released, some of them are subject to Congressional review. The review procedure here is similar to that for licensed commercial sales, in that letters of offer for $25 million or more in defense articles or services, or for $7 million or more in major defense equipment, must be signed by the service commander or vice commander and must be submitted to the Speaker of the House of Representatives and to the Senate Committee on Foreign Relations for approval before they are issued.

On request from the House Committee on International Relations, detailed information must also be submitted describing the weapons proposed for sale in such letters of offer, naming the manufacturers that would supply them, explaining the reasons why a foreign government has requested them, and assessing the likely impact of their transfer on our own military needs, our relations with other countries in the region for which they are destined, and their effect on the balance of power in that region.

It is true that this information need only be submitted upon request, but in fairness to those members of the committee authorized to request it, they have at least done so from time to time.

Section 36(b) of the Arms Export Control Act states:

*The letter of offer shall not be issued if the Congress, within thirty calendar days after receiving such certification, adopts a concurrent resolution stating that it objects to the proposed sale, unless the President states in his certification that an emergency exists which requires such sale in the national security interests of the United States.*

In practice, DSAA gives Congress even more time—a total of fifty days in which to review those letters of offer over which it has review authority. The first twenty days are a period in which committee members can examine a letter of offer on an informal basis, and during that time they are enjoined to keep the matter confidential. For the subsequent formal thirty-day review period, the proposed sale is open to public debate.

Once the review period has expired, however, and Congress has stated no objection to the sale, the letter of offer is countersigned by DSAA and released, and the United States commitment is made.

While the President, by declaring a state of emergency, might on occasion overrule Congressional objection to a particular sale, it would still appear that the veto authority granted to Congress affords it a substantial measure of control over Foreign Military Sales.

However, no formal Congressional resolution of disapproval of an arms sale has ever been passed. Congress has never once used its power of veto.

Moreover, that power is sharply restricted, in a manner exactly parallel to the limits imposed on Congressional authority over commercial arms licenses. For it is clear that those letters of offer the Pentagon is not required to submit for prior Congressional approval include all offers for less than $7 million in major defense equipment and even all offers for less than $25 million that do not happen to include major defense equipment. Thus, many of the 8,000 FMS agreements processed each year are never reviewed in advance by Congress. While these are certainly fewer in number than the commercial licenses that escape review, they account for a considerable volume of sales.

DSAA holds that smaller sales of significant combat equipment to sensitive areas of the world are also reviewed in advance by Congress, whenever the President, the State Department or the Department of Defense feels it wise to consult with Congressional leaders about the impact of such a sale. But such consultations may or may not take place. They are left up to the initiative of the Executive Branch, and the Legislature, which consequently may or may not hear of such sales in advance, has no authority in any case to stop them. These consultations, when they occur, take place outside the arena of Congressional jurisdiction.

DSAA points out that there have been times when proposed arms sales have been revised on the basis of consultation with Congressional leaders. If we could rely on the Executive Branch voluntarily to submit itself to Congressional advice and act accordingly each time, then Congress would need no vested authority of any kind.

DSAA also points out that Congress has the opportunity to review all FMS agreements for sales of $1 million or more, because complete reports of such sales are given to Congress on a quarterly basis, showing all FMS agreements in that amount or above concluded in the previous three months and listing all sales of major defense equipment in that amount or above planned in the next three months.

It is too late for Congress to act on sales agreements already concluded, but the suggestion lingers that since members of Congress are informed in advance of sales of $1 million or more of major defense equipment, there is time for them to take whatever action they may wish.

Whatever action Congress might wish to take, it can take none. Simply to learn in advance of sales of this size may be to review them, but it is to review them without the authority to veto them. Thus, informing Congress of such sales may appear to be a responsible gesture, but it is an empty gesture.

Finally, in the same way that commercial licenses for sales of less than $1 million are not reported, FMS agreements for sales of less than $1 million are not reported. They are signed and released from DSAA without countersignature by a service commander. While again there are certainly fewer of these than of unreported commercial licenses, the fact remains that there is a further number of FMS agreements which Congress not only has no authority to question, but about which it is not even informed.

Early in 1977 President Carter indicated that he intended to review arms sales more closely than his predecessors had. But in fact he reviews only those sales requiring advance approval from Congress. Lesser sales are reviewed if, in the judgment of the Department of State or the Office of the Secretary of Defense, their sensitivity warrants it. Again, it is up to these offices, not the President, to interpret the guidelines determining which sales are sensitive.

Once a letter of offer and availability has been released, and is received by the foreign government whose original request it answers, a contract is signed between that government and the American prime contractor for the weapon system under order. A procedure has been established through which the foreign government now makes an initial advance payment to the military service normally in charge of procurement for that weapon system. This money is deposited in the service logistics control office, where a trust fund is set up on behalf of the foreign purchaser.

Three months prior to each progress payment due under the terms of the contract, the service finance office draws a check against the United States Treasury and sends it to the contractor. The foreign government's trust fund is then billed to reimburse the Treasury for the amount drawn. Periodically, the trust fund is replenished by further prepayments from abroad. In this way the contractor receives all payments from the Treasury rather than from abroad, and Treasury funds are covered well in advance of their disbursement.

There results what is known as Treasury float, or an excess of advance payments from foreign arms purchasers. In recent years the sum of such prepayments has generally exceeded the value of the contractual work and deliveries they anticipate by an average of approximately $5 billion. From this, the Treasury benefits by between $250 million and $300 million a year in savings on interest payments on its debt.

### Financed Sales

Lending facilities for the purchase of arms have existed in this country since 1934, when the Export-Import Bank was established to finance loans for commercial exports, some of which included military equipment. But until the 1960s loans for this purpose were seldom given by the United States government.

It was then that we began to respond to notions of sounder fiscal policy, determining thereafter to recover the value of what we exported abroad as often as it was possible. We gradually reduced grant aid under MAP, and began actively to encourage an increase in cash purchases of military equipment. Many of our allies, who up until that time had received American arms free, were unable to pay for them. Loans became more popular. While sales under the FMS program have steadily grown in the past decade, the proportion of credit to cash sales has also steadily grown.

Credit extended to governments abroad in 1970 amounted to only $70 million, representing 7.2 percent of the $967.5 million in Foreign Military Sales agreements concluded that year. In 1973 a total of $5.76 billion in arms was sold under the FMS program. A slightly larger proportion of this, $541 million equivalent to 9.3 percent of total sales, was financed by credit loans. By 1976, the proportion of credit to cash sales had grown to the point where credit purchases of $2.192 billion accounted for 25.3 percent of the year's total in FMS sales of $8.66 billion.

During the 1960s the Export-Import Bank, which came to be known as Eximbank, made loans directly to foreign countries for the purchase of military equipment at interest rates averaging 5.5 percent. In addition to its direct loans Eximbank also made what were known as Country-X loans, paying specific amounts of money on request to an account held by the Department of Defense. The Pentagon would then transfer the funds abroad without identifying the recipient countries for the bank.

According to the importance of the loan and the recipient country's solvency, interest rates charged by the Department of Defense were sometimes higher, sometimes lower than those it paid to Eximbank for Country-X funds. The rates varied from 5.5 percent to as little as 3.5 percent, and the Pentagon accordingly would make a profit or absorb the loss.

Direct loans from Eximbank between 1963 and 1967 totalled $1 billion, while Country-X loans accounted for $604 million from 1965 through 1967, and then increased to approximately $500 million each year in 1968 and 1969. Many of the countries which received the

Country-X loans have still not been identified. Nor is it known whether this practice continues.

In 1974 the Federal Financing Bank was established as a division of the Treasury, and took charge of the bulk of FMS credit lending. According to the Defense Department this bank handles only those loans guaranteed by the United States government, while commercial banks continue to handle direct loans to foreign purchasers. This is true, but in recent years most of our loans to countries purchasing arms and military equipment have been guaranteed.

Of $2.192 billion in FMS credit extended by our government in 1976, repayment was waived for $750 million in loans to Israel. Of the balance of $1.442 billion only $31 million was provided by direct loans, while the remaining 98 percent of loans were guaranteed. These were all funded by the Federal Financing Bank.

United States government guaranteed loans are offered for limited periods of time. Purchasers of defense equipment are normally given two years in which to accept a loan before the offer of funds is withdrawn. This would seem a responsible policy for the use of Treasury money. It also inspires the borrower to a rapid commitment.

Interest rates from the Federal Financing Bank vary, because they are based on the actual trading of outstanding issues in the Treasury Securities market. According to the Defense Department the current rates of interest charged for guaranteed loans for the purchase of defense equipment are one eighth of a percent higher than Treasury borrowing rates for loans of comparable terms. This would seem to discourage borrowing.

However, these rates remain well below the level of commercial interest rates. This, too, provides certain incentives, as the Presidential report to Congress on arms control notes:

*Interest rates, based on the cost of money to the United States Government, are lower than available commercial rates, especially for most developing countries. It is possible that*

*offers of loans on these attractive terms and with expiration dates on their availability are an inducement for some lesser developed countries to order military equipment they might otherwise do without.*

Loans need to be financed, and the money for this is requested each year by the Pentagon and authorized by Congress. In 1975 $300 million in authorized appropriations financed $850.3 million in loans, and the total of $2.192 billion in credit extended in 1976 was financed by appropriations of $1.065 billion.

The level of funding authorized each year to finance loans is usually close to the level of funding requested. For example, the administration requested $707.7 million to finance FMS sales credits totalling $2.217 billion in 1978, and received authorization to appropriate $677 million in that year to finance a credit program of up to $2.102 billion.

Because our loans to foreign purchasers of military equipment are much in demand, those loans that are offered each year are normally accepted. Consequently, the limit of each year's authorized credit allowance is generally reached, and the available funds to finance FMS credit loans are generally expended.

If, in keeping with this pattern, all of the credit made available in 1978 is used, then credit purchases in 1978 will represent 23 percent of that year's anticipated FMS sales of $8.8 billion. This would remain close to the 1976 ratio of credit to cash sales.

Actual figures for sales and credit extended in 1977 will not be made available until well into 1978, but total sales for Fiscal Year 1977—through the end of September of 1977—were at first estimated to be about $9.9 billion. General Fish estimated that only 10 percent of FMS sales in 1977 would be financed. In view of the fact that the Pentagon has appropriated $880 million to finance loans in 1977—substantially more than the $677 million that will be used to finance 23 percent of anticipated FMS sales of $8.8 billion in 1978—the estimate of total 1977 FMS sales seemed rather low. When in November of 1977 the Pentagon announced it had made an error in bookkeeping procedure, and had underestimated 1977 sales by $1.4 billion, the true 1977 figure, $11.3 billion in sales, made the large financing appropriation more understandable. General Fish said, "Estimates are extremely dif-

ficult to make, and you don't get a good fix until now." But the financing appropriation had been made at the *beginning* of the year.

The money used to finance FMS loans is placed into the Military Assistance Credit account, a revolving account under Defense Department control, which is fed not only by yearly appropriations but also by interest payments on previous loans. Funds are drawn from this account as needed to finance future loans.

Since no loans are financed beyond the year's limit of authorized credit, and since fresh appropriations each year fully purchase the credit for that year's loans, the repaid interest from abroad on previous loans accumulates untouched.

Instead of reducing appropriations each year, and using the year's accumulation of repaid interest to purchase as much new credit as possible, the Pentagon continues to appropriate the full amount required for that credit, allowing the surplus of interest repayments from abroad to grow in the Military Assistance Credit account.

This is unfortunate, inasmuch as each year's appropriation of funds to finance loans, while not adding to the value of the military equipment exported that year, adds to the government's cost in exporting it. The profit in interest which accrues from previous loans, and which is the basis for commercial lending operations, is not passed back to the government, which bears the cost of new loans each year.

It is not known how large a fund has accumulated in the Military Assistance Credit account. It is clear that the interest charged by the bank to extend loans eventually returns with the loan repayments. It is clear that since these interest charges were covered by appropriated funds, only the principal need be repaid to the bank while the repaid interest remains in the Military Assistance Credit account. Assuming that on an average the Pentagon charges the same interest as it originally paid to secure the funds on loan, then it is also

clear that as each loan is fully repaid an amount equal or close to the amount originally appropriated to finance that loan has been added to the Military Assistance Credit account.

The record of repayment for FMS loans is excellent. General Fish points out that "in twenty-seven years we have had no defaults."

Section 208 of the Arms Export Control Act increased the repayment terms for FMS loans from ten to twelve years. What this means is that in twelve years from 1977, interest payments equivalent to the $880 million in 1977 loan financing appropriations will have accumulated in the Military Assistance Credit account. Each preceding year will have added additional sums, just as interest payments on all of the FMS loans extended in past years make up the balance of what is in that account right now. At the probable rate of return of interest payments on those older loans, whose yearly value has been a good deal lower than the volume of credit currently extended, between $200 million and $300 million per year is estimated now to be flowing into the Military Assistance Credit account from those sources.

If any of these surplus funds are ever transferred from this account, it is not known for what purpose. But it would be naive not to consider that some of this money might be used to tender additional loans on a confidential basis, rather like the old Country-X loans, to arms purchasers abroad.

One very reasonable use of the Military Assistance Credit account, which does not involve the transfer of funds but involves their implied presence, is to support the United States government guarantee that stands behind most FMS loans. A 1964 amendment to the Foreign Assistance Act gave the Department of Defense the authority to guarantee 100 percent of all credit extended on arms sales while only obligating 25 percent of the total as a reserve. Thus, a reserve of only $525 million will put the full guarantee of the United States government behind $2.102 billion in credits in 1978.

Under these exceptional conditions, a bank cannot feel it risks the loss of money when it extends credit. Just as the purchaser of arms is encouraged to borrow, so is the bank encouraged to lend.

We must next consider the practice of waiving repayment of certain loans. As we have seen, repayment of $750 million in credit to Israel was waived in 1976. This was the balance of a loan of $1.5 billion granted to that country under Section 210 of the Arms Export Control Act, which also gave Israel a grace period of ten years on repayment of principal and a term of twenty years on full repayment of the other $750 million portion of that loan.

Similarly, under the Emergency Security Assistance Act of 1973, a loan of $2.482 billion was made to Israel, and repayment of $1.5 billion of that amount was waived. $1 billion of credit has been authorized for Israel in 1977, with a waiver of repayment of $500 million.

Aside from the question of whether or not it pleases us to see credit of this magnitude extended in support of a country almost certainly doomed without it, we must still understand what happens when repayment of a sizeable share of that credit is waived.

The 1976 loan to Israel of $750 million, repayment of which was waived, is listed by DSAA among the FMS loan agreements concluded in 1976. These, in turn, make up the credit portion of total Foreign Military Sales of $8.66 billion tallied by the DSAA comptroller for that year.

Of this $8.66 billion, the value of arms and equipment sold on a cash basis is promptly returned to industry and our economy. Normal billing procedure requires full payment of the balance due within 60 days after the arms are delivered, though the President may extend this period to 120 days in an emergency. The value of equipment purchased on credit is returned to industry within the same period of time, and the funding which made the sale possible is eventually returned to the Treasury or a commercial bank on completion of the term of the loan, now a maximum of twelve years.

But the value of $750 million in arms and equipment sold on credit in 1976, and repayment of which is waived, is never returned at all. Nothing comes back. This money becomes in effect a form of grant aid.

Thus, actual FMS sales for 1976 were not $8.66 billion but $7.91 billion. Actual grant aid in 1976 was not $210 million chargeable that year to the Military Assistance Program, together with $63 million in excess defense articles whose cost was not included under MAP. It was the sum of those amounts added to $750 million, or a total of $1.023 billion.

It may be argued that it doesn't matter whether this $750 million is regarded as a loan or as grant aid. That is not quite true. For even though the waiver on repayment of that money does nothing to affect the total value of arms and equipment exported from this country in 1976, it substantially increases the government's cost in making those arms available. Whether funds for grant aid are appropriated by the Department of Defense, or drawn from the Treasury in the form of a loan, repayment of which is waived, it all comes out of the taxpayer's pocket and none of it comes back. In 1976 we spent $750 million more than most of us were aware.

## Military Education and Training

Training is an essential accompaniment to most arms transfers. Aircraft, especially, require of their pilots an intense and prolonged familiarization not only with the aerodynamic behavior of a particular aircraft's frame and propulsion systems, but also with the many mechanical and electronic procedures involved in operating its associated navigational, targeting, sighting, ranging, weapons release, weapons guidance, radar and counter measures systems. It takes up to three years, with accumulated costs running as high as $500 thousand, to train a pilot to the point where he can engage in combat with some of our more sophisticated aircraft. It takes from six to eight weeks and between $70 and $100 thousand merely to train a pilot experienced in one type of aircraft to fly another.

While training is often included in the cost of the sale of a major weapon system abroad, just as often it is not. When it is not, we still provide training services under the International Military Education and Training Program (IMET). Since the program's inception 30 years ago, IMET has trained 456,000 foreign military personnel at a total cost of $1.874 billion. By the end of 1977 we will have trained 5,200 more personnel from 46 countries, spending $5.6 million on flying instruction alone. The total cost of the 1977 IMET program will run to $30.2 million.

Section 106 of the Arms Export Control Act required that after 30 June 1976 all training of foreign military personnel be conducted within the United States. In 1976 the IMET program cost was $22.8 million. An appropriation of $35 million has been requested for IMET in 1978.

When a foreign country can pay for the costs of training its personnel, those costs are included among the contracts in the Foreign Military Sales program, and the training may be conducted in this country or on foreign soil. Foreign countries whose personnel are trained under IMET, however, do not pay the costs. We do. Therefore, the IMET program is another form of grant aid. The money for the program is appropriated yearly, and was once included as part of the appropriation for the Military Assistance Program.

Beginning in 1976, however, the IMET costs have not been included in the reported MAP expenditure. Thus, in order to obtain a complete accounting of the costs of military equipment and services we provide free each year, we must add the IMET costs to the MAP expenditure, along with the acquisition costs of excess defense articles shipped under the MAP program that year, and along with the disbursement of loans for which repayment has been waived. In 1976, therefore, another $22.8 million was spent to provide training under IMET.

By combining the training of foreign personnel simultaneously with military personnel of our own in the use of certain weapon systems, and thus spreading the costs of training over a larger number of recipients than are being paid for by the IMET appropriation, the Pentagon is able to achieve a saving in training costs equivalent to two percent of the yearly IMET expenditure. In 1976, therefore, the Pentagon saved through combined training under IMET appropriations an additional $456 thousand.

## Costs, Savings and the True Value of Exports

From examining the procedures our government currently follows for the review, approval or licensing of arms export agreements, we can see that the total yearly value of our arms exports is somewhat higher than their reported value. We can see that in a variety of ways the Federal budget bears the costs of exporting defense equipment and services abroad. We can also see that in a variety of ways the Department of Defense, through its administration of programs of sales, credit, training and grant aid to support or facilitate arms exports, as well as by encouraging the extended production of arms to meet export requirements, saves substantial amounts of money.

Aside from its savings through combined training under IMET, through the research and development surcharges and administrative fees it adds to FMS contracts, through its recoupment of interest payments on FMS credit loans and through MAP appropriations that exceed the original costs of excess defense articles and their rehabilitation, the Pentagon achieves a major saving in lowered unit procurement costs for many weapons which, due to export orders, are produced in greater numbers than are required for our own inventory.

The Congressional Budget Office has estimated that the economies of scale realized through the increased production of these weapons reduce the Pentagon's total costs for weapons acquisitions sufficiently to save the equivalent of between 10 and 16 percent of the average yearly value of our arms exports.

Even at the lower 10 percent ratio of savings to sales, this amounts to a saving, in constant 1975 dollars, of $604.4 million per year.

Using that estimate, together with estimates we have earlier made of other savings, the Pentagon currently saves a total of approximately $1.126 billion per year through the production and export of defense equipment.

The costs to the Federal budget of our export of defense equipment and services in 1976 included $750 million in loans, repayment of which was waived, $210 million in MAP appropriations, $63 million in original acquisitions costs of excess defense articles shipped under MAP, $1.065 billion in FMS credit financing appropriations, and $22.8 million for IMET. The total cost of these programs was $2.110 billion.

Finally, based on our analysis of licensing and review procedures for arms sales agreements, the true value of our exports of arms and related equipment and services in 1976 appears to have been not $9.992 billion, as reported from official sources, but, at the most conservative estimate, close to $11.455 billion.

The following table compares the reported value of our arms exports in 1976 with an estimate of their actual value, and also illustrates how the government incurs costs in the export of arms, and

how the Department of Defense makes savings.

## The Need for Controls

One concludes that the export of arms from this country follows a path of largely unobstructed growth, and that the rate of growth is a little higher than most of us supposed. This results from a combination of powerful economic momentum, the frequent coincidence of economic and recognized political priorities, the broad authority granted to the military establishment to create and implement policy, a close interdependence between that establishment and industry to serve each other's needs, a Congress too often indulgent, and procedures for the review, approval and reporting of arms sales that are hopelessly inadequate.

The Presidential report to Congress on arms control recognizes the inadequacy of existing controls:

*The laws presently governing arms transfers are extremely complicated, and are presently scattered among several Acts of Congress which are not entirely consistent in their requirements.*

The report also recognizes that the continued export of arms from this country has its liabilities:

*Arms transfer programs have also entailed costs (implied commitments, extensive United States presence) and risks (arming*

**1976 United States Exports of Arms and Related Defense Equipment and Services ($ in millions)**

| | Reported Export Value | Excess Defense Articles Costs | Actual Export Value | Cost to Government | Cost to Defense Dept. | Savings to Defense Dept | Savings to Treasury |
|---|---|---|---|---|---|---|---|
| Licensed Commercial Sales | 1,100 | | 2,500 | | | | |
| Cash Foreign Military Sales | 6,468 | | 6,468 | | | | |
| Foreign Military Credit Sales | 2,192 | | 1,442 | | | | |
| Repayment Waived FMS Credit Sales | | | 750 | 750 | | | |
| Military Assistance Appropriations | 210 | 63 | 273 | 273 | 63 | 100 | |
| FMS Credit Financing Appropriations | | | | 1,065 | | | |
| Interest on Prior FMS Loans (Average) | | | | | | 200 | |
| International Military Education & Training | 22.8 | | 22.8 | 22.8 | | .456 | |
| FMS Administrative Fees (Average) | | | | | | 30 | |
| Research & Development Surcharge FMS Sales (Average) | | | | | | 191.7 | |
| Unit Cost Savings Through FMS Sales (Average) | | | | | | 604.4 | |
| Treasury Float on Advance FMS Payments (Average) | | | | | | | 250 |
| | 9,992.8 | 63 | 11,455.8 | 2,110.8 | 63 | 1,126.456 | 250 |

*countries whose policies and objectives may change radically and suddenly).*

It is clear, the study notes, that a restraint on United States arms transfers would have a number of beneficial effects, including the following:

*Encourage a general reduction in world arms transfers and reliance on military might as an essential element in a more peaceful and stable world order, curtail the potential for arms races and limit the intensity of conflict if it occurs, reduce reliance on arms transfers as a means of implementing our diplomacy to the detriment of alternative non-military instruments, protect United States military capabilities by limiting the dispersion of military technology, limit the diversion of monies and skills in developing nations away from fundamental economic needs, and permit United States resources to be shifted away from financing arms transfers to supporting economic development.*

This is an important acknowledgement by the National Security Council that such conditions exist and need to be relieved, and that tighter arms controls in this country would help serve that need.

President Carter, too, has acknowledged that need, and on 19 May he issued a statement on arms control announcing his intention to reduce the volume of our arms exports. "We cannot," he said, "be both the world's leading champion of peace and the world's leading supplier of weapons of war." Presumably he felt that he must choose for us one role or the other. The question remains which role he has chosen.

In his statement on arms control the President promised a reduction in dollar volume, in constant 1976 dollars, of 1978 arms exports under the FMS and MAP programs from their 1977 level. We have seen, however, that FMS sales alone in 1978 are expected to reach $8.8 billion. In order to reflect a reduction in 1978 volume, 1977 FMS sales would have to be higher than this amount. But that would be higher than anyone, for the first ten months of 1977, had expected.

It was also in the President's interest to raise the 1977 figures by pushing through as many large sales as possible, including the sale of E-3A AWACS aircraft to Iran, before the end of Fiscal Year 1977. This he tried to do. While it was a direct contradiction of the spirit of his intent, it certainly would have helped serve the letter of his intent, and make

his promise of reduced sales in 1978 come true.

Unfortunately, the AWACS sale did not go through in time. On the other hand, in November of 1977, a new accounting by the Pentagon of 1977 sales, made because a "bookkeeping error" had been discovered, raised the true figure for 1977 sales, previously estimated at $9.9 billion, to $11.3 billion. The discrepancy of $1.4 billion exceeds the value of the Iranian AWACS sale—now included in the 1978 total—by only $170 million. But this may make it a bit easier for the President to live up to his promise after all.

The President said that no weapons would again be produced solely for export (as were the Northrop F-5 series of fighter aircraft, and FMC Corporation's Armoured Infantry Fighting Vehicle), and that the United States would not again be the first supplier to introduce higher levels of military technology into any region of the world than currently exist there. Yet the proposed sale of F-15 fighter aircraft to Saudi Arabia, and the recently concluded AWACS sale to Iran, constitute precisely such escalations of technology, and both proposals have had the support of the Carter administra-

**FMC Corporation's AIFV for Netherlands Army**

tion. In the case of the AWACS sale this advocacy was difficult to abandon when the sale was not approved in time for inclusion in the 1977 sales figures.

Further, the President said that coproduction agreements for significant weapons would be prohibited. Perhaps an understanding should be reached about which weapons are to be considered significant, in view of the current Israeli proposal to coproduce in Israel

**F-16 Fighter Aircraft**

our new F-16 air combat fighter, which is already under coproduction in The Netherlands and in Belgium, and in view of the negotiations now in progress between the Japanese firm of Kawasaki and Lockheed Aircraft Corporation for the coproduction in Japan of the P-3C Orion anti-submarine and reconnaissance aircraft.

The President added that commitments for the sale or coproduction of advanced weapons would be prohibited until those weapons were operationally deployed with United States forces, "thus removing the incentive to promote foreign sales in an effort to lower unit costs for Defense procurement."

The incentive remains. A foreign sale can lower our unit procurement cost of a weapon just as effectively after we have deployed it as before. A total of 135 F-15 Eagle fighter interceptor aircraft are now operationally deployed by the Tactical Air Command. 21 of these have been operationally deployed at Bitburg, West Germany, since they flew there from Langley Air Force Base on 27 April 1977. They will soon be joined by two more squadrons of F-15s. Four additional F-15s have been delivered thus far to Israel, out of a sale to that country of 25 of the aircraft which took place before the F-15 had entered our own inventory. That helped to lower our unit procurement costs, as did the sale of 100 F-15s to Japan. The proposed sale of F-15s to the Saudis would help further, and that is the main reason for it. The F-15, as we have seen, still "has a cost problem."

In addition, President Carter said his administration would not entertain any requests for the retransfer of arms, and that prior State Department authorization would be required before agents of private manufacturers or the United States government could take any action that might promote the sale of arms abroad. We have seen how difficult these restrictions are to enforce.

Moreover, in response to industry criticism that has taken place in the months since the President announced these restrictions, there has been a relaxation in the language defining what kinds of industry contacts with potential export customers require prior approval. In May it was understood that these would be contacts that "design to influence a decision to purchase." Now prior approval is only required if the contact is "designed to constitute a basis for a decision to purchase."

The President also added that since we dominate the world market to such

**P-3 Orion Patrol Aircraft**

a degree, he believed that the United States can and should take the first step in seeking multilateral cooperation from other major suppliers for the reduction of worldwide arms transfers.

Finally, the President said he would continue to utilize arms transfers to promote the security of the United States and its allies, that we would honor all of our defense treaty obligations, as well as our responsibility to assure the security of the state of Israel, and that only those countries with which we have major defense treaties would be exempt from the new policy of arms export restraints.

This means that a good many countries are exempt. The Southeast Asia Collective Defense Treaty Organization (SEATO) expired on 30 June 1977, but we still have a separate defense treaty (ANZUS) with two of its original seven members, Australia and New Zealand, and we also have a mutual defense treaty with Japan. The Central Treaty Organiza-

tion (CENTO), which grew from the Baghdad Pact, originally included France and Pakistan, but those two countries have since disassociated themselves from it. The only additional signatory to CENTO which is not also a member of NATO is Iran. Finally, there is NATO itself, with 14 member nations aside from the United States. Adding Israel, we have at the outset a total of 19 major developed countries understood to be exempt from any restraint on United States arms exports under the new Carter policy.

Furthermore President Carter announced four days later, on 21 May, that he felt NATO was too exclusive an organization, and that the United States would seek broader defense alliances involving more countries as our allies—countries which, presumably, would also be free from restrictions on American arms exports.

On 11 July the President, who six weeks earlier had indicated he felt the United States should take the first step in reducing worldwide arms transfers, said that this country would find it difficult to take the first step. A key problem in limiting international arms sales, he indicated, is dissuading other suppliers, such as the Communist nations, from moving aggressively into the arms market once the United States has reduced its sales. He added:

*Our ability to restrain international arms transfers will in many cases depend upon our ability to gain cooperation of potential alternative suppliers. It will be most difficult to achieve the cooperation of Communist suppliers whose support for neighboring countries motivates increased acquisitions by some of the largest purchasers of United States arms.*

The Presidential report to Congress on arms control defined similar problems:

*The prospect that other countries will voluntarily and spontaneously follow our model of restraint is unlikely. If others begin to fill the vacuum we leave, the pressures in this country to loosen the bonds of restraint could become substantial.*

At the present time there is a backlog of Foreign Military Sales agreements signed and approved by the current or previous administrations for a total of $30.1 billion in undelivered defense equipment, including $11 billion in weapons, all of which has been scheduled for delivery within the next four to seven years. It is within Presiden-

tial authority to rescind any of these agreements. But that is not likely to happen. The report tells why:

*Cancellation of existing contracts by the United States (which would have to pay substantial termination costs) or refusal to support items previously sold would understandably provoke sharp reactions from the purchasing countries.*

Accordingly, there is no plan with the Carter administration either to cancel such contracts or to refuse to enter into subsequent contracts for the supply of ammunition, spare parts, maintenance, training and other support for the weapons previously sold.

So it is clear that President Carter's policy on arms control will not yield a significant reduction in the flow of American arms abroad. Existing contracts create obligations reaching far into the future. Defense alliances exempt many of our most important client countries from a restraint on arms sales. There is continuing pressure from industry to produce arms and find a market for them, and there is a concurrent pressure from the Pentagon to reduce its costs by facilitating access to that market. It is impossible to enforce restrictions on sales activities as long as the sale of arms continues to be allowed. It is equally impossible to enforce restrictions on the retransfer of arms once they have been freed from direct United States control.

No wonder General Fish said to me, "We'd all like to see the total volume of sales lowered, but the margin of decision is narrow." No wonder Vice-President Mondale said: "America is no longer an arsenal of democracy; it is quite simply an arsenal."

## Solutions

In seeking some means to impose realistic restraints on the flow of arms, the National Security Council studied the effects of placing a ceiling on the dollar volume of our military exports, either on a quota basis for each country eligible to purchase or receive arms, or by giving priority to requests in the order of their submission.

The NSC saw that the latter system would break down. We would tend to delay our decisions on whether or not to meet certain arms requests "until late in the year when competing demands (among which trade-offs would be necessary) were better known," but it was clear that we would still be able to honor many requests in sequence while making sure that certain weapons went where we wanted them to go.

However, the NSC found several other disadvantages to a ceiling. Among them:

*If ceilings were administered on a quota basis, the United States Government would have to make explicit, and eventually public, distinctions among categories of recipients.*

We already do this. We favor those countries that participate with us in defense alliances. Understandably enough, we favor those countries whose security promotes our own. Countries that are eligible for FMS sales are broken down into two groups, as we have seen, and sales to one of those groups need no prior review by the State Department and are restricted in size and composition. We also clearly favor major buyers like Iran.

But the NSC has other objections:

*Announcement of a ceiling, in combination with apprehension that the ceiling could be lowered in subsequent years, might encourage buyers to place orders that otherwise would have been deferred.*

This presupposes that buyers have shown a measure of restraint, which the imposition of a ceiling would eliminate. There has never been any indication of such voluntary restraint. Buyers are already ordering every article of military equipment they can afford, whether or not they need it. Even if a ceiling did increase their appetite for arms, the purpose of imposing a ceiling is to curb exports regardless of demand. The growth of demand is not the issue. The volume of sales is the issue.

A further objection from the NSC:

*Competition among United States firms and, perhaps, their respective promotional activities could become more intense as they worked to ensure that their interests were accomodated within the ceiling.*

This may be evidence that the free enterprise system does not really believe in competition after all. It is difficult to imagine how competition between our major arms firms could become any more intense than it already is. But if it were to become so, it would not be able to stimulate sales—so long as a ceiling had been imposed on the volume of sales.

Finally, the Council's major objection to a ceiling:

*Recipients would tend to utilize their full share of the ceiling each year to avoid risks of unmet demands in subsequent years. The arms transfer ceiling could become a floor. A ceiling which included commercial sales may tend to increase the proportion of licenses that result in sales.*

This, again, implies that the volume of sales might be lower when no ceiling exists. But we do not run the risk of discouraging some sort of voluntary incentive to reduce sales. We run the risk of a steady increase in the volume of sales. Even if a ceiling becomes a floor, it also remains a ceiling. Even if there is an increase in the proportion of licenses that result in sales, the total volume of sales in which they result will be lower. That is the purpose of a ceiling.

In view of the quality of these objections, the establishment of a ceiling reducing the dollar volume of arms exports remains an effective option of policy.

The NSC also considered restraints on the export of certain types of weapons as

**M-47 Dragon Antitank Missile**

well as restraints on exports to certain countries. Among the weapons considered were those that could effectively be operated by terrorists, including man-portable air defense systems like RED-EYE and anti-tank systems like DRAG-ON. It was also thought valuable to consider restraints on the export of police equipment:

*Weapons that might associate the United States undesirably with the internal affairs of a foreign country (riot control weapons, equipment, and agents). None are sold through FMS procedures, but commercial licenses may be authorized.*

A good many such licenses have been authorized. From 1973 through 1976 the United States sold to Third World countries alone a total of 49,936 police revolvers and automatic pistols, 9,720 carbines, submachine guns and semi-automatic rifles, 5,225 shotguns, gas guns and riot guns, 6,633 canisters of Mace, 155,835 tear gas grenades, over seven million rounds of ammunition and a vast assortment of electrified cattle prods, truncheons, metal detectors, sensors, eavesdropping and surveillance equipment, most of it licensed by the Office of Munitions Control, some of it not licensed at all.

**Cadillac Gage V-150 Commando**

This equipment was purchased by police, internal security and regular army organizations of more than 50 nations. This raises the question of restraints on the export of such equipment to countries whose use of it is clearly to support or expand programs of internal repression. The NSC concedes:

*The hard fact is that most nations of the world today engage to some degree in repressive practices. A number of countries with deplorable records of human rights observance are also countries where we have important security and foreign policy interests.*

This trend has not gone unnoticed by some of our major arms manufacturers, who in the past decade have developed weapons ill-suited for use against regular military forces but highly effective in counterinsurgency missions against undefended targets or resistance groups equipped only with small arms.

Thus, Cadillac Gage Corporation developed the V-150 Commando armoured car, and has in the past five years sold 296 of these vehicles to police organizations abroad, variously equipped with smoke and tear gas dischargers, fire hoses, loudspeakers, and 7.62mm and 20mm gun turrets. The Haitian Palace Guard purchased six. The Bravia Cgaim-

**A-37B Dragonfly**

ite, an unlicensed copy of the V-150 Commando, is manufactured in Portugal, and numbers of these are believed to have been sold to South Africa.

Similarly, the Cessna A-37 Dragonfly and Rockwell OV-10 Bronco aircraft, whose respective top speeds are only 507 and 281 mph, were both developed in the mid-1960s specifically for counterinsurgency use, and were well-tested against undefended targets in Vietnam. Highly vulnerable to any sophisticated form of air defense, these aircraft can take off and land on short jungle clearings, are equipped with grenade launchers and high-speed automatic cannon, and can deliver remarkably heavy loads of ordnance, including a variety of newly-developed anti-personnel bomblets, cluster and flechette mines, fuel air explosives, and gas and napalm bombs.

While we retain large numbers of both of these aircraft in our own inventories, we have exported to date 794 of 891 Cessna A-37B or T-37 aircraft scheduled for delivery, and 66 of 82 Rockwell OV-10A Broncos. Recipient countries include Brazil, Chile, Colombia, Greece, Cambodia, Pakistan, Peru, Portugal, Thailand, Turkey, Venezuela, West Germany, and Zimbabwe when it was still Rhodesia.

It is true that we have expressed our disapproval of repressive regimes by supporting arms embargoes against South Africa, Rhodesia and the Portuguese colonies in Africa, and that Congress has legislated embargoes on arms to Chile and Uruguay in response to alleged violations of human rights in those countries. But we have seen how simple it is to violate these embargoes, and how difficult to enforce them. The

**OV-10A Bronco**

fact also remains that, by making available police equipment, military grant aid and training services to some of these same countries, and by supplying those services and the arms and equipment just described to more than 50 other countries, we are supporting far more political repression in the world than we discourage.

According to Amnesty International of London, the countries most frequently accused of violations of human rights are Argentina, Brazil, Chile, Ethiopia, Indonesia, Iran, the Philippines, South Korea, Thailand and Uruguay. In the past five years those countries alone have purchased $17.5 billion in United States

defense equipment, and received $1.1 billion more in grant aid, accounting for 30 percent of all United States arms transfers during that period.

In the same period 12,732 officers from those same countries, including members of Chile's Carabineros and DINA secret police, Iran's SAVAK, the Presidential Security Force of South Korea and the Thai National Police and Border Patrol—all organizations notorious for their disregard of human rights—received military, counterinsurgency and internal security training in the United States under IMET and other programs.

The NSC concludes:

*United States arms that seem especially likely to be used for repression can be systematically denied. However, widespread use of the blunt instruments of program termination and arms embargoes is likely to result in arms transfer cutoffs in geographic patterns involving small countries whose individual importance for our security interests may not be great, but whose collective importance may be.*

If there is any collective importance in all of those countries engaged in the repeated violation of human rights, it is not in how they may affect our security interests, but in how our continued association with them and our continued support of their regimes corrupts the principles of human dignity and political freedom to which the United States once dedicated itself. To place all these countries under an arms embargo would be, at last, to reaffirm those principles.

Ceilings on the dollar volume of our arms exports, embargoes against selected countries, prohibitions on the export of certain types of weapons suited only for police or internal security operations would all be effective steps to take in forming a policy of arms control. But none of these steps could be taken without economic repercussions regarded as undesirable.

Early in 1977 the Department of the Treasury prepared an assessment of how various arms control policies would affect our economy.* The most serious of the hypothetical situations it examined

*Study of the Economic Effects of Restraint in Arms Transfers, Department of the Treasury, 1977.

was an immediate cutback of 40 percent in the volume of our military exports, taking place in 1977 and carried on through 1983. It was found that this would have a rather modest impact on aggregate economic indicators.

Such a cutback, the Treasury determined, would produce a drop in real Gross National Product equal, in constant 1975 dollars, to $2 billion, with a reduction of 10 percent per year in the rate of decline, resulting in a loss of only $1.8 billion in GNP by 1983.

The relative change in the current account of the United States balance of payments was found to be much greater than the computed changes in other economic indicators. By 1983 our balance of payments under the 40 percent cutback would have deteriorated by about $5 billion, in current dollars, or by $4.1 billion if grant aid exports are included in the cutback. On a trade-weighted basis, there would be a requisite 2.1 percent depreciation of the dollar.

Another result of the cutback would be a decline in the Treasury float, comprised of the excess of advance payments from foreign purchasers of military equipment. For each $1 billion decline in the float, interest payments of the Treasury would increase, with an appropriate lag, by about $50 million per year.

As we have seen, our current level of arms exports affords the Department of Defense a variety of savings. Those which accrue from research and development surcharges and lower unit procurement costs total almost $800 million per year, in 1975 dollars. The Treasury estimates that by 1983 the effects of a 40 percent cutback would have reduced those savings by about $310 million per year.

The estimated percentage decline in total employment under the cutback would reach only one tenth of one percent by 1983. This would have an effect on the Treasury, which collects about eight percent of the total value of foreign sales of military items in corporate and personal income taxes.

The reduced military export bill would cause a drop in corporate profits and personal income resulting in a loss to the Treasury of tax revenues amounting to less than $500 million, in current dollars, by 1983. The aggregate loss in tax revenues during the intervening five years would total $4.2 billion, in current dollars, if the dollar were to remain unchanged, and $1.2 billion if the dollar were to depreciate at the predicted rate.

There would be other budgetary effects on the Treasury. Higher unemployment would mean losses in Social Security taxes, increased government disbursements for compensation outlays, and possibly stepped-up expenditures under public assistance programs.

In computing these effects, the Treasury used the DRI Longtrend model of the economy. The report acknowledges that the economic impact of the cutback would be about 50 percent larger if based on the Wharton model of the United States economy, but it sums up its assessment as follows:

*Any plausible degree of restraint in exporting defense goods and services is likely to affect broad economic aggregates, except, perhaps, the trade balance, rather moderately. Moreover, even these moderate adverse effects may be easily countered by slightly more expansionary monetary and fiscal policies.*

From the viewpoint of public administration, then, a cutback in our arms exports appears to be manageable. From the viewpoint of the work force, however, it is quite a different matter. The unemployment problem created could be a good deal more serious than it might seem. An increase in total unemployment of one tenth of one percent means the displacement of 132,000 workers. Under a 40 percent cutback in arms exports, the aerospace, communications and ordnance industries would suffer the most. The states that would sustain the greatest rise in unemployment, in order of severity, are Connecticut, Washington, California, Indiana, Kansas, Michigan, Missouri, Ohio, Vermont and New Jersey.

Among occupational categories, the most severely affected, of course, would be the technical and professional jobs, employing aerospace designers, electronic and mechanical engineers, and accounting for 17.5 percent of the workers displaced. Most of these people are highly skilled, motivated towards only one specialization, trained for only one job. The higher the level of skill and the narrower the specialization of a particular occupational group, the more intractable the problem of reemployment.

These people would not be happy. Their representatives would fight in Congress to protect their jobs. But what those Congressmen would really be fighting to protect, whether or not they knew it, are the more powerful elements of their constituencies, the defense corporations which employ these workers, and whose margin of profit might be retained by eliminating their jobs but whose volume of sales would surely decline in the event of any cutback in arms exports. These companies, with powerful lobby groups and strong allies in the Pentagon and other government agencies, would form the heart of resistance to any attempt to reduce the volume of our arms exports abroad. Which is certainly part of the reason why there has never been a successful attempt to restrain such exports in the past.

In comparison with the enormous influence wielded by the defense and aerospace manufacturers and the whole establishment of interests that support them, the workers these companies employ would be of little consequence in affecting policy by themselves, if they ever had to act for themselves, even though the loss of their jobs would be the only genuine tragedy in a shift of economic priorities. Job security, that basic right implicitly offered and constantly threatened in our land of opportunity, is not something we have learned to provide. Nor will we ever provide it, without a fundamental change in the distribution of wealth.

Implicit in this discussion has been the vision not of a mere cutback in arms exports but of a day when there are few if any exports of military equipment to purchasers abroad, other than of articles essential to our security and that of our allies. As we have seen, an understanding of what that security truly requires can never be unbiased as long as there is pressure from industry to continue producing what it produces now.

We are confronting some of the basic commitments of our economy. These are the commitments to self-perpetuation and growth. Whatever we now produce, it is felt, we must continue to produce. Otherwise, enormous investments of capital in tooling, castings and forgings, designs and production assembly systems may be lost. If we can produce more than we are producing now, then we must do so because it will increase profits. If there is something else we can produce with a minimum of additional investment, then we must do that too. It is a wise course to follow. But it is wise only in order to maximize the corporate return on investment. It may not produce what the world—or even the military—needs.

We do not need many more military aircraft. Nor do we need, as has been suggested, more commercial airliners instead. We need safer airliners, with a greater tolerance for metal fatigue, more reliable landing gear, more effective navigational and communications equipment. We need more efficient airliners, costing less to produce and consuming less fuel, and consequently costing less, for both owners and passengers, to use.

We need safer and more efficient urban transport systems. We need more effective and less costly waste disposal systems. We need alternate supplies of cheap energy. We need to employ technology not to continue the proliferation of unneeded goods, but to improve the efficiency and safety and utility—and to cut to a fraction the cost—of what we already have.

We need a shift in national priorities. The defense establishment may have played a large part in creating existing priorities, but its role would rapidly change, and along with that change its assessment of our security interest would change, as we changed our economic commitments. We must abandon the commitment to growth.

We need to protect the jobs that exist, and we need to create more jobs. There are jobs for the most highly specialized of our systems analysts, computer technicians and aerospace engineers, challenging all of their inventiveness and brilliance. But these are challenges of quality, not of growth. Those people must be directed to these challenges. They must be trained for them. They should be de-

manding that training now.

We need some of the public assistance programs the Treasury foresaw. We need to care for the workers who are laid off while factories are being retooled to make tractors instead of tanks. We need to find the work for them to do. The work will not exist until we recognize that it needs to be done.

We cannot look to the institutions basically in need of change to initiate that change and voluntarily restructure their ratios of profit to overhead, abandon their plans for expansion, relinquish their claims to a steady increase in volume of sales. The corporations will not stop what they are doing until it becomes illegal to do it any longer. The legislation to make them stop will not be drafted until, one day, an administration and a Congress realize it must be done. That day will not come until those who read this and all of those who already know this feel the effects of what is happening around them sufficiently to recognize that they can no longer endure it. Ours can still be a government by the people and for the people. It just needs the people. It needs their voice. Until that time the United States will continue to manufacture and distribute the weapons of war, and these will grow deadlier and more abundant with each passing year.

## The Weapons in This Book
Of the thousands of articles of defense equipment and related items covered by the United States Munitions List, this book describes less than six hundred. It does not, for example, include entries on strategic nuclear weapons and their delivery systems. With the exception of 102 Polaris missiles sold to England (without nuclear warheads) under the FMS program, such weapons have not so far been offered to any other country. Regulations fully prohibit the transfer of nuclear warheads and bombs to a foreign government's control, and are also far more strict, though not entirely effective, in preventing the transfer of nuclear technology and materials which might have military application.

However, since these conditions may change, our current major strategic nuclear weapons, as well as those we regard to be tactical nuclear weapons, are covered in a separate appendix to the book, along with a discussion of whether any useful distinction can be

made between strategic and tactical nuclear weapons.

Nor will one find here the vast assortment of military articles, from helmets, boots, uniforms, canteens and tents to radio equipment, surgical equipment, tractors and cranes, machine tools and transport vehicles, all of which are as essential as weapons themselves to the creation and maintenance of a combat-ready military force.

What the book does attempt to provide is coverage of all the major American weapons—those items capable of causing any form of destruction to man or materials—that are currently in service with other nations or available for sale or transfer to them. Since few such items of equipment manufactured in America, save those which employ fission or fusion, are not now or soon to be in service abroad, the book becomes a survey of the full range of conventional—or nonnuclear—arms produced in the United States.

Consequently, the book includes all of the major weapons currently in service with our own armed forces, those about to enter service, those now regarded by our services as obsolete or undergoing replacement—though still available for production or transfer, and assured of a long life in foreign forces, and major weapons from the World War II and postwar eras that remain in service abroad today.

An attempt has been made to cover all of our current front-line combat and support aircraft, helicopters and counterinsurgency aircraft, the variety of new aircraft weapons pods and armament systems, tanks and armoured vehicles, destroyers, missile frigates, minesweepers, submarines, riverine warfare craft and other naval vessels, our full range of guided missiles with conventional high-explosive warheads, infantry weapons of every type, mortars and machine guns, recoilless rifles, bombs, torpedoes, mines, grenades, howitzers, all calibers of field artillery, and a representative sampling of the current types of ammunition these many different weapons fire.

Weapons developed solely for export are covered here too. Some of these, like FMC Corporation's Armoured Infantry Fighting Vehicle, 850 of which were delivered to the Netherlands Army, have been private production ventures. Others were conscious instruments of our foreign policy, fully backed by our government—such as Northrop's F-5A Freedom Fighter and F-5E Tiger II, a series of fighter-bomber aircraft presently serving in more than fifteen air forces overseas and strengthening what we fancy continues to be, in President Roosevelt's words, our "arsenal of democracy."

There are also notes on weapons now in development. It is likely that many of these new weapons will be made available to our allies. They include the flechette dart, 25 or 30 of which can be loaded into a 12-gauge shotgun round, the XM19 5.56mm flechette rifle, the ring aerofoil grenade, the Copperhead 105mm cannon-launched guided projectile, and Astrolite—a liquid mine.

Included are comparisons of the lethality and destructive power of different types of projectiles and fragmentation devices, with descriptions of what they do to the human target.

Among the appendices are summaries of the current state of the art in the design and production of fire control systems, electronic warfare equipment, drones and remotely piloted vehicles, radar, sonar, range finding and sighting equipment, and sensors.

The criteria for selection remain arbitrary. Military transport aircraft, for example, are included while ground transport vehicles are not. We transfer a large quantity of jeeps, trucks and unarmed specialized vehicles abroad for military use. There is in fact such a variety of this equipment that inclusion of it would have made the book unwieldy. Another reason for deleting these items was their relative availability. Most countries can readily acquire or even build their own military

F-5F of Imperial Iranian Air Force

ground transport at a reasonable cost, while the acquisition of air transport requires a major expenditure and usually involves procurement from a major supplier like the United States.

In addition to describing a weapon and its capabilities, each entry identifies its manufacturer and gives production figures when this information is available. When it has not been possible to obtain verifiable figures an estimate of production is made—but only in those cases where it is reasonable to do so. For example, in view of the variety of types of hand grenade currently produced in America or produced here in the past, and in view of the number of manufacturers involved who have since changed their business or gone out of business or merged with other companies, and whose records are lost or incomplete, any estimate of the total number of hand grenades that have been produced to date in the United States could be wrong by too great a margin to be of significance. Such estimates have therefore been avoided.

Each entry also gives the numbers of a weapon deployed by our own armed forces, the quantity transferred abroad, the foreign countries to which it has been supplied, and an indication of whether it has been supplied as grant aid through the Military Assistance Program (MAP) or sold through the Foreign Military Sales Program (FMS). When a weapon is reported in a certain country, but was not supplied through FMS or MAP, it is evident that it found its way to that country by commercial sale or some other means. When the alternate source and means of transfer are known, that is stated. Sometimes that is not known, though the weapon is still known to be

present in a country. When the presence of a weapon in a certain country is only suspected but has not been verified, that is stated too. This information is reasonably complete, and includes proposed transfers that, at the time this book went to press, had not yet taken place. Such transfers are identified as pending.

### A Note on Prices

Prices are given for more than 200 of the weapons covered in this book, including all of those items of major defense equipment that are currently in production, currently in service with our own military forces, or in high demand abroad. These prices are the unit costs of weapons to the United States government. They are equivalent to what our government charges when selling the weapons abroad. In order to give a sense of comparative values between our government acquisitions costs and the open market, current open market prices are also given for some of these weapons, as well as for some older weapons no longer in production but still in service around the world.

Government acquisitions costs are generally lower than open market prices for the same weapon. This usually is due to the large quantities in which our government purchases most weapons, though as we have seen there are certain weapons it cannot afford to purchase in the quantities it desires. The M60E2 7.62mm machine gun, manufactured by the Maremont Corporation and other firms, cost our government $707 per unit in 1977. The open market price for the same weapon ranges between $1,500 and $2,000.

Yet occasionally, due to its availability from other sources, a weapon can be purchased more cheaply on the open market than from our government. The M40A1 106mm recoilless rifle, a weapon in great demand due to its portability and high firepower, currently costs our gov-

**M40A1 106mm Recoilless Rifle of Italian Army**

ernment $47,000 per unit. Perfect copies are now made in several countries. The weapon was available in Taiwan for $11,640 per unit in 1976. In 1977 the Israelis offered it for between $18,000 and $21,150. Current open market prices for the M40A1, new from stock, peak at $32,500. Thus competition from other sources of supply can have a substantial effect on value.

The value of a weapon, and consequently its price, fluctuates not only due to supply and demand, but also due to the conflicting forces of depreciation on the one hand and inflation on the other.

New weapons have a fairly stable value, and sharp rises in inflation over the past decade have acted to raise their prices substantially. Since the government acquisitions costs cited in this book are taken from the most recent year in which each weapon was purchased, and since not every weapon was most recently purchased in the same year, the year of acquisition is always cited here along with the unit cost. In this way, allowance can be made for the probable effects of inflation. The Cessna A-37B Dragonfly aircraft, for instance, was most recently purchased by our government in 1975. At that time the unit procurement cost was $534,000 per aircraft. If A-37Bs were sold today, they would undoubtedly be sold at a higher price.

Older weapons have a less stable value, depending to a large degree on their usefulness, which may vary greatly from one part of the world to another. Obsolete aircraft, no longer sufficiently swift or maneuverable to play any useful role in the United States Air Force, may remain of significant value to a foreign air force operating in an environment where much lower levels of technological sophistication suffice to meet combat demands. While the value of these aircraft may have depreciated considerably in our own eyes, the demand for them in certain regions of the world may be enormous—assuring their sale at a high price.

Due to their proliferation throughout the world, the weapons whose values remain most constant and least subject to fluctuations of supply and demand are small arms. With the exception of special circumstances, like those which obtained in Beirut in 1975, when sudden large demands rose at the mercy of very few suppliers, the prices of small arms have generally increased only in step with inflation. A Smith & Wesson M28 .357 Magnum revolver, which sold for $98.00 in 1970, cost $123.00 in 1975, and $140.00 in 1977. The M-1 Garand rifle, which sold for $31.00 in 1946, was

**Smith & Wesson Model 28 .357 Magnum revolver**

priced at $79.95 in 1975, and can be bought second-hand today for $75.00. Black market prices are higher, but keep the same relative pace with inflation.

Sometimes the effects of depreciation and inflation appear to balance each other out. The famous North American

P-51 Mustang fighter, a piston-engined aircraft recently manufactured by Cavalier as the F-51D, and used today as a counterinsurgency fighter-bomber by several countries in Latin America, Africa and Asia, originally cost $50,985 with its Packard-Merlin engine. That was during World War II. Today, P-51 airframes occasionally appear on the market, and can be purchased for $7,500. But to fit the aircraft with a new engine, strengthened wings and new landing gear, and to otherwise rehabilitate and reequip it for combat duty, would cost at least another $35,000. Installation of a basic armament system, for example two .50 Caliber aircraft machine guns, would bring the total cost up to amost exactly $50,000. The use of a modern armament system, such as the Emerson Minitat 5.56mm machine gun (currently available for $55,000 installed), could nearly double that cost. The addition of modern avionics and other electronic equipment would raise the cost further.

Prices quoted in the book are identified not only by the year in which they occurred but also as open market prices or prices to the United States government. Open market prices are those obtained by independent dealers or foreign governments, acting as brokers between other governments or individuals either on an open or a confidential basis. Prices to the United States government are its acquisition costs. These are given as the unit procurement cost of each weapon, equivalent to the base price we charge another government through the Foreign Military Sales program, before adding a surcharge for research and development costs.

Unit procurement costs should not be confused with various other officially standardized computations of a weapon's cost, each one of which includes a different number of its cost components. The various different quotations of unit cost which result, and which are frequently made by manufacturers and military procurement officers when referring to the same weapon at the same time, have led to a considerable amount of confusion. In the case of aircraft, for example, costs are computed and cited by four different standards. There is the aircraft's Unit Flyaway Cost, its Weapon System Cost, its Unit Procurement Cost, and its Program Acquisition Cost.

The Flyaway Cost includes the cost of the airframe, propulsion equipment, electronics, armament, other equipment furnished by the government and installed, further non-recurring costs, and an allowance for engineering change orders. The Weapon System Cost of the aircraft adds to its Flyway Cost the further costs of ground support equipment, training equipment, technical data, training manuals and other publications, and factory training, installation, checkout and technical services provided by the contractor. The Unit Procurement Cost adds to this total the cost of initial spares. Finally, the Program Acquisition Cost combines the Unit Procurement Cost with a certain amount of the costs of research, development, testing and evaluation of the aircraft, the total of which is apportioned equally

**A-10 Close Air Support Aircraft**

among the number of aircraft being produced.

There is frequently a dramatic variance. In the case of the A-10 Close Air Support Aircraft, developed by Fairchild Industries and now in production, the Unit Flyaway Cost has been cited as $4.82 million, the Unit Procurement Cost as $5.62 million, and the Program Cost as $6.12 million.

Research and development costs themselves also vary greatly from one weapon to another, involving many millions of dollars spent over several years in some cases, and comparatively minor expenditures, over short periods of

time, in others. Sometimes the development of a new weapon involves only minor modifications of another weapon before it. The degree to which the costs of research and development raise the unit cost of a weapon also varies greatly according to the total number of units of each weapon under manufacture, which in some cases may be large, in others small. Finally, surcharges for research and development may be added to the export bill for some weapons but not for others. For all of these reasons, it was thought best to eliminate such a variable in citing costs in this book. The costs given are therefore Unit Procurement Costs. These reflect the base prices at which, discounting the possible effects of inflation, the costs of weapons will eventually stabilize after research and development have been paid out.

Program Acquisitions Costs are occasionally also cited in the book—but always clearly identified as such—when they provide interesting comparisons with the Unit Procurement Costs, showing how much difference the costs of research and development can sometimes make.

One must keep these differences in mind when examining the prices of arms sales quoted by public officials or cited in the press. As we have seen, the differences in price between two separate sales of the same quantity of the same weapon may be due to the fact that in one case, but not in the other, the sale includes training or construction or the supply of technical assistance or spare parts. Another reason for such differences may be that one source quotes Unit Procurement Costs while another quotes Program Acquisitions Costs.

In truth, of course, while research and development costs are variables, they remain a part of what we pay before a weapon is placed in active inventory. They are part of the extraordinary costs of military preparedness. Nor does it stop there. If we want, for instance, an accurate idea of what it finally costs to place a single combat-ready aircraft in

the sky, we must add to the cost of the aircraft itself the cost of equipping it with a typical load of ordnance and the cost of training the pilot who flies it.

**F-4D Phantom Fighter-Bomber**

The Unit Procurement Cost of the F-14A Tomcat fighter interceptor aircraft will be $20.620 million in 1978, when 44 of the aircraft will be delivered to the United States Navy. The Unit Program Cost that year will be $21.379 million. We now have the cost of an aircraft sitting on the tarmac—a very sophisticated aircraft but an empty one, and not yet equipped with its normal complement of Phoenix air-to-air missiles. The 1978 Unit Procurement Cost of an AIM-54A Phoenix missile will be $406,190. Six Phoenix missiles, the normal load, will therefore cost $2.437 million. Add to that the cost of the aircraft, and add $500,000 to train the pilot flying it. Thus a combat-ready F-14A Tomcat, airborne,

**MIM-23A HAWK Missile at moment of launch**

**CVN-68 USS Nimitz aircraft carrier**

will cost a total of $24.316 million.

This still leaves out the substantial costs of operation and maintenance, including repairs, replacement parts and fuel. It costs $900,000 to keep six Bell UH-1B Iroquois helicopters flying for one year. The operational costs for a single B-52 bomber during the air raids conducted over North Vietnam were $41,000 for each sortie. According to the Tactical Air Command, it cost $22.9 million, in 1976 dollars, to keep one squadron of 24 F-4 Phantom aircraft flying for one year. This included, among other costs, $1.8 million in replenishment spares, $2.9 million in depot maintenance, $4.3 million in fuel, and $7.5 million in personnel pay, together with costs for support equipment, safety or logistics modifications, base material support, operating support, munitions and missile training, transfers and medical expenses.

These are peacetime costs. Similar expenditures are currently being undertaken for the operation and maintenance of an additional 4,976 combat aircraft and 664 transport aircraft in our Tactical Air Command, Military Airlift Command, Pacific Air Forces and United States Air Force in Europe, the 463 bombers and 615 tanker aircraft in our Strategic Air Command, the 374 combat aircraft in

our Aerospace Defense Command, 650 combat aircraft in our Air National Guard and 420 combat aircraft in our Air Force Reserve, the 800 combat aircraft in the United States Army and the 2,610 combat aircraft and 2,638 other types of aircraft in the United States Navy and Marine Corps, our 9,704 Army and 1,359 Navy helicopters, our 1,054 intercontinental ballistic missiles, our 41 strategic ballistic missile submarines and 91 additional attack submarines, our 21 aircraft carriers—13 of them on active duty in three major fleets—309

**NIKE HERCULES Air Defense Missiles based on Taiwan**

major surface combatants and 932 ships and craft of other types in the Navy, the 8,930 main battle tanks, 1,600 reconnaissance tanks and 16,950 armoured personnel carriers deployed by the Army and Marine Corps in three Marine Corps divisions and fourteen Army divisions, three armoured cavalry regiments and one brigade, our Army's 900 HAWK and Nike-Hercules missiles and sixteen battalions of Lance and Honest John mis-

siles, the Marine Corps's 35 battalions of HAWK missiles, and the Army's 2,700 self-propelled guns and howitzers, 2,200 towed 105mm and 155mm field artillery pieces, 5,700 mortars, 6,000 90mm and 106mm recoilless rifles, 2,400 TOW and Dragon anti-tank missiles, 600 20mm and 40mm anti-aircraft guns and 20,000 Vulcan guns and anti-aircraft missiles, together with a variety of other weapons too numerous to list here, but all of which are kept in constant readiness for war.

Nor does this include the costs of having acquired this staggering array of weaponry, costs which are constantly increasing. It cost approximately $55 million to construct and outfit an aircraft carrier during World War II. In the 1960s the cost of a nuclear-powered aircraft carrier ranged between $500 million and $600 million. By 1974 this cost had risen to $1 billion. Today an additional Nimitz class nuclear-powered attack carrier, which has been proposed, would cost $2.2 billion to build. Its complement of aircraft would cost another $2.8 billion, and the variety of destroyers, cruisers, frigates and other ships which accompany it would cost another $2 billion. A new carrier strike force, added to the 13 we now have on active service, would therefore cost a minimum of another $7 billion.

Then there are the costs of all the other additions we plan to make each year to our arsenal. Among the 82 programs listed in the Pentagon's latest Selected Acquisitions Report, 44 have an estimated cost to completion of $178 billion. This includes $40 billion for four different fighter aircraft programs, $48 billion for a five-year program to build 157 new Navy vessels, and $9 billion to equip 10 Navy destroyers with the new Aegis air defense system.

Finally, we have not considered the costs of engaging in war itself, costs impossible to compute in dollars—let alone by more meaningful standards.

# COMBAT AIRCRAFT

The design and development of combat aircraft in the United States has closely followed specific requirements set by our military services. These requirements are for aircraft that can meet certain standards in performing one or more distinct combat roles either established as a current tactical need or envisioned as an impending need for the future. In recent years our requirements have broadened, in response not only, as before, to advances in Soviet military technology, or to changes in the geopolitical balance of power that have proliferated that technology, but also to changes in the social and political structure of the Third World.

The growing consolidation of power over the last decade by military and other elites in the developing countries of Asia, Africa and Latin America, and their increased reliance on repressive solutions to political unrest, has given rise to a considerable demand for various types of counterinsurgency aircraft to perform internal security missions. Because of our frequent desire to lend support to such regimes, and our growing anticipation of the possible need, in cases where it appears to further our interests, for direct American involvement of the kind we demonstrated in Vietnam, we have responded to this demand with a variety of new aircraft.

The Rockwell OV-10A Bronco, the Helio AU-24A Stallion and the Cessna A-37B Dragonfly were all developed in the 1960s specifically for counterinsurgency (COIN) missions. They are light, adaptable, comparatively inexpensive, and capable of delivering substantial loads of sophisticated munitions on target. Their designs sacrifice speed and maneuverability for stability and a maximum weapons load, and therefore they can operate only in an environment where full control of the airspace is retained.

A number of light utility aircraft and trainers, fitted out with armament and wing hardpoints to accept ordnance, have also recently been adapted for the COIN role, and have performed successfully. They include the Cessna T-41 Mescalero, the Beechcraft T-34 Mentor, the North American T-6 Texan, the Cessna O-2A, the Piper PA-28 Cherokee, the North American Rockwell T-28 Trojan, the Fairchild AC-119, and the Rockwell International T-2E Buckeye. These aircraft have been purchased in quantity by a large number of countries.

The major influence on the design of our combat aircraft continues, of course, to emanate from our planning for the variety of tactical needs foreseen in any kind of confrontation with the Soviet sphere, notably the contingency of a NATO war with Soviet and Warsaw Pact forces in Europe. The Soviet superiority in tank strength, with 26,250 tanks currently deployed in 38 fully-mobilized Soviet and Warsaw Pact armoured divisions and 54 mechanized divisions in Eastern Europe, confronting 11,310 main battle tanks in NATO and French forces, has led to our increased production and deployment of TOW and other manportable anti-tank systems, as well as to various strategies for defense in depth. It has also led to the development of the Fairchild A-10 Close Air Support Aircraft, three wings of which, comprising 216 aircraft, are now scheduled for deployment at Sembach and Ramstein Air Bases in West Germany, and probably at Brentwaters in the United Kingdom.

Heavily armoured to protect it from Soviet 23mm antiaircraft cannon, the A-10 has been designed to approach targets at very low altitudes in order to avoid Soviet radar and antiaircraft missile defenses. It will soon be fitted with Pave Penny laser target designators, and it can carry up to 16,000 lbs of a variety of ordnance, including Mk 82 and Mk 84 laser-guided and electro-optically guided bombs, Rockeye cluster munitions, and as many as nine AGM-65A Maverick electro-optically guided air-to-surface missiles. An infrared imaging version of the Maverick has also become available for the A-10, as pilots who have tested it believe that infrared homing is far superior to electro-optical guidance in the hazy atmospheric conditions prevalent in Europe. The infrared Maverick has been designated AGM-65D.

The A-10's most formidable weapon, however, is its General Electric GAU-8 30mm cannon which, at variable rates of from 2,100 to 4,200 rounds per minute, spews rounds of a special projectile whose density has been increased by use of a depleted uranium core. This sustains the velocity of the projectile, and its force of impact is such as to penetrate the heaviest armour plate that now exists and even most armoured turret castings. It is expensive, however, at $11.00 per round. The Air Force, which hopes eventually to reduce the cost per round to about $3.50, has meanwhile ordered 20 million rounds of 30mm armour-piercing incendiary ammunition for the GAU-8 system. Of the A-10 aircraft itself, a total of 733 is planned.

Close air support of ground forces is only one of the major roles of tactical air. Another is the maintenance of air superiority over an enemy's air forces. This requires aircraft capable of great speed and maneuverability, and for this role we have designed the Grumman F-14 Tomcat and the McDonnell Douglas F-15 Eagle, both of which exceed speeds of Mach 2 and have more sophisticated weapons systems and electronics than their Soviet counterparts.

There is currently some concern over the latest Soviet fighter interceptor, the MIG-25, which NATO has codenamed Foxbat. Even though this aircraft was designed in the

1960s, and employs electronic systems so simple (though perfectly reliable) as to utilize vacuum tubes, its fighter version can reach speeds close to Mach 2.8, which is rather faster than our F-14 and F-15 aircraft. Foxbat-B, the reconnaissance version of the MIG-25, is reliably reported to have exceeded speeds of Mach 3, and flies today with impunity over areas of Europe and the Middle East. During the 1973 Middle Eastern war Israeli F-4 Phantom aircraft encountered some of the Foxbat-B models, and were never able to close any distance between them.

As we have seen, the F-14 and F-15 are expensive aircraft to acquire, and are only slowly coming into inventory. The Navy plans procurement of 390 F-14 aircraft through 1981. To date 270 have been delivered. The Air Force plans procurement of 729 F-15 aircraft, of which less than 150 have been delivered thus far. 24 of the aircraft form the 29th Tactical Fighter Squadron at Nellis Air Force Base. Another 72 form the First Tactical Fighter Wing at Langley Air Force Base, from which 21 of the aircraft have so far been transferred to the 36th Tactical Fighter Wing at Bitburg Air Base, West Germany.

Because of their cost and their slow entry into service, these twin-engined fighter interceptors will have to be supplemented by less costly and more easily accumulated types of aircraft, like the single-engined General Dynamics F-16, and possibly the McDonnell Douglas F-18 and A-18 Hornet and the Northrop F-18L Cobra. The 1978 Unit Procurement Cost of the F-16 is $12.322 million, as compared with the 1978 Unit Procurement Cost of the F-15 Eagle, $17.367 million. Aircraft like the F-16 will be counted on to make up a force of adequate size, augmenting and balancing available air superiority forces by performing both ground support and air interception missions—but only over areas of the battlefield that remain under allied command and control.

A third major mission for tactical air is interdiction, the deep penetration of hostile airspace to attack supply lines and installations based at the enemy's rear. Range and reasonable speed are required for this, and while no new aircraft have been designed for

such missions some existing types, including the General Dynamics F-111, with a combat radius of over 1,500 miles, the Grumman A-6 Intruder, whose operational radius with maximum payload exceeds 900 miles, and the venerable McDonnell Douglas F-4 Phantom, with an operational ground attack radius of over 1,000 miles, can perform this role adequately.

The design of aircraft to meet these varying missions is not an easy matter. It is complicated by the fact that Soviet air defenses and air forces are rapidly improving in quality and increasing in quantity. Our response to this, with fewer aircraft on hand, has been a tendency to mix forces, in the belief that it is most efficient and economical to design only a portion of our aircraft for specific missions, while requiring that a large number of other types be capable of performing more than one mission—so that they may be used as changing tactical situations demand.

Our Navy, in fact, has been criticized for keeping in service too great a variety of aircraft, most of which are highly specialized, and has been asked to review its needs and try to acquire aircraft used by other services or to combine its tactical missions among fewer aircraft types.

There are dangers in this policy. It creates a tendency to ask a given weapon system to do too much. Designers and manufacturers are encouraged to respond by trying to satisfy conflicting requirements. Commonality of equipment is sensible only so long as it meets a commonality of requirements. Naval aircraft, for example, must be designed to meet the additional needs for compact storage and operation from aircraft carriers. Compensations in design to meet these needs always run the risk of increasing an aircraft's weight, and sometimes also its cost, while reducing its speed, range and maneuverability. It could be folly to ask the same design to meet the needs of other services at the same time.

The ambition to maximize the efficiency of carrier-based aircraft operations, the anticipation of preemptive enemy air strikes against airfield runways to obstruct their use, and the growing need to operate counterinsurgency aircraft in the most primitive conditions without conventional landing strips, have all led to increased interest in STOL (Short Take Off and Landing) and V/STOL (Vertical or Short Take Off and Landing) aircraft, the latter type able to operate from a space no larger than the aircraft itself occupies. Our Air Force and Navy both have STOL and V/STOL development programs under way, although Defense Secretary Harold Brown recently ordered a $666 million cutback in one of these programs, a $1.45 billion joint Navy and Marine Corps development program for a new generation of V/STOL aircraft.

In the meanwhile the Marine Corps operates the Hawker-Siddeley Harrier V/STOL fighter-bomber, 102 of which it procured in 1971, together with 8 TA-8A V/STOL trainer aircraft, and it plans further procurement of 350 McDonnell Douglas AV-8B Harriers, an improved version of the British aircraft with increased range and load capacity. The AV-8A has experienced a number of difficulties, most of them in low-level flight training, that have resulted in 26 crashes to date with the loss of 10 pilots and 24 aircraft. However, the AV-8B has shown remarkable maneuverability, through skillful use in forward flight of its vectored thrust turbofan engine. Upward or downward vertical thrusts of the engine, designed to enable the aircraft to take off and land vertically, can also be applied while it is in forward motion. The resulting movement, known as vectoring in forward flight (VIFF), causes the aircraft literally to jump rather than slide into new flight paths, which can prevent sophisticated homing missiles and their guidance radars from locking onto them as targets. In combat simulations using VIFF techniques, the AV-8B outfought the Navy's F-14A in six out of sixteen encounters, fought it to a draw in another seven, and lost only three. V/STOL aircraft, despite the Navy's present setback in further development, appear to have an important role in the future.

This is the current production model of a jet attack aircraft derived from the T-37 jet trainer, and used in counterinsurgency (COIN) missions for the destruction of ground targets. With a crew of two seated in tandem, dual controls and full blind-flying instrumentation, the Dragonfly first flew in 1963 and went into service with the United States Air Force in 1967. It was heavily used in the COIN role in support of ground operations in Vietnam. In 1968 over 100 Vietnamese pilots were trained to fly the A-37 at England Air Force Base, Louisiana.

The Dragonfly's two powerful turbojet engines give it exceptional lift and impressive STOL (Short Take Off and Landing) capabilities. It can carry two thirds of its own weight in bombs and air munitions externally mounted, take off in as little as 1,800 feet and, with normal loads, land in the same amount of space. It can also fly as slowly as 95 mph without stalling. Such relatively moderate speed enables its crew more easily to locate and keep visual track of targets on the ground, and makes the aircraft an unusually stable weapons platform with a high margin of accuracy for strafing and bombing missions.

The Dragonfly's fixed armament, a GAU-2B/A six-barreled 7.62mm Minigun, is installed in the forward fuselage with a drum magazine of 1,500 rounds of standard NATO ammunition on a linkless feed system, and achieves variable rates of fire of either 3,000 or 6,000 rounds per minute.

In April of 1968, during riverine warfare operations in the Mekong Delta, Vietnam, one of the A-37A Dragonfly aircraft attached to the 604th Special Operations Squadron at Bien Hoa Air Base attacked as a target of opportunity the rural hamlets of Loc Trang I,

Loc Trang II and Loc Trang III in an area designated a free-fire zone because of its presumed use as a refuge for Viet Cong. The Dragonfly was carrying six M47A2 white phosphorous bombs, six CBU-24B cluster canisters and two SUU-11A gun pods, each pod weighing 323 lbs and mounting a 7.62mm Minigun identical to the aircraft's fixed armament. In a single sortie the Dragonfly was able to level to the ground all but three or four of the approximately 100 huts and other small buildings that comprised the Loc Trang group.

In its first pass, approaching the nearest village in line, the aircraft opened fire with a simultaneous two-second burst from all three Miniguns. The shattering and splintering effect of these 600 rounds on the buildings in line of fire made the village look to the pilot like "hay going through a threshing machine."

As the aircraft passed over the village it dropped two cluster canisters, each weighing 718 lbs and containing 600 bomblets. Released by compressed air in a closely-spaced pattern approximately two hundred yards across by fifty yards long, and almost perfectly bracketing the length and breadth of

## CESSNA A-37B DRAGONFLY

the village, the bomblets burst at a variety of heights or on impact with the ground. Each bomblet weighed one lb, and as it burst it released, with the equivalent explosive force of a hand grenade, 250 steel shards at high velocity. This meant that within the area 1,200 bomblets released a total of 300,000 steel shards, densely meshing in all directions at hundreds of feet per second, cracking stone, deeply pitting wood, and shattering into fragments any less sturdy or less pliable materials, all in a matter of ten seconds. To the aircrew above, it looked like "hundreds of sparklers going off."

People were seen running from the next two villages as the Dragonfly approached, but the pilot believed that the first village had been taken fully by surprise. The subsequent villages were struck in the same manner, and on their second pass the crew dropped their phosphorous bombs. As each bomb hit, the ground structures at the explosion's epicenter collapsed in a cloud of brilliant white smoke, and long trails of phosphorous shot out of the cloud and arched for hundreds of feet in the air. Wherever they landed, and all along the length of their trails, the particles of phosphorous stuck to buildings, trees, vegetation and anything else with which they came into contact, immediately setting it afire. When the aircraft turned for base, the entire area was in flames. The attack had taken about three minutes.

A total of 329 Dragonfly aircraft are operational today with the United States Air Force. Our most recent purchase of 89 A-37B Dragonfly aircraft in 1975, well after USAF operations ceased in Vietnam, indicates our continued planning for COIN contingencies elsewhere in the world.

**Maximum Weight:** 14,000 lbs

**Maximum Speed:** 507 mph

**Power Plant:** 2 x General Electric J85-GE-17A turbojet engines

**Operational Range:** 460 miles

**Armament:** 1 x GAU-2B/A 7.62mm Minigun

**Ordance Capacity:** 5,680 lbs on eight external hardpoints

**Compatible Stores:** SUU-20 bomb/rocket pod, SUU-11A gun pod, LAU-3A/32A/59A rocket pod, Mk 81, Mk 82 or M-117 bomb, BLU-1C/B or BLU-32B fire bomb, CBU-12A/14A/22A/24B/25A dispenser and bombs, CBU-19A cluster canister and SUU-25A flare launcher.

USAF
14823

**Produced to date:** 878 A-37A and A-37B

**Manufacturer:** Cessna Aircraft Company. Their first jet aircraft. In production.

**Exported under FMS:** 54 (82 more on order)

**Exported under MAP:** 301 (1 more on order)

**In US Service:** 329, of a total of 487 procured by USAF. Includes 40 A-37B in 2 Air National Guard squadrons and 51 in 4 Air Force Reserve squadrons.

**In Service Abroad:** Cambodia (24), Chile (34), Ecuador (12), Guatemala (8), Honduras (4), Iran (12), Peru (36), Thailand (16), Uruguay (8), and Vietnam (194, about 30 of which have been lost in combat).

**Price:** $534,000 (1975 Unit Procurement Cost to U.S. government for 89 aircraft).

**Recent Transfers:** 34 to Chile at unit cost of $323,500 in 1974, shortly after fall of Allende regime. Chile's order later increased to 52 aircraft. 24 to Peru at unit cost of $750,000, including armament, spares and pilot training, in 1974. 12 to Iran at unit cost of $2.5 million, including armament, spares, training, and contribution to R&D, in 1974. 1974 unit procurement cost to USAF was approximately $400,000. 12 to Ecuador at unit cost of $600,000@ in 1975. 12 planned for Ethiopia were not delivered.

# CESSNA T-37C JET TRAINER

To the thousands of pilots who were trained in it, this aircraft was affectionately known as the "Tweety Bird," owing to the characteristic high-pitched whistle of its engines. The progenitor of the A-37 Dragonfly, it first flew in 1954. With provision for armament and wingtip fuel tanks, the T-37C Tweety Bird has become an effective and popular COIN aircraft in more than a dozen countries. It is used by our Air Force for basic jet training before graduation to the Northrop T-38 Talon and other aircraft, and it is also used by the Luftwaffe for its flight training programs at Sheppard Air Force Base, Texas (where pilots from other countries are also trained).

**Maximum Weight:** 7,500 lbs

**Maximum Speed:** 402 mph

**Operational Range:** 850 miles

**Ordnance Capacity:** 2 x 250 lb bomb, or 4 x AIM-9 Sidewinder AAM

**Produced to date:** 1,272, including 444 T-37A, 552-T-37B and 273 T-37C

**Manufacturer:** Cessna Aircraft Company. In production.

**Exported under FMS:** 222 (7 more on order)

**Exported under MAP:** 217 (7 more on order)

**In US Service:** 885 T-37A and T-37B (of a total of 957 procured by USAF)

**T-37B/C in Service Abroad:** Brazil (65), Chile (32), Colombia (10), Greece (24), Jordan (12), Cambodia (9), Peru (32), Pakistan (63), Portugal (30), South Korea (25), Thailand (16), Turkey (50), Vietnam (24), West Germany (43 of 47 procured), and Burma.

**Cessna T-37C with Sidewinder missiles**

## CONVAIR F-102A DELTA DAGGER

The first Delta-winged aircraft designed in the United States, this supersonic single-seat fighter interceptor entered service in 1956, equipping 25 squadrons of the Air Defense Command. As McDonnell F-101B and Convair F-106 aircraft replaced it, the F-102A took up a decade of service with our Air Force in Europe and the Pacific. Now largely withdrawn from service, the F-102A is becoming available in quantity for transfer to foreign countries. 200 are being retained and converted for use in this country as target drones, simulating Soviet fighter aircraft.

**Maximum weight:** 32,000 lbs

**Maximum speed:** Mach 1.25 (825 mph)

**Operational Range:** 1,100 miles

**Armament:** 3 x AIM 4-A/E Falcon AAMs and 3 x AIM-4C/F Falcon AAMs or 2 x AIM-26A/B Super Falcon AAMs (AIM-26A has a nuclear warhead) or, in early versions, 24 x 2.75 inch unguided aerial rockets.

**Produced:** 875 F-102A and 111 TF-102A two-seat trainer aircraft

**Manufacturer:** Convair. Production completed.

**Exported under MAP:** 73

**In US Service:** 38 F-102A in 2 Air National Guard squadrons

**In service Abroad:** Greece (20), and Turkey (40)

## CONVAIR F-106 DELTA DART

Developed as an improvement upon the F-102A, the F-106 Delta Dart has a similar range but much greater speed. Production of the aircraft was completed in 1960, but a number have been retrofitted with the M61A1 Vulcan 20mm cannon, and still serve today with our Aerospace Defense Command and Air National Guard. They are soon to be replaced in these units by McDonnell Douglas F-4 and other aircraft, and consequently the F-106 will also become available for sale or grant aid overseas.

**Maximum weight:** 35,000 lbs

**Maximum speed:** Mach 2.3 (1,525 mph)

**Operational Range:** 1,150 miles

**Armament:** 1 x M61A1 Vulcan 20mm cannon, 4 x AIM-4F/G Super Falcon AAMs in weapons bay, 1 x AIR-2A Genie or AIR-2B Super Genie AAM externally mounted.

**Produced:** 274 F-106 and 63 F-106B two-seat trainers.

**Manufacturer:** Convair. Production completed.

**In US Service:** 230 F-106, 140 in 6 Aerospace Defense Command squadrons and 90 in 6 Air National Guard squadrons

## DOUGLAS A-1 SKYRAIDER

This is perhaps the most sophisticated and versatile single piston-engined aircraft ever built. Its range and load capacity are greater than those of many aircraft developed after it first entered service in 1946. It has been flown with a load of underwing stores surpassing its own empty weight. These capabilities have extended the Skyraider's life through the jet age, and it remains today one of the most effective COIN aircraft available.

The Skyraider equipped United States Navy aircraft carriers and provided close air support to the Marine Corps well into the 1960s. It served in the Korean War, and was used with effect throughout the war in Vietnam—where the USAF two-seat version, the A-1E, became known as the "Spad." Several squadrons of A-1E aircraft were flown in Vietnam by the First Air Commando Wing of our Tactical Air Command. In ground support operations, a flight of four of these aircraft could deliver the destructive force equivalent to a broadside salvo of six-inch guns from a naval cruiser.

Electronic counter measures versions of the Skyraider, the EA-1E and EA-1F, were also developed, along with a low altitude single-seat model, the A-1H. About 150 A-1H and

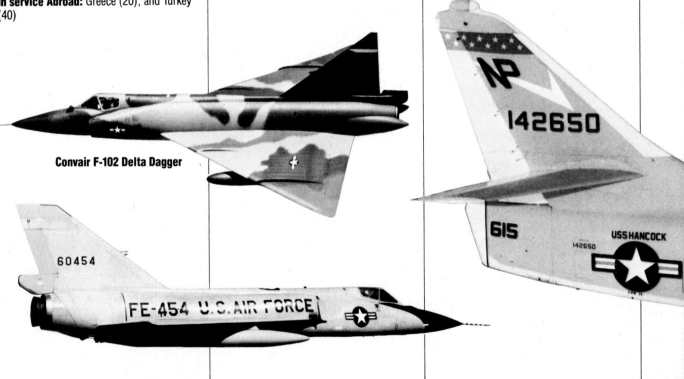

**Convair F-102 Delta Dagger**

**Convair F-106 Delta Dart**

A-1G aircraft were supplied to South Vietnam, and became the country's principal operational aircraft. Vietnamese Air Vice Marshal Nguyen Cao Ky's infamous Coup Squadron, painted black with tigerskin markings and based at Tan Son Nhut airfield, was comprised of A-1H Skyraiders.

Numbers of A-1D aircraft were flown by the French Air Force in Algeria, Madagascar and Somaliland, and some of these aircraft were transferred to Cambodia after the Algerian war. Britain's Royal Navy has also used a version of the EA-1D, then designated AD-4U, to perform airborne early warning missions.

**Maximum Weight:** 25,000 lbs

**Maximum Speed:** 318 mph

**Operational Range:** 3,000 miles

**Armament:** 4 x 20mm cannon wing-mounted

**Ordnance Capacity:** 8,000 lbs, on fifteen underwing pylons

**Produced:** 3,180, including all variants

**Manufacturer:** Douglas Aircraft Company. Production completed in 1957.

**Exported under MAP:** 331

**In US Service:** 1,455, for USAF AND USN, including 670 A-1E and EA-1E, 713 A-1H and 72 A-1J

**In Service Abroad:** France (88), Cambodia (14), Vietnam (100), United Kingdom (51), Chad, Central African Republic.

# DOUGLAS A-3 SKYWARRIOR

When it first entered service in 1956, the Skywarrior was the largest as well as the first fully jet-powered aircraft to operate from a carrier deck. The A-3B version served as the Navy's front-line nuclear strike aircraft, equipping six squadrons. A reconnaissance version, the RA-3B, was produced with twelve cameras in the weapons bay, and a further variant, the EA-3B, was one of the first to be fitted with side-looking airborne radar (SLAR). Many of the A-3s have been transferred to training squadrons, but further conversions of the A-3B are still deployed by the Navy, including the KA-3B flight refuelling tanker and the EKA-3B tanker countermeasures strike (TACOS) aircraft, which accompanies strike formations on long-range missions, performing the dual functions of providing them with fuel and with radar jamming and other electronic defense suppression as they near the target area. These will gradually be replaced as greater numbers of the lighter and more advanced Grumman KA-6 Intruder and EA-6 Prowler aircraft become available.

**Maximum Weight:** 73,000 lbs

**Maximum Speed:** 610 mph

**Operational Range:** 2,900 miles

**Armament:** 2 x 20mm cannon in radar-controlled tail mounting (A-3B only)

**Produced:** 285, including all variants. 50 A-3A, of which 5 converted to EA-3A, 168 A-3B, with conversions to KA-3B and EKA-3B, 24 EA-3B, 31 RA-3B, and 12 TA-3B training aircraft.

**Manufacturer:** Douglas Aircraft Corporation. Production complete.

**In US Service:** United States Navy only.

Douglas A-1J Skyraider

Douglas EKA-3B Skywarrior

# FAIRCHILD REPUBLIC A-10A CLOSE AIR SUPPORT AIRCRAFT

The result of a major development program to meet what the Air Force regards as one of our most urgent tactical requirements for the 1980s, this single-seat attack aircraft, powered by twin turbofan engines, is the first Air Force system ever designed specifically to provide close air support of ground forces, most especially against the masses of Warsaw Pact heavy armour anticipated in the event of a European land war.

Production of the first 54 A-10 aircraft was approved in July of 1954, and the procurement of 22 additional A-10s was authorized in 1975. The first production A-10 was delivered in February of 1976 to the 355th Tactical Fighter Training Wing at Davis-Monthan Air Force Base in Arizona, and by July of 1977 the 354th Tactical Fighter Wing at Myrtle Beach Air Force Base, South Carolina, was fully operational with 72 A-10 aircraft. Additional A-10s are now being delivered to air bases in West Germany. Procurement was funded for another 100 of the aircraft in 1977, and funds have been approved for a further 96 in 1978. The Air Force plans to purchase a total of 733.

The design of the A-10 has attempted to optimize STOL performance, ensuring a high degree of maneuverability and the flexibility to operate from forward air strips, while at the same time seeking a heavy load capacity and the endurance to remain over the battle area for extended periods of time. As may be seen from the specifications that follow,

these objectives have been largely achieved, though at the sacrifice of optimum airspeed. While 95 percent of its airframe is constructed of aluminum, weight was added to the A-10 in order to protect it against the Soviet 23mm cannon and other low altitude air defense systems it is expected to encounter. The pilot's cockpit area, the flight control system and the engines have been encased in titanium armourplate.

To provide it with resistance against more sophisticated air defense systems the A-10 will be fitted with electronic counter measures equipment that includes the Westinghouse ALQ-119 jamming system and the Sanders Associates ALQ-132 infrared jammer.

All A-10s are also being fitted with the Pave Penny laser target identification system, a detachable pod weighing 32 lbs produced by Martin Marietta. It can automatically detect a target illuminated by a laser on the ground or in another aircraft, lock onto that target, and give its precise range and bearing in the pilot's head-up display, so that he can read this information while he locates the target visually.

Tests with the seven-barreled GAU-8 30mm high-velocity Gatling gun, mounted in the A-10's nose, have been impressive. Its

special ammunition, plastic-banded to reduce barrel wear, aluminum-cased to reduce its weight, and utilizing a depleted uranium core to increase its density on impact, has been able to destroy most armoured targets, including heavy Soviet tanks, with bursts of one or two seconds in the first strafing pass. The cannon fires at selectable rates of 2,100 or 4,200 rounds per minute.

Nevertheless, the A-10 has had its problems. The first A-10 crash occurred on June 3, 1977, at the Paris Air Show, when it struck the ground while completing a loop. The pilot, Howard Nelson, director of Fairchild flight operations, was killed. The second A-10 crash occurred the following week, while the aircraft was making a low-level pass over the gunnery range at Myrtle Beach Air Force Base. Again the pilot died. These events confirmed the opinion of several pilots who had flown the aircraft that its sluggish response to controls could be dangerous in certain tactical situations requiring low-level flight—the very situations in which it was expected to perform its primary mission.

One former Army officer has called the A-10 "nothing better than a Stuka" (the World War II German JU-87 dive bomber, known for its poor maneuverability).

During early stages of production in September of 1975, metal fatigue was found in the A-10 fuselage frame. It turned out that stress loads had not been correctly estimated in the design. Further stress surveys were made. Ordinarily, a change in the original forging is required to correct a structural weakness due to errors in design. However, in his Report to Congress for Fiscal Year 1977 the Secretary of Defense noted that engineers were able to retrofit new parts for the weak section of the fuselage and simultaneously redesign those parts for future production, without making any changes in the original forging design. It is not clear how this was accomplished. The Secretary added, "It is believed that the remaining risk is sufficiently small to warrant proceeding into full production."

If any structural weakness now remains in the A-10's fuselage, it still could not account for the aircraft's sluggish response to pilot handling. That is probably due to its unusual distribution of weight, with its two large turbofan engines—each weighing 1,427 lbs dry—located well aft of the wings, and to its unsatisfactory ratio of weight to lift power. But urgent maneuvers to compensate for poor lift place a maximum strain on the airframe, and it is at such moments of stress that a structural weakness could prove fatal. Whether this is the reason for the crashes is not known.

No A-10 aircraft have been sold abroad to date, though we are actively seeking sales. In addition to the NATO countries Israel, Korea and Thailand are thought to be likely customers. The Air Force is presently quoting a price of $6 million per aircraft for a minimum sale of 42 aircraft. This represents a $4 million purchase price together with a $2 million recoupment in research and development costs.

**Maximum Weight:** 47,400 lbs

**Maximum Speed:** 449 mph

**Power Plant:** 2 General Electric TF34-GE-100 high bypass ratio turbofans

**Operational Range:** 288 miles (combat radius)

**Time Over Target:** 1.8 hours

**Key Electronics:** ALR-46 Baseline Radar Warning, ALQ-119 Baseline Jamming, ALQ-132 Infrared CM, Pave Penny Laser Designator

**Armament:** 1 x GAU-8 30mm cannon with 1,350 rounds

**Ordnance Capacity:** 16,000 lbs on eleven external hardpoints

**Compatible Stores:** Mk 82 GP/LDGP/LG (laser-guided) bomb, Mk 84 GP/LDGP/LG/EO (electro-optically guided) bomb, M-117 demolition bomb, BLU-1 or BLU-27/8 Incendiary bomb, SUU-25/42 flare launcher, Rockeye II cluster munition, CBU-24/42/49/60 dispenser, SUU-23 gun pod

**Stores Combinations:** 24 x 500 lb bomb, 16 x 750 lb bomb, 4 x 2,000 lb bomb, 9 x AGM-65A Maverick ASM and 2 x AIM-9E/J Sidewinder AAM

**Produced to date:** 90 of 733 planned for USAF

**Manufacturer:** Fairchild Industries. In production.

**In US Service:** United States Air Force only.

**In Service Abroad:** No sales to date, but future sales expected.

**Price:** $5.679 million (1978 Unit Procurement Cost to U.S. government for 96 aircraft. Original request had been for 144 aircraft, on which scale the unit cost would have dropped to $5.520 million. 1977 unit cost for 100 aircraft was $5.579 million). $6.000 million (Price quoted for FMS sales in 1978, on a minimum purchase of 42 aircraft).

This is one of the aircraft that were heavily used in the bombing of North Vietnam. Originally designed as a high-speed, long-range strategic strike fighter-bomber, it was fitted with an internal weapons bay to carry its nuclear bombs. Alternatively, however, it could carry up to 13,000 lbs of conventional bombs and other munitions on external pylons, and in the end it was used to deliver these types of ordnance while its two-seat version was modified to perform specialized defense suppression missions.

Prototypes of the F-105 first flew in 1955, and the aircraft became operational in 1958. In March of 1965 two squadrons of 50 Thunderchiefs joined in one of the opening raids of the air war over North Vietnam, and by June of 1966 two fully operational wings of F-105s, the 355th Tactical Fighter Wing (TFW) and the 388th TFW, comprising a total of 144 aircraft and based, respectively, at Takhli and Korat Royal Thai Air Force Bases in Thailand, were flying bombing sorties at a monthly average of over sixty hours per aircraft. The 355th TFW alone flew more than 101,000 sorties for more than 263,000 combat hours, delivering 202,586 tons of bombs and other ordnance on 12,675 targets.

The F-105 is equipped with the multi-barreled General Electric M-61 Vulcan 20mm cannon, which can fire its load of 1,029 rounds at the rate of 100 rounds per second. The aircraft's extensive electronic systems include expanded radar scopes and a toss bombing computer, retained to this day in most of the aircraft, for nuclear weapons delivery. Thirty of the F-105D models were also equipped with Thunderstick II, a navigation and weapons delivery system that automatically guides the aircraft to its target, selects angles of attack, times bomb releases and simultaneously maneuvers to avoid enemy fire. These aircraft literally fly themselves.

Due to its weight, which exceeds that of most World War II medium bombers, the Thunderchief has been nicknamed the "Thud" by those pilots who flew it. It has an extravagant take-off roll—using up more than 8,000 feet of runway in the warmest weather—and it does not turn quickly in the air. But for all of its size and complexity it was found to be one of the simplest and most reliable aircraft to fly. Its endurance in combat is legion. Severely battle-damaged F-105s have continued to fly for hours with all of their oil lines shot away. Pilots used to say its engine was so tough that you could put a rock in one end and get sand out the other.

When loaded down with bombs the Thunderchief lost a substantial amount of

airspeed, making it vulnerable to attack by other aircraft. Once freed of its ordnance, however, it could move at rates of 952 mph "on the deck" (the pilots's term for sea level) or as much as 1,485 mph (Mach 2.25) at 38,000 feet, faster than both the MIG-21 and the MIG-23. This meant that on the return leg of a bombing mission the F-105 turned hunter. During the air war in Vietnam Thunderchiefs brought down a total of 29 enemy MIG aircraft. However, over the months of the war the Thunderchief losses accumulated, due to SAM missiles and other ground fire, and to MIG attacks on their incoming bomb runs. After Operation Linebacker II brought the air war to a close in January of 1969, more than 400 F-105s—nearly half of the aircraft's total production run—had been destroyed.

The growing threat of radar-guided SAM missile sites in North Vietnam called for new tactics of defense suppression, an inevitable step in the development of electronic warfare which produced a significant variant of the F-105. The 143 two-seat versions of the aircraft, originally intended for use as trainers, were converted to F-105F defense suppression aircraft. They were loaded with a variety

# FAIRCHILD REPUBLIC F-105 THUNDERCHIEF

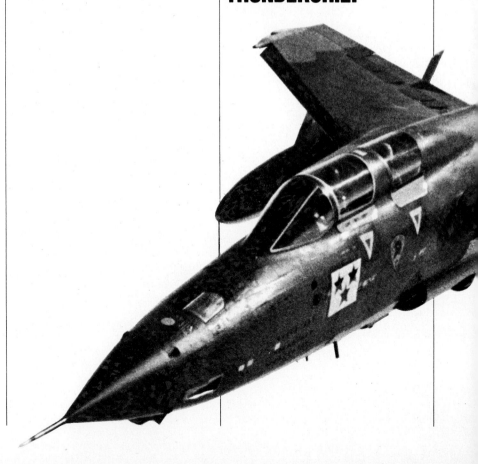

of radar detection and jamming equipment, and armed either with four AGM-45 Shrike or two AGM-78 Standard ARM anti-radiation missiles.

The electronics warfare officer, who sat behind the pilot of the F-105F, would search with his equipment for emissions from any of the Fansong radars that guided the SAM missile sites. When he found one he would give its position to the pilot, who would fire one of the aircraft's Shrike or other radar-homing missiles. The missile would ride in on the radar pulse and obliterate the radar installation at its source. Without its radar the SAM site could not track or lock onto a target. While missiles could still be fired blind, they posed only a minimal threat.

Fansong radar operators soon learned to turn on their radar for only the briefest moment to fix a target. If the F-105F could not detect the emission and fix the radar position during that moment, the site was safe. The F-105F pilots, in turn, would try deliberately to provoke radar operators into turning on their equipment, in order to expose their position, and this kind of tactic, similar to the behavior of weasels and other hunting animals, earned the F-105F the nickname of Wild Weasel.

Up to the end of the war in Vietnam two squadrons of these aircraft, the 17th Wild Weasel Squadron and the 561st Tactical Fighter Squadron, flew from Korat to provide defense suppression for fighters and bombers engaged in the raids. The 561st TFS flew more than 1,900 sorties. Along with some single-seat F-105Ds, 50 of the F-105Fs were converted to F-105G Wild Weasels with ECM (electronic counter measures) pods built into their fuselages.

Today two Wild Weasel squadrons, the 561st at George Air Force, California, and the 66th Fighter Weapons Squadron at Nellis Air Force Base, Nevada, remain operational with the Tactical Air Command. Both are equipped with the F-105G, and a few additional F-105Gs operate with the Pacific Air Forces. Of the approximately 350 surviving F-105s of other types, 120 F-105Ds are incorporated in five squadrons of the Air National Guard and 50 F-105Bs are assigned to three squadrons of the Air Force Reserve.

**Maximum Weight:** 54,000 lbs

**Maximum Speed:** 1,485 mph (Mach 2.25)

**Power Plant:** 1 x Pratt & Whitney J75-P-19W turbojet

**Operational Range:** 1,840 miles (combat radius of 920 miles)

**Armament:** 1 x GE M-61 Vulcan 20mm cannon, with 1,029 rds

**Ordnance Capacity:** 13,000 lbs on 17 external hardpoints.

**Stores Combinations:** 4 x AGM-12 Bullpup ASM, or 2 x AGM-12 Bullpup ASM and 2 x AIM-9H Infrared Sidewinder AAM, or 16 x 750 lb bomb, or 9 x 1,000 lb bomb, or 3 x 3,000 lb bomb (F-105B/D), 4 x AGM-45 Shrike ARM, or 2 x AGM-78 Standard ARM (F-105F/G)

**Produced to date:** 833 of all types, including 2 prototype YF-105A, 15 F-105B, 3 RF-105B reconnaissance aircraft, 610 F-105D (of which some modified to F-105G), and 143 F-105F (50 of which modified to F-105G).

**Manufacturer:** Fairchild Republic. No further production planned.

**In US Service:** 120 F-105D with Air National Guard, 50 F-105B with Air Force Reserve, approximately 70 F-105G with Tactical Air Command and Pacific Air Forces. Approximately 400 lost in Vietnam.

**In Service Abroad:** None at present.

**Price:** $2.287 million. (Unit Procurement Cost in 1964 for 130 aircraft)

# REPUBLIC F-84G THUNDERJET, F-84F THUNDER-STREAK, AND RF-84F THUNDERFLASH

A sturdy series of fighter-bombers which served in both our Tactical and Strategic Air Commands, the F-84 was provided in large numbers to fourteen foreign air forces under the Military Assistance Program during the middle and late 1950s. Through that period these aircraft formed the backbone of NATO air defense, and various models continue to operate today in at least four air forces overseas.

The first prototype F-84 flew in 1947, and by December of 1950 early production aircraft were flying combat missions with the 27th Fighter-Escort Wing in Korea. In all, six USAF wings were equipped with the F-84, which had an impressive external ordnance capacity, in view of its own light weight, of up to 4,000 lbs. During the Korean War F-84s flew 86,408 sorties and delivered 55,987 tons of ordnance.

The F-84G Thunderjet was the first operational fighter-bomber equipped for mid-air refueling, and also the first to carry the atomic bomb. With four external fuel tanks it had a combat radius of 1,000 miles, and its in-flight refueling capability gave it global range.

Unfortunately, the straight-winged Thunderjet lacked maneuverability, and 355 of the F-84G and earlier models were lost to enemy flak, and in some cases, to the more versatile MiG-15 in combat over Korea.

An improved swept-wing version, the F-84F Thunderstreak, had in the meanwhile been designed, substituting a more powerful Wright Sapphire J65 engine. It matched in maneuverability any other aircraft then flying, and it became operational in 1954. Like its predecessor, the F-84F mounted four M-3 .50 Cal machine guns in its nose and a further gun in each wing. It could carry 6,000 lbs of external ordnance, in twenty different combinations of stores. The F-84F became one of our front-line fighter-bombers, and over 1,300 were produced specifically for NATO countries.

By lengthening the nose of the F-84F, and by replacing the nose engine air intake with wing-root intakes, a reconnaissance version of the aircraft, the RF-84F Thunderflash, was produced. The space provided in the nose allowed the installation of a variety of cameras, radar and other electronic equipment. The four nose machine guns were kept, and the addition of underwing magnesium flare cartridges made the RF-84F the first reconnaissance aircraft capable of night photography.

The Belgian, Dutch, Italian and Iranian air forces retired their F-84s only a few years ago, replacing them for the most part with

**F-84F Thunderstreak**

**RF-84F Thunderflash**

F-104 and F-5 aircraft. Our Air National Guard and Air Force Reserve units have also retired their remaining F-84s, though a few are still used as target drones. As these aircraft are phased out by the more sophisticated air forces, it is likely that they will begin to appear as inexpensive replacements for older piston-engined aircraft still flown by the air forces of a number of less developed countries in Central and South America, Africa and Asia. This likelihood will not be diminished, as some contend, by a shortage of replacement parts, for there are now companies which specialize in manufacturing and providing parts for any aircraft in the world.

**Maximum Weight:** 26,000 lbs (F-84G); 28,000 lbs (F-84F)

**Maximum Speed:** 658 mph

**Operational Range:** 2,000 miles (with external tanks) (Combat Radius: 1,000 miles)

**Armament:** 6 x M-3 .50 Cal MG (F-84G and F-84F), 4 x M-3 .50 Cal MG (RF-84F).

**Ordnance Capacity:** 4,000 lbs (F-84G) 6,000 lbs (F-84F)

**Produced:** 7,919 of all variants, including 1,465 earlier models, 3,025 F-84G, 2,711 F-84F, and 718 RF-84F.

**Manufacturer:** Fairchild Republic. Production completed.

**Exported under FMS:** 19 RF-84F

**Exported under MAP:** 3,936, including 1,646 F-84G, 1,301 F-84F, and 449 RF-84F

**In US Service:** Few, as target drones. 355 lost in Korean combat.

**In Service Abroad:** Greece (54 F-84F), Portugal (80 F-84G), Turkey (75 F-84F) and 30 RF-84F), and Yugoslavia (60 F-84G)

**Formerly in Service:** Belgium, Denmark, France, Italy, Iran, Netherlands, Norway, Taiwan, Thailand, West Germany. (Of 450 F-84F, Germany transferred 65 to Greece and 153 to Turkey. Of 108 RF-84F, Germany transferred 22 to Greece, 36 to Turkey and 4 to Belgium).

**Price:** F-84G: $210,965 (Unit Procurement Cost in 1952 for 1,937 aircraft). F-84F: $396,352 (Unit Procurement Cost in 1953 for 1,039 aircraft). RF-84F: $546,112 (Unit Procurement Cost in 1954 for 589 aircraft).

F-84 Thunderjet

# FAIRCHILD AC-119G SHADOW AND AC-119K STINGER

Developed in 1967 to provide added firepower for ground defense suppression missions in Vietnam, this is an armed version of the famous C-119 Flying Boxcar. Conversions of 26 C-119F transport aircraft to AC-119G gunships were made by fitting each aircraft with four General Electric GAU-2B/A 7.62mm Miniguns to fire from its port side, and by adding night illumination systems, image intensifiers, flare launchers and an analog fire-control computer. Another 26 of the aircraft were coverted to AC-119Ks by adding two J85-GE-17 auxiliary jet engines in pods under the wings, and by increasing the armament to include two side-firing M61A1 Vulcan 20mm cannon. Further modifications to the AC-119K included the installation of side-looking airborne radar (SLAR) and forward-looking infra-red (FLIR) target acquisition systems, and the Westinghouse low-light-level television (LLLTV) target-viewing system. The addition of the SLAR, FLIR and LLLTV systems gave the AC-119K the ability by day or night to locate and destroy targets invisible to the naked eye with pinpoint accuracy.

In combat the pilot would bank the aircraft in a slow, wide arc, tilting it to the left to bring its firepower to bear on the target selected. The two M61A1 Vulcan cannon of the AC-119K fire at rates of 4,000 to 6,000 rpm, and its four GAU-2B/A Miniguns fire at rates of 3,000 or 6,000 rpm. This means that the aircraft can deliver as much as 600 rounds per second of assorted projectiles into an area as tightly confined as fifty square yards. Areas struck by this intensity of fire, no matter how thickly vegetated—or inhabited—before the attack, often give the appearance afterwards of cleared and freshly-plowed earth.

In view of their value for COIN operations in areas relatively free of air defense, these 52 aircraft remain operational with our Tactical Air Command.

A total of 476 C-119G, C-119J and C-119K transport aircraft have also been sold or transferred under MAP to Brazil, Belgium, Ethiopia, Jordan, India, Italy, Morocco, Taiwan and South Vietnam, and they remain operational in all but the first of those countries. While none were transferred with fixed armament or other modifications, it is likely that in their recipient countries a number of these slow-moving, stable aircraft have been fitted with other weapons for a similar ground defense suppression role. Two of Belgium's 30 C-119Gs have been transferred to Ethiopia which, with its eight C-119Ks supplied by the United States through MAP, now has ten of the aircraft type. Of her 48 C-119Gs and C-119Js, Italy has converted three to EC-119 electronic counter measures aircraft.

**Maximum Weight:** 80,400 lbs

**Maximum Speed:** 250 mph

**Operational Range:** 1,980 miles

**Key Electronics:** SLAR/FLIR/LLLTV (AC-119K only)

**Armament:** AC-119G: 4 x GAU-2B/A 7.62mm Minigun; AC-119K: 4 x GAU-2B/A 7.62mm Minigun and 2 x M61A1 20mm Vulcan cannon

**Produced to date:** 52 aircraft, including 26 AC-119G and 26 AC-119K

**Manufacturer:** Fairchild Republic. Available for production.

**In US Service:** 52 aircraft in USAF.

**In Service Abroad:** Vietnam (24 AC-119G).

**Price:** AC-119G: $1.316 million (1967 Unit Procurement Cost for 26 C-119F with conversion costs of $423 thousand per aircraft for electronics and $230 thousand per aircraft for armament). AC-119K: $2.218 million (1967 Unit Procurement Cost for 26 C-119F with conversion costs of $1.025 million per aircraft for electronics, $362 thousand per aircraft for armament and $168 thousand per aircraft for auxiliary jet engines).

# FAIRCHILD AU-23A PEACEMAKER

Produced in the United States under license from the Swiss firm of Pilatus Flugzeugwerke AG, this is a piston-engined aircraft which, due to its light weight and STOL performance, is ideally suited for COIN operations. Developed from the Pilatus Porter, a utility aircraft that can carry up to ten passengers, the AU-23A Peacemaker can carry eight fully-equipped troops. Alternatively, it can carry up to 2,000 lbs of cluster bombs, gun pods, flare dispensers, rocket launchers, napalm canisters or smoke grenades on external hardpoints, with either a manually-operated side-firing 20mm cannon or two 7.62mm Miniguns mounted in its cabin.

**Maximum Weight:** 6,100 lbs

**Maximum Speed:** 174 mph

**Operational Range:** 1,116 miles (combat radius of 558 miles)

**Armament:** 1 x XM-197 20mm cannon firing 700 rpm, or 2 x 7.62mm Minigun, firing 2,000 or 4,000 rpm

**Take-Off Run:** 510 ft

**Landing Run:** 295 ft

**Ordnance Capacity:** 2,000 lbs on five external hardpoints

**Produced to date:** 66, including 51 for export and 15 for USAF

**Exported under FMS:** 20 (5 more on order)

**Exported under MAP:** 13

**Manufacturer:** Fairchild Republic. In production.

**In US Service:** 1 AU-23A. 15 originally procured by USAF. 1 lost. 13 transferred under MAP to Thailand.

**In Service Abroad:** Thailand (33, with 5 on order). Israel, Colombia and Ecuador expected to purchase. Swiss Pilatus Porter operated in COIN role by Australia, Peru, Sierra Leone and Sudan.

**Price:** $600,000 (Unit Program Cost for 20 aircraft transferred under FMS to Thailand in 1974). Swiss Pilatus Porter currently priced at $170,000 @.

One of the prototypes in our Air Force's Lightweight Fighter program, originally designed not for production but only to test the feasibility of highly advanced aerodynamic technologies and new materials, the F-16 succeeded so well in combining speed and maneuverability with modest size and what appeared at the time to be low cost that, partly for this reason, it was selected in January of 1975 as our new Air Combat Fighter for the 1980s.

The weight of the F-16 was kept low by extensive use of graphite-epoxy materials on the tailplane surfaces and a fibreglass fin tip, and by choice of a single, powerful engine, the Pratt & Whitney F100-PW-100 twin-shaft afterburning turbofan, the same as that used in the F-15. The engine's 25,000 lbs of thrust applied to the aircraft's gross weight of only 22,800 lbs gives it, with normal loads, a thrust-to-weight ratio of nearly 1.5 to 1. This enhances its ability to maneuver and accelerate.

To provide maximum lift with minimum drag, the aircraft's wing area was reduced as much as possible, and compensated for by flaring its fuselage sides to prominent edges beginning just aft of its nose. These edges blend the body to the wings by sweeping outwards at the wing roots. There are no sharp angles. The consequent thickening of the wing roots also gives the aircraft a more rigid structure.

On the leading edges of its wings the F-16 incorporates maneuver flaps which, in order to obtain optimum lift coefficients at high angles of attack, are programmed automatically to adjust the wing camber—the angle of the wing's curve into the air—according to the aircraft's speed and angle of attack. This ensures higher lift, lower drag at any lift, and maximum directional stability.

The resulting high maneuverability of the F-16 would be to no avail if its pilot could not withstand the gravitational forces created by the rapid accelerations of speed and tight turns of which it is capable. Therefore, use has been made of what designers call fly-by-wire technology. All of the aircraft's control surfaces are moved by servo-mechanism actuated by electrical signals. These signals are transmitted by wire from rubber pedals for directional changes, and by hand pressure to a side-arm control stick for accelera-

# GENERAL DYNAMICS F-16 AIR COMBAT FIGHTER

tion, longitudinal pitch and latitudinal roll. The control stick sits in an arm rest. The pilot is set back at an angle of 30 degrees, rather than the normal 13 degrees, and he is set high in a polycarbonate bubble canopy that affords him visibility of 360 degrees. He doesn't have to move. He is consequently freed of the effort to work against gravitational pull during the aircraft's maneuvers, and he need not restrict the aircraft's movements in order to make his own movements possible. Almost anything the aircraft can do, he can do. A pilot in the cockpit of the F-16 can withstand gravitational forces up to 9 Gs.

The F-16 is equipped with the Westinghouse X-band multimode pulse-Doppler range and angle attack radar, with its planar array in the aircraft's nose. The radar has a lookdown range in ground clutter of from 17 to 23 miles, and a lookup range of from 23 to 29 miles. Also included as standard equipment in the USAF F-16 are the Itek AN/ALR-46 radar warning system with a Dalmo-Victor CM-442/ALR digital radar warning processor, a Singer-Kearfott inertial navigation system, Transco threat warning and beacon an-

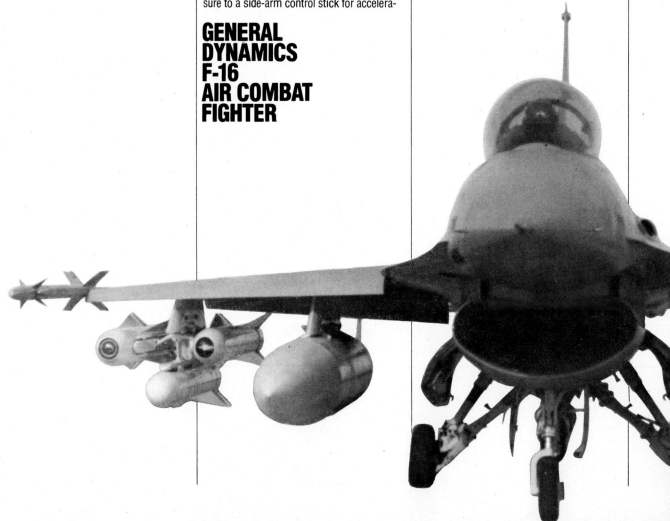

tennae, Lear Siegler stick force sensors, a Teledyne angle-of-attack transmitter, a Delco fire control computer, a Photo-Sonics gun camera, a Kaiser radar electro-optical display, the Rockwell/Collins AN/AR-118 TACAN system, a Sperry Flight Systems central air data computer, and a General Electric M61A1 Vulcan 20mm cannon with 500 rounds.

Perhaps the most remarkable piece of equipment aboard the F-16, however, is its HUDWAS (Head-Up Display with Automatic Simulation) unit, built by Marconi-Elliott Avionic Systems. It superimposes on the pilot's view of the target a continuous simulated tracerline display of the path his cannon projectiles will take if he fires the weapon, instantaneously adjusting that simulated path to show the precise effects of even the most sudden changes in the aircraft's speed, direction of flight, range from the target and angle of attack. It is presently the only air-to-air gunsight tracerline display in the world. The pilot need only make sure the end of the tracerline path touches the target, and he cannot miss with even the shortest burst of fire. This conserves ammunition, and increases combat efficiency.

As our new Air Combat Fighter, the F-16 will complement the more expensive and more sophisticated F-14 and F-15 aircraft in the air superiority role, but because of its smaller radius of action compared with those aircraft, it will be expected to engage enemy air forces for control of the airspace only over battlefield areas. At the same time, it will be expected to supplement the F-4, A-10 and other aircraft in the ground attack and close air support roles.

The Air Force had originally planned procurement of 650 aircraft, including 96 F-16B two-seat versions. Observations gained from the 1973 Middle Eastern war, however, suggested to tactical planners that the quantity of aircraft deployed in combat was as crucial to the maintenance of air superiority as the quality of their performance. As a result, USAF increased its F-16 procurement level to 1,388 aircraft, including another 73 F-16Bs. In October of 1977 the Defense Systems Acquisitions Review Council approved commencement of full production of the first 105 F-16s. Initial deliveries are expected early in 1979.

Aside from the F-16's high performance and promise of low cost, the other major factor in its selection by USAF was a growing need among several NATO countries for a new interceptor aircraft to replace those in current use. Six months following its selection by USAF, a major agreement was reached with a NATO consortium comprised of Belgium, Denmark, the Netherlands and Norway for coproduction of the F-16 and for the initial procurement of 348 aircraft to replace the aging F-104Gs in their own air force inventories.

The firms of Fairey and SABCA in Belgium and Fokker-VFW in the Netherlands will each assemble 174 of the F-16 aircraft, in cooperation with Denmark's Per Udsen, and the massive coproduction agreement will involve more than 56 subcontracting agreements, including a $32 million contract with Norway's Nera Bergen for production of the AN/ALR-46 radar warning system under license from Itek/ATI and Dalmo-Victor and, under license from Pratt & Whitney, contracts for $38 million with Denmark's Dansk Industri Syndikat, $142 million with N. V. Philips in the Netherlands, $163 million with Kongsberg Vapenfabrikk in Norway and $836

**General Dynamics F-16 Air Combat Fighter with two underwing fuel tanks, six AGM-65 Maverick air-to-ground missiles (including television-guided and scene magnification models) and an AIM-9L Sidewinder air-to-air missile mounted at either wingtip. (USAF)**

million with Belgium's Fabrique Nationale for components of 348 F100-PW-100 jet engines.

Under the terms of the agreement the European consortium will produce 10 percent of the components for USAF aircraft, 40 percent of the components for its own aircraft, and 15 percent of the components for aircraft sold to other countries.

Sales of the F-16 to several other countries are pending.

Turkey has requested 100 F-16s, with an option on the purchase of another 50 to 100. Israel would like to purchase 75 of the aircraft and coproduce 200 more, with options on a further 150 to 200. 90 F-16s have been proposed for sale to South Korea. Spain would like to purchase 72. Greece has unofficially requested price information on 150 to 200

F-16s. The European consortium itself may eventually purchase another 297. Australia has a requirement for 160 new aircraft, and Saudi Arabia for 150. Both are considering the F-16, though the Saudis have stated a preference for the F-15. Canada will soon select 100 to 125 of a new aircraft to replace its CF-101 Voodoos and CF-104Ds in the immediate future, with 200 more aircraft to be added in time. The F-16 is a leading contender. Taiwan, too, is a likely F-16 purchaser.

In all, Pentagon analysts estimate a total of $15 billion in F-16 sales over the next decade. The aircraft seems bound for widespread use in the remaining years of this century.

A good share of the earnings, this time, will go to the European coproducers. Belgian industry alone stands to gain more than $1 billion in earnings from existing contracts. Owing to higher European tooling and labor costs, components supplied from Europe may, according to the General Accounting Office, raise the cost of the first 650 USAF F-16s by as much as $241 million. Yet it seems unlikely that the European consortium would have agreed to take the F-16 in the first place without a coproduction agreement. The full costs of development and production would

then have been borne singly by the United States government, and this would have raised the unit cost of the aircraft even further. The incentive was therefore strong to accede to the European desire for coproduction, in order to obtain sufficient sales to reduce the unit costs more substantially than the European charges for components will raise them.

Nonetheless, costs for the F-16 have soared. Its Unit Flyaway Cost had originally been estimated at $4.6 million, but by 1975 it exceeded $6 million. Under the terms of the multinational agreement the Flyaway Cost was not to exceed a ceiling of $6.091 million in 1975 dollars, but that cost, too, has been exceeded by costs of duplicate tooling in Europe. The participating European governments have agreed to absorb these increased costs along with the cost of inflation. Even so, the Unit Procurement Costs are now estimated at $7.597 million for each of Norway's 72 aircraft, $8.152 million for each of

Denmark's 48 aircraft, $8.333 million for each of Belgium's 116 aircraft, and $9.245 million for each of 102 aircraft for the Netherlands.

As for the USAF F-16, which includes a variety of additional electronic systems, such as the National Security Agency's KIT-1A/TSEC cryptographic coding and decoding communications system, the unit cost based on full procurement of 1,388 aircraft now stands at $9.659 million in current dollars, and the 1978 Unit Procurement Cost of 105 aircraft is $12.322 million.

The General Accounting Office maintains that some of the cost increase has resulted from the European consortium's requirement for an aircraft capable of both air-to-air and ground attack missions, and the need for the F-16 to meet these dual criteria. However, these are the same criteria as those set by USAF for the Air Combat Fighter. Perhaps all that can be said is what the GAO report concluded: "It is not realistic to attempt to establish not-to-exceed prices at a point very early in any acquisition program." When dealing with our defense industry, that is certainly true.

**Maximum Weight:** 22,800 lbs gross, 33,000 lbs fully loaded.

**Maximum Speed:** 1,400 mph (Mach 2.12)

**Power Plant:** 1 x Pratt & Whitney F100-PW-100 turbofan, 25,000 lb thrust

**Operational Range:** 1,300 miles as interceptor, with ground attack radius of from 120 to 575 miles

**Ceiling:** 60,000 ft

**Key Electronics:** HUDWAS/AN/AR118 TACAN/AN/ALR-46 radar warning system/Westinghouse X-band multimode pulse-Doppler range and angle attack radar/NSA KIT-1A/TSEC crypto comm system/AN/ALQ-119 ECM jamming pod

**Armament:** 1 x M61A1 Vulcan 20mm cannon with 500 rounds

**Ordnance Capacity:** 2 x AIM-9J/L Sidewinder AAM on wingtips (500 lbs) with 10,200 lbs additional stores on five external hardpoints

**Manufacturer:** General Dynamics. In production.

**In US Service:** 1,388 planned, including total of 168 F-16B, with deliveries of first 105 scheduled for 1979.

**Soon to be in Service Abroad:** By 1979: Belgium (104 F-16A and 12 F-16B), Denmark (36 F-16A and 12 F-16B), Netherlands (80 F-16A and 22 F-16B) and Norway (60 F-16A and 12 F-16B), coproduced under license. By 1982: Egypt (50) and Israel (75).

**Probable Future Markets:** Australia (75), Belgium (additional 14 to 100), Greece (150 to 200), Israel (additional 55 to 200), Netherlands (additional 30 to 121), Norway (additional 72), People's Republic of China (200, proposed by Henry Kissinger), Saudi Arabia (150), South Korea (90), Spain (72), Turkey (100 to 250), Taiwan (50), and Venezuela (16 to 24).

**Price:** $12.322 million (1978 Unit Procurement Cost to USAF for 105 aircraft). $6.091 million (Unit Flyaway Cost for European consortium. For procurement costs see text).

The first aircraft designed in an attempt to meet joint Navy and Air Force requirements, the F-111, originally known as the TFX (Tactical Fighter, Experimental), was also the first aircraft produced in any quantity to employ variable-sweep wings. These have the advantage, when swept at their minimum angle of only 16 degrees, of providing the aircraft with its largest surface area, maximizing lift so that it can take off in no more than 3,100 feet and land in 3,000, and of substantially reducing that surface area when fully swept back at their maximum angle of 72.5 degrees, enabling the aircraft in flight to reach its highest speeds—which at altitudes of over 36,000 feet exceed Mach 2.5 (1,650 mph).

The mechanism controlling the sweep of the wings is no more complicated than an automobile jack. The wings pivot on steel bars set into a geared assembly at their roots. Large screws, hydraulically powered, extend to move the gears and push the wings back or to contract and pull them forward.

The development of the F-111, while originally intended to save more than $1 billion in estimated additional costs for separate Navy and Air Force fighter programs, was plagued by heavy cost overruns and serious defects in construction. This resulted in the loss of several early aircraft and most of their pilots, a full Senate investigation, charges of favoritism in the awarding of contracts, a failure to meet joint service requirements, the cancellation of contracts by the Navy and the United Kingdom, a reduction of orders to 582 aircraft—less than 25 percent of the number originally planned—and the expenditure for this smaller number of $3.5 billion more than had been anticipated for the procurement of all of the original 2,400.

In November of 1962, concluding a competition with Boeing aircraft, the firm of General Dynamics was awarded a production contract for the F-111, and 18 F-111A and 5 F-111B prototype aircraft were ordered for the Air Force and the Navy respectively. When Congress learned shortly thereafter that the consensus of Defense Department evaluation reports had been that selection of the Boeing design would have led to an aircraft less expensive than the F-111 and superior to it in performance, a Senate subcommittee opened an investigation into the award of the contract. The investigation would continue for the next nine years. Even though it was underway in 1963, work continued on the prototypes and the first of these, an F-111A, was delivered and flew in December of 1964.

By 1967 the subcommittee, chaired by Senator John McClellan, had discovered that program costs for the Navy's F-111B had doubled from $5.8 billion in 1962 to $11.6 billion, even though the number of aircraft the Navy sought had been reduced from 1,700 to 1,300.

It was then learned that the Department of Defense had hired the Performance Technology Corporation, an independent consulting firm, to examine the F-111 program and determine whether, due to inefficient manufacturing operations, costs were higher than they should be. Using this "should-cost" method of audit, the independent consultants found that the Pratt & Whitney TF30-P-12 engines for the F-111 were costing 50 percent more than they should. As a result, the Defense Department renegotiated the contract with Pratt & Whitney and reduced its value by more than $100 million.

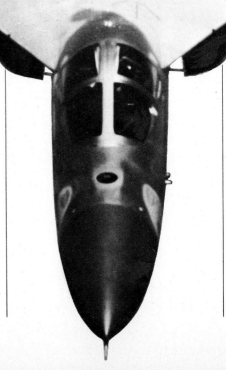

# GENERAL DYNAMICS F-111 AND FB-111A

This, of course, suggested the possibility of further reforms in defense contracting. Although the Proxmire Committee Report on the Economics of Military Procurement has strongly recommended that the General Accounting Office study how the "should-cost" method could be made standard procedure in all defense contract auditing, the Defense Department seems determined to avoid it. Only once since that time has the method been used, when in 1970 the Army authorized a "should-cost" audit of Raytheon's HAWK missile program and found it was running 30 percent above its possible cost.

Other components of the F-111 program, including the airframe built by General Dynamics and the aircraft's avionic systems, supplied by North American, were also suffering from cost overruns but were not subjected to "should-cost" audits.

Meanwhile Great Britain, in a series of arms trade agreements that may have led to the devaluation of the pound, contracted in 1967 to purchase 50 F-111 aircraft for $20 million each—but only on the understanding that the United States, within the next few years, would purchase $325 million in arms from Great Britain. In view of the spirit behind our Buy American Act, this indicated an unusual degree of cooperation on our part.

Unfortunately the understanding included our purchase of 16 minesweepers from the British at $5 million each. In September of 1967 Congressman John W. Byrnes of Wisconsin successfully introduced an amendment to a defense appropriations bill requiring that all United States naval vessels be built in American shipyards. That, along with further disclosures of defects in the F-111, caused Great Britain in January of 1968 to cancel her order for the aircraft.

In July of 1968 the Navy, after delivery of just seven prototype F-111Bs, cancelled its entire order for 1,300 of the aircraft, leaving only Air Force orders for slightly more than 500 F-111s. Among its other deficiencies the F-111B was more than eight tons overweight, a condition that wholly precluded its use in the carrier operations for which it had been intended.

The Navy's cancellation of its contract was what is termed a cancellation of convenience. Such cancellations technically occur only when the military service reverses its decision about the requirement for a weapon system. They allow for a reimbursement to the manufacturer of costs incurred in development together with a portion of the program's anticipated profits, and thus they protect the manufacturer from loss. If, however, the manufacturer fails to perform by the terms of contract, then the contract may be cancelled for default, and considerable losses may be

incurred. Even though the F-111B failed to meet the Navy's requirements due to defects in its construction, and even though the Navy still needed 1,300 aircraft, the option of cancellation for default was not taken.

Indeed, the Navy's final cancellation terms included payment to General Dynamics of $1 million for research and development on behalf of the Air Force version of the F-111. The negotiations for cancellation of the contract, completed in November of 1968, were handled between Paul Nitze, Deputy Secretary of Defense, who is today a member of the Committee on the Present Danger, and Roger Lewis, chairman of General Dynamics—and a former Assistant Secretary of the Air Force under Eisenhower.

The McClellan Permanent Investigating Subcommittee had meanwhile discovered other links between General Dynamics and the Department of Defense. It turned out that Roswell Gilpatrick, Undersecretary of the Air Force from 1951 to 1952 and Deputy Secretary of Defense from 1961 to 1964, had during the latter period played a leading role in the evaluation of the F-111 and had recommended that the contract be awarded to General Dynamics. This would have gone unnoticed save for the fact that before he re-joined the Defense Department Gilpatrick worked with the Wall Street law firm of Cravath, Swain and Moore—the firm which represented General Dynamics at the time.

Furthermore, one of that firm's partners, Moore, joined the board of directors of General Dynamics one month after the contract was awarded.

At about this time, early production F-111As were being delivered to the Air Force for evaluation in Vietnam. They first saw combat there in March of 1968. Within two weeks three of the first eight F-111As had crashed, due not to hostile action but to mechanical failures. Further crashes occurred and the aircraft were periodically grounded. By 1970 there had been a total of 15 F-111A crashes due to causes other than enemy fire, with seven pilot fatalities and a further six pilots missing.

Investigations finally led to a structural failure in the carry-through box which held the pivots in place for the aircraft's movable wings. While sound in design and reliable in subsequent aircraft like the F-14, this mechanical innovation had been poorly executed by the contractor. Under the emergency program IRAN (Inspect and Repair As Needed), a boron-epoxy doubler was applied to the wing pivots of all Tactical Air Command F-111s. This involved 223 aircraft already delivered by the time IRAN went into effect in 1970, together with 250 more under construction. The cost of these repairs was then estimated at $80 million.

By 1970 the unit cost of the F-111 itself, originally estimated at $4.5 million, had soared to $13.7 million. It would continue to rise, with inflation and with various improvements in engines and electronics added to subsequent models.

A total of 508 of the aircraft were produced for the Tactical Air Command, and two of these were converted to FB-111A fighter-bombers for evaluation by the Strategic Air Command (SAC), which had a requirement for 210 new bombers to replace its aging B-58A Hustlers and its early B-52C and B-52F Stratofortresses. But by 1971 the cost of an FB-111A, with its improved TF30-P-7 engines, its Mk IIB advanced electronics and its wingspan increased by seven feet, was $16 million. Funding cuts limited SAC procurement to 74 new aircraft. Including the two converted fighter aircraft, these 76 FB-111As were assigned to SAC's 340th Bomb Wing at Carswell Air Force Base, Texas, and are now with the 509th Bomb Wing at Pease AFB, New Hampshire and the 380th Bomb Wing at Plattsburgh AFB, New York. 72 of the aircraft are this year completing modifications with the AN/ALQ-137 automatic Self-Protection deceptive electronic counter measures (ECM) system.

Of Tactical Air Command aircraft, a total of 18 prototype F-111As and 141 production F-111As were built with Mk I electronics and TF30-P-12 engines. The eleventh production F-111A was converted to an RF-111A recon-naissance aircraft. The thirteenth was fitted with the M61A1 Vulcan 20mm cannon, as was every aircraft thereafter. Early production F-111As were assigned to the 347th Tactical Fighter Wing at Takhli Air Base, Thailand, moving to Korat Air Base when Takhli was closed in 1974. Today the remaining F-111As are assigned to the 474th Tactical Fighter Wing and the 422nd Fighter Weapons Squadron at Nellis AFB, Nevada.

In addition to the seven prototype F-111B aircraft for the Navy's cancelled program, two F-111K prototypes were produced for evaluation by Great Britain, and are now used by USAF as research and development aircraft under the new designation YF-111A. In addition, 24 F-111C aircraft were built with Mk I electronics and TF30-P-3 engines to replace the old Canberra bombers in the First and Sixth Squadrons of the Royal Australian Air Force. By the time they were delivered in 1976, after seven years in storage, the cost of each of these aircraft was $22.239 million.

There followed 96 F-111Ds with TF30-P-9 engines, assigned today to the 27th Tactical Fighter Wing at Cannon AFB, New Mexico, and 94 F-111Es with Mk II electronics, assigned to the 20th Tactical Fighter Wing at Upper Heyford, England and the 474th Tactical Fighter Wing at Nellis AFB, Nevada.

The final production aircraft were 126 F-111Fs, equipped with Mk IIB electronics, including the AN/ALQ-94 deceptive ECM system, and TF30-P-100 engines that provided 25 percent more thrust. With these last aircraft a reliable bomber had finally evolved from what continues to be viewed as a fighter design, even though it led to an aircraft more powerful and heavier than the four-engined bombers of World War II. The F-111Fs serve today with the 366th Tactical Fighter Wing at Mountain Home AFB, Idaho.

A total of 42 F-111As will be converted to EF-111A TJS (Tactical Jamming System) aircraft. To be organized in two squadrons, they are intended to accompany tactical bombers over hostile territory and protect them by locating enemy emitting radars and providing effective jamming. They will carry three tons of electronic counter measures equipment, including a pallet-mounted AN/ALQ-99A system. The same system that is installed on the Grumman EA-6B Prowler, this comprises an AN/ALQ-137 automatic Self-Protection de-

EF-111A

ceptive ECM system, an AN/ALR-62 Terminal Threat Warning System, and a fin tip pod that houses the ECM receiver system and antennae. The conversion work is being carried out by Grumman Aircraft, which completed the first two EF-111As in May of 1977 at a cost per aircraft of $41.922 million. When their conversion costs are added to their original procurement costs, these 42 aircraft will be among the most expensive in our arsenal. Unfortunately, according to one officer, "the Air Force needs more like a hundred."

Nor does the troubled history of the F-111 end there. As far back as 1964, General Dynamics had designed the FB-111G, an improvement on SAC's FB-111A fighter-bomber, and the F-111X-7, a stretched version of the FB-111A proposed as a substitute for the B-1 strategic penetrating bomber.

After the recent cancellation of the B-1 program, the old proposal for the F-111X-7 was resurfaced in an attempt by the Air Force to regain the option of a new penetrating bomber—even though that was precisely what the Carter administration had determined was not needed. The F-111X-7 proposal was now called the FB-111H, and the Air Force requirement was for 165 of these aircraft with an increased weapons load over that of the FB-111A, and with their potential range increased from 4,100 to 5,700 nautical miles. 65 FB-111As were to be converted at a cost of $34.876 million per aircraft, and 100 new FB-111H models were to be built at a cost per aircraft of $41.880 million.

What made the proposal attractive was that, at an average unit procurement cost of $39.121 million, and an average unit program cost, including research and development, of $42.424 million as compared with $101 million for each B-1, the FB-111H program would cost less than a third of the anticipated program cost of the B-1.

This development rekindled hopes for the B-1, as it may also have been intended to do. Some Congressmen reasoned that if the administration attempted to obtain funds for the FB-111H, then it must believe that a new penetrating strategic bomber was needed after all. If so, why not the best? Cost was no longer a consideration if the need was real. Either the administration meant what it said or it did not. After some equivocation from the White House and Department of Defense, Congress reassured itself that the administration really did not believe any kind of new penetrating bomber was needed, and so killed the FB-111H proposal in October of 1977.

**Maximum Weight:** 91,500 lbs. FB-111A: 119,000 lbs

**Maximum Speed:** 1,650 mph (Mach 2.5) 915 mph at sea level

**Power Plant:** 2 x Pratt & Whitney TF30-P-12 turbofan engines (A and B models), P-3 (C), P-9 (D and E models), P-100 (F) and P-7 (FB-111A)

**Operational Range:** 3,800 miles. FB-111A: 4,700 miles

**Ceiling:** Over 60,000 ft

**Key Electronics:** In Pods: AN/ALQ-87 ECM or AN/ALQ-131 Defensive Jamming ECM. Internally: AN/APS-107/109 Radar Warning, AN/ALQ-109 ECM, Pave Tack Laser Designator, AN/ALQ-94 ECM (F-111A/D/E/F only), AN/AVA-9 Integrated Display (D only), AN/ALR-62 Radar Warning and AN/ALQ-137 Deception ECM (EF-111A and FB-111A only), and AN/ALQ-99A (EF-111A only).

**Armament:** 1 x M61A1 Vulcan 20mm cannon on #13 and subsequent models (none on FB-111A)

**Ordnance Capacity:** 33,000 lbs on eight external hardpoints and in weapons bay. FB-111A: 37,500 lbs.

**Stores Combinations:** 42 x 750 lb bomb and 2 x 750 lb bomb in weapons bay (only 20 externally at full wing sweep). FB-111A: 48 x 750 lb bomb and 2 x 750 lb bomb in weapons bay, or 6 x B-61 nuclear gravity bomb or 6 x AGM-69A SRAM missile. FB-111H: 12 x AGM-69A SRAM.

**Produced to date:** 158 F-111A, 1 RF-111A, 7 F-111B, 24 F-111C, 96 F-111D, 94 F-111E, 126 F-111F, 2 F-111K (now YF-111A) and 76 FB-111A (including 2 converted F-111A). 42 F-111A undergoing conversion to EF-111A.

**Manufacturer:** General Dynamics. Available for production. Grumman produced F-111B.

**Exported under FMS:** 24 F-111C.

**In US Service:** Approximately 380 of 506 F-111A/B/D/E/F and K models in USAF's Tactical Air Command, and 72 of 76 FB-111A in Strategic Air Command.

**In Service Abroad:** Australia (24)

**Price:** $22.238 million (1976 Unit Program Cost for 24 F-111C transferred under FMS to Australia); $17.125 million (1975 Unit Procurement Cost for 12 F-111F); $9.722 million (1972 Unit Procurement Cost for 96 F-111D). FB-111A: $16.319 million (1971 Unit Procurement Cost). EF-111A: $57.522 million (Total unit cost including 1977 unit conversion cost of $41.922 million and 1962 Unit Procurement Cost of $15.6 million for F-111A model under conversion)

Currently forming the backbone of our Navy's carrier-based bomber force, this twin-engined two-seat strike and reconnaissance aircraft has a combat range, fully loaded, of more than 1,800 miles. It is fitted with Digital Integrated Attack Navigation Equipment (DIANE), a computerized ground mapping radar system which flies it to preselected targets at altitudes as low as treetop level, times the release of its bombload with pin-point accuracy, and returns it to its carrier deck without the use of any external navigation aids. The pilot never has to look outside the cockpit. The DIANE system is so effective in flying the aircraft by day or night, in any kind of weather, that the A-6 Intruders which carry it are frequently flown with other aircraft in order to provide them with its superior guidance.

The A-6A Intruder entered service in February of 1963, and first saw combat in July of 1965 when a squadron of 12 of the aircraft, the Sunday Punchers (VA-75), flew a mission over North Vietnam from the carrier *Independence.* During the years of the air war in Southeast Asia, A-6 squadrons flew most of the Navy's deep interdiction bombing missions. A single squadron, the Tigers (VA-65), flew 1,239 sorties during its operational cycle aboard the carrier *Constellation.*

A total of 488 A-6As were produced, and many of these were modified to other standards, including 19 A-6B, fitted to fire the AGM-78A Standard ARM anti-radiation missile, 12 A-6C, housing FLIR (Forward Looking Infra Red) sensors and LLLTV (Low Light Level Television) cameras in a turret under their fuselages to locate targets not identifiable by radar, and 62 KA-6D, a tanker version with its DIANE equipment removed, and which can deliver as much as 21,000 lbs of fuel. A further six A-6As were converted to EA-6A electronic defense suppression aircraft, with more than 30 antennae that acquire, locate, classify and jam enemy radar signals. These and 21 new aircraft built to EA-6A standard were allocated to the Marine Corps.

The more advanced A-6E, the current production model of the aircraft, first entered service in December of 1972. It incorporates a series of sophisticated improvements on the DIANE system, including an IBM AN/ASQ-133 digital computer, a Fairchild signal data converter which translates analogue information from sensors to digital information for display and for comparison with the computer's memory, a Conrac armament control unit, a Norden AN/APQ-148 multi-mode radar which locates, tracks and computes the range of fixed or moving targets while simultaneously navigating the aircraft by ground mapping its flight, and a Kaiser AN/AVA-1 Vertical Display Indicator (VDI), which electronically duplicates the shape and propor-

tions of terrain and other objects over which the aircraft flies by using information from externally-mounted sensors, and displays its simulation of that terrain in correct motion and perspective according to the aircraft's speed and altitude, just as it would all be seen—if weather and other conditions did not frequently block visibility—through the pilot's windscreen. The VDI superimposes on this picture the aircraft's planned course and target points, and also provides bomb release and maneuvering information.

192 A-6As have been converted to A-6E standard, and 189 new A-6E aircraft are planned. Of the latter, approximately 141 have been delivered to date. With continuing deliveries at the rate of about 12 per year, the Navy will have its full allotment of 381 A-6E aircraft by 1982.

Four A-6Es have undergone further modifications that include the Hughes Target Recognition and Attack Multisensor (TRAM), a turreted electro-optical and infrared sensor system that provides target acquisition, tracking and weapons guidance data for laser-guided and electro-optically guided munitions. The aircraft have also been modified to accept the AGM-53A Condor TV-guided air-to-surface missile.

# GRUMMAN A-6E INTRUDER AND EA-6B PROWLER

**EA-6B Prowler with ALQ-99 ECM Pods**

A highly sophisticated and costly derivation of the A-6 is the EA-6B Prowler electronic counter measures aircraft. Not a conversion of the A-6 but a newly built aircraft, it follows the A-6 design but has an extended nose section to provide room for two additional crew members who operate its ECM equipment. This includes the AN/ALQ-92 Communications Jammer and the AN/ALQ-126 Deception ECM Jamming System, both built by Sanders, as well as the AN/ALQ-99A Tactical Jamming System built by AIL/Raytheon. An Extended Capability (EXCAP) version of the aircraft, which doubles the jamming power of the original EA-6B, carries a complement of four AN/ALQ-99A TJS systems in pods under its wings. Each pod is independently powered by a Garret-AiResearch four-bladed axial flow ram-air turbine, which by itself generates enough power to light a city of 100,000 people.

The EXCAP EA-6B Prowler is now operational with the Sixth Fleet in the Mediterranean and the Seventh Fleet in the Western Pacific. Four of the aircraft are normally as-signed to each carrier. An Improved Capability (ICAP) version of the Prowler is also planned, with further ECM equipment that includes digital tuning for a more rapid response time in jamming enemy signals after their detection. A test version of the ICAP Prowler first flew in July of 1975. Of the EA-6B aircraft of all types, a total of 77 is planned. Approximately 50 have been delivered thus far.

**Maximum Weight:** 60,600 lbs. EA-6B: 58,500 lbs.

**Maximum Speed:** 685 mph.

**Powered by:** 2 x Pratt & Whitney J52-P-8A/B turbojets. EA-6B: 2 x P&W J52-P-408 turbojets.

**Operational Range:** Over 1,800 miles. Combat radius of over 900 miles. Ferry range: 3,225 miles.

**Key Electronics:** DIANE (A-6A), FLIR and LLLTV (A-6C only). A-6E: AN/ASQ-133, Conrac ACU, AN/APQ-148 multi-mode radar, Kaiser AN/AVA-1 VDI, and TRAM (four aircraft to date). E-6B: AN/ALQ-92 jammer, AN/ALQ-126 Deception ECM, AN/ALQ-99A TJS.

**Crew:** Two. Four on EA-6B.

**Armament:** Provision for 4 x GE M134 7.62mm Minigun pods or 4 x AIM-9 Sidewinder AAM

**Ordnance Capacity:** 18,000 lbs on five external hardpoints.

**Stores Combinations:** 4 x AGM-12A/B/C Bullpup ASM, or 4 x AGM-78A Standard ARM (A-6B only), or 4 x AGM-53B Condor ASM (A-6E TRAM only), or 20 x 500 lb bomb, or 13 x 1,000 lb bomb, or 5 x 2,000 lb bomb

**Produced to date:** 488 A-6A, of which 19 converted to A-6B, 12 to A-6C, 62 to KA-6D, 6 to EA-6A and 192 to A-6E. 21 additional EA-6A, 50 of 77 planned EA-6B, and 141 of planned 189 A-6E also delivered to date.

**Manufacturer:** Grumman Aerospace Corporation. In production.

**In US Service:** A-6A/B/C and KA-6D in 15 USN and 11 USMC squadrons. EA-6B in 10 USN squadrons.

**Price:** $14.866 million (1978 Unit Procurement Cost for 12 A-6E aircraft). $22.966 million (1978 Unit Procurement Cost for 6 EA-6B Prowler aircraft) TRAM conversion Cost: $1.416 million@ for 36 aircraft in 1979.

**A-6E TRAM**

**A-6E Intruder**

This is one of the fastest and most maneuverable aircraft in our inventory. A two-seat, long-range interceptor, it is fitted with equipment representing some of our most advanced technology. The result of a development competition begun after cancellation of the Navy's F-111B program, it incorporates some of the systems originally developed for that aircraft, including the Hughes AN/AWG-9 Fire Control Radar. Like the F-111B, it also employs variable-sweep wings, but with rather more success.

More than 24 percent of the F-14 is constructed of titanium, as compared with nine percent in the F-4 Phantom and even less in most other aircraft. The extensive use of this alloy, lighter but stronger than steel, together with electron beam welding and a boron-epoxy composite for the tailplane skins, achieves for the aircraft an optimum ratio of strength to weight. This, combined with the high thrust of its two engines, gives the F-14 extraordinary agility. It remains fully controllable at angles of attack as steep as 90 degrees.

With its wings extended fully forward at 20 degrees the F-14 can take off in less than 1,000 feet and land in 1,500. Its tailplanes assume primary control of the aircraft when the wings are swept back for speed at their maximum angle of 68 degrees. The sweep of the wings is automatically adjusted by a Mach Sweep Programmer to achieve maximum speed with minimum drag. As the wings change their position the aircraft's center of pressure changes, and movable glove vanes at its leading-edge wing roots automatically adjust to stabilize pitch. At altitude, with maximum wing sweep, the F-14 reaches its top speed of 1,560 mph (Mach 2.34).

In addition to its M61A1 Vulcan 20mm cannon, situated in the portside fuselage with 675 rounds, the F-14 fires the Hughes AIM-54A Phoenix air-to-air missile, whose range is close to 100 miles. The AN/AWG-9 fire control and target illuminating radar, which can operate in either pulse-doppler or conventional pulse modes, provides target detection, tracking and ranging functions for the Vulcan gun and various combinations of AIM-54A Phoenix, AIM-7E/F Sparrow and AIM-9G Sidewinder missiles. It can track up to 24 targets while simultaneously guiding as many as six Phoenix missiles to separate targets at distances of more than 50 miles.

Intended as an eventual replacement for the F-4 Phantom as the Navy's primary carrier-borne fighter, the F-14 is expected to perform a variety of air superiority roles, including combat air patrol and air interception, fighter escort and strike force protection, and secondary attack of tactical ground targets. It is capable of very low flight and has a fast rate of climb. Combined with its maneuverability, range, speed and advanced weapons systems, these qualities would appear to make it suitable for all of its assigned missions.

The first development F-14A flew on December 21, 1970, piloted by USN Commander George W. White, Jr. It crashed nine days later, during its second flight, after a complete failure of its hydraulic system. The tenth development aircraft also crashed in June of 1972, from similar causes. Exactly one year later a third F-14 literally shot itself down with a Sparrow missile which failed to clear the aircraft and struck its fuselage.

There have been 13 crashes of F-14 aircraft to date, and many are still under investigation. The Navy believes that three were due to spins which the pilots might have controlled, and that another four were due to the aircraft's engine fan blades, which have had a tendency to fly off. Engine shafts will have to be strengthened on the 231 F-14s delivered to the Navy thus far, and the installation of retainers is also planned to prevent the fan blades from flying off. These repairs will cost approximately $823,000 per aircraft.

The House Armed Services Committee has reluctantly voted $67 million to begin this repair program, and has little choice but to vote, in time, the remaining $123 million required. Members of the Committee feel that the engine was poorly designed in the first place, but the problem now is that these aircraft already exist and were very expensive to acquire. "The issue is simple," said Representative Robert E. Badham of California. "Either we protect our men out there who are flying them or we don't."

Aside from these setbacks, the aircraft has made a smooth transition into service, with early deliveries beginning in 1974. By September of 1974 two squadrons, VF-1 (Wolfpack) and VF-2 (Bounty Hunters), had been formed and assigned to the carrier USS Enterprise. They flew their first operational sorties in the spring of 1975 on fighter escort missions during the evacuation from Southeast Asia. By July 1975 VF-14 (Tophatters) and VF-32 were operational aboard the USS John F. Kennedy, and in April of 1976 squadrons VF-142 (Ghostriders) and VF-143 (Pukin Dogs) were assigned to the USS America. USS Nimitz received VF-41 (Black Aces) and VF-84 (Jolly Rogers) in January of 1977, and shortly thereafter USS Constellation received VF-211 (Checkmates) and USS Kitty Hawk received VF-114 (Aardvarks). VF-101 (Grim Reapers) is now forming at Naval Air Station Oceana for carrier assignment in the near future.

While the Navy had originally planned to acquire 722 F-14s, a prodigious rise in the aircraft's cost, from $11.3 million in 1974 to $19.025 million in 1977, forced a substantial reduction in the program. The additional cost of the engine repair program has further reduced the planned procurement. With funds

# GRUMMAN F-14A TOMCAT

in hand for 306 aircraft, the Navy now plans a total of only 390 F-14s, all of which should be operational by 1981. Only 24 carrier-borne squadrons are planned, and six of these may be equipped with the less costly F-18 Hornet. The Marine Corps has also dropped its plan to purchase the F-14A and will take the F-18 instead.

By 1977 a total of 243 F-14 Tomcats had been delivered, including 12 to Iran. That country had purchased 80 F-14s, and its first three were delivered to Khatami Air Force Base in January of 1976. The original agreement had scheduled delivery of 61 aircraft to Iran by the end of 1977, with the balance due in the first six months of 1978. Delivery of all aircraft was completed three months ahead of this schedule, mainly because their manufacturer, Grumman Aerospace Corporation, owed its solvency to this order.

In 1974, as a result of heavy cost overruns and consequent losses in the early stages of its F-14 contract with the Navy, Grumman found itself in a critical state of undercapitalization, and lost its credit standing with American banks. The Melli bank of Iran loaned the company $75 million, and persuaded nine American banks to lend it $125 million more. The Iranian government had already agreed to the purchase of the F-14s, and now it wanted to be sure the aircraft were produced and delivered. The $200 million in loans saved Grumman from financial ruin, and the company is now making a profit on F-14 deliveries.

In July of 1974, when Grumman concluded its agreement with Iran for the sale of the F-14s, it planned to pay a total of $28 million in fees to the firm of Houshang Lavi and his brothers, Iranian commission agents living in the United States, and the firm of former United States Army Colonel Albert J. Fuge, another Grumman commission agent. The company had already paid out $6 million of that amount when General Hassan Toufa-

nian, Iran's vice minister of war for armaments, vigorously objected, pointing out that Iran had never agreed to having part of its payment for the aircraft turned over to any agent as a commission, that when commissions on any sale exceeded $1 million Foreign Military Sales regulations required approval from the Department of Defense—which in this case had not been obtained, that Houshang Lavi and one of his brothers were *persona non grata* in Iran due to allegations of earlier fraudulent activities on their part, that the use of agents was in any case against Iranian government policy, that Grumman knew this, that Grumman's conduct seemed especially inappropriate in view of Iran's earlier assistance in keeping the F-14 program alive and Grumman out of bankruptcy, that at that time no one in Iran would have dreamed Grumman capable even of planning to pay commissions of this magnitude, that the aircraft would be less expensive if the money planned for commissions were deducted from the total Iranian purchase price, and that Iran was therefore entitled to deduct $28 million from bills submitted by the United States government under the F-14 contract.

In December of 1977 Grumman reached a compromise agreement with Iran whereby the purchase price of the contract will remain the same but Grumman will add to it $24 million worth of spare parts and replacement equipment for the F-14 aircraft, to be shipped over the next three years.

In the meanwhile Houshang Lavi has brought suit against Colonel Fuge and Grumman Aircraft for damages, charging that Fuge attempted to bribe Grumman and that those two parties "conspired" with Ira-

nian officials to sign away his original rights to 35 percent of the anticipated commissions.

The seventh and thirty-first production F-14As were modified to F-14B standard by fitting them with improved lightweight engines designed to accelerate the aircraft from 533 mph to 1,066 mph (Mach 1.6) in 83 seconds. Tests were not successful, and the planned procurement of 179 F-14Bs was dropped. An F-14C with new avionics and weapons systems has been designed, but to date no further development has taken place.

**Maximum Weight:** 55,000 lbs for interceptor mission, 72,000 lbs fully loaded

**Maximum Speed:** 1,544 mph (Mach 2.34) 910 mph (Mach 1.36) at sea level.

**Power Plant:** 2 x Pratt & Whitney TF30-P-412A afterburning turbofan engines. 2 x F401-PW-400 (F-14B only)

**Operational Range:** 2,000 miles

**Key Electronics:** AN/AWG-9 Fire Control Radar, AN/5400-B Weapon Control Computer, AN/ALR-45 Radar Warning System, AN/ALQ-100 Deception ECM, AN/ALQ-129 Track Breaker, AN/CP-1113/AWG Central Computer.

**Armament:** 1 x M61A1 Vulcan 20mm cannon with 675 rds.

**Ceiling:** 60,000 feet

**Ordnance Capacity:** 14,500 lbs on 2 wing pylons and 1 fuselage pallet.

**Stores Combinations:** 6 x AIM-54A Phoenix AAM and 4 x AIM-9G Sidewinder AAM, or 4 x AIM-7E/F Sparrow AAM and 4 x AIM-9G Sidewinder AAM.

**Produced to Date:** 430 F-14A, including 350 of a total of 390 planned for USN (two of which converted to F-14B) and 80 for Iran.

**Manufacturer:** Grumman Aerospace Corporation. In production.

**Exported Under FMS:** 80.

**In US Service:** 231 F-14A in 14 USN squadrons. From 4 to 14 additional squadrons planned.

**In Service Abroad:** Iran (77 of 80 delivered)

**Price:** $20.624 million (1978 Unit Procurement Cost for 44 aircraft). $19.025 million (1977 Unit Procurement Cost for 36 aircraft). $23.750 million (1974 Unit Program Cost for 80 aircraft sold under FMS to Iran, including unit procurement cost of $11.3 million and research and development surcharge)

# GRUMMAN OV-1 MOHAWK

A twin turboprop STOL aircraft, with side-by-side seating for a crew of two, the Mohawk was intended primarily for tactical reconnaissance and surveillance missions, operating from forward airstrips in close conjunction with ground forces. But the first three versions of the aircraft, the OV-1A, OV-1B and OV-1C, were all flown during the initial years of our involvement in Southeast Asia armed with a variety of weapons, including grenade launchers, napalm and fragmentation bombs, 500 lb demolition bombs, 2.75 inch FFAR rocket pods, and pods mounting multi-barreled 7.62mm Miniguns or .50 Caliber machine guns.

The United States Army, our only service using the OV-1, no longer flies armed Mohawks due to a 1965 Defense Department ruling that all ground support missions assigned to fixed-wing aircraft were to be flown by the Air Force or other services. Israel, however, flies the armed reconnaissance version of the Mohawk, designated JOV-1A.

A rugged and stable aircraft, with full-span wing slats and triple tail fins and rudders, the Mohawk first entered service in February of 1961. Key reconnaissance models are the OV-1B, with a long pod mounted under its fuselage containing an AN/APS-94D SLAR (Side Looking Airborne Radar) system for terrain-mapping, and capable of producing an almost instantaneous permanent film record of the radar image below and to either side of the aircraft's flight path, the OV-1C, which mounts the AN/AAS-24 Infrared Mapping System, a KA-76 serial frame camera and a KA-60C panoramic camera with a focal width of 180 degrees, and the OV-1D, which can quickly convert to carry either the SLAR pod or the Infrared Mapping System by use of a pallet mount.

86 OV-1B and OV-1C were converted to OV-1D standard, and 37 new OV-1D were built. Under the Quick Look II program, 16 OV-1B were also converted in 1974 to EV-1E electronic warfare aircraft with pod-mounted AN/ALQ-133 radar target locators. A few additional conversions were made to RV-1C and RV-1D ECM reconnaissance aircraft.

**Maximum Weight:** With SLAR: 18,109 lbs With IR: 17,912 lbs

**Maximum Speed:** With SLAR: 289 mph With IR: 305 mph

**Operational Range:** With SLAR: 944 miles With IR: 1,011 miles

**Key Electronics:** AN/APS-94 (OV-1B), AN/UPE-3 SLAR and AN/UAS-4 (OV-1D), AN/AAS-24 (OV-1C), AN/APQ-142 (RV-1D only), AN/ALQ-133 ECM (EV-1E only), and AN/ALQ-147 IRCM/DECM pod.

**Ordnance Capacity:** 3,740 lbs on six external hardpoints

**Stores Combinations:** 6 x 500 lb bomb, or 4 x 500 lb bomb and 2 x SUU-11A gun pod, LAU-3A/32A/59A rocket pod or CBU-19A cluster canister.

**Produced:** 375 of all types, including 9 development and 64 production OV-1A, 101 OV-1B, 133 OV-1C and 37 OV-1D. 16 OV-1B converted to EV-1E, and 86 B and C models converted to OV-1D and RV-1D.

**Manufacturer:** Grumman Aerospace Corporation. Available for production.

**Exported under FMS:** 28 JOV-1A.

**In US Service:** 45 OV-1A, 132 OV-1B/C and RV-1C, 123 OV-1D and RV-1D, and 16 EV-1E in US Army.

**In Service Abroad:** Israel (28) (2 OV-1D have also been on loan to West German Luftwaffe from US Army).

**Conversion Costs:** $1.666 million (Unit conversion cost of 12 OV-1C to RV-1D standard in 1977) $2.102 million (Unit conversion cost of 16 OV-1B to EV-1E standard in 1977)

**OV-1B with AN/APS-94D SLAR System**

# HELIO
# AU-24A STALLION

The Helio Aircraft Company, formerly a division of General Aircraft Corporation and now owned by John Roberts, Ltd., designed some of the most outstanding STOL aircraft ever to be produced. The company's first aircraft took off from a tennis court at Harvard University in 1948, and is now in the Smithsonian Museum. The AU-24A, with a single turboprop engine, fixed landing gear, high, cantilevered wings, full-span leading-edge flaps and a swept-back tail fin, takes off with a full load in just 320 feet and lands in no more than 250.

Military modifications, including the addition of M4A4 bomb racks on five external hardpoints, a gunsight and armament control panel, and a cabin mounting for side-firing weapons, were made by Kaman Aerospace. Under the Credible Chase program, an Air Force competiton to develop a STOL counterinsurgency aircraft, 15 AU-24A Stallions were procured for evaluation along with 15

Fairchild AU-23A Peacemakers. Like the Peacemaker, the Stallion can carry a variety of external stores, including gun or rocket pods, flare dispensers and small bombs, or alternatively it can carry eight combat troops, a crew of two and a gunner who fires a pintle-mounted multi-barreled 7.62mm Minigun or M-197 Vulcan 20mm cannon from the cabin.

14 of each of the aircraft under evaluation were eventually transferred from the Air Force under the Military Assistance Program, the AU-23A Peacemakers to Thailand and the AU-24A Stallions to Cambodia. Thailand ordered and received an additional 20 Peacemakers, and has another 5 on order. Further orders are expected for the Stallion from a number of countries when production resumes under new ownership in 1978.

**Maximum Weight:** 6,300 lbs

**Maximum Speed:** 218 mph

**Operational Range:** 1,090 miles (combat radius of 545 miles)

**Take-Off Run:** 320 feet

**Landing Run:** 250 feet

**Armament:** 1 x XM-197 20mm cannon firing 700 rpm, or 1 x 7.62mm Minigun, firing 2,000 or 4,000 rpm

**Ordnance Capacity:** 2,300 lbs on five external hardpoints

**Produced to date:** 20, including 2 prototype, 1 evaluation and 2 demonstrator AU-24A, and 15 for USAF

**Manufacturer:** John Roberts, Ltd. (formerly Helio Aircraft). Production to resume in 1978.

**Exported under MAP:** 14

**In US Service:** 2 with USAF, including 1 on lease from manufacturer.

**In Service Abroad:** Cambodia (14)

**Price:** $585,928 (1974 Unit Procurement Cost for 15 aircraft to USAF)

# LOCKHEED F-80C SHOOTING STAR AND T-33A TRAINER

One of the earliest jet aircraft designed, the F-80 Shooting Star became this country's first operational jet fighter. Though it entered service more than thirty years ago it is still used widely throughout the world. Its three basic versions, the F-80 fighter, a T-33A trainer created by adding three feet to the aircraft's fuselage length in order to seat two in tandem, and an armed attack trainer, the AT-33A, were all supplied in quantity to 39 foreign air forces. The aircraft are still being transferred abroad, and at least 800 fly today with 35 nations.

Designed and placed in production before the end of World War II, but too late to participate in that conflict, the F-80 entered USAF service in 1946. By the beginning of the Korean War five F-80 fighter wings were operational with our Far East Air Force, and during the war they flew 98,515 sorties, dropping 33,266 tons of bombs and 8,327 tons of napalm. The first jet fighter battle in history took place in November of 1950 when an F-80 flown by Lieutenant Russel J. Brown shot down a MiG-15 as it crossed the Yalu River. In time, however, the MiG aircraft proved to be more maneuverable, and against it the F-80 sustained a ratio in air combat losses of 7 to 6. By 1953 the North American F-86 Sabre had replaced the Shooting Star as our front-line fighter, but the trainer and armed attack trainer versions of the older aircraft still fly with our Air Force and Navy, and have trained more jet pilots, here and abroad, than any other aircraft to date.

The basic difference in armament between the fighter and armed attack trainer versions of the Shooting Star is that the AT-33A has two M-3 .50 Caliber aircraft machine guns mounted in its nose while the F-80C has six. Both are capable of delivering 2,000 lbs of bombs or other air munitions. The T-33A trainer is easily modified to AT-33A standard, and has undergone such modifications in many recipient countries.

1,715 F-80 fighters were built, including 677 F-80A and 240 F-80B models, most of them supplied to the Air Force with some conversions to RF-80A reconnaissance aircraft, and 798 F-80C models, 50 of which were supplied to the Navy and Marine Corps as TV-1 trainers, while 685 were assigned to the Air Force and 113 were transferred under the Military Assistance Plan to seven Latin American air forces.

Of the T-33 trainer 5,819 were built, including 699 T-33B for the Navy and Marine Corps as TV-2 trainers. The balance were supplied to the Air Force and to a large number of foreign air forces as trainers or armed attack trainers. 87 were converted to RT-33A photo-reconnaissance aircraft for seven foreign countries, and a few were converted to DT-33A drone aircraft and QT-33A radio drone aircraft for target training in this country.

Under license, an additional 656 T-33A were built by Canadair as CL-30 Silver Stars. Canada still flies 158 of these, and has supplied them to several other countries including Greece and, most recently, Bolivia. Lockheed also supplied parts for another 210 T-33A to be assembled by Kawasaki in Japan, where 186 are still in service. The United States is still transferring T-33A trainers abroad under the MAP and FMS programs, including a total of 265 of the aircraft under MAP since 1974, and with current FMS orders outstanding for another 33.

An improvement on the F-80, incorporating the first jet engine afterburner and a stretched nose to accomodate airborne weather radar, and substituting armament of 24 internally-mounted Mighty Mouse rockets for the original M-3 aircraft machine guns, was developed by Lockheed during the Korean War and designated the F-94 Starfire. A total of 466 F-94A and F-94B aircraft were procured by the Air Force, together with 110 F-94C models, the first fighters to be equipped with the Hughes automatic fire control system. These aircraft served with USAF in the late 1950s, and to date none have been transferred abroad.

**Maximum Weight:** 16,000 lbs.

**Maximum Speed:** 610 mph (set world speed record of 623.9 mph in 1947)

**Power Plant:** 1 x Allison J33-A-35 turbojet engine.

**Operational Range:** 1,345 miles

**Ceiling:** 47,500 feet

**Armament:** 6 x M-3 .50 Cal MG (F-80) or 2 x M-3 .50 Cal MG (AT-33A)

**Ordnance Capacity:** 2,000 lbs on external hardpoints

**Produced:** 1,715 F-80, including 677 F-80A, 240 F-80B and 798 F-80C, and 6,685 T-33, including 656 Canadair CL-30, 210 Kawasaki T-33A, 87 RT-33A, many AT-33A and few DT-33A and QT-33A. 576 F-94 also produced, including 110 F-94C.

**Manufacturer:** Lockheed Aircraft Corporation. Production complete.

**Exported under MAP:** 113 F-80, 87 RT-33A, and 1,323 AT-33A and T-33A.

**Exported under FMS:** 334 AT-33A and T-33A (33 more on order).

**In US Service:** Approximately 300 T-33A in Aerospace Defense Command, few AT-33A in USAF, and T-33B in USN. Few DT-33A and QT-33A in USAF and USN.

**F-80C in Service Abroad:** Chile (10), Ecuador (9), Uruguay (6). Formerly also in Brazil, Peru and Venezuela.

**AT-33A in Service Abroad:** Brazil (54), Burma (12), Colombia (16), Indonesia (31), Mexico (15), Peru (10), South Korea (44), Venezuela (12), and Uruguay (6).

**RT-33A in Service Abroad:** Ethiopia (2), Iran (16), Italy (12), Pakistan (3), Thailand (2), and Yugoslavia (20). Formerly also in the Netherlands and Turkey.

**T-33A in Service Abroad:** Belgium (15), Bolivia (13), Brazil (18), Canada (158), Chile (8), Colombia (10), Cuba (10), Denmark (18), Ecuador (12), Ethiopia (10), France (150), Greece (60), Guatemala (5), Honduras (3), Indonesia (10), Iran (25), Italy (25), Japan (186), Laos (3), Libya (3), the Netherlands (50), Nicaragua (4), Pakistan (26), Philippines (10), Peru (8), Portugal (24), Saudi Arabia (13), South Korea (30), Spain (75), Taiwan (18), Thailand (6), Turkey (60), Yugoslavia (70) and West Germany (192). Formerly also in Norway.

**Price:** $307,692 (1973 unit cost for sale of 13 aircraft from Canada to Bolivia).

**T-33A of West German Bundesluftwaffe**

Far ahead of its time when it first entered service almost twenty years ago, the Starfighter offered NATO air forces a significant tactical edge over existing Soviet aircraft in the early 1960s, and was consequently the subject of a major multinational coproduction effort, the first of its kind, that involved seven nations and turned out 2,780 of the new fighter in its interceptor, fighter-bomber, trainer and reconnaissance versions. In many NATO air forces the Starfighter replaced F-84 Thunderjets and F-86 Sabres, which in turn were transferred to other countries.

Intended only as a high-speed interceptor, the Starfighter was required to perform in a variety of other roles to which it proved ill-suited. As a result, 531 Starfighter aircraft to date have been lost in crashes, in which almost 100 pilots have lost their lives. These incidents, which appeared to gain frequency in the mid-1960s, provoked bitter controversy throughout the NATO organization, led to the discovery of excessive commissions and other questionable payments in connection with the Starfighter's initial sale, became the focus of a major scandal in the European press—with decisive political consequences for some of those in power, precipitated official investigations in West Germany and the Netherlands, and culminated in a series of international lawsuits involving millions of dollars in reparations.

Yet the Starfighter remains a front-line interceptor in most NATO countries, being only gradually replaced by the F-4 Phantom and other aircraft of European design. It serves today with the air forces of fourteen nations as well as with our own Air National Guard.

The design of the Starfighter grew from discussion with USAF pilots who had fought in Korea, and who believed that the decisive factor in air combat was speed. The Starfighter became the first aircraft capable of climbing faster than the speed of sound. It reaches level speeds of 1,450 mph (Mach 2.2). This capability, however, was achieved at the sacrifice of range, flexibility and endurance.

Like a nervous thoroughbred horse, the Starfighter is what pilots call an "unforgiving" aircraft. Designed to achieve high thrust and low drag, it incorporates a powerful engine, short, stubby wings like the fins of a missile, and a slim fuselage whose narrow diameter reduces air resistance. Because its wings, only seven and a half feet long, afford little surface area they have been placed close to the aircraft's tailplane, so that between them these two horizontal surfaces provide a concentration of lift sufficient to take the Starfighter off the ground and bring it safely down again.

Normally, however, a decent space is required between an aircraft's wing and tailplane surfaces, so that one can balance the other to control movements of pitch in the vertical plane. Otherwise, when the pilot attempted to raise or lower the aircraft's nose, it would respond either too slowly or too suddenly. To restore to this aircraft some measure of control over vertical movement, its entire tailplane, a proportionately large horizontal area, was designed to move as a single flap.

However, the jolting effect of a change in the tailplane cant, without sufficient wing area to provide stabilizing control, easily causes the Starfighter to roll. Therefore its wings, their leading edges machined razor thin to further reduce air resistance, have been angled downwards at an anhedral of

10 degrees. This somewhat counters its tendency to roll, though pilots have still found it difficult to keep the Starfighter upright and level in the horizontal plane.

The Starfighter is literally kept in the air by the forward thrust of its engine, and it becomes more stable as it increases speed. Many of the aircraft have been lost simply as a result of an engine flameout, for it has no stability at glide speed. Highly sensitive to controls, the Starfighter requires the precision and steady hand of an experienced pilot.

The first of two XF-104 Starfighter prototypes flew in February of 1954. They were followed by 17 YF-104 aircraft, built for evaluation by the Aerospace Defense and Tactical Air Commands. The initial production aircraft, a single-seat F-104A powered by a General Electric J79-GE-3B engine, first flew in February of 1956. Of the F-104A 153 were built. They first entered service with the 83rd Fighter Interceptor Squadron in January of 1968, and also flew with the Aerospace Defense Command in Spain. But due to a series of accidents, the aircraft's poor range and its inability to fly under a variety of weather conditions, it was withdrawn from service late in 1959. Under the Military Assistance Plan 14 F-104As were supplied to Pakistan and 36 to Jordan, while the balance were reassigned to the Air National Guard, where they served from 1963 to 1966. Today only one squadron of Starfighters, the 198th Tactical Fighter Squadron at Muniz, Puerto Rico, remains in service with the ANG, equipped with the later F-104C.

26 two-seat F-104B Starfighters were built, together with 77 single-seat F-104C fighter-bombers. Undre MAP, 22 of the F-104Bs were transferred to Taiwan, 2 to Jordan and 2 to Pakistan. The F-104Cs were assigned to the 479th Tactical Fighter Wing, one squadron of which was sent in 1965 to Vietnam to counter the anticipated threat of the MiG-21. That aircraft, however, failed immediately to appear. The F-104Cs were

# LOCKHEED F-104 STARFIGHTER

used, instead, in the ground attack role for a brief period, withdrawn from Vietnam, and then sent back at the end of that year when the MiG-21 finally entered combat. Little air combat took place between the two aircraft types.

Two further two-seat versions of the Starfighter, the F-104D and F-104F, were produced by Lockheed for transfer abroad. Parts for 20 of the D model were shipped to Japan for assembly by Mitsubishi, and 30 of the F model were built for West Germany, where they were later to be used as trainers.

In 1955, NATO announced its decision to adopt a common aircraft that would serve in the strike, interceptor and reconnaissance roles, and requested bids for a suitable design from several manufacturers, including Grumman, Convair, Northrop, Lockheed, the Swedish firm of SAAB, and the French firm of Dassault. By October of 1968, when the competition had narrowed between Lockheed's F-104 Starfighter and Dassault's Mirage III, West German Defense Minister Franz-Josef Strauss selected the Starfighter, and in March of 1959 a contract was signed with Lockheed for the purchase of the first 96 aircraft. West Germany was by far the most important market for the Starfighter, having the largest requirement of any of the NATO countries, initially projected at 670 aircraft, and then increased to 866. In the end, West German procurement would total 1,128 Starfighters, employed variously as interceptor, fighter-bomber, trainer and reconnaissance aircraft.

In an attempt to meet the many requirements of these highly divergent roles, the Starfighter was subjected to a number of structural modifications, including a strengthened fuselage frame to resist the added stress of maneuver, and some additional fin area to increase its stability for low-level weapons delivery. This became the F-104G, or Super Starfighter. Incorporating a J79-GE-11A engine that produced 15,800 lbs of thrust with afterburner, the aircraft was capable of short sprint speeds of Mach 2.2. One of the first aircraft to be fitted with the M61 Vulcan multi-barreled 20mm cannon as

standard equipment, it also carried a Litton LN-3 inertial navigation system, and the F-15A-41B multimode North American Search and Range Radar (NASARR).

In 1959 the Netherlands also selected the F-104G, and within the next two years Belgium, Italy, Canada and Japan followed. All of these countries became party to massive coproduction agreements, and Canada in particular produced trainer and fighter-bomber versions of the F-104 to equip its own and five other NATO air forces.

A West German production consortium, comprising the firms of Messerschmitt, Heinkel, Dornier and Siebel, produced an initial 210 F-104Gs in the early 1960s and, under the new name of Messerschmitt-Bölkow-Blohm, another 100 from 1970 to 1972. All of these were delivered to the Luftwaffe. In Belgium the firms of SABCA and Avions Fairey combined to produce 187 aircraft, 99 for the Belgian air force and the balance of 88 for the Luftwaffe. Licenses were similarly granted by Lockheed in Holland for the firms of Fokker, Aviolanda, Focke-Wulf, Hamburger Flugzeugbau and Weser Flugzeugbau to produce a total of 350 F-104Gs, 95 for the Netherlands and the balance of 255 for the Luftwaffe. In Italy Fiat, Aermacchi, Piaggio, SACA and SIAI-Marchetti joined to produce 199 F-104Gs, 124 for the Italian air force, 25 for the Netherlands, and another 50 for the Luftwaffe.

In Koblenz, a NATO Starfighter Management Organization employed 150 people to coordinate the production schedules of more than 45 manufacturers.

To the same F-104G standard, Canadair of Canada produced 140 aircraft, wholly financed by the United States, for transfer under MAP to Greece, Spain, Denmark, Norway and Turkey. 200 of a Canadian CF-104A, similar to the F-104G but with improved navigational instrumentation and missile fire control, and without the M61 Vulcan cannon, were produced by Canadair for the Canadian air force, and 15 of these were sold to Denmark and 22 to Norway.

Lockheed itself initially produced 98 F-104Gs, 96 to meet the first Luftwaffe order

and one each for evaluation by Italy and Belgium. These were followed by 50 more F-104Gs in the early 1970s as replacement aircraft for the Luftwaffe. In addition, Lockheed built three F-104J aircraft to the G standard for Japan, and licensed production there of another 207 F-104Js by Mitsubishi.

Two-seat trainers were also produced, including 20 TF-104Js for assembly by Mitsubishi, 38 licensed Canadair CF-104Ds, 7 of which were transferred to Denmark, and 350 Lockheed TF-104Gs. Many of these went to West Germany's Luftwaffe too, as well as to seven other countries, and 147 were converted to RF-104G photo-reconnaissance aircraft, some of them mounting SLAR (Side Looking Airborne Radar) equipment, for West Germany, Taiwan and the Netherlands.

After receiving new aircraft from Lockheed and MBB in the early 1970s, partially to replace those that had crashed, the Luftwaffe retired some of its older Starfighters. A number were scrapped at Erding. In 1973, 44 F-104Gs and 12 RF-104Gs were sold to a private dealer in Memmingen for transfer to South Africa. This was in violation of a standing United States embargo on the sale or retransfer of weapons to that country.

The latest development of the Starfighter is the Aeritalia F-104S, which is fitted with a more powerful J79-GE-19 engine, nine wing hardpoints for external stores, the Autonetics R21G radar, and the ORPHEUS multi-sensor ECM reconnaissance pod. It is also the first Starfighter capable of firing the AIM-7 Sparrow series of air-to-air missile. To date, Aeritalia has built 245 F-104S aircraft, 205 of them for the Italian air force and 40 for Turkey, a country which also received several West German F-104Gs in 1978.

The agreement for the sale of the 40 Aeritalia F-104S aircraft to Turkey was signed in 1974, during a United States embargo on the sale of arms to that country. The embargo had been imposed by Congress in response to Turkey's use of American weapons in the invasion of Cyprus. The sales agreement, like any other agreement for the sale of weapons produced abroad under license from the United States, required the approval of our State Department. Even though the embargo was then in force, that approval was given. Since the sale was a violation of the embargo, the approval was given in secret.

Spares for the first 18 aircraft, to be delivered in 1975, were paid for by the government of Libya as a loan to Turkey.

In January of 1962 the first Luftwaffe Starfighter crashed. In June of the same year four Luftwaffe Starfighters flying in close formation over Eifel collided and crashed, and all four pilots were killed. By the end of that year seven aircraft had been lost. Another 11 crashed in 1964. The crashes became more frequent. By the end of 1967 the Luftwaffe could count 73 Starfighters lost due to crashes, and that total continued to mount, reaching 91 by 1969 and 121 by 1970. Pilots began to call the aircraft the "flying coffin." *Captain Lockheed and the Starfighter,* a popular record album in the early 1970s, included such songs as "The Widow Maker" and "Catch a Falling Starfighter."

To date the Luftwaffe has lost 177 Starfighter aircraft and more than 40 pilots. In 1974 the families of 32 of these men filed a $20 million negligence suit against Lockheed. The company made settlement payments out of court the following year that totalled $12 million.

As the Starfighter crashes began to increase in frequency in 1965, and public resentment with Lockheed began to rise in West Germany, some suspicion was inevitably cast on the wisdom of the aircraft's original selection for the Luftwaffe. Lockheed's rather blatant lobbying to obtain the sale was also recalled. A team of no less than 20 Lockheed sales representatives had installed themselves in Bonn's Kaiserhof Hotel in 1957, throwing parties for members of the Bundestag and giving interviews to the press that stirred up fears about the threat

from the East and how best to counter it. Defense Minister Strauss had later been forced to resign, in 1962, chiefly as a result of his excessive zeal in raiding the offices of *Der Spiegel* magazine. But the Starfighter scandal did play an important political role in the 1966 West German elections, helping to embarrass and bring about the fall of Chancellor Ludwig Erhard.

To make matters worse Ernest Hauser, a former Austrian intelligence officer who had helped Franz-Josef Strauss to find a job after the end of World War II, and who in turn had been employed by Lockheed, at Strauss's request, in their Koblenz office, published his memoirs in which he claimed that Lockheed, in order to encourage Strauss to select the Starfighter, had paid a total of $12 million to the political party supporting him. This could never be proved. When Strauss left office he removed or destroyed most of the pertinent records dealing with the Lockheed negotiations.

However, in August of 1975 Lockheed, in response to growing pressure from Congress and the media, published a report conceding that since 1970 the company had paid a total of $22 million to political organizations and government officials in foreign countries, in order to further its sales programs abroad. In May 1977 Lockheed revised this figure to $38 million, refusing, however, to give the names of any of the money's recipients, on the grounds that this would "gravely damage goodwill, jeopardize valuable existing contracts and injure prospects for future sales." In one case, in the words of the report, funds were paid "to a special consultant

as compensation for preparation of false receipts used to document other currency payments."

Some recipients were finally identified. Fred Meuser, head of the Lockheed office in Geneva, had received, it turned out, a commission of $900,000 from Lockheed for his assistance in arranging the sale of the first 96 F-104Gs to West Germany in 1959.

Seventeen years following that sale, Senator Frank Church convened his Subcommittee on Multinational Corporations, and in February of 1976 Lockheed Chairman Daniel J. Haughton, who would resign shortly thereafter, told the Subcommittee that, for his assistance in arranging the sale of the Starfighter to his country, Lockheed had paid $1 million to Prince Bernhard of the Netherlands.

This revelation caused an immediate sensation in the Netherlands, whose prime minister ordered an investigation, appointing for that purpose a committee of three distinguished jurists headed by A. M. Donner. The Donner committee spent the next six months collecting what evidence it could find. Fred Meuser refused to testify or cooperate in any way, though it turned out that it was he who had originally suggested to Lockheed that Prince Bernhard be paid. The Prince himself had at first a poor memory of what had transpired, but finally acknowledged having received $100,000 from Lockheed, which he said he gave to friends as "Christmas presents."

In the end, however, the Donner committee retrieved two letters written by the Prince to Lockheed requesting money. Though the Donner Report was able to confirm three payments made to the Prince from 1960 through 1962, and totalling $1 million, it pointed out that these payments were made long after the Starfighter was sold to the Netherlands in 1959, and that therefore there was "no evidence of improper attempts by the aircraft industry to influence the decision-making."

The release of the Donner Report made it necessary for the Prince to relinquish his post as inspector general of the Dutch armed forces, and to resign his seats on the boards of Fokker Aircraft, the Hoogovens steel company, and KLM. He also gave up his position as head of the World Wildlife Fund. Nonetheless, a criminal investigation was ruled out. A Dutch official recently suggested that "the Prince made a stupid error, but nothing beyond what businessmen do all the time." Prince Bernhard just won the 1977 man-of-the-year award, given by an association of Dutch exporting firms.

While the selection of the Starfighter in West Germany and the Netherlands may have been encouraged by excessive commissions, bribes or the prospect of such payments, it

would be a mistake to conclude that therefore it was bound to have been a poor selection to fill the requirements at hand. It was a poor selection for other reasons. It would also be wrong to assume that, because the Luftwaffe suffered so many Starfighter crashes, it was making mistakes that were not being made by other air forces. The main reason why so many Luftwaffe Starfighters crashed is because the Luftwaffe had a great many more of the aircraft to begin with. A comparison of Starfighter crashes in other countries shows that the aircraft brought just as much disaster to most of them as it did to the country where it became a scandal. In addition to the 121 F-104s lost in Germany through 1970, 64 had by that time crashed in the United States, 58 in Canada, 35 in Italy, 13 in Belgium and 80 in Holland. The ratio of these losses to the total of Starfighter aircraft in each country's inventory was actually higher in the United States, Canada and Italy than it was in West Germany, averaging between 22 and 24 percent as compared with the Luftwaffe's 14 percent. The aircraft are still crashing. The most recent crash, a midair collision of four Italian air force F-104S Starfighters as they took off from Bitburg Air Base, Germany, occurred in September of 1975.

It is true that many of the German pilots were young and inexperienced, that for eleven years after the war West Germany was not permitted to fly military aircraft of any kind, that the Starfighter was a complex weapon system for which the six-week training course at Luke Air Force Base, Arizona, barely qualified the Luftwaffe pilots, that training and flying conditions were far less favorable in the crowded European airspace than over the Arizona desert, and that the Luftwaffe increased the complexity and weight of its F-104s by loading them down with additional equipment. But comparative records suggest that the Luftwaffe pilots met the challenge of this aircraft better than pilots in most other countries.

The real error made by every air force that used this aircraft was in expecting it to perform strike, reconnaissance and other low-level or long-range missions, merely because those were the requirements at hand. They were asking the Starfighter to do what it was not designed to do. The price they had to pay was severe.

**Maximum Weight:** 28,780 lbs

**Maximum Speed:** 1,452 mph (Mach 2.2)

**Power Plant:** 1 x J79-GE-11A engine (F-104G), 1 x J79-GE-19 engine (F-104S)

**Operational Range:** 300 miles. Without weapons, and with 4 drop tanks: 1,380 miles.

**Ceiling:** 58,000 feet

**Armament:** 1 x M61 Vulcan 20mm cannon

**Ordnance Capacity:** 4,000 lbs.

**Stores Combinations:** 3 x 1,000 lb bomb, or 2 x 1,000 lb bomb and 1 x 2,000 lb bomb, or 4 x AIM-9 Sidewinder AAM, or 2 x AIM-9 amd 2 x AGM-12 Bullpup ASM or 2 x FFAR 2.75" rocket pod. F-104S only: 2 x AIM-9 and 2 x AIM-7 Sparrow AAM.

**Produced:** 2,782 of all types to date, including 2 XF-104, 17 YF-104, 153 F-104A, 26 F-104B, 77 F-104C, 80 F-104D, 30 F-104F, 1,334 F-104G, 210 F-104J (to G standard), 200 CF-104A (to G standard), 350 TF-104G (of which 147 converted to RF-104G), 20 TF-104J, 38 CF-104D and 245 F-104S.

**Manufacturer:** Lockheed Aircraft Corporation. Licensed production in six foreign countries (see text). F-104S currently under licensed production by Aeritalia in Italy.

**Exported under MAP:** 394 F-104A/B/D and TF-104G, and 24 RF-104G.

**Exported under FMS:** 239 F-104D/F/G/J and 56 TF-104G/J, and 112 RF-104G. 6 aircraft delivered in 1976.

**In US Service:** 19 F-104C of 198th TFG of Puerto Rico ANG, now phased out.

**F-104A/B/D/F/G/J/S in Service Abroad:** Belgium (100), Canada (201), Denmark (40), Greece (36), Italy (330), Japan (230), Jordan (38), the Netherlands (120), Norway (22), Pakistan (16), South Africa (44), Spain (25), Taiwan (100), Turkey (90), and West Germany (867). (NB: aircraft that have crashed or been transferred must be subtracted from these totals).

**TF-104G/J in Service Abroad:** Canada (31), Denmark (10), Italy (28), Japan (20), the Netherlands (18), Norway (2), Spain (3), Taiwan (5), Turkey (7) and West Germany (137).

**RF-104G in Service Abroad:** The Netherlands (20), South Africa (12), Taiwan (20), and West Germany (112).

**Price:** $1.300 million (Unit Price for 96 F-104G to West Germany in 1959). $1.486 million (Average Unit Procurement Cost of F-104A and F-104C to USAF in 1963). $1.949 million (Average European consortium price for F-104G fully equipped in 1965). $2.074 million (Unit FMS Cost for F-104G in 1972). $3.777 million (Unit Cost for first 18 of Aeritalia F-104S to Turkey in 1974). $4.100 million (Unit Cost for balance of 40 Aeritalia F-104S to Turkey in 1975 and 1976).

# MARTIN B-57 AND GENERAL DYNAMICS RB-57F

The first military aircraft of foreign design to be chosen by the United States since 1918, the Martin B-57 was based on the original William Petter design for Britain's first jet-engined bomber, the English Electric Aviation Canberra. A twin-engined light tactical bomber with a crew of two seated in tandem, it was first produced in the United States in 1953. Eight B-57A and 67 RB-57A photo reconnaissance aircraft were built by the Martin Company of Baltimore under license from English Electric. These were followed by 202 B-57B, 38 B-57C and 68 B-57E bombers, most of which had eight wing-mounted .50 caliber machine guns, though a small number were fitted instead with four 20mm cannon in their noses. The B-57Cs had dual controls for training use, and all of the B, C and E models were capable of delivering 6,000 lbs of bombs and other air munitions, 4,000 lbs from an internal rotary weapons bay and 2,000 lbs from four wing pylons, or up to 5,000 lbs internally and 2,000 lbs underwing.

These bombers served with our Tactical Air Command from 1955 to 1969, after which they were assigned to Air National Guard units. They were recalled, however, in 1964 for combat service in Vietnam, and during the following years many were modified as reconnaissance, weather reconnaissance and electronic countermeasures aircraft, performing target identification, pathfinding and defense suppression missions alongside our force of Douglas B-66 and EB-66 Destroyers (the Air Force version of the Douglas A-3 Skywarrior, 214 of which were produced). Most of the B, C and E models of the B-57 have been reassigned to the Air National Guard and to Aerospace Defense Command, though 30 B-57Bs were transferred to Pakistan and four were supplied to South Vietnam.

A major redesign of the B-57 for strategic reconnaissance involved a substantial increase in the aircraft's wingspan from 64 to 106 feet, the use of more powerful dual-shaft J57-P-37A turbojet engines and the addition of a fuselage radome. This was the RB-57D, 20 of which were built, 14 as single-seat and 6 as two-seat aircraft. Two were transferred to Taiwan.

General Dynamics of Fort Worth also converted 21 B-57Bs and RB-57Ds to the RB-57F configuration for high-altitude reconnaissance, further increasing the wingspan to 122 feet, replacing the turbojet engines with TF33-11A turbofans, and adding two auxiliary turbojet engines in underwing pods. With U-2 and SR-71A aircraft, the RB-57F has flown reconnaissance and surveillance missions from bases in Alaska, Norway, the United Kingdom, West Germany, Spain, Turkey, Iran and Argentina. Five of these aircraft were converted to WB-57F weather reconnaissance craft.

Sixteen additional B-57Bs were converted by General Dynamics to B-57G all-weather and night interdiction aircraft, equipped with multifunction radar and a pod under the nose that houses infrared sensors, a laser rangefinder and a low-light-level TV camera. They are capable of delivering laser-guided bombs and of guiding other aircraft for the precision bombing of targets wholly obscured by darkness or cloud cover.

In addition to these 16 B-57Gs, and to our remaining 15 RB-57F strategic reconnaissance aircraft, all of which are kept in active inventory, earlier conversions of the B-57 operate today fitted with a variety of ECM and ECCM (electronic counter counter measures) equipment, including EB-57Ds with the 17th Defense Systems Evaluation Squadron (DSES), EB-57Es with the 134th DSES in Burlington, Vermont, and EB-57Bs with the 117th DSES at Forbes Air Force Base, Kansas.

Of the English Electric Canberra from which the B-57 was derived, Great Britain built 926 aircraft and Australia 49. Twelve of these serve today in Argentina, 54 in Australia, 6 in Ecuador, 4 in Ethiopia, 6 in France, 106 in India, 28 in Peru, 18 in Rhodesia, 9 in South Africa, 2 in Sweden, 191 in the United Kingdom, 30 in Venezuela, and 4 in West Germany.

**Maximum Weight:** 51,000 lbs (A), 55,000 lbs (B/C/E/G), 46,000 lbs (D), 63,000 lbs (F)

**Maximum Speed:** 582 mph

**Power Plant:** 2 x J65-W-5 turbojet (A/B/C/E/G) 2 x J57-PW-37A turbojet (D only) 2 x TF33-PW-11A turbofan and 2 x J60-P-9 turbojet (F only)

**Operational Range:** 2,100 miles (A/B/C/E/G) 3,700 miles (F only)

**Armament:** 8 x .50 cal MG wing-mounted, or 4 x 20mm cannon, wing or nose-mounted (B/C/E/G only. None on RB or WB models).

**Ordnance Capacity:** 4,000 lbs in internal weapons bay and 2,000 lbs on wing pylons, or 5,000 lbs internally and 1,000 lbs under wings.

**Manufacturer:** The Martin Company. Production completed. Conversions by General Dynamics.

**Produced:** 403 of all models, including 8 B-57A, 67 RB-57A, 202 B-57B, 38 B-57C, 20 RB-57D and 68 B-57E. Many conversions to EB-57B/D/E, to RB-57B/C/D/E, to TB-57C/E and to WB-57C. 21 conversions to RB-57F, of which some converted to WB-57F. 16 conversions to B-57G.

**Exported under FMS:** 30 B-57B

**Exported under MAP:** 2 RB-57D and 4 B-57B

**In US Service:** 20 EB-57 in Aerospace Defense Command, 25 EB-57 in Air National Guard, 15 RB-57F in Strategic Air Command, 16 B-57G in Tactical Air Command, additional WB-57s with Military Airlift Command and EB-57s with three DSES squadrons.

**In Service Abroad:** Pakistan (30 B-57B), Taiwan (2 RB-57D) and South Vietnam (4 B-57B)

# McDONNELL F-101 VOODOO

In 1951 our Strategic Air Command (SAC) ordered production of a long-range fighter interceptor that had been envisaged as a protective escort for the front-line strategic penetrating bomber of that period, the B-36. Development ensued from the twin-engined McDonnell XF-88, two prototypes of which had first flown in 1948. The production aircraft, the F-101 Voodoo, had a range of 1,700 miles and a speed at 40,000 feet of Mach 1.85 (1,220 mph). It could carry 2,700 lbs of ordnance on two wing pylons, as well as two retractable pods each mounting twelve 2.75'' spin-stabilized aerial rockets (SSAR). Mounted in its nose were either three or, with its TACAN navigational equipment removed, four M-39 20mm cannon. In 1952 the first 29 F-101A fighters were delivered not to SAC, which had in the meanwhile eliminated the requirement for a bomber escort, but to the Tactical Air Command to serve in the fighter-bomber role. With 48 additional F-101As ordered in 1953, these early aircraft equipped three TAC squadrons.

For the Air Defense Command, 478 F-101B interceptors were built, including some TF-101B trainers with full dual controls. Equipped with more powerful J57-P-55 engines and the MG-13 radar fire control system—which gives the aircraft an all-weather capability—the F-101B substitutes a rotary missile bay for the earlier 20mm nose armament, and carries in it three AIM-4D or AIM-26 Falcon air-to-air missiles. It is also a two-seat fighter, with a radar fire control officer seated in tandem behind the pilot. This provision reduces the aircraft's fuel load capacity, and consequently cuts its range to 1,550 miles.

The F-101B, which entered service in 1961, was followed by the F-101C, 47 of which were built as single-seat fighters with strengthened airframes for low-level bombing and in-flight refueling, and with a centerline fuselage hardpoint fitted to carry a one-megaton nuclear bomb. Reconnaissance versions of the Voodoo were also produced, including 36 RF-101As and 166 RF-101Cs. These aircraft eliminated all armament, substituting six cameras, two in a

fuselage well and four in an extended nose. RF-101Cs of the 363rd Tactical Reconnaissance Wing at Shaw Air Force Base, South Carolina, provided many of the photographs that identified Soviet intermediate range ballistic missile sites in Cuba in 1962. Most of the RF-101As and RF-101Cs of Tactical Air Command have been replaced today by the RF-4C Phantom II, which began entering service in 1965. Taiwan was supplied with 25 RF-101Cs, four of which remain operational with the Nationalist Chinese Air Force today.

In October of 1965 three squadrons of F-101As were converted to RF-101G standard for the Air National Guard, and in 1967 and 1968 all 47 F-101Cs were converted to RF-101H standard and assigned to Air National Guard units.

Of the F-101B aircraft, 56 were converted to carry two AIR-2A Genie air to-air missiles with nuclear warheads, and were transferred to Canada as CF-101Bs, along with 10 TF-101B trainers as CF-101Fs. The Canadian Armed Forces flew these aircraft for ten years, and in 1971 exchanged its 58 surviving Voodoos for 66 refurbished F-101Bs of our Air Defense Command, with updated electronics and other improvements. These aircraft, designated F-101F and TF-101F, make up the front line of Canada's early warning interceptor force today, though the Canadian government has recently decided on a new aircraft—the McDonnell-Douglas F-18 Hornet—to replace them.

Until 1974, 124 F-101Bs remained operational with the Aerospace Defense Command, when they began to be withdrawn and replaced by F-4 and RF-4 Phantoms. Today, 134 F-101Bs and 64 RF-101Gs and RF-101Hs make up 7 interceptor and 4 reconnaissance squadrons of the Air National Guard, including the 132nd, 136th, 178th, 116th, 123rd, 111th and 179th Fighter Interceptor Squadrons. The 111th FIS is part of the 147th Fighter Interceptor Group, which is shortly scheduled to re-equip with RF-4C Phantom aircraft and move from Ellington to Bergstrom Air Force Base, Texas, as the 147th Tactical Reconnaissance Group.

**Maximum Weight:** 46,7000 lbs.

**Maximum Speed:** 1,220 mph (Mach 1.85) at 40,000 feet. 720 mph (Mach .95) at sea level.

**Ceiling:** 52,000 feet.

**Power Plant:** 2 x J57-PW-13 (A models) 2 x J57-PW-55 (Subsequent models).

**Operational Range:** 1,700 miles (A and C). 1,550 miles (B).

**Armament:** 3 or 4 x M-39 20mm cannon in nose (A and C). 3 x AIM-4D or AIM-26 Falcon AAM and 2 x AIR-2A Genie AAM (B). None on RF models.

**Ordnance Capacity:** 2,700 lbs on two wing pylons. 1 x one-megaton nuclear bomb (C model only).

**Stores Combinations:** 2 x 2,000 lbs bomb and 2 x 12-round 2.75" SSAR pod, or 4 x 680 lb aerial mine.

**Manufacturer:** McDonnell-Douglas. Production completed in 1961.

**Produced:** 806 of all types, including 2 XF-88 prototypes, 77 F-101A, 478 F-101B, 47 F-101C, 36 RF-101A and 166 RF-101C. Conversions of F-101A/C to RF-101G/H, and of F-101B and TF-101B to CF-101B/F and F/TF-101F.

**Exported under FMS:** 17RF-101C to Taiwan, 56 F-101B to Canada as CF-101B, (1961), 56 F-101B to Canada as F-101F (1971), 10 TF-101B to Canada as CF-101F (1961), 10 TF-101B to Canada as TF-101F (1971).

**Exported under MAP:** 8 RF-101C to Taiwan.

**In US Service:** The last RF-101s of 186th Tactical Reconnaissance Squadron, Mississippi ANG, were phased out in January of 1979.

**In Service Abroad:** Canada (66 F-101F and 10 TF-101F), Taiwan (4 RF-101C).

**Price:** $1.8 million (Unit Procurement Cost for 478 F-101Bs in 1961).

In 1957 Stanley Hooker of the Camm engineering group in Bristol, England, began work on the design for a vectored-thrust aircraft engine, the direction of whose jet exhaust could be adjusted to push the aircraft up as well as forward. By 1959 he had successfully completed work on a chain drive system, powered by a pneumatic motor, which could tilt four engine exhaust nozzles at a variety of angles, forcing through them the fan and core gases from a twin-shaft turbofan engine. When the nozzles were tilted directly downward, the aircraft to which they were fitted would achieve full vertical lift, and when tilted to the rear they would allow the exhaust to push the aircraft forward in the conventional manner.

The tactical advantages of aircraft fitted with such an engine were obvious. They would substantially reduce the operational space required to mount combat air missions. Ideal for naval carrier operations, such aircraft would make more feasible the plans that have lately gained support in our Navy for small aircraft carriers weighing about 22,000 tons, far less expensive at $400 million each than the $2.2 billion Nimitz class carriers, but able to carry as many vertical lift aircraft as do the larger carriers of more conventional aircraft types. In ground operations, vertical lift aircraft could operate from spaces no larger than they occupy, expanding our combat strike capability from forward unimproved airstrips and retaining that capability from airfields damaged by enemy action.

Consequently, Stanley Hooker's design was pushed forward in development. The engine was built by Rolls Royce as the Pegasus 101, and it was adopted by the British firm of Hawker Siddeley to power the world's first VSTOL (Vertical or Short Take Off and Landing) aircraft, the P1127, six prototypes of which were built and had successfully hovered and performed vertical ascent and descent maneuvers by 1961. Within a few years a joint British, American and West German evaluation squadron was formed to test and fly the aircraft, nine more prototypes of which were built as the Kestrel FGA Mk 1. The Kestrel Squadron flew its aircraft from 1964 through 1965, and its work resulted in Royal Air Force orders for 92 GR Mk 1, Mk 1A and Mk 3 Harriers and 15 T Mk 2, Mk 2A and Mk 4 twin-seat Harrier trainers, as well as United States Marine Corps orders for 102 AV-8A Harriers and 8 TAV-8A twin-seat Harrier trainers. Deliveries of production aircraft from Hawker Siddeley began in 1969, equipping No. 1 Squadron, No. 38 Group of the Royal Air Force Strike Command. By 1974 RAF Squadrons 3, 4 and 20 in West Germany had been equipped with Harriers, as had USMC Squadrons VMA-542 and VMA-513 in Beaufort Marine Corps Air Station, South Carolina, and

VMA-231 at Cherry Point MCAS, North Carolina.

With a top speed of 737 mph (Mach .972) and an unrefuelled range of over 2,000 miles, the AV-8A Harrier can carry a normal load of 5,300 lbs and a maximum load of 7,740 lbs of mixed ordance on five fuselage and underwing hardpoints, including three 1,000 lbs bombs, two 30mm Aden gun pods each with 150 rounds, and two Matra 155 rocket pods each with nineteen 68mm SNEB rockets. In addition, it can carry two AIM-9 Sidewinder air-to-air missiles on wingtip points, and when armed only with Sidewinders for the air interceptor role it has a combat radius of 400 miles with a one-hour loiter time. It carries a fixed reconnaissance camera and can mount a belly reconnaissance pod with five more cameras. The aircraft is therefore suitable for a variety of tactical attack and reconnaissance roles.

As a ship-based multirole aircraft, the Harrier has also met expectations. In 1976 the USMC deployed some AV-8As on the Sixth Fleet's *USS Franklin D. Roosevelt* in attack, reconnaissance, limited air defense and superiority roles. Britain's Royal Navy has ordered 24 Harriers to deploy in groups of five each together with large complements of helicopters on its Invincible class light aircraft carriers, five of which are planned. Through our Navy, the Spanish Navy purchased 6 AV-8As and 2 TAV-8As in 1973, and they now deploy the aircraft, which they call the Matador, on the carrier PH-01 *Dedalo*, a former Cleveland class cruiser built in 1942 and converted as a carrier and supplied to Spain by the USN in 1973.

Improvements are meanwhile continuing on the basic aircraft. The Pegasus 101 en-

# BRITISH AEROSPACE HARRIER, AV-8A, AND McDONNELL DOUGLAS AV-8B

gine, which equipped 10 of the first 90 AV-8As delivered to the USMC, has been replaced by the Pegasus 103, whose export designation is MK 50 and whose American designation, as built by Pratt & Whitney in this country, is F402-RR-401. It has about 2,500 lbs more thrust than the original engine. In vertical lift aircraft this is crucial. The thrust required for a fully vertical liftoff is a good deal more than that for short takeoffs in an angled forward direction, consuming proportionally more fuel. Consequently, an aircraft capable of carrying a substantial load of ordnance on short takeoffs must sacrifice a portion of that load for vertical takeoffs, or else sacrifice fuel, reducing its range.

The firm of McDonnell Douglas has developed an improved Harrier, the AV-8B, which will use the F402 engine but makes extensive use of graphite-epoxy construction, a larger wing area with a longer span and somewhat less sweep, single slotted flaps and drooping ailerons. These modifications will increase the Harrier's unrefuelled range to 3,000 miles and its maximum weight from 26,000 to 29,000 lbs, and will give it a top speed of over Mach 1. But the aircraft will still be capable of greater loads—and greater ranges—on short rather than vertical takeoffs. On vertical takeoffs,

**AV-8A OF USMC**

with 8,000 lbs of fuel, it is rated for a maximum ordnance load of 6,000 lbs and a combat radius of 115 miles, while short takeoffs with the same amount of fuel will increase the ordnance load capacity to 7,800 lbs and the combat radius to 172 miles. With 9,000 lbs of fuel and 3,500 lbs of ordnance, its combat radius is dramatically increased to 748 miles. It is clear from this that the direction of further development will be not toward VSTOL but toward STOVL (Short Take Off and Vertical Landing) aircraft that will maximize the advantages of vertical lift and minimize its disadvantages.

Other improvements on the AV-8B will be the substitution of two 20mm Mk 12 cannon for the British 30mm Aden guns, the addition of an Angle Rate Bombing System and passive ECM, and the incorporation of a dual-mode television and laser target seeker linked to the pilot's Marconi-Elliott HUD (Head-Up Display) by an IBM digital computer.

The Marine Corps has planned procurement of 360 AV-8B Harriers, originally conceived as a joint production venture by McDonnell Douglas and British Aerospace Corporation, each firm producing 50 aircraft in the first production year. A number of factors have slowed progress of the AV-8B program. To date, 26 AV-8A Harriers have crashed, with the loss of 10 pilots and 24 aircraft. Most of these accidents have occurred during low-level flight training, and cannot be traced to maintenance problems or flaws in the aircraft's design. But they have helped to strengthen the Navy's case against further development of the AV-8B.

That service would prefer the Marine Corps to purchase the A-18 attack version of its F-18 Hornet, 800 of which are planned. If instead of the AV-8B the USMC purchased 360 F-18s, a total of 1,160 basically similar aircraft would be produced with identical engines and airframe, similar avionics, and a high commonality of other parts. This would considerably reduce the Navy's unit procurement cost for the F-18. As well as procuring a new attack aircraft, the USMC will also eventually have to consider adoption of the A-18 anyway, as a replacement fighter for its aging F-4 Phantom aircraft.

Defense Secretary Harold Brown, in his continuing effort to reduce the number of different aircraft types in active inventory among the services, would also prefer the USMC to take the A-18. He has delayed full-scale development of the AV-8B by fifteen months, cutting in half the Marine Corp's $198.5 million request for AV-8B development funds in Fiscal Year 1979. Two development AV-8Bs will be built with 1978 research and development funds.

Secretary Brown also recently ordered a $666 million cutback in a joint Navy and Marine Corps program of $1.45 billion for the development of a wholly new generation of VSTOL aircraft. Despite these setbacks, vertical lift aircraft continue to offer valuable capabilities. The use of VIFF (vectoring in forward flight) techniques—shifts in the directional thrust of its engine while the aircraft is in flight—have successfully jumped the Harrier into new flight paths, breaking the lock of a hostile radar or the weapons guidance and homing locks, respectively, of enemy aircraft and missiles. This high degree of maneuverability, the capacity for rapid deployment and the ability to operate from limited space would appear to assure a large role in the future for VSTOL or STOVL aircraft.

**Maximum Weight:** 26,000 lbs (A) 29,000 lbs (B)

**Maximum Speed:** A: 737 mph (Mach .972) B: 760 mph (Mach 1+)

**Ceiling:** 50,000 feet

**Power Plant:** 1 x F402-RR-401 vector-thrust turbofan engine.

**Operational Range:** 2,070 miles (A) 3,000 miles (B)

**Combat Radius:** 260 to 400 miles (A) 115 miles with VTO, or 172 to 748 miles with STO (B).

**Armament:** No fixed armament. 2 x Aden 30mm cannon in underbelly pods (A), or 2 x Mk 12 20mm cannon in pods (B). 2 x AIM-9D Sidewinder AAMs at wingtip points (A and B).

**Ordnance Capacity:** 5,300 to 7,740 lbs on 3 fuselage and 2 underwing pylons.

**Stores Combinations:** 3 x Mk 83 1,000 lb bomb and 2 x Matra 155 with 19 68mm SNEB rockets @ (A) 12 x Mk 82 500 lb Snakeye (with 8,000 lbs fuel) or 7 x Mk 82 500 lb Snakeye (with 9,000 lbs fuel) (B), plus gun pods and AIM-9 Sidewinder AAMs.

**Manufacturer:** British Aerospace Corp. BAC (AV-8A). In production. McDonnell-Douglas AV-8B now in development.

**Produced:** 241 of all types, including 6 P1127, 9 Kestrel FGA Mk 1, 92 GR Mk 1, Mk 1A and Mk 3, 15 T Mk 2, Mk 2A and Mk 4, 102 AV-8A Harrier, 8 TAV-8A Harrier, 6 AV-8A Matador, 2 TAV-8A Matador, and 1 Mk 52 demonstration aircraft. 24 FRS Sea Harrier on order for Royal Navy. 2 AV-8B built and 2 on order. USMC plans total of 360 AV-8B.

**In US Service:** 90 of 110 AV-8A and TAV-8A originally procured, in three USMC squadrons at Yuma, Arizona (VMA-513) and Cherry Point, North Carolina (VMA-231 and VMA-542), and one training squadron (VMAT-203) at Cherry Point.

**In Service Abroad:** Spain (6 AV-8A and TAV-8A) and United Kingdom (92 GR Mk 1, Mk 1A, Mk 3 and 15 T Mk 2, Mk 2A, Mk 4.

**Price:** AV-8A: $646,000 (1969 Unit Procurement Cost for 90 AV-8A to USMC). AV-8A: $4.3 million (1974 Unit Procurement Cost for 12 AV-8A to USMC). TAV-8A: $7.55 million (1974 Unit Procurement Cost for 8 TAV-8A to USMC). AV-8B: $7 million (Estimated Unit Procurement Cost for 360 AV-8B to USMC, 1977).

**Recent Transfers:** 8 AV-8A and TAV-8A to Spain through U.S. Navy in 1973 for $3.75 million @.

**Future Sales:** Argentina, Australia, Brazil, Chile, Iran, Israel, Jordan, Lebanon (prior to its civil war), Japan, Singapore, Taiwan and New Zealand have all expressed interest in the AV-8B.

One of the fastest, most versatile and powerful aircraft ever built, the F-4 Phantom can match in almost every respect the performance of any of the latest generation of combat aircraft now in production. With twin turbojet engines, it is capable of short sprint speeds as high as 1,606 mph (Mach 2.43) and can carry up to 16,000 lbs of air munitions—more than the bomb load of a World War II B-29 Superfortress. Already in active service for more than eighteen years, it is the subject of major U.S. Navy and U.S. Air Force modification and rebuilding programs that will extend the life of several hundred of its type to serve alongside newer aircraft through the 1980s.

Still in production, with more than 5,153 units built to date, the Phantom is used in greater numbers than any other aircraft in the Western world. Flown in combat in the Middle East and Southeast Asia, land-based or carrier-based, assigned to nuclear strike or tactical roles, it serves today not only with our Air Force, Navy, Marine Corps and Air National Guard but also as a front-line fighter interceptor, fighter-bomber and reconnaissance aircraft in Iran, Israel, Spain, Greece, Turkey, West Germany, the United Kingdom, Japan and South Korea, and it has recently been acquired by Egypt and Singapore as well. Phantoms also flew for several years on lease to the Royal Australian Air Force, pending delivery of F-111Cs to that country.

Development of the twin-seat Phantom as a radar-controlled fighter interceptor, with a radar intercept officer (RIO) seated in tandem behind the pilot, began in 1953. The fire control radar, guiding six AIM-7 Sparrow or four AIM-7 and four AIM-9 Sidewinder air-to-air missiles, was to be housed in the nose and a fairing for an infrared sensor mounted in a tube just beneath it. The first development aircraft, the XF4H-1, flew in May of 1958. 47 additional prototype aircraft, later designated F-4A, followed and by 1960 deliveries had begun of 649 F-4B Phantoms for the USN and USMC. Fitted with J79-GE-8 engines and the AN/APQ-72 radar, these aircraft soon equipped 29 USN squadrons. 178 would later be uprated as F-4N with improved avionics for the Navy, 44 would be converted as QF-4B supersonic target drones, and a few as DF-4B drone control aircraft.

# McDONNELL DOUGLAS F-4 PHANTOM

The Navy also fitted 12 F-4Bs with the AN/ASW-21 digital data link communications system, designated them F-4Gs, and assigned them in 1966 to USN Squadron VF-213 aboard the *USS Kitty Hawk*, from which they flew a number of combat missions over Vietnam. 46 RF-4Bs were also produced without armament in 1965 to perform photographic and electronic reconnaissance for the Marine Corps.

By May of 1963 the F-4C was in service with USAF. 583 were built. With AN/APQ-100 fire control radar, the Litton LN-12A/B inertial navigation system, GAM-83 controls and a Lear-Siegler AJB-7 bombing system, these aircraft equipped 16 of the 23 wings in Tactical Air Command. 36 were later sold to Spain as C-12 fighter-bombers, and 24 were modified as EF-4C Wild Weasel aircraft, equipped with ECM warning sensors, chaff dispensers, jamming pods and anti-radiation missiles. Some F-4Cs were delivered to the Air National Guard in January of

1972, and serve today with the Guard's 183rd Tactical Fighter Group in Springfield, Illinois. The remainder equip our 401st Tactical Fighter Wing at Torrejon, Spain, and our 81st Tactical Fighter Squadron at Spangdahlem Air Base, West Germany, as well as serving with several squadrons of the 12th Air Force based in Arizona and California.

For the Air Force, 505 unarmed RF-4C reconnaissance aircraft were built with FLIR (Forward Looking Infra Red) detection sensors, the AN/AVD-2 laser line scan camera, SLAR (Side Looking Airborne Radar) high-definition film equipment, and special panoramic cameras whose moving lens elements afford pictures with coverage from horizon to horizon. Large numbers of the RF-4C were turned over to the Air National Guard in February of 1972, today equipping 7 of its Tactical Reconnaissance Groups, but the aircraft also serves with the 10th Tactical Reconnaissance Wing, RAF Alconbury, Great Britain, the 26th TRW at Zweibrucken Air Base, Germany, and the 67th TRW at Bergstrom AFB, Texas.

The Air Force continued production with 843 F-4Ds, equipped with J79-GE-15 engines, improved avionics including a new inertial navigation and attack system, and the AN/APQ-109 radar. 18 F-4Ds were later transferred to South Korea under MAP, and 64 were sold to Iran. During the war in Southeast Asia F-4Ds and some F-4Cs served with our 5th Air Force, flying from bases at Kadena and Yokuta, Japan, and at Osan, South Korea. The F-4D now equips the 48th and 84th Tactical Fighter Wings of our 3rd Air Force based in the United Kingdom, as well as our 10th and 23rd Tactical Fighter Squadrons based in West Germany. F-4Ds have also just been delivered to the Air National Guard's 108th Tactical Fighter Group, and to the 154th TFG at Hickham AFB, Hawaii, finally phasing out of service the latter unit's F-102A Delta Dagger interceptors.

The F-4E was the first version of the Phantom to carry, along with its complement of AIM-7 and AIM-9 air-to-air missiles, an internal armament system, the M61A1 Vulcan 20mm cannon with 640 rounds. It is also equipped with TISEO (Target Identification System, Electro-Optical), a Vidicon television camera with a zoom lens to distinguish long-range targets, and with the AN/APQ-120 radar, which gives it a much-improved target intercept capability. More powerful J79-GE-17 engines have been provided, and while these increase the aircraft's weight by about 3,600 lbs they also increase its ferry range from 1,860 to 2,600 miles.

Retrofitted with leading-edge wing slats for greater maneuverability, the F-4E has been for several years the most sophisticated aircraft in our inventory. Sensibly enough, it is also the version of the Phantom that has been produced and exported in the greatest numbers. Of a total of 1,302 F-4Es produced, 295 had originally been intended for export, but to date 846 have been transferred abroad, along with 133 RF-4E multisensor reconnaissance aircraft fitted with the Honeywell AAD-5 infrared line scan camera. The 456 F-4Es that remain in active USAF inventory now equip not only 26 home-based fighter squadrons of our Tactical Air Command but, along with some F-4Ds and F-4Cs, 9 fighter squadrons of our 17th Air Force in West Germany as well.

Large numbers of the F-4E were supplied to Iran and to Israel, those to the latter country specially fitted with a solid state version of the AN/APQ-120 fire control radar. Israel now seeks a new inertial navigation and weapons delivery system for 160 of its F-4Es and its 15 RF-4Es, and has requested competing bids for the supply of the Lear-Siegler ARN-101, the Litton LW-33 and the Singer Kearfott SKN-2400 in a system compatible with existing equipment aboard these aircraft, and on the condition that 25 percent of the value of the contract be awarded in licensed production to the electronics firm of Tamam, a subsidiary of Israeli Aircraft Industries.

Further versions of the Phantom similar to the F-4E were produced in this country especially for export. The F-4F, an F-4E with modified electronics, was built for the West German Bundesluftwaffe, and 175 of these aircraft together with an additional 10 complete F-4F airframes without engines were delivered to West Germany between 1973 and 1976. For the Japanese Air Self-Defense Force, parts for another 158 F-4Es equipped with J/APR-1 and J/APR-2 tail warning radars were delivered for assembly in Japan by Mitsubishi, and these aircraft were designated F-4EJ. The F-4K was produced for Britain's Royal Navy, and the F-4M for her Royal Air Force. Both types of aircraft were fitted with Rolls Royce Spey engines and the AN/APG-59 fire control radar. The F-4K, also equipped with the AWG-10 radome, was built with a foldable nose to permit its use on Royal Navy aircraft carriers, and the first 28 F-4Ks to be delivered today equip the Royal Navy's No. 892 Squadron. The remaining 20 F-4Ks and all 118 of the F-4Ms were delivered to the Royal Air Force, the

F-4Ms fitted with AWG-12 radars and reconnaissance pods, and these aircraft fly today with No. 6 and No. 54 Groups of RAF Air Support Command in England and West Germany.

After the F-4E and its export variants, production continued with 518 F-4J aircraft for the Navy and Marine Corps. These incorporated the AN/AWG-10 pulse-doppler fire control radar and the AJB-7 bombing system, and they were built with slotted tails and a droop of 16.5 degrees in the ailerons to reduce their landing speeds. These and the Navy's original F-4Bs, including those uprated to F-4N standard, serve today in eighteen Navy and twelve Marine Corps squadrons.

Aside from the F-4N improvement program for 178 of the Navy's F-4Bs, a series of other improvement and conversion programs have been undertaken in order to enhance the capabilities and extend the service life of the Phantom, providing an increase in the overall numerical inventory of up-to-date United States combat aircraft. Over 1,200 USAF Phantoms have been retrofitted with leading-edge wing slats to improve maneuverability and turn performance, and to provide an added margin of safety in stalls. Over 600 USAF Phantoms have been refitted with the Pave Tack pod, carrying FLIR target detection and laser designator systems, or with the Westinghouse AN/ASQ-153 Pave Spike pod, which carries electro-optical target detection and laser designator systems.

At a cost of $4.5 million per aircraft, 30 of the Marine Corp's RF-4Bs will be refur-

bished to give them eight added years of service life, and will be uprated with the installation of AN/AAD-5 infrared target detection equipment, the AN/APD-10 side-looking radar, the AN/ASW-25 carrier automatic landing system and the AN/ASN-92 carrier inertial navigation system.

116 F-4Es are being converted to EF-4E standard as Wild Weasel defense suppression aircraft, fitted with the AN/APR-38 tail radar warning system and armed with RIM-66D Standard ARM, AGM-88A Harm or AGM-45A Shrike anti-radiation missiles. The first two EF-4Es were completed in 1976, and another 15 were delivered in 1977. To complete the program, 60 more EF-4Es will be delivered in 1978, and 39 in 1979. These aircraft will form four squadrons, replacing two EF-4C and two F-105G Wild Weasel squadrons.

90 of the Marine Corp's F-4Js are being rebuilt to extend their service life. Another 260 F-4Js are being converted to F-4S standard, with leading-edge slats and modified low-smoke J79-GE-10B engines. The F-4S will also incorporate the Westinghouse AN/AWG-10 weapon control system. With additional structural improvements to extend the service life of these aircraft another 10 years, the F-4S program will cost $1.9 million per aircraft. Thus, in a variety of roles the Phantom will remain in service with our own armed forces and abroad for at least another decade.

**Maximum Weight:** 57,400 lbs (A/B/C/D/J/K/M) 60,630 lbs (E/EJ/F)

**Maximum Speed:** 1,450 mph (Mach 2.2) Short sprint capability of 1,606 mph (Mach 2.43)

**Power Plant:** 2 x J79-GE-2/2A (A), J79-8 (B/C/G), J79-10 (J/N), J79-10B (S), J79-15 (D), J79)17 (E/EJ/F), 2 x Rolls Royce Spey (K/M) EJ engines built to J79-17 standard by Ishikawajima-Harima.

**Operational Range:** 1,860 miles, or 2,600 miles for E/EJ/F. Attack combat radius of 1,000 miles. Air intercept combat radius of 900 miles.

**Ceiling:** 71,000 feet.

**Key Electronics:** See text for the variety of progressive improvements.

**Armament:** 6 x AIM-7E Sparrow AAM, or 4 x AIM-7E and 4 x AIM-9D/L Sidewinder AAM. 1 x M61A1 Vulcan 20mm cannon with 640 rds (E only). No armament on DF/QF/RF models.

**EF Armament:** 2 x RIM-66D Standard, AGM-88A Harm or AGM-45A/B Shrike ARM (EF-4C/E).

**Ordnance Capacity:** 16,000 lbs, on one fuselage and four wing pylons.

**Stores Combinations:** 18 x M117 750 lb bomb, or 15 x MLU-10/B aerial mine, or 15 x LAU-3A/10A rocket pod, or 11 x Mk 83 1,000 lb bomb, or 24 x Mk 82 500 lb bomb, or 4 x AGM-12A Bullpup ASM.

**Manufacturer:** McDonnell Douglas, In production.

**Produced:** 5,153 of all types, including 47 F-4A, 649 F-4b (of which 12 converted to F-4G, 178 to F-4N, 44 to QF-4B and some to DF-4B), 46 RF-4B, 583 F-4C (of which 24 converted to EF-4C), 505 RF-4C, 843 F-4D, 1,302 F-4E (of which 116 under conversion to EF-4E), 133 RF-4E, 158 F-4EJ, 14 RF-4EJ, 185 F-4F, 52 F-4K, 118 F-4M, and 518 F-4J (of which 260 under conversion to F-4S). 1 F-4C also converted to F-4CCV R&D aircraft.

**Exported under FMS:** 1,580 aircraft, including 36 F-4C, 64 F-4D, 822 F-4E, 133 RF-4E, 158 F-4EJ, 12 RF-4EJ, 185 F-4F, 52 F-4K and 118 F-4M.

**Exported under MAP:** 18 F-4D to South Korea in 1969, and 2 RF-4EJ to Japan.

**In US Service:** Approximately 2,605 aircraft in 88 squadrons of Tactical Air Command, 18 USN and 12 USMC squadrons, and 30 squadrons of Air National Guard. Over 100 aircraft lost in stalls, and additional hundreds in combat in Southeast Asia.

**In Service Abroad:** Greece (52 F-4E and 8 RF-4E), Iran (32 F-4D, 177 F-4E and 16 RF-4E), Israel (After combat losses, 269 of 298 F-4E, and 15 RF-4E), Japan (158 F-4EJ and 14 RF-4EJ), Singapore (34 F-4E), South Korea (18 F-4D and 36 F-4E), Spain (36 F-4C, 18 F-4E and 6 RF-4E), Turkey (80 F-4E), United Kingdom (52 F-4K and 118 F-4M) and West Germany (185 F-4F and 88 RF-4E)

**USN Carrier Deployment:** F-4Js of VF-21 and VF-154 on CVW-2 *USS Ranger.* F-4Js of VF-31 and VF-103 on CVW-3 *USS Saratoga.* F-4Ns of VF-151 and VF-161 on CVW-5 *USS Midway.* F-4Ns of VF-41 and VF-84 on CVW-6 *USS America.* F-4Js of VF-33 and VF-102 on CVW-7 *USS Independence.* F-4Js of VF-31 and VMPA-333 on CVW-8 *USS Nimitz.* F-4Js of VF-114 and VF-213 on CVW-11 *USS Kitty Hawk.* F-4Ns of VF-51 and VF-111 on CVW-15 *USS Coral Sea.* F-4Js of VF-11 and VF-74 on CVW-17 *USS Forrestal.*

**Price:** F-4B: $2.191 million (1963 Unit Procurement Cost for 649 aircraft). F-4C: $1.704 million (1965 Unit Procurement Cost for 583 aircraft). F-4E: $4.108 million (1974 Unit Procurement Cost for 835 aircraft, based on production of an additional 295 aircraft for export, and on delivery of 24 aircraft that year).

**Conversion Costs:** F-4S: $1.9 million (1978 Unit Conversion Cost for 260 F-4J aircraft) RF-4B: $4.5 million (1978 unit cost to update and rebuild 30 aircraft)

**Some Major Sales:** 104 F-4EJ in parts to Japan for assembly in 1968 for $12.8 million @. 175 F-4F to West Germany in 1971 for $8 million @. 32 F-4D to Iran in 1972 for $3.31 million @. 40 F-4E to Turkey in 1972 for $6.25 million @ (16 of these delivered before the embargo in February of 1975, and the remainder after the embargo in October of 1975). 48 F-4E to Israel, during the Yom Kippur War in 1973, for $2.1 million @. 36 F-4E to Iran in 1974 for $4.166 million @. 18 F-4D, on loan to South Korea since 1972, purchased by that country in 1975 for $2.563 million @. 18 F-4E to South Korea in 1975 for $9.888 million @. 8 RF-4E to Greece in 1975 for $11.375 million @. 12 RF-4E to Iran in 1975 for $11.916 million @. 40 F-4E to Turkey under MAP in 1978 at a cost to the U.S. Government of $7.73 million @.

Known as the "Bantam Bomber" and still in production after 22 years in service, the Skyhawk was originally planned as a jet-engined successor to the A-1 Skyraider, and was produced to meet a Navy requirement for a light attack aircraft that could deliver a nuclear bomb within the Soviet Union from naval carriers brought to its perimeters. The Navy wanted an aircraft weighing no more than 30,000 lbs fully loaded, and with wings sufficiently small that they would not be required to fold for carrier operations. These specifications were met. In fact Ed Heinemann, chief engineer for what was then the Douglas Aircraft Company of El Segundo, thought he could build an aircraft weighing half the amount the Navy allowed. He almost did. Early versions of the Skyhawk, the A-4A and A-4B, weighed 7,700 lbs empty and, with 5,000 lbs of ordnance and varying amounts of fuel, from as little as 17,000 to no more than 22,000 lbs. Reaching a top speed of 676 mph, these early aircraft had a combat radius of 920 miles.

Prototypes of the A-4 flew in 1954, and 166 A-4As were subsequently built, first entering service in 1956 with USN Squadron VA-72, the Hawks. These were followed by 542 A-4Bs and 638 A-4Cs, which during the 1960s equipped 12 Marine Corps and 30 Navy squadrons, including two or three squadrons on every aircraft carrier in the fleet. Several of these squadrons flew combat missions in Southeast Asia, the best-known having been VA-113, which operated from the *USS Enterprise* in the Tonkin Gulf in 1968.

To date more than 3,024 Skyhawks have been built in progressively improved versions. While the newest versions are still in production, either for export or to equip a number of active Marine Corps attack squadrons, the Navy has withdrawn most of its Skyhawks from front-line combat service. Most recently, the *USS Ticonderoga's* VA-55, VA-76 from the *USS Independence,* and the *USS Bon Homme Richard's* VA-144 have replaced their Skyhawks with newer aircraft, leaving the A-4 in active service only with VA-59 and VA-216 aboard the *USS Hancock.* Many of the Navy's Skyhawks have been transferred to the Naval reserve or to training units, while many more have been transferred abroad. The Skyhawk remains a principal aircraft of the Israeli Air Force, and serves in increasing numbers in Southeast Asian and Latin American countries, despite our stated intent to avoid the transfer of sophisticated weapon systems to the latter part of the world.

Substantial improvements to each successive model of the Skyhawk have continued to increase its sophistication and enhance its combat capabilities. The A-4B and subsequent models were fitted with a refuel-ing probe along the aircraft's starboard side, providing it with a midair refueling capability. This and the substitution of a more powerful J65-W-16A engine greatly increased the aircraft's range. Armed with two Mk 12 20mm cannon in its wing roots, the A-4B could also be fitted with AGM-12A Bullpup air-to-ground missiles.

In addition to the 542 A-4Bs built for the USN and USMC, 30 were built for Thailand, 45 for the Argentine Air Force as A-4Ps, and 16 for the Argentine Navy as A-4Qs. For the Republic of Singapore, 32 A-4Bs armed with twin 30mm Aden cannon and 4 TA-4Bs were built under license by Lockheed Aircraft Services of Singapore, and designated A-4S and TA-4S respectively. In this country, the Lockheed Aircraft Service Company recently rebuilt 43 former USN A-4Bs, 40 of them as A-4S and 3 as twin-canopied two-seat TA-4S trainers, for delivery to Singapore in 1977. Another 45 former USN A-4Bs have been refurbished and delivered to Argentina as additional A-4Ps, and serve today with the Grupo de Ataque Halcon at Villa Mercedes. 12 more former USN A-4Bs were delivered to Chile in 1975.

The A-4C was the first Skyhawk with an all-weather capability, and many were modified for the Naval reserve as A-4Ls with improved electronics and a computerized bombing system. By adding two more underwing pylons and substituting a still more powerful J52-P-6A engine, the A-4E increased the aircraft's external ordnance capacity from 5,000 to 8,600 lbs. In addition to the 499 A-4Es built for the USN and USMC, a total of 188 aircraft have been built

# McDONNELL DOUGLAS A-4 SKYHAWK

to the same standard for Israel as A-4Hs, equipped with two 30mm DEFA cannon, each with 150 rounds, and delivered to that country in three lots, 48 in 1967, 60 in 1972, and 100 in 1974. For tactical air combat training, four of the Navy's A-4Es were converted to "Mongoose" aggressor aircraft, with flight characteristics and radar and infrared signatures similar to advanced Soviet aircraft. In addition to its 188 A-4Hs, Israel was also provided in 1973 with 43 former USMC A-4E aircraft, specially uprated to the more advanced A-4F standard.

The A-4F, with the J52-P-8A engine, was the first of the Skyhawks to appear with a humped dorsal fairing behind the cockpit to house the aircraft's additional electronic equipment. It had increased armor protection for the pilot, a zero-zero pilot ejection seat, and wing spoilers to shorten the aircraft's landing run by 1,000 feet.

Of the A-4F 146 were built for the Navy and Marine Corps, along with 146 twin-seat TA-4F trainers and 185 TA-4J trainers—the latter with simplified electronics, eliminating the external ordnance pylons, gun pod, weapons delivery computer, radar and low-altitude bombing systems. First delivered in 1966, the TA-4J is still in production. An additional 8 A-4Fs were built for Australia as A-4Gs and 10 were built for New Zealand as A-4Ks, serving today with No. 75 Squadron of the Royal New Zealand Air Force at Ohakea. These aircraft, delivered in 1966 and 1967, were equipped with the AIM-9 Sidewinder missile. Two TA-4G trainers for Australia and four TA-4K trainers for New Zealand were also built and delivered at the same time, along with six TA-4KU trainers built to the same standard for Kuwait.

In 1970 8 additional A-4Gs and 2 TA-4Gs were rebuilt from former Navy A-4F and TA-4F aircraft for delivery to Australia, where they serve with Squadron VF-805 of the Royal Australian Navy aboard *HMAS Melbourne*. In 1974, 15 former USN A-4Fs were sold to Brazil. A few additional Navy A-4Fs have been modified as EA-4Fs for EW (Electronic Warfare) training, and serve today with VAQ-33 and FEW-56.

Known as the Skyhawk II, the A-4M, which first entered service with the USMC in 1970, was equipped with the J52-P-408A engine and a braking parachute, and had an increased ammunition capacity of 200 rounds for each of its Mk 12 20mm cannon, and an increased external ordnance capacity of 9,155 lbs. Today it equips USMC Squadrons VMA-121, VMA-223 at Naha Air Base, Okinawa, VMA-224, VMA-255, VMA-324 and VMA-543 at Glenview Naval Air Station. With over 187 deliveries thus far, the A-4M is expected to continue in production for the Marine Corps at the rate of 18 aircraft per year through 1984. The Marine Corps will maintain its A-4M squadrons until that time, when it expects to receive delivery of substantial numbers of the new AV-8B and

other aircraft. All A-4Ms in service and in production are also undergoing conversion to A-4Y standard, with updated pilot HUD systems and the addition of the Hughes ARBS (Angle Rate Bombing System).

In addition to the A-4M, 36 of which have been sold to Kuwait, 116 A-4N aircraft have also been built to the same standard for Israel, with the addition of two 30mm DEFA cannon and the advanced AN/APG-53A fire control radar.

Pending deliveries of Skyhawk aircraft abroad include orders from Thailand and Greece. France, Lebanon, Peru, the Philippines, Tunisia and Zaire have also expressed interest in purchasing quantities of the aircraft.

**Maximum Weight:** 22,000 lbs (A/B). (All other models: 24,500 lbs carrier-based, or 27,420 lbs land-based).

**Maximum Speed:** 676 mph. 865 mph (E only).

**Power Plant:** 1 x J65-W-4 (A), J65-W-16A (B/C/D/P/Q/S/L), J52-P-6A (E/H), J52-P-8A (F/G/K/KU), J52-P-408A (M/N).

**Operational Range:** Combat radius of 335 miles with minimum fuel, 920 miles with maximum fuel. Ferry range of 2,055 miles.

**Ceiling:** 49,000 feet.

**Key Electronics:** AN/APX-72 IFF, Marconi-Elliott AN/AVQ-34 HUD, AN/ASN-41 navigational computer, AN/APN-153(V) radar navigation equipment, AN/ARN-84 TACAN, AN/APN-94 radar altimeter, Goodyear AN/ALE-39 chaff dispenser, Raytheon AN/ALQ-76 ECM jammer, Sanders Assoc. AN/ALQ-100/126 Deception ECM, Itek AN/ALR-45 radar warning receiver, Magnavox AN/ALR-50 launch warning receiver, Sanders Assoc. AN/ALQ-19 ECM, Schoniger Assoc. AN/ALQ-23 ECM.

**Armament:** 2 x Mk 12 20mm cannon with 200 rpg. 2 x 30mm Aden gun (S only) or 2 x 30mm DEFA cannon (H/N only).

**Ordnance Capacity:** 5,000 lbs on three external hardpoints (A/B/C/D). 8,600 lbs on five external hardpoints (E/F/H/G/K), 9,155 lbs (M/N).

**Stores Combinations:** 4 x AGM-12A Bullpup AGM, or 3 x 2,000 lb bomb, or 6 x 500 lb bomb, or 12 x 250 lb bomb and 2 x AGM-12A Bullpup AGM.

**Manufacturer:** McDonnell-Douglas. In production.

**Produced:** 3,024 of all models, including 2 XA4D-1 prototypes, 166 A-4A, 572 A-4B (of which 50 converted to A-4P, 40 to A-4S and 3 to TA-4S), 635 A-4C (some of which converted to A-4L), 4 A-4D, 499 A-4E (of which 4 converted to Mongoose, 43 to A-4F), 2 TA-4E, 146 A-4F (of which 8 converted to A-4G and some to EA-4F), 146 TA-4F (of which 2 converted to TA-4G), 8 A-4G, 2 TA-4G, 188 A-4H, 10 TA-4H, 185 TA-4J to date, 10 A-4K, 4 TA-4K, 6 TA-4KU, 223 A-4M to date (of which 187 to be converted to A-4Y), 116 A-4N, 45 A-4P, 16 A-4Q, 32 A-4S and 4 TA-4S. A minimum of 72 additional A-4M to be produced.

**Exported under FMS:** 680 of all models. (48 more on order).

**Exported under MAP:** None to date.

**In US Service:** Approximately 566 aircraft, including 42 A-4F in 3 USN squadrons, 243 A-4E, a-4F and A-4m in 15 USMC squadrons, 48 A-4E and A-4F in two Naval Air Reserve squadrons, and 233 TA-4F and TA-4J in 14 Naval Air and Marine Air Reserve training squadrons.

**In Service Abroad:** Argentina (95 A-4P and 16 A-4Q), Australia (16 A-4G and 4 TA-4G), Brazil (15 A-4F), Chile (12 A-4B), Israel (43 A-4F, 188 A-4H, 10 TA-4H, and 116 A--4N), Kuwait (36 A-4M and 6 TA-4KU), New Zealand (10 A-4K and 4 TA-4K), Thailand (30 A-4B), and Singapore (72 A-4S and 7 TA-4S).

**Price:** $6.28 million (1978 Unit Procurement Cost for 18 A-4M for USMC). $4.176 million (1977 Unit Procurement Cost for 21 A-4M for USMC).

**Recent Transfers:** 36 A-4N to Israel in 1973 for $3.311 million@. 36 A-4M to Kuwait in 1974 for $6.944 million@.

# McDONNELL DOUGLAS F-15 EAGLE

This is probably the most sophisticated combat aircraft yet designed. Powered by two Pratt & Whitney F100 engines, it can easily reach speeds of Mach 2.54 (1,676 mph). In the air interceptor role, with four AIM-7F Sparrow air-to-air missiles, three external fuel tanks and two additional FAST Pack conformal fuel pallets now being specially built for the F-15 to extend its range, the aircraft can carry a total of 31,376 lbs of fuel, giving it a maximum potential range of 3,362 miles, or a maximum combat radius of 1,681 miles. Its peak altitude is 103,000 feet, and when an early F-15 first climbed to 98,425 feet (more than 18 miles above the earth's surface) in just 3 minutes and 43 seconds, it broke 8 world time-to-climb records including, by more than 36 seconds, the previous record held for that height by the Soviet MiG-25.

Since that time the E-266M (Modfikatsirovanny) version of the MiG-25 has reclaimed three of these records, but in several other respects the Eagle's performance is unmatched. At combat weight with half its internal fuel (about 5,572 lbs), the aircraft's powerful turbofan engines, each with 26,000 lbs of thrust, give it a thrust-to-weight ratio of 4.1 to 1, the highest ratio for any aircraft in the world. As a result, the Eagle can pull a turn of more than 14 degrees per second, as compared with a maximum of 11 degrees per second in the F-5E, and during that turn it can sustain gravitational forces of more than five times its own weight (5 g) without losing airspeed. On full afterburner at 15,000 feet, it will accept forces of more than 7 g while at the same time maintaining an airspeed of 460 mph. This makes it the most maneuverable aircraft flying, able to climb faster and turn more sharply than any other, and giving the pilot who flies it "a distinct edge," according to General Robert Dixon, head of USAF's Tactical Air Command. "There is no air superiority fighter in existence," he added, "that can match its combat capability."

The F-15 is both a fighter interceptor and a fighter-bomber. Mounting a multi-barreled General Electric M61A1 Vulcan 20mm cannon, which fires at variable rates of from 4,000 to 6,000 rounds per minute, it can fly an air interceptor mission with a combat radius of just under 600 miles on internal fuel alone (about 11,146 lbs), carrying with it four each of the latest AIM-9L infrared homing Sidewinder and AIM-7F Sparrow air-to-air missiles. By adding two FAST Pack conformal fuel pallets, which add another 8,800 lbs of fuel, it can carry the same load of ordnance to an increased combat radius of 1,068 miles. For mixed air-to-air and air-to-ground missions, it can retain its Spar-

row missiles and 950 rounds of 20mm ammunition for its gun, while also carrying a variety of alternate bomb loads for the same distances. These loads include eighteen Mk 82 560-lb Snakeye demolition bombs, or three Mk 84 2,054-lb demolition bombs, or nine BLU-27/B fire bombs, each with 790 lbs (100 gallons) of Napalm or fifteen CBU-52/B 680-lb anti-personnel fragmentation bomblet dispensers.

For an increased combat radius of 1,209 miles in the fighter-bomber role, the F-15 can exchange its FAST Pack fuel pallets for three external fuel tanks, giving it a total of 22,576 lbs of fuel, the weight of which somewhat reduces the ordnance it could carry. But its load could still include its 20mm ammunition, its four Sparrow missiles, two ECM (Electronic Counter Measures) pods to jam the homing mechanisms of hostile air defense missiles, along with three 2,276-lb Mk 84 electro-optically guided precision bombs, or instead of those bombs 7,000 lbs of any other type of bomb previously mentioned.

The heart of the Eagle's fire control system is the Hughes AN/APG-63 fire control radar, which has a target detection range of more than 100 miles and has been described by Air Force General John Vogt as "a decade ahead of anything else." In combat simulations with the F-4 Phantom in May, 1974, the F-15's radar was able to detect, identify and lock on to Phantoms flying in ground clutter at altitudes of no more than 50 feet off the ground, and in 46 out of 47 simulated engagements it was able successfully to intercept these targets with a theoretical missile launch.

As a result of the recent joint Air Force and Navy AIMVAL (Air Intercept Missile Evaluation) and ACEVAL (Air Combat Evaluation) exercises, more than 20 improvements are planned for the AN/APG-63 fire control radar system, in order to provide better missile and gun shoot cues on the pilot's HUD (Head Up Display), enhance the radar's vertical scanning capability, and endow the system with the ability to reacquire targets while at the same time remaining in an automatic scanning mode. The pilot will be given an armament select switch, with which he may choose any one of three variable radar scanning modes most appropriate for the weapon he intends to use. For the M61A1 Vulcan 20mm cannon the radar will operate at a range scale of 10 miles, at which distance it automatically acquires the target, displaying elevation and azimuth on the HUD field of view. For the AIM-9L Sidewinder, a short-range missile, the radar will search at the normal range of 20 miles at medium PRF (Pulse Repetition Frequency), 60 degrees of vertical scan in azimuth, and four horizontal bars of elevation. For the medium-range AIM-7F Sparrow missile, the radar would extend its

search range to 40 miles at high PRF, with 30 degrees of scan and four bars of elevation. While high PRF is desirable to acquire and determine the speed and bearing of targets at longer ranges, it somewhat reduces the radar's "look-down" ability to distinguish low-flying targets from ground clutter.

An AIM-9L boresight switch will also be provided, permitting the pilot to fire this missile at a short-range target already acquired, while the radar simultaneously continues to illuminate a target at longer range for the AIM-7F. By June of 1978, all of these improvements, standard on F-15s now in production, will have been retrofitted to aircraft delivered earlier.

Subsequent improvements will include the addition of a programmable 24,000 word solid-state memory computer and signal processor, to increase the flexibility of the F-15's radar processing and to "sharpen" its radar Doppler beam, approximating a condition known to specialists as "synthetic aperture radar." This is the use of data processing to synthetically project a larger radar antenna than in fact exists on the aircraft. While that cannot increase the radar's range, which is already impressive enough, it does substantially improve its accuracy of azimuth and range resolution.

The F-15 now carries the Northrop Defense Systems AN/ALQ-135 (V) countermeasures set which, unlike the Westinghouse AN/ALQ-119 and AN/ALQ-131 TJS (Tactical Jamming System) pods, is internally installed on the aircraft. In a $48 million program for improving the F-15's airborne and ground support equipment a radar warning receiver, tail warning set and additional internal countermeasures equipment will be installed on all F-15 aircraft, including the AN/ALR-56 threat warning system, a warning receiver which will control all the F-15's countermeasures activities. Produced by the Loral Corporation, the AN/ALR-56 is the first standard production item of USAF countermeasures equipment involving the concept of countermeasures power management, a technique for automatically determining the priority of threats from hostile aircraft or ground air defense artillery and missile sites, and for automatically assigning and concentrating available jammer power on each hostile radar or weapon guidance system according to the immediacy of its threat.

The AN/ALR-56 and its generation of radar warning receivers, such as the Dalmo-Victor AN/ALR-62 for the F-111 aircraft and Itek Corporation's AN/ALR-69 for the F-4, F-16, A-7 and A-10, represent a substantial advance in technology over the early radar warning receivers used on our aircraft in Vietnam. Those systems, such as the Applied Technology AN/APR-25/26 and

AN/APR-36/37, utilized hard-wired analog processors, and displayed their information on small cathode ray tubes. Threats would appear on the tubes as a series of strobe lines, their points of departure indicating the position of the radar site relative to the aircraft's bearing.

The new generation of radar warning system, the first of which was the AN/ALR-46, substitutes digital for analog data processing, and it displays its information in alphanumerics. Thus, recognizable characteristics of missile guidance radars such as the Soviet SAM-2, SAM-3 and SAM-4 are interpreted, together with their emission points, and displayed on the pilot's screen with appropriate suffix numerals to identify them. Missile site locations appear on these screens with circles around them, and once a missile is launched the circle begins to blink steadily. Aircraft are identified by an aircraft symbol, antiaircraft artillery by the letter A, and unidentifiable threats by the letter U. The most immediate threat is enclosed by a diamond. In response to these threats the AN/ALR-56 then allocates the jamming power generated by the F-15's ICS (Internal Countermeasures System), the AN/ALQ-135, drowning out or distorting command guidance signals to hostile missiles and other weapons.

The AN/ALQ-135 costs $376,500, a good deal less than the externally-mounted AN/ALQ-131 TJS pod. The latter, originally estimated at approximately $350,000 per unit, is being procured by USAF in 1978 for $650,000 each. Even the cost of the AN/ALQ-119 TJS pod, which when paired with the AN/ALR-69 radar threat warning receiver is called the Compass Tie system, has risen to $400,000 per unit.

After one year of pilot training at Luke AFB, Arizona, production F-15s first entered USAF service on 9 January 1976 to equip the 27th, 71st and 94th Tactical Fighter Squadrons, 1st Tactical Fighter Wing, at Langley AFB, Virginia. By July of 1978, the 49th TFW at Holloman ARB, New Mexico, will have completed conversion from the F-4 to the F-15. In addition to the 72 aircraft to be stationed at Holloman by July and the 72 F-15s already at Langley, a further 79 F-15s are now stationed at Bitburg Air Base, West Germany, with the 36th TFW. By October of 1978 another 18 F-15s will be stationed at Soesterberg Air Base, West Germany, and by December of 1978 the 32nd Tactical Fighter Squadron will have been deployed with 18 F-15s at Camp New Amsterdam, the Netherlands. By January of 1979 an additional wing of 54 F-15s is scheduled to be operational at Eglin AFB, Florida.

In all, USAF plans procurement of 729 F-15s, though production may be increased to meet requirements for strengthening NATO air defenses. A two-seat, Wild Weasel version of the aircraft is also under consid-

eration for ground attack and defense suppression missions.

The first F-15s to enter service abroad, on 10 December 1976, were 5 aircraft out of a total order of 25 for the Israeli Air Force. That country has requested another 25 F-15s, and will receive at least 15 of these as part of an arms transfer package worked out in February of 1978 by President Carter. The package will include 75 of the new General Dynamics F-16 for Israel, out of a total of 250 requested, 50 F-5Es for Egypt, out of a total of 200 requested by President Sadat, and 60 F-15s for Saudi Arabia. The decision to sell to Saudi Arabia an aircraft of the F-15's sophistication has caused a great deal of controversy since its announcement. It is clear to most observers that such an aircraft in Saudi hands will change the balance of power in the Middle East, as well as introduce the F-15 to a wholly new region of the world, the Indian Ocean, and that therefore it contradicts one of the guidelines President Carter laid down in his arms control statement of May, 1977, when he said: "The United States will not be the first supplier to introduce into a region newly-developed, advanced weapons systems which would create a new or significantly higher combat capability."

It appeared that Carter had introduced the new arms proposal in order to fulfill promises of arms made to the three heads of state involved, in return for which, it has been surmised, the President hoped to ensure that Saudi Arabia would continue to make oil available to the West, use her predominant influence in OPEC to keep the price of oil from rising, and continue to lend her financial support to Egypt. The Saudis, in fact, were to pay for the F-5Es reserved for Egypt, but later postponed.

The Israelis have reacted to the Saudi sale with alarm. Israeli Foreign Minister Moshe Dayan has called it "a serious threat to Israel's security." They fear that such a strengthening of the Saudi air force will make it even more imperative to retain Israeli air bases at Eilat, Yamit and Sharm-el-Sheikh, some of the very occupied zones they have been asked to leave, their reluctance to do so having already become one of the major obstacles in the peace negotiations. They fear that, in the event of a new war, the Saudis could transfer their F-15s to Arab confrontation states engaged in active fighting with Israel, and have indicated, in fact, that the danger of their possible use or transfer for use in such a war would require the Israeli Air Force to take pre-emptive strikes against these aircraft and their bases even if the Saudis had not yet committed themselves to the conflict.

Israeli Prime Minister Menachem Begin, calling the F-15 "the latest aircraft on earth," asked Washington to "reappraise'' its decision. He and other critics were met with a number of assurances. President Carter said that ''Saudi Arabia has never had any active aggression with Israel,'' although the Israelis, of course, recall that the Saudis supported Egypt in a past war with their country. Carter also pointed out that the F-15s would not be delivered to the Saudis until 1981, as though the years before that time were the only period during which Israel need be concerned with her security.

Administration officials added that Saudi F-15s would not be transferred to another Arab air force in the event of war. The aircraft, they asserted, required many hours of specialized training in expensive ground simulators and a formidable amount of ground support equipment for effective operations. In any case, they concluded, the Saudis would not be able to train other Arab pilots on the F-15 without detection by Israel and the United States.

While all these assertions are correct, the transfer of F-15s from the Saudi Air Force to another in time of war remains entirely feasible. In the Saudi sale, for $2.5 billion, just over $1.620 billion will pay for the aircraft themselves which, with administrative fees and a surcharge for a portion of the original F-15 research and development costs, have a Foreign Military Sales price of $27 million each. The remaining $880 million in the sale is for ground simulators, produced by Goodyear Aerospace Corporation, all the support equipment required, a variety of air munitions compatible with the aircraft, and an accelerated training program for Saudi pilots in the United States.

The simulators could certainly be used to train pilots from other Arab countries in Saudi Arabia. While this activity would certainly be detected, it remains unclear what Israel could do about it, or what the United States *would* do about it. Nor, in order to transfer the F-15 to another Arab air force, would the array of ground support equipment have to be transferred to other Arab air bases. It would suffice to allow Jordanian, Egyptian or Syrian pilots to fly the F-15 from existing Saudi bases, where all the support equipment would be maintained.

Certainly, from Saudi bases the F-15 would have no trouble reaching Israel. Tabuq, one of three bases being completed along the northwestern Saudi border with Jordan, is just 300 miles from Jerusalem and Tel Aviv, only 125 miles (a ten-minute flight) from Eilat on the Gulf of Aqaba, and 140 miles from Sharm-el-Sheikh at the Straits of Tiran. Even if the aircraft were operated from bases near Riyadh, 800 miles to the southeast, that is still within easy striking distance.

But in truth, Israeli territory is within easy striking distance even for the F-5E, which may soon be added to the Egyptian arsenal

and based at Cairo, only 200 miles from Tel Aviv, or at forward Egyptian air bases even nearer. For that matter, Israel is well within range of existing Egyptian MiG-23s and MiG-27s, Sukhoi Su-7s, Mirage IIIEs and Tupolev TU-16s, Jordanian F-5As and F-104As, Syrian Mig-23s, SU-7s, MiG-17s and F-86Fs, Iraqi MiG-21s, MiG-23Bs and Hawker Hunter bombers, Iranian F-4Es and F-5Es, and BAC Lighting bombers and F-5Es already in the Saudi inventory.

When referring to the Saudi sale, administration officials have been careful to talk of the F-15 as an ''air-to-air fighter,'' as though it could pose a threat to Israel only as a fighter-bomber. As we have seen, it is a formidable fighter-bomber, but as we have also seen, the Israelis are much accustomed to living with this kind of threat. What concerns Israel is the other of this aircraft's dual capabilities, precisely the capability the Carter administration concedes it has, as an ''air-to-air fighter.''

In the air interceptor role and in the hands of an Arab pilot at war with Israel, the F-15 becomes a new form of threat not present in that region before. With its speed and agility, its sophisticated fire control radar and air-to-air ordnance, it is capable of outfighting and destroying in the air most other Israeli aircraft, which could not adequately be defended by Israel's own limited force of F-15s. For the first time, Israel's air supremacy in the Middle East, the key factor in her ability to conduct a successful defense of her territory, would be seriously challenged.

President Carter adhered to the letter if not the spirit of his earlier statement on arms control when he said, ''We are not introducing new weapons in the Middle East. F-15s are already being delivered into the Middle East.'' The F-15s he meant are Israel's own, delivered to her by an agreement reached in 1975. This helped to sustain an already established factor in the Middle Eastern balance of power: Israel's air superiority. To deliver F-15s to a second country in the Middle East and challenge that *status quo* departs both from the letter *and* the spirit of Carter's original intent, for it results in a very large change in the existing balance of power.

Additionally, Carter contradicts his policy in another way. For he is avoiding the introduction of new weapons into a region, as promised, only when he refers to the region of the Middle East. Through Saudi Arabia, F-15s will be introduced to another region, that of the Indian Ocean and Horn of Africa, far from the reach of Israeli F-15s.

Operating from Israel's southernmost air base at Sharm-el-Sheikh, Israeli F-15s would just be able to reach the Ethiopian city of Asmara. Addis Ababa, a good deal further south, would be well out of their range. From bases at Jiddah, however, Saudi

F-15s could reach not only Addis Ababa but most of the Ogaden region where Ethiopian forces, with Cuban and Soviet assistance, have been fighting with Ogaden separatist insurgents supported by Somalia. From the Saudi base of Sabya most of Somalia as well, including its capital city Mogadishu, could be reached in the aircraft. From positions along the Saudi Arabian border with Oman the F-15 could even reach Karachi and Bombay. Clearly the aircraft will have been introduced into a new region that daily grows in its strategic implications.

In defense of the Saudi sale, administration officials have implied that President Ford had committed the United States to providing the Saudis with ''the aircraft of their choice,'' and that the Saudis had subsequently settled on the F-15. When he visited Saudi Arabia in January of 1978, President Carter promised Crown Prince Fahd that he would recommend the sale, and on his return indicated that he felt he could not refuse them the aircraft, because by that time they had come to regard its sale as a test of United States friendship.

No doubt the Saudis have regarded this sale as a test of our friendship, ever since the F-15 was promised to them. But in fact they did not select the aircraft. The United States did. In May of 1977, when Crown Prince Fahd visited the United States, he had, according to *The New York Times,* ''no shopping list.'' When asked about arms he listed several aircraft of interest, but only the F-15 was offered by the Air Force. Throughout the summer of 1977 the Pentagon continued quietly urging the Carter administration to choose the F-15 for the Saudis. In October of that year Defense Secretary Harold Brown formally recommended its sale. At that point, however, the President still had not made up his mind, and was considering an offer instead of the ''less-advanced'' F-16, an aircraft whose transfer to the Saudis would not have affected the balance of power in the Middle East.

As a last reassurance to the Israelis, President Carter declared, ''Our commitment to Israel's security has been and remains firm,'' although in presenting the combination of aircraft sales to Israel, Egypt and Saudi Arabia he made it clear that Congress was expected to regard all three sales as a single ''package,'' and let it be known that if the Saudi sale were disapproved, then the sale of aircraft to Israel might have to be ''reconsidered.'' This threat to deny aircraft to Israel appeared to be gambling with her security, or at the very least attempting to pass the responsibility for it to Congress, and has thus brought into question how firm the President's commitment to Israel's security really is.

The reason the administration chose the F-15 for the Saudis over other available aircraft lay in the urgency of F-15 procurement for our own Air Force, the rising costs of the F-15 program, and the Pentagon's desire to offset those costs by increased production which would inevitably involve foreign sales.

The F-15 is not without its problems. Its engines are so powerful that pilots tend to get carried away and push the aircraft to its limits. This consumes precious fuel too rapidly, and dramatically reduces the F-15's operational range. As a result, the Air Force has instituted the PEP 2000 program to increase the aircraft's fuel capacity by installing two detachable underwing fuel pallets called FAST (Fuel and Sensor, Tactical) Packs, specially shaped to conform with the F-15's airframe design so as not to create a drag and affect its aerodynamic performance. This program will cost $160 million, including $12.2 million to retrofit FAST Packs on F-15s already delivered.

There has also been trouble with the F100 engine. Due to obstruction by metallic debris, its fuel nozzle would stick in the open position, burning a hole through an engine vane and damaging turbine blades. Some of the blades themselves resonated at the same frequency as the engine, and would crack under the consequent stress. The digital engine electronic control, used to fine-trim the engine at intermediate and higher power, would shut itself off because it was not being effectively cooled, as planned, by the flow of fuel, which itself became too hot. The result was engine overspeed and turbine blade failure, which accounted for three accidents in the F-15 from July through September of 1977, each of which cost more than $200,000 in repairs.

A $50 million program is underway in 1978 to correct these deficiencies, adding a strainer to engine fuel nozzles to clear them of metallic debris, developing procedures to test and discard turbine blades resonating at the wrong frequencies, installing more reliable clock oscillators, developing a thicker turbine case, and developing either an engine overspeed control, that will automatically reduce the flow of fuel when overspeed is sensed, or a system to bypass the heat exchanger and engine electronic control, by taking fuel directly from the boost stage of the main fuel pump. There is also a continuing $4 million engine diagnostic program scheduled for Fiscal Year 1979.

Finally, there have been the inevitable contract cost overruns, $57 million worth in the past three years. These costs, together with the costs of the PEP 2000 and engine repair programs, raise by $370,000 the unit program cost for each F-15 in our Air Force, from $17.960 million to $18.330 million per aircraft.

In 1976, the unit procurement cost of an F-15, fully-equipped but without a share of research and development costs or the costs of spares, was $12.768 million, based on the purchase of 132 aircraft. In 1977 we purchased 108 F-15s at a unit procurement cost of $13.181 million. We planned to purchase another 108 of the aircraft in 1978 at a unit procurement cost of $15.899 million, but Congress would not vote the additional funds required. As a result, we reduced the 1978 procurement to 78 aircraft. A consequence of this, however, was that the unit procurement cost shot up to $17.367 million.

Therefore, while inflation, cost overruns, design deficiencies and programs to correct them drive up the base cost of an F-15, they are plainly not the only forces at work in determining its final cost. The number of aircraft produced matters too. As we have seen, the higher the production run, the lower the unit cost. In order, with limited funds, to acquire the number of F-15s we need, we must do all we can to reduce their unit cost. In the case of this aircraft it is already clear that this will mean producing far more F-15s than our Air Force plans for itself. As one Air Force colonel put it, "The F-15 has a cost problem, and to a degree it makes sense to amortize the overrun with a big sale to the Saudis."

It makes so much sense that the Air Force is doing all it can to help McDonnell Douglas sell the F-15 abroad. Japan has agreed to take 100 of the aircraft over the next six years at a current cost of about $27.480 million each, importing some, assembling others from kits, and coproducing the remainder under a license obtained by Mitsubishi. This will include the acquisition of the first 23 F-15s for Japan in Fiscal Year 1978. McDonnell Douglas have had expressions of interest from Australia, West Germany, even France, and anticipate an export

for a total of about 400 F-15s. They will all have to be sold in order to keep the goal of our own requirements within reach.

As it is, the Air Force is unhappy with the reduced 1978 domestic procurement program, which will make our own F-15s available too slowly to meet force expansion schedules in our effort to prepare for an Armageddon on the battlefields of NATO. Air Force procurement of the F-15 has already been deferred four times, and USAF officials estimate that by 1980 we will have 190 less F-15s than had originally been planned for completion by that time. Without the Saudi sale unit costs would rise even further, and our own procurement schedule would consequently fall even further behind.

The Saudi F-15 episode has perhaps been useful to the Carter administration in clarifying the conflicts between economic fact and the President's desire, under current practices and regulations, to control the proliferation of arms. At the same time, it illustrates a growing conflict between this country's very real need to build alliances with the Arab countries and Israel's very real need to depend upon us for her security.

**Maximum Air Interceptor Weight:** 64,191 lbs (with three external fuel tanks and 2 FAST Pack fuel pallets, 4 x AIM-7F and 950 rds 20mm ammo).

**Maximum Ground Attack Weight:** 61,351 lbs (with 2 x FAST Pack fuel pallet, 4 x AIM-7F, 950 rds 20mm ammo, 2 x ECM Pod and 9,558 lbs bombs).

**Air Interceptor Takeoff Weight:** 40,113 lbs (with 4 x AIM-7F and 950 rds 20mm ammo), or 40,893 lbs (with addition of 4 x AIM-9L).

**Air Interceptor Takeoff Weight:** 34,540 lbs (half internal fuel, AIM-7F and 20mm ammo only).

**Fuel Capacity:** 11,146 lbs (internal), or 19,946 lbs (with 2 x FAST Pack fuel pallet), or 22,576 lbs (with 3 x external fuel tank), or 31,376 lbs (with 3 x external tank and 2 x FAST Pack).

**Maximum Speed:** 1,676 mph (Mach 2.54)

**Powered by:** 2 x Pratt & Whitney F100 turbofan engines, each with 26,000 lbs thrust.

**Maximum Air Interceptor Range:** 3,362 miles, or combat radius of 1,681 miles (with 31,376 lbs fuel, 4 x AIM-7F and 950 rds 20mm ammo).

**Normal Air Interceptor Range:** 2,137 miles, or combat radius of 1,068 miles (19,946 lbs fuel, 4 x AIM-7F, 4 x AIM-9L and 950 rds 20mm ammo).

**Maximum Ground Attack Range:** 2,419 miles, or combat radius of 1,209 miles (22,576 lbs fuel, 4 x AIM-7F, 950 rds 20mm ammo and 7,000 lbs bombs).

**Normal Ground Attack Range:** 2,137 miles, or combat radius of 1,068 miles (19,946 lbs fuel, 4 x AIM-7F, 950 rds 20mm ammo and 10,508 lbs bombs).

**Key Electronics:** Hughes AN/APG-63 fire control radar/Loral AN/ALR-56 threat warning system/Northrop AN/ALQ-135(V) ICS, Magnavox AN/ALQ-108 IFF and launch warning system/IBM 4-Pi Central Computer/Cincinatti Electronics AN/AAR-38 infrared warning system/Litton AN/ASN-109 Inertial Navigation Sensor.

**Ceiling:** 103,000 feet.

**Armament:** 1 x GE M61A1 Vulcan 20mm cannon with 950 rds.

**Air Interceptor Stores:** 4 x AIM-7F Sparrow and 4 x AIM-9E or AIM-9L Sidewinder.

**Maximum Ordnance Capacity:** 12,000 lbs (internal fuel only, for range of 1,194 miles, or combat radius of 597 miles.

**Ground Attack Stores Combinations:** 18 x Mk 82 560 lb Snakeye bomb, or 9 x BLU-27/B fire bomb, or 15 x CBU-52/B bomb dispenser, or 12 x CBU-24B/B bomb dispenser, or 9 x CBU-42/A bomb dispenser, or 18 x Mk 20 Rockeye, or 3 x Mk 84 laser guided, infra-red guided or electro-optically guided bomb

**Manufacturer:** McDonnell Douglas. In production.

**Produced:** Approximately 160 aircraft to date.

**Exported under FMS:** 25.

**In US Service:** 600 of 729 planned for USAF had been delivered by the summer of 1981.

**In Service Abroad:** Israel (25, with 40 more on order), and Japan (2, with 98 more on order).

**Price:** $17.367 million (1978 Unit Procurement Cost for 78 aircraft to USAF). $13.181 million (1977 Unit Procurement Cost for 108 aircraft to USAF). $18.330 million (1978 Unit Procurement Cost for F-15 with costs of PEP 2000 and F100 engine repair programs added). $24 million (1975 unit FMS price for 25 aircraft sold to Israel). $27.48 million (1978 unit FMS price for first 23 of 100 aircraft sold to Japan).

**Deliveries Pending:** Israel (40, including 15 ordered in February 1978 and 25 ordered in November 1978), Japan (98 F-15CJ and F-15DJ from coproduction by Mitsubishi, with deliveries through 1987), and Saudi Arabia (60 F-15 and TF-15, ordered in February 1980, with delivery by the end of 1982).

**Future Sales:** Australia, France and West Germany have expressed interest.

# NORTH AMERICAN F-86 SABRE

Produced in larger quantities than any other aircraft since the end of World War II, the F-86 Sabre was the pride of the United States Air Force during the Korean War, and the front-line interceptor in most NATO and SEATO countries during the 1950s. Produced under license in Australia, Canada, Italy and Japan, it has also been heavily traded and retransferred throughout the world, and continues to serve today in no less than 34 countries.

A swept-wing version of the Navy's straight-winged FJ-1 Fury, the Sabre first flew in 1947, and entered service with USAF in 1949. Together with 3 prototype XP-86 fighters and 33 F-86A1 straight-winged fighters, redesignated FJ-1 Fury, 521 F-86A and 2 F-86C aircraft were produced by North American Aviation through 1950. The 33 Furies entered service with USN Squadron VF-5A, and were the first Navy jet aircraft to complete an operational tour at sea. These early versions were armed with six M-3 .50 Caliber machine guns, each with 267 rounds, mounted forward on either side of the aircraft's nose. They could also carry eight 5'' rockets or two 1,000 lb bombs.

The first all-weather version of the Sabre, the F-86D, was fitted with an engine afterburner and a nose-mounted radome. For the machine guns on earlier models it substituted a retractable pack of 24 2.75'' rockets, and it was one of the first combat aircraft to employ radar as an aid to target acquisition, together with head-on combat tactics. Of the 2,504 F-86Ds produced by North American, 981 were later converted to F-86L standard with improved avionics for compatibility with our SAGE (Semi-Automatic Ground Environment) defense system. 457 F-86Ds were transferred under MAP to eight countries in Europe and the Far East, and 20 F-86Ls were supplied to Thailand.

Subsequent production by North American included 571 FJ-2, FJ-3 and FJ-4 Furies, all of them by this time with swept wings, for the USN and USMC, and 336 F-86E and 2,254 F-86F aircraft for USAF and 13 air forces abroad. The E and F models of the Sabre were favorites with our pilots in Korea. Though unable to climb as rapidly or to as high an altitude as the Soviet MiG-15, they were rugged and versatile, and quickly established their superior maneuverability, in the hands of a good pilot, with a kill ratio of 7 to 3 against the Soviet aircraft. By the war's end, Sabres had shot down a total of 814 enemy aircraft. The F-86 was the favorite of other pilots who fought in Korea, too. No 2 Squadron of the South African Air Forces, attached to the United States 12th Fighter Interceptor Wing in Korea, was equipped by March of 1953 with F-86Fs,

and by the end of that year had flown 1,457 sorties in the aircraft. As a result of their familiarity with the Sabre, the South Africans subsequently ordered a large quantity of the aircraft for their own Air Forces.

North American followed with production of 473 F-86H models, 60 of them armed with four M39 20mm aircraft cannon, each with 132 rounds, and 120 F-86Ks armed with four M24A1 20mm cannon and capable, also, of carrying the early AIM-9B Sidewinder air-to-air missile. Specially built for NATO, the F-86K had a simpler fire control system than the D model, but retained the AN/APG-37 radar. With a climb rate of 12,000 feet per minute, it reached a top speed of 693 mph, slightly faster than some of the earlier models. 60 of these aircraft were supplied to Norway and the other 60 to the Netherlands, which later transferred all of its Sabres to Turkey.

In Italy, 221 additional F-86Ks were produced under license by Fiat, for delivery to the Italian Air Force, France, West Germany, the Netherlands and Norway. In Japan, Mitsubishi produced 300 F-86F aircraft under license, and converted 38 of them to RF-86F reconnaissance aircraft for the Japanese, South Korean and Yugoslavian air forces. In Australia the Commonwealth Aircraft Corporation undertook licensed production of 111 Sabres, designated CA-27, and fitted with Rolls-Royce Avon engines and two 30mm Aden cannon, each with 150 rounds. First entering service with the Royal Australian Air Force in 1951, these Sabres have since been partially replaced by Mirage IIIs. 16 have been transferred to Malaysia and another 16 to Indonesia.

In Canada, between 1950 and 1958, a total of 1,815 Sabres were produced by Canadair to various standards, including Mk 2, Mk 4, CL-13 Mk 5 and CL-13 Mk 6, the last 655 aircraft with Orenda turbojet engines. Some of this production was undertaken for the Royal Canadian Air Force, some for export, including 90 Mk 6 to South Africa and 125 Mk 2 and Mk 4 to Yugoslavia, and some for the United States, including deliveries to USAF.

The Sabres whose history has been most interesting were those supplied to the Federal Republic of Germany, which received 88 F-86Ks produced in Italy by Fiat, 55 F-86Ks built by North American, and 330 Canadair Mk 5 and Mk 6. They have had an extraordinary career. As the Bundesluftwaffe rearmed itself in the 1960s with the F-104 Starfighter, 50 of the old Canadair Mk 6 Sabres were transferred to Portugal, which subsequently used them in Angola and Mozambique.

Through the offices of the arms brokers Merex A.G. of Bonn, in cooperation with the firm of Interarms owned by Samuel Cummings, 74 of the Bundesluftwaffe's F-86Ks, which originally had cost $232,000 each, were purchased for $46,400 each and sold to Venezuela for $140,000 each, yielding a total profit of $6.926 million, which Mr. Cummings asserts was all turned over to Merex. Venezuela subsequently retransferred 24 of these aircraft to Rhodesia and 4 to Honduras.

Merex A.G. also arranged for the sale of 90 former Bundesluftwaffe Mk 6 Sabres to Iran for $75,000 each. That country, in turn, sold them for an unknown amount to Pakistan. In one of the few instances in which the United States has stepped in to enforce its restrictions against the retransfer of arms of American manufacture or design, Washington demanded that Pakistan return these aircraft to Iran. Eventually all but seven were returned, at a cost to Iran of $111,000 each.

**Maximum Weight:** 20,610 lbs.

**Maximum Speed:** 687 mph.

**Powered by:** 1 x General Electric J47-GE-27 turbojet. 1 x Rolls-Royce Avon turbojet (CA-27 only). 1 x Orenda turbojet (CL-13 Mk 6 only).

**Operational Range:** 925 miles, or combat radius 460 miles.

**Armament:** 6 x M-3 .50 Cal MG. 24 x 2.75" rocket (D only). 4 x M39 20mm cannon (some H models only). 4 x M24A1 20mm cannon (K only).

**Ordnance Capacity:** 8 x 5" rocket or 2 x 1,000 lb bomb, and 2 x AIM-9 Sidewinder AAM only).

**Manufacturer:** North American Aviation/Fiat/Mitsubishi/Commonwealth Aircraft Corporation/Canadair. Production completed.

**Produced:** 9,263 of all types, including 3 XP-86 prototypes, 33 FJ-1 Fury, 521 F-86A, 2 F-86C, 2,504 F-86D (of which 981 converted to F-86L), 200 FJ-2, 149 FJ-3, 222 FJ-4, 336 F-86E, 2,254 F-86F, 2 TF-86F, 300 Mitsubishi

F-86F (of which 38 converted to RF-86F), 473 F-86H, 120 F-86K, 221 Fiat F-86K, 111 CA-27, 350 Canadair Mk 2, 438 Mk 4, 370 Mk 5 and 655 Mk 6.

**Exported under FMS:** 375.

**Exported under MAP:** 2,804 F-86 and 17 RF-86.

**In US Service:** Some, as QF-86 target drones.

**In Service Abroad:** Argentina (28 F-86F), Australia (79 CA-27), Bangladesh (3 ex-Pakistani F-86F), Bolivia (6 F-86F), Burma (12 F-86F), Colombia (6 Mk 6 and 5 F-86F), Denmark (38 F-86D), Ethiopia (14 F-86F), France (60 Fiat F-86K), Greece (50 F-86D and 12 Mk 6), Indonesia (16 CA-27), Italy (63 Fiat F-86K), Iran (83 Mk 6), Honduras (4 ex-Venezuelan/ex-West German F-86K), Japan (106 F-86D, 146 F-86F, 262 Mitsubishi F-86F and 18 RF-86F), Jordan (4 F-86F), Malaysia (16 CA-27), Norway (64 F-86K and 90 F-86F), Pakistan (35 F-86F of 120 originally delivered, and 7 Mk 6), Peru (14 F-86F), Philippines (18 F-86D and 40 F-86F), Portugal (18 F-86F and 50 ex-West German Mk 6), Rhodesia (24 ex-Venezuelan/ex-West German F-86K), Saudi Arabia (20 F-86F), South Africa (34 Mk 6), South Korea (40 F-86D, 122 F-86F and 10 RF-86F), Spain (244 F-86F), Syria (12 F-86F), Taiwan (25 F-86D, 320 F-86F and 7 RF-86F), Thailand (47 F-86F and 17 F-86L), Tunisia (12 F-86F), Turkey (66 ex-Dutch F-86K and 50 F-86D), Venezuela (19 ex-West German F-86K, 38 North American F-86K and 22 F-86F), and Yugoslavia (130 F-86D, 121 Mk 4, and 10 RF-86F).

**Formerly in Service:** Canada (906 Mk 2, Mk 4, Mk 5, Mk 6), Italy (180 Mk 4), the Netherlands (66 F-86K), USAF (4, 900 F-86A/D/E/F/H/L), USN (3,233 FJ-1/2), USMC (371 FJ-3/4) and West Germany (88 Fiat F-86K, 55 North American F-86K, 75 Mk5 and 225 Mk 6).

**Price:** $232,000@ (1959 unit cost for 55 North American F-86K to West Germany). $46,400@ (1966 dealer's unit discount cost, at 20 percent of original price, for 74 former West German F-86K to Interarms-Merex). $140,000@ (1966 second-hand unit cost for identical 74 former West German F-86K to Venezuela). $90,000@ (1966 unit cost for 90 former West German Mk 6 to Iran).

North American
F-100 Super Sabre

# NORTH AMERICAN F-100 SUPER SABRE

A direct descendant of the F-86 Sabre, the F-100 was the first USAF aircraft capable of sustained supersonic performance, reaching a top speed of 864 mph (Mach 1.31). It first flew in 1953, and during the late 1950s and early 1960s it served as a primary interceptor with our Tactical Air Command as well as with the air forces of Denmark, France, Taiwan and Turkey. From 1966 through 1971 the F-100D and F-100F models saw heavy service in Vietnam, performing both fighter interceptor and ground attack missions. The aircraft still flies today in all of the countries to which it was originally supplied, as well as with our own Air National Guard.

**Maximum Weight:** 34-832 lbs.

**Maximum Speed:** 864 mph (Mach 1.31).

**Powered by:** 1 x Pratt & Whitney J57-P-21A turbojet engine.

**Operational Range:** 1,100 miles, or combat radius of 550 miles. Maximum 1,500 miles with two external fuel tanks.

**Crew:** 1. (F-100F only: 2).

**Ceiling:** 50,000 feet.

**Armament:** 4 x M39E 20mm cannon, 200 rounds per gun, firing 1,500 round per minute. 2 x M39E 20mm cannon (F-100F only). 4 x AIM-9 Sidewinder AAM (all models).

**Ordnance Capacity:** 7,500 lbs on six external hardpoints, including 4 x AIM-9 and 6 x 1,000 lb bomb, or 4 x AIM-9, 2 x 1,000 lb bomb and 2 x AGM-12 Bullpup ASM.

**Manufacturer:** North American Aviation. Production completed.

**Produced:** 2,294 of all types, including 2 YF-100A prototypes, 203 F-100A (of which 80 converted to F-100D), 476 F-100C, 1,274 F-100D, and 339 twin-seat F-100F.

**In US Service:** 423 F-100C, F-100D and F-100F in 18 Air National Guard squadrons.

**Exported under FMS:** 37 (including 6 F-100F to Turkey in 1977).

**Exported under MAP:** 505 F-100 and 4 RF-100.

**In Service Abroad:** Denmark (48 F-100D and 24 F-100F), France (75 F-100D and 7 F-100F), Taiwan (80 F-100A, partially converted to F-100D, and 20 F-100F), and Turkey (40 F-100D and 16 F-100F). A proposed sale of 260 F-100C to Turkey was never consummated.

**Price:** $663,354@ (1955 unit conversion cost for 80 F-100A to D standard, for transfer under MAP to Taiwan).

Flown today in the air forces of thirty nations, and about to join another three, this lightweight, twin-engined supersonic fighter was specifically designed in the late 1950s for export. It is easy to maintain, and for its relatively low cost it offers a high performance both as a fighter interceptor and as a ground attack aircraft. Armed with two M39 20mm cannon, each with 280 rounds, and two AIM-9 Sidewinder air-to-air missiles at wingtip points, it can simultaneously carry from 5,200 to 7,000 lbs of ordnance on five pylons, two under either wing and one beneath its fuselage, including four 1,000 lb bombs or four AGM-12 Bullpup air-to-surface missiles.

The newest version of this aircraft, the F-5E, is equipped with a lead-computing optical gunsight and, for ground attack mission, a manually-depressible roll-stabilized bombsight reticle. An advanced inertial navigation system and fire control radar are standard on most export models, including the Emerson AN/APQ-153/157 fire control radar and the General Electric AN/APQ-113/114 attack radar. With a more powerful engine, extended wing leading edges and modified flaps for increased maneuverability, the F-5E has a top speed of 1,056 mph (Mach 1.6), a ground attack radius of 190 miles and an air interceptor radius of 987 miles.

Reconnaissance and twin-seat trainer versions have been produced as well, including the RF-5A equipped with four KS-92 cameras, the twin-seat F-5B trainer variant of the F-5A, the F-5F trainer variant of the F-5E and the RF-5E reconnaissance aircraft, fitted with four KS-121 cameras. All of these versions retain the full combat capabilities of the standard F-5 including internal armament, with the exception of the F-5F, which mounts only a single M39A2 20mm cannon.

F-5A and F-5B aircraft were made available in large quantities abroad in the early 1960s. To Iran alone, 233 of the aircraft were transferred, 12 of them on lease, together with 16 RF-5As, and since that time Iran has sold or given away her F-5As and F-5Bs, including 50 to Pakistan in 1972, 48 to Ethiopia in 1974, 36 to Jordan, 65 to Turkey and 15 to Kenya. These last aircraft were purchased in 1976 for $330,000 each, financed by a one-year $5 million loan to the Kenyan government from the United States. The 12 Iranian F-5As on lease were purchased in 1974 from the United States by Greece. In addition to the aircraft supplied to her by Iran, Turkey acquired a large number of other F-5As, including 7 as a gift from Libya in 1975.

While retaining her RF-5As, Iran subsequently replaced her earlier F-5 aircraft with 141 of the newer F-5Es and 28 F-5Fs. Another 69 F-5Es and F-5Fs had been on order for Iran until the Shah's removal. In these later sales, which took place in 1973 and 1975, Northrop, the aircraft's maker, paid a total of $2 million in commissions to

its sales agents. When the Iranian government pointed out that this had needlessly increased the cost of its aircraft by $2 million, and demanded that the money be repaid to Iran, Northrop did so, but the firm insisted that there had been nothing illegal in paying such commissions in the first place.

Another large Middle Eastern purchaser of the F-5 was Saudi Arabia, which bought 28 F-5Bs in 1972, 30 F-5Es in 1974, 20 F-5Fs in 1975, and another 110 F-5Es and 5 F-5Fs toward the end of 1975. Northrop has admitted paying $450,000 to its Saudi Arabian agent to bribe two Saudi generals in connection with the last of these sales.

Licensed production of the F-5 series has been undertaken in Taiwan by the Aero Industry Development Center, which has thus far produced 120 F-5Es and may produce another 60, in Spain by CASA, which produced 36 SF-5A, 34 SF-5B and 10 SRF-5A, and in Canada by Canadair. The Canadian firm produced 75 NF-5A and 30 NF-5B for the Netherlands, as well as 89 CF-5A and 44 CF-5D, the latter to B standard, for its own air force. When 18 of Canada's CF-5A and 2 of her CF-5D were subsequently sold to Venezuela in 1971 without payment to Northrop of its normal commission on licensed sales, that company sued Canadair for $17.5 million in damages. The Cana-

# NORTHROP F-5A FREEDOM FIGHTER AND F-5E TIGER II

**Northrop F-5A**

dians then filed a countersuit for $26 million based on delays by Northrop in releasing technical data required for the manufacture of aircraft for Canada and the Netherlands, licenses for which had already been obtained. In the end the matter was settled with a payment to Northrop of $9 million.

To date, 734 F-5A and F-5B aircraft and 192 F-5Es and F-5Fs have been transferred abroad under MAP, including 16 F-5As and 4 F-5Bs to the Philippines, 36 F-5Es and 5 F-5Bs to Jordan, 72 F-5Es to South Korea in 1972, and in 1975 30 F-5Es to Thailand and 14 F-5Es and 2 F-5Bs to Malaysia.

Based on the F-5 airframe, the T-38A Talon supersonic basic trainer was developed for the Air Force, which purchased 1,112 of the aircraft. With General Electric J85-GE-5 turbojet engines and weighing only 12,093 lbs, the Talon was in other respects similar to the twin-seat versions of the F-5. 46 were purchased by the West German Luftwaffe, 24 for the National Aeronautics and Space Administration, and 5 for the Navy, which uses them as air combat trainers for pilots graduating to the F-4 Phantom or F-14 Tomcat.

But the Air Force also wanted a heavier aircraft, closer in performance to the characteristics of Soviet interceptors, for air combat simulations. It went back to the F-5, whose weight, speed and size very nearly matched the Soviet MiG-21. In 1972 the Air Force purchased 71 F-5Es. With aircrews specially trained in Soviet tactics, these aircraft today form several aggressor squadrons to fly simulated aerial combat in regular training exercises with units throughout our Tactical Air Command. 12 of the aircraft are stationed with the 26th Tactical Fighter Aggressor Training Squadron at Clark Air Base in the Philippines. Another 18 are based with the 527th Tactical Fighter Aggressor Training Squadron at Alconbury Royal Air Force Base in England, with a unit frequently deployed to Zaragosa, Spain. The remaining USAF aggressor F-5Es are attached to the 64th and 65th Fighter Weapons Squadrons, 57th Tactical Training Wing at Nellis AFB, Nevada.

Out of the simulated combat exercises over Dogbone Lake at Nellis AFB, including the recent AIMVAL (Air Intercept Missile Evaluation) and ACEVAL (Air Combat Evaluation) program, some startling lessons have been learned about the future of air combat. Two of our fastest and most maneuverable aircraft, the F-14 Tomcat and F-15 Eagle, were pitted in simulated combat against aggressor F-5Es. All were similarly armed with short-range AIM-9L Sidewinder and medium-range AIM-7F Sparrow missiles, or with various test missiles offering equivalent ranges with higher degrees of sensitivity and maneuverability. In hundreds of test dogfights, preserved by computer for study, the ratio of F-5Es shot down by the far more expensive and complex aircraft remained consistently between 1.3 and 1.4 to 1.

The reasons for this soon became apparent. In order to guide their missiles to their targets, or in order merely to identify their targets, the F-14 and F-15 both had to bring themselves within visual range of the F-5E. The aggressor aircraft was therefore able to identify a target and launch its own missile before it was shot down. Over and over again, the other aircraft was shot down too.

With its Northrop TVSU (Television Sighting Unit), the F-14 was able to identify the F-5E at a range of 10 miles, and at that point launch its Sparrow missile. This was still out of visual range of the F-5E. But in order to *guide* its missile to the target the F-14 had to remain on an approach course, keeping the missile within a radar guidance cone no more than 65 degrees off boresight—the angle from an imaginary line extending directly in front of the aircraft. As a result the F-14 was sighted, and before its Sparrow missile hit home a missile was launched against it. Both aircraft were destroyed.

For all its sophistication the F-15, due to program cost overruns, has been fitted neither with TVSU nor TISEO, the two medium-range electro-optical sighting devices currently available. It had to approach closer to its target, and consequently fared even worse.

Acquiring moving objects over a range of 100 miles, the radars of both of these prized aircraft have proved highly capable, though the F-14's AN/AWG-9, designed with a high PRF (Pulse Repetition Frequency) for use over the open sea, has a good deal more trouble than the F-15's AN/APG-63, with a lower PRF, in distinguishing low-flying targets from ground clutter. But while these radars could lock onto targets at great distances they still could not identify them. Longer-range missiles, like the F-14's AGM-54A Phoenix, have a guided range of 50 miles and, using their own homing radar, an additional self-guided range of 10 miles. But without positive identification of the target, these capabilities are of little value. Thus, all of the superior performance capabilities of highly complex and sophisticated aircraft have been found, in these recent tests, to be nullified in actual air combat.

It is a stalemate, created by the current limitations of technology. In order to break it, not only must a means be developed of making positive identification of a target at much longer ranges. A self-guided missile must also be developed. Variously referred to as a "fire-and-forget" or "launch-and-leave" missile, this weapon would have to be capable of guiding itself over a range of 20 or 30 miles to its target, so that the aircraft launching it would not have to remain in the area, risking identification by the target, to guide it. Programs to develop such missiles have now been stepped up, as have programs for improving and extending the range of electro-optical and other means of target identification before a missile is launched.

Improvements in radar offer one possibility for long-range target identification, such as a far more compact version, suitable for fighter aircraft, of the highly classified technology in the Westinghouse AN/APY-1 radar and its associated data processing system aboard the Boeing E-3A AWACS. The AWACS has a startling ability to fully interpret large numbers of targets at very long ranges, but the technology to compress the contents of a radome measuring thirty feet across and of an aircraft weighing 325,000 lbs to a feasible size and weight for a fighter is presently not at hand.

Musketeer, a top secret program conducted by Hughes Aircraft, has for several years attempted to develop a means of identifying aircraft at long range from their engine harmonics, interpreted by the instantaneous measurement of minute changes in the frequency of reflected milimeter wavelength radar. Another possibility lies in the improvement of infrared sensors. Various tones and shades of aircraft paint yield different levels of heat, and eventually it may be possible, with improved sensors, to compare the infrared "signature" of a target with data preprogrammed in the attacking aircraft's computer. Already, USAF technicians have found that the bright red and yellow panels on our aircraft, giving operating instructions and marking engine exhausts and emergency equipment, increase their infrared signatures for hostile sensors. These familiar markings will consequently soon disappear from our aircraft.

But until the time that a technological advance may break the current stalemate, it is clear that in any future air combat, the moment one pilot comes within range of an opponent's missiles, both pilots will probably die. This grim fact has been well-suppressed until after pilots have been recruited. However, it certainly explains this country's current emphasis on building up large forces of comparatively inexpensive aircraft like the F-16, for in the foreseeable future numerical superiority appears to be the only factor that will decide the outcome of air combat. The United States is attempting to prepare for, and survive, massive losses in the sky.

**Maximum Weight:** 20,677 lbs (A/B) 24,080 lbs (E/F) 12,093 lbs (T-38A)

**Maximum Speed:** A/B: 925 mph (Mach 1.4). E/F: 1,056 mph (Mach 1.6). T-38A: 811 mph (Mach 1.23).

**Powered by:** 2 x GE J85-GE-13 turbojets (A/B) 2 x GE J85-GE-21 turbojets (E/F) 2 x GE J85-GE-5 turbojets¹ (T-31A)

**Operational Range:** A/B: Air intercept radius of 195 miles, ground attack radius of 635 miles. E/F: Air intercept radius of 987 miles, ground attack radius of 190 miles.

**Ceiling:** A/B: 50,500 feet, E/F: 54,000 feet.

**Armament:** 2 M39A2 20mm cannon (only 1 on F-5F). T-38A: none.

**Ordnance Capacity:** On five external pylons, 5,200 lbs (A/B) or 7,000 lbs (E/F).

**Stores Combinations:** 2 x AIM-9 Sidewinder AAM and 4 x 1,000 lb bomb or 4 x AGM-12 Bullpup ASM.

**Manufacturer:** Northrop. In production.

**Produced:** 4,256 of all types to date, including 1,040 F-5A, F-5B, RF-5A and variants, 2,029 F-5E, F-5F, and RF-5E, and 1,187 T-38A Talon trainers.

**Exported under FMS:** 180 F-5A and F-5B, and 398 F-5E and F-5F, with 69 more on order.

**Exported under MAP:** 734 F-5A and F-5B, and 192 F-5E and F-5F.

**In US Service:** 66 F-5E in two USAF TFAT squadrons and two USAF Fighter Weapons squadrons, 1,112 T-38A in USAF, 24 in NASA, and 5 in USN.

**In Service Abroad:** Brazil (6F-5B and 36 F-5E), Canada (71 CF-5A and 42 CF-5D), Chile (15 F-5E and 3 F-5F), Ethiopia (60 F-5A, including 48 ex-Iranian F-5A, and 2 F-5B), Greece (75 F-5A, including 12 ex-Iranian F-5A, 24 F-5B, 18 RF-5A and 36 F-5E), Indonesia (12 F-5E and 4 F-5F), Iran (16 RF-5A, 141 F-5E and 28 F-5F. An order for 69 more was cancelled), Jordan (30 ex-Iranian F-5A, 11 F-5B, including 6 ex-Iranian F-5B, and 66 F-5E), Kenya (15 ex-Iranian F-5A, 10 F-5Eand 2 F-5F), Libya (45 F-5A and 4 F-5B), Malaysia (14 F-5E and 2 F-5B), Morocco (16 F-5A, 4 F-5B and 2 RF-5B), Netherlands (75 NF-5A and 30 NF-5B), Norway (75 F-5A, 32 F-5G to RF-5A standard, and 12 F-5B), Pakistan (50 ex-Iranian F-5A), Peru (20 F-5E and 4 F-5F), Philippines (16 F-5A, 4 F-5B and 11 F-5E), Saudi Arabia (28 F-5B, 140 F-5E and 25 F-5F), Singapore (18 F-5E and 3 F-5F), South Korea (45 F-5A, 10 RF-5A, 4 F-5B, 126 F-5E and 6 F-5F), South Vietnam (68 F-5A, 2 F-5B and 22 F-5E, of which 51 F-5A and 22 F-5E left abandoned by American forces), Spain (36 SF-5A, 10 SRF-5A and 34 F-5B), Switzerland (72 F-5E), Taiwan (70 F-5A, 4 F-5B and to date 120 F-5E), Thailand (25 F-5A, 2 F-5B, 43 F-5E and 3 F-5F), Tunisia (10 F-5E and 2 F-5F), Turkey (140 F-5A, including 65 ex-Iranian and 7 ex-Libyan F-5A, 40 RF-5A and 12 F-5B), Venezuela (18 ex-Canadian CF-5A, 2 ex-Canadian CF-5D and 14 F-5E), West Germany (46 T-38A Talon), and Yemen (24 F-5E).

**Recent Transfers:** 28 F-5B to Saudi Arabia in 1972 for $1.43 million@. 141 F-5E to Iran in 1973 for $1.16 million@. 6 F-5B and 36 F-5E to Brazil in 1973 for $2.738 million@. Unit Procurement Cost for @. 15 F-5E and 3 F-5F to Chile in 1974 for $2.857 million@. 20 F-5E and 4 F-5F to Peru in 1974 for $2.92 million@. 30 F-5E to Jordan in 1974 for $2.7 million@. 30 F-5E to Saudi Arabia in 1974 for $2.92 million@. 54 F-5E and 6 F-5F to South Korea in 1975 for $3.416 million@. 20 F-5F to Saudi Arabia in 1975 for $4.43 million@. 13 F-5E and 3 F-5F to Thailand in 1975 for $4.38 million@. 10 F-5E and 2 F-5F to Tunisia in 1975 for $4.5 million@. 14 F-5E to Venezuela in 1975 for $2.142 million@. 110 F-5E and 5 F-5F to Saudi Arabia in 1975 for 6.872 million@. 11 F-5E to the Philippines in 1976 for $5.545 million@. 18 F-5E and 3 F-5F to Singapore in 1976 for $5.238 million@. 72 F-5E to Switzerland in 1976 for $6.388 million@. 24 F-5E to Yemen in 1976 for $4.166 million@. 10 F-5E and 2 F-5F to Kenya in 1976 for $6.25 million@. 15 ex-Iranian F-5A to Kenya in 1976 for $330,000@. 12 F-5E and 4 F-5F to Indonesia in 1977 for $7.5 million@.

**FMS Sales Pending:** Argentina (28 F-5E and 3 F-5F), Egypt (50 F-5E for $8 million@, including spares, training and support, to be paid by Saudi Arabia, but currently postponed), Indonesia (12 F-5E and 4 F-5F for $7.812 million@ for delivery in 1980).

**Sales Lost:** The United States offered the F-5E to Ecuador, but that country opted instead for the Israeli Kfir jet fighter, which is faster and has a longer ranger than the F-5E. The Kfir, however, employs the General Electric J79 engine, an item of equipment on our Major Defense Equipment List. On the grounds that we had to restrict the transfer of such equipment, we refused to allow the Israelis to sell 24 Kfir aircraft to Ecuador. The F-5E employs the J85 engine, which is also on the Major Defense Equipment List. In July of 1979, France sold Ecuador 20 Mirage F-1 interceptor aircraft.

**Price:** $1.6 million@ (Unit procurement cost to USAF in 1973).

**Northrop F-5E Tiger II**

# ROCKWELL OV-10 BRONCO

Developed in the early 1960s, the OV-10 was the winning design in a LARA (Light Armed Reconnaissance Aircraft) competition to meet USAF and USMC requirements for an inexpensive aircraft to perform forward air control, observation and secondary ground support missions. It has since emerged as one of the deadliest and most versatile light strike and counterinsurgency aircraft in the world. Powered by twin turboprops, it has a top speed of 281 mph, or can loiter at only 55 mph. Normally armed with four M60C 7.62mm machine guns in sponsons under its fuselage, it can simultaneously carry two AIM-9 Sidewinder missiles at either wingtip for air defense, 2,400 lbs of a variety of air munitions, guns or rocket pods slung under its sponsons, and another 1,200 lbs of ordnance on a centerline fuselage hardpoint.

With twin booms and a high tail to permit rear loading of its fuselage, the Bronco can also carry five fully equipped combat troops or, on MEDEVAC (Medical Evacuation) missions, two stretchers, for a total load of 3,200 lbs internally.

The OV-10 first entered service in Vietnam in 1966. 157 OV-10A were ordered by the Air Force, and under the Pave Nail program, 15 were modified with laser rangefinders and night sighting equipment to perform night air control and target designation duties. The Marine Corps ordered another 114 of the aircraft, loaned 18 to the USN for light armed reconnaissance, forward air control and helicopter escort service, and modified 2 to YOV-10D standard, adding a FLIR (Forward Looking Infra Red) sensor under the nose and substituting for the fuselage sponsons a turret with two M197 three-barreled 20mm cannon. These became known as NOGS (Night Observation Gunship System), and 24 more USMC OV-10A were converted to this standard as OV-10D.

Many OV-10A and OV-10D remain in service today with the Marine Corps and USAF's Tactical Air Command, including those with the 601st Tactical Control Wing at Sembach Air Base, West Germany. But to date 134 have also been transferred abroad, including 32 OV-10C built for Thailand, 16 OV-10E built for Venezuela, 16 OV-10F built for Indonesia, and 18 OV-10B built for West Germany as target towing aircraft, 12 of which were subsequently modified to OV-10Z standard by adding an auxiliary General Electric J85-GE-4 turbojet engine above the aircraft's fuselage to boost its speed to 393 mph. Under MAP and FMS, additional OV-10As have subsequently been supplied to Thailand, South Korea and Venezuela, and a request from Morocco for 24 of the aircraft was reduced to 6. Four OV-10F are also believed to have been transferred illegally to Rhodesia in 1978.

**Maximum Weight:** 14,466 lbs.

**Maximum Speed:** 281 mph.

**Powered by:** 2 x Garrett AiResearch T76-G-410/411 715 shp turboprops.

**Operational Range:** Fully loaded combat radius of 288 miles. Ferry range: 1,200 miles.

**Ceiling:** 30,000 feet.

**Crew:** 2.

**Electronics:** NOGS only: FLIR/LLLTV

**Armament:** *A/C/E/F:* 4 x 460C 7.62mm MG in sponsons. OV-10D NOGS: 2 x M197 three-barreled 20mm cannon in turret.

**Air Defense Armament:** 2 x AIM-9 Sidewinder AAM.

**Ordnance Capacity:** 3,600 lbs on one centerline and two sponson hardpoints, including 1 x 1,200 lb bomb and 4 x 600 lb bomb or 4 x " Zuni rocket pod or 4 x 2.75" FFAR pod.

**Manufacturer:** Rockwell International. Production for USAF and USMC completed in 1969, but available for production.

**Produced:** 376 of all types, including 7 YOV-10A prototypes, 287 OV-10A (of which 15 converted to Pave Nail and 26 converted to OV-10D NOGS), 18 OV-10B (of which 12 converted to OV-10Z), 32 OV-10C, 16 OV-10E and 16 OV-10F.

**Exported under FMS:** 88.

**Exported under MAP:** 52.

**In US Service:** 85 OV-10A in USAF, 10 OV-10A and 26 OV-10D NOGS in USMC, and 9 OV-10A in USMC Reserve.

**In Service Abroad:** Indonesia (16 OV-10F), Morocco (6 OV-10A), South Korea (24 OV-10A), Thailand (32 OV-10C and 24 OV-10A), Venezuela (16 OV-10E and 4 OV-10A), West Germany (6 OV-10B and 12 OV-10Z) and Zimbabwe (4 OV-10F?).

**Recent Transfers:** 6 OV-10C to Thailand in 1973 for $2.333 million@. 24 OV-10A to South Korea in 1975 for $2.43 million@.

# VOUGHT A-7 CORSAIR II

Developed in 1963 for the Navy as a light-weight attack aircraft to replace the A-4 Skyhawk, the A-7 is similar in appearance to the F-8 Crusader, from which it was derived. It has the same characteristic chin air intake, but is more than eight feet shorter than the Crusader, earning for it among Navy pilots the nickname SLUF (Short, Little, Ugly Fellow). With a top speed of 698 mph and a combat radius of 715 miles, it can carry 4,000 lbs of ordnance or, for shorter distances, a maximum of 15,000 lbs on two fuselage and six underwing hardpoints. Late versions of the aircraft, the A-7D and A-7E, can carry up to 18,400 lbs.

The A-7A, of which the Navy ordered 199, first entered service with USN Squadron VA-147 (Argonauts) in 1967, and on December 3 of that year the aircraft was introduced into combat for the first time in the Tonkin Gulf off Vietnam. 196 A-7B aircraft followed, with deliveries to the Navy beginning in 1968. Both of these early versions were armed with two Colt Mk 12 20mm cannon and four AIM-9 Sidewinder air-to-air missiles fixed on pylons at either side of the aircraft's nose.

For the Air Force, the A-7D was ordered in 1966 and first entered service in 1968. It was the first all-weather version of the bomber, incorporating an IBM AN/ASN-91 digital computer and the AN/APG-126 forward-looking radar. For the Mk 12 20mm cannon it substituted one General Electric M61A1 multi-barreled Vulcan 20mm cannon

with 1,000 rounds, and it was also the first aircraft in the world to provide for the pilot a HUD (Head Up Display) system, projecting data from its radar, inertial navigation system and other sensors on a clear glass plate overlaid on the windshield directly in front of the pilot without obscuring his vision of the airspace ahead.

This aircraft, of which 435 were built, remains in service today in 12 squadrons of USAF's Tactical Air Command, including 3 squadrons of the 23rd TFW at England AFB, Louisiana, 4 squadrons of the 354th TFW at Myrtle Beach AFB, South Carolina, 4 squadrons of the 355th TFW at Davis-Monthan AFB, Arizona, and the 65th Fighter Weapons Squadron at Nellis AFB, Nevada. The 354th TFW's aircraft are undergoing replacement by Fairchild A-10s, and will be transferred to the Air National Guard, which already operates more than 100 A-7Ds. Various improvement programs for the A-7D have included the installation of automatic wing maneuvering flaps on 384 of the aircraft, and the addition of Pave Penny laser target designators on 350 aircraft. All A-7Ds are now equipped to carry four AGM-65 Maverick air-to-surface missiles.

Subsequently, the Navy ordered the A-7E as an all-weather and night fighter-bomber, with improved avionics similar to those aboard the A-7D, including intertial navigation and HUD systems, and also including a FLIR (Forward Looking Infra Red) system.

Like the A-7D, it is equipped with the M61A1 Vulcan 20mm cannon. Most of the A-7Es have been fitted with an uprated Allison TF41-A-2 engine similar to that on the A-7D, but 67 were built with a Pratt & Whitney TF30-P-8 engine, the same kind used on the earlier A-7B. To avoid confusion, these 67 aircraft have been designated A-7C. 41 of these A-7Cs, along with 40 A-7Bs, have been converted to TA-7C two-seat trainers.

The Navy has received the 666 A-7Es it originally required, but Vought would like to keep its production line open, and has been getting considerable assistance from Congress. In 1976, the Defense Department eliminated 24 planned A-7Es from the budget. At that time the aircraft each cost $5.597 million, so this represented a saving of over $134 million. But in May of 1977 the Senate Armed Services Committee voted funds to procure another 12 aircraft, and in November of 1977 the funding was approved. By that time the aircraft each cost $8.58 million, for a total expenditure of over $102 million. For an increase of more than 50 percent of the unit cost of an A-7E in 1976, the Navy was getting only half of the aircraft it deferred at that time, aircraft which it believes it no longer requires.

A number of Vought proposals to keep production going have involved possible variants of the A-7, including an RA-7E reconnaissance version to replace the RA-5C Vigilante, a KA-7F tanker version, and an A-7D/ER equipped with the GAU-8/A 30mm cannon to fulfill an Air Force requirement for a close air support aircraft. This last requirement has been met by the Fairchild A-10, and the tanker subsequently selected was the KA-6D version of the Grumman Intruder, while tactical reconnaissance missions are currently being performed by various versions of the RF-4 Phantom.

Grumman Aircraft, in an effort to counter the threat to their own F-14 production, which they envision in the Navy's current planned procurement of the new McDonnell Douglas F-18 Hornet, also came up with a proposal involving the Vought A-7. At one point, the Navy had planned to cancel the F-18 program, but the new aircraft was to be equipped with the General Electric F404 engine, made at a General Electric plant in Lynn, Massachusetts. Massachusetts Congressmen vigorously campaigned to keep the F-18 program alive in order to protect General Electric's investment at Lynn, and they succeeded.

Grumman engineers then obtained plans for the F404 engine and redesigned the Vought A-7 to provide for two of these engines, creating an aircraft that would fulfill the original USN mission requirements met by the F-18. They subsequently circulated a briefing paper in Washington showing how much less expensive it would be to use the existing Vought airframe than invest in a wholly new aircraft, and claimed that the administration could save $1 billion by killing the F-18 program, building more Grumman F-14 fighter aircraft to fulfill the Navy's fighter requirements, and building the new twin-engined design of the Vought A-7 to fill the Navy's bomber requirements.

This campaign failed, mostly because the Navy was looking for a less expensive fighter aircraft than the F-14 which, at an estimated $15.630 million each, the F-18 promises to be, and also because the F-18 design can easily be adapted to the A-18 strike aircraft configuration, filling the bomber requirement as well. This would help to achieve one of Defense Secretary Harold Brown's goals of commonality, and it is why the Marine Corps is under considerable pressure to abandon the AV-8B Harrier and adopt the A-18 instead, for the increased production of the basic F-18 aircraft would further reduce its unit procurement cost.

Vought, which has also sold 60 A-7H aircraft, built to E standard, to Greece, together with 6 TA-7H trainers, also hoped to sell 110 of these aircraft to Pakistan. In one of the few instances in which the Carter administration has met the promise of its announced arms control policy, this sale was cancelled in May of 1977—but not, it turns out, in an attempt to reduce the flow of arms abroad. Rather, we had insisted that Pakistan not proceed with an agreement with France to build a nuclear fuel processing plant in Pakistan. This agreement was signed, and work on the plant is now under way. At that point, the United States cancelled the A-7 sale. Pakistan is now negotiating with the United Kingdom for the purchase of the BAC Jaguar.

**Maximum Weight:** 42,000 lbs.

**Powered by:** 1 x P&W TF30-P-6 nonafterburning turbofan (A), TF30-P-8 (B/C), Allison TF41)A)1 (Rolls Royce Spey) (D), TF41-A-2 (E).

**Operational Range:** Ferry range of 2.871 miles, combat radius of 715 miles with 4,000 lbs external ordnance.

**Armament:** 2 x Colt Mk 12 20mm cannon (A/B), 1 x GE M61A1 Vulcan 20mm cannon (D/E)

**Air Defense Armament:** 4 x AIM-9 Sidewinder AAM on cheek pylons.

**Ordnance Capacity:** On two fuselage and six underwing hardpoints, 15,000 lbs (A/B) or 18,400 lbs (D/E).

**Stores Combinations:** 15 x 750 lb bomb, or 10 x 1,000 lb bomb, or 4 x 3,100 lb bomb or 4 x AGM-65 Maverick ASM.

**Manufacturer:** LTV Aerospace. In production for USN, and available for production.

**Produced:** 1,565 of all types, including 3 prototypes, 199 A-7A, 196 A-7B (of which 40 converted to TA)7C) 67 A)7C (of which 41 converted to TA-7C), 435 A-7D (of which 1 converted to YA-7H), 599 A-7E, 60 A-7H and 6 TA-7H.

**Exported under FMS:** 66.

**Exported under MAP:** 16.

**In US Service:** 334 A-7D in 12 squadrons of USAF Tactical Air Command, 101 A-7D in 6 Air National Guard squadrons, 324 A-7A/B/C/E in 24 USN squadrons, and 48 A-7A/B in USN Air Reserve.

**US Carrier Deployment:** A-7Bs of VA-46 and VA-72 on CVW-1 *USS John F. Kennedy,* A-7Es of VA-25 (Fist of the Fleet) and VA-113 on CVW-2 *USS Ranger,* A-7Es of VA-37 (Bulls) and VA-105 on CVW-3 *USS Saratoga,* A-7As of VA-56 and VA-93 on CVW-5 *USS Midway,* A-7Bs of VA-15 and VA-87 on CVW-6 *USS America,* A-7Es of VA-12 and VA-6 on CVW-7 *USS Independence,* A-7Es of VA-82 and VA-86 on CVW-8 *USS Nimitz,* A-7Es of VA-146 and VA-147 (Argonauts) on CVW-9 *USS Constellation,* A-7Es of VA-192 and VA-195 on CVW-11 *USS Kitty Hawk,* A-7Es of VA-27 (Royal Maces) and VA-97 on CVW-14 *USS Enterprise,* A-7Es of VA-22 and VA-94 on CVW-15 *USS Coral Sea,* A-7Es of VA-81 and VA-83 on CVW-17 *USS Forrestal.*

**In Service Abroad:** Greece (60 A-7H and 6 TA-7H), and Indonesia (16 A-7A).

**Price:** $8.58 million (1978 Unit Procurement Cost for 12 A-7E to USN). $7.667 million (1977 Unit Procurement Cost for 30 A-7E to USN). $5.597 million (1976 Unit Procurement Cost for 30 A-7E to USN). $4.171 million (1975 Unit Procurement Cost for 24 A-7D to USAF).

**Recent Transfers:** 60 A-7H to Greece in 1974 for $3.8 million@, increased to $4.316 million@ in negotiations reached before delivery in 1976.

# VOUGHT F-8 CRUSADER

Designed in 1953 to meet a Navy requirement for a fighter aircraft able to land and take off from a carrier deck but also capable of supersonic speeds, the F-8 incorporated an ingenious principle, that of the variable-incidence wing, which pivots upwards at an angle of 7 degrees to provide drag for lower approach speeds and lift for carrier takeoffs while at the same time keeping the aircraft horizontal so that the pilot has a clear view of the carrier deck. Early models of the F-8 reached speeds of 1,013 mph (Mach 1.53), while the later F-8D has a top speed of 1,230 mph (Mach 1.86).

The F-8A first entered service in 1957 with USN Squadron VF-32 aboard the *USS Saratoga.* 318 F-8As, 130 F-8Bs and 187 F-8Cs were produced, powered by a single Pratt & Whitney J57 turbojet engine and armed with four Colt Mk 12 20mm cannon, each with 84 rounds. On fuselage side rails aft of the cockpit two AIM-9 Sidewinder air-to-air missiles could be carried, or alternatively, four Zuni 5'' (127mm) unguided rockets, while simultaneously 5,000 lbs of ordnance could be carried underwing. These aircraft became the Navy's standard carrier-based day fighter until the F-4 Phantom II entered service in the 1960s. Even then, F-8 Crusaders continued to fly from the smaller carriers *USS Hancock* and *USS Oriskany,* from which the F-4 could not operate, until those vessels were decommissioned in 1976. Consequently, a good many Crusaders saw action in Vietnam, and by the time we had withdrawn from that conflict had accumulated a record of 18 MiG-21 aircraft shot down, as compared with a total of 11 shot down by all other USN and USMC aircraft combined.

144 of an unarmed photo reconnaissance version of the Crusader were also produced, equipped with five cameras, and enough of these aircraft had entered service in time to provide the major portion of our reconnais-sance information on Cuba during the missile crisis of 1962. Many of these RF-8As, most of them rebuilt to RF-8G standard, remain in service today.

The first Crusader with a limited all-weather capability was the F-8D, of which 152 were produced. With a Vought push-button auto-pilot and the AN/APQ-83 radar, they also had an increased armament capacity of 144 rounds for each cannon and up to four AIM-9 Sidewinder or eight Zuni rockets on side rails. They were followed by 286 F-8Es, similarly armed, but with a nose radome 3 inches longer to house the AN/APQ-94 radar and an AN/AAS-15 infrared sensor.

Two F-8A were subsequently converted to DF-8A drone control aircraft for the Regulus missile program, and one was converted to a twin-seat armed trainer. But for the other models of the Crusader an extensive re-manufacturing program was undertaken, including the conversion of 63 F-8B to F-8L, 73 RF-8A to RF-8G, 87 F-8C to F-8K, 89 F-8D to F-8H, and 136 F-8E to F-8J. In all, 448 aircraft were rebuilt to extend their service life, most of the modifications involving structural reinforcement, improved avionics and new landing gear, but in the case of the F-8J more than 100 aircraft were reengined as well, with the TF30-P-420 afterburning turbofan. After twenty years in front-line service to date, many of these rebuilt Crusaders are expected to reach a flight life of more than three million hours. Many continue to serve in the Navy, Marine Corps and Naval Air Reserve.

Many more Crusaders are also becoming available for export abroad. 35 F-8H aircraft have recently been refurbished, at a cost of $920,000 each, for transfer to the Philippines, under MAP. This has been criticized as jeopardizing the credibility of the administration's human rights program, under which arms and military aid would be restricted to those countries that appear, as the Philippines prominently does, on the State Department's list of nations that have continued to demonstrate serious violations of human rights.

While aid, as a consequence of the State Department's report, has been cut or dramatically reduced to such countries as Bolivia, Colombia, Haiti, Honduras, Nicaragua, Paraguay and Peru, the $36.6 million in military aid and credits originally allocated to the Philippines remains in the budget for Fiscal Year 1979, and it is exactly the same amount as had been approved for the previous year. In February of 1978, President Carter even specifically asked that no cut in arms aid be made to the Philippines, despite the negative human rights report on the Marcos regime. This compromise of our human rights program, which in turn becomes a compromise of our belief in the value of upholding human rights, may be due to the priority requirements of maintaining good relations with the Marcos regime in order not to jeopardize the stability of our military base rights in that country. Clark Air Force Base, and the naval base of Subic Bay are both regarded by the military as crucial to the maintenance of our security in the Far East, most especially in the face of our planned withdrawal of forces from South Korea.

In addition to the Crusaders soon to be supplied to the Philippines, which may be only the first of many future transfers of this aircraft, an additional 42 F-8E aircraft were produced in 1946 for the French Navy. Subsequently upgraded to F-8J standard, they serve today with Flotille 12F aboard the carrier Clemenceau and Flotille 14F on the carrier Foch.

**Maximum Weight:** 34,000 lbs.

**Maximum Speed:** A/B/C: 1,013 mph (Mach 1.53). D/E: 1,230 mph (Mach 1.86

**Powered by:** 1 x P&W J57-P-12 (A), or J57-P-4A (B/L), or J57-P-16 (C/K), or J57-P-20 (D/H), or J57-P-20A (E/J), or 1 x P&W TF30-p-420 turbofan (100 J). RF-8G: 1 x J57-P-22.

**Operational Range:** Combat radius of 440 miles (A/B/C), or 455 miles (D/E) K/L/H/J).

**Ceiling:** 42,900 feet.

**Armament:** 4 x Colt Mk 12 20mm cannon with 84 rpg (A/B/C), or 144 rpg (D/E/K/L/H/J).

**Air Interceptor Stores:** 2 x AIM-9 Sidewinder AAM or 4 x 5" (127mm Zuni rocket (A/B/C), or 4 x AIM-9 Sidewinder AAM or 8 x 5" Zuni rocket (all other versions).

**Ordnance Capacity:** 5,000 lbs on underwing hardpoints, including 12 x Mk 81 250 lb bomb, or 8 x Mk 82 500 lb bomb, or 4 x Mk 83 1,000 1 bomb, or 2 x AGM-12 Bullpup ASM, or 16 x Zuni 5" rocket.

**Manufacturer:** LTV Aerospace. Production completed.

**Produced:** 1,261 of all types, including 2 XF8U-1 prototypes, 318 F-8A (of which 1 converted to NTF-8A, 2 converted to DF-8A and some to QF-8A), 130 F-8B (of which 63 converted to F-8L), 144 RF-8A (of which 73 converted to RF-8G), 187 F-8C (of which 87 converted to F-8K), 152 F-8D (of which 89 converted to F-8H), 281 F-8E (of which 136 converted to F-8J), 42 F-8E(FN) and 1 TF-8E.

**Exported under FMS:** 36 F-8E and TF-8E.

**Exported under MAP:** 35 F-8H.

**In US Service:** 48 F-8J and 15 RF-8G in USN, 48 F-8J and 8 RF-8G in USN Air Reserve, and 24 F-8J in USMC Reserve.

**In Service Abroad:** France (42 F-8J) and the Philippines (25 F-8H. Of the 35 delivered, 10 will be broken up and used for spares).

**Conversion Costs:** $920,000 @ LTV price for rebuilding 25 F-8H for transfer to the Philippines).

# IN DEVELOPMENT:
# McDONNELL DOUGLAS/NORTHROP F-18 HORNET AND A-18 COBRA

The Navy has ordered 800 of this powerful, twin-engined aircraft as its new primary carrier-based fighter for the 1980s, and would also like the Marine Corps to take an additional 360 in place of the AV-8B Harrier now under consideration. Somewhat modified as a carrier-based strike aircraft, the USMC version of the Navy's F-18 Hornet would be designated A-18 Cobra, and the increased production of a total of 1,160 aircraft with a high commonality of parts would considerably reduce the Navy's unit procurement cost for the F-18, currently estimated at $15.630 million. The F-18 might also serve the Marine Corps as an eventual replacement fighter aircraft for its F-4 Phantoms.

Based on the prototype YF-17, the losing contender against the General Dynamics F-16 in the Air Force competition for a lightweight combat fighter, the F-18 design was originally developed by Northrop. McDonnell Douglas, because of its greater experience in developing carrier-based aircraft for the Navy, has assumed the prime contractor role in fulfilling the Navy contract, and will be responsible for 60 percent of the aircraft's airframe and for its assembly. Northrop, however, in performing the balance of the work, will profit both from domestic and foreign sales of the aircraft, and has at the same time developed a land-based version, the F-18L or Cobra II, specifically for export. 7,000 lbs lighter than the F-18, and with its fuel capacity reduced by 3,500 lbs, the F-18L will have neither folding wings nor the wing slots required for high-angle carrier landing approaches. Northrop has planned a flat export price of $16 million each for the F-18L Cobra II.

**Maximum Weight:** 44,000 lbs (F-18/A-18) 30,500 lbs (F-18L)

**Maximum Speed:** Above Mach 2.

**Powered by:** 2 x General Electric F404-GE-400 afterburning turbojets.

**Anticipated Combat Radius:** 460 miles.

**Manufacturer:** McDonnell Douglas/Northrop.

**In US Service:** 800 F-18 planned for USN, and possibly 360 A-18 for USMC.

**Price:** $15.630 million@ (1978 estimated unit procurement cost for 800 F-18 to USN). $16 million@ (1978 Northrop estimate of unit FMS price for export sale of F-18L).

**Sold Abroad:** Canada (137 CF-18, for $18.248 million@ for delivery between 1982 and 1989).

# COMBAT SUPPORT AND SPECIAL MISSION AIRCRAFT

Included in this section are aircraft designed for specialized combat or combat support missions, and military or commercial transport aircraft adapted for such uses. These missions include anti-submarine warfare (ASW), maritime and coastal patrol, command and battlefield control, airborne early warning (AEW) and fighter direction, reconnaissance and observation, aerial refuelling for long-range strike and interception missions, forward air control of ground artillery or of aircraft flying ground support missions, liaison duties and, of course, pilot training.

Aircraft used exclusively for the transport of cargo or personnel are covered in the section following this one, but those which are used as tankers, trainers, observation or command aircraft are also mentioned here. There have been many uses, for example, of the Boeing 707, well-known as a commercial airliner. As a cargo aircraft its military designation is C-135, and it has been adapted for aerial tanker (KC-135), airborne communications (ED-135) and electronic reconnaissance (RC-135) missions. The 707 airframe is also the basis for the E-3A AWACS (Airborne Warning and Control System). The larger Boeing 747 is being used for the E-4A AABNCP (Advanced Airborne National Command Post), only one of which is now planned at an estimated cost of $177 million.

Training variants of combat aircraft, such as the T-33, have been covered in the previous section, along with a major combat variant of the T-37 trainer, the A-37 Dragonfly. The trainers in this section serve primarily in the role for which they were designed, but in many parts of the world such aircraft have frequently been modified and equipped for COIN (counterinsurgency) missions, as have a variety of light commercial transport aircraft manufactured by such firms as Piper, Beechcraft and Cessna. Such modifications and uses are mentioned wherever they are known to exist.

Conversely, some former combat aircraft, such as the Grumman F-9F Panther, are used today primarily as trainers, and are therefore included in this section.

Many reconnaissance variants of combat aircraft, such as the RF-4 Phantom and the RF-5, have been covered in the previous section. Included here are those aircraft used solely for reconnaissance purposes, among them the Lockheed U-2 and SR-71A Blackbird, even though one such aircraft, the North American Rockwell RA-5C Vigilante, retains a significant combat capability of its own.

The effectiveness of the S-3 Viking, the P-3 Orion and other aircraft assigned to the highly specialized role of anti-submarine warfare lies less in the specialized weapons they carry—aerial mines, depth charges and torpedoes—than in the quality and versatility of their radar and underwater detection gear, including sonobuoys, sonobuoy reference systems and magnetic anomaly detection (MAD) equipment. This equipment has therefore been emphasized.

Some light observation and utility aircraft, used for close reconnaissance and forward air control, have also been heavily modified to fly a variety of electronic reconnaissance missions—in one case by remote control. Such versions are also listed here.

Though equally important to the successful execution of combat missions, combat support aircraft, as a category of equipment, are generally regarded to be less lethal than combat aircraft themselves. Consequently they have been made available in even greater numbers around the world. Those in use today span a period of development and production of over thirty years. Since these aircraft, like all other weapons, have been used and will continue to be used as instruments of foreign policy, their pattern of distribution provides a fascinating glimpse into what parts of the world, and to what degree, and at what moments in history, we have sought and continue to seek to extend our sphere of influence.

Thus, aircraft of the 1950s, obsolete by our standards, equip the air forces of Latin and Central America, along with many aircraft of World War II vintage. More modern aircraft have been supplied to the wealthier nations in that part of the world, Argentina, Brazil and Venezuela, or to nations in whose affairs we have become politically involved, like Chile. Aircraft of the late 1950s and early 1960s, such as the F-86 and F-100, have been supplied in large numbers to Japan, Taiwan and South Korea, marking our effort to strengthen our network of influence in the Far East at the close of the Korean War. In the middle and late 1960s the F-104 Starfighter, and then the F-5E, began to appear in the inventories of most NATO nations, as we worked to bolster the strength of that organization. During our involvement in Southeast Asia in the late 1960s and early 1970s, the OV-10 Bronco, T-41 Mescalero, T-28 Trojan and other COIN aircraft developed during that period were supplied to the air forces of Laos, Thailand and Indonesia, which fly them today.

The most advanced and most expensive aircraft now in production already equip or will soon equip the air forces of the Middle East, where the vast wealth from oil revenues makes them easily affordable, or where—in at least the case of Israel—they may be genuinely needed for survival.

Several of the aircraft types manufactured by Cessna have been licensed for production to Reims Aviation in France. The distribution of these licensed models suddenly reveals a whole new sphere of influence, compatible with our own, as the French attempt to maintain ties with their former African empire, exporting aircraft to Benin, Chad, Mauritania, Gabon, Cote d'Ivoire, Niger and Senegal.

## BEECH F-33 BONANZA/QU-22

Light observation and forward air control aircraft. Based on the commercial Beech Model 35B, formerly the Beech Model A36 Debonair. Subject of a 1967 USAF adaptation, the Model PD 249 Pave Coin Bonanza, for counterinsurgency reconnaissance in Vietnam. Several purchased by USAF and US Army as QU-22. Under USAF's Pave Eagle program, six QU-22 were modified to QU-22B standard, equipped with a slow-turning quiet propeller, for low-level electronic surveillance, locating Viet Cong positions by monitoring their radio transmissions. Though manned by personnel operating signals intelligence equipment, these aircraft were flown by remote control.

**Type:** Prop-driven single-engined monoplane, seating 4 to 6.

**Weight:** 3,600 lbs.

**Speed:** 209 mph.

**Range:** 824 miles.

**Produced:** more than 13,000 of all types, including 9,823 Bonanzas.

**In Service Abroad:** Iran (45 F-33A/C), Mexico (20 F-33C), Spain (24 F-33C/E), West Germany (21 QU-22A).

**Price:** $65,000@(1965 Unit Cost for 20 to Mexico in 1974). $51,612@(Unit cost for 31 to Iran in 1974).

## BEECH MODEL B55 BARON/T-42A COCHISE AND VC-6A

Instrument trainer and transport aircraft, based on the Beech Model 95/55 Baron. 70 were purchased by the US Army as T-42A Cochise trainers, and 1 was purchased by USAF as a VIP transport aircraft, designated VC-6A, for the 1254th Special Air Missions Wing of MATS (Military Air Transport Service). Five T-42A aircraft were subsequently supplied to Turkey under MAP.

**Type:** Prop-driven twin-engined monoplane, seating 4 to 6.

**Weight:** 5,100 lbs.

**Speed:** 236 mph.

**Range:** 1,225 miles.

**Produced:** 1,996 of all types, including 1,784 Baron B55/E55/E58/E58P.

**In US Service:** 61 T-42A in US Army and 1 VC-6A in USAF/MATS.

**In Service Abroad:** Japan (6 Baron), Rhodesia (1 Baron), Spain (15 Baron), Turkey (5 T-42A).

**Price:** $45,545@ (1965 Unit Procurement Cost for 55 aircraft to US Army).

## BEECH MODEL B80 QUEEN AIR/U-8 SEMINOLE (FORMER L-23)

A utility aircraft used for reconnaissance and liaison. First developed in 1950 as the commercial Beech Model 50 Twin Bonanza, it later became the Beech Model A65 Queen Air. During the Korean War the US Army purchased 258 of these aircraft and operated them under the designation L-23, converting 8 of them to RL-23D standard with AN/APQ-86 SLAR (Side Looking Airborne Radar) equipment for wide-area reconnaissance. The designation of all aircraft was later changed to U-8, and 93 former L-23A and L-23B were converted to U-8D standard, while the RL-23D aircraft became RU-8D. An additional 77 U-8D were purchased, along with 12 more RU-8D. These were followed by 6 U-8E and 71 U-8F. The U-8Es and six RU-8Ds have since been converted to U-8G standard with additional electronic modifications.

**Type:** Prop-driven twin-engined monoplane, seating 8 to 10.

**Weight:** 7,700 lbs.

**Speed:** 239 mph.

**Range:** 1,220 miles.

**Produced:** Over 1,000 of all types, including Model 50 Twin Bonanza, Models A65 and B80 Queen Air, and 424 L-23 and U-8 aircraft.

**In US Service:** 152 U-8D/F and 12 U-8G in US Army, 29 U-8D/F in Army National Guard, and 1 U-8D and 8 RU-8D in Army Reserve.

**In Service Abroad:** Argentina (5 Queen Air), Chile (5 Twin Bonanza), Israel (9 L-23 and 20 Queen Air), Japan (29 Queen Air), Morocco (2 Twin Bonanza), Pakistan (6 L-23 and 1 Twin Bonanza), Peru (21 Queen Air), Switzerland (3 Twin Bonanza), Venezuela (20 U-8 and 6 Queen Air), and Uruguay (6 U-8 and 2 Queen Air).

**Beech F-33A Bonanza**

## BEECH MODEL C90 KING AIR/T-44A AND VC-6B

A US Navy trainer, based on the commercial Beech Model C90. To date the Navy has purchased 71 of these aircraft as T-44A VTAMX (Advanced Multi-Engine Trainers), and USAF has purchased 1 as a VC-6B VIP transport aircraft assigned to the 1254th Special Air Missions Wing of MATS. USN T-44As are based at Corpus Christi Naval Air Station.

**Type:** Twin-turboprop monoplane, seating 10.

**Weight:** 9,650 lbs.

**Speed:** 240 mph.

**Range:** 1,265 miles.

**Ceiling:** 29,500 ft.

**Produced:** Over 1,500 of all types to date.

**In US Service:** 71 T-44A in USN and 1 VC-6B in USAF/MATS.

**In Service Abroad:** Chile (2 King Air 90), Japan (7 King Air 90), Spain (12 King Air 90).

**Price:** $769,500@ (1976 Unit Procurement Cost for 23 aircraft to USN). $510,000@ (1974 Unit Procurement Cost for 23 to USN).

## BEECH MODEL B100 KING AIR/U-21 UTE AND RU-21

A utility aircraft used for reconnaissance and surveillance, and as a light transport for up to 10 fully-equipped combat troops. Of a total of 172 of these aircraft purchased by the US Army since 1963, and designated U-21 Ute, 70 have been converted to various RU-21 standards for electronic surveillance, and are operated today by the Army Security Agency. These include 4 RU-21A, 3 JU-21A, 3 RU-21B, 2 RU-21C, 18 RU-21D, 16 RU-21E, 8 RU-21F, 4 RU-21G, and 12 RU-21H.

**Type:** Twin-turboprop monoplane, seating 8 to 15.

**Weight:** 11,000 lbs.

**Speed:** 285 mph.

**Range:** 1,395 miles.

**Ceiling:** 24,850 ft.

**Produced:** Over 240 to date, including 172 for US Army.

**In US Service:** 102 U-21 Ute in US Army and 70 RU-21A/B/C/D/E/F/G/H in Army/ASA.

**In Service Abroad:** Algeria (1 King Air 100), Canada (1 King Air 100), Belgium (1 King Air 100), Chile (1 King Air 100), Indonesia (2 King Air 100), Jamaica (1 King Air 100), Malaysia (3 King Air 100), Mexico (2 King Air 100), Saudi Arabia (2 King Air 100), Thailand (2 King Air 100).

**Price:** $39,900@ (Unit cost for 2 King Air 100 to Indonesia in 1975). $500,000@ (Unit Procurement Cost for 5 RU-21F, fully equipped for electronic surveillance, to Army Security Agency in 1975).

## BEECH MODEL 200 SUPER KING AIR/C-12A HURON AND RU-21J

A transport and utility aircraft for the US Army and USAF, and a highly sophisticated electronic surveillance aircraft for the Army Security Agency. Most of the transport versions are stationed abroad today, performing staff liaison work for United States military missions in the Middle East. Under the Army's top secret Cefly Lancer program, three Beech Super King Air 200s were ordered in 1974 for electronic reconnaissance work in Vietnam. Similar to the less powerfully-engined RU-21 series based on the King Air 100 and flown by the ASA, they have now been turned over to that organization. The Navy is now considering the purchase of 22 C-12As as support aircraft, and to the consternation of several members of Congress including Senator Barry Goldwater, the Navy has planned its procurement without the normal competitive bidding required by law, contending that since the Army and Air Force have made earlier purchases of the same aircraft this requirement is inapplicable. Senator Goldwater and his colleagues suspect, however, that the price Beechcraft is asking for the Navy's aircraft is rather high, at $981,000 each, as compared with a unit cost of $642,000 when the Army and Air Force purchased C-12As in 1974.

For coastal patrol and marine reconnaissance duties, the Irish Air Force has leased a Super King Air 200 from British Eagle Air Services, and two Super King Air 200s have been sold to the French Air Force equipped with cameras for reconnaissance work.

**RU-21J of U.S. Army**

**Type:** Twin-turboprop monoplane, seating 8 to 10.

**Weight:** 12,000 lbs.

**Speed:** 310 mph.

**Range:** 2,000 miles.

**Produced:** Over 1,250 to date, including 70 for USAF and US Army as C-12A and 3 for US Army as RU-21J.

**In US Service:** 36 C-12A in US Army and 34 C-12A in USAF, all based with MAAG groups in Iran and Saudi Arabia. 3 RU-21J based in USA With ASA.

**In Service Abroad:** France (2 Super King Air 200), Ireland (1 Super King Air 200).

**Price:** $642,000@ (1974 Unit Procurement Cost for 34 C-12A, 20 for US Army and 14 for USAF). $830,000@ (1977 Unit Procurement Cost for 20 C-12A). $981,000@ (Proposed 1978 Unit Procurement Cost for 22 C-12A for USN).

# BEECH MODEL 45/T-34A/B MENTOR AND T-34C TURBO MENTOR

A powerful and versatile trainer based on the Beech Model 45 Bonanza, and used as an attack bomber and COIN aircraft in several countries. The Model 45 first flew in 1948. USAF took delivery of 353 of the aircraft in 1953. They were designated T-34A Mentor. The following year, 423 T-34B Mentors were delivered to the USN, which still has 134 in service. By 1958 Beechcraft had produced 1,094 of the civilian and military versions of the Model 45, together with another 318 for export. Chile purchased 66 T-34A aircraft for $15,150 each. The Mentor was produced under license by RACA in Argentina, which built 75 for the Argentine Air Force, by the Canadian Car and Foundry Company, which produced 100 of the USAF T-34As and another 25 for the Royal Canadian Air Force, and by Fuji Industries in Japan, which produced 36 for the Philippines, 40 for Indonesia and 195 for its own armed forces.

A more powerful turbine-engined version, the T-34C Turbo Mentor, was developed in 1973, and is now in production to replace the Navy's T-34B as a basic and intermediate trainer. The USN anticipates procurement of a total of 400 T-34Cs. Deliveries of the T-34C began in 1976, by which time we had reached sales agreements to provide 18 of the new aircraft for Ecuador, 16 for Ethiopia and, in our first export sale to that country, 12 for Morocco.

**Type:** (T-34C) Single-engined turboprop monoplane, seating 2.

**Weight:** 2,950 lbs (A/B), 4,274 lbs (C).

**Speed:** 189 mph (A/B), 247 mph (C).

**Range:** 735 miles (A/B), 749 miles (C).

**Ordnance Capacity:** (T-34C) 1,800 lbs, including FFAR 2.75'' rocket pods, SUU-11/A 7.62mm Minigun pods, Mk 81 250 lb Snakeye or Mk 82 500 lb Snakeye bombs.

**Produced:** 1,412 Model 45 Bonanzas, including 353 T-34A for USAF and 423 T-34B for USN. Estimated production of 400 T-34C planned for USN.

**In US Service:** 134 T-34B in USN, and approximately 70 T-34C.

**Exported under FMS:** 10 T-34C (32 more on order).

**Exported under MAP:** 71 T-34A/B.

**In Service Abroad:** Argentina (91), Canada (25), Chile (66), Colombia (41), Ecuador (12 T-34C with 8 on order), El Salvador (3), Ethiopia (16 T-34C on order), Greece (12), Indonesia (16 and 40 Fuji), Japan (195 Fuji T-34), Mexico (4), Morocco (10 T-34C, with 2 on order), Peru (6), Philippines (36 Fuji T-34), Saudi Arabia (18), Spain (25), Turkey (24), Uruguay (1), Venezuela (34).

**Price:** $395,900@ (1976 Unit Procurement Cost for 98 aircraft to USN). $844,100@ (1978 Unit Procurement Cost for 34 aircraft to USN).

**Recent Transfers:** 12 to Morocco in 1975 for $458,000@.

**Beech T-34C Turbo Mentor**

# BOEING KC-97L STRATOFREIGHTER

This is a tanker version of the C-97 Strato-freighter, which was the transport version of the B-29 Superfortress. Of the 888 C-97s produced, 219 were KC-97F tankers and 592 were KC-97Gs, the latter group forming our Strategic Air Command's aerial refuelling tanker force from the beginning of production in 1951 through 1957, when they began to be replaced by the KC-135. The KC-97L is a further conversion of the G and F models, with the addition of two auxiliary jet engines in pods under each wing. These aircraft today equip our Air National Guard.

**Type:** Prop-driven four-engined tanker aircraft with two auxiliary jet engines in underwing pods.

**Maximum Weight:** 175,000 lbs.

**Fuel Transfer Capacity:** 90,000 lbs.

**Speed:** 375 mph.

**Range:** 4,300 miles.

**Produced:** 811, including 219 KC-97F and 592 KC-97G. 622 conversions of F and G to KC-97L. Remaining 189 Fs converted to 135 C-97G, 26 C-97K, and 28 HC-97G.

**In US Service:** 75 KC-97L in Air National Guard.

**In Service Abroad:** Israel (11 C-97 and KC-97), and Spain (3 KC-97L).

**Price:** Approximately $610,000@ in 1952.

# BOEING KC-135 STRATOTANKER/EC-135 and RC-135

A jet-engined aerial refuelling tanker, based on the commercial Boeing 707. A total of 732 KC-135s were produced, 3 of which, by deleting their tanker refuelling booms and other equipment, were converted into C-135A transports. An additional 15 C-135A and 30 C-135B were produced, along with 12 C-135F tankers for France. Further variants on the KC-135 were 14 EC-135C and 3 EC-135J ACP (Airborne Command Post) aircraft for the Strategic Air Command, 4 RC-135A photographic reconnaissance aircraft, 10 RC-135B electronic reconnaissance aircraft, 10 WC-135B weather reconnaissance aircraft, 8 EC-135N advanced range instrumentation aircraft, 6 KC-135Q/R/T tanker aircraft with special modifications to refuel U-2, SR-71A and other strategic reconnaissance aircraft, 8 RC-135C/D/E/M/S/U electronic reconnaissance aircraft, and 25 EC-135G/H/K/L/P signals intelligence, airborne relay and command and communications aircraft. Deliveries of the KC-135A began in 1957, and 610 of these aircraft today equip our Strategic Air Command.

**Type:** Four-engined turbojet tanker aircraft.

**Maximum Weight:** 297,000 lbs.

**Fuel Transfer Capacity:** 198,000 lbs (31,200 gallons).

**Speed:** 585 mph.

**Range:** 1,150 miles.

**Produced:** 877 of all types, including 732 KC-135A (of which 3 converted to C-135A), 15 C-135A, 30 C-135B, 12 C-135F, 14 EC-135C, 3 EC-135J, 4 RC-135A, 10 RC-135B, 10 EC-135B, 8 EC-135N, 6 KC-135Q/R/T, 8 RC-135C/D/E/M/S/U, and 25 EC-135G/H/K/L/P.

**In US Service:** 610 KC-135A in SAC, 37 EC-135 and 16 RC-135 in USAF, and 4 KC-135 in Air National Guard.

**In Service Abroad:** France (16 KC-135F).

# BOEING E-3A AWACS

Based on the commercial Boeing 707-320C, the AWACS (Airborne Warning and Control System) is planned as an aerial battlefield command center which combines the functions of airborne early warning, battlefield surveillance and tactical control. Its Westinghouse AN/APY-1 surveillance radar is installed in pressurized vessels in the aircraft's aft lower deck, and the radar's antenna is housed in a thirty-foot rotating dome mounted above the aircraft on two struts. Completing a full revolution every 10 seconds, the antenna scans through a radius of 360 degrees and returns high-PRF (Pulse Repetition Frequency) signals to the aircraft's IBM System 4-Pi CC-1 central computer and data processor. At a normal operating height of 40,000 feet, the AWACS has an effective target detection range of over 250 miles. Its radar can track 600 targets simultaneously, successfully distinguishing them, at altitudes below its own, from what radar operators call "ground clutter," and its computer and data processor can identify and fully interpret over 240 targets simultaneously, measuring the dimensions of each, computing its altitude, speed and directional bearing, and visually displaying this information in digital and alphanumeric form on MPC (Multi-Purpose Display) consoles in the aircraft's operations center.

The military implications of this newly-developed capability are enormous. Commanders may be provided with immediate and accurate information on a very large number of moving targets within an immense area of air space. Their warning time for approaching targets is vastly increased. The AWACS, unarmed, may protect itself by sending fighter aircraft to an approaching threat well before it comes within range. Tactical ground units benefit from the aircraft's ability to detect targets hundreds of

**Boeing KC-135 refuelling a B-52 bomber**

miles beyond the ground horizon. The threat of low-level air penetration below the scanning lobes of ground radar defenses is eliminated.

Unfortunately, this technology is also exorbitantly expensive. One of the least expensive sets of equipment aboard the AWACS is its Northrop Omega radio navigation receiver and computer which, with Delco inertial platforms and a Ryan Doppler velocity sensor, provides the aircraft with precise positioning data. Each system costs $780,000. The Westinghouse AN/APY-1 surveillance radar cost $6.824 million per unit in 1977. USAF procurement costs for the complete aircraft have risen from $65.6 million each at the program's inception to $78.1 million per aircraft in 1978, during which year the Air Force plans procurement of three.

The Air Force has planned on a total of 34 AWACS aircraft. It is a priority program which most senior Air Force officials regard as crucial to the national security. Unfortunately, funding had existed for only 25 of these aircraft, until the Carter administration was able to obtain Congressional approval of a sale of 7 AWACS to Iran for $1.229 billion. This substantially reduced the share of research and development costs that had to be apportioned to each AWACS aircraft in the USAF procurement program. Before the sale, the unit procurement cost for three of the aircraft in 1978 had risen to $80.9 million each. After the sale, this cost was reduced by $2.8 million per aircraft. It appeared that the Air Force would eventually be able to procure all 34 of the aircraft planned, but then the Khomeini government cancelled Iran's order.

$510.2 million of the Iranian sale was for spares, maintenance support, site surveys and training. This left a total "end item" cost of $718.7 million for the seven

aircraft themselves, or $102.671 million each. Some of this, of course, is a share of the AWACS research and development costs, to which the Iranians were making a fair contribution. Despite these costs, the Shah wanted to purchase another 3 AWACS. It should be noted that those versions of the E-3A AWACS planned for Iran would not have been equipped with some systems standard on the USAF version, including United States government enciphering gear, JTIDS (Joint Tactical Information Distribution System) equipment, USAF signal intelligence equipment, electronic ECCM circuitry and secure mode IFF (Interrogation Friend or Foe) circuitry.

While the Iranian sale, easing financial pressure on the Air Force AWACS program, had somewhat relaxed United States government pressure on NATO, in turn, to adopt the AWACS as its own early warning system, that organization may yet purchase from 16 to 18 of the aircraft. Many NATO commanders argue that there is no need for such a large aircraft. Their requirement is simply for a system to pass tracking and targeting information to ground operations centers. They had never planned on an operations center in the air. What they may not have realized is that the United States has planned for a mobile airborne operations center so that it would survive in the event that nuclear weapons are introduced on the battlefields of NATO, a contingency which NATO planners are hardly prepared to accept. Theirs may in the end be the more intelligent attitude, for in regarding nuclear war as unacceptable, they may make it that much less feasible.

One NATO country, Great Britain, has meanwhile decided not to purchase the AWACS but to develop its own airborne early warning system based on the Hawker-Siddeley Nimrod long-range reconnaissance aircraft. A great deal of American electronic equipment will be used on the

Nimrod, including a digitally-based ESM system supplied by Loral Electronic Systems.

The first six USAF AWACS aircraft are now operational with the Tactical Air Command's 552nd Airborne Warning and Control Wing at Tinker Air Force Base, Oklahoma, where 16 of the aircraft will eventually be based. A total of 14 should be delivered by the end of 1978. USAF's 966th Airborne Warning and Control Training Squadron is also based at Tinker AFB, and is now training the first operational AWACS crews with a simulator that cost $12 million. Further AWACS aircraft will be deployed to Europe, Alaska and air bases in the Pacific.

**Type:** Airborne warning and battlefield control aircraft, powered by four jet turbofan engines.

**Maximum Weight:** 325,000 lbs.

**Speed:** 600 mph.

**Endurance:** 12 hours without refuelling.

**Operating Height:** 40,000 feet.

**Radar Target Detection Range:** Over 250 miles.

**Capacity:** Track 600 targets, interpret 240 simultaneously.

**Produced:** Six of 34 on order for USAF.

**In US Service:** Six E-3A with 552nd AWCW at Tinker AFB.

**Pending Exports:** 18 to be delivered to NATO, and 5 to Saudi Arabia.

**Price:** $78.1 million@ (1978 Unit Procurement Cost for 3 aircraft to USAF). $102.671 million@ (Unit FMS price for 7 aircraft to Iran in 1977).

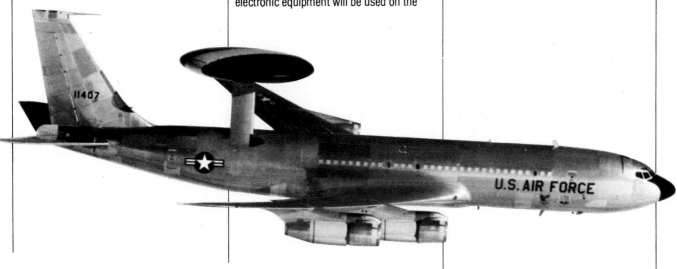

**Boeing E-3A AWACS**

## CESSNA O-1 BIRD DOG L-19 AND SIAI MARCHETTI SM-1019

A light observation and forward air control aircraft, originally designated the L-19. First produced in 1950, and used extensively by the US Army and USMC in Korea and Vietnam. Versions have also been produced in Pakistan, in Japan by Fuji, and in Italy by SIAI Marchetti as the SM-1019. Many lightly-armed versions exist.

**Type:** Prop-driven single-engined monoplane.

**Weight:** 2,430 lbs.

**Speed:** 115 mph.

**Range:** 530 miles.

**Produced:** 3,431 of all types, including 3 XL-19B/L prototypes, 14 commercial aircraft, 2,428 O-1A (some of which converted to G), 310 TO-1D, 591 O-1E, 60 O-1B and 25 O-1C.

**Foreign Production:** 36 Fuji O-1E, 100 SIAI Marchetti SM-1019, and approximately 22 O-1E in Pakistan.

**In US Service:** 1,265 O-1A/G and 310 TO-1D and 110 O-1E in US Army, and 60 O-1B and 25 O-1C in USMC.

**Exported under FMS:** 10.

**Exported under MAP:** 1,634.

**In Service Abroad:** Austria (19 O-1A/E), Brazil (20 O-1E), Canada (22 O-1E), Cambodia (10 O-1E), Chile (4 O-1E), France (110 O-1E), Italy (100 O-1E and 100 SM-1019), Japan (87 O-1A and 36 Fuji O-1E), Laos (20 O-1E), Lebanon (6 O-1E), Norway (26 O-1E), Pakistan (70 O-1E including 10 locally produced), Spain (8 O-1E), Taiwan (22 O-1E), Thailand (20 O-1E), and South Vietnam (60 O-1A/E supplied under MAP and 119 O-1E abandoned by US forces).

## CESSNA MODEL 337 SUPER SKYMASTER/O-2

A twin-engined forward air control aircraft frequently used as an attack bomber and COIN aircraft, and produced under license by Reims Aviation of France as the FTB 337G. For its very light weight its two engines, one in the nose and one behind the front fuselage compartment, give it exceptional lift and speed. Developed from the commercial Cessna Models 336 and P337, it was first delivered in 1966 to USAF, which ordered a total of 501 O-2As. In 1967, 31 O-2Bs were also delivered, equipped with high-power aerial broadcast systems for psychological warfare missions in Vietnam. Many of the USAF O-2As and O-2Bs were fitted with hardpoints for underwing FFAR 2.75'' rocket pods and 7.62 mm SUU-11/A minigun pods for COIN use. USAF has since received another 100 O-2B, and to date over 325 FTB 337G aircraft have been produced, many for export, by Reims Aviation, which has also developed an FTMA Milirole STOL version.

**Type:** Prop-driven twin-engined twin-tailed monoplane with dual controls, seating 4 to 6.

**Weight:** 4,630 lbs.

**Speed:** 199 mph.

**Range:** 1,120 miles.

**Ordnance Capacity:** 1,400 lbs, including 2.75'' FFAR rocket pods, SUU-11/A 7.62mm gun pods, Mk 81 250 lb Snakeye or Mk 82 500 lb Snakeye bombs.

**Produced:** Over 2,112 of all types, including 325 FTB 337G by Reims Aviation and 1,787 by Cessna, of which 501 O-2A and 131 O-2B delivered to USAF, and 12 O-2A delivered to Iran.

**In US Service:** 80 O-2A/B in Air Training Command, and 155 O-2A/B in Air National Guard.

**Exported under MAP:** 35.

**Exported under FMS:** 12.

**In Service Abroad:** Argentina (2 Cessna 337), Benin (2 Reims FTB 337G), Ecuador (3 Cessna 337), Ethiopia (1 Cessna 337), Gabon (1 Reims FR-337), Iran (12 O-2A), Ivory Coast (3 Reims FR-337) Malagasy (3 Reims FTB 337G), Mauritania (4 Reims FR-337), Niger (2 Reims FR-337), Senegal (4 Reims FTB 337G), Sri Lanka (4 Cessna 337), Togo (3 Reims FR-337), Venezuela (8 Cessna 337), and Vietnam (40 O-2A/B abandoned by US forces).

## CESSNA MODEL 310/U-3A/B (FORMER L-27A)

A light observation and liaison aircraft, based on the commercial Cessna Model 310. In 1957 USAF procured 160 of these, which were popularly known in that service as the "Blue Canoe," and designated them L-27A. The designation was later changed to U-3A, and an order for 36 U-3Bs with all-weather avionics followed in 1962. The commercial Model 310 and several models following it, including the 340, 340B, 402, 402B and 411, have been widely adopted by several foreign military services for use as trainers and lightly-armed COIN aircraft.

**Type:** Prop-driven twin-engined monoplane, seating 5 (310/340/340B) or 8 (402/402B/411).

**Weight:** (U-3A) 4,700 lbs, (U-3B) 5,500 lbs.

**Speed:** 223 mph.

**Range:** 1,740 miles.

**Produced:** 4,268 commercial and military versions, including 196 U03A/B.

**In US Service:** 130 U-3A and 36 U-3B in USAF.

**Exported under MAP:** 6 U-3A.

**In Service Abroad:** Bolivia (3 Cessna 402), France (14 Cessna 31ON and 12 Cessna 411), Finland (4 Cessna 402), Haiti (1 Cessna 310), Indonesia (7 Cessna 402B), Malaysia (12 Cessna 402B), Saudi Arabia (12 Cessna 310K), Tanzania (3 Cessna 310), Thailand (6 U-3A), and Zaire (36 Cessna 310).

**Recent Transfers:** 12 Cessna 402B to Malaysia in 1974. 15 Cessna 310 to Zaire in 1975.

# CESSNA MODEL 185 SKYWAGON/U-17

A light single-engined aircraft used for reconnaissance and forward air control, and based on the commercial Cessna Model 185. It is popular in many countries as a utility and COIN aircraft, and when fitted with underwing hardpoints can carry a substantial amount, for its size, of external ordnance stores. In 1963 the Air Force purchased 265 U-17As, followed by 215 U-17Bs and 17 U-17Cs. A large number have been transferred abroad under MAP, and many commercial Cessna Models 185, 206 and 207 have been purchased directly from the manufacturer for subsequent military modification abroad.

**Type:** Prop-driven single-engined monoplane, seating 4 to 6.

**Weight:** 3,300 lbs.

**Speed:** 178 mph.

**Range:** 1,075 miles.

**Produced:** More than 2,334 commercial and 497 military versions to date, including 265 U-17A, 215 U-17B and 17 U-17C.

**Ordnance Capacity:** 1,500 lbs on two external hardpoints, including SUU-11/A 7.62mm gun pods, Mk 81 250 lb and Mk 82 500 lb Snakeye bombs, rocket and flare pods.

**Exported under FMS:** 3.

**Exported under MAP:** 517.

**Un US Service:** 169 U-17A and 136 U-17B in USAF.

**In Service Abroad:** Argentina (20 Cessna 207), Bolivia (15 U-17A), Costa Rica (7 Cessna 185), Greece (10 U-17A), Honduras (3 Cessna 185), Indonesia (6 Cessna 207), Iran (45 Cessna 185), Jamaica (3 Cessna 185), Laos (4 U-17A), Guatemala (4 Cessna 207), Panama (12 Cessna 185), Paraguay (10 Cessna 185), Peru (5 Cessna 185), South Africa (16 Cessna 185), South Korea (34 U-17A/B), Turkey (22 U-17A/B), Uruguay (6 U-17A), and Vietnam (41 U-17A and 3 Cessna 206).

# CESSNA MODEL 180 SKYWAGON AND MODEL 182 SKYLANE

Earlier versions of the Model 185 Skywagon, these two commercial aircraft have also gained popularity abroad for military reconnaissance and transport service. One of them, the Model 182 Skylane, is manufactured in France by Reims Aviation as the F-182.

**Type:** Prop-driven single-engined monoplane, seating 4 to 6.

**Weight:** 3,200 lbs.

**Speed:** 164 mph.

**Range:** 1,022 miles.

**Produced:** More than 5,648 Model 180 and 15,452 Model 182.

**In Service Abroad:** Burma (10 Cessna 180), Chile (6 Cessna 180), Guatemala (3 Cessna 180), Honduras (1 Cessna 180), Nicaragua (10 Cessna 180), Venezuela (5 Cessna 180 and 12 Cessna 182N).

# CESSNA MODEL 150/A 150 AEROBAT

Observation and forward air control aircraft, based on the commercial Cessna Model 150 and later Model 170, and manufactured in France by Reims Aviation as the F-150. Over 21,771 of this aircraft have been produced.

**Type:** Prop-driven single-engined monoplane, seating 2 to 4.

**Weight:** 1,600 lbs.

**Speed:** 124 mph.

**Range:** 656 miles.

**Produced:** 21,771 of all types to date.

**In Service Abroad:** Dominica (3 Cessna 170), Ecuador (24 Cessna 150), Guatemala (6 Cessna 150), Ivory Coast (2 Reims F-150), and Sri Lanka (6 Cessna 150).

# CESSNA MODEL 172 SKYHAWK T-41 MESCALERO

A basic trainer frequently used abroad in the COIN role, and based on the commercial Cessna Model 172 Skyhawk, formerly the Model 172 Cardinal. Over 24,822 of all types have been produced to date, and the aircraft is also produced under license in Pakistan and in France by Reims Aviation as the R172E and Model 551 Reims Rocket. USAF ordered 170 of this aircraft in 1964, designated T-41A, and later increased the order to 237. The US Army followed with orders for 255 T-41B Mescalero, which were delivered in 1967 and followed by a second USAF order for 52 T-41C. A more powerful T-41D was subsequently developed to equip air forces abroad with a basic trainer, and large numbers of the T-41D have been transferred under MAP.

**Type:** Prop-driven single-engined monoplane, seating 2 to 4.

**Weight:** 2,300 lbs.

**Speed:** 138 mph.

**Range:** 720 miles.

**Ordnance Capacity:** 900 lbs on two underwing hardpoints.

**Produced:** 24,822 of all types to date, including 1,234 F-172 by Reims Aviation, 60 T-41D at Cambellpur in Pakistan, and 544 T-41A/B/C and over 340 T-41D.

**In US Service:** 240 T-41A and 52 T-41C in USAF, and 255 T-41B in US Army.

**Exported under FMS:** 49.

**Exported under MAP:** 275.

**In Service Abroad:** Argentina (6 T-41D), Cambodia (12 T-41D), Colombia (30 T-41D), Ecuador (8 T-41A and 10 T-41D), Greece (8 T-41D), Honduras (5 T-41D), Iran (30 T-41D), Laos (6 T-41D), Pakistan (60 T-41D locally produced), Peru (40 T-41D), Philippines (22 T-41D), Saudi Arabia (6 T-41D and 8 Cessna 172), Singapore (6 Cessna 172), Thailand (30 T-41D), and Turkey (16 T-41D).

**Price:** $500,000@ (1974 Unit Procurement Cost for 250 T-41D to USAF).

Cessna O-2

USAF 21360

# GRUMMAN
# E-2 HAWKEYE

An airborne early warning and fighter direction aircraft, usually operated from naval carriers but soon to be used by the Israelis for ground-based operations. The Hawkeye is under consideration by a number of other countries, including Australia and Japan, and it has also been considered by NATO as a less expensive airborne early warning system as an alternative to the E-3A AWACS. Because the Air Force has preferred NATO to consider the AWACS, Grumman Aircraft has been unable to demonstrate the Hawkeye system to NATO commanders, and no formal evaluations of the aircraft by NATO had taken place up to March of 1978.

The Navy's first airborne early warning aircraft was the E-1 Tracer, adapted from the S-2 Tracker anti-submarine aircraft. The E-2 Hawkeye, however, was the first aircraft specifically designed as an airborne warning and fighter control system. Replacing the earlier Tracers, the Hawkeye first entered service in 1966, equipping USN Squadrons VAW-11 and VAW-12. 59 E-2A were built with an AN/APS-96 radar system, and by 1971 these had all been updated to E-2B standard with the improved AN/APS-120 long-range surveillance radar, AN/APA-171 radar antenna, AN/OL-93/APA signal processor and Litton AN/OL-77/ASQ computer. The E-2B equipped 14 USN squadrons of four aircraft each. Operating together, the aircraft in each squadron are able to collect information on all moving targets within an area of more than 125,000 square miles, identifying and monitoring a number of such targets for the ATDS (Airborne Tactical Data System) and relaying this information, in turn, to ship-board and ground-based NTDS

(Naval Tactical Data System) operations centers, which coordinate the operations of all USN air and naval forces.

Equipped with secure mode data link systems, including an AN/APX-72 IFF (Interrogation Friend or Foe) transponder, the Hazeltine AN/RT-988/APX IFF interrogator and a Magnavox AN/ALQ-108 IFF ECM Deception Set, the Hawkeye can also vector fighter aircraft into position to intercept enemy aircraft. By shutting down their own radar and communicating with the Hawkeye solely by data link, our fighter aircraft are more difficult to track, and they can also avoid missiles fired by hostile aircraft which home on radar emissions.

In 1971 the first improved E-2C Hawkeye flew, equipped with the AN/APS-125 Advanced Radar Processing System which, like the Westinghouse AN/APY-1 surveillance radar aboard the E-3A AWACS, has the ability to distinguish targets in radar ground clutter. With improved target memory capability in a microelectronic computer, a more powerful ADP (Automatic Data Processing) system, and the Litton-Amecon AN/ALR-59 ESM Passive Detection System, the E-2C is now able, operating at a height of about 30,000 feet, to track as many as 300 targets at once and fully interpret 30 of them. In view of the Hawkeye's much lower unit cost as compared with the Boeing AWACS, this capability compares favorably with that of the AWACS, even though the latter aircraft can track 600 targets at once and interpret up to 240. Both aircraft have a target detection range of over 250 miles.

The first deliveries of the E-2C Hawkeye were to USN Squadrons VAW-123 at Norfolk Naval Air Station, Virginia, and VAW-

125 aboard the *USS Constellation*. The Navy has a total requirement for 49 of these aircraft, with funds now in hand for procurement of 34 to equip 6 AEW squadrons. E-2Bs currently in service will also be retrofitted with the AN/APS-125 radar system, bringing them up to C standard.

**Type:** Carrier-based airborne warning and control aircraft, powered by twin turbo-props, with crew of 5.

**Maximum Weight:** (E-2C) 51,569 lbs.

**Speed:** 374 mph.

**Range:** 1,700 miles.

**Endurance:** 7 hours without refuelling.

**Operating Height:** 30,000 feet.

**Radar Target Detection Range:** Over 250 miles.

**Capacity:** Track 300 targets, interpret 30 simultaneously.

**Produced:** 59 E-2A, all of which converted to E-2B, and 16 of 53 E-2C planned, including 4 for Israel.

**In US Service:** 59 E-2B and 16 E-2C in 18 USN AEW squadrons.

**Exported under FMS:** 4 to Israel.

**In Service Abroad:** Israel (4).

**Price:** $32.433 million@ (1978 Unit Procurement Cost for 6 aircraft to USN). $24.416 million @ (1977 Unit Procurement Cost for 6 aircraft to USN). $42.5 million@ (Unit cost for 4 aircraft to Israel under FMS in 1976).

# GRUMMAN TF-9J COUGAR

A basic Navy jet trainer, derived from the Grumman F-9F Panther, the first jet fighter built by Grumman for the Navy. The two-seat trainer version has swept wings, and first entered service in 1956. A number of these aircraft were used in combat in Vietnam, with two 20mm cannon installed in their noses and provision for up to 2,000 lbs of external ordnance.

**Type:** Single-engined jet trainer, seating 2.

**Weight:** 20,600 lbs.

**Speed:** 705 mph.

**Range:** 1,000 miles.

**Produced:** 3,370 of all types, including 1,385 F-9F Panthers and 1,985 F-9J Cougars, of which 399 were converted to TF-9J.

**In US Service:** 110 TF-9J in USN.

**In Service Abroad:** Argentina (2).

**Grumman E-2C Hawkeye**

# GRUMMAN TC-4 ACADEME/VC-4 GULFSTREAM

A specialized aircrew trainer derived from the commercial Grumman Gulfstream transport aircraft. The US Navy has fitted out the TC-4C with a complete A-6A Intruder avionics system in an aft cabin, with a training pilot cockpit and radar computer consoles to train Intruder aircrews. The Gulfstream is also used as a VIP transport and patrol aircraft by our Coast Guard.

**Type:** Twin-engined turboprop trainer, seating 9.

**Weight:** 36,000 lbs.

**Speed:** 334 mph.

**Range:** 2,205 miles.

**In US Service:** 9 TC-4C in US Navy, and 1 VC-4A and 1 VC-11A in Coast Guard.

**In Service Abroad:** Greece (1 VC-4).

**Price:** $8.1 million@ (1978 UPC to USMC).

# HELIO U-10 SUPER COURIER

A light utility aircraft used in the COIN role and, like all Helio aircraft, possessing remarkable STOL capabilities. With leading-edge slats spanning the full length of its wings and a large slow-turning propeller, the U-10 can take off in less than 350 feet and travel as slowly as 30 mph without stalling. Fitted with underwing pylons, it can carry up to 1,000 lbs of external ordnance. The aircraft became quite popular among Special Forces and other elite units in Vietnam, and an improved U-10B was developed with a paradrop door and room to carry five combat troops.

**Type:** Prop-driven single-engine monoplane, seating 5.

**Weight:** 3,400 lbs.

**Speed:** 167 mph.

**Range:** 1,380 miles.

**Ordnance Capacity:** 1,000 lbs, including 4 Mk 81 250 lb Snakeye bombs or 2 Mk 82 500 lb Snakeye bombs, or 2 FFAR 2.75'' rocket pods, or 2 SUU-11/A 7.62mm Minigun pods.

**Produced:** More than 525 Super Couriers of all types, including 136 U-10A, U-10B and U-10D to USAF.

**In US Service:** 100 U-10A/B/D in USAF Tactical Air Command.

**Exported under MAP:** 36 U-10A.

**In Service Abroad:** Peru: (5 Super Courier), South Africa (2), Thailand (36 U-10A).

# LOCKHEED AL-60 AERMACCHI AM-3C

A light utility aircraft heavily used in a number of countries as a tactical support and COIN fighter, and based on a Lockheed design first flown in 1959. Production of the aircraft has been licensed to Lockheed-Azcarate in Mexico and Aermacchi in Italy. From the basic AL-60 design Aermacchi produced the AM-3C in cooperation with Aeritalia, and deliveries of the AM-3C began in 1967, including 40 to South Africa, where they are called the Bosbok. South Africa's Atlas Aircraft, in turn, was licensed to produced the AM-3C as the C4M Kudu, and has produced to date an additional 160 of the aircraft. The Rhodesian Air Force has received a few of the Aermacchi Al-60s, which it calls the Trojan despite the confusion of nomenclature between this aircraft and the North American Rockwell T-28 Trojan, five of which are also in Rhodesia operating in the COIN role. South Africa's Bosboks equip the 41st Squadron at Johannesburg and the 42nd Squadron at Potchefstroom.

**Type:** Prop-driven single-engined monoplane, seating 6 (AL-60), 3 (AM-3C) or 8 (C4M).

**Weight:** (AL-60) 4,500 lbs, (AM-3C/C4M) 3,860 lbs.

**Speed:** (AL-60) 156 mph, (AM-3C/C4M) 173 mph.

**Range:** (AL-60) 645 miles, (AM-3C/C4M) 615 miles.

**Ordnance Capacity:** Up to 750 lbs on two to four underwing pylons, including 2 Mk 81 250 lb Snakeye bombs, or two AN/M1A2 cluster bombs with six 20 lb fragmentation bombs each, or two AN/M4A1 cluster bombs with three 25 lb fragmentation bombs each, or two AN/M 1A2 cluster bombs with six 20 lb fragmentation bombs each, or two M28A2 cluster bombs with 24 5 lb butterfly bombs each, or two Matra gun pods, each with two 7.62mm machine guns with 2,000 rounds, or two SUU-11/A 7.62mm Minigun pods with 1,500 rounds each, or two Matra 125 rocket pods with six 2.75'' rockets each, or two Matra 122 rocket pods with seven BPD 50mm rockets each, or two Nord AS-11/12 wire-guided missiles. Parachute flares, photoflash bombs and target markers may also be carried.

**Produced:** Over 250 of all types.

**In Service Abroad:** Central African Republic (10 Aermacchi AL-60C5 Conestogas), Italy (40 Aermacchi AM-3C), Mexico (18 Azcarate AL-60), Rhodesia (12 Aermacchi AL-60F5 Trojans), and South Africa (40 Aeritalia AM-3C Bosboks and 150 Atlas C4M Kudu), Mauritania (2).

# GRUMMAN S-2 TRACKER E-1 TRACER AND C-1 TRADER

Carrier-borne anti-submarine patrol and attack aircraft, from which an airborne early warning aircraft and a light COD (Carrier Onboard Delivery) transport aircraft were also derived. Still equipping a number of USN Air Reserve squadrons, the S-2 Tracker serves as a front-line ASW aircraft in several foreign navies. With a crew of four, including two radar plotters, the S-2 was the first ASW aircraft to carry both submarine detection equipment and ASW weapons. The S-2A is fitted with the AN/APS-38 search radar, a MAD (Magnetic Anomaly Detection) boom extending behind its tail, a 70 million candlepower searchlight slung beneath its starboard wing, and 32 active or passive sonobuoys fitted in wing nacelles.

The MAD boom registers disturbances caused to the Earth's magnetic field by large masses of metal beneath the surface of the sea. Sonobuoys, dropped into the water at preselected depths, leave on the surface a small float fitted with a transmitter that beams each buoy's position to the mother aircraft. The passive sonobuoy detects the hydrodynamic disturbances caused within a radius of several miles by the movement of submarines, or the sounds of submarine machinery and propellers turning over even greater distances. The active sonobuoy, some varieties of which remain operational for several hours, employs continuous wave sonar to detect the presence of large objects under water, even when they are silent and still. When contact is made, the aircraft uses the sonobuoy's position as the center of its search radius.

The S-2 Tracker is equipped to carry the Mk 101 or Mk 57 ''Big Betty'' nuclear depth charge, as well as 60 echo-sounding depth charges, two electric acoustic-homing torpedoes and a variety of other ordnance on six underwing pylons.

A total of 1,163 S-2 Trackers were produced. Large numbers were exported, and several modifications were made to US-2 utility and target towing aircraft and some RS-2 photographic survey aircraft. 100 Trackers were also produced under license by De Havilland of Canada. From the basic S-2 airframe design, the first airborne early warning aircraft, the E-1 Tracer, was developed, equipped with the AN/APS-82 search radar. Of these, 88 were produced. A final variant was the C-1 Trader transport aircraft for Carrier Onboard Delivery of cargo and personnel.

**Type:** Prop-driven twin-engined ASW/AEW/COD aircraft.

**Weight:** (S-2A) 17,357 lbs, (S-2E)29, 150 lbs, (C-1A and E-1B) 27,00 lbs.

**Speed:** 287 mph.

**Range:** (S-2A) 900 miles, (S-2E) 1,300 miles.

**Ordnance Capacity:** (S-2 only) 1,500 lbs, including 2 electric acoustic-homing torpedoes, 60 echo-sounding depth charges, two Mk 101 or Mk 57 nuclear depth charges, four 385 lb depth charges, or six 250 lb bombs, in addition to 6 2.75'' FFAR or 5'' Zuni rocket pods or 4 7.62mm SUU-11/A gun pods on underwing pylons.

**Search Radar:** (S-2A) AN/APS-38, (S-2E) AN/APS-88, (E-1B) AN-APS-82.

**Produced:** A total of 1,438 of all types, including 755 S-2A (of which some conversions to TS-2A/US-2A/S-2B/US-2B/S-2F), 60 S-2C (of which some conversions to US-2C/RS-2C), 121 S-2D, 227 S-2E, 43 De Havilland CS2F-1 and 57 De Havilland CS2F-2, together with 87 C-1A and 88 E-1B.

**In US Service:** 30 S-2E, 9 E-1B and 30 C-1A in USN, and 16 S-2E, 8 E-1B in USN Air Reserve.

**Exported under FMS:** 108.

**Exported under MAP:** 165.

**In Service Abroad:** Argentina (6 S-2A), Australia (2 S-2E), Brazil (13 CS2F-1), Canada (13 CS2F-1 and 57 CS2F-2/3), Italy (48 S-2A), Japan (60 S-2A), the Netherlands (24 S-2A and 17 CS2F-1), Taiwan (9 S-2A), Thailand (5 S-2A), Turkey (12 S-2E and 2 TS-2A), Uruguay (3 S-2A), Venezuela (12 S-2E) and Israel (2 E-1B as EV-1).

**Price:** $8.765 million@ (1968 Unit Procurement Cost for 22 S-2E aircraft to USN).

**Pending Orders:** Australia, which already had an order pending for 6 additional S-2Es, lost 12 aircraft of the original 14 S-2E trackers belonging to Royal Australian Navy Squadrons VS 816 and VT 851 in a fire at RAN Air Station Nowra, near Sydney, on 5 December 1976. RAN may order additional S-2Es to replace those lost.

**Lockheed P-2E**

# LOCKHEED P-2 NEPTUNE

A land-based anti-submarine attack and maritime patrol aircraft. Designed toward the end of World War II, it did not enter service until 1947, but since that time it has been produced and used in greater quantities than any other ASW aircraft. While it has been replaced in the USN by the P-3 Orion, it still serves in our Naval Reserve, and in 11 foreign countries.

Early versions of the Neptune were armed with twin .50 Caliber machine guns in the nose and tail and in a dorsal turret, and with wingtip fuel tanks could carry 8,000 lbs of mixed ordnance in an internal weapons bay, including ASW torpedoes, mines, depth charges and bombs, as well as 16 5″ Zuni rockets underwing, for a range of over 2,500 miles. A searchlight was normally fixed in the starboard wingtip tank. Other versions had solid noses fitted with six 20mm cannon, and substituted 20 mm cannon in the tail and dorsal turret as well.

One of the early P2V-1 aircraft, later redesignated P-2A, was stripped for long-distance patrol under the *Truculent Turtle* program. Of the 83 P2V-3 aircraft, later redesignated P-2C, 12 were equipped to deliver nuclear weapons from aircraft carriers, though never deployed in this role, another 2 were modified as P2V-3Z armoured transports, and 30 were fitted with the AN/APS-20 search radar in a belly radome. These were followed by 52 P-2D, also equipped with the AN/APS-20, and by 424 P-2E.

The P-2E, which appeared in 1950, was the first Neptune to be fitted with a MAD (Magnetic Anomaly Detection) boom in its tail, as were all Neptunes and indeed all ASW aircraft thereafter. It was also equipped with two Westinghouse J34-WE-34 auxiliary turbojets, which boosted its speed to 403 mph. Twelve of these aircraft were modified to Sp-2E standard with Jezebel passive detection systems, while others were converted to

EP-2E early warning and DP-2E drone control aircraft. In Vietnam, the U.S. Army used some modified P-2Es as AP-2E and OP-2E tactical reconnaissance aircraft equipped with sensors and SIGINT(signals intelligence) systems. Six P-2E aircraft were subsequently transferred to Argentina, 12 to France, 14 to Brazil, 36 to Britain's Royal Air Force, and 20 P-2E and 12 SP-2E to the Netherlands where they equipped four ASW squadrons. Twelve British P-2E were later retransferred to Portugal, as were twelve Dutch P-2E, while the twelve Dutch SP-2E were retransferred, in an apparent violation of United States policy, to South Africa.

Of the 83 P-2F that followed only a few were equipped with auxiliary turbojet engines. These were redesignated P-2G. Others were modified as TP-2F trainers or equipped, as MP-2Fs, to carry the Petrel AUM-N-2 air-to-surface ASW missile. Twelve P-2Fs were transferred to France.

The P-2H, which first entered service in 1959, was the final Lockheed production model of the Neptune. All were equipped with auxiliary jet engines, and while early production models carried twin .50 Caliber machine guns in their tail and dorsal turret, later models substituted twin 20mm cannon and final models dropped this armament entirely. Seven of these aircraft were modified for USAF as RB-69A electronic testbeds, one for the USN as an EP-2H experimental aircraft with UHF telemetry equipment, and a few were equipped as LP-2J arctic photo reconnaissance aircraft. The Army also used a few AP-2H aircraft for low-level ground and coastal interdiction in Vietnam. Large numbers of the P-2H, however, were converted to SP-2H standard with the addition of Jezebel/Julie echo-ranging detection equipment, and it is this conversion that has been transferred in quantity abroad, including 2 to Argentina, 16 to the Netherlands, 16 to Australia, 4 to Chile, 24 to France and 28 to Japan.

In addition to its 28 P-2H produced by Lockheed, the Japanese Marine Self Defense Force has also been provided with 48 P-2H produced under license by Kawasaki between 1959 and 1965. These were followed by the Kawasaki P-2J, a lengthened version of the Neptune fitted with twin turboprop engines and with radar, sensor and data processing equipment so advanced, including the AN/APS-80J search radar, as to give it an ASW detection capability almost equal to that of the P-3 Orion, the Neptune's successor.

**Type:** Prop-driven twin-engined ASW aircraft, E/G/H models with auxiliary jet engines, or twin turboprop aircraft (P-2J).

**Crew:** Seven (P-2J: eight).

**Weight:** 79,895 lbs.

**Speed:** 356 mph (A/B/C/D/F) or 403 mph (E/G/H/J).

**Range:** 2,765 miles. Maximum ferry range of 3,685 miles.

**Armament:** 6 x .50 Cal MG in nose, tail, dorsal turret, or 6 x 20mm cannon in nose and 4 x 20mm cannon in tail and dorsal turret. (None in later H and J models).

**Ordnance Capacity:** 10,000 lbs, including 8,000 lbs internally and 2,000 lbs underwing.

**Stores Combinations:** 2 x 2,165 lb ASW Torpedo or 2 x 2,000 lb Mk 55 mine, or 8 x 1,000 lb Mk 52 mine, or 12 x 325 lb depth charge or 8 x 1,000 lb bomb or 4 x 2,000 lb bomb, and 16 x 5″ Zuni rocket underwing.

**Produced:** 1,188 of all types, including 2 prototype aircraft, 15 P-2A, 81 P-2B, 83 P-2C, 52 P-2D, 424 P-2E, 83 P-2F, 359 P-2H (including 48 Kawasaki P-2H), and 89 P-2J. See text for conversions.

**Exported under FMS:** 72.

**Exported under MAP:** 186.

**In US Service:** 36 SP-2H in Naval Air Reserve.

**In Service Abroad:** Argentina (8 ex-RAF P-2E and 10 SP-2H), Australia (16 SP-2H in No. 10 Squadron of RAAF, Townsville, Queensland), Brazil (14 P-2E), Chile (4 SP-2H), France (12 P-2E, 12 P-2F of 26 originally delivered, and 12 SP-2H of 29 delivered), Japan (89 P-2J and 40 P-2H of 76 delivered), the Netherlands (8 P-2E and 15 SP-2H of 19 delivered, in No. 320 Squadron of the Royal Netherlands Navy), Portugal (12 ex-Dutch P-2E and 12 ex-British P-2E) and South Africa (12 ex-Dutch SP-2E).

**Formerly in Service:** Australia (12 P-2E and 12 P-2H), Canada (25 P-2H), France (29 P-2H of 33 delivered), the Netherlands (4 ex-French P-2H) and United Kingdom (52 P-2E).

**Price:** $10.1 million@ (1976 Unit Procurement Cost to Japanese Marine Self Defense Force for 89 P-2J).

Based on the Lockheed Electra commercial airliner, this is the most sophisticated ASW aircraft flying. It is currently in production and in service with the USN and seven foreign navies, and is soon to join an eighth. Early versions, carrying two and a half tons of highly advanced electronics and submarine detection equipment, had a range of 1,500 miles with three hours of time over target, and could carry a total of 20,000 lbs of mixed ASW ordnance in an internal weapons bay and on ten underwing pylons. They were capable of patrolling 322,000 square miles of ocean at a cost, Lockheed claimed, of less than a penny per square mile. Since that time the aircraft's capabilities have been greatly increased, along with its costs.

The Orion first entered service in 1962 with USN Squadrons VP-8 and VP-44. Replacing the P-2 Neptune and other ASW aircraft, 157 P-3As were built, of which 10 were converted to EP-3E electronic reconnaissance aircraft, 4 to WP-3A weather reconnaissance aircraft, and 2 to specialized RP-3A aircraft, one of them, under Project Outpost Season, for a worldwide environmental study codenamed *El Coyote* and the other, under Project Birdseye, for an arctic environmental study codenamed *Arctic Fox*. Three P-3As were subsequently transferred to Spain.

The P-3B, of which 144 were built for the USN and 20 for export, had an increased range of 2,380 miles and, while its greater fuel load reduced its ordnance capacity to about 15,000 lbs, it was equipped to carry the AGM-12 Bullpup air-to-surface missile. Ten of the 20 export models were supplied to No. 11 Squadron of the Royal Australian Air Force, 5 to No. 5 Squadron of the Royal New Zealand Air Force, and 5 to No. 333 Squadron of the Norwegian Navy.

The P-3C, the current production model of the Orion, first entered service in 1968, and has since been the subject of several progressive programs to update and increase its submarine detection capabilities. With an AN/APS-115 search radar with 240 degrees of forward scan and 120 degrees of rearward scan, an AN/ASA-64 MAD boom capable of detecting the magnetic disturbances caused by submarines submerged to their maximum depths, 52 acoustic sonobuoy chutes and a maximum load of 88 sonobuoys, and an AN/ASQ-114 general purpose digital computer capable of automatically flying the aircraft to target interception points it predicts from data supplied by these detection systems, and of automatically selecting and releasing sonobuoys for search, and mines, depth charges and torpedoes when a target has been fixed, the P-3C can carry up to 7,252 lbs of internal ASW ordnance, including two depth charges and four Mk 44 acoustic homing torpedoes, and has an air endurance

of 17 hours, or an operational radius of 1,266 miles while remaining on station or in search patterns for up to seven hours.

It is an awesome weapon system, which the Navy has been steadily refining. An early improvement program, called *Update I*, gave the aircraft's computer seven times its former memory capacity. *Update II* added a Texas Instruments FLIR (Forward Looking Infra Red) sensor mounted in a chin turret, and capable of detecting heat sources (such as those left by submarine engines) *under* water; a Cubic Corporation sonobuoy reference system which employs a series of 10 antennae spaced along the aircraft's fuselage to provide a base length from which to triangulate the exact position of each sonobuoy from its VHF radio signals, as well as the relative positions of sonobuoys to one another; a Precision Data acoustic recorder for sonobuoy signals, providing 28 channels as compared with 14 on earlier aircraft; and the capability to carry AGM-84 Harpoon missiles on any of three outboard stations under either wing.

The sonobuoy reference system represented a significant advance in ASW technology, as it no longer required an aircraft to fly directly over a sonobuoy's position in order to fix its location. But improvements in submarine technology have continued to require compensatory improvements in the sensitivity of sonobuoy detection equipment, and in the speed and accuracy of acoustic signal processing. Most especially, substantial reductions in the noise of submarine engines have made their acoustic detection more difficult. The AN/SSQ-57 sonobuoy has therefore been developed, with an ambient noise meter to read the pressure spectrum of sea noise from 50 to 1,700 cycles. Once the level of ambient sea noise has been established and compared with the frequency spectrum, other active sonobuoys can then be spaced

# LOCKHEED P-3 ORION

apart in the water at distances which minimize the interference of ambient noise and maximize sensitivity to other frequencies in the spectrum. The ambient noise in any given area of the sea varies greatly, and is affected by several factors including pressure, the depth and contours of the sea floor, the variable presence of thermal layers caused by shifting currents or climatic conditions, and the salinity of the water. The higher the salinity, for example, the more quickly sound travels. Once these differences have been accounted for, more accurate acoustic sensing can take place.

The current Orion improvement program, *Update III*, will substitute a Hazeltine Corporation sonobuoy receiver increasing the available radio channels to 99, and an IBM acoustic signal processor with 32 channels. Its computer memory will be increased from 65,000 to 393,000 words, and it will employ the new OMEGA Worldwide Navigation System, which intercepts signals from eight well-separated low frequency stations to provide a fix on the aircraft's position that is accurate, at any given moment of time, within one nautical mile. The *Update III ER* (Extended Range) program will actually rebuild the aircraft, increasing its wingspan by 10 feet and its length by more than six, adding a capacity for 17,960 more lbs of fuel and extending its range to 3,165 miles.

The first *Update III* P-3Cs will be delivered in 1980. Along with current deliveries to the USN, ten *Update II* P-3Cs will be delivered in 1978 to Australia. The Navy plans a total of 257 P-3Cs and has thus far received 163 of the aircraft, including 12 in 1977. 14 are planned in 1978, 12 in 1979, 16 in 1980, 24 in 1981, and completing the program, 16 aircraft in 1982.

In addition to the P-3C, six P-3F aircraft were built without active sonar or MAD gear, but equipped to carry AGM-84 Harpoon missiles, and sold to Iran with a complement of those missiles in 1972. They were delivered in 1975. Under Project Magnet, codenamed *Roadrunner*, one RP-3D aircraft was built to fully map the Earth's magnetic field, as well as two WP-3D aircraft for the United States National Oceanographic and Atmospheric Administration, for cloud seeding experiments in an attempt to reduce the destructive force of hurricanes.

In Canada, licensed coproduction of the P-3C has also been undertaken by Canadair, which expects to supply wing sets and forward fuselage sections for a total of 150 aircraft, including 96 for the USN. The balance of Canadair production will be for its own version of the P-3C, the CP-140 which, fitted with many of the ASW systems of the S-3 Viking, is similar in standard to *Update II* versions of the Orion. 36 CP-140 LRMPA (Long Range Maritime Patrol Aircraft) have so far been produced for the Canadian Armed Forces, together with 8 for Australia. Canadair anticipates orders from Australia for 4 additional aircraft, and an order from the Netherlands for thirteen.

The Japanese Marine Self Defense Force has also decided to purchase the Orion, having originally set a requirement for 100 to 120 of the aircraft in 1976, when the unit program cost was estimated at $13 million each. By December of that year the program cost had risen to $20.75 million each, and by January of 1977 it was up to $33.33 million@. At that point, the requirement was reduced to 60 aircraft, and by January of 1978, when the program cost had reached $34.2 million@, the acquisition was fixed at 45 aircraft. These will be purchased, assembled or coproduced by the Japanese over the next 11 years, including a procurement of 8 P-3Cs in 1978 at a unit procurement cost of $21.88 million@. Three

of these aircraft will be directly imported, four assembled in Japan from kits, and 1 will be built under license by Kawasaki Heavy Industries. They may not, however, include all the equipment aboard USN versions of the aircraft, such as the Loral Electronics AN/ALQ-78 ESM (Electronic Support Measures) pod fixed on the port inboard wing pylon, the AN/ASN-84 inertial navigation sets, the AN/APN-178 Doppler navigator to measure drift and ground speed velocity, the AN/AJN-15 flight director system, or the highly advanced tactical display systems such as the AN/ASS-66 or the AN/ASA-70 multipurpose displays, which use alphanumerics, tactical symbols, scan-converted radar, variable cursors and conics on a 7.5" cathode ray tube to indicate sonobuoy positions, target positions and bearings computed from any two consecutive signals, the aircraft's position, bearing and ground speed, range scales and predicted target intercept points, and steering commands for new bearings to track and intercept targets. These displays will also identify a target when analyzed signals from the aircraft's FLIR, MAD, radar and sonobuoy systems favorably compare with the computer's memory, which has been preprogrammed with all known signal characteristics of identifiable targets.

Lockheed also attempted to sell the P-3C to Italy, but failed due to competition from the French firm of Breguet, 18 of whose Atlantique maritime patrol aircraft were sold to that country instead. Lockheed officials claim that Breuguet bribed Italian officials. In connection with the Lockheed sale of the P-3C to Japan, as well as of the Lockheed L-1011 airliner to All Nippon Airways, a total of $1.7 million in questionable payments was disbursed by Lockheed through the former chairman of the Marubeni Company, Hiro Hiyama. Mr. Hiyama is now under arrest, and the Japanese government, in an attempt to determine the final destination of these funds, has requested testimony from former Lockheed president Carl Kotchian and the company's current and former directors of sales for the Far East. The United States district Court in Los Angeles has refused to allow these gentlemen to testify without a guarantee of their immunity from trial, which so far the Japanese government has not seen fit to promise.

**Type:** Land-based four-engined turboprop ASW and reconnaissance aircraft.

**Crew:** 10 (A/B) or 12 (C).

**Weight:** 103,000 lbs (A/B/C), 135,000 lbs (*Update III* P-3C), 142,000 lbs (*Update III ER* P-3C).

**Speed:** 473 mph.

**Range:** 1,500 miles and 3 hour loiter (A), 2,380 miles (B), 2,532 miles and 7 hour lioter (C), 3,165 miles (*Update III ER* P-3C).

**Stores Combinations:** 1 x 2,000 lb mine or 3 x 1,000 lb mine or 8 x 325 lb depth charge or 4 x Mk 44 acoustic homing torpedo internally, and 6 x 2,000 lb mine and 2 x 1,000 lb mine or 4 x Mk 44 torpedo or 4 x AGM-84 Harpoon missile on underwing pylons.

**Key ASW Equipment:** AN/APS-115 radar, Texas Instruments FLIR turret, AN/ASA-64 MAD boom, 52 sonobuoy chutes with maximum load of 88 sonobuoys, Cubic Corporation (Update II) or Hazeltine (Update III) sonobuoy reference receiver.

**Produced:** 518 of all types to date, including 1 YP3V-1 prototype, 157 P-3A (of which 4 converted to WP-3A, 10 to EP-3E and 2 to RP-3A), 144 P-3B (of which some converted to EP-3B and 2 to EP-3E), 163 of 257 P-3C planned, 6 P-3F, 1 RP-3D, 2 WP-3D, and 44 Canadair CP-140.

**In US Service:** 307 P-3C and P-3B, and 12 EP-3E in USN, 1 RP-3D in USN, and 81 P-3A in USN Air Reserve.

**Exported under FMS:** 30, with 55 on order.

**Exported under MAP:** 3 P-3A.

**In Service Abroad:** Australia (10 P-3B and 8 CP-140), Canada (36 CP-140), Iran (6 P-3F), the Netherlands (4 P-3C), Norway (5 P-3B), New Zealand (5 P-3B) and Spain (3 P-3A).

**FMS Deliveries Pending:** 10 P-3C *Update II* to Australia, 45 P-3C to Japan.

**Sales Pending:** 4 CP-140 to Australia, 13 CP-140 to the Netherlands.

**Price:** $22.56 million@ (1978 Unit Procurement Cost for 14 P-3C to USN). $26.8 million@ (1979 Unit Procurement Cost for 12 P-3C to USN). $19.708 million@ (1977 Unit Procurement Cost for 12 P-3C to USN). $15.535 million@ (1976 Unit Procurement Cost for 14 P-3C to USN).

**Recent Transfers:** 6 P-3F to Iran in 1972, for delivery in 1975, for $12.166 million@. 4 P-3C to the Netherlands in 1974 for $20.5 million@. 8 CP-140 to Australia in 1975 for $20 million@. 10 P-3C to Australia in 1975, for delivery in 1978, for $25 million@. 3 P-3B to Norway in 1977 for $6 million@. 8 P-3C to Japan in 1977, for delivery in 1978, for $21.88 million@.

# LOCKHEED S-3 VIKING

This is a carrier-based jet-engined ASW aircraft designed in 1972 as a replacement for the S-2 Tracker. Lighter in weight than its land-based counterpart, the P-3 Orion, the Viking has a shorter air endurance time of only 7.5 hours, as compared with the Orion's 17. That, however, is still more than adequate for carrier-based operations, and it still provides the Viking with a range of 2,500 miles, or a combat radius of 460 miles with five hours on station. What the Viking also offers is maneuverability. With a top speed of 518 mph it can loiter at only 184 mph. From an altitude of more than 30,000 feet it can dive to sea level, using speed brakes, in less than two minutes.

The Viking is equipped with CAINS (Carrier Aircraft Inertial Navigation System) and a Univac AN/AYK-10 1832A digital computer, which has a memory capacity of 65,000 words. Its sensor systems, controlled by the computer, include a retractable Texas Instruments AN/ASQ-81 MAD boom, a Texas Instruments FLIR turret with 360 degrees of scan and two sets of lenses, wide angle and zoom, 60 sonobuoys, an AN/APS-116 high-resolution search radar, also produced by Texas Instruments, and an IBM AN/ALR-47 passive electronic surveillance system. Computer-directed and independent of ambient light, the FLIR turret can penetrate light fog and haze and will pick up heat traces by day or by night. Sonobuoy signals are received by a 32 channel acoustic recorder and a data processor, integrated with the central computer. The AN/APS-116 radar, with 240 degrees of scan, operates in three modes: a high PRF (Pulse Repetition Frequency) and quick antenna rotation for small targets out to 35 miles, a lower PRF and slower antenna rotation for surface search and reconnaissance out to 175 miles, and a high PRF and slow rotation for a long-range search beyond that distance. In a small aircraft of the Viking's size, all of this equipment costs twice as much as the airframe itself.

The Viking first entered service with USN training Squadron VS-41 in 1974. The first operational squadrons were VS-21 aboard the *USS John F. Kennedy*, VS-22 on the *USS Saratoga*, and VS-28 on the *USS America*. The Navy plans a total of 187 S-3A Vikings to equip 12 carrier squadrons of 10 aircraft each, with spares, and may adapt some for electronic countermeasures support missions as ES-3A aircraft with TASES (Tactical Airborne Signal Exploitation Systems), as KS-3A tanker aircraft, or as US-3A cargo and utility craft. 30 S-3A have been offered for sale to the Federal Republic of Germany.

**AN/SSQ-47B Active Sonobuoy** with automatic keyed continuous wave sonar. Maximum Depth: 800 ft. Weight: 32 lbs. One of 168,400 such units produced to date by Sparton Electronics.

**Type:** Carrier-based twin-engined jet turbofan ASW aircraft.

**Crew:** 4.

**Weight:** 52.539 lbs.

**Speed:** 518 mph, or loiter at 184 mph.

**Range:** 2,303 miles or 7.5 hours maximum air endurance. Typical combat radius of 460 miles with 5 hours time over target.

**Ordnance Capacity:** Over 7,000 lbs, including 4 x Mk 82 500 lb bomb and 4 x Mk 46 torpedo, or 4 x Mk 54 depth charge or 4 x Mk 53 mine in internal weapons bays, and 6 x Mk 82 or Mk 36 destructor bomb, Mk 20 cluster bomb or LAU-68/A, LAU-69/A or LAU-61/A 2.75″ FFAR rocket pods with, respectively, 7 or 19 rockets each, or LAU-10/A rocket pods each with four 5″ FFAR or Zuni rockets, on TER-7 triple ejector racks underwing.

**Produced:** 165 of all types to date, including 8 research and development prototypes, 146 of 187 S-3A planned for USN.

**In US Service:** 146 S-3A in 12 USN squadrons.

**Price:** $11.585 million@ (1976 Unit Procurement Cost for 41 S-3A to USN). $10.4 million@ (1975 Unit Procurement Cost estimate for 187 S-3A to USN).

**FMS Sales Pending:** 30 S-3A to West Germany, the first 15 of which were offered in 1975 for $21.133 million@.

# LOCKHEED EC-121 WARNING STAR CONSTELLATION

An electronic reconnaissance, airborne early warning, fighter control and submarine detection aircraft adapted from the commercial Lockheed Super Constellation airliner. Before the existence of more specialized aircraft like the E-3A AWACS for airborne early warning, and the P-3 Orion for antisubmarine warfare, the EC-121 fulfilled these and a variety of other specialized missions, and small numbers of the aircraft remain in service today.

The military version of the Super Constellation first entered service as a transport aircraft, capable of carrying 106 passengers or 72 combat troops. Some USAF C-121C transport aircraft were subsequently rebuilt as EC-121S electronic reconnaissance aircraft with more than six tons of electronic signals intelligence and other equipment aboard. Early USN transports, including the R7V-1, were later transferred to the Military Airlift Command as C-121G transports and subsequently rebuilt as C-121J airborne communications relay aircraft.

By the early 1950s the value of the Constellation in the reconnaissance role became significant. With its range of 4,600 miles and an air endurance of 20 hours, and with its capacity for 40,000 lbs of specialized cargo, it became one of the first airborne platforms for the rapidly emerging electronic technol-

ogy that was destined to have an immense impact on military capabilities by the end of that decade. The Air Force ordered 10 RC-121C, later redesignated EC-121C, as airborne early warning aircraft, and 70 RC-121D. These first entered service in 1954. They had a distinctive appearance. Above the fuselage was a radome eight feet high and shaped rather like the conning tower of a submarine, housing the most powerful search radar of its time. Beneath the fuselage was another bowl-shaped radome carrying additional radar and other equipment designed to determine the speed and directional bearing of targets detected by the radar above. Some of these aircraft were later redesignated EC-121D, or rebuilt with wingtip tanks as EC-121H, and transferred to the Aerospace Defense Command.

For the Navy, 121 EC-121K were built, and 8 were modified to WC-121N for weather reconnaissance. Subsequent modifications of the EC-121K were one EC-121L with a rotating UHF radome, some EC-121M electronic counter measures aircraft, the EC-121P for submarine detection, and the EC-121R, extensively used by the Navy in Vietnam during Operation Igloo White, and fitted with relay requipment to monitor ground sensors along the Ho Chi Minh Trail. The EC-121Rs would relay the signals to a base in Thailand, where a computer would fix their position and direct air attacks to those points where targets had been detected.

The Indian Navy purchased nine L-1049G Constellations from Air India, and today uses eight for maritime patrol and one as a transport. Until recently, the French Air Force also used the Constellation. The USN continues to use the NC-121K, an EC-121K modified for ELINT (Electronic Intelligence) missions with

a Litton AN/ALQ-124 ECM system and pulse analysers, while rebuilt USAF EC-121H and EC-121T Warning Stars still serve with the Aerospace Defense Command, the Air National Guard, and the 79th Squadron of the Air Force Reserve at Homestead AFB, Florida.

**Type:** Four-engined prop-driven AEW and ELINT aircraft.

**Crew:** From 16 to 31 depending on mission.

**Weight:** 143,600 lbs.

**Speed:** 321 mph.

**Range:** 4,600 miles.

**Produced:** 358 of all types, including 15 C-69A for USAF, 9 PC-121A, 1 VC-121B, 4 C-121A, 33 C-121C (some of which converted to EC-121S), 32 R7V-1 for USN (redesignated C-121G and some of which converted to C-121J), 10 RC-121C (redesignated EC-121C), 70 RC-121D (many of which converted to EC-121H and later rebuilt as EC-121D and EC-121T), 142 EC-121K (8 of which converted to WC-121N, 1 to EC-121L, and many to EC-121M/P/Q/R), and 42 EC-121T delivered in 1973. (Some USN EC-121K/Q later modified to NC-121K).

**In US Service:** 6 NC-121K in USN Squadron VAQ-33, 10 EC-121T in USAF Aerospace Defense Command, 4 EC-121H in ANG and 4 in USAF Reserve.

**In Service Abroad:** France (6 L-749A), India (9 L-1049G) and Israel (1 L-1049).

# LOCKHEED U-2

This is the aircraft in which Francis Gary Powers was shot down over Sverdlovsk in the Soviet Union on 1 May 1960. His aircraft bore no markings, because the U-2 was intended for clandestine surveillance over the Soviet Union and the People's Republic of China at altitudes above 100,000 feet, which we rightly assumed were safe from the reach of surface-to-air missiles, whose maximum bursting altitude at that time was 60,000 feet. However, the engine on the U-2 Powers flew that day flamed out, and he could not reignite it. The aircraft was hit by a missile only after it had lost 43,000 feet.

First developed in secret at Lockheed's "Skunk Works" in California, the U-2 entered service in 1955 with deliveries of early aircraft to Watertown Strip in Nevada, where its CIA pilots were trained. From 1956 through 1960 the U-2s, equipped with high-resolution long-range cameras, flew from bases in Alaska, Japan, Taiwan and Turkey, Lakenheath in England, Wiesbaden in West Germany, and Peshawar in Pakistan (from which Powers flew), mapping the Soviet Union and mainland China in photographs. Nationalist Chinese pilots were trained to fly the aircraft in the United States and several U-2s were transferred for their use to Taiwan. After four of them were shot down over mainland China, these aircraft were withdrawn from service in 1966. Another American U-2, piloted by Major Rudolf Anderson, Jr., had also been shot down over Cuba during the missile crisis in October of 1962.

Francis Gary Powers was later returned to this country in exchange for the Soviet spy Colonel Rudolf Abel. Powers recently died in a helicopter accident. After the diplomatic discomfiture caused by his capture, the U-2s were withdrawn from clandestine service, painted with normal USAF markings, and transferred to the 4028th and 4080th Strategic Reconnaissance Wings of our Strategic Air Command, where they openly perform the same function. Some were modified to WU-2A and WU-2C high altitude weather reconnaissance aircraft, two were transferred to NASA for research, and two have been used by the Defense Atomic Support Agency in its HASP (High Altitude Sampling Program) effort to collect data on the upper atmosphere.

The latest version of the U-2 was the U-2R, with a wingspan increased from 80 to 103 feet. USAF may reopen the U-2 production line for 100 additional U-2Rs to fulfill a NATO TR-1 tactical reconnaissance requirement. From altitudes of over 85,000 feet, these aircraft would use the UPD-X standoff SLAR (Side Looking Airborne Radar) to provide imagery of ground areas 35 miles long by several miles wide, deep within Warsaw Pact countries, and with a clarity of resolution capable of distinguishing objects ten feet apart on the ground. An additional requirement for 60 aircraft to carry the Lockheed PLSS (Precision Location Strike System) target designator may also be met by the U-2R.

**Type:** Jet-engined high-altitude strategic reconnaissance aircraft.

**Crew:** 1, or 2 /U-2D and U-2CT only).

**Weight:** 20,000 lbs.

**Speed:** 520 mph.

**Powered by:** 1 x J57-PW-37A turbojet (A only),  1 x J75-P-13 (B/C/D/R).

**Ceiling:** 70,000 feet (A), or 85,000 feet (B/C/D/R).

**Range:** 2,600 miles (A), or 4,000 miles (B/C/D/R).

**Produced:** 65 of all types to date, including 20 U-2A, 3 U-2B, 25 U-2C, 5 U-2D, and 12 U-2R. Some conversions to WU-2A and WU-2C, and 1 conversion to U-2CT twin-seat trainer.

**In US Service:** 40 U-2C/D/R in 2 SAC strategic reconnaissance squadrons, some WU-2A/C, 1 U-2CT in USAF, and 2 U-2C in NASA.

**Exported under MAP:** 6 U-2A to Taiwan, four of which subsequently shot down and 2 withdrawn from service.

**Price:** $22.06 million@ (1978 estimated Unit Procurement Cost for 25 U-2R equipped as TR-1 with UPD-X SLAR for USAF).

# LOCKHEED SR-71A BLACKBIRD

This is the fastest aircraft in the world. Developed in the early 1960s for many of the same clandestine reconnaissance missions that had earlier been assigned to the U-2, and subsequently used over the Soviet Union, mainland China, the Middle East and Southeast Asia, it proved far more difficult to shoot down than the aircraft preceding it, because it moved at more than three times the speed of sound. In May of 1965 the SR-71 set an absolute world speed record of 2,070 mph (Mach 3.14) at 80,000 feet, and in July of 1976 it set a new record of 2,189 mph (Mach 3.32). That is faster than the muzzle velocity of a bullet fired from a 30.06 Caliber rifle.

The SR-71 is also our original "stealth" aircraft, whose curved surfaces and narrow fuselage weaken the radar signals it reflects, offering a minimum radar "signature." As it approaches, it is often visible to the naked eye before it is seen on a radar screen.

Constructed largely of a titanium alloy, and carrying 80,000 lbs of JP-7 high-temperature fuel, the SR-71 can map with its cameras over 100,000 square miles of the Earth's surface in less than an hour—the time it takes this aircraft to fly from California to Florida. It has been nicknamed the Blackbird because its surfaces are painted a deep indigo blue, a color with a high rate of heat emission to retard overheating during

sustained supersonic flight, which at altitudes of 80,000 feet can raise the aircraft's surface temperatures as high as 1,100 degrees Fahrenheit. This special paint also absorbs radar energy, further weakening the signals it reflects.

Three A-11 development aircraft, later converted to YF-12A prototypes of the Blackbird, first flew in 1964. Converted that year for the USAF IMI (Improved Manned Interceptor) program, they were fitted with the Hughes AN/ASG-18 fire control radar in a nose radome, infrared sensors and two weapons bays to carry a total of four Hughes AIM-47A Falcon long-range air-to-air missiles. The Air Force subsequently dropped its requirement for this aircraft, and the three YF-12As, along with one YF-12C, were transferred to NASA for its Advanced Supersonic Technology Program. A strategic reconnaissance requirement, however, was kept, and in 1966 the first of 33 SR-71A aircraft were delivered to the 4200th Strategic Reconnaissance Wing of SAC, later redesignated the 9th Strategic Reconnaissance Wing, at Beale AFB, California, It is the only USAF unit that has flown these aircraft, and it continues to operate them today. Two SR-71B trainers were also built with twin cockpits, and after one crashed an SR-71A was rebuilt with twin cockpits and redesignated SR-71C.

To date, none of the SR-71A have been sold or offered abroad, but the Shah of Iran, of course, once requested them.

**Type:** Twin-engined jet-powered strategic reconnaissance aircraft.

**Crew:** 2.

**Weight:** 170,000 lbs.

**Speed:** 2,189 mph (Mach 3.32) at 86,000 feet. Has reportedly reached speeds up to 2,310 mph (Mach 3.5).

**Range:** 2,982 miles.

**Powered by:** 2 x Pratt & Whitney J58 turbojet engine.

**Produced:** 39 aircraft to date, including 3 YF-12A prototypes (formerly A-11), one YF-12C, 33 SR-71A (one of which converted to SR-71C), and 2 SR-71B. Production ended in 1968.

**In US Service:** 32 SR-71A, 1 SR-71B and 1 SR-71C in one SAC strategic reconnaisance wing, and 4 YF-12A/C in NASA.

**Price:** $24.616 million@ (1972 Unit Procurement Cost for 6 SR-71A to USAF).

## GENERAL DYNAMICS CONVAIR T-29

A navigation, radar and bombing trainer based on the C-131 military transport aircraft, which in turn was based on the Convair commercial airliner models 240, 340 and 440. For the Air Force, a total of 365 T-29 trainers were built, with early deliveries in 1949. Ten T-29Bs were transferred to the Navy, which also took delivery of 143 C-131 aircraft, including the C-131A Samaritan, used for MEDEVAC (Medical Evacuation) missions, C-131B, D, F and G transport versions, and the C-131E electronic counter measures trainers, some of which were later converted to RC-131F standard for photographic surveillance. The aircraft has also been used by the air forces of Bolivia, Canada, Italy, Spain and West Germany.

**Type:** Twin-engined prop-driven specialized trainer and transport aircraft.

**Weight:** 47,000 lbs.

**Speed:** 293 mph.

**Range:** 450 miles.

**Produced:** Over 520 aircraft to date for military use, including 48 T-29A, 105 T-29B, 119 T-29C (some of which converted to ET-29C), 93 T-29D, 26 C-131A, 36 C-131B, 33 C-131D, 10 C-131E (6 of which converted to RC-131F), 36 C-131F, 2 C-131G, 4 VC-131H and 8 CC-109.

**In US Service:** Over 60 T-29B/C/D in USAF, 14 C-131A, 12 C-131F and 6 RC-131F in USN.

**In Service Abroad:** Bolivia (5 Convair 440), Canada (7 CC-109), Italy (4 Convair 440), Spain (6 Convair CV-440), and West Germany (2 Convair 440).

## NORTH AMERICAN T-6 TEXAN

A two-seat basic trainer produced in the United States, Canada and Australia from 1938 through 1954, and still in use in 39 countries as a trainer, light COIN and close air support aircraft, capable of carrying up to 1,500 lbs of bombs, rocket and gun pods. In 1949, 2,068 of the more than 10,000 T-6 trainers produced were converted to T-6G standard especially for the COIN role. In South Africa, which acquired 100 of the original T-6G, another 150 of the aircraft have been locally produced.

**Type:** Single-engined prop-driven trainer and light COIN aircraft.

**Weight:** 5,617 lbs.

**Speed:** 215 mph.

**Range:** 870 miles.

**Produced:** More than 10,000 of all types, including 2,068 T-6G COIN conversions.

**Exported under FMS:** 691.

**Exported under MAP:** 1,099.

**In Service Abroad:** Argentina (6 T-6G), Bolivia 23 T-6G), Brazil (30 AT-6G), Cambodia (6 T-6), Chile (6 T-6G), Dominican Republic (4 T-6), Ecuador (16 T-6G), El Salvador (10 T-6), Greece (20 T-6D/G), Gautemala (7 T-6G), Haiti (3 T-6), Honduras /6 T-6), India (130 T-6G), Indonesia (25 T-6G), Iran (42 T-6G), Israel (12 T-6G), Italy (54 T-6C/D/F/G), Laos (10 T-6G), Mexico (45 AT-6G), Morocco (50 T-6G), New Zealand (19 T-6C/D), Nicaragua (4 AT-6G), Pakistan (30 T-6G), Paraguay (14 T-6G), including 10 ex-Brazilian T-6G), Peru (15 T-6D), Portugal (288 T-6G), South Africa (250 T-6G, including 150 locally produced), South Korea (16 T-6), Spain (200 T-6D/G), Taiwan (22 T-6), Thailand (140 T-6G), Tunisia (12 T-6G), Turkey (40 T-6J), Uruguay (13 T-6), United Kingdom (3 T-6), Venezuela (24 T-6G), West Germany (65 T-6G), Zaire (32 T-6G) and Zambia (8 T-6G).

## NORTH AMERICAN T-28 TROJAN

A very popular single-engined COIN aircraft first developed in 1948 as a two-seat basic trainer. The most powerful primary trainer of its time, it was adopted by both our Air Force and Navy, and it is still operated by the latter service. Capable of carrying up to 2,000 lbs of bombs and other air munitions underwing, early versions of the T-28 were used as close air support aircraft in the Congo and in Vietnam. By the early 1960s large numbers of the T-28A were being converted to T-28D standard specifically for COIN operations, including 321 aircraft in 1962, another 72 in 1970, and 160 more, fitted with wing armament and ammunition, in 1973. These aircraft were capable of carrying up to 4,000 lbs of ordnance underwing, and were supplied in large numbers to several countries abroad under MAP, including South Vietnam, Laos, Cambodia and Thailand.

After various conversions to T-28D standard by North American and Fairchild, licensed production continued in this country with the Hamilton T-28R Nomad, and subsequently the PacAir Nomad, both specifically designed for export sales as light strike aircraft especially equipped for desert warfare operations. Some of them were sold to Morocco, Rhodesia, Zaire and Ethiopia. Under sublicense, Sud Aviation of France had meanwhile produced another 245 of this aircraft as the T-28R Fennec, or "Desert Rat." Some of Sud Aviation's production aircraft were sold to Morocco, Tunisia, Argentina and Cuba. France had earlier converted 130 T-28A from the United States to T-28D standard, and used that aircraft in Algeria.

In 1963 prototypes of a YAT-28E were produced, with an increased ordnance capacity of 7,000 lbs, for export. After three prototypes were built the program was cancelled. In 1973, Taiwan's Aero Industry Development Center produced an XT-CH-1A prototype identical to the T-28, and has since constructed small quantities of the aircraft. The various versions of the T-28 remain in service today in 25 countries.

**Type:** Single-engined prop-driven twin-seat primary trainer and COIN strike aircraft.

**Weight:** 8,495 lbs (A/B/C), 9,200 lbs (XT-CH-1A), or 12,000 lbs (D).

**Speed:** 380 mph (A/B/C), 368 mph (XT-CH-1A), or 352 mph (D and variants).

**Range:** 1,250 miles, or fully-loaded combat radius of 500 miles.

**Ordnance Capacity:** 2,000 lbs on six underwing pylons (A/B/C), or 4,000 lbs (D), or 7,000 lbs on 12 pylons (YAT-28E).

**Typical Stores:** 2 x .50 Caliber MG pod on inner pylons, and 2 x 750 lb bomb and 2 x 2.75" FFAR pod on outer pylons.

**Produced:** Over 3,000 of all types, including 1,194 T-28A (of which 553 converted to T-28D), 489 T-28B, 299 T-28C, 411 T-28D and T-28R, 3 YAT-28E, 245 T-28R Fennec, and approximately 20 XT-CH-1A.

**Exported under FMS:** 310.

**Exported under MAP:** 654.

**In US Service:** 182 T-28B/C in USN.

**In Service Abroad:** Argentina (34 T-28D and 40 Fennec), Bolivia (4 T-28D), Brazil (12 T-28C), Cambodia (60 T-28D and 14 AT-28), Congo Republic (12 T-28D), Cuba (25 Fennec), Dominican Republic (6 T-28D), Ecuador (9 T-28D), Ethiopia (12 T-28D and 12 T-28R), France (130 T-28D and 140 Fennec), Haiti (6 T-28D), Honduras (4 T-28D), Japan (40 T-28A), Laos (60 AT-28D), Mexico (32 T-28D), Morocco (6 T-28R and 25 Fennec), Nicaragua (6 T-28D), Philippines (12 T-28A), Rhodesia (5 T-28R), South Korea (6 T-28A and 42 T-28D), Taiwan (10 T-28D and approximately 20 XT-CH-1A), Thailand (55 T-28D), Tunisia (12 Fennec), and Zaire (16 T-28D and 5 T-28R).

# NORTH AMERICAN ROCKWELL RA-5C VIGILANTE

A carrier-based all-weather reconnaissance and strike aircraft developed from an original Navy requirement for a supersonic carrier-based nuclear attack bomber. One of the most advanced reconnaissance aircraft flying, capable of a top speed of 1,385 mph, with a range of 3,000 miles and able to carry up to 10,000 lbs of bombs and other air munitions, the RA-5C is equipped with a long pod under its fuselage that houses several high-speed, high-resolution cameras, SLAR (Side Looking Airborne Radar), infrared sensors and ECM equipment, and has also been fitted with REINS (Radar Equipped Inertial Navigation System), which allows it to fly its missions in any weather, at any altitude, by day or by night. Incorporating a number of advanced aerodynamic principles, including differential slab tailplanes and boundary layer wing control, it is likely to continue in active service in our Navy for a number of years, and will not immediately become available for transfer abroad.

After two prototype YA3J-1 aircraft were developed in 1958, a total of 57 A-5A Vigilantes were produced for the USN as supersonic attack bombers, first entering service in 1962 with USN Squadron VAH-7 aboard the *USS Enterprise*. These were followed by six A-5B aircraft designed for longer-range missions with extra fuel in a fuselage hump aft of the cockpit. But while the B model was in production the Navy's requirement for an attack bomber was cancelled, and a reconnaissance version of the aircraft was ordered instead. Between 1962 and 1966, 63 RA-5C were produced, first entering service in 1964 with USN Squadron RVAN-5 on the *USS Ranger*. Another 46 of the aircraft were produced between 1969 and 1971, while 53 of the original A-5A and the six A-5B aircraft were also rebuilt to RA-5C standard, giving the Navy a total of 168 of the aircraft.

**Type:** Twin-engined supersonic reconnaissance and strike aircraft, seating 2.

**Powered by:** 2 x General Electric J79-GE-10 turbojet engines.

**Weight:** 80,000 lbs.

**Speed:** 1,385 mph (Mach 2.1)

**Range:** 3.000 miles.

**Ordnance Capacity:** Up to 10,000 lbs, including 8,000 lbs on four underwing hardpoints.

**Stores Combinations:** 4 x 2,000 lb bomb or 4 x AGM-12 Bullpup ASM.

**Produced:** 174 of all types, including 2 YA3J-1 prototypes, 57 A-5A (53 of which converted to RA-5C), 6 A-5B (all converted to RA-5C), and 109 RA-5C.

**In US Service:** 168 RA-5C in 24 USN Squadrons.

# PIPER MODEL PA-18 CUB/L-4/L-18 AND MODEL 150 SUPER CUB/L-21/U-7A

A light observation aircraft, based on the commercial Piper Model PA-18 Cub and Model 150 Super Cub, and used in great numbers throughout the world for liaison, forward air control and light strike missions. Over 40,000 have been produced since 1940, at least half of them for military use under various designations, including the L-4 in 1941, the L-18 in 1949, and in 1951 the L-21, later redesignated U-7.

**Type:** Single-engined prop-driven monoplane, seating 2.

**Weight:** 1,580 lbs.

**Speed:** 123 mph.

**Range:** 770 miles.

**Produced:** Over 40,000 of all types, Military versions include over 2,000 L-4, 105 L-18B, 838 L-18C, 150 L-21A (later redesignated U-7A) and 582 U-7B.

**Exported under MAP:** 603.

**In US Service:** 105 L-18B, 120 U-7A, 582 U-7B and 243 PA-18 in USAF, and 838 L-18C and 30 U-7A in US Army.

**In Service Abroad:** Belgium (4 L-18C), Denmark (15 L-18C), France (12 L-18C and L-21A), Greece (21 L-21A), Indonesia (12 L-4J), Iran (38 L-18C), Israel (60 L-18C), Italy (50 L-18 and L-21A), the Netherlands (65 L-21A), Norway (24 L-18C), Paraguay (4 L-4A), Portugal (27 L-21B), Switzerland (12 L-18C), Thailand (44 L-21A), Turkey (105 L-18B), Uganda (16 L-18C), Uruguay (3 L-21A), and West Germany (40 L-18C).

**North American Rockwell RA-5C Vigilante**

# PIPER MODEL PA-28 CHEROKEE

A light military trainer adapted from the commercial Piper Model PA-28 Cherokee and Model 140 Cherokee Lance.

**Type:** Single-engined prop-driven monoplane, seating, 2, 4, 6 or 7.

**Weight:** 2,550 lbs.

**Speed:** 147 mph.

**Range:** 1,160 miles.

**Produced:** Over 1,714 of all types to date, including 186 Cherokee Lance. Arrow II, Warrior, Pathfinder, Archer II and Cherokee VI are currently in production.

**In Service Abroad:** Finland (5 Cherokee Arrow), Chile (2 Cherokee VI), Tanzania (6 Cherokee 140 Lance).

**Price:** $37,850@ (1978 Manufacturer's Price for Cherokee Arrow III). $44,610@ (1978 Manufacturer's Price for Cherokee VI 300). $54,640@ (1978 Manufacturer's Price for Cherokee 140 Lance).

# ROCKWELL T-2 BUCKEYE

A basic jet trainer first developed in 1958 and capable of carrying up to 3,500 lbs of bombs, gun pods and rocket pods in the COIN role. It continues in service today with the USN as a primary jet trainer, capable of qualifying pilots through levels of skill that include carrier landings and takeoffs. As the Navy changes to more modern training aircraft, the T-2 promises to become increasingly popular abroad as a light, high-speed COIN aircraft. Specially equipped for this purpose, 40 T-2C aircraft were supplied in 1974 to Greece, rebuilt as T-2Es with six underwing stores pylons. The following year, in a sale not publicly announced, Morocco purchased 20 T-2E. Of the 24 T-2Ds supplied to Venezuela, without carrier landing equipment and standard USN avionics, 12 were similarly equipped for ground attack missions.

**Type:** Twin-engined jet-powered primary trainer and COIN aircraft, seating 2.

**Weight:** 13,799 lbs.

**Speed:** 540 mph.

**Range:** 1,047 miles.

**Ordnance Capacity:** 3,500 lbs on 6 underwing pylons (E standard and any earlier models with appropriate modifications).

**Produced:** Over 600 of all types, including 1 XT2J-1 prototype, 217 T-2A (of which 2 converted to YT-2B prototypes), 97 T-2B (of which 1 converted to YT-2C prototype), 255 T-2C (of which 40 converted to T-2E), 24 T-2D and 20 T-2E to date.

**Exported under FMS:** 84.

**In US Service:** 97 T-2B and 215 T-2C in USN.

**In Service Abroad:** Greece (40 T-2E), Morocco (20 T-2E), Venezuela (24 T-2D, 12 of which equipped to E standard).

**Price:** $4.45 million@ (1975 unit FMS cost for 20 T-2E to Morocco).

**Sales Pending:** Indonesia (12).

**Rockwell T-2 Buckeye**

# WORLD WAR II AIRCRAFT REMAINING IN SERVICE

A surprising number of aircraft produced by the United States in World War II remain in service today in Latin America, Asia and Africa, where nations with less-developed economies can ill afford more expensive military equipment. These aircraft are kept operational through continuous rebuilding programs, and by replenishment with spare parts and replacement items locally produced, saved from original stocks, or purchased from international firms which specialize, today, in making any part for any aircraft. The fact that such companies exist and now serve a booming market is a reminder that no piece of military equipment, obsolete by our standards, need go out of service. It all gets passed on. Somewhere there will be a demand for it. Thus, the output of military production over the years is not subject to control, as has been suggested, by deterioration and time. It merely accumulates.

In the vast "Boneyard" at Davis-Monthan Air Force Base, Arizona, thousands of aircraft produced in World War II sit in neat rows awaiting potential transfer, along with many thousands of aircraft produced in the postwar period, including such discarded Navy jet fighters as the Grumman F-11A Tiger, the McDonnell Douglas F-3 Demon, and the North American AF-1E Fury, some of which were the pride of our forces in Korea. Occasionally the Pentagon will receive a request for some of these. Auctions of surplus equipment are regularly held by the Defense Supply Agency, and now and then some remarkably new aircraft will appear in them, though always stripped, as required by law, of their warmaking potential.

What has been taken out, however, can be replaced, often with more advanced equipment, when these aircraft reach their destination. What often happens is that a private firm will offer to purchase a quantity of one type of aircraft or another, and will then rebuild and reequip them for export. In one case, that of the P-51 Mustang, the Cavalier Aircraft Corporation was offered a contract to do so, in order to meet some of our security commitments abroad under MAP, and in 1967 began building a far more lethal and powerful version of the famous World War II fighter, known as the Cavalier F-51D, and later as the Piper Enforcer.

The costs of these aircraft vary, and have little relationship to their original costs. A North American P-51 Mustang originally cost just over $54,000, and a Republic P-47 Thunderbolt $30,600, which later increased to $89,000 at the close of production. A Boeing B-17 Flying Fortress originally cost $218,000, a B-29 Superfortress $680,000, the postwar B-47 $2 million, and the B-36 $3.7 million. Many of these airframes could be purchased today for their scrap metal value, from $5,000 for a fighter aircraft to $30,000 for a large bomber. The demand has mostly been for fighters and twin-engined bombers, though five B-17 bombers have been transferred abroad under MAP and 19 sold under FMS, while no less than 88 of the larger B-29s have also been supplied to the United Kingdom under MAP.

To reinforce these old aircraft and reequip them with new engines and modern avionics, and to install whatever armament suits the role for which their new owners intend them, may cost from four to twenty times the cost of the airframe itself. But that is still a fraction of the cost of aircraft coming off the assembly lines today. Hence, we find them in use, and are likely to find more of them in use in the future. There follows a list of the major types of World War II aircraft currently in service.

**BEECH AT-10 AND AT-11 KANSAN.** Armed versions of the Beech Models 26 and 18 respectively, and used as light attack bombers. 1,771 of the Model 26 were produced for the U.S. Army as AT-10s, and of 7,091 of the Model 18 produced, 5,257 were AT-11 Kansans or C-45 military transports. The AT-11 is flown today by Chile (3), Honduras (6), Mexico (15), Nicaragua (4), and Uruguay (13).

**Chance-Vought F4U Corsair**

ADAK
137919

137919

**BEECH C-43 and C-45 EXPEDITOR.** Twin-engined transport versions of the Beech Models 17 and 18. 448 of the C-43 were produced, together with 5,204 of the very similar C-45, which remains a popular transport aircraft today. Between 1952 and 1961 2,263 C-45s were rebuilt, and 388 were delivered to Canada. An additional 78 C-45s were sold abroad under FMS, and 94 were supplied under MAP. Users of the C-45 today are Bolivia (5), Burma (4), Canada (100), Chile (3), Ecuador (6), Haiti (2), Japan (65), Nicaragua (4), Portugal (15), Somalia (1), Thailand (5), and Turkey (6).

**CHANCE VOUGHT F-4U CORSAIR.** The famous Navy and Marine Corps fighter aircraft. Still flown today by El Salvador (6) and Honduras (10).

**CONVAIR PBY-5 CATALINA.** The very graceful twin-engined flying boat, used for maritime patrol. Flown today by Argentina (6), Brazil (12), Chile (3), Dominican Republic (2), Ecuador (2), Indonesia (3) and Mexico (5).

**DOUGLAS B-26 INVADER.** Twin-engined bomber later redesignated A-26. Heavily used in the COIN role in Africa and in Vietnam. Several supplied by the CIA to fly ground support in our attempted invasion of Cuba in 1961, and some shot down over the Bay of Pigs. Contract pilots attempted to fly 20 of these aircraft to Portugal for clandestine use in her African colonies, and managed to deliver 7 before the operation was exposed. 109 exported under FMS, and 173 under MAP. Flown today in Brazil (15), Chile (15), Colombia (6), Dominican Republic (7), Honduras (6), Indonesia (2), Nicaragua (6), Portugal (7) and West Germany (3).

**CURTISS-WRIGHT C-46 COMMANDO.** Twin-engined military transport. 3,180 produced. 24 exported under FMS and 84 under MAP. Flown today in Brazil (12), Dominican Republic (6), Honduras (8), Japan (11), People's Republic of China (42), Peru (2), South Korea (30), Taiwan (30), and Uruguay (5).

**GRUMMAN HU-16 ALBATROSS.** A twin-engined maritime patrol aircraft, still in service with our own Coast Guard. Widely-used abroad as a front-line ASW aircraft. 569 produced, including 296 HU-16A and 138 HU-16B to USAF, and 135 HU-16C to USN, of which 51 later converted to HU-16D. 45 exported under FMS, and 99 under MAP. 26 used by the United States Coast Guard for search and rescue missions. Users abroad today include Argentina (6), Brazil (14), Canada (10), Chile (6), Greece (8), Indonesia (13), Italy (13), Japan (6), Norway (16), Pakistan (5), Peru (4), the Philippines (4), Portugal (8), Spain (21), Taiwan (10), Thailand (2), Venezuela (5) and West Germany (10). Three Spanish HU-16s are being replaced by Fokker F-27 aircraft, modernized with Litton AN/APS-504 (V-2) search radar and Litton LTN-27 inertial navigation systems.

**NORTH AMERICAN B-25 MITCHELL.** Twin-engined bomber. 80 exported under FMS and 6 under MAP. The People's Republic of China today maintains and flies 43 captured B-25J and 6 B-25H bombers, together with 1 four-engined heavy B-24J Liberator bomber—probably the only Liberator flying today (with the exception of those maintained by India, and by our Confederate Air Force, an organization of former pilots which preserves many World War II aircraft), among the 18,000 originally produced.

**NORTH AMERICAN P-51 MUSTANG/ CAVALIER F-51D.** Single-engined fighter aircraft capable of speeds over 450 mph. Last in USAF service with the 18th Fighter Bomber Wing at Osan, Korea, in 1953. Over 14,000 produced, 7,956 of which were rebuilt and modified by Cavalier and other firms as F-51Ds. Our Air Force keeps 2 of these to test new air munitions and armament for counterinsurgency use. 118 exported under FMS, and 335 under MAP. A total of 383 were transferred to Taiwan. Israel purchased 25 F-51Ds from Sweden in 1950. Currently flown by Bolivia (12), Dominican Republic (20), El Salvador (6), Guatemala (10), Haiti (6), Israel (11), Indonesia (19), Nicaragua (12), People's Republic of China (90), and South Africa (21).

**LOCKHEED PV-2 HARPOON.** Maritime patrol aircraft. Used by Portugal for bombing missions in Angola. Still flown by Peru (4) and Portugal (6).

**REPUBLIC P-47 THUNDERBOLT.** Single-engined fighter aircraft. 57 exported under FMS, and 525 under MAP. The People's Republic of China operates 36 P-47Ds.

**Grumman HU-16 Albatross**

# TRANSPORT AND UTILITY AIRCRAFT

Mobility is no less important than firepower The most advanced weapons and the most disciplined troops, highly skilled in their use, are of little value without the ability to bring those resources to bear as quickly as possible, and in the greatest possible numbers, over considerable distances, as well as the ability thereafter to keep combat units continuously and securely supplied once they have been committed to battle.

Transport aircraft are therefore an essential tactical and strategic element in the modern arsenal, determining both the distance over which one country may become militarily involved in another's affairs, and the potential degree of that involvement. The military establishments of every nation measure each other's might partly in terms of the size of their air transport fleets, and of the types of aircraft deployed, their range and capacities.

Similarly, the numbers of such aircraft that a country amasses, as well as the types it chooses, can tell a great deal about the contingencies for which it plans. In 1972, for example, our Air Force announced a requirement for 277 of an aircraft it called the Advanced Medium STOL (Short Take Off and Landing) Transport, or AMST. the AMST was expected to carry 150 troops or 30,000 lbs of cargo over a distance of 1,200 miles, fly at top speeds of 500 mph and slow down to less than 100 mph in order to land in less than 500 feet or, employing highly advanced technology, take off fully loaded in less than 1,000 feet.

Since all of those countries in Europe, the Middle East and other parts of the world to which we have openly bound ourselves in mutual security agreements have numerous modern airfields capable of handling the heaviest aircraft flying, and STOL capabilities are therefore not a prerequisite for their use, the AMST program indicates planning for a sizeable airlift capability in different parts of the world—the less-developed nations of Africa and Asia where shorter, unimproved landing strips would have to be relied upon in order to intervene quickly and in force. It is clear that we mean to be prepared for such contingencies.

Two ingenious AMST prototypes were developed, the McDonnell Douglas YC-15, using an externally-blown flap system, wing spoilers, and the powerful reverse thrust of its engines to slow the aircraft down upon landing, and the Boeing YC-14, which for the same purpose uses a system of upper surface blowing and downward-turning trailing-edge flaps to take advantage of the tendency of a jet flow to follow the surface over which it passes. However, neither of these prototypes could perform sufficiently well to meet USAF requirements. In addition, the costs of the program, initially estimated at $1.4 billion, rose to $5.5 billion in 1977 and $6.3 billion by 1978. The Air Force had originally planned to spend no more than $5 million per aircraft, approximately the cost in 1972 of the C-130 Hercules transport it was said to be intended to replace. But the AMST had risen to $22.74 million per aircraft by 1978.

The Carter administration recently cancelled the AMST program. The decision appears to have been on the grounds that neither prototype met USAF requirements, rather than on the grounds of costs, for we are now preparing to spend even more money for fewer aircraft in another program, that for the ATCA (Advanced Tanker Cargo Aircraft), which may be expanded to fill part of the requirement the AMST had been intended to meet. The initial ATCA program involved the conversion, for dual cargo or tanker use, of either 41 commercial Boeing 747s at a cost of $77.56 million each, or of 41 DC-10 aircraft for $63.41 million each. This time presumably on the grounds of costs, the DC-10 was chosen. If more of these aircraft are later ordered to make up for the cancelled AMST (though not to fill the requirement for a STOL transport), then the unit cost may drop somewhat—though never much below $40 million each, still almost twice the cost of the AMST in 1978.

Another option is to create a Civil Reserve Air Fleet (CRAF) by modifying for military cargo use 81 wide-body aircraft now flown by commercial airlines, and using these aircraft only in case of need. The modifications would cost approximately $5.67 million per aircraft, and adding payments to the airlines to cover the increased operating costs of the aircraft after their weight had been increased by conversion, a total of $6.07 million per aircraft. It seems a comparatively economical plan, in view of our apparent need for an expanded transport fleet.

One might wonder why we need more such aircraft, when we already have an impressive inventory of gigantic transports, none of which was inexpensive itself when originally procured, nor any of which is proving inexpensive to maintain, including in our Military Airlift Command more than 400 C-130 Hercules aircraft, 284 C-141 Starlifters and 81 of an aircraft called the C-5A Galaxy. Each Galaxy cost $55 million new, and each is capable of carrying a cargo load of 265,000 lbs, or up to 345 combat troops, or two M-60 main battle tanks together with sixteen 3/4 ton trucks. A stretched fuselage is being built for 275 of our C-141s at a cost of $2.48 million each. 76 of our C-5A Galaxies are being fitted with entirely new, strengthened wings, at a cost of $14.34 million each. These two improvement programs will cost the Air Force a total of $1.772 billion. The full Military Airlift Command fleet could transport an entire armoured division and most of its equipment in one trip. But all of that capability, and all of its cost, would still appear not to suffice.

## BEECH B99

A twin-engined turboprop airliner seating 17, and in military use as a small troop carrier or VIP transport. First developed in 1968. Over 164 produced to date.

**Weight: 10,400 lbs.**

**Speed:** 254 mph.

**Range:** 1,170 miles.

**In Service Abroad:** Chile (9), Thailand (1).

**Price:** $3.587 million@ (1978 manufacturer's price).

## BOEING C-135

A four-engined jet transport aircraft based on the commercial Boeing model 707. The 707 was also the basis for the KC-135 jet tanker aircraft, delivered earlier than the C-135 transports, and for the E-3A AWACS now in production. 15 C-135A and 30 C-135B aircraft were produced, with deliveries beginning in 1961. Among other conversions of the KC-135 tanker, discussed in the previous section, 3 were modified to C-135A standard. There followed modifications of 11 C-135B to VC-135B as VIP transports, and conversions of three commercial 707-120s as VC-137B transports. Two of the somewhat larger commercial 707-320Bs were converted to VC-137C, and one of these operates today with the 89th Military Airlift Wing as Air Force One for the President of the United States. Iran has purchased six 707-320C aircraft and ten 707-320Ls fitted with refuelling booms as tanker aircraft, and has another 707-320C on order. 12 C-135F, similarly equipped, were produced for France as tankers, and redesignated KC-135F. Of its five 707-320Cs, redesignated CC-137s, Canada uses two as tanker aircraft.

**Weight:** 333,000 lbs.

**Speed:** 600 mph.

**Range:** 4,300 miles (C-135A/B/707 variants), 7,000 miles (VC-137C).

**Capacity:** 87,100 lbs of cargo or 126 combat troops. (VC-137 variants seat 49).

**Produced:** 65 aircraft, including 18 C-135A (including three converted from KC-135A), 30 C-135B (11 of which converted to VC-135B), 3 VC-137B, 2 VC-137C and 12 C-135F (redesignated KC-135F).

**Exported under FMS:** 12 C-135F

**In US Service:** 18 C-135A and 19 C-135B in USAF MAC, 11 VC-135B and 3 VC-137B in MATS, 2 VC-137C in 89th MAW.

**In Service Abroad:** Argentina (1 707-320B), Canada (5 707-320C), Egypt (1 707-320C), France (12 C-135F, redesignated KC-135F), Iran (6 707-320C and 10 707-320L), Israel (10 707-320L), Portugal (4 707-320C), Taiwan (1 707-320B), Saudi Arabia (1 707-320C) and West Germany (4 707-320C).

**Price:** $21.307 million@ (1974 unit cost for 6 707-320C to Iran, equipped with refuelling booms).

## BOEING KC-97 STRATOFREIGHTER

A four-engined, prop-driven transport version of the B-29 Superfortress, first developed in 1944. Only 77 of the transport version were built before the design was modified to produce 811 KC-97 tanker aircraft. Only the tanker version is in service today with our Air National Guard.

**Weight:** 175,000 lbs.

**Speed:** 375 mph.

**Range:** 4,300 miles.

**Capacity:** 92,500 lbs of cargo, 96 combat troops or 69 casualty litters.

**Produced:** 77 C-97A/C, YC-97, YC-97A/B, and VC-97A/d.

**Exported under FMS:** 7.

**In Service Abroad:** Israel (12), Spain (3).

## BOEING T-43

A twin-engined jet transport and trainer, based on the commercial Boeing model 737. Fitted with Honeywell T-45 electronic simulators, LORAN and a variety of radar and inertial navigation systems, 19 of these aircraft were ordered by USAF in 1971 to replace the Convair T-29 as a navigation trainer. The aircraft is anticipated to become a popular short-range military transport abroad.

**Weight:** 115,500 lbs.

**Speed:** 586 mph.

**Range:** 2,995 miles.

**Capacity:** 42 combat troops or 25 casualty litters.

**Produced:** 19 T-43A to date.

**In US Service:** 19 T-43A in USAF.

## CONVAIR C-131 SAMARITAN

A twin-engined prop-driven short-range transport and MEDEVAC (Medical Evacuation) aircraft for the Navy, based on the Convair commercial airliner models 240, 340 and 440, and a version of which was also adopted by USAF as the T-29 trainer (see Combat Support Aircraft section). A total of 143 C-131 and 4 VC-131 aircraft were produced for the Navy, some as C-131E electronic counter measures trainers, six of which were subsequently converted to RC-131F photographic surveillance aircraft. Commercial versions of the Convair airliner in military service abroad are covered in the entry for the T-29.

**Weight:** 47,000 lbs.

**Speed:** 293 mph.

**Range:** 450 miles.

**Capacity:** 16,000 lbs of cargo, 60 combat troops or 42 casualty litters.

**Produced:** 147 of all types, including 26 C-131A, 36 C-131B, 33 C-131D, 10 C-131E (of which 6 converted to RC-131F), 36 C-131F, 2 C-131G and 4 VC-131H.

**Exported under MAP:** Bolivia (1).

**In US Service:** 12 C-131A, 12 C-131F and 6 RC-131F in USN, and 1 C-131F in USMC.

**Convair C-131 Samaritan**

# CESSNA MODEL 177 CARDINAL/V206C STATIONAIR/207 SKYWAGON

A number of these commercial Cessna models, seating from four to ten passengers, have been purchased for military service abroad as light utility and transport aircraft. A total of 4,147 Cardinals have been produced to date, including 886 of the Cardinal RG and RGII versions, 134 of which have been produced under license by Reims Aviation in France. In addition, 3,724 of the V206C Stationair and 319 of the 207 Skywagon, a Stationair with a somewhat longer fuselage, have been produced.

**In Service Abroad:** Argentina (6 Skywagon 207), Ecuador (1 Cardinal 177), Gautemala (2 V206C), Indonesia (5 Skywagon 207), Israel (25 V206C).

# CESSNA MODEL 500 CITATION

A newly developed short-range jet transport aircraft, powered by twin turbofans and seating 8 to 10. Cessna has to date produced 300, one of which has been purchased by the Venezuelan air force.

**In Service Abroad:** Venezuela (1).

# DOUGLAS C-47 SKYTRAIN AND C-117

Based on the commercial Douglas DC-3 airliner, which first flew in 1936 and entered service with major airlines in 1938, this became the most widely-used military transport aircraft in history. After forty years, it is still used by smaller airlines throughout the world and remains in military service in no less than 90 countries. Known in England as the Dakota and nicknamed the *Gooney Bird* by our own Air Force, it was used as a troop and cargo transport, a paradrop aircraft for men and supplies, and during the Normandy invasion as a paratroop glider tug. Normally seating 28 combat troops, it has been known to carry as many as 74. It is powered by two Pratt & Whitney prop-driven radial engines.

After 416 DC-3s were delivered to commercial airlines, the Air Force began to take delivery of the C-47 Skytrain, and later of the C-53 Skytrooper, the same aircraft fitted with paradrop doors. Production of both types totalled 9,520. Some of these were subsequently converted as R4D aircraft for the Navy, and later redesignated C-117. A Super DC-3 followed, with squared wingtips and tail, and conversions of 98 of these for the Navy were designated C-117D. Navy procurement totalled 850 of all types.

The C-47 has the distinction of being the only military aircraft of American design licensed for production in the Soviet Union, where Lisunov built a total of 1,700 Li-2s, many of which are still used. 571 additional C-47s were built under license in Japan by Showa and Nakajima.

Of the several conversions of the C-47 remaining in service, two are of note, including the EC-47, equipped with radar and infrared sensors and passive ESM (Electronic Support Measures) equipment for electronic reconnaissance, and the AC-47D, a close air support aircraft developed for use in Vietnam. Early models of the AC-47D were equipped with .30 Caliber and .50 Caliber machine guns fixed in the aircraft's port side, but these were replaced by the General Electric M134 7.62mm six-barreled Minigun when that item of equipment became available. The normal complement of Miniguns fixed in the port side of the AC-47D is three, each carrying 1,500 rounds, with an additional 15 or 18 thousand rounds of 7.62mm ammunition stored aboard the aircraft. With each gun firing up to 6,000 rounds per minute, the AC-47D can deliver a combined rate of fire of 18,000 rounds per minute, the intensity of which is such that its extraordinary rattling has given it the radio call sign *Spooky*, and the smoke from its fire the nickname, *Puff the Magic Dragon*. Consequently, the AC-47D is known today as the *Dragon Ship*. 53 AC-47D conversions were made, and some remain in service today with USAF, while others were left in Vietnam or transferred to Laos and Cambodia.

**Weight:** 26,000 lbs, or 29,000 lbs (AC-47D).

**Speed:** 299 mph, or 230 mph (AC-47D).

**Range:** 2,125 miles.

**Capacity:** 7,500 lbs of cargo, 28 combat troops or 18 casualty litters. Maximum overload: 74 combat troops.

**Produced:** 14,062 of all types, including 413 DC-3 and DC-3A, 4 DC-3B, 953 C-47DL, 2,832 C-47ADL, 2,099 C-47ADK, 300 C-47BDL, 2,808 C-47BDK, 133 TC-47BDK, 193 C-53, 1 XC-53A, 8 C-53B, 17 C-53C, 159 C-53D, 17 C-117A, 98 C-117D, 1 C-48, 3 C-48A, 2,700 Li-2 and 571 C-47J. Conversions include 1 XD-47C, 120 R4D-1, 2 R4D-2, 20 R4D-3, 10 R4D-4, 238 R4D-5, 148 R4D-6, 86 R4D-7, 101 R4D-8 (later redesignated C-117D), 53 AC-47D, 51 YC-47F, 11 C-117C and 16 C-48B.

**Exported under FMS:** 119.

**Exported under MAP:** 702.

**In US Service:** Of 9,520 originally procured by USAF, and 850 by USN, 19 C-47 and 9 AC-47D remain in USAF/TAC.

**In Service Abroad:** Angola (2), Argentina (24), Australia (6), Belgium (14), Bolivia (18), Brazil (59, including 2 EC-47), Bulgaria (24 Li-2), Burma (12), Cambodia (11, including 6 AC-47D), Cameroun (5), Canada (47, as CC-129), Central African Republic (3), Chad (1), Chile (28), Colombia (8), Congo Republic (2), Dahomey (2), Denmark (8), Dominican Republic (6), East Germany (12 Li-2), Ecuador (12), El Salvador (5), Ethiopia (4), Finland (8), France (20), Gabon (3) Greece (30), Guatemala (8), Haiti (3), Honduras (6), India (90), Indonesia (12), Iran (10), Israel (10), Italy (9, including 2 EC-47), Ivory Coast (3), Japan (4), Jordan (4), Laos (30, including 10 AC-47D), Libya (9), Malagasy Republic (5), Malawi (4), Mali (2), Mauritania (3), Mexico (6), Morocco (10), Nepal (2), New Zealand (6), Nicaragua (3), Niger (4), Nigeria (9), North Yemen (2), Norway (4), Oman (3), Pakistan (18), Panama (4), Papua-New Guinea (4), Paraguay (10), People's Republic of China (60), Peru (19), Philippines (30), Poland (8 Li-2), Portugal (40), Rhodesia (4), Rwanda (2), Senegal (6), Somalia (3), South Africa (48), South Yemen (4), Soviet Union (80 Li-2), Spain (50), Sri Lanka (2), Sweden (10), Sudan (2), Syria (50), Taiwan (50), Thailand (25), Togo (2), Turkey (50), Uganda (6), United Kingdom (2), Upper Volta (3), Uruguay (13), Venezuela (24), West Germany (20), Vietnam (11 Li-2, 20 C-47, 2 EC-47, 20 AC-47 and 8 RC-47, including 36 abandoned by United States forces), Yugoslavia (15), Zaire (10), and Zambia (10).

**Price:** $94,000@ (1941 Unit Procurement Cost for 300 C-47B to USAF). $21,500@ (1977 US government surplus price).

# DOUGLAS C-54 SKYMASTER C-118 LIFTMASTER

Based on the commercial Douglas DC-4 and DC-6 airliners, these four-engined prop-driven transports carry up to 50 combat troops and were first delivered to the Air Force and Navy in the early 1940s. They still serve with the USN, and in 33 countries abroad.

**Weight:** 73,000 lbs (C-54). 102,000 lbs (C-118).

**Speed:** 274 mph (C-54). 360 mph (C-118).

**Range:** 1,500 miles (C-54). 3,860 miles (C-118).

**Capacity:** 32,000 lbs (C-54) or 27,000 lbs (C-118) of cargo, or 50 combat troops.

**Produced:** Over 1,000 C-54 for USAF and USN, and 101 C-118A for USAF and 65 C-118B to USN (of which 4 converted to VC-118B).

**Exported under FMS:** 10 C-54 and 3 C-118.

**Exported under MAP:** 70 C-54 and 5 C-118.

**In US Service:** 1 C-54Q and 12 C-118B in USN, and 30 C-118B in USN Air Reserve.

**In Service Abroad:** Argentina (6 C-54, 4 C-118 and 2 DC-6), Belgium (4 DC-6B), Bolivia (1 C-54), Brazil (4 C-118 and 4 DC-6), Cambodia (6 C-54), Central African Republic (1 C-54), Chile (4 C-118 and 2 DC-6B), Colombia (10 C-54), Denmark (6 C-54), Ecuador (4 DC-6B), France (4 C-54, 10 DC-6B), Gabon (1 DC-6B), Guatemala (1 C-54), Honduras (1 C-54), Italy (2 DC-6B), Mexico (5 C-54, 2 C-118), Niger (2 DC-6B), Nigeria (1 DC-6B), Panama (1 DC-6B), Paraguay (2 C-54), Peru (4 C-54, 6 DC-6), Portugal (19 C-54, 11 DC-6B), South Africa (5 DC-4), South Korea (12 C-54), Spain (20 C-54), Taiwan (1 DC-6B), Thailand (2 C-54), Turkey (3 C-54), Venezuela (3 C-54), Vietnam (1 DC-6B), West Germany (4 DC-6B), Yugoslavia (4 DC-6B), and Zaire (4 C-54 and 1 DC-6).

**Price:** $102,681 @(1946 Unit Procurement Cost for 261 C-54 to USAF).

# DOUGLAS C-124 GLOBEMASTER II

A four-engined prop-driven long-range transport aircraft with nose-loading doors, developed from the C-54. Preceded by 15 C-74 Globemasters delivered in 1947, 204 C-124A Globemaster IIs were ordered by USAF, followed by 243 C-124Cs with AN/APS-42 weather radar fitted in their noses. Deliveries of the Globemaster II began in 1949 and ended in 1955. The aircraft equipped the Military Airlift Command until 1968, when they were transferred to the Air Force Reserve and the Air National Guard.

**Weight:** 194,500 lbs.

**Speed:** 304 mph.

**Range:** 4,030 miles.

**Capacity:** 68,500 lbs of cargo, or 200 combat troops or 127 casualty litters.

**Produced:** 462 of all types, including 15 C-74 Globemaster, 204 C-124A Globemaster II, and 243 C-124C Globemaster II.

**In US Service:** 160 C-124C in Air National Guard and Air Force Reserve.

# DOUGLAS C-133 CARGOMASTER

A four-engined prop-driven long-range strategic transport specially designed to carry missile transporters and other large Army vehicles. 35 C-135As were delivered to USAF from 1956 to 1958, and 15 C-133Bs, with rear-loading clam-shell doors to permit carriage of the Titan missile, followed in 1959. A few have been sold as heavy freighters to commercial airlines, and the remainder have been assigned to the Air Force Reserve.

**Weight:** 286,000 lbs.

**Speed:** 359 mph.

**Range:** 4,030 miles.

**Capacity:** 110,000 lbs of cargo, or 200 combat troops.

**Produced:** 50, including 35 C-133A and 15 c-133B.

**In US Service:** 25 C-133A and C-133B.

# FAIRCHILD C-119 FLYING BOXCAR AND C-119K PACKET

A twin-engined prop-driven medium-range transport, first developed in 1947. The aircraft is built with high twin tail booms to permit rear-loading access to the fuselage. A total of 1,051 Flying Boxcars were produced, including conversions of many C-119Gs to C-119K Packets by the addition of two General Electric J85-GE-17 auxiliary turbojets in pods under the wings. 39 C-119Bs were delivered to the Navy, followed by production of 318 C-119Cs for export to several countries abroad under MAP. USAF ordered a total of 694 C-119F and C-119G models, and 58 of the C-119Fs were subsequently transferred to the USN, while 68 C-119Fs were converted to C-119J standard for USAF with larger rear-loading doors to carry light tanks and other heavy vehicles. Of the C-119G, 26 were converted to AC-119G Shadows armed with four M134 7.62mm Miniguns, whose Air Force designation is GAU-2B/A, firing from the aircraft's port side, and were heavily used for defense suppression in Vietnam (see Combat Aircraft section). Another 26 of the C-119K Packet conversions, with auxiliary jet engines, were modified to AC-119K Stingers, equipped with four Miniguns and two rapid-firing M61A1 Vulcan 20mm can-

**Fairchild C-119 Flying Boxcar**

non as well. These 52 aircraft are still in service with USAF's Tactical Air Command. Eight C-119Gs were also converted to C-119K Packets, unarmed, and transferred to Ethiopia under MAP.

**Weight:** 77,000 lbs.

**Speed:** 243 mph (C-119K).

**Range:** 990 miles.

**Capacity:** 20,000 lbs of cargo, or 62 combat troops.

**Produced:** 1,051 of all types, including 39 C-119B, 318 C-119C, and 694 C-119F and C-119G (of which many converted to C-119K, 58 to C-119J, 26 to AC-119G and 26 to AC-119K).

**Exported under FMS:** 137.

**Exported under MAP:** 339.

**In US Service:** 26 AC-119G and 26 AC-119K in USAF/TAC, 10 C-119J in ANG and 4 in USMC Reserve.

**In Service Abroad:** Belgium (28 C-119G), Brazil (12 C-119G), Ethiopia (8 C-119K and 2 ex-Belgian C-119G), Italy (48 C-119G/J, of which 3 converted to EC-119 ECM aircraft), Jordan (3 C-119K), Morocco (8 C-119G), Taiwan (50 C-119G), and Vietnam (56 C-119G, including 40 abandoned by United States forces).

**Price:** $663,000@ (1949 Unit Procurement Cost for 39 C-119B to USN).

# FAIRCHILD C-123 PROVIDER

A twin-engined prop-driven medium-range transport aircraft developed in 1949 from the design for a World War II cargo glider. One XC-123 Avitruc prototype aircraft was built by Chase Aircraft, followed by five pre-production C-123Bs manufactured by the Kaiser-Frazer Corporation. Full production, undertaken by Fairchild, began in 1954, and ended with 300 additional C-123Bs for USAF, 185 of which were subsequently modified to C-123K standard with the addition of two General Electric J85-GE-17 turbojets in pods under the wings, while a further 10 were modified to C-123J with Fairchild J44 jet engines in wingtip pods. In Vietnam, a few C-123Ks were modified as AC-123K gunships, and then reconverted to cargo aircraft as NC-123Ks, while others were fitted with defoliation equipment as UC-123Js. Some of the aircraft remain in our Air National Guard and Air Force Reserve.

**Weight:** 60,000 lbs.

**Speed:** 228 mph.

**Range:** 1,035 miles.

**Capacity:** 24,000 lbs of cargo, 61 combat troops or 50 casualty litters.

**Produced:** 306 of all types, including 1 XC-123, and 305 C-123B, 185 of which converted to C-123K, to to C-123J, some to UC-123K and some to AC-123K with reconversion to NC-123K.

**Exported under FMS:** 24.

**Exported under MAP:** 160.

**In US Service:** 8 C-123J in Air National Guard and 47 C-123K in Air Force Reserve.

**In Service Abroad:** Cambodia (40 C-123K), Taiwan (15 C-123B), Thailand (13 C-123B), Saudi Arabia (6 C-123B), Venezuela (18 C-123B), and Vietnam (50 C-123K).

**Fairchild C-123B Provider**

# GRUMMAN C-1 TRADER

Twin-engined, prop-driven carrier-based COD (Carrier Onboard Delivery) transport and utility aircraft, derived from the Grumman S-2 Trackser ASW aircraft (see Combat Support Aircraft section). 87 C-1As were produced, with deliveries beginning in 1955, and 4 were subsequently converted to EC-1A electronic surveillance aircraft.

| | |
|---|---|
| **Weight:** | 27,000 lbs. |
| **Speed:** | 287 mph. |
| **Range:** | 900 miles. |
| **Capacity:** | 8,250 lbs of cargo, or nine passengers. |
| **Produced:** | 87 C-1A, four of which converted to EC-1A. |
| **In US Service:** | 30 C-1A in USN. |

# GRUMMAN C-2A GREYHOUND

A twin-engined turboprop COD (Carrier Onboard Delivery) aircraft based on the design for the Grumman E-2 Hawkeye (see Combat Support Aircraft section). It is capable of carrying small vehicles, spare jet engines and other aircraft parts needed aboard aircraft carriers, or can seat up to 39 passengers. Deliveries to the USN began in 1966, and totalled 25 aircraft. They all remain in service.

| | |
|---|---|
| **Weight:** | 54,830 lbs. |
| **Speed:** | 352 mph. |
| **Range:** | 1,650 miles. |
| **Capacity:** | 10,000 lbs of cargo, 39 combat troops or 20 casualty litters. |
| **Produced:** | 25 C-2A. |
| **In US Service:** | 25 C-2A in USN. |

# GRUMMAN VC-4 GULFSTREAM

A twin-engined turboprop transport aircraft, a version of which has been adopted by the USN as the TC-4 Academe, a specialized trainer for Grumman A-6 Intruder aircrews. The VC-4 Gulfstream is in service with our Coast Guard.

| | |
|---|---|
| **Weight:** | 36,000 lbs. |
| **Speed:** | 334 mph. |
| **Range:** | 2,205 miles. |
| **Capacity:** | 9 passengers. |
| **Produced:** | 9 TC-4C, 2 VC-4A and 1 VC-11A. |
| **In US Service:** | 1 VC-4A and 1 VC-11A in United States Coast Guard. |

**In Service Abroad:** Greece (1 VC-4A).

**Price:** $6 million @(1972 Unit Procurement Cost for 1 VC-4A to Coast Guard).

# LOCKHEED C-5A GALAXY

A long-range strategic heavy transport aircraft powered by four General Electric TF39-GE-1 turbofan engines, and originally developed in 1965 to meet an Air Force requirement for a heavy transport able to carry all the components of an Army division.

The C-5A contract was awarded to Lockheed after that firm submitted a proposal underbidding a Douglas design by $100 million and a Boeing design by $400 million. With a total value of $3.4 billion, the contract obligated the Air Force to procurement of 58 C-5As through 1969, with an option for the purchase of another 62. The cost per aircraft was estimated at the time at $28.33 million each.

In November of 1968, three years after the contract was signed, Ernest A. Fitzgerald, Air Force Deputy for Management Systems, testified to the Proxmire Committee that the C-5A program had sustained cost overruns totalling $1.9 billion, raising the program cost of each aircraft to $44.17 million, and that Defense Secretary Robert McNamara, who testified earlier that same year that the C-5A program had remained well within the limits of estimated costs, had known otherwise since at least November of 1967, when he received a memorandum from the Comptroller of the Department of Defense informing him of a C-5A cost overrun of $420 million.

Further, Mr. Fitzgerald reported that *he* had known of the overruns since November of 1966, that he had reported them to his superiors at that time, and that thereafter, he had observed, the routine cost accounting reports issued in the Pentagon for major weapon systems deleted all overrun figures for the C-5A program. He also reported that he had found a clause in the original contract with Lockheed containing a repricing formula, whereby that portion of the costs of the first 58 aircraft which exceeded the amount originally estimated would be included in the higher costs of aircraft purchased thereafter, at a price to be negotiated between the Air Force and Lockheed. Having signed a contract that had appeared to set strict limits on cost, performance and delivery, we were in effect giving a guarantee of government approval of any cost overruns in the program.

Two weeks after Mr. Fitzgerald testified, the Air Force informed him that his job had been "reclassified." Formerly in charge of systems management for almost every major Air Force weapon program, including the Minuteman missile and the F-111 fighter aircraft, he was reassigned to supervising construction of a bowling alley in Thailand. At the same time he was disqualified for tenure, in which new status he was subject to dismissal without cause.

Senator Proxmire demanded an investigation into the C-5A program by the Defense Department and the General Accounting Office, and also asked that the Air Force not act on its option to purchase further C-5A aircraft until the investigations were completed. However, Lockheed would not give the GAO its figures on cost overruns, and referred all inquiries to the Air Force. The Air Force, in turn, made no figures available until the day before the new Proxmire hearings reconvened.

Yet the investigation turned up some interesting documents, including a memo from Air Force Secretary Alexander Flax stating that the C-5A program was well "within

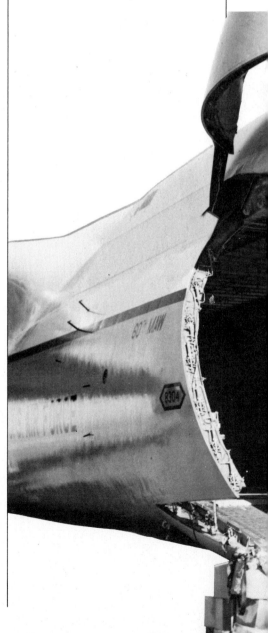

the range between target and ceiling costs," and dated in March of 1968, six months *after* the Defense Comptroller's Office had informed Secretary McNamara, Secretary Flax and everyone else in the Pentagon otherwise. There was also a memorandum to the new Secretary of the Air Force, Harold Brown, outlining the ways in which Ernest Fitzgerald could be dismissed.

It turned out that the Air Force had tried to prevent Fitzgerald from testifying, then had tried to change the figures in his report to the Proxmire Committee, and had finally attempted to delay the Committee's access to the report, by holding it for several weeks on the desk of Robert H. Charles, assistant secretary of the Air Force.

In his testimony before the Committee, Mr. Charles refused to concede that the Air Force had tried to conceal the C-5A cost overruns, despite overwhelming documentary evidence to the contrary, and even denied that any disciplinary action had been taken against Ernest Fitzgerald.

In November of 1969, Ernest Fitzgerald was fired. His job was abolished in a reduction of the work force—one of the methods suggested in the memo to Secretary Brown.

Four additional Congressional hearings were opened to investigate the C-5A. It was eventually established that the Air Force had decided to falsify its own records of the C-5A program in order to protect Lockheed's image, even though the result was to corroborate a false picture of that firm's financial condition, misleading not only Congressional investigators but also, in probable violation of the Securities and Exchange Act, Lockheed's investors and shareholders.

Senator Proxmire introduced an amendment to the Military Procurement Authorization Act deleting the funding requested by USAF for the procurement of a fourth squadron of 23 additional C-5As. The Air Force warned that if these funds were denied and financing of the C-5A program were interrupted, Lockheed might then be unable to deliver any of the aircraft—even though the first 58 had presumably been paid for. Senator Proxmire called this "political extortion," but he was defeated on the Senate floor by a vote of 64 to 23. The additional 23 C-5As were purchased, and the program closed with a total of 81 aircraft delivered—though far later than originally scheduled—at a unit program cost of $55 million each.

In four squadrons of 19 aircraft each, these C-5As are assigned to the 436th Military Airlift Wing, Dover AFB, Delaware, and the 60th Military Airlift Wing at Travis AFB, California. Four additional C-5As make up the 56th Military Airlift Training Squadron at Altus AFB, Oklahoma. The 76 C-5As not assigned to training service are being fitted with new, reinforced wings to extend their service life, at a cost of $14.34 million each. This will raise the total cost for each of those aircraft to $69.34 million each.

In 1975, the government of Iran requested 10 C-5As, and a price of $58 million each was agreed upon. To date, no letter of offer has been issued indicating approval of that sale.

---

**Weight:** 764,500 lbs.

**Speed:** 571 mph.

**Range:** 6,333 miles (with 112,600 lbs cargo), 3,512 miles (with 220,000 lbs cargo).

**Capacity:** 265,000 lbs of cargo, or 345 fully-equipped combat troops, or two M-60A1 or M-48A3 main battle tanks and sixteen ¾ ton trucks, or three M-41A3 or M-551 tanks and sixteen ¾ ton trucks, or one M-60A1 or M-48A3 tank and two UH-1B helicopters, or three CH-47C helicopters, or six M-113A1 armoured personnel carriers, or 10 Lance missiles with towing and launch vehicles. Nose-loading doors.

**Produced:** 81 C-5A.

**In US Service:** 76 C-5A in four USAF/MAC squadrons, and 4 C-5A in one MAT squadron.

**Price:** $55 million @(1973 Unit Program Cost of 81 C-5A to USAF). $44.17 million @(1968 Unit Program Cost of 58 C-5A to USAF). $28.33 million @(1965 Estimated Unit Program Cost for 120 C-5A to USAF). $69.34 million @(1978 total Unit Program Cost of 76 C-5A to USAF, including cost of $14.32 million per aircraft to rebuild with new wings and center sections).

**Future Sales:** 10 C-5A requested in 1975 by Iran for $58 million @. No action taken.

# LOCKHEED C-141 STARLIFTER

This is the aircraft that flew most of our soldiers to Vietnam. A four-engined long-range strategic freighter and troop transport, powered by Pratt & Whitney TF33-P-7 turbofans, it is the first jet-powered transport from which United States Army paratroops ever jumped, and it also holds a world paradrop record of 70,195 lbs of cargo. With rear-loading doors, the C-141 was built to fill a USAF requirement for a large jet transport to replace the existing prop-driven types in the Military Airlift Command fleet. The contract with Lockheed was signed in 1961, originally calling for 132 aircraft, but procurement was later increased for a total of 284. Deliveries of operational C-141s began in 1965, and the aircraft today equip the 437th Military Airlift Wing at Charleston AFB, South Carolina, the 438th MAW at McGuire AFB, New Jersey, two squadrons of the 60th MAW at Travis AFB, California, the 62nd MAW at McChord AFB, Washington, and the 63rd MAW at Norton AFB, California.

The C-141A originally cost $6.3 million each. A program to convert 275 of the aircraft to C-141B standard with a stretched fuselage is now underway at a cost of $2.48 million per aircraft, bringing the total procurement cost of each C-141B up to $8.78 million.

**Weight:** 323,100 lbs.

**Speed:** 564 mph.

**Powered by:** 4 x Pratt & Whitney TF33 turbofan engine.

**Range:** 6,140 miles.

**Capacity:** 70,847 lbs of cargo (86,207 lbs for C-141s modified to carry the Minuteman ICBM), or 154 combat troops, or 80 casualty litters.

**Produced:** 284 C-141A (of which 275 to be converted to C-141B).

**In US Service:** 284 C-141S in 14 USAF/MAC squadrons and one MAT squadron.

**Price:** $6.3 million @(1972 Unit Procurement Cost for 132 C-141A to USAF). $8.78 million @(1978 estimated Unit Procurement Cost for 275 C-141B, adding $2.48 million per aircraft for conversion cost of each C-141A).

# LOCKHEED C-130 HERCULES

A rugged and versatile medium-range transport aircraft, powered by four turboprop engines, the C-130 has proved to be one of the most popular items of military equipment available for export from this country. After 23 years in service, it continues in production, with deliveries of more than 1,600 aircraft to date and orders outstanding for many more. It serves today as a standard transport and special equipment platform in 46 foreign air forces. The Israelis used it in their raid on Entebbe. The Turkish Air Force used it to paradrop troops over Cyprus. Egyptian commandos used it in their raid on Cyprus in February of 1978. The United States used it in the unsuccessful attempt to rescue 53 American hostages in Iran in April of 1980. The Canadians used it to search for radioactive debris from the fallen Soviet Cosmos 954 naval reconnaissance satellite. It is continuously being transferred and retransferred around the world. Through the new government in Saigon, Libya recently acquired ten C-130A aircraft out of 42 of that type left abandoned by United States forces in Vietnam.

Though the larger jet-powered C-5A Galaxy and C-141 Starlifter were intended to replace the Hercules in our own Air Force, 325 C-130E transports remain in front-line service with our Military Airlift Command, along with several hundred others equipped for a variety of special missions in almost every branch of our military services.

With deliveries beginning in 1956, Lockheed produced 461 C-130A and C-130B aircraft with pressurized fuselages, reinforced landing gear for operation from unimproved airfields, and full-section rear doors. They

**Lockheed C-141A Starlifter**

were equipped with a Sperry AN/APN-59 radar. These were followed by 503 C-130Es for USAF's Military Airlift Command.

Several of the A and E models of the Hercules have been converted to DC-130 drone control aircraft, equipped to carry various types of RPV (Remotely Piloted Vehicle) such as the Teledyne-Ryan BQM-34 Firebee. As the technology of drone control rapidly expands, the DC-130 may come to play an important tactical role in the three-stage delivery of air munitions, approaching to within a ''standoff'' distance from its target, beyond the reach of enemy ground air defenses, releasing its RPVs and directing their flight toward the target and, when they have reached it, signalling them to release their ordnance—all without the exposure of personnel to enemy fire.

Additional conversions of the early C-130s include 16 RC-130A reconnaissance aircraft for USAF, later converted to RC-130s standard, equipped for photogrammetric mapping and electronic geodetic surveillance, 10 JC-130Bs equipped with nose booms for the aerial recovery of satellites, 12 C-130Ds for USAF equipped with skis for Arctic operations, the LC-130R, similarly equipped with skis, for the USN, a single NC-130B experimental STOL aircraft, utilizing air-blown surface controls, 20 HC-130B search and rescue aircraft for our Coast Guard, the WC-130E weather reconnaissance aircraft for USAF, 46 KC-130F, 8 KC-130H and 20 KC-130R assault transport tanker aircraft for the Marine Corps, an EC-130E for the Coast Guard, using the LORAN electronic navigation system, 15 HC-130N aircraft fitted with direction-finding equipment, and 66 HC-130H aerial recovery aircraft, 20 of which were subsequently converted to HC-130P standard, specially equipped for the inflight refuelling of helicopters.

The Air Force has also equipped 8 EC-130E aircraft as ABCCC (Airborne Battlefield Command and Control Centers). In coordination with ground-based TACC (Tactical Air Control Centers), these aircraft are planned as airborne operations centers, providing command and control for the immediate battlefield area, relaying target information, monitoring air strikes and deep interdiction sorties, receiving and processing ground requests for immediate air strikes, and directing the aircraft required in response. The heart of the ABCCC is LTV Corporation's USC-15 modular airborne command center, a pod forty feet long and weighing 20,000 lbs which fits into the cargo hold of the EC-130E, seats from 12 to 16 people and, but for heating and cooling systems and radio antennae, operates independently of the aircraft with self-contained equipment that includes tactical displays and twenty HF, UHF and VHF radio communications sets.

These eight aircraft, together with seven USC-15 pods, are attached to the 7th Airborne Command and Control Squadron at Keesler AFB, Mississippi, reporting to the 552nd Airborne Warning and Control Wing (which operates the E-3A AWACS), at Tinker AFB, Oklahoma. The 7th ACCS was first formed in September of 1965 at Tan Son Nhut Air Base, Vietnam, and subsequently performed airborne mission control for the evacuations of Saigon and Pnom Penh, as well as battlefield control during the recovery of the SS Mayaguez. Operating in conjunction with the E-3A and flying at altitudes of from 17,000 to 23,000 feet, each EC-130E ABCCC will be equipped to perform battlefield control on a multidivision front, handling 300 missions every eight hours.

USN Squadron VQ-4 also operates the EC-130G and EC-130Q TACAMO tactical airborne command and communications aircraft, of which 24 were originally planned in 1975 at a cost of $18.3 million each. Equipped with TACAMO III or TACAMO IVB airborne communications systems (TACAMO stands for Take Charge And Move Out), these aircraft perform the essential function of backup radio relays for strategic missile submarines. Procurement has been reduced to 14 aircraft, due to the rising costs of the advanced TACAMO communications equipment. A single EC-130Q planned for delivery in 1978 will cost $31.7 million.

Some little-known conversions of the C-130 are the AC-130H Spectre gunship and the MC-130E Combat Talon Blackbird. The Air Force operates 9 AC-130H and 14 MC-130E, under the control of the 1st Special Operations Wing of Tactical Air Command, based at Hulbert Field, Eglin AFB, Florida.

The AC-130H Spectre grew from the need for an improved counterinsurgency gunship to replace the AC-47D Dragon Ship and the AC-119K Stinger. Those aircraft, due to the limited range of their own 7.62mm and 20mm armament, had to orbit their targets at altitudes no greater than 3,500 feet, and consequently exposed themselves to effective ground fire from weapons of similar caliber. Heavier armament was decided upon, and after initial tests with an AC-130E equipped with four M61A1 20mm Vulcan cannon and four M134 7.62mm Miniguns, the AC-130H was developed.

Along with two 20mm Vulcan cannon and provision for two 7.62mm Miniguns, the AC-130H is equipped with a 40mm Bofors gun and a 105mm howitzer, both of which are capable of minor adjustments in elevation and azimuth for final aimpoint corrections. All of the armament is fixed in the port side of the aircraft, which orbits at considerably higher altitudes, out of reach of small arms fire from the ground, and all armament is controlled by a fire control computer.

In addition, the Spectre is fitted with FLIR (Forward Looking Infra Red) sensors for target detection by day or night, through haze or battle smoke, a gated-laser illuminator for covert illumination whose source is invisible to ground troops, a laser target designator and laser rangefinder, a 2 kw searchlight, four AN/ALQ-87 ECM jamming pods, the AN/ARN-92 inertial navigation system, LORAN-C and Doppler radar, a Black Crow sensor to detect ground radio emissions, a special radar to pick up coded ground radar beacons, and two LLLTV (Low Light Level Television) cameras on a gimballed platform, one with a wide-angle and the other with a high-resolution lens. Grenade launchers can also be fitted, and gun and rocket pods or other air munitions can

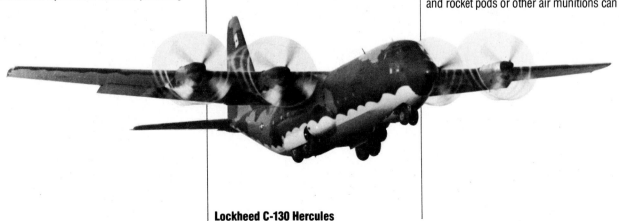

**Lockheed C-130 Hercules**

be carried underwing. Video tape recorders are also on board, for post-mission analysis. Of the 10 AC-130H conversions, one aircraft was lost on a mission over North Vietnam.

The MC-130E Combat Talon Blackbird grew out of a very different requirement—that for an aircraft to carry Special Forces or Navy SEAL teams on clandestine missions, and to recover them from hostile territory afterwards. Equipped with FLIR for night operations, with terrain-following radar that enables them to fly only 250 feet above ground, a K-band radar for high-resolution ground-mapping, an inertial navigation system and a LORAN-C receiver, the Combat Talons have also been fitted with inflight refuelling equipment, considerably extending their operational range. They carry a variety of ECM gear, including the AN/ALR-46 radar warning receiver, AN/ALE-27 chaff dispensers, and the AN/AAQ-8 infrared decoy system, which misleads the heat-seeking guidance mechanisms of missiles fired at the aircraft.

Perhaps the most interesting piece of equipment aboard the Combat Talon is its Personnel Recovery System, made by the Robert Fulton Company. An inflatable baloon, nylon line, gas bottle and harness are dropped to the ground. The user straps on the harness, attaches the line to the harness and baloon, inflates the baloon and releases it, carrying the line several hundred feet aloft. The MC-130E is fitted with a nose boom which intercepts the line, secures it, snaps the man in the harness off the ground and eventually hauls him in. The system can simultaneously recover two men or 500 lbs of cargo.

In view of the mission for which the MC-130E has been designed, it is interesting to note that while six of the fourteen existing Combat Talons are based with the 1st SOW in its 8th Special Operations Squadron at

Eglin AFB, four are also regularly stationed with the 7th SOS in West Germany, and four with the 1st SOS in Okinawa.

The current production model of the Hercules is the C-130H, 292 of which were originally planned in 1973 at a cost of $4.8 million each, 131 for delivery to USAF and 161 for export. But the export orders increased. In 1975 the planned production run was expanded to 378 aircraft, 217 of them for export, which kept the cost per aircraft to about $5 million. Production, however, continues. Lockheed has been embarked for several years on a vigorous sales campaign for the aircraft throughout the world, and the orders continue coming in. 66 C-130Ks were specially built for Britain's Royal Air Force. Seven C-130Bs were sold to South Africa before the embargo on arms sales to that country could be implemented, and today these aircraft equip No. 28 Squadron of the South African Air Force, based at Waterkloof.

As with its sales of the F-104 Starfighter and the P-3 Orion, Lockheed has exhibited a somewhat excessive zeal in promoting the C-130 Hercules. In 1971, fourteen C-130E were sold to Italy for $60 million, after an investment of $2 million in commissions and fees. It was later determined, during hearings of the Senate Subcommittee on Multinational Corporations in 1976, that most of that $2 million had been used to bribe Italian officials. In May of 1977, at about the same time that Lockheed publicly announced an increase in its estimate of past payments to public officials and political organizations in order to further sales of its aircraft abroad, raising the total of such payments to $38 million, an Italian par-

liamentary inquiry commission formally indicted Italian Premier Mariano Rumor and two former defense ministers, Mario Tanassi and Luigi Gui, on charges of corruption in connection with the Hercules sale.

In 1976, Iraq had entered into an agreement with Lockheed for the purchase of 10 L-100-20s, civil versions of the C-130. But after exposure that year and the following year of Lockheed's record of questionable payments abroad, the Iraqi government failed to make further payments toward purchase of the aircraft. Lockheed representatives have since been unable to make contact with Iraqi officials.

Syria has ordered four C-130H, but so far this sale has not been approved by the State Department.

**Weight:** 175,000 lbs.

**Speed:** 384 mph.

**Range:** 2,487 miles with maximum payload, or 5,135 miles with maximum fuel.

**Capacity:** 45,000 lbs of cargo, or 92 combat troops, or 64 paratroops, or 74 casualty litters.

**Produced:** Over 1,600 of all types to date, including 461 C-130A and C-130B, 503 C-130E, 12 C-130D, 7 C-130F, 46 KC-130F, 8 KC-130H, 20 KC-130R, 66 C-130K, and 477 C-130H to date. Conversions include 8 EC-130E ABCCC for USAF, 14 EC-130G and EC-130Q TACAMO for USN, 10 AC-130H Spectre and 14 MC-130E Combat Talon Blackbird for USAF/TAC. For other conversions see text.

**Lockheed DC-130A Hercules with 3 Ryan BQM-34 Firebee target drones**

**Exported under FMS:** 211.

**Exported under MAP:** 52.

**In US Service:** 325 C-130E in USAF/MAC, some RC-130A and WC-130E in MAC, 8 EC-130E, 9 AC-130H and 14 MC-130E in USAF/TAC, 170 C-130A/B/E and 14 EC-130G/Q in USN, 46 KC-130F, 8 KC-130H and 20 KC-130R in USMC, 170 C-130A/B/E, 8 HC-130H and 20 HC-130P in Air National Guard, 100 C-130A/B/E in Air Force Reserve, 24 HC-130H and 1 EC-130E in United States Coast Guard.

**In Service Abroad:** Abu Dhabi (2 C-130E), Argentina (3 C-130E and 8 C-130H), Australia (12 C-130A and 12 C-130E), Belgium (12 C-130H), Bolivia (2 C-130H), Brazil (11 C-130E and 8 C-130H), Cameroun (2 C-130E), Canada (24 C-130E and 5 C-130H), Chile (2 C-130E and 2 C-130H), Colombia (3 C-130B and 2 C-130E), Denmark (3 C-130H), Ecuador (2 C-130E), Egypt (3 C-130H and 2 EC-130H), Greece (12 C-130H fitted with ELINT equipment),

Gabon (3 L-100-30), Indonesia (8 C-130B), Iran (15 C-130E and 49 C-130H), Israel (4 C-130E, 20 C-130H and 2 KC-130H), Italy (14 C-130E, of which 1 converted to EC-130E), Jordan (4 C-130B), Kuwait (2 C-130H), Libya (8 C-130E and 10 C-130A from abandoned United States Vietnam stocks acquired through Saigon), Malaysia (6 C-130H), Mexico (3 C-130H), Morocco (6 C-130A), New Zealand (5 C-130H), Nigeria (6 C-130H), Norway (6 C-130H), Pakistan (7 C-130B and 8 C-130E), Peru (6 L-100-20), Portugal (5 C-130H), Philippines (4 C-130H and 4 L-100-20), Saudi Arabia (10 C-130E, 29 C-130H, 4 HC-130P and 4 KC-130H), South Africa (7 C-130B), Singapore (2 C-130H), Spain (6 C-130H and 3 KC-130H), Sweden (4 C-130E), Turkey (10 C-130E), United Arab emirates (2 C-130H), United Kingdom (66 C-130K), Venezuela (6 C-130H), Vietnam (42 C-130A, many of which left abandoned by United States forces, and 10 of

which recently transferred to Libya), West Germany (10 C-130H, some of which to be transferred to Portugal), and Zaire (6 C-130H).

**Price:** $8.825 million @ (1975 Unit Procurement Cost for 4 C-130H to USAF). $5.014 million @ (1974 Unit Procurement Cost for 42 C-130H to USAF). $9.859 million (1977 Unit Procurement Cost for 4 KC-130R to USMC). $31.7 million@ (1978 Unit Procurement Cost for 1 EC-130Q to USN). $18.3 million@ (1975 estimated Unite Procurement Cost for 24 EC-130G to USN).

**Recent Transfers:** 14 C-130E to Italy in 1971 for $4.285 million@. 2 C-130H to United Arab Emirates in 1973 for $5 million@. 6 C-130A to Morocco in 1973 for $4.8 million@. 4 L-100-20 to the Philippines in 1973 for $5 million@. 3 C-130H to Denmark in 1973 for $6.666 million@. 1 C-130E to Sweden in 1974 for $6.9 million. 6 C-130H to Malaysia in 1974 for $7.833 million @. 6 C-130H to Nigeria in 1974 for $7.833 million@. 8 C-130H to Libya in 1974 for $8.125 million@. 5 C-130H to Canada in 1974 for $5.28 million@. 8 C-130H to Greece in 1975 for $5.84 million@. 8 C-130E to Australia ni 1975 for $6.3 million@. 3 L-100-20 to Peru in 1975 for $6.666 million@. 10 C-130H to Saudi Arabia in 1975 for $9 million@. 3 C-130H to Portugal in 1975 for $6.666 million@. 3 KC-130H to Spain in 1975 for $9 million@. 6 C-130H to Egypt in 1976 for $6.666 million@. (2 subsequently converted to EC-130H, and 1 C-130H destroyed in Cyprus raid on 19 February 1978). 12 C-130H to Australia in 1976 for $9.583 million@. 6 C-130H to Sudan in 1977 for $9.1 million@. 1 C-130H to Zaire in 1977 for $9 million.

**FMS Deliveries Pending:** Australia (12 C-130H), Kuwait (2 L-100-20), Jordan (2 C-130H), Morocco (6 C-130H), Philippines (2 C-130H), Sudan (6 C-130H).

**FMS Sales Pending:** Egypt (14 C-130H for $13.17 million @, requested for delivery in 1979), Syria (4 C-130H, awaiting State Department approval).

167

## LOCKHEED C-140 JETSTAR

A four-engined jet-powered medium-range transport gaining popularity for military use abroad, and based on the commercial Lockheed JetStar airliner. Of the sixteen C-140s purchased by USAF, eleven have been converted as VC-140B VIP transports, and five are assigned to the Air Force Communications Service to minotor and maintain world-wide military navigation systems.

**Weight:** 42,000 lbs.

**Speed:** 570 mph.

**Range:** 2,235 miles.

**Capacity:** 13 passengers and crew of 3.

**Exported under FMS:** 3.

**In US Service:** 5 C-140A and 11 VC-140B.

**In Service Abroad:** Indonesia (1), Libya (1), Mexico (1), Saudi Arabia (2), West Germany (4).

## McDONNELL DOUGLAS C-9 NIGHTINGALE SKYTRAIN II

A twin-engined jet-powered medium-range transport aircraft, used by USAF as an aeromedical transport, and based on the commercial DC-9 airliner.

**Weight:** 98,000 lbs.

**Speed:** 565 mph.

**Range:** 1,484 miles.

**Capacity:** 40 passengers, or 40 casualty litters.

**Exported under FMS:** 2.

**In US Service:** 21 C-9A in USAF and 3 VC-9B and 11 C-9B Skytrain II in USN.

**In Service Abroad:** Italy (2 DC-9), Kuwait (2 DC-9).

**Price:** $7.350 million@ (1975 Unit Procurement Cost for 9 C-9B to USN). $21 million@ (1975 Unit FMS Price for 2 DC-9 to Kuwait).

## PIPER U-11A AZTEC AND TURBO AZTEC

A prop-driven twin-engined light utility aircraft, seating five, and developed from the Piper Apache Twin. Over 4,000 of the commercial model have been produced.

**Weight:** 5,200 lbs.

**Speed:** 253 mph.

**Range:** 1,310 miles.

**Capacity:** 5 or 6 passengers, or pilot and 1 casualty litter.

**In US Service:** 20 U-11A in USN.

**In Service Abroad:** Argentina (6), France (2), and Spain (8, including 6 Turbo Aztec E).

**Price:** $110,100 @ (1978 Manufacturer's List Price).

## PIPER NAVAJO TURBO NAVAJO NAVAJO CHIEFTAIN

A twin-engined light utility and transport aircraft, prop-driven and in later models equipped with turboprop engines, seating from six to ten passengers.

**Weight:** 7,060 lbs (Navajo) or 6,500 lbs (Turbo Navajo).

**Speed:** 147 mph (Navajo), or 261 mph (Turbo Navajo).

**Range:** 950 miles (Navajo) or 1,730 miles (Turbo Navajo).

**Capacity:** 6 to 10 passengers.

**In Service Abroad:** Argentina (5 Turbo Navajo), Chile (1 Turbo Navajo), France (10 Turbo Navajo), Nigeria (2 Turbo Navajo) and 1 Navajo Chieftain), Spain (8 Turbo Navajo, including 1 PA-31P Pressurized Navajo), and Syria (2 Navajo Chieftains).

**Price:** $179,790 @ (1978 Manufacturer's List Price for Navajo). $191,440 @ (1978 Manufacturer's List Price for Turbo Navajo). $204,430 @ (1978 Manufacturer's List Price for Navajo Chieftain).

**Rockwell International T-39 Sabreliner**

## ROCKWELL INTERNATIONAL T-39 SABRELINER

A twin-engined jet-powered transport aircraft and aircrew trainer, based on the commercial Rockwell Sabreliner 40, and used in both our Air Force and Navy. In addition to 143 T-39As and six T-39Bs delivered to USAF, the Navy ordered 42 T-39Ds for maritime radar training, nine CT-39Es, and five CT-39Gs with an extended fuselage. USAF's T-39Bs were equipped with NASARR (North American Search and Range Radar) and Doppler radar to train aircrews for the F-105 Thunderchief, which uses the same equipment, and some of these aircraft were later converted to T-39F standard, with special equipment to train F-105G Wild Weasel aircrews.

**Weight:** 18,650 lbs.

**Speed:** 563 mph.

**Range:** 2,118 miles.

**Capacity:** 2,500 lbs of cargo, or 9 passengers.

**In US Service:** 143 T-39A and six T-39B (of which 3 converted to T-39F) in USAF, and 42 T-39D, 9 CT-39E and 5 CT-39G in USN.

**Price:** $1.750 million @ (1975 Unit Procurement Cost for 6 T-39D to USN).

## ROCKWELL INTERNATIONAL U-4B AERO COMMANDER TURBO COMMANDER SHRIKE COMMANDER

A prop-driven twin-engined light transport aircraft seating nine, including crew, and used by our Air Force and Army for short-range utility and transport service, and by fourteen foreign air forces.

**Weight:** 6,750 lbs.

**Speed:** 203 mph.

**Range:** 948 miles.

**Capacity:** 500 lbs of cargo, or seven passengers.

**In Service Abroad:** Argentina (14 Shrike Commander), Colombia (1 Aero Commander 560), Dahomey (1 Aero Commander 500B), Dominica (1 Aero Commander 500), Greece (1 Aero Commander 500 and 2 Aero Commander 680FL), Guatemala (1 Turbo Commander), Indonesia (3 Grand Commander), Iran (6 Shrike Commander, 3 Aero Commander, 3 Turbo Commander), Ivory Coast (1 Aero Commander 500), Kenya (1 Turbo Commander), Laos (4 Aero Commander 520), Pakistan (1 Aero Commander), Philippines (1 Aero Commander), and South Korea (3 Aero Commander).

**Price:** $800,000 @ (1977 Unit Procurement Cost for 2 U-4B to USAF).

## COMMERCIAL AIRCRAFT IN MILITARY USE

A number of additional commercial airliner designs have come into limited use for military service abroad, including the Boeing 727 and 747, the Lockheed L-188, and the McDonnell-Douglas DC-8. The Boeing 747, whose design was originally conceived to compete for the Air Force heavy transport requirement filled by the Lockheed C-5A Galaxy, went into commercial service in 1969, at which time the aircraft's price was approximately $22 million each. In 1974 and 1975, Iran purchased twelve 747s, and uses them today as aerial refuelling tankers. West Germany has purchased three Boeing 727s for $11 million each. In 1973 Argentina purchased three Lockheed L-188s for $1.666 million each. The Bolivian Air Force has two L-188s, and Ecuador operates 3 Gates Learjets. France uses three DC-8s as ECM aircraft, one of which she purchased from the United Kingdom in 1973 for $8.7 million, and another of which was obtained from the United States in 1975 for $11.2 million.

In 1978 the price of a Learjet was $1.895 million@, and of a Swearingen Merlin $2.084 million@.

# HELICOPTERS

The concept of a rotary wing aircraft is as old as that for any other type of flying machine, but the technology to realize it was not fully developed until toward the end of World War II. Today, the helicopter has added a new dimension to the mobility of ground forces, enabling them to occupy and control areas previously inaccessible. At the same time, it has provided far greater firepower and maneuverability than previously available in rendering close air support of ground forces. Capable of vertical movement, able to change direction immediately by turning on its own axis, a helicopter can take more effective evasive action. Rising up over ridges or treelines and dropping down again out of sight, it can achieve surprise. Descending quickly into narrow valleys, able to reduce its speed without stalling, or even to hover motionless, it can provide a more stable weapons platform, approach to within much closer range of its target, and bring a much greater variety of powerful weapons to bear on that target, for longer periods of time, than any fixed-wing aircraft.

Taking advantage of these capabilities, every military service in the world has built up its helicopter forces. The Bell Models 204 and 205, both with the military designation of UH-1 Iroquois, exist in greater numbers throughout the world than any other aircraft currently in service. More than 8,000 have been produced. It is licensed for production by Fuji in Japan, Agusta-Bell in Italy and the Aero Industry Development Corporation in Taiwan. Over 4,300 are now in service with our own armed forces, and are used both as gunships and basic transport in the air cavalry squadrons and air mobile divisions whose organization they made possible.

Specialized attack helicopters, including the AH-1 Cobra and the new Hughes AH-64, will be produced in increasing numbers to perform an expanded role for close air support and antitank defense. From the armament, already formidable, that it carried in its early days of service in Vietnam, the AH-1 Cobra has undergone a series of conversions to heavier armament, from Minigun turrets, grenade launchers, gun and rocket pods to the TOW antitank missile. The Army's successive AH-1 modernization programs, which have already involved conversion of 93 AH-1G to AH-1Q standard, equipping them to carry eight TOW missiles, and conversion of these AH-1Qs, together with an additional 197 AH-1Gs, to AH-1S standard, equipped not only with TOW but also with a new Lycoming T53-L-703 engine to improve the aircraft's ability to hover, will be accompanied by increased production of the Cobra, including 100 AH-1S in 1978, 98 upgunned AH-1S in 1979, with new chin turrets capable of carrying 20mm and even 30mm cannon, and 107 fully modernized AH-1S in 1981. These final aircraft will be fitted with a variety of improvements, including a new fire control computer, laser rangefinder and infrared jamming equipment.

Together with the conversion of all existing Cobras, including the balance of 400 AH-1Gs, to modernized AH-1S standard, the additional production in the next three years will raise our force of these attack helicopters from 690 such aircraft now available to 995 AH-1S by 1981. 210 of these Cobras will be assigned to our Seventh Army in Europe, organized into 10 attack helicopter companies of 21 aircraft each, two of them equipping the air combat battalions in each of our four Army divisions, and one assigned to each of our two armoured cavalry regiments.

Eventually these Cobras will be joined by the 536 Hughes AH-64 (Armed Attack Helicopter) now planned for production,

each of which will carry TOW or the new Hellfire antitank missile, as well as the Hughes XM-230E1 30mm chain gun. They are expected to provide an antitank defense capability sufficiently formidable to offset the disproportionate tank strength currently favoring Soviet and Warsaw Pact forces, whose 26,250 tanks are opposed, at this time, by 11,310 tanks in NATO and French forces.

Meanwhile, helicopter technology has continued to improve. The turboshaft engine was introduced, substantially reducing noise and heat emission, the latter improvement affording the aircraft greater protection against heat-seeking missiles by reducing its infrared signature. The Bell Model 212, or UH-1N, a twin-turboshaft version of the UH-1B single-engined Iroquois, was introduced in 1969, providing greater power and range, and of course greater safety.

As we continue to build up our own helicopter forces, countries abroad do the same. Enormous orders have come from Iran, including a $367 million sale in 1972 of 202 AH-1J Sea Cobra attack helicopters, all of them equipped with electrically-driven chin turrets mounting a three-barreled XM-197 20mm cannon, and 65 of them equipped to AH-1T standard (the Marine Corp's equivalent of our Army's AH-1S) carrying eight TOW missiles each, as well as an even larger sale in 1973, worth $497 million, for 287 of the Bell Model 214A Isfahan, a version of the UH-1 Iroquois, which was later increased to 293 and finally to 326 aircraft, and further details of which will be found in the following pages.

# BELL MODEL 206 JET RANGER OH-58 KIOWA TH-57 SEA RANGER

A light observation and training helicopter, the U.S. Army version of which is known as the OH-58 Kiowa and the Navy version of which is the TH-57 Jet Ranger. It first flew in 1962, and deliveries of 2,200 to the Army began in 1969. The Kiowa was heavily used in combat in VIetnam, equipping scout platoons of the armoured cavalry regiments, and armed either with the M-8 system, mounting an XM-129 40mm grenade launcher with 156 rounds, or the M-27 system with a General Electric M-134 six-barreled 7.62mm Minigun carrying 2,000 rounds. The Navy has used its TH-57A Sea Rangers as trainers. Over 5,500 of all types have been produced to date, including more than 500 AB206 helicopters produced under license in Italy by Agusta-Bell. Australia's Commonwealth Aircraft Industries has also assembled 44 Bell 206Bs from kits.

**Weight:** 3,000 lbs (OH-58A), or 3,200 lbs (OH-58C conversion), or 3,350 lbs (AB206).

**Speed:** 140 mph (OH-58A/TH-57A), or 138 mph (AB206).

**Range:** 388 miles.

**Capacity:** 5 passengers, or 7 passengers (Bell 206L), and 1,200 lbs external ordance.

**Armament:** M-8 system with XM-129 40mm grenade launcher and 156 rounds, 300 to 450 rpm and range of 1,625 yards. M-27 system with M-134 7.62mm Minigun and 2,200 rounds, 2,200 to 4,000 rpm and range of 1,250 yards.

**Produced:** Over 5,500 to date, including 2,200 OH-58A (many of which converted to OH-58C), 40 TH-57A, 74 CUH-58A and 22 TH-58A for Canada, and more than 500 AB206.

**Exported under FMS:** 104.

**Exported under MAP:** 3.

**In US Service:** 1,350 OH-58A/C in U.S. Army, 587 OH-58A in Army National Guard, 122 OH-58A in Army Reserve, and 31 TH-57A in USN.

**In Service Abroad:** Abu Dhabi (5 AB206), Argentina (6 OH-58A), Australia (12 Bell 206B and 44 Bell/CAI 206B), Austria (13 AB206B and 12 OH-58A), Brazil (25 Bell 206A), Brunei (4 Bell 206), Canada (74 CUH-58A, designated CH-136, and 22 TH-58A), Chile (6 Bell 206), Colombia (10 OH-58A), Dubai (2 AB206), Finland (1 AB206), Indonesia (2 Bell 206B), Iran (164 AB206), Israel (12 Bell 206), Italy (110 AB206), Jamaica (4 Bell 206B), Japan (12 Bell 206), Liberia (2 AB206), Malta (4 AB206), Mexico (5 Bell 206A), Morocco (24 OH-58A), Malaysia (5 Bell 206B), Oman (4 AB206), Peru (10 OH-58A), Saudi Arabia (16 AB206), Spain (16 AB206 and 18 OH-58A), Sri Lanka (7 Bell 206), Sweden (10 AB206), Switzerland (2 AB206), Tanzania (2 AB206), Thailand (3 Bell 206), Turkey (12 AB206), Uganda (4 AB206), United Arab Emirates (6 AB206), and Venezuela (6 Bell 206B).

**Price:** $233,333 @ (1976 FMS Price for 12 OH-58A to Austria). $500,000 @ (1974 Agusta-Bell Price for 10 AB206 equipped for ASW, with HKP 6 torpedoes, to Sweden).

**Bell OH-58C Kiowa**

# BELL MODELS 204 AND 205 UH-1 IROQUOIS MODEL 214A ISFAHAN

In service in 46 countries throughout the world, and used in greater numbers than any other aircraft flying today, the UH-1 Iroquois is the military version of several successively more powerful commercial Bell helicopters, the first of which was the Model 204, which flew for the first time in 1956. Originally designated HU-1 (Helicopter, Utility), accounting for the nickname of *Huey* by which it would continue to be known long after those two letters were reversed, the UH-1A, UH-1B and UH-1C military variants for the U.S. Army were all based on the Model 204, as was the TH-1L Seawolf trainer for the USN. Deliveries of these aircraft began in 1959.

The helicopter's potential for close air support was quickly understood, and in Vietnam the UH-1B was heavily armed, first with the M-5 system, an M-75 40mm grenade launcher with 315 rounds, and then with the M-21, which provided two M-134 six-barreled 7.62mm Miniguns on sponsons, each with 600 rounds, and two M-158 rocket pods, each with seven 2.75″ FFARs (Folding Fin Aerial Rockets), which could be launched in six seconds to a range of 3,750 yards. Occasionally, both systems were used simultaneously, and in some variants the two M-134 Miniguns were replaced by eight .30 Caliber machine guns, four mounted on each sponson. The M-134 Miniguns, or their longer-barreled M-139 versions, were sometimes fitted on Sagami pintle mounts at either or both of the aircraft's cabin doors, or instead of them two M60 7.62mm machine guns could be used, either pintle-mounted or held by hand. This early version of the helicopter gunship, precursor of the AH-1 Cobra, offered a withering amount of firepower.

In 1963 the Bell Model 205 appeared, along with its key military variants, the UH-1D and UH-1H, of which latter version over 1,200 were produced. 625 of them were transferred to South Vietnam in 1967. Somewhat heavier than its predecessor, the Model 205 could carry up to 15 combat troops and 5,000 lbs of external ordnance. The UH-1H became one of our Army's standard helicopter transport aircraft, and while many UH-1Ds also served in the transport role a number were armed as gunships, either with the M-23 system, providing two M60D 7.62mm machine guns with 600 rounds, or the M-16 system, a pair of M60 machine guns with a much higher rate of fire and 6,000 rounds, and two M-158 2.75″ rocket pods. Several other military variants of the Model 205 were produced, including the UH-1E assault helicopter for the Marine

Corps, the UH-1F support gunship for USAF, the Navy's TH-1L trainer, UH-1L utility helicopter, and HH-1K marine patrol and rescue craft, the Army's UH-1M helicopter gunship fitted with infrared sensors for night operations, the TH-1F and UH-1P psywar versions for USAF, fitted with loudspeakers and other equipment for the pacification programs in Vietnam, and the Air Force's HH-1H search and rescue helicopter.

In 1972 development began on the Model 214 which, fitted with a more powerful Lycoming T5508D engine, raised the aircraft's speed from 127 mph to over 150 mph. This model was also equipped with a Noda-Matic vibration damping system and a high-rated transmission system, and in 1973 the government of Iran placed an initial order for 287 of these aircraft, to be designated the Bell 214A Isfahan, for $1.52 million each. The order was later increased to 293 and then to 326 Isfahans, 38 of them Bell Model 214C.

In connection with this sale, worth over $495 million, Bell Helicopter, a major subsidiary of Textron, paid $2.9 million as a commission to its sales agency in Iran, the firm of Air Taxi. Air Taxi was founded in 1953 by General Mohammed Khatemi, chief of the Imperial Iranian Air Force. In the early 1960s, in order to eliminate possible con-

flicts of interest, the Shah of Iran, General Khatemi's brother-in-law, issued a directive that no officials in his government should be involved in business enterprises. General Khatemi realized he could no longer be publicly associated with Air Taxi, the firm through which many aircraft were being sold to his own Air Force. He therefore arranged for two of his friends to list themselves in his place as holders of his Air Taxi stock. But he did not divest himself of that stock. He also arranged to have William French, Bell's previous agent in Iran, expelled from the country—in order, Mr. French claims, to eliminate competition.

In December of 1977 President Carter nominated G. William Miller, chairman of Textron, Inc., to replace Arthur Burns as chairman of the Federal Reserve Board, and two months later the Senate Banking Committee convened to consider whether to recommend confirmation of Miller's nomination. Textron had meanwhile been under investigation by the Securities and Exchange Commission due to a series of allegations of illegal activities, including false billings, kickbacks, bribes and other questionable payments. The $2.9 million payment to Air Taxi in 1973 was one of these, and the Senate Committee was forced to consider it. If it could be established that General Khatemi had remained a secret partner in Air Taxi, Bell's sole agent in Iran by that time, then

**Bell UH-1B with M-5 40mm grenade launcher in nose turret, 2 M-159 2.75″ rocket pods, and quad .30 cal. machine guns**

his selection of the Bell Model 214A for his country's Air Force was a clear case of conflicting interests. If it could further be established that Bell knew of the General's continuing involvement with Air Taxi, then the $2.9 million payment had not been a commission but a bribe.

In its investigation the Committee was able to verify General Khatemi's covert ownership of Air Taxi stock at the time the Bell sale was concluded, but unable to ascertain whether Miller knew of it. In his testimony Miller denied having had such knowledge, though he did acknowledge that Textron had engaged in other questionable practices which were under investigation by the SEC, and that Textron officials had always brought these to his attention.

In view of the fact that three Bell sales executives were sent to Iran in November of 1969, precisely in order to determine whether Air Taxi's representation of Bell in that country would create any conflict of interest, and that according to Dr. Hassan Safavi, a former Iranian government official, the three did learn of General Khatemi's involvement in Air Taxi—because Dr. Safavi himself told them of it—Senator Proxmire, the Committee chairman, found it curious that this information had not been passed on to Miller as so much else was.

General Khatemi died in a glider accident in 1975. One of the three Bell executives who had visited Iran in 1969 also subsequently died. The Committee could not locate a second. The third would comment on the matter no further than to say he had heard "allegations and rumors" of General Khatemi's involvement. He would not clarify, however, whether he had reported even these "rumors" to Miller.

In its own investigation of this and several other incidents, the Securities and Exchange Commission had expected that Textron records might show whether or not Miller and other company officials had known they were paying a bribe in 1973. But Textron had refused to produce its records, and the SEC then filed an action in Federal District Court to force the company's compliance with their subpoena.

The SEC investigation promised to be thorough, and was anticipated to last for over six months. But before Textron records could be made available, the Senate Banking Committee, in response to considerable pressure from the White House, recommended Miller's nomination by a vote of 14 to 1, and early in March of 1978 the full Senate confirmed his nomination as the new chairman of the Federal Reserve Board.

The UH-1 is also in production under license in Taiwan by the Aero Industry Development Corporation, which to date has produced 118 UH-1H, in Japan by the firm of Fuji, which first produced 90 UH-1B and has now produced to date 81 UH-1H, and in

Italy by Agusta-Bell, which has so far produced over 350 of the AB204 and AB205, including 170 for its own armed forces, many of them equipped for ASW service with AN/AQS-13B variable-depth sonar and the AN/APS-195 search radar, and carrying Mk 44 homing torpedoes.

**Weight:** 9,500 lbs (Model 204/UH-1A/B/C), 10,500 lbs (Model 205/UH-1D/N and variants).

**Speed:** 127 mph (Models 204/205), or 150 mph (Model 214). AB204AS: 104 mph.

**Range:** 248 miles (Model 204), or 318 miles (Models 205/214).

**Capacity:** 3,880 lbs of cargo, 8 to 10 combat troops, or 2 casualty litters (Model 204). 5,000 lbs of cargo, up to 15 combat troops, or 6 casualty litters (Models 205/212).

**Armament:** UH-1B: M-5 system with 1 x M-75 40mm grenade launcher and 315 rounds, 230 rpm and range of 1,875 yards, or M-21 system with 2 x M-134 7.62mm Minigun and 600 rounds, 4,800 rpm and range of 1,250 yards, and 2 x M-158 2.75″ rocket pod, each with 7 FFAR and range of 3,750 yards. Variants of M-21 substitute 8 x .30 Cal. MG for M-134. Additional pintle-mounted M-134 or hand-held M60C MG often carried. UH-1D: M-23 system with 2 x M60D 7.62mm MG with 600 rounds, 550 to 600 rpm and range of 1,250 yards, or M-16 system with 2 x M60C MG with 6,000 rounds, 2,000 to 2,600 rpm and range of 1,250 yards, and 2 x M-158 2.75″ rocket pods, each with 7 FFAR and range of 3,750 yards. Additional armament frequently carried in cabin, pintle-mounted or hand-held.

**Produced:** More than 8,000 of all types to date, including over 2,500 Bell Model 204 and military variants UH-1A/B/C, over 3,000 Bell Model 205, including UH-1D and more than 1,200 UH-1H, several hundred Bell Model 214, including 100 214A Isfahan for Iran, out of a total order of 288 Model 214A and 38 Model 214C, 118 Uh-1H by AIDC in Taiwan, 90 UH-1B and 81 UH-1H to date by Fuji in Japan (with engines built by Kawasaki), and over 350 AB204 and AB205 by Agusta-Bell in Italy, including many ASW versions for Italian forces and export.

**Exported under FMS:** 383.

**Exported under MAP:** 1,628.

**In US Service:** 82 UH-1H in USAF/MAC, 2,350 UH-1B/D/H and 300 UH-1C in U.S. Army, 1,135 UH-1B/D/H in Army National Guard, 285 UH-1B/C/H in Army Reserve, 62 TH-1L in USN, 19 UH-1E in USN Reserve, 86 UH-1E in USMC, 16 HH-1H in USAF Reserve, some UH-1F, TH-1F and UH-1P in USAF, some UH-1L and HH-1K in USN, some UH-1M in U.S. Army.

**In Service Abroad:** Argentina (5 UH-1D and 19 UH-1H), Australia (24 UH-1B, 67 UH-1D

and 41 UH-1H), Austria (12 UH-1B and 23 AB204B), Bolivia (2 UH-1H), Brazil (33 UH-1D, of which 6 converted to SH-1D, and 36 UH-1H), Brunei (2 Bell 205A), Burma (18 Bell 205A), Canada (25 UH-1H, designated CH-118), Cambodia (32 UH-1H), Chile (3 UH-1D and 5 UH-1H), Colombia (6 UH-1B), Dubai (4 AB205A equipped with TOW), El Salvador (6 UH-1H), Ethiopia (6 UH-1H and 6 AB204B), Greece (36 AB204B, 6 AB205, 10 UH-1D and 35 UH-1H), Guatemala (6 UH-1D), Indonesia (2 Bell 204B), Iran (4 Bell 205A and 90 AB205A), Israel (30 UH-1D, 25 Bell 205 and 40 AB205A), Italy (110 AB204B, 30 AB204AS and 30 AB205), Jamaica (6 Bell 205), Japan (90 Fuji UH-1B and 81 Fuji UH-1H), Kuwait (6 AB204B and 4 AB205), Ghana (6 AB205), Laos (16 UH-1D), Lebanon (4 AB204), Malaysia (10 Bell 205), Mexico (3 UH-1B and 6 Bell 205), Morocco (24 AB205), Netherlands (7 AB204B), Nicaragua (2 UH-1H), New Zealand (5 UH-1D and 13 UH-1H), Norway (32 UH-1B and 6 AB205), Oman (5 AB205), Panama (7 Bell 204 and 2 UH-1B), Peru (22 Bell 205), Philippines (12 UH-1D), Saudi Arabia (1 AB204B and 25 AB205), Somalia (8 AB205), South Africa (25 AB205A), South Korea (5 UH-1D), Spain (12 AB204B, 4 AB204AS, 12 UH-1B and 16 UH-1H), Sweden (18 AB204B), Switzerland (12 AB204B), Taiwan (54 UH-1D and 118 AIDC UH-1H), Thailand (20 UH-1B/D and 50 UH-1H), Turkey (10 UH-1D, 16 AB204B, 4 AB204AS and 23 AB205), Uganda (6 AB205), United Arab Emirates (8 AB205), Uruguay (2 UH-1H), Venezuela (12 UH-1D and 9 UH-1H), Vietnam (625 UH-1H, and 196 UH-1B left abandoned by American forces), West Germany (354 UH-1D, including 352 assembled by Dornier), Yugoslavia (16 UH-1D and 17 AB205), and Zaire (4 UH1H and 28 AB205).

**Bell Model 214 In Service Abroad:** Iran (28 Model 214A and 39 Model 214C Isfahan, out of a total of 288 214A and 38 214C ordered), and Oman (5 Model 214A).

**Price:** $219.512 @ (1961 Unit Procurement Cost for 106 UH-1B to U.S. Army). $344,423 @ (1965 Unit Procurement Cost for 221 UH-1H to U.S. Army). $1.1 million @ (1974 Unit Procurement Cost for 55 Fuji UH-1H for Japanese Ground Self Defense Force).

**Recent Transfers of Model 205:** 14 UH-1H to Brazil in 1974 for $428,571 @. 13 UH-1H to Thailand in 1974 for $807,692 @. 35 UH-1H to Greece in 1975 for $785,714 @.

**Recent Transfers of Model 214:** 287 Model 214A Isfahan to Iran in 1972 for $1.524 million @. Order later increased to 288 Model 214A and 38 Model 214C.

**FMS Deliveries Pending:** Argentina (12 UH-1H), and Australia (12 UH-1H).

# BELL MODEL 212 UH-1N IROQUOIS

The current production model of the UH-1, a twin-engined version powered by a Pratt & Whitney PT6T-6 Turbo Twin Pac, and first developed in 1969 under Canadian sponsorship. Safer and more powerful and with a greater range, it was planned primarily for use as a transport. Almost 700 have so far been produced, including 250 commercial versions, 70 CUH-1N for the Canadian Armed Forces, 65 for the U.S. Army, 79 for the Air Force, 149 for the Navy and Marine Corps, and approximately 40 under license by Agusta-Bell in Italy. Many of the Italian versions are equipped for ASW service, carrying Mk 44 homing torpedoes, Mk 46 depth charges and other weapons.

**Weight:** 11,200 lbs.

**Speed:** 126 mph.

**Range:** 414 miles.

**Capacity:** 15 combat troops, or 6 casualty litters, and 3,382 lbs of cargo or external stores.

**Produced:** Over 650 to date, including 70 CUH-1N, 293 UH-1N for United States forces, and 40 AB212 or AB212AS.

**Exported under FMS:** 101.

**In US Service:** 79 UH-1N IN USAF/MAC, 65 UH-1N in U.S. Army, 69 UH-1N in USN and 80 UH-1N in USMC.

**In service Abroad:** Brunei (4 Bell 212), Canada (70 CUH-1N, designated CH-135), Colombia (1 Bell 212), Ghana (2 Bell 212), Iran (11 AB212), Italy (28 AB212AS), Lebanon (2 AB212), Mexico (1 Bell 212), Oman (1 AB212), Peru (17 Bell 212), Spain (4 AB212), Turkey (6 AB212AS), Uganda (1 Bell 212), United Arab Emirates (3 AB212), West Germany (3 Bell 212), and Zaire (1 AB212).

**Price:** $1.027 million @ (1976 Unit Procurement Cost for 15 UH-1N to U.S. Army). $1.333 million @ (1976 Unit Procurement Cost for 30 UH-1N to USMC). $1.541 million @ (1977 Unit Procurement Cost for 12 UH-1N to U.S. Army).

**Recent Transfers:** 3 Bell 212 to West Germany in 1976 for $1.333 million @. 3 AB212AS ASW Helicopters to Turkey from Italy in 1976 for $1.8 million @.

**Deliveries Pending:** Argentina (2 Bell 212), Peru (6 AB212AS), Spain (4 AB212AS), United Arab Emirates (1 AB212), Japan (14 Bell 212, sold in 1978).

# BELL MODEL 47 OH-13 SIOUX

One of the earliest helicopters to enter service, the Bell Model 47 was designed in 1943, first flew in 1945, and was initially delivered to the U.S. Army in 1946 under the designation UH-13 for use as a light observation and scout aircraft. After 28 years in service, it still flies in the armed forces of 36 countries, including our own. More than 2,500 of the Model 47 have been produced, including over 1,000 by Bell, 1,100 in Italy by Agusta-Bell under a license obtained in 1952, 240 under a license obtained the following year by the Japanese firm of Kawasaki, which designated the aircraft KH-4, and 250 produced under license by Westland in the United Kingdom and designated AH Mk 1 and HT Mk 2.

**Weight:** 2,950 lbs.

**Speed:** 84 mph, or 105 mph (AB47G).

**Range:** 247 miles, or 214 miles (Kawasaki KH-4), or 210 miles (AB47G).

**Capacity:** 3 passengers, or 4 in KH-4 and AB47G.

**Produced:** Over 2,500 of all types, including 1,100 Bell 47B/D/G/H/J, 1,100 Agusta-Bell 47G/J (including some equipped for ASW with 1 x Mk 44 torpedo), 240 Kawasaki 47G, designated KH-4, and 250 Westland 47G, designated AH Mk 1 and HT Mk 2.

**Exported under FMS:** 132 OH-13 and 15 TH-13.

**Bell twin-engined UH-IN Iroquois**

# BELL AH-1 COBRA

Developed in 1965 as a specialized gunship version of the UH-1 Iroquois, and nick-named the *HueyCobra,* the AH-1 Cobra first entered service in Vietnam in 1967. With a crew of two seated in tandem, the gunner in front and the pilot behind him, the Cobra has a fuselage only three feet and two inches wide, making it a more difficult target to hit from the ground than were the armed versions of the UH-1. With a formidable variety of armament, progressively strengthened over the years, the Cobra has developed into one of this country's major antitank systems, armed with the TOW missile.

The AH-1G Cobra, of which 1,124 were produced, was initially armed with the Emerson TAT (Tactical Armament Turret) 101, carrying an M60C 7.62mm machine gun with a rate of fire of from 500 to 750 rounds per minute. This was replaced by the TAT 102, mounting a six-barreled General Electric M-134 7.62mm Minigun with 1,500 rounds, firing at a rate of from 1,300 to 4,000 rounds per minute, to a range of 1,250 yards.

The TAT 102 was eventually replaced by the M-28 turret, also developed by Emerson, and now standard on the AH-1G and all subsequent versions for the U.S. Army, including the AH-1Q and AH-1S. The M-28 turret holds either one or two M-134 Miniguns with 4,000 rounds of 7.62mm ammunition, or two M-129 40mm grenade launchers with 300 rounds, firing grenades at a rate of from 230 to 450 rounds per minute to a range of 1,875 yards, or one M-134 Minigun and one M-129 grenade launcher each.

In addition to the M-28 turret, Emerson Electric also developed the standard M-6 pylon to carry additional M-134 Miniguns in pods on inboard stations, and rocket pods or other ordnance on outboard stations. A common arrangement accompanying the M-28 turret is the M-21 armament system, consisting of two M-18 gun pods, each with an M-134 Minigun and 600 rounds, firing at a rate of 4,800 rounds per minute, and on outboard stations two M-158 2.75" rocket pods, each carrying 7 rockets which can all be fired in six seconds to a range of 3,750 yards. A heavier load, keeping the M-18 gun pods on inboard stations, fits two M-200 rocket pods on the outboard stations along with two M-158 pods. The M-200 pod carries nineteen 2.75" rockets, and in this configuration the Cobra carries a total of 52 rockets.

To witness one of these aircraft in action, thus armed, is a frightening experience. Appearing remarkably like a dragonfly in the distance, the aircraft approaches its target flying at a low level over the treeline. Suddenly it belches smoke and fire while still 3,000 yards off. These are the rockets, equipped either with HE (high explosive) or WP (white phosphorous) warheads. A few plunge into the ground in steps toward the target, sending up brilliant white plumes, but most converge on the target in a dense series of nearly simultaneous explosions. Each of these rockets, nicknamed *Tiny Tim,* has the equivalent explosive force of an 81mm mortar shell, and those with WP warheads nearly match the force of a 4.2" (107mm) mortar shell. The curious sound of them all going off almost at once has been likened to a large pair of cymbals being clashed a few inches from one's ear.

While the forces of these blasts are still being felt, smoke is billowing up, earth, stone and fragments of other materials are heaved into the air, and fires are beginning to light within an area almost one hundred yards across, the Cobra is still 2,000 yards away. An odd, rapid coughing sound is heard. These are the 40mm grenades, sputtering out of the aircraft's turret in short bursts of six or seven each second. Almost immediately after this comes the high-pitched rattle of three Miniguns, one in the turret and two on either inboard station. The grenades begin to burst in short, snakelike patterns on the ground, each one, with a popping sound and a brief flash, fragmenting into more than a hundred shards.

As the aircraft dashes forward over its target, hovers, rears back and dashes forward again, it resembles a snake repeatedly striking.

There is a distinct change, now, in the rattle of the Miniguns, which has gone to a higher pitch. This means the gunner has obtained his range. With a trigger control, he has automatically selected higher rates of fire for the guns, and is firing for effect. The three guns are throwing more than 200 rounds per second into the target area, and their smoke is such that it partly obscures the aircraft from view.

Hovering near the target, the Cobra begins to swing back and forth from side to side, as though suspended on a wire from above. The electrically-driven turret has a turning radius of 230 degrees, and is automatically guided by the gunner's helmet sight subsystem. A fire control computer automatically adjusts the gunner's lead angle, compensating for the motion of aircraft and target. Thus, while the Cobra's nose points slightly out of the target area at either end of its swinging arc, the turret itself remains fixed directly on the target, and 7.62mm rounds continue to hose it down.

Of the AH-1Gs originally produced, 34 have been converted by the Army as trainers, another 38 were supplied to the USMC as trainers for the Marine Corp's AH-1J and AH-1T Sea Cobras, 20 have been transferred to Spain and 12 to Israel, and 66 were

175

left abandoned by American forces in Vietnam, including 30 of the aircraft in mint condition, unassembled and crated in their original packing grease. An additional 70 AH-1Gs are now being offered on the open market in Europe, through private arms brokers, for $1.7 million each. These aircraft are each fully-equipped with the Norton Company's NOROC armour, protecting the crew seats and side panels, and each is armed with two M-18 Minigun pods, two M-157 rocket pods with seven 2.75″ rockets each, and a special turret with one M-29 40mm grenade launcher and a General Electric M61A1 Vulcan six-barreled 20mm cannon.

Three additional AH-1Gs were specially fitted in 1970 with SMASH (Southeast Asia Multisensor Armament System for Huey Cobra), including Emerson Electric's MTI (Moving Target Indicator), an AN/APQ-137B high-resolution radar, and the Aerojet SSPI (Sensor System, Passive Infrared). Other AH-1Gs have been equipped with Aeronutronic-Ford's ATAFCS (Airborne Target Acquisition and Fire Control System), a 400 lb electro-optical target acquisition and designation pod mounted in the aircraft's nose to provide target illumination for the Martin-Marietta laser-guided Copperhead 155mm howitzer round. The ATAFCS incorporates an International Laser Systems laser designator and rangefinder, a Rockwell International laser spot tracker to acquire remotely-designated targets, an autotracker with both day and night capability, and a Texas Instruments FLIR (Forward Looking Infra Red) sensor.

In 1977 the U.S. Army converted 93 of its AH-1Gs to AH-1Q standard, equipped to carry eight TOW antitank missiles. The conversion work, carried out by Hughes Aircraft and the Univac Division of Sperry Rand, cost $586,138 per aircraft. At a higher cost, 197 additional AH-1Gs will be converted in 1978 to AH-1S standard, incorporating the AN/APR-39 radar warning set, a flat-plate canopy to reduce glare, improved navigation equipment, modified control linkages, the capacity for an additional 500 lbs of gross weight, and a new Lycoming T53-L-703 engine to improve the aircraft's ability to hover. At the same time, the 93 converted AH-1Qs will be reworked again to bring them up to AH-1S standard, while 100 wholly new AH-1S aircraft will also be produced. This will give the Army a total of 390 AH-1S aircraft equipped with the TOW missile by the end of 1978.

In 1979, 98 new AH-1S aircraft will be produced to an upgunned standard, with improved electrical and communications systems, a new armament management system for pylon-mounted weapons, and a new chin turret capable of carrying the M-61A1 Vulcan six-barreled 20mm cannon, the M-197 three-barreled flexible 20mm weapon system, the M-188 three-barreled 30mm cannon, or the Hughes XM-230 multi-barreled 30mm chain gun. The previous 390 AH-1S aircraft will be upgraded to this same standard. By 1981 all of these aircraft will have been reworked again, together with 400 additional AH-1Gs, to a modernized AH-1S standard, with a laser rangefinder, laser target detector and autotracker as standard equipment, together with a closed circuit refueling system, a new air data system and an omnidirectional airspeed indicator, a Doppler navigation system, secure voice communications, a HUD (Head Up Display) for the pilot, ECM

equipment including an AN/ALQ-44 infrared jammer and hot metal and infrared plume suppressors, and most important of all, a new Marconi-Elliott Avionic Systems fire control computer. Another 107 modernized AH-1S aircraft will be produced in 1981, giving the Army by the end of that year a total of 995 AH-1S aircraft so equipped, each capable of carrying eight TOW missiles.

210 of these aircraft will be assigned to our Seventh Army in Europe, organized into 10 attack helicopter companies of 21 aircraft each, two of them equipping the air combat battalions in each of our four Army Divisions, and one assigned to each of our two armoured cavalry regiments. An additional 126 AH-1S may also be organized into two attack helicopter battalions of three companies each, for assignment to the Seventh Army at corps level, bringing the total strength of TOW-equipped AH-1S in Europe to 336 helicopters. They are expected to provide an antitank defense capability sufficient to offset the current superiority in Soviet and Warsaw Pact tank strength.

For the Marine Corps, the twin-engined AH-1J Sea Cobra has been developed, with deliveries of the first 69 aircraft in 1970 and 1971. Powered by a Pratt & Whitney T400-TP-400 Twin Pac coupled turboshaft, the AH-1J incorporates a standard turret with the M-197 three-barreled 20mm cannon, and can be armed on its pylon stations with a variety of air munitions, including M-18 gun pods, Mk 115 bombs, CBU-55/B Fuel Air Explosive dispensers, Mk 45 parachute flares and SUU-44 flare dispensers, and either the LAU-68/A 2.75″ rocket pod with 7 rockets, similar to the Army's M-158, or the LAU-61/A and LAU-69/A rocket pod with 19 rockets, similar to the Army's M-200. A new version, the AH-1T, of which 59 have thus far been delivered, is equipped to carry the TOW missile.

In 1972 Iran ordered 137 of these twin-engined AH-1Js, together with 65 AH-1Ts equipped with TOW missiles, for $1.82 million each, All 202 of these aircraft have been delivered. In an even larger sale not publicly announced, Saudi Arabia purchased 440 AH-1J Sea Cobras the following year, and so far has received 200. Japan has ordered 50 AH-1Js, and may order another 50. In 1977, Israel purchased 20 AH-1Js for $1.61 million each, together with a supply of 4,500 air-launched TOW missiles, in a sale worth $64 million. These aircraft should be delivered by the end of 1978, as will be the balance of Iran's order.

Having purchased $367 million worth of AH-1Js and AH-1Ts, and $497 million worth of Bell 214A/C transport helicopters, Iran has also signed FMS contracts with the United States worth an additional total of $613 million, including creation of a $57 million logistics support system for the AH-1J, a $139 million logistics support and depot maintenance system for the 214A, a $250 million construction and training program to build and operate four helicopter area support centers, and a $167 million training program for 1,550 helicopter pilots and 4,500 mechanics. Thus, in acquiring this sizeable helicopter force and in preparing to operate and maintain it, Iran is spending a total of $1.477 billion.

In 1977, in response to Saudi, Iranian and Egyptian urgings, the government of Morocco decided to take a more active role in the future against Soviet penetration of Africa, a role for which the United States has already prepared that country better than is commonly known. In preparation for this, and also to meet specific needs in its fight

for control over the Western Sahara, Morocco has requested 24 AH-1G Cobras, along with 24 Rockwell OV-10A Bronco aircraft. The $100 million sale would be offset by FMS military credits to that country that have currently averaged $45 million per year. Due to the fact that a United Nations mission and a ruling of the World Court have both denied Moroccan claims to the Western Sahara, public reaction to this sale's announcement has delayed its consummation. United States interests in that country, however, include our desire to continue operating a naval air station at Kenittra and a secret communications station at Sidi Yahya.

**Weight:** 9,500 lbs (G/Q), or 10,000 lbs (S/J), or 13,928 lbs (T).

**Speed:** 207 mph (G/Q/S), or 219 mph (J/T).

**Range:** 359 miles.

**Turret Armament:** M-28 turret with 1 or 2 x M-134 7.62mm Minigun, or 2 x M-129 40mm grenade launcher, or 1 x M-134 and 1 x M-129 (G/Q). M-28 turret with 1 x M-61A1 Vulcan 20mm cannon, or 1 x M-197 20mm cannon, or 1 x M-188 30mm cannon, or 1 x XM-230 Hughes 30mm chain gun (S). M-197 three-barreled 20mm cannon (J/T).

**Pylon Armament:** 2 x M-18 Minigun pod and 2 x M-158 rocket pod, or 2 x M-158 and 2 x M-200 rocket pod, or 2 x M-18 and 2 x M-118 smoke grenade dispenser, or 2 x M-18, 2 x M-158 and 2 x M-200, or 4 x M-200, or 1 x XM-35 20mm cannon on port inboard station /AH-1G). 2 x M-158 and 2 x M-200, or 2 x M-200 and 4 x TOW missile, or 2 x M-158 and 8 x TOW missile, or 2 x M-18 Minigun pod and 8 x TOW missile, or 8 x TOW missile. /AH-1Q/S). 4 x LAU-68/A rocket pod, or 2 x LAU-68B/A and 2 x M-18 gun pod, or 2 x LAU-68B/A and 2 x Mk 45 parachute flare, or 2 x LAU-68B/A and 2 x Mk 115 bomb, or 4 x LAU-61/A or LAU-69/A rocket pod, or 2 x M-18 gun pod and 2 x M-118 smoke grenade dispenser, or 4 x

SUU-44 flare dispenser, or 4 x CBU-55/B Fuel Air Explosive dispenser (J). 4 x TOW missile, or 8 x TOW missile, or 8 x TOW missile and 2 x LAU-68/A rocket pod (T).

**Produced:** 2,114 of all types to date, including 1,124 AH-1G (of which 34 converted to TH-1G, 93 to AH-1Q for reconversion to AH-1S, 197 to AH-1S of total of 597 planned, 3 to AH-1G SMASH, and 3 to AH-1G (ATAFCS), 459 AH-1J to date of a planned production of approximately 900, 100 AH-1S (to be followed by 98 in 1979 and 107 in 1981), and 59 AH-1T.

**Exported under FMS:** 398.

**Exported under MAP:** 4.

**In US Service:** 400 AH-1G, 390 AH-1S and 34 TH-1G in U.S. Army, 5 AH-1G in Army National Guard, 32 AH-1G, 69 AH-1J and 59 AH-1T in USMC, and 6 AH-1G in USMC Reserve.

**In Service Abroad:** Iran (202 AH-1J/T), Israel (12 AH-1G and 20 AH-1J), Japan (50 AH-1J), Saudi Arabia (200 AH-1J), Spain (20 AH-1G), and Vietnam (66 AH-1G left abandoned by United States forces).

**FMS Deliveries Pending:** Iran (17 AH-1J and 65 AH-1T), and Saudi Arabia (220 AH-1J).

**FMS Sales Pending:** Japan (50 AH-1J), Morocco (24 AH-1G).

**Price:** (AH-1G) $1.550 million@ (1975 Unit Procurement Cost for 56 AH-1G to U.S. Army). $1.256 million@ (1976 Unit Procurement Cost for 60 AH-1G to U.S. Army). (AH-1S) $1.397 million@ (1977 Unit Procurement Cost for 82 AH-1S to U.S. Army). $1.489 million@ (1978 Unit Procurement Cost for 83 AH-1S to U.S. Army). (AH-1J) $1.590 million@ (1973 Unit Procurement Cost for 20 AH-1J to USMC). $3.371 million@ (1976 Unit Procurement Cost for 7 AH-1J to USMC). $2.683 million@ (1977 Unit Procurement Cost for 23 AH-1J to USMC). (AH-1T) $2.714 million@ (1976 Unit Procurement Cost for 14 AH-1T to USMC). $2.682 million@ (1977 Unit Procurement Cost for 23 AH-1T to USMC). $3.650 million@ (1978 Unit Procurement Cost for 8 AH-1T to USMC).

**Conversion Costs:** $586,138@ (1977 cost of converting 93 AH-1G to AH-1Q). $1.060 million@ (Estimated 1979 cost for conversion of 200 AH-1G to modernized AH-1S standard).

**Recent Transfers:** 202 AH-1J/T to Iran in 1972 for $1.82 million@ . 440 AH-1J to Saudi Arabia in 1973 for $1.2 million@. 20 AH-1J to Israel in 1977 for $1.61 million@.

# BOEING VERTOL CH-47 CHINOOK

Well-known as a troop carrier, the Chinook was developed in 1956 to meet an Army requirement for a battlefield mobility helicopter capable of carrying two tons of cargo internally and eight tons externally. In the latter role it has performed prodigious work, airlifting far more than the maximum rated weight of cargo slung under its fuselage and retrieving more than 11,400 disabled aircraft, valued at approximately $3 billion, during the war in Vietnam. With a rear-loading ramp, the CH-47 was designed for all-weather operation, and deliveries of the first CH-47As to the U.S. Army began in 1962. Four were converted to armed ACH-47As with the XM-41 armament system, a pintle-mounted M60D 7.62mm heavy machine gun at the aircraft's rear ramp. This was supplemented by additional .50 Caliber or 7.62mm machine guns mounted at either window aft of the pilot's bay. In 1971, 49 CH-47A were supplied under MAP to South Vietnam.

In response to a new Army requirement for an improved HLH (Heavy Lift Helicopter), capable of an increased cargo load of 28,000 lbs and with advanced flight controls, 361 of the Army's CH-47A and CH-47B aircraft are planned for conversion to CH-47D standard, meeting these requirements, at an estimated cost of $4.67 million each, including engine and rotor blade development funding. An additional 190 new CH-47D aircraft will be built, equipped with Honeywell advanced flight controls, at a cost of $6.32 million each, giving the Army a force of 551 CH-47Ds by 1985.

Since 1970, the CH-47C has been manufactured under license in Italy by Elicotteri Meridionali, which has supplied quantities of this aircraft to the Italian army and to Iran, and which now has orders on hand from Libya and Syria.

**Weight:** 46,000 lbs.

**Speed:** 189 mph.

**Range:** 230 miles fully loaded, ferry range of 1,420 miles.

**Capacity:** 44 combat troops, 27 casualty litters, or 13,212 lbs internal cargo, or 23,212 lbs external cargo (CH-47A/B/C). 28,000 lbs external cargo (CH-47D). Hot-weather maximum lift capacity of 9,000 lbs (CH-47A/B/C), or 15,000 lbs (CH-47D).

**Produced:** Over 868 of all types to date, including 550 CH-47A/B (of which 4 converted to ACH-47A and 361 planned for conversion to CH-47D), and 250 Boeing CH-47C, together with 68 Meridionali CH-47C to date and production planned for at least 80 more. New production of 190 CH-47D planned.

**Exported under FMS:** 20.

**Exported under MAP:** 79.

**In US Service:** 361 CH-47A/B, 214 CH-47C and 4 ACH-47A in U.S. Army, 50 CH-47A/B in Army National Guard, and 31 CH-47A/B in Army Reserve.

**In Service Abroad:** Australia (12 CH-47C), Canada (8 CH-47C, designated CH-147), Iran (42 Meridionali CH-47C), Israel (8 CH-47C), Italy (26 Meridionali CH-47C and 2 Boeing CH-47C), Libya (8 Meridionali CH-47C), Spain (7 CH-47C), Thailand (4 CH-47C), Turkey (12 CH-47C), and Vietnam (49 CH-47A and 36 CH-47C left abandoned by United States forces).

**Price:** $6.67 million @ (1977 Unit FMS Cost for 30 CH-47C to United Kingdom). $6.32 million @ (1978 estimate of Unit Procurement Cost of 190 CH-47D produced through 1985 for U.S. Army). $1.00 million @ (1978 U.S. Army estimate of unit residual value of 361 CH-47A/B). $5.67 million @ (1978 estimate of unit value for conversion of 361 CH-47A/B to CH-47D, at Unit Program Conversion Cost of $4.67 million @). $3.003 million @ (1976 Unit Procurement Cost for 12 CH-47C to U.S. Army). $2.008 million @ (1974 Unit Procurement Cost for 24 CH-47C to U.S. Army).

**Recent Transfers:** 6 CH-47C to Spain in 1972 for $3 million @. 12 CH-47C to Australia in 1972 for $3.683 million @. 8 CH-47C to Canada in 1974 for $3.75 million @. 22 Meridionali CH-47C to Iran in 1975 for $5 million @. 30 CH-47C to United Kingdom in 1977 for $6.67 million @.

**Deliveries Pending:** Iran (50 Meridionali CH-47C), Libya (16 Meridionali CH-47C), Syria (6 Meridionali CH-47C), United Kingdom (30 Boeing CH-47C).

# BOEING VERTOL MODEL 107/H-46 SEA KNIGHT

Nearly identical in appearance to the CH-47 Chinook, but only half its size, the H-46 Sea Knight was developed in 1959 to fill a USN and USMC requirement for a VERTREP (Vertical Replenishment) helicopter to airlift stores, parts, munitions, troops and small vehicles from logistic support ships to combatant ships and beachheads. Over 1,200 Sea Knights have been produced, including 134 to date under license by Kawasaki in Japan, with deliveries of 600 CH-46A to the USMC beginning in 1962. Since then, the aircraft has been used in a variety of specialized roles, including long-range search and rescue and mine countermeasures missions. In 1974, 300 of a more powerful CH-46E, with six times the range of previous models, were delivered to the Marine Corps.

**Weight:** 19,000 lbs (A/D/F and Kawasaki models), or 21,000 lbs (CH-46E).

**Speed:** 168 mph.

**Range:** 109 miles (A/D/F and Kawasaki models), or 663 miles (CH-46E).

**Capacity:** 25 combat troops or 4,000 lbs of cargo.

**Produced:** Over 1,200 of all types, including 600 CH-46A, 3 CH-46C, 24 UH-46A, 300 CH-46E, and several hundred UH-46D for USN, CH-46D for USMC, and CH-46F with improved avionics for USMC, together with 134 Kawasaki KV-107 aircraft to date.

**Exported under FMS:** 2.

**In US Service:** 24 in USN, 186 in USMC, and 40 in USMC Reserve.

**In Service Abroad:** Canada (18 Boeing Model 107, 6 as CH-113 Labrador and 12 as CH-113A Voyageur), Japan (122 Kawasaki KV-107), Sweden (21 Boeing Model 107, designated HKP-7, and 8 Kawasaki KV-107, designated HKP-4C), and Thailand (4 Kawasaki KV-107).

**Price:** $3.7 million @ (1975 Unit Procurement Cost for 122 Kawasaki KV-107 to Japanese Air, Ground and Maritime Self Defense Forces).

**Boeing H-46 Sea Knight**

# FAIRCHILD HILLER FH-1100/OH-5

Designed in 1963 to compete for the Army's LOH (Light Observation Helicopter) requirement, subsequently filled by the Hughes OH-6A Cayuse, the Hiller OH-5 continued in production for commercial use but has been adapted for military service by several countries abroad.

**Weight:** 2,750 lbs.

**Speed:** 127 mph.

**Range:** 348 miles.

**Capacity:** 5 passengers, or 1,000 lbs of cargo.

**In Service Abroad:** Argentina (10 FH-1100), Brazil (6 FH-1100), Chile (2 FH-1100), Ecuador (1 FH-1100), El Salvador (1 FH-1100), Philippines (8 FH-1100), and Thailand (16 FH-1100).

# BOEING VERTOL MODELS 43 AND 44/H-21 SHAWNEE

First developed in 1949, the design for the H-21 was originally derived from the Piasecki "flying banana" transport and cargo helicopter. Five CH-21s were delivered to the Marine Corps in 1949 as cargo and utility craft, and they were followed in 1952 by 18 YH-21s for USAF. 32 H-21A and 153 H-21B followed. When the firm of Piasecki changed its name to Vertol in 1956, the H-21A and H-21B were redesignated Model 42, and in that same year Models 43 and 44 were developed. Over the course of the next few years a total of 321 H-21Cs based on the Model 43 were delivered to the U.S. Army or countries abroad, including 98 for France. The H-21C performed most of the Army's supply helilifts during the early years of our involvement in Vietnam. The Model 44, a further development of the H-21 design, was not used by our own services, but was supplied in small numbers abroad.

**Weight:** 13,500 lbs (Model 43), or 15,000 lbs (Model 44).

**Speed:** Speed: 127 mph.

**Range:** 450 miles (Model 43), or 360 miles (Model 44).

**Capacity:** 2,500 lbs of cargo or external ASW ordnance, 20 combat troops, or 12 casualty litters.

**Produced:** Over 600 of all types, including 5 CH-21, 18 YH-21, 32 H-21A, 153 H-21B and 321 H-21C.

**Exported under FMS:** 14.

**Exported under MAP:** 28.

**In Service Abroad:** Canada (5 H-21A, 6 H-21C and 3 Model 44A), France (20 H-21C, of 98 originally delivered), Japan (6 H-21B and 2 Model 44A), Soviet Union (1 Model 44B and 1 Model 44C), Sweden (9 Model 44A, designated HKP-1 and used for ASW), and West Germany (3 H-21C of 42 originally delivered).

## HILLER MODEL 12E RAVEN/OH-23 AND MODEL 360/UH-12

A light general-purpose helicopter designed in the late 1950s. Over 2,000 were produced, 1,471 of which were delivered to the U.S. Army, USN and USAF. The final military version, the OH-23G, was transferred in small quantities to the United Kingdom, where the Royal Navy used it as the HT Mk 2 trainer, and to Canada, where 24 of the aircraft fly under the designation of CH-112 Nomad.

**Weight:** 3,100 lbs.

**Speed:** 90 mph.

**Range:** 439 miles.

**Capacity:** 3 passengers.

**Produced:** Over 2,000 of all types, including 100 H-23A for the U.S. Army, 16 HTE-1 trainers for USN, 5 H-23A for USAF, 273 OH-23B for the U.S. Army, 35 HTE-2 trainers for USN, 145 OH-23C, 483 OH-23D, 22 OH-23F and 392 OH-23G.

**In Service Abroad:** Canada (24 OH-23G, designated CH-112 Nomad), Chile (6 Hiller 12E and 6 Hiller SL-6), Colombia (4 H-23A), Dominican Republic (2 Hiller 12E), Guatemala (1 OH-23G), Mexico (1 Hiller 12E), Paraguay (3 Hiller 12E), Thailand (6 OH-23F), United Kingdom (21 OH-23G, designated HT Mk2).

## HUGHES MODELS 269 AND 300 TH-55A OSAGE

A light general-purpose helicopter developed in 1955, 792 of which were delivered to the U.S. Army as TH-55A Osage beginning in 1964. Since 1974 the improved Model 300 has been under licensed production in Italy by BredaNardi and in Japan by Kawasaki.

**Weight:** 1,850 lbs.

**Speed:** 86 mph.

**Range:** 204 miles.

**Capacity:** 2 passengers (Model 269), or 3 passengers (Model 300).

**Produced:** Over 2,463 to date, including 792 TH-55A Osage for U.S. Army.

**In U.S. Service:** 653 TH-55A Osage in U.S. Army.

**In Service Abroad:** Algeria (14 BredaNardi 300), Brazil (6 Hughes 300), Colombia (60 TH-55A), Ghana (2 BredaNardi 300), India (4 Hughes 300), Japan (48 Kawasaki TH-55J), Kenya (19 Hughes 269), Nicaragua (1 Hughes 269), and Switzerland (7 Hughes 269A).

**Price:** $90,000 @ (1975 Unit Procurement Cost for 35 TH-55J to Japanese Ground Self Defense Force).

## HUGHES MODEL 500 OH-6 CAYUSE

The winner in 1961 of the Army's LOH (Light Observation Helicopter) competition, whose acronym led to the aircraft's popular nickname of *Loach,* the OH-6 equipped the scout platoons of our cavalry regiments in Vietnam, where they were armed on a portside pylon either with the M-8 system, providing an M-129 40mm grenade launcher, or the M-27E1, an M-134 7.62mm Minigun with a fixed azimuth but adjustable in elevation to move through 25 degrees, carrying 2,000 rounds and capable of a rate of fire of 2,000 rpm. 1,434 OH-6As were delivered to the U.S. Army by 1970, and these were followed by the OH-6C, whose more powerful engine increased the aircraft's speed from 150 to 200 mph. 192 OH-6A/Cs are planned for assignment to the sixteen attack helicopter companies now being organized to equip our Seventh Army in Europe, 12 of them, along with 21 AH-1S Cobra gunships, in each company.

Hughes Aircraft, which has proposed an OH-6D Advanced Scout Helicopter based on the same airframe, has also developed a special version of the OH-6 with five main rotor blades instead of four, four tail rotor blades instead of two, a blanketed engine assembly and an engine exhaust muffler, features all of which greatly reduce the aircraft's noise. Hughes calls it "the Quiet One." In 1968 the company also developed the Model 500M for export to several countries, and at the Paris Air Show in 1977 Hughes exhibited the new Model 500M Defender, equipped to carry up to four TOW missiles, with hinged debris deflectors to permit reloading of the TOW launchers, and incorporating some of the features of "the Quiet One." These various versions have been licensed for production in Argentina, Indonesia, Italy and Japan. Kiyushki International has just been licensed to produce the Model 500 in Pakistan, and arrangements have just been completed for licensed production of the Model 500M Defender in South Korea, where 100 of the aircraft will be built.

**Weight:** 2,400 lbs.

**Speed:** 150 mph (OH-6A), or 200 mph (OH-6C), or 175 mph (Model 500M Defender).

**Range:** 380 miles.

**Capacity:** 2,000 lbs of cargo or external ordnance, or 2 to 4 passengers (OH-6A/C and Model 500M), or up to 7 passengers (Model 500M Defender).

**Armament:** M-8 system with 1 x M-129 40mm grenade launcher or M-27E1 system with 1 x M-134 7.62mm Minigun with 2,000 rounds (OH-6A/C). ASW equipment including MAD gear and 2 x Mk 44 torpedo (Model 500M in some versions manufactured by BredaNardi in Italy and Kawasaki in Japan). 2 x M-18 gun pod and 2 x M-158 2.75" rocket pod, or 4 x TOW antitank missile (Model 500M Defender).

**Produced:** Over 2,000 of all types to date, including 1,434 OH-6A, 135 OH-6J by Kawasaki in Japan, 120 Model 500M by BredaNardi in Italy, 44 Model 500M in Indonesia, and 145 Model 500M by RACA in Argentina. Continued export production of Model 500M and Model 500M Defender by Hughes anticipated, together with production of 50 Model 500M by Kiyushki International, in cooperation with Cessna Aircraft, in Pakistan and 100 Model 500M Defender in South Korea.

**Exported under FMS:** 31.

**Exported under MAP:** 23.

**In US Service:** 76 OH-6A/C in U.S. Army and 349 OH-6A in Army National Guard. 192 Army and Guard aircraft to be transferred to Seventh Army in West Germany, by 1981.

**In Service Abroad:** Argentina (14 OH-6A, 6 Hughes 500M, and 145 RACA 500M), Austria (12 Hughes 500M), Bolivia (12 Hughes 500M), Colombia (12 OH-6A), Congo Republic (2 BredaNardi NH-500M), Denmark (12 Hughes 500M), Dominican Republic (7 OH-6A), Japan (135 Kawasaki OH-6J), Indonesia (44 Hughes 500M locally assembled), Italy (48 BredaNardi NH-500M and 12 BredaNardi 500M-ASW), Mexico (13 Hughes 500M), Nicaragua (4 OH-6A), Pakistan (2 Hughes 500M), Philippines (12 Hughes 500M), Sierra Leone (2 Hughes 500M), Spain (12 Hughes 500M and 4 BredaNardi NH-500M-ASW), Taiwan (6 Hughes 500M).

**Production Pending:** Pakistan (50 Kiyushki 500M), South Korea (100 500M Defender).

**Price:** $450,000 @ (1975 Unit Procurement Cost for 135 Kawasaki OH-6J to Japanese Ground and Marine Self Defense Forces). $700,000 @ (1977 Unit Procurement Cost for 145 RACA 500M to Argentine Air Force). $766,670@ (1978 unit cost for 30 500 M-D to Israel, equipped with stabilized TOW sight and launchers).

**Hughes OH-6 Cayuse
with M-27E1 Armament System.**

# KAMAN SH-2D AND SH-2F SEASPRITE

A ship-based utility helicopter, first delivered to the USN in 1962 as the UH-2A for VERTREP (Vertical Replenishment) cargo service, and modified by a series of subsequent conversions into one of the most sophisticated multi-purpose helicopters flying, fulfilling an interim USN requirement for a LAMPS (Light Airborne Multi-Purpose System) aircraft until the Sikorsky LAMPS Mk III helicopter enters service in the early 1980s.

The initial 88 UH-2As were followed in 1963 by delivery of 102 UH-2Bs, and by 1967 all 190 of these aircraft had been converted to UH-2C standard, equipped with two General Electric T58 turboshaft engines. One UH-2C was subsequently modified to NUH-2C standard to test a helicopter platform for launching AIM-7 Sparrow and AIM-9 Sidewinder air-to-air missiles, and then it was modified again under the designation NHH-2D to evaluate ship landing techniques. Six UH-2Cs were armed with chin-mounted 7.62mm Minigun turrets and waist-mounted M60C 7.62mm machine guns for search and rescue operations in Vietnam, and at the same time they were given a new four-blade tail rotor. A further 67 were equipped with the same rotor but not armed, and were designated HH-2D.

In 1967 two of these new HH-2D conversions were equipped to evaluate ASMD (Anti-Ship Missile Defense) systems under the Navy's LAMPS program, and a further 20 were remodified to SH-2D LAMPS configuration as anti-submarine attack aircraft, equipped with towable MAD (Magnetic Anomaly Detection) gear, sonobuoys, flares, smoke markers, torpedoes and a Marconi LN-66 high-power surface search radar. After a final 2 HH-2Ds were converted to advanced LAMPS aircraft equipped for both ASW and ASMD roles, the Navy decided to convert the remaining 116 UH-2Cs and 43 HH-2Ds to SH-2F LAMPS Mk I standard, installing a more advanced LN-66HP radar, replacing its three-foot radome with a five-foot radome housing a larger antenna to substantially increase its range, adding a sixty-gallon external fuel tank for increased flight range, equipping the aircraft to operate either the Mk 44 or Mk 46 acoustic-homing anti-submarine torpedo, and substituting a high-performance rotor which gives the SH-2F the lowest vibration level of any helicopter flying.

While it is equally adept at SAR (Search And Rescue), MEDEVAC and VERTREP missions, the SH-2F LAMPS Mk I Seasprite has been assigned the primary respon-

sibilities of fleet protection as an ASW and ASMD aircraft, and, as an extension of the sensor and weapons systems of surface vessels, serves a subsidiary function by using its radar to provide over-the-horizon targeting for ship-launched missiles.

---

**Weight:** 12,800 lbs (SH-2D), or 13,300 lbs (SH-2F).

**Speed:** 168 mph.

**Range:** 445 miles.

**Armament:** 2 x Mk 44 or Mk 46 torpedo.

**Produced:** 88 UH-2A and 102 Uh-2B, all of which converted to UH-2C. Of 190 UH-2C, 1 converted to NUH-2C and subsequently to NHH-2C, 6 to HH-2C and 67 to HH-2D, of which 1 subsequently converted to HH-2D ASMD aircraft, 20 to SH-2D LAMPS and 2 to YSH-2E LAMPS Mk III prototypes. 116 UH-2C and 43 HH-2D subsequently converted to SH-2F LAMPS Mk I in 1975.

**In US Service:** 20 SH-2D and 159 SH-2F in USN.

**Kaman H-2 Seasprite recovering a Navy UDT (Underwater Demolition Team) member**

## KAMAN HH-43 HUSKIE

Developed in 1950 for patrol, search and rescue and utility service, the HH-43 was first used by the USMC in Korea as the OH-43D, a designation later changed to UH-43C. USAF became the major user of this helicopter, taking delivery of 18 HH-43A and 193 HH-43Bs, all with the distinctive ''bear paw'' landing feet. 40 HH-43Fs were also produced for export, though some were converted to QH-43G drones for the USN.

**Weight:** 9,150 lbs.

**Speed:** 120 mph.

**Range:** 504 miles.

**Capacity:** 1,000 lbs of cargo, or 5 passengers, or 4 casualty litters.

**Produced:** Over 230, including 18 HH-43A, 193 HH-43B and 40 HH-43F, some of which converted to QH-43G.

**Exported under FMS:** 12.

**Exported under MAP:** 58.

**In US Service:** 12 HH-43F in USAF/MAC.

**In Service Abroad:** Burma (12 HH-43B), Colombia (6 HH-43B), Morocco (4 HH-43B), Iran (17 HH-43F), Pakistan (6 HH-43B), and Thailand (3 HH-43B).

## SIKORSKY MODEL S-58/H-34 CHOCTAW SH-34 SEA BAT UH-34 SEA HORSE

First developed in 1954 to meet a Navy requirement for an ASW helicopter, the Model 58 entered service in 1955 as the SH-34G Sea Bat, equipped for ASW search but not for strike operations. The SH-34J with automatic stabilization equipment followed, together with the LH-34D equipped for cold-weather operations. Over 1,000 UH-34D/and UH-34E Sea Horses were purchased by the Marine Corps for cargo and amphibious utility service, together with a few VH-34D transport helicopters for command groups. These were followed by 437 CH-34 Choctaws for the Army, and six HH-34F search and rescue aircraft for the Coast Guard. 145 CH-34As were subsequently transferred to West Germany, 94 of them under MAP, and the West German government later retransferred 24 of these to Israel. Licensed production was undertaken in the United Kingdom by Westland, which named its version the Wessex, and in France by Sud Aviation, which built 12 SH-34s equipped for ASW service and 154 CH-34As for the French Army. Many of the latter aircraft were used extensively in combat in the Algerian War and in Indochina.

Of the 1,821 S-58s built by Sikorsky, most of them for military service, many are being rebuilt with the PT6T Twin Pac set of turbine engines, and some of these are now available on the open market through independent arms brokers.

**Weight:** 13,000 lbs.

**Speed:** 138 mph.

**Range:** 278 miles.

**Capacity:** 10 passengers, or 6 casualty litters, or 2,000 lbs of cargo.

**Produced:** Over 2,200 of all types, including 370 SH-34G, SH-34J and LH-34D to USN (some of which converted to UH-34G and UH-34J), 1,008 UH-34D/E and VH-34D to USMC, 6 HH-34F to USCG, 437 CH-34A/B/C to U.S. Army, 255 Westland Wessex, 154 Sud Aviation CH-34A and 12 Sud Aviation SH-34.

**Exported under FMS:** 97 CH-34 and 22 SH-34.

**Exported under MAP:** 153 CH-34, 24 SH-34 and 27 UH-34.

**In US Service:** None remain. USMC Sea Horse has been replaced by Boeing Vertol CH-46 Sea Knight and Sikorsky CH-53 Sea Stallion. USN Sea Bat has been replaced by Kaman SH-2D/F Seasprite and Sikorsky H-3 Sea King. Army Choctaws have been replaced by Boeing Vertol CH-47 Chinook and Bell UH-1H/N Iroquois.

**In Service Abroad:** Argentina (12 SH-34G), Australia (27 Wessex), Bangla Desh (2 Wessex), Brazil (7 S-58 and 6 CH-34A), Brunei (1 Wessex), Cambodia (3 CH-43A), Canada (24 UH-34G), Central African Republic (4 CH-34A), Chad (6 Ch-34A), Chile (15 CH-34A), France (154 Sud Aviation CH-34A and 12 Sud Aviation SH-34), Ghana (3 Wessex), Haiti (4 CH-34A), Indonesia (7 S-58), Israel (24 CH-34A), Italy (9 SH-34J), Iraq (12 Wessex), Japan (14 SH-34G), Laos (4 UH-34D), Netherlands (6 UH-34J), Nicaragua (4 CH-34A), Philippines (2 CH-34A), South Vietnam (40 CH-34A), Taiwan (18 CH-34A), Thailand (20 CH-34A), United Kingdom (210 Wessex in RAF and RN), Uruguay (1 SH-34J), and West Germany (121 CH-34A).

**Price:** $125,000 @ (1978 open market price for S-58 powered by original single Wright R-1820-84B/D piston engine, second-hand). $750,000 @ (1978 open market price for rebuilt S-58T with PT6T Twin Pac set of turbine engines).

# HUGHES AH-64 ADVANCED ATTACK HELICOPTER

The winner in 1976 of an Army competition for a new AAH (Advanced Attack Helicopter), the Hughes AH-64 has been designed primarily for the antitank role, and will be able to carry up to sixteen TOW missiles or sixteen of the new Rockwell International Hellfire laser-seeking antitank missile, together with two M-158 2.75" rocket pods and a Hughes XM-230 30mm chain gun in a collapsible turret under the aircraft's fuselage, with up to 1,200 rounds of 30mm Aden/DEFA ammunition. Alternatively, in a close air support role, it will be able to carry four M-200 rocket pods, each carrying nineteen 2.75" rockets, while retaining all of its 30mm ammunition. The XM-230 chain gun, incorporating a new Hughes chain drive system and rotary bolt action, is anticipated to cost approximately $10,000 less than comparable guns of its caliber.

Heavily armoured to protect it from Soviet 12.7mm and 23mm antiaircraft fire, the AH-64 is equipped with an advanced infrared suppression system reducing heat from its engines, a Singer Doppler Navigator to improve NOE (Nap Of the Earth) flying, so that the aircraft remains as close as safely possible to the contours of the terrain below it, a Teledyne Systems fire control computer, a Honeywell helmet sight for the gunner, a Martin Marietta PNVS (Pilot's Night Vision System), and the Northrop TADS (Target Acquisition and Designation System) incorporating FLIR (Forward Looking Infra Red) sensors, a visible-light sight and a laser ranging and target designation unit.

Far more agile than any previous helicopter, the AH-64 will be able to land longitudinally on slopes of up to 12 degrees and latitudinally on slopes of up to 15 degrees.

The Army has planned delivery of 536 AH-64s by 1985, and 363 of these, together with 872 of the 995 modernized AH-1S Cobra attack helicopters then available, will provide full front-line strength for a force of sixteen divisions.

**Weight:** 17,400 lbs.

**Speed:** 197 mph.

**Range:** 424 miles.

**Armament:** 1 x Hughes XM-230 30mm chain gun with 1,200 rounds. 4 x M-200 rocket pod with total of 76 2.75" rockets, or 16 x TOW antitank missile, or 16 x Hellfire laser-seeking antitank missile, and 2 x M-158 rocket pod with total of 14 2.75" rockets.

**Produced:** 536 planned for U.S. Army by 1985. Program is now in engineering development.

**Price:** $4,200 million @ (1978 estimate of Unit Procurement Cost of 536 aircraft to U.S. Army, in 1976 dollars). $6.216 million @ (1978 estimate of Unit Program Cost of 536 aircraft to U.S. Army, in 1976 dollars).

# SIKORSKY MODEL S-55/H-19 CHICKASAW

A multi-purpose transport and utility helicopter, first delivered in 1950, and used by all branches of our military services as well as by 26 countries abroad. It has been licensed for production by Mitsubishi in Japan, by SNCA in France, and in the United Kingdom by Westland, whose version is called the Whirlwind.

**Weight:** 7,900 lbs.

**Speed:** 112 mph.

**Range:** 360 miles.

**Capacity:** 10 passengers, or 6 casualty litters, or ASW armament of 1 x Mk 44 or Mk 46 torpedo.

**Produced:** Over 1,700 of all types, including 5 YH-19 for USAF, 10 UH-19A for USN and 60 for USMC as HRS-1, 270 UH-19B for USAF (some of which converted to HH-18B), 50 UH-19C and 338 UH-19D for U.S. Army, 91 CH-19E for USN and USMC (together with 10 for Britain's Royal Navy), 145 UH-19F for USN and USMC (30 of which converted to HH-19G for USCG), 15 UH-19F for Britain's Royal Navy, 44 Mitsubishi S-55, 25 SNCA S-58, and 400 Westland Whirlwind.

**Exported under MAP:** 23.

**In Service Abroad:** Argentina (5 S-55 and 6 UH-19), Brazil (5 Whirlwind), Canada (3 S-55T), Chile (6 S-55T and 4 UH-19), Cuba (10 Whirlwind), Dominican Republic (2 H-19), Ghana (6 Whirlwind), Greece (12 H-19D), Guatemala (3 H-19D), Honduras (3 H-19D), Iran (22 Whirlwind), Israel (12 H-19D), Japan (44 Mitsubishi S-55), Jordan (6 Whirlwind), Kuwait (2 Whirlwind), Nigeria (3 Whirlwind), Pakistan (8 UH-19D), Philippines (5 CH-19E), Qatar (2 Whirlwind), Spain (18 H-19D), Taiwan (7 CH-19E), Thailand (13 CH-19E), Turkey (26 H-19D), United Kingdom (10 CH-19E, 15 UH-19F and 56 Whirlwind), Venezuela (10 CH-19E), and Yugoslavia (10 Whirlwind).

# SIKORSKY MODELS S-61A AND S-61B H-3 SEA KING

Developed in 1957 to fill a Navy requirement for an ASW helicopter capable of both search and strike operations, the Sikorsky S-61A incorporated twin turbine engines, advanced avionics and an amphibious hull. Not only did it carry MAD (Magnetic Anomaly Detection) equipment, radar and other sensors for submarine detection, but it could also be armed with four Mk 44 or Mk 46 torpedoes, or 4 Mk 11 depth charges or other munitions. Deliveries of 255 SH-3A Sea Kings to the Navy began in 1961, and were followed by nine specially-equipped RH-3A mine counter measures craft, 12 HH-3A search and rescue craft, 105 SH-3G utility helicopters, and the SH-3H equipped both for ASW and ASMD (Anti-Ship Missile Defense) roles. Ten VH-3A and eleven VH-3D VIP transport helicopters have been delivered to the U.S. Army and Marine Corps, for the emergency evacuation of key United States government officials from Washington. A recent test evacuation with one of these aircraft, prior to which the Secret Service had not been informed, caught its White House agents totally by surprise, removing the President's wife and his national security advisor before they could prevent it from taking off.

In 1963, Canada purchased 41 S-61A aircraft, built to SH-3A standard, and redesignated them CH-124. 36 of these aircraft were assembled in Canada. In 1964, six CH-3Bs were delivered to USAF for missile site support and drone recovery duties, and in 1965 the most advanced ASW version of the aircraft, the SH-3D, appeared. 72 of these today equip ten Navy squadrons, and another 22 have been delivered to Spain, 4 to Brazil and 4 to Argentina, together with 9 Sikorsky S-61A for Denmark and 16 for Malaysia.

In 1964 Agusta-Bell undertook licensed production of the S-61A, supplying SH-3D ASW versions to the Italian and Iranian navies. The aircraft has also been licensed for production in Japan by Mitsubishi, which to date has produced 107 SH-3A and SH-3D versions for its own Marine Self Defense Force, and in the United Kingdom by Westland, which has produced 149 Sea Kings, 69 for the Royal Navy, 15 for the RAF, 10 for Australia, 5 for Belgium, 12 for India, 10 for Norway, 6 for Pakistan and 22 for West Germany.

**Weight:** 18,626 lbs.

**Speed:** 166 mph.

**Range:** 724 miles.

**Capacity:** 22 to 31 combat troops, 9 to 15 casualty litters, or 6,000 lbs of internal cargo, or 8,000 lbs of external cargo.

**Armament:** 840 lbs of external ordnance, including 4 x Mk 44 or Mk 46 torpedo, or 4 x Mk 11 depth charge or other munitions, and provision for waist-mounted M60C 7.62mm or other machine gun.

**Produced:** Over 875 of all types, including 255 SH-3A 9 RH-3A, 12 HH-3A, 105 SH-3G, 24 SH-3H, 10 VH-3A, 11 VH-3D, 6 CH-3B, 41 CH-124, 102 SH-3D (72 of them for the USN), 107 Mitsubishi SH-3A and SH-3D, 42 Agusta-Bell SH-3D, 149 Westland Sea King, and many Sikorsky S-61A/B adapted for military use.

**Exported under FMS:** 11.

**Exported under MAP:** 2.

**In US Service:** 72 SH-3D and 60 SH-3G/H in USN, 32 SH-3A in USN Air Reserve, 6 CH-3B in USAF, 5 VH-3A and 5 VH-3D in U.S. Army, and 5 VH-3A and 6 VH-3D in USMC.

**In Service Abroad:** Argentina (4 SH-3D and 2 S-61N), Australia (10 Westland Mk 50 Sea King), Belgium (5 S-61N and 5 Westland Mk 48 Sea King), Brazil (4 SH-3D and 2 S-61N), Canada (41 SH-3A designated CH-124), Denmark (9 S-61A), Egypt (6 S-61A), Indonesia (1 S-61A), Iran (18 ABSH-3D), Israel (12 S-61N), Italy (24 ABSH-3D), Japan (59 Mitsubishi SH-3A and 48 Mitsubishi SH-3D), Malaysia (16 S-61A), Norway (10 Westland Mk 43 Sea King), Pakistan (6 Westland Mk 45 Sea King), South Korea (10 SH-3A), Spain (24 SH-3D), United Kingdom (56 Westland Mk 1 and 13 Mk 2 in Royal Navy, and 15 Westland Mk 3 in RAF), and West Germany (22 Westland Mk 1 Sea King and 1 S-61A).

**Price:** $5.212 million @ (1975 Unit Procurement Cost for 59 SH-3A to Japanese Marine Self Defense Force).

**Recent Transfers:** 18 Agusta-Bell SH-3D to Iran in 1975, fully-equipped with Sistel Marte anti-ship weapon system and Sea Killer Mk 2 missiles, for $20.166 million @.

**Deliveries Pending:** Iran (2 Agusta-Bell SH-3D).

**Orders Pending:** France, which has tested 2 S-61As for its Navy.

# SIKORSKY S-61R/HH-3E JOLLY GREEN GIANT

A further development of the Sikorsky Model S-61A, the S-61R was produced in 1963 to meet an Air Force requirement for a multi-purpose assault transport and SAR (Search and Rescue) helicopter. With sponsons added for stabilization, an auxiliary gas-turbine power unit, and a rear-loading ramp hydraulically-powered, the first of 41 CH-3Cs was delivered to USAF in December of 1963. These were followed in 1966 by 42 CH-3E armed assault helicopters with an Emerson Electric TAT-102 turret mounted in a pod on both the port and starboard sponsons, each turret holding a General Electric M-134 7.62mm six-barreled Minigun, whose USAF designation is GAU-2B/A. One or two M-60D 7.62mm machine guns could also be mounted at the doors aft of the pilot's cabin. As these aircraft were delivered, the same armament was added to USAF's 41 CH-3Cs, converting them to CH-3E standard.

Shortly thereafter, an additional 50 S-61Rs were ordered for USAF's Aerospace Rescue and Recovery Service, similarly armed but with added armour plating and self-sealing jettisonable fuel tanks. These were the famous HH-3E Jolly Green Giants, which rescued hundreds of Air Force and Navy pilots in Southeast Asia. For the Coast Guard an unarmed version, the HH-3F Pelican, was produced. Licensed production of the S-61R has been undertaken in Italy by Agusta-Bell, which to date has produced 20 of the aircraft for the Italian Navy and the export market.

**Weight:** 22,050 lbs.

**Speed:** 162 mph.

**Range:** 465 miles.

**Capacity:** 5,000 lbs of cargo, 30 combat troops, or 15 casualty litters.

**Armament:** 2 x TAT-102, each with 1 x GAU-2B/A 7.62mm Minigun, and 1 or 2 x M60D waistmounted M60D 7.62mm MG.

**Produced:** Over 200, including 41 CH-3C (all of which converted to CH-3E), 42 CH-3E, 50 HH-3E, 40 HH-3F, 20 Agusta-Bell ABHH-3F, and many S-61R.

**In US Service:** 39 CH-3E and 23 HH-3E in USAF, 5 HH-3E in Air National Guard, and 34 HH-3F in Coast Guard.

**In Service Abroad:** Israel (12 ABHH-3F), and Italy (8 ABHH-3F).

# SIKORSKY MODEL S-62/HH-52A

With a flying-boat hull and two outrigged stabilizing floats, the S-62 was Sikorsky's first fully amphibious helicopter. It entered service in 1958. 99 were ordered by our Coast Guard as HH-52A long-range search and rescue aircraft, and several S-62s have been supplied aboard for military or police use. It has been licensed for production by Mitsubishi in Japan.

**Weight:** 8,100 lbs.

**Speed:** 109 mph.

**Range:** 474 miles.

**Capacity:** 12 passengers, or 600 lbs of internal cargo, or up to 3,000 lbs externally.

**Produced:** Over 170 to date, including 99 HH-52A for USCG, 25 Mitsubishi S-62, and over 50 Sikorsky S-62.

**Exported under FMS:** 1.

**In US Service:** 88 HH-52A in USCG.

**In Service Abroad:** India (2 S-62C), Japan (17 S-62A), Philippines (2 S-62A), Taiwan (2 S-62C), and Thailand (2 S-62A).

**Sikorsky HH-3E Jolly Green Giant**

# SIKORSKY MODEL S-64 SKYCRANE CH-54 TARHE

Powered by two Pratt & Whitney T73-P-1 turboshafts, and with a six-blade main rotor 76 feet in diameter (which increases to 88 feet when the rotor is turning), the CH-54A weighs only 19,234 lbs but can carry more than its own weight, up to a maximum overall load of 42,000 lbs. After five prototypes flew in 1962, the U.S. Army ordered 66 CH-54A Tarhes which were delivered in 1964. In 1969 the first two of a total of 36 CH-54Bs were ordered, with T73-P-700 turboshafts which increased the aircraft's lift capacity to a maximum load of 47,000 lbs. Able to carry light armoured vehicles and artillery pieces slung from its long fuselage boom, the CH-54 has also been designed to accommodate the Universal Military Pod, a prefabricated steel compartment weighing 20,000 lbs which can carry 45 combat troops, 24 casualty litters, a complete field surgery unit or a fully-equipped field communications and command post. In Vietnam the CH-54s were able to retrieve a total of 380 crashed aircraft. Two of the original S-64 prototypes were transferred to the West German Bundesluftwaffe.

**Weight:** 19,234 lbs. Loaded weight of 42,000 lbs (CH-54A), or 47,000 lbs (CH-54B).

**Speed:** 126 mph.

**Range:** 230 miles.

**Capacity:** 1 x Universal Military Pod with 45 combat troops or 24 casualty litters, or maximum loads of 22,766 lbs of cargo (CH-54A), or 27,766 lbs (CH-54B).

**Produced:** Over 100 aircraft, including 5 S-64 prototypes, 66 CH-54A, 36 CH-54B, and many production S-64 for commercial or military use.

**In US Service:** 18 CH-54A and 36 CH-54B in U.S. Army, and 22 CH-54A in Army National Guard.

**In Service Abroad:** West Germany (2 S-64).

# SIKORSKY MODEL S-65/H-53 SEA STALLION

Developed in 1964 to meet a Marine Corps requirement for a heavy assault transport helicopter, and utilizing the design of the Sikorsky Model S-61 and the engine technology of the S-64, the twin-engined Sea Stallion became one of the most powerful helicopters ever built. Designed with a sealed fuselage and sponson floats for amphibious landing, it was also equipped with the Integrated Helicopter Avionics System which enabled it in 1968, one year after it first entered service in Vietnam, to perform the first automatic terrain-avoidance flight by a helicopter. Amazingly agile for its size and weight, it was also able to perform loops and rolls in the manner of fixed-wing aircraft.

By 1972 a total of 265 CH-53A and CH-53D Sea Stallions had been delivered to the USMC. These were followed in 1967 by eight HH-53Bs for USAF's Aerospace Rescue and Recovery Service. Known as Super Jolly Green Giants, and with armament similar to that of the earlier S-61R, the HH-53B was equipped with external jettisonable fuel tanks and a retractable inflight refueling probe. In 1968,

**Sikorsky CH-54 Tarhe**

the Air Force took delivery of 64 HH-53C unarmed utility Sea Stallions, capable of lifting an external load of 20,000 lbs.

Procurement for the Navy followed in 1973 with 30 RH-53D mine sweeping helicopters, and with the conversion that year of 15 USMC CH-53A to RH-53A mine sweeping craft, similarly equipped to handle mechanical, acoustic or magnetic mines. Both the conversion and new production models were armed with twin .50 Caliber machine guns to detonate surface mines. In 1975, Iran purchased six new RH-53Ds. Two will be delivered to Japan in 1978. Because Iran already had this type of aircraft, the RH-53D was picked over the CH-47 for the hostage rescue attempt in Iran in April of 1980, in the belief that it would arouse fewer suspicions if detected.

The CH-53G, an export version of the Sea Stallion built to CH-53A standard, was also developed, and in 1969 three were sent to West Germany for evaluation. Subsequently the West German firm of VFW-Fokker built 110 CH-53G under license, for delivery to the Heeresflieger (Army Air Corps) between 1971 and 1975. Israel has purchased a total of 28 CH-53Gs to date.

In 1975 the first prototype three-engined YCH-53E flew. With an increased lift capacity of 37,700 lbs, it introduced a more advanced automatic flight control system, an all-weather navigation system, long-range fuel tanks and a main rotor with seven blades constructed of titanium. The Navy currently plans a force of 72 of these aircraft to support amphibious assault operations. Transporting heavy weapons, construction equipment and cargo to Marine

Corps beachheads, and retrieving damaged aircraft, the CH-53E will be able to airlift 93 percent of the combat gear of a division. Originally estimated to cost $6.5 million each, the CH-53E has become expensive. Ten were purchased in 1976 for $9.66 million each, and six more were purchased in 1977 for $15.583 million each. Procurement funds were eliminated in 1978, but the CH-53E is back in the budget for Fiscal Year 1979, when 14 will be purchased for $12.01 million each.

**Weight:** 23,485 lbs or 42,000 lbs fully loaded (CH-53A/D). 32,049 lbs empty, or 69,750 lbs fully loaded (CH-53E). RH-53D: 50,000 lbs.

**Speed:** 196 mph (CH-53A/D), or 200 mph (CH-53E).

**Range:** 306 miles (CH-53A/D), or 540 miles (CH-53E).

**Capacity:** 55 combat troops or 24 casualty litters. Maximum CH-53A/D and HH-53C cargo load: from 18,500 to 20,000 lbs externally. Maximum CH-53E cargo load: from 28,800 to 37,700 lbs externally. Typical external loads: 1 x 105mm howitzer or 1 x 28,000 lb bulldozer. Typical internal loads: 1 x 1½ ton truck or 2 x M-151 jeep or 2 x HAWK missile and launcher, up to maximum of 16,000 lbs (all models).

**Armament:** 2 x TAT-102 turret with GAU-2B/A 7.62mm Minigun (HH-53B only). 2 x .50 Caliber MG (RH-53A and RH-53D only).

**Produced:** Over 550 of all types to date, including 143 CH-53A (15 of which converted to RH-53A), 8 HH-53B, 64 HH-53C, 122 CH-53D, 38 RH-53D, 141 CH-53G, 4 prototype and 1 static testframe YCH-53E, 16 CH-53E, and several S-65.

**Exported under FMS:** 39.

**In US Service:** 8 HH-53B and 64 HH-53C in USAF/MAC, 15 RH-53A and 30 RH-53D in USN, 16 CH-53E and 110 CH-53D in USMC, and 12 CH-53D and 128 CH-53A in USMC Reserve.

**In Service Abroad:** Austria (2 S-650), Iran (6 RH-53D and 6 S-65A), Israel (28 CH-53G and 16 S-65C), Japan (2 RH-53D), and West Germany (113 CH-53G, 110 produced by VFW-Fokker).

**Price:** $5 million @ (1976 Unit Procurement Cost for 6 RH-53D to USMC). $4.7 million @ (1977 Unit Procurement Cost for 4 HH-53C to USAF). $9.66 million @ (1976 Unit Procurement Cost for 10 CH-53E to USMC). $15.583 million @ (1977 Unit Procurement Cost for 6 CH-53E to USMC). $12.01 million @ (1979 Unit Procurement Cost for 14 CH-53E to USMC). $10.67 million @ (1978 anticipated Unit Cost for total of 72 CH-53E through 1983). $14.8 million@ (1978 Unit Procurement Cost for 6 CH-53E to USMC). $500,000@ (1978 open market second-hand price for S-65).

**FMS Sales Pending:** 12 HH-53C to Iran, requested in 1976.

**Sikorsky H-53 Sea Stallion**

# SIKORSKY MODEL S-70/UH-60 BLACKHAWK LAMPS MK III

The winner in 1976 of the Army's UTTAS (Utility Tactical Transport Aircraft System) competition, and in 1977 of the Navy's LAMPS (Light Amphibious Multi-Purpose System) Mk III competition, the Sikorsky S-70, powered by two General Electric T700 turboshafts, incorporates advanced fly-by-wire technology, extensive fiberglass construction, and a main rotor with titanium spars, and has been designed in a compact, boxlike shape, with a much lower silhouette than the Bell UH-1 Iroquois series, which enables it to fit in the cargo hold of a C-130 Hercules. Six of the aircraft can fit in the hold of a C-5A Galaxy. Derived from the Sikorsky Model S-67, which holds the world helicopter speed record of 220.8 mph, the S-70 is agile enough to bank at angles of more than 90 degrees.

Supplementing and eventually replacing the Army's UH-1 series of transport helicopters, the UH-60A Blackhawk will be able to carry a crew of three and an assault squad of 11 fully-equipped combat troops, and will be armed with its own side-firing M60 7.62mm machine gun. The Army, with 15 pre-production aircraft in hand, plans procurement of a total of 1,107 UH-60s, with the first 56 in production in 1978.

For the Navy, 200 ship-based LAMPS MK III helicopters are planned, sharing a common airframe and engines with the UH-60, but with folding rotor blades and provision for all of the highly-specialized ASW, ASMD (Anti-Ship Missile Defense) and ECM equipment the Navy requires. This will include a Texas Instruments AN/APS-115 surface search radar, a Texas Instruments AN/ASQ-81 magnetic anomaly detector, a Bendix AN/AQS-13 dipping sonar and transponder, a General Dynamics AN/ARR-52 sonobuoy receiver, a Bowmar/Loral AN/AYK-1 LAMPS computer, an IBM laser rangefinder, a Honeywell AN/APN-171 radar altimeter, a Teledyne Ryan AN/APN-182 Doppler navigation sensor, an AN/SLQ-31/32(V) LAMPS MK III ESM (Electronic Support Measures) system for the aircraft's ASMD mission, and two Mk 44 or Mk 46 acoustic-homing torpedoes.

**Weight:** 22,000 lbs.

**Speed:** 198 mph.

**Range:** 416 miles.

**Capacity:** 11 combat troops, or 4 casualty litters, or 7,000 lbs cargo (UH-60). 2 x Mk 44 torpedo, or 2 x Mk 46 torpedo, or up to 7,000 lbs of other ordnance (LAMPS MK III).

**Produced:** 3 UH-60 and 1 LAMPS MK III prototypes, and 15 pre-production UH-60A. Total of 1,107 UH-60 and 200 LAMPS MK III planned.

**In US Service:** 153 UH-60 to be in service by 1982, and 200 SH-60 LAMPS MK III by 1984.

**Price:** $3,646 million @ (1978 Unit Procurement Cost of 56 UH-60 to U.S. Army). $4.839 million @ (1978 Unit Program Cost of 56 UH-60 to U.S. Army). $8.207 million @ (1977 Unit Program COst of 15 pre-production UH-60 to U.S. Army). $3.750 million @ (1978 estimate of Unit Procurement Cost of 200 LAMPS MK III to USN, in 1978 dollars).

**Future Sales:** Japan and Jordan have both expressed interest in UH-60.

**Sikorsky UH-60 Blackhawk**

# AIRCRAFT AND HELICOPTER ARMAMENT SYSTEMS

In the past twenty years the evolution of aircraft armament in the United States has followed three distinct paths. There has been a continuing development of more powerful internal gun systems, primarily for use as air-to-air weapons in high-performance fixed-wing aircraft. A wholly new weapon system, the gun pod, has been developed, primarily for air-to-ground use. A self-contained gun with a high rate of fire and its own ammunition supply, the pod can be mounted on underwing pylons or helicopter sponsons precisely like a bomb or any other type of air munition, and is then electrically connected to the aircraft's fire control system. Most aircraft and helicopters are built today with electrical connections and fire control systems capable of performing all the electronic functions required to arm and fire a wide variety of gun and rocket pods and other weapons, and pods have been developed with guns of every major caliber. The number of pods an aircraft may carry is limited only by their weight and the aircraft's load capacity. The gun pod is most effectively used in the close air support or COIN (counterinsurgency) role, operating at close range in secure airspace, and in conditions of high visibility.

The final major development effort has focused on creating higher firepower and greater flexibility in the fixed armament of helicopters, which operate at lower speeds and closer ranges than fixed-wing aircraft, and has led directly to the automatic grenade launcher with selectable rates of fire, and the nose-mounted helicopter turret. In all three areas of development the firms of General Electric, Emerson Electric and Hughes Aircraft have been leaders, working in close cooperation and using each other's systems.

The highly capable scientific minds that have always been available to improve the efficiency of weapon systems realized many years ago that in air-to-air combat, if a sufficient number of rounds fired from a gun could be made to converge at a given moment of time in an area of airspace sufficiently small, a target passing through that space at that moment could not survive its effects. This condition they called "lethal density." They also realized that it was important for a gun system to achieve lethal density as quickly as possible, for as a pilot maneuvered to obtain his target, his opportunities to fire his guns were fleeting and few, and the less time he spent locked onto that target in order to fire, the less time he would have in which to become a target himself.

During World War II and the Korean War, pilots learned to achieve lethal density by developing tactics of mutual support, in which the guns of two or more aircraft were brought to bear on a single target. They also learned to close on the target, reducing their range from it, for they knew that the density of a group of projectiles was directly proportional to the distance they travelled. The further they had to go, the more they became spread out in space.

One method for increasing the number of guns brought to bear on a target was to install more guns on each aircraft. Another was to increase the rate of fire of each gun, so that at any given moment a single gun threw as many projectiles into one area of space as could several guns with lower rates of fire. The caliber of the guns could also be increased, so that each projectile, larger in diameter, occupied more space.

An early step to increase lethal density was to remove guns from their wing positions and group them close together around the aircraft's nose. This tightened the density of a group of projectiles at the starting point from which they began their trajectories, so that at a given range they remained more densely packed than they would have been had they started at points spread out along the aircraft's wings.

But the decisive development in aircraft armament, which achieved lethal density by several of these means at once, was a return to the principle of the Gatling gun, in which several barrels, once mechanically cranked by hand but now electrically-driven at very high speeds, would turn, load and fire on a single axis. This led to the General Electric Minigun, a six-barreled 7.62mm weapon which achieved lethal density through an increased number of guns, a close grouping of the guns, and extremely high rates of fire of up to 4,000 rounds per minute.

High rates of fire have also been achieved through improvements in the chambering of ammunition, in belting or other linking systems, including linkless feed systems, and in the means by which empty casings are expended from the gun chamber. Caseless ammunition is now being developed, and is bound even further to increase the rates of fire of standard gun systems.

Utilizing the same multi-barreled principle of its 7.62mm Minigun, General Electric next developed the six-barreled 20mm Vulcan cannon, now standard on most United States high-performance combat aircraft, and used in a variety of other applications, including the Vulcan Air Defense System (VADS), an antiaircraft artillery piece on a towed mount, designated M-167, or on a self-propelled turret mount, using the M-113 armoured personnel carrier and designated M-163. The Navy has also developed a CIWS (Close-In Weapons System) employing the Vulcan cannon in a ship-board turret mount for anti-ship missile defense.

Further increases in gun caliber have been developed, both by General Electric, which now manufactures the GAU-8/A 30mm multi-barreled cannon using the Gatling principle, and by Hughes Aircraft, whose XM-230 gun uses a chain system to drive a rotating bolt mechanism in a single 30mm cannon barrel at rates of fire up to 1,000 rounds per minute.

Following is a summary of the major United States internal aircraft guns, gun pods and helicopter armament systems currently available.

# GENERAL ELECTRIC 7.62MM MINIGUN M-134/GAU/2B/A

A six-barreled cluster of guns rotating on a single axis, and firing standard NATO 7.62mm ammunition on a linked or linkless feed system. Each barrel fires only once in a full revolution of the cluster, reducing barrel wear and the likelihood of overheating. Externally powered, and normally installed with 1,500 rounds of ammunition, the gun achieves variable rates of fire of from 2,000 to 6,000 rpm, and is effective at ranges of up to 1,250 yards (3,750 feet).

The U.S. Army designation of the 7.62mm Minigun is M-134, and its USAF/USMC designation is GAU-2B/A. There is also a somewhat longer-barreled M-139 version. Installed as fixed armament in the A-37A and A-37B Dragonfly, the Minigun is also used in the Army's M-18E1 gun pod, whose USAF designation is SUU-11B/A. Three Miniguns are normally mounted in the AC-47A gunship versions of the Douglas C-47, and four are mounted in the AC-119G Shadow and AC-119K Stinger gunship versins of the Fairchild C-119, as well as in the AC-130H Spectre gunship version of the Lockheed Hercules. This provides sufficient firepower to cover an area the size of a city block in a single second with a round per square foot. In Southeast Asia, the Vietnamese came to call the Minigun ''the muttering death.''

The Minigun is also employed in several helicopter armament systems, including the Emerson TAT-102, XM-53 and M-28 turrets, the Emerson Minitat system, the M-21 and M-27E1 pylon-mounted systems, and the XM-93 and XM-94 pintle-mounted systems. 1978 open market price for the Minigun, without installation, is $57,550 @.

# GENERAL ELECTRIC 5.56MM XM-214

A six-barreled automatic gun based on the Gatling principle of the Minigun, firing the same light 5.56mm ammunition developed for the M-16 rifle, at a muzzle velocity of 3,250 feet per second. Externally-powered, either by a hydraulic motor or by the electrical power from a set of nickel-cadmium batteries, the XM-214 has selectable rates of fire of from 400 to 6,000 rpm, and can fire as few as three rounds or as many as 1,500 in a single burst. The weight of the system is 28 lbs. While it has not yet been adopted for specific applications by any of our military services, it has been anticipated for use on aircraft, helicopters and ground vehicles. One of the advantages it offers is that the weight of the 5.56mm round is about half that of the 7.62mm round, allowing storage of twice as much ammunition, under identical load restrictions, as can be carried for the 7.62mm Minigun.

# GENERAL ELECTRIC M-61A1 VULCAN 20MM CANNON

The standard internal armament of most high-performance combat aircraft produced in the United States today, the Vulcan gun is a cluster of six cannon barrels rotating in sequence, firing the standard M-50 series of electrically-primed 20mm ammunition at rates of up to 6,000 rpm, with a muzzle velocity of 3,380 feet per second. Externally powered and weighing 255 lbs, the gun is normally installed with a linkless feed ammunition drum containing over 1,000 rounds, but the number of rounds carried varies according to the aircraft's load capacity. Thus, only 500 rounds are carried on the General Dynamics F-16, 676 rounds on the Grumman F-14A Tomcat, 950 rounds on the McDonnell Douglas F-15 Eagle, 725 rounds on the Lockheed F-104 Starfighter, 640 rounds on the McDonnell Douglas F-4E Phantom, 1,020 rounds on the Vought A-7E and A-7D Corsair II, 1,015 rounds on the Convair F-106 Delta Dart, 1,029 rounds on the Fairchild Republic F-105 Thunderchief, and 2,084 rounds on the General Dynamics F-111. The Vulcan gun on the F-111 also has a fixed rate of fire of 5,000 rpm. 1978 open market price for the M-61A1, without installation, is $66,320 @.

**GAU 2B/A 7.62mm Minigun**

**M61A1 20mm Vulcan Gun**

## HUGHES MK 11 MOD 5 TWIN 20MM CANNON

A twin-barreled air-cooled automatic cannon firing electrically-primed M-50 or Mk 100 series 20mm ammunition from a revolving cylinder with eight chambers fed by two belts of Mk 6 ammunition links simultaneously advanced by a single sprocket. Operated by gun-gas and recoil, the system achieves rates of fire of from 700 to 4,200 rpm. It is used by the USN and USMC, and has been in service since 1966.

## GENERAL ELECTRIC M-197 20MM GUN

A three-barreled, externally powered lightweight version of the M-61A1 Vulcan Gun, operating on the Gatling principle with rates of fire of from 400 to 1,500 rpm. It is the standard turret armament on the Marine Corp's AH-1J and AH-1T Cobra helicopter gunships, and has been supplied to Iran, Japan and Saudi Arabia to arm the AH-1Js ordered by those countries. The M-197 weighs 146.2 lbs.

## GENERAL ELECTRIC XM-188 30MM GUN

A three-barreled 30mm gun firing percussion-primed XM-552 HEDP ammunition at rates of from 200 to 2,000 rpm with a muzzle velocity of 2,200 feet per second. Designed to be fully interchangeable with the M-107 20mm gun in aircraft and helicopter applications, it weighs only 108 lbs, offering heavier firepower without any increase in weight over that of other systems.

## GENERAL ELECTRIC GAU-8/A 30MM AVENGER

A seven-barreled rotating cluster of guns operating on the Gatling principle of its predecessors of lighter caliber, the 20mm Vulcan Gun and 7.62mm Minigun, and firing specially-developed 30mm API (Armour Piercing Incendiary) and HEI (High Explosive Incendiary) ammunition at rates of fire of from 2,100 to 4,200 rpm. The Avenger has been developed specifically as an antitank weapon for installation on the Fairchild A-10 Close Air Support Aircraft, and is fitted in the aircraft's nose with a drive system of dual hydraulic motors and 1,350 rounds of 30mm ammunition on a double-ended linkless feed. The total weight of the gun with its controls and ammunition is 4,029 lbs.

The high muzzle velocities of the Avenger's 30mm API and HEI projectiles, 3,240 and 3,450 feet per second respectively, reduce their flight time to the target by about 30 percent as compared with that of most 20mm projectiles, resulting in a proportional decrease in aiming error. On impact, the 30mm HEI projectile produces six times the energy of a 20mm projectile.

With plastic rotating bands to reduce barrel wear, and with an aluminum cartridge case substantially lighter than brass or steel cases, the GAU-8/A 30mm API round has its weight concentrated in a high-density penetrating core comprised of depleted uranium. It thus incorporates a principle similar to that of the APDS (Armour Piercing Discarding Sabot) round fired by tank guns and antitank artillery, using a large caliber barrel for maximum propellant force and maximum velocity, and a subcaliber

penetrating core for maximum density, resulting in a high kinetic energy at its point of impact with the target.

The 30mm Avenger system has been designed for ten bursts of two seconds each, with a minute of cooling time between bursts. Each two-second burst releases approximately 135 rounds, sufficient to hit most targets several times. Recent USAF tests conducted with the gun have found that, when fired at a 4,000 foot slant range, the 30mm API round has fourteen times the kinetic energy of 20mm projectiles at its point of impact, and can penetrate all known thicknesses of armour on medium and heavy tanks.

## EMERSON XM-140 30MM AUTOMATIC GUN

A single-barreled lightweight 30mm gun specifically designed for attack helicopter gunships, the XM-140 has a low recoil force and a rate of fire of no more than 315 rpm, but its effective range is more than 11,000 feet, giving the helicopter from which it fires a ''stand-off'' capability to engage targets from distances nearly invulnerable to ground fire. It also employs ammunition with a dual-purpose shaped charge, enabling it to engage both ''hard'' targets, such as armoured vehicles and concrete bunkers, and ''soft'' targets, such as open trenches, trucks and wooden buildings, with equal effect.

**GAU-8/A 30mm Gun**

# HUGHES XM-230 CHAIN GUN

A single-barreled 30mm lightweight gun, externally powered, which fires at rates of from 100 to 1,000 rpm, in bursts of only a single shot or up to 100 rounds. It operates by means of a rotating bolt mechanism turned by a simple chain drive, and because of its simplicity, with only 97 parts in the production model, it is highly reliable and comparatively inexpensive for its caliber. Weighing less than 100 lbs, it will be installed as standard armament, with 1,200 rounds of WECOM 30 aluminum-cased ammunition, on the new Hughes AH-64 AAH (Advanced Attack Helicopter). While originally anticipated to have a production cost of only half that of other heavy caliber automatic guns, its unit procurement cost is now expected to reach $56,000 by 1979. That, however, is still approximately $10,000 less than the cost of comparable systems.

# GENERAL ELECTRIC 7.62MM GUN POD SUU-11B/A/M-18E1

A pod containing the General Electric 7.62mm Minigun with 1,500 rounds of ammunition in a drum magazine on a linkless feed system, and attachable with standard bomb lugs to the weapon pylons of a variety of aircraft and helicopters. It can be operated at airspeeds up to Mach 1.2 (792 mph). Spent cartridge cases are ejected through a port in the pod floor. The U.S. Army version of the Minigun pod, the M-18E1, has pre-set rates of fire of 2,000 or 4,000 rpm, and is frequently carried on inboard stations as part of the armament system of the AH-1 Cobra attack helicopter. The USAF version, designated SUU-11B/A, has pre-set rates of fire of 3,000 or 6,000 rpm. Both versions of the pod weigh 324 lbs fully loaded.

# GENERAL ELECTRIC 20MM VULCAN GUN POD/SUU-16/A/XM-12

A pod containing the General Electric M-61A1 20mm Vulcan Gun with 1,200 rounds of M-50 series 20mm ammunition. Operated by a self-contained ram air turbine drive system, the gun fires at a fixed rate of 6,000 rpm, and can fire all of its ammunition in a single burst without overheating. Weighing 1,650 lbs with its ammunition, the SUU-16/A is a heavy load for helicopters and smaller fixed-wing aircraft such as the A-1 Skyraider or the T-28 Trojan. Its ram air turbine, which must be lowered into the airstream in preparation for firing, also requires speeds above 400 mph, beyond the capabilities of those aircraft, in order to achieve its full rate of fire. In Vietnam, its use was therefore restricted to high-performance aircraft types like the F-100 Super Sabre and the F-105 Thunderchief, flying in the ground support role. It is also compatible with the A-4D Skyhawk, the F-111, and the F-4 Phantom.

# GENERAL ELECTRIC 20MM VULCAN GUN POD/SUU-23/A/XM-25

A pod containing the GAU-4 version of the General Electric M-61A1 20mm Vulcan Gun, with 1,200 rounds of M-50 series 20mm ammunition. The GAU-4 is a self-powered version of the Vulcan Gun, driven not by electrical power but by its own gun gas passing into a piston and cam mechanism to rotate the barrels. This retains the capability for high rates of fire even at speeds under 400 mph—insufficient to drive the ram air turbine of the other Vulcan 20mm Gun Pod, the SUU-16/A. Fully loaded, the SUU-23/A weighs 1,730 lbs, and it fires at a fixed rate of 6,000 rpm. In service with USAF's Tactical Air Command, it has also been sold in quantity to Iran, the United Kingdom and West Germany.

# HUGHES MK 4 MOD 0 20MM GUN POD

A pod containing the Hughes twin-barreled 20mm Mk 11 Mod 5 gun, which fires at rates of from 700 to 4,200 rpm with an effective range of over 1,000 yards. Weighing 1,389 lbs fully loaded, it can be operated at all airspeeds, and has been used by the Navy and the Marine Corps on the A-4 Skyhawk, the F-4 Phantom, the A-6 Intruder, the A-7 Corsair II, and the OV-10 Bronco. Production of 800 pods was completed in 1968.

**SUU-23/A 20mm Vulcan Gun Pod**

## GENERAL ELECTRIC XM-214 5.56 MM GUN POD

A pod containing the General Electric XM-214 5.56mm automatic gun and 1,500 rounds of ammunition. Its very light weight, less than 100 lbs fully loaded, makes it suitable for use on helicopters and a wide range of light fixed-wing aircraft.

## GENERAL ELECTRIC GPU-2/A 20MM LIGHT-WEIGHT GUN POD

A pod containing the General Electric M-197 three-barreled 20mm cannon and 300 rounds, and firing at pre-selected rates of either 750 or 1,500 rpm. It offers very heavy firepower for its weight, which is only 586 lbs fully loaded. Simple to maintain (the barrels can be replaced without removing the pod from the aircraft), and powered by a self-contained nickel cadmium battery, it can be mounted on a variety of aircraft of United States or foreign manufacture, and it is now in production for the U.S. Navy.

## M-75 40MM GRENADE LAUNCHER

An automatic grenade launcher which fires 40mm explosive projectiles to a range of 1,875 yards at a rate of 230 rpm. With a complement of 300 rounds of 40mm grenades, it is used in the M-5 helicopter turret system for the armed Bell UH-1B and UH-1C Iroquois aircraft.

## M-129 40MM GRENADE LAUNCHER

A lightweight automatic grenade launcher, externally-powered, which fires M-384 and M-385 high-velocity 40mm explosive projectiles at rates of from 230 to 450 rpm, with an effective range of from 1,875 to 2,750 yards. It is now replacing the M-75 grenade launcher in the M-5 turret system, and it is also used in the M-8 system for the OH-6A and OH-58A helicopters, the standard M-28E1 turret system for the AH-1G and AH-1S Cobra attack helicopters, and the pintle-mounted XM-93 and XM-94 waist-ramp armament systems for the UH-1N. The entire launching mechanism, which fires grenades with a muzzle velocity of 790 feet per second, weighs just 54.5 lbs. Grenades are belt-fed from a supply of up to 156 rounds in the M-8 system and 300 rounds in the M-28E1 system. The M-129 grenade launcher is now in full production by the Maremont Corporation.

## EMERSON XM-120 UNIVERSAL TURRET

A standard armament turret for the AH-1 Cobra and other helicopters, accommodating grenade launchers and guns of several calibers, including the M-60 7.62mm machine gun, the six-barreled 7.62mm Minigun, and three-barreled 20mm and 30mm cannon.

## EMERSON TAT-101

The first in a series of Emerson TAT (Tactical Armament Turret) systems, lightweight hydraulically-powered turrets with a variety of armament for use by the AH-1 Cobra and other helicopters. The TAT-101 has two belt-fed M-60C 7.62mm machine guns firing at a rate of 600 rpm with 15 degrees of vertical elevation above the line of boresight and 45 degrees below it, in a turret turning through a full 180 degrees of horizontal azimuth at a maximum slew rate of 45 degrees per second.

## EMERSON TAT-102

Similar to the TAT-101, the TAT-102 turret substitutes a single General Electric M-134 7.62mm Minigun for one or both of the M-60 machine guns. With an elevation of 25 degrees above boresight and up to 90 degrees below it, and capable of elevation adjustments of 60 degrees per second, the Minigun, with or without a single M-60C machine gun, is situated in a turret moving through a maximum of 180 degrees of azimuth at a higher slew rate than that of the TAT-101, 80 degrees per second.

## EMERSON TAT-161

A turret mounting the General Electric M-61A1 20mm Vulcan Gun, firing at a rate of 750 rpm. It can also be adapted for three-barreled 20mm and 30mm cannon, and has a slew rate of 45 degrees per second, moving through 180 degrees of azimuth, with 15 degrees of elevation above boresight and 45 degrees below it.

## EMERSON TAT-140

Using the Emerson XM-120 Universal Turret, the TAT-140 mounts an Emerson XM-140 single-barreled 30mm cannon firing at a rate of 315 rpm. The turret moves through 180 degrees of azimuth, and affords the gun 25 degrees of elevation above boresight and 90 degrees below it.

**M-28E1 Turret**

**Maremont M-129 40mm Grenade Launcher**

# EMERSON M-28E1 TURRET

The standard turret armament for the AH-1G, AH-1Q and AH-1S Cobra attack helicopters of the U.S. Army, the M-28E1 carries two M-129 40mm grenade launchers, or two M-134 7.62mm Miniguns, or one of each, and moves through 110 degrees of azimuth, affording its guns or grenade launchers 20 degrees of elevation above boresight and 50 degrees below it. The Miniguns in this system can fire at selectable rates of 2,000 or 4,000 rpm, and the grenade launchers at 400 rpm. Each Minigun is equipped with 4,000 rounds, and each grenade launcher with 300 rounds. With one M-134 Minigun and one M-129 grenade launcher, the weight of the turret and its full load of ammunition is 916 lbs.

# M-5 TURRET SYSTEM

A small turret for the UH-1B or UH-1C armed transport helicopter, mounting one M-75 40mm grenade launcher with 300 rounds, firing at 230 rpm.

# GENERAL ELECTRIC M-97 20/30MM FLEXIBLE ARMAMENT SYSTEM

The standard turret armament for the AH-1J and AH-1T Cobra attack helicopters of the Marine Corps, the M-97 employs either the General Electric M-197 three-barreled 20mm cannon or that company's XM-188 three-barreled 30mm cannon, coupled with a stabilized pantograph sight and a linked ammunition storage and feed system. Driven by two servo motors, one to move it through 110 degrees of forward azimuth, the other to give its gun 21 degrees of elevation above boresight and 50 degrees below it, the turret receives its position commands from the pantograph sight operated by the aircraft's gunner. Slewing in azimuth at a rate of 80 degrees per second, and in elevation at 60 degrees per second, the turret automatically follows the pantograph line of sight, which maintains a proper lead angle according to input from the aircraft's airspeed indicator, and simultaneously compensates for aircraft vibration and torque due to the recoil forces of the gun when firing.

In this system, the M-197 gun is supplied with 750 rounds of 20mm ammunition, and fires at a rate of 750 rpm, while the XM-188 gun is supplied with 500 rounds of XM-552 HEDP (High Explosive Dual Purpose) 30mm ammunition, and fires at a rate of 2,000 rpm. The weight of the full system, when armed with the M-197, is 1,032 lbs. The M-197 can be interchanged with the XM-188 gun, chuting and feed system in less than 30 minutes without any modification to the aircraft. This turret, armed with the M-197 gun, has also been supplied with export models of the AH-1J Cobra purchased by Iran, Israel, Japan and Saudi Arabia. It is also fitted on the Marine Corps' YOV-10D NOG Night Observation Gunship) version of the OV-10 Bronco, coupled with a FLIR (Forward Looking Infra Red) sensor.

**M-97 Weapon System
with M-197 20mm Gun**

# EMERSON XM-51 SUPPRESSIVE FIRE SUBSYSTEM

A nose turret with one M-129 40mm grenade launcher and 300 rounds, originally developed for the cancelled AH-56A Cheyenne attack helicopter, and now used as a replacement for the M-5 turret system on the UH-1B and UH-1C helicopters.

# EMERSON XM-53 SUPPRESSIVE FIRE SUBSYSTEM

Also developed for the AH-56A Cheyenne attack helicopter, this is a nose turret with one GAU-2B/A 7.62mm Minigun, and is suitable for use on the UH-1B and UH-1C helicopters.

# EMERSON XM-52 AREA FIRE SUBSYSTEM

A helicopter belly turret with one Emerson XM-140 single-barreled 30mm gun. Together with the XM-51 and XM-53 subsystems, the XM-52 comprises the AAFSS (Advanced Aerial Fire Support System) developed for the AH-56A Cheyenne attack helicopter. Although the Cheyenne program was cancelled the XM-52, like the other two subsystems in the AAFSS, has a wide variety of other helicopter applications.

# GENERAL ELECTRIC XM-35 ARMAMENT SUBSYSTEM

Specifically developed for the AH-1 Cobra attack helicopter, this is a 20mm armament system utilizing the XM-195 version of the General Electric M-61A1 Vulcan Gun, with blast deflectors, and mounted on the aircraft's inner port pylon station as supplementary armament to the guns in its nose turret. 950 rounds of 20mm ammunition are supplied from containers mounted outside the aircraft's fuselage, and the total weight of the gun and its ammunition is 980 lbs. The XM-195 fires at a fixed rate of 750 rpm, and produces a muzzle velocity of 3,380 feet per second.

# XM-30 ARMAMENT SUBSYSTEM

A heavy armament subsystem for the UH-1B helicopter, comprised of two Emerson XM-140 single-barreled 30mm guns mounted on either side of the aircraft, and firing at a combined rate of 850 rpm. The total weight of the system, including ammunition stored inside the aircraft, is 1,800 lbs.

**Emerson 7.62mm Mini-Tat beneath an Iranian OH-58 Helicopter**

# EMERSON MINI-TAT

Specifically designed for light observation and reconnaissance helicopters, the Emerson Mini-Tat incorporates the General Electric GAU-2B/A 7.62mm Minigun on a retractable arm and swivel mount which can be installed in 30 minutes on either side or beneath the fuselage of a wide variety of helicopters of both domestic and foreign manufacture, as well as under the wings of several fixed-wing aircraft including the Pilatus Turbo Porter and the SM-1019. Weighing 247 lbs with 1,000 rounds of standard NATO 7.62mm ammunition, the Mini-Tat can move through 180 degrees of azimuth, 10 degrees of elevation above boresight and 70 degrees of depression, slewing at a rate of 80 degrees per second, and firing at selectable rates of 750 or 1,500 rpm. It can be fully retracted when not in use. In production since 1973, the Mini-Tat is now in service in Canada, Chile, France, Iran, Saudi Arabia, South Africa and Thailand. The 1978 open market price for the Mini-Tat, installed with 1,000 rounds of ammunition, is $55,000 @.

# MAMEE AMMUNITION MODULE

MAMEE (Meyer Ammunition Module, Emerson Electric) is an externally-mounted drum ammunition storage and feed system for helicopters in which linked ammunition is folded in cylindrical drums at a much higher density than that of other systems, permit-

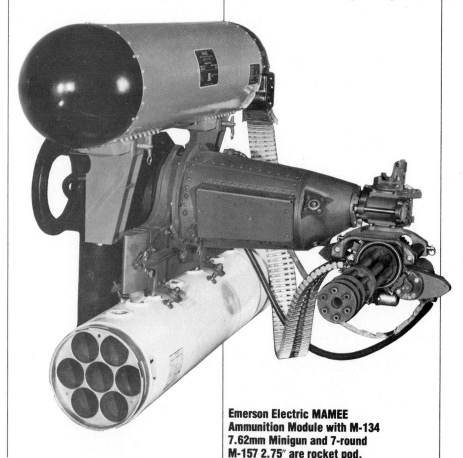

**Emerson Electric MAMEE Ammunition Module with M-134 7.62mm Minigun and 7-round M-157 2.75″ are rocket pod.**

ting storage of up to 3,000 rounds of 7.62mm ammunition in rotary drums on either side of the aircraft's fuselage, serving Emerson Mini-Tat or other weapons of this caliber.

# M-8
# ARMAMENT SYSTEM

For the Hughes OH-6A and Bell OH-58A light observation helicopters, this is an M-129 40mm grenade launcher mounted on a standard M-6 pylon on the port side of the aircraft. With a fixed azimuth, 10 degrees of elevation and 24 degrees of depression, and an adjustment rate of up to 30 degrees per second, the M-8 system launches grenades from the M-129 at variable rates of from 300 to 450 rpm. The full weight of the system, with a maximum of 156 rounds of linked 40mm cartridges, is 236 lbs.

# M-27E1
# ARMAMENT SYSTEM

For the Hughes OH-6A and Bell OH-58A light observation helicopters, this system mounts one M-134 7.62mm Minigun on a standard M-6 pylon on the port side of the aircraft, with storage for 2,000 rounds of ammunition. A twin-speed electric motor fires the gun at rates of 2,000 or 4,000 rpm. Fixed in azimuth, the Minigun has 10 degrees of elevation and 24 of depression when mounted on the OH-6A, and 5.5 degrees of elevation and 20 of depression when mounted on the OH-58A. Full weight of the system, with 2,000 rounds of 7.62mm ammunition, is 234 lbs.

# M-16
# ARMAMENT SYSTEM

For the UH-1B and UH-1C helicopters, the M-16 system mounts two M-60C 7.62mm machine guns on rack and support assemblies on either side of the aircraft, together with two M-158 rocket pods, each with seven 2.75″ FFAR (Folding Fin Aerial Rockets). With an elevation of 11 degrees and a depression of 63, and with traverse of 12 degrees inboard and 70 degrees outboard, the two M-60C machine guns fire at rates of 2,000 to 2,600 rpm, and are automatically disengaged when their target track leads the boresight too close to the aircraft itself. 6,000 rounds of 7.62mm ammunition are supplied. Effective range of the M-60C is 1,250 yards (3,750 feet), and the range of the 2.75″ rockets, all of which can be fired in six seconds, is 3,750 yards (11,250 feet).

# M-21
# ARMAMENT SYSTEM

For the UH-1B helicopter, the M-21 system mounts two General Electric M-134 7.62mm miniguns on rack and support assemblies on either side of the aircraft, together with two M-158 rocket pods. With an elevation of 10 degrees and a depression of 85, an inboard traverse of 12 degrees and an outboard traverse of 70, the Miniguns fire at rates of 2,400 and 4,000 rpm. When either gun tracks inboard sufficiently, it is disengaged and the other gun automatically increases its rate of fire on the target from 2,400 to 4,000 rpm to compensate for the disengaged gun. The M-21 system is in service with the United States and Italian Armies.

# M-23
# ARMAMENT SYSTEM

Two pintle-mounted M-60D 7.62mm machine guns, one at either cargo door of the UH-1D helicopter, with 600 rounds of ammunition per gun and a rate of fire of from 550 to 600 rpm. With unlimited traverse, the guns may be depressed 82 degrees, or elevated 3.5 degrees forward and 6.5 degrees aft.

# M-24
# ARMAMENT SYSTEM

Two pintle-mounted M-60D 7.62mm machine guns, one at the forward port escape hatch and the other at the forward starboard door of the CH-47 Chinook helicopter, firing at rates of 550 to 600 rpm, belt-fed from ammunition boxes, 200 rounds to a box, which can be stowed in any quantity for which there is space.

# XM-41
# ARMAMENT SYSTEM

One pintle-mounted M-60D 7.62mm machine gun positioned at the rear loading ramp of the CH-47 Chinook helicopter, with a safety harness for the gunner. May be used in conjunction with the M-24 system.

# XM-59
# ARMAMENT SYSTEM

For the UH-1D or UH-1H helicopter, this system is similar to the M-23, but substitutes for one of the M-60D machine guns of that system an M-2 .50 Caliber (12.7mm) heavy machine gun at either cargo door. In this system, the two guns have a traverse of 88 degrees, a depression of 80 degrees and an elevation of 6.5 degrees fore and aft.

# XM-93 AND XM-94
# ARMAMENT
# SUBSYSTEMS

The XM-93 subsystem provides a pintle-mounted M-134 7.62mm Minigun at the port and starboard cargo doors of the Army's twin-engined Bell UH-1N Iroquois transport helicopter, while the XM-94 subsystem substitutes a pintle-mounted M-129 40mm grenade launcher at each door. Both subsystems have a fixed traverse of 90 degrees forward and 70 degrees aft, a depression of 70 degrees, and an elevation of 5.5 degrees. Fired from the cockpit by remote control, the Miniguns of the XM-93 subsystem have a fixed rate of fire of 2,000 rpm, but under manual control their rate of fire can be increased to 4,000 rpm. The M-129 grenade launchers in the XM-94 subsystem have a fixed rate of fire of 400 rpm.

The pintle mount for the M-129 grenade launcher is similar to that used for the same weapon on U.S. Navy Swift Boats and other riverine warfare craft. For the Miniguns of the XM-93 subsystem, the Sagami pintle mount was often used in Vietnam, with a heavy steel frame axis on which the weapon would move in elevation, and a steel rack grip for the gunner, providing greater stability in azimuth.

# EMERSON TOW
# ANTITANK MISSILE
# LAUNCHER

The standard TOW missile launcher for the Army's AH-1S Cobra attack helicopter and the Marine Corps' AH-1T Cobra, mounted singly or in pairs on both the inboard and the outboard stations of the M-6 pylon, for a maximum load of four TOW launchers on each pylon, or a total of eight on the aircraft. It has also been mounted in trios on the rack and support assemblies of the UH-1 helicopter. Each launcher weighs 271 lbs. 1978 open market price for the launcher, installed but unloaded, is $42,040 @.

# BOMBS AND AIR MUNITIONS

Estimates of the number of casualties resulting from a nuclear war between the superpowers vary from only a few hundred million in a successful preemptive attack to as much as 25 percent of the Earth's population in a more intensive and prolonged exchange. In a nuclear war, a major objective is the swift reduction of an opponent's retaliatory capabilities, and therefore primary targets include nuclear weapons themselves. Were it not for that fact, these casualty estimates would be much higher. The United States alone has a formidable nuclear arsenal, sufficient at this point to obliterate all human life several times over.

Aside from its nuclear weapons, however, the United States has also produced hundreds of millions of bombs of the "conventional" variety, including high-explosive demolition bombs, chemical bombs, incendiary and fire bombs, aerial mines and depth charges, fragmentation bombs and bomb clusters, unguided aerial rockets, glide bombs guided by laser-seekers or electro-optical sights, and a powerful new breed of fuel air explosives. Some chemical bombs are filled with toxins so deadly that the release of a single one could take as many lives as the blast, heat and radiation from a one-megaton nuclear bomb.

Leaving aside such special weapons, too, there remains a vast proliferation of bombs of American manufacture in all of the other

conventional categories, hundreds of thousands in production today, and many hundreds of thousands more produced years ago and stockpiled in great quantities for service throughout the world. It has been estimated that if all of these bombs were dropped in the appropriate places at the appropriate times, they could destroy 10 percent of the Earth's inhabitable surface and 35 percent of the Earth's population along with it. If all of the conventional bombs produced in other countries were added to this weight, the casualty figures would nearly double.

Such considerations make it difficult to distinguish between "conventional" weapons and those that are unconventional. Chemical bombs filled with nerve gas can be said to be unconventional because, to our knowledge, they have not been used. A nuclear bomb has been used only twice. The concept of precedence thus affects our notion of what is conventional, along with our

sense of whether the destructive power of an individual weapon falls within acceptable limits. Since the lethality of a nuclear bomb can be matched or even surpassed by the combined force of many nonnuclear bombs, it is clear that "conventional" weapons can achieve unconventional effects, either by their increasing degree of sophistication or through the unprecedented extent of their use. The first firestorm occurred not at Hiroshima but in Dresden.

To determine whether the use of a weapon has had or may have unconventional effects, there is little value in finding out if these effects are regarded as unacceptable. They are never acceptable to their victims and they are always acceptable to their users. Instead, we need only establish whether the extent of their use, and their consequent effects, break with precedent.

The United States broke with precedent in Southeast Asia, where we dropped more than four and a half million tons of bombs, well over the total tonnage of bombs dropped throughout World War II, and equivalent to 36 tons for every square mile in North and South Vietnam. We were, of course, fighting an "unconventional" war by another use of that term. We achieved

**Grumann F-14A Tomcat** with its fixed and some of its alternate armament loads. Foremost are four AIM-9L Sidewinder missiles, and behind them 676 rounds of 20mm ammunition for Tomcat's M61A1 Vulcan Gun and six AIM-7E Sparrow missiles. Behind these are six AIM-54A Phoenix long-range missiles and two wing fuel tanks. In the next row are 14 Mk 81 250-lb. Snakeye bombs, and behind them an alternate load of eight Mk 82 500-lb. bombs. At the wingtips are another alternate load of four M117 750-lb. bombs and eight AGM-65A Maverick air-to-surface missiles on racks.

unprecedented, and therefore unconventional, effects. We might just as well have dropped unconventional, or nuclear, bombs—as a number of planners even suggested at the time.

Today, research to improve the efficiency of conventional bombs, achieving unprecedented levels of lethality, proceeds at an unparalleled pace, and procurement continues along with it. In the peacetime years of 1976 and 1977, our combined military services spent $359.6 million in the procurement of free-fall and guided air munitions, including $10.6 million for the Navy's CBU-72/B Fuel Air Explosives, $6.2 million for Navy CBU-59/B APAM cluster bomb units, a combined Air Force and Navy procurement of $188.4 million in MK 20 ROCKEYE antitank cluster munitions, $33.1 million for 2.75″ aerial rockets for the Army and

Navy, $37.2 million for the Air Force's MK 84 2,000-lb bomb, and $26.9 million for the Navy's WALLEYE guided bomb.

The prices for these munitions currently vary from $300 to $1,000 each according to their size, weight, complexity of construction, the type of filler involved, and the quantity ordered. Usually, the production runs are substantial. Small cluster bomblets weighing one or two lbs, several hundred of which fill many of our new CBU (Cluster Bomb Unit) dispensers, cost very little per unit. In 1963, four million BLU-3/B bomblets were purchased for $6.50 each, and today most simple bomblet types cost $9.50 to $16.00 each for a similar quantity. The only expensive bombs are those modified with laser-guidance and electro-optical sighting kits. The KMU-351A/B laser-guided version of the MK 84 2,000-lb bomb, for example, cost $3,100 each in 1977, and the KMU-353A/B electro-optically guided version of the same bomb cost $13,000 each in the same year.

Large numbers of these air munitions are sold to almost every country that has trade with the United States, with restrictions only on fuel air explosives and bombs with advanced guidance mechanisms. Israel was

**Mk 81 Snakeye before and after release.**

refused the CBU-55/B Fuel Air Explosive munition in 1976, but she still purchased $72.8 million worth of MK 20 ROCKEYE, MK 82 SNAKEYE, M117 DESTRUCTOR and other air munitions that year, or about 180,000 bombs.

Self-powered munitions delivered by air are covered in the section on guided missiles which follows this one. Here is a summary of the major categories of free-fall and guided air munitions, with a list of the types of each now in production or remaining in service.

# GENERAL PURPOSE DEMOLITION BOMBS

Intended primarily for the destruction of buildings, concrete bunkers and other fixed military installations, this type of bomb is often used to incapacitate or destroy tanks and armoured vehicles. To achieve its effects it relies primarily on the blast forces of its explosive filler, and secondarily on the shrapnel produced by disintegration of its case. A 100-lb bomb will make a crater in the earth six feet deep and 20 feet in diameter, displacing approximately 225 cubic feet of soil and other material. It can penetrate more than two feet of concrete and more than four inches of steel, and its shrapnel is lethal to a radius of 200 feet. The power of such a weapon is proportional to its size. A 2,000-lb bomb with the identical explosive filler will make a crater 36 feet deep and 50 feet in diameter, displacing 8,500 cubic feet of soil, penetrating more than 11 feet of concrete and up to 15 inches of steel. Its shrapnel is lethal to a radius of 1,200 feet. Here are some major general purpose and demoliton bombs developed before 1960 and still in service.

**AN-M30A1 100-LB GENERAL PURPOSE BOMB**: A cast steel case with 54.2 lbs of Tritonal, Amatol or TNT. Total weight: 101 lbs.

**MK I 100-LB DEMOLITION BOMB**: A welded, cast or sheet steel case with 55 lbs of Amatol or Lyconite, or 59 lbs of TNT. Total weight: 112 lbs.

**M38A2 100-LB PRACTICE BOMB**: A cast steel case with 80 lbs of sand and a spotting charge of 3 lbs of Black Powder. Total weight: 100 lbs.

**AN-M57A1 250-LB GENERAL PURPOSE BOMB**: A cast steel case with 132 lbs of Tritonal, Amatol or TNT. Total Weight: 261 lbs.

**AN-M58A2 500-LB SEMI-ARMOUR-PIERCING BOMB**: A cast steel case with 143.1 lbs of Picratol. Total weight: 536.5 lbs.

**AN-M64A1 500-LB GENERAL PURPOSE BOMB**: A cast steel case with 262 lbs of Tritonal, Amatol, TNT or Compostion B. Total weight: 535 lbs.

**M52A1 1,000-LB ARMOUR-PIERCING BOMB**: A converted artillery shell with 58 lbs of Explosive D. Total weight: 1,078 lbs.

**AN-M59 1,000-LB SEMI-ARMOUR-PIERCING BOMB**: A cast steel case with 315 lbs of Amatol or 313 lbs of Picratol. Total weight: 990 lbs.

**AN-M65A1 1,000-LB GENERAL PURPOSE BOMB**: A cast steel case with 572 lbs of Tritonal, Amatol, TNT or Composition B. Total weight: 1,081 lbs.

**AN-MK 33 1,000-LB ARMOUR-PIERCING BOMB**: A cast steel case with 140 lbs of Explosive D. Total weight: 1,008 lbs.

**MK III 1,100-LB DEMOLITION BOMB**: A welded, cast or sheet steel case with 632 lbs of TNT. Total weight: 1,130 lbs.

**AN-MK I 1,600-LB ARMOUR-PIERCING BOMB**: A cast steel case with 209 lbs of Explosive D. Total weight: 1,590 lbs.

**MK I 2,000-LB DEMOLITION BOMB**: A forged steel case with 1,060 lbs of TNT. Total weight: 2,030 lbs.

**AN-M66A1 2,000-LB GENERAL PURPOSE BOMB**: A cast steel case with 1,036 lbs of Tritonal, Amatol or TNT. Total weight: 2,053 lbs.

**M103 2,000-LB SEMI-ARMOUR-PIERCING BOMB**: A cast steel case with 556.5 lbs of Picratol. Total weight: 2,039 lbs.

**AN-M56A2 4,000-LB LIGHT CASE BOMB**: A sheet steel case with 3,515 lbs of Tritonal. Total weight: 4,535 lbs.

Bombs developed after 1960 became more compact and slender, and as research into the chemistry of explosives advanced, more powerful fillers like Minol replaced the TNT of earlier days, increasing the destructive forces of blast. To increase the precision of bomb delivery by high-speed aircraft, the Snakeye bomb was developed by fitting a TRD (Tail Retarding Device) to a standard bomb to increase its drag and slow its descent. Springing open after the bomb is released from the aircraft, the TRD allows a pilot to make his bomb run at a very low level, with a high increase in accuracy, by giving him time to escape its blast. Here are the major general purpose bombs now in production and service:

**MK 81 250-LB GENERAL PURPOSE BOMB**: A cast steel case with 96 lbs of Minol, Tritonal or H6 Explosive. Total weight: 262 lbs.

**MK 81 Snakeye 250-LB GENERAL PURPOSE HIGH-DRAG BOMB**: The MK 81 bomb fitted with a MK 14 TRD. Total weight: 302 lbs.

**MK 82 500-LB GENERAL PURPOSE BOMB**: A cast steel case with 192 lbs of Minol 2, Tritonal or H6 Explosive. Total weight: 531 lbs.

**MK 82 SNAKEYE 500-LB GENERAL PURPOSE HIGH-DRAG BOMB**: The MK 82 bomb fitted with a MK 15 TRD. Total weight: 571 lbs.

**M117 750-LB GENERAL PURPOSE BOMB**: A cast steel case with 403 lbs of Minol 2 or Tritonal. Total weight: 823 lbs.

---

**Left to Right**
M52 1000-lb AP, AN-MK 33 1000-lb AP, MK II 1100-lb AP, AN-MK 1 1600-lb AP, MK I 2000-lb Demo, KMU-370/B 3000-lb LGB, MK 84 Mod 0 2000-lb GP, MK 88 Mod 0 1000-lb Practice, MK 83 Mod 0 1000-lb GP, M117 750-lb GP, MK 82 Mod 0 500-lb GP, MK 81 Mod 1 250-lb GP.

**M117D DESTRUCTOR 750-LB GENERAL PURPOSE HIGH-DRAG BOMB**: The M117 bomb fitted with the MAU-91A/B TRD. Total weight: 863 lbs.

**MK 83 1,000-LB GENERAL PURPOSE BOMB**: A cast steel case with 445 lbs of Minol 2, Tritonal or H6 Explosive. Total weight: 985 lbs.

**MK 83 DESTRUCTOR 1,000-LB GENERAL PURPOSE HIGH-DRAG BOMB**: The MK 83 bomb fitted with the MAU-91A/B TRD. Total weight: 1,025 lbs.

**MK 84 2,000-LB GENERAL PURPOSE BOMB**: A cast steel case with 945 lbs of Minol 2, Tritonal or H6 Explosive. Total weight: 1,970 lbs.

**M118 3,000-LB GENERAL PURPOSE BOMB**: A cast steel case with 1,975 lbs of Tritonal. Total weight: 3,049 lbs.

While these bombs were not designed as anti-personnel weapons, their effects can be devastating for those who have not found cover. The chance direct hit, of course, literally tears the human body limb from limb. Shrapnel will shear off an arm, leg or head within its lethal radius, and wound severely at greater distances. Those untouched by fragments of blast may still fall prey to concussion. As the shock waves of blast snap through the earth, those sufficiently close will feel as though they were hit in the chest with the end of a log, and may suffer precisely the same effects. Ribs crack. Lungs collapse. Bodies bounce from the earth like

dolls. For those physically unhurt, the noise and concussion may ring in the ears for hours, sometimes days. The experience has turned many minds.

In Vietnam, the B-52s would fly their bomb runs over the countryside at an altitude of 20,000 feet, too high to be seen or heard from the ground. Each aircraft would release its load of fifty M117 750-lb bombs, weighing more than 18 tons. For the people on the ground, the sudden terror and confusion of having the earth erupt without warning before their eyes, and the anticipation of further such attacks, was profoundly demoralizing.

# CHEMICAL BOMBS

The Geneva Protocol of 17 June 1925 prohibited the use of asphyxiating, poisonous and other gases in warfare, but the United States did not ratify the Protocol until 22 January 1975. Even then, ratification was signed on the proviso that the prohibition of gases ''shall cease to be binding on the government of the United States'' if ''an enemy state...fails to respect the prohibitions laid down in the Protocol.'' Not to be unprepared for the failings of others, we have continued to produce and stockpile a variety of chemical bombs filled with nerve gases and other agents. In Vietnam we used great quantities of chemical defoliants and incapacitating gases, though none were used against us.

Phosphorous is a chemical whose brilliant white smoke first prompted its use in munitions as an artillery marking device. It is now used in bombs, mortar shells and artillery projectiles throughout the world, both to mark artillery fire and as an incendiary agent. It has also proved effective as an anti-personnel weapon. On exposure to air, phosphorous ignites spontaneously, and burns at a heat of 280.5 degrees Centigrade until it is spent. People hit by phosphorous cannot prevent it from continuing to burn. It cannot be smothered, because contact with flesh makes it burn too. It must be scraped off, or dug out of the flesh.

These are some of our chemical bombs, most of them currently in service:

**AN-M46 100-LB PHOTOFLASH BOMB**: A cast steel case with 25 lbs of Photoflash powder, yielding 500 million candlepower for battlefield illumination and night reconnaissance photography. Total weight: 51.9 lbs.

**AN-M47A2 100-LB ALL-PURPOSE CHEMICAL BOMB**: A smoke, incendiary or non-persistent gas bomb with a cast steel case and filled with varying weights of White Phosphorous, Mustard Gas, Phosgene, Hydrocyanic Gas or oil gel. Approximate weight depending on filler: 100 lbs.

**M125A1 10-LB NON-PERSISTENT GAS BOMB**: A sheet steel cylinder with a 14'' drop parachute, filled with 2.6 lbs of GB (Sarin) nerve gas. Total weight: 8.5 lbs.

**M34 CLUSTER**: A sheet steel cluster dispenser holding 76 M125A1 Non/Persistent Gas Bombs. 2,115 of these clusters were assembled, containing a total of more than 200 tons of nerve gas. All had allegedly been destroyed by deactivation or neutralization by 1973. But newer bombs containing the same filler were subsequently produced. Total weight of loaded dispenser: 1,130 lbs.

**M70 115-LB GAS BOMB**: A cast steel case with 57 lbs of White Phosphorous, Mustard Gas or gas gel. Total weight: 122.5 lbs.

**BLU-52/B 350-LB CHEMICAL BOMB**: An aluminum case with 615 lbs of CS-1 powder which produces tear gas on exposure to air. Total weight: 697 lbs.

**MK 94 Mod 0 500-LB NON-PERSISTENT GAS BOMB**: A standard Mk 82 bomb modified with a burster charge and filled with 108 lbs of GB (Sarin) nerve gas. Total weight: 441 lbs.

**MK 116 MOD 0 WETEYE 750-LB CHEMICAL BOMB**: An aluminum alloy case with 403 lbs of GB (Sarin) nerve gas. Total weight: 701 lbs.

**MC-1 750-LB NON-PERSISTENT GAS BOMB**: A standard M117 bomb modified with 220 lbs of GB (Sarin) nerve gas. Total weight: 725 lbs.

**AN-M79 1,000-LB CHEMICAL BOMB**: A cast steel case with varying weights of AC (Hydrocyanic Gas), CK Cyanogen Chloride or CG(Phosgene) incapacitating agents. Approximate weight depending on filler: 960 lbs.

Mustard Gas (HD/G/T/HN3) is persistent and often lethal. It evaporates slowly, retaining an effective concentration for several hours after initial dispersion. It attacks the skin—causing blisters, the eyes—causing inflammation, ulceration and blindness, and the lungs. Inhaled in concentrations of 300 to 1,000 parts per million of air, its burning effect on the lungs causes death. In the Prussic Acid family, Phosgene (CG), Cyanogen Chloride (CK) and Hydrocyanic Acid (AD) yield a less persistent vapor which, inhaled in concentrations of 3,200 to 5,000 parts per million, attacks the lungs, causing coughing, retching, asphyxia, pneumonia and, after a period of several hours, death. Sarin (GB) is a form of nerve gas, derived from phosphine oxide. It has no smell and can be absorbed through the skin and eyes as well as by inhalation. In concentrations of only 70 parts per million, it attacks the central nervous system and is lethal in 10 to 30 minutes. Symptoms are a dimming of vision and difficulty in breathing, intense perspiration, drooling, headache, confusion and drowsiness. In the next stage there is nausea, retching, cramps and loss of control of the bladder and rectal ring muscle. Finally, motor ataxis sets in, with involuntary twitching, jerking and convulsion. This is followed by coma, paralysis of the heart and lungs, and death.

In the 1960s and 1970s the United States continued development of more refined forms of nerve gas (GD/GE/GF/VE/VX) which are more difficult to treat than GB. In view of the fact that these gases work very much like the proposed neutron bomb, which has been praised because it attacks only people without destroying buildings, equipment and other capital assets, they are likely to remain in inventory.

# AERIAL MINES

This is a relatively new family of munitions developed during the Vietnam war. Delivered by air, these weapons must be distinguished from bombs with delayed-action fuses, for they are detonated only on activation of one or several of a variety of acoustic, seismic, magnetic, heat or pressure sensors. They are usually provided also with a self-destruct mechanism, detonating automatically after a pre-determined period of hours or days to allow the passage of friendly forces over the ground they guarded. Here are some of the latest types in service or soon to be placed in inventory:

**MLU-10/B 750-LB LAND MINE**: A cylindrical steel casing with an explosive filler of Destex, equipped with seismic, magnetic and infrared sensors to determine, respectively, the weight of an oncoming object, the presence of metal in its construction, and the heat of an internal combustion engine. It is thus designed in order to destroy only vehicles passing over it, and will not detonate if a man passes by on foot. The infrared sensor had to be added after early versions of the mine were detonated by farmers carrying scythes, shovels and other metallic objects. Total weight: 766 lbs.

**BLU-31/B 750-LB DEMOLITION BOMB**: The MUL-10/B Land Mine equipped with an improved seismic sensor to distinguish the weight of an armoured vehicle from that of a truck, and with an acoustic sensor responsive to the frequencies of engines used in tanks.

**MK 36 DESTRUCTOR 500-LB DEMOLITION BOMB**: A standard Mk 82 bomb fitted with the Snakeye MK 15 TRD and with acoustic, seismic and infrared sensors to detonate at the approach of an oncoming vehicle. During Operation Igloo White in Southeast Asia, many of these were dropped along the Ho Chi Minh Trail to interrupt supply columns bound for the Viet Cong and North Vietnamese regular forces. A number of separate sensing devices were also dropped with transmitting equipment to alert our forces to the presence of trucks along the Trail. We would then assign air strikes at the appropriate coordinates. The Vietnamese found they could frequently neutralize these sensing mechanisms by urinating on them. Total weight: 576 lbs.

**MK 7 GATOR MINE SYSTEM**: An anti-tank and anti-personnel mine system, jointly sponsored by USAF and USN, using a cluster dispenser and small ASP (All-altitude Spin Projectile) bomblets aerodynamically shaped to spin outwards on release from their container, providing a wide dispersion. The projectiles have a shaped charge designed to penetrate the underside of a tank. The system will be operational in 1979.

**GRASSHOPPER MINE SYSTEM**: An anti-personnel mine with an infrared sensor sufficiently sensitive to respond to the heat of human bodies. When activated, it jumps from the ground and explodes at a height of three feet, sending shrapnel in all directions to a lethal radius of 350 feet. Total weight: 65 lbs.

**BLU-42 WAAPM (WIDE AREA ANTI-PERSONNEL MINE)**: A cluster dispenser munition with 180 bomblets. Each of these, on landing, sends out several feet of wire which, when tripped, detonates the bomblet with a lethal radius of 200 feet. The cluster is composed of 10 cans, each with 18 bomblets, to ensure wide dispersion.

**BLU-54 WAAPM**: The BLU-42 with an improved bomblet which jumps into the air before detonation, thus increasing by 180 degrees its arc of lethal penetration.

**XM-22 GRAVEL MINE/XM-27/XM-45E1**: Incorporating the latest advances in high explosive chemistry, this tiny mine weighs only .07 ozs, but is capable of blowing off a foot. Also known as Dragonteeth or Button Bomblets, 4,800 of them are packed into 25-lb cluster containers, which in turn are packed into cluster bomb units of 12 and 16 containers, densely seeding a wide area. Gravel Mines have been produced by the Trenton Textile Corporation, Lowenthal Manufacturing, Southeastern Distributing Company, the Hercules and Susquehanna Corporations, the Bemis Company, and duPont.

# UNGUIDED AERIAL ROCKETS

Two basic types continue in service after long use, the 5'' (121.8mm) Zuni rocket, and the 2.75'' (67mm) FFAR (Folding Fin Aerial Rocket) known as Mighty Mouse or Tiny Tim (the latter name was originally given to a larger 11.75'' rocket now obsolete). Of these, the 2.75'' FFAR is the most popular, though procurement of the Zuni continues. $11.5 million was spent in FY 1977 for Zuni procurement, as compared with $15 million for the 2.75'' FFAR in the same year. The Zuni is also being used to deliver the Pave Pat Blue 73 warhead in the Army's SLUFAE (Surface Launched Unit, Fuel Air Explosive) mineclearance system.

The 2.75'' rocket is launched either from the M-157 or M-158 pod (whose USAF designation is LAU-68B/A) containing seven rockets each, or from the larger M-159 and M-200 pod (whose USAF designations are LAU-61/A and LAU-69/A) with nineteen rockets each. Combinations of two or four of either type of pod, with as few as 14 or as many as 76 rockets, are a part of several standard United States helicopter armament systems. The rockets can all be fired within 6 seconds, and have an effective range of 3,750 yards (11,250 feet).

Several warheads are available for the 2.75'' rocket, including the M-156 10-lb chemical warhead, the M-151 10-lb HE (High Explosive), WP (White Phosphorous) or APERS (Anti-Personnel) fragmentation warhead, and the M-229 17-lb HE, WP or APERS warhead. The M-151, which has been made by several firms including the American Electric Division of City Investing Corporation and the Aerojet General Division of General Tire and Rubber, has the equivalent explosive force of an 81mm mortar round. The M-229, which has been made by Medico Industries and Lehigh, Inc., has nearly the explosive force of a 4.2'' (107mm) mortar round.

There is also Northrop Corporation's WDU-4A/A warhead for the 2.75'' rocket. This is a flechette warhead. A result of the Beehive Project to develop a new type of

anti-personnel munition for the 90mm and 105mm artillery projectiles, the flechette is a small, slender needle from two to three inches long, with a barbed point and a tail stabilizer to prevent it from tumbling in flight. It has an effective range of several hundred feet. Mass-produced from aluminum at a very low cost, by an embossing process developed at the Picatinny Arsenal, flechettes can be packed to a quantity of more than 3,000 in each WDU-4A/A warhead. Bursting in a highly dense pattern, they shred human flesh. Soldiers in Vietnam have reported seeing their victims pinned to trees. Flechettes have been made by the Kissell Company, Norris Industries, the Skagit Corporation, Northrop and Whirlpool.

The 1978 Unit Procurement Cost of a complete 2.75'' rocket is $101.

# AIRCRAFT DEPTH BOMBS

Used for underwater targets and equipped with hydrostatic fuses, depth bombs and mines of serveral types are produced in this country for aerial delivery to their targets, which are usually submarines. These include the AN-MK 54 and AN-MK 41 Depth Bombs, the MK 57 and MK 101 Nuclear Depth Bombs, and the MK 52, MK 53, MK 55 and MK 56 Mines. The AN/MK 54 Mod 1 Depth Bomb, for example, consists of a thin sheet steel case with either 226 lbs of TNT or 248 lbs of HBX Explosive, with a total weight that accordingly varies from 324 to 346 lbs.

**Left to Right**
M83 4-lb Frag, AN-M41A1 20-lb Frag, MK II-B 25-lb Frag, MK II-A 25-lb Frag, M72A1 23-lb Frag, M82 90-lb Frag, AN-M81 260-lb Frag, AN-M88 220-lb Frag, M28A2 100-lb Cluster, AN-M57A1 250-lb GP, M38A2 100-lb Practice, AN-M46 100-lb Photoflash, AN-M47 100-lb Chemical, M70A1 115-lb Chemical, MK III 100-lb Demo, MK I 100-lb Demo, MK 1 Mod 4 100-lb Demo, AN-M30A1 100-lb GP, MK I 40-lb Incendiary, AN-M50A2 4-lb Incendiary.

# INCENDIARY AND FIRE BOMBS

Early incendiary bombs were filled with thermite, magnesium powder, metallic sodium and various oil and gas gels to produce intense and persistent fires that would complete the process of destruction begun by demolition bombs. They were, of course, a terrifying anti-personnel weapon as well. Napalm, a mixture of 25 percent gasoline, 25 percent benzene, and 50 percent aluminum or polystyrene soap as a thickener, improved on these agents by spreading the fire more evenly and thoroughly over greater areas. It was also found to be of great value applied to tunnel works and concrete bunkers impenetrable by high explosive or armour-piercing munitions, for its fire would consume all the air available to the personnel within, sucking the oxygen out of their lungs and causing asphyxiation and death. Troops in the open were transformed into living torches. Heavily used in Vietnam, Napalm inflicted severe burns on very large numbers of people, most of whom did not survive. During the 1960s the Dow Chemical Corporation was well known as a producer of Napalm. Less well-known is the firm which continued production of Napalm in subsequent years, the American Electric Company of Los Angeles, a subsidiary of City Investing Corporation. Napalm and other incendiary bombs are stocked in substantial quantities in the United States and in NATO countries. Here are the major types of incendiary and fire bombs in production or in service:

**AN-M50A3 4-LB INCENDIARY BOMB:** A hexagonal sheet steel case filled with 1.75 lbs of Magnesium Thermite, and with spring-loaded stabilizing fins. Total weight:3.7 lbs.

**M36 INCENDIARY CLUSTER:** A sheet steel container with 182 AN-M50A3 Incendiary Bombs. The container breaks apart in the air, spreading the individual bombs over an area of several hundred yards, depending on the altitude at which it is released. Total weight: 722 lbs.

**MK I 40-LB INCENDIARY BOMB:** A cast steel case with an oil emulsion containing Thermite and metallic sodium. Total weight: 40 lbs.

**BLU-10A/B 250-LB FIRE BOMB:** An aluminum case with 211 lbs (33 gallons) of Napalm. Total weight: 250 lbs.

**BLU-23/B 500-LB FIRE BOMB:** An aluminum case with 430 lbs (67 gallons) of Napalm. Total weight: 490 lbs.

**BLU-32/B 500-LB FIRE BOMB:** A welded aluminum case with 529 lbs (67 gallons) of the considerably heavier Napalm B. Total weight: 589 lbs.

**AN-M76 500-LB INCENDIARY BOMB:** A cast steel case with 180 lbs of Gas Gel and Magnesium. Total weight: 475 lbs.

**MK 77 MOD 1 FIRE BOMB:** An aluminum case with 75 gallons of Napalm. Total weight: 520 lbs.

**M116A2 750-LB FIRE BOMB:** An aluminum case with 80 gallons of Napalm or thickened fuel. Total weight: 685 lbs.

**MK 77 MOD 0 750-LB FIRE BOMB:** An aluminum case with 110 gallons of Gas Gel. Total weight: 760 lbs.

**MK 78 MOD 2 750-LB FIRE BOMB:** A welded sheet steel case with 110 gallons of Napalm. Total weight: 760 lbs.

**BLU-1/B 750-LB FIRE BOMB:** A reinforced aluminum case with 615 lbs (90 gallons) of Napalm. Total weight: 697 lbs.

**BLU-27/B 750-LB FIRE BOMB:** A welded aluminum case with 790 lbs (100 gallons) of Napalm B. Total weight: 873 lbs.

**MK 79 MOD 0 1,000-LB FIRE BOMB:** A sheet steel case with 112 gallons of Napalm. Total weight: 912 lbs.

# FRAGMENTATION AND CLUSTER BOMBS

This type of bomb was originally developed as an anti-personnel weapon, but its explosive force and the velocity and penetrating ability of its shrapnel have been increased to such an extraordinary extent in recent years that a highly effective new type of anti-tank weapon, the Rockeye cluster munition, has been engendered as an outgrowth of this research. Needless to say, the increased velocity of fragments, together with advanced techniques for multiplying the number of lethal fragments, ensuring their even dispersion over a wide area, and ensuring detonation at the optimum altitudes for maximum effect, have given modern anti-personnel fragmentation bombs a capability for efficient, controlled devastation not even anticipated twenty years ago. Fragments moving at speeds sufficient to penetrate the armour of a tank are clearly not impeded by steel helmets. A larger number of fragments

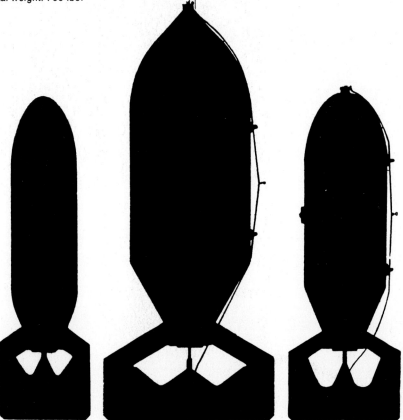

spread over a larger area will be more lethal to far many more people.

One of the first steps, taken in the early 1960s, to increase the number of lethal fragments from munitions of a given weight and size was the introduction of the BLU (Bomb, Live Unit), an individual bomblet case weighing one or two lbs with its own explosive filler, and packed by the hundreds into a larger container, the SUU (Suspended Underwing Unit). The fully assembled container with bomblets is called the CBU (Cluster Bomb Unit). No larger in overall size than a single demolition bomb in one of the standard categories of weight, the SUU breaks apart in the air, releasing the individual BLU bomblets. Where there had been only one large explosion before, there are now several hundred individual explosions, vastly increasing the number of fragments produced by the release of a single air munition.

To ensure wide dispersion, the bomblet cases are cast with aerodynamic vanes to spin them outwards upon release. Another technique, developed in the SUU-7 series, is to eject the bomblets sequentially by compressed air in a long trail behind the aircraft, discarding the SUU dispenser when it is empty.

The consequence of these improvements is that a single one of our latest CBU munitions has the equivalent effect of a well-aimed barrage of 600 simultaneous rounds of 81mm mortar fire. Here are the basic types of fragmentation and cluster bombs now in service:

**M83 4-LB FRAGMENTATION BOMB**: A cylindrical steel case with 1.2 lbs of cast TNT and spring-loaded case covers which open like wings to increase drag and retard its fall. It is thus nicknamed the Butterfly Bomb. Total weight: 4 lbs.

**M28A2 100-LB FRAGMENTATION BOMB**: A sheet metal case with 24 M83 Fragmentation Bombs. Total weight: 100 lbs.

**M29A1 500-LB FRAGMENTATION CLUSTER**: A sheet metal case with 90 M83 Fragmentation Bombs. Total weight: 415 lbs.

**MK II-A 17-LB FRAGMENTATION BOMB**: A 3'' artillery shell modified with a filler of 1.5 lbs of TNT. No longer in service in the United States. Total weight: 16.8 lbs.

**MK II-B 25-LB FRAGMENTATION BOMB**: A cast steel case with 5.5 lbs of TNT. No longer in service in the United States. Total weight: 23.4 lbs.

**AN-M41A1 20-LB FRAGMENTATION BOMB**: A light sheet steel case with square steel wire wound spirally over it, and filled with 2.7 lbs of TNT. Total weight: 19.8 lbs.

**M1A2 100-LB FRAGMENTATION CLUSTER**: A suspended rod and adaptor rings to hold six AN-M41A1 20-lb Fragmentation Bombs. Total weight: 122 lbs.

**AN-M26A2 500-LB FRAGMENTATION CLUSTER**: An assembly of rods, braces and adaptors to hold 20 AN-M41A1 20-lb Fragmentation Bombs. Total weight: 418 lbs.

**M72A1 23-LB FRAGMENTATION BOMB**: A cast steel case with 2.9 lbs of TNT, and with a retarding parachute. Dropped in clusters of three or more. Total weight: 24.6 lbs.

**AN-M81 260-LB FRAGMENTATION BOMB**: A cast steel case with square steel wire wound spirally over it, and filled with 36 lbs of Composition B Explosive. Total weight: 262 lbs.

**M82 90-LB FRAGMENTATION BOMB**: A cast steel case with square steel wire wound spirally over it, and filled with 61.2 lbs of TNT or Composition B Explosive. Total weight: 88.5 lbs.

---

**Left to Right**
MK III 300-lb Demo, MK III 600-lb Demo, MK III 1100-lb Demo, M103 2000-lb SAP, AN-M56 4000-lb Demo, AN-M66A2 2000-lb GP, AN-M79 1000-lb Chemical, AN-M59A1 1000-lb SAP, AN-M76 500-lb Incendiary, M58A2 500-lb SAP, AN-MK 54 Mod 1 Depth Charge, AN-MK 41 Depth Charge.

**M27A1 500-LB FRAGMENTATION CLUSTER**: An assembly and tail fin to hold six M82 90-lb Fragmentation Bombs. Total weight: 585 lbs.

**MK 44 MOD 0 550-LB LAZY DOG MISSILE CLUSTER**: A sheet steel case with an airburst explosive charge of 21.8 lbs of TNT, and filled with 10,000 two-inch pointed iron nails. These, travelling at the velocity of bullets from a rifle, silently plunge into an area of about 100 square yards, and have the equivalent effect of several hundred 12-gauge shotgun rounds fired downwards from a height of 50 feet above the head. Total weight: 560 lbs.

**BLU-26/B SADEYE 1-LB FRAGMENTATION BOMB**: A cast steel shell with aerodynamic vanes and a filler of .7 lbs of TNT in which 600 steel shards have been embedded. Variously equipped with a proximity fuse to explode at a height of 30 feet, an impact-fuse to explode on hitting the ground, or a delayed-action fuse to explode one minute or more after hitting the ground. Shards are lethal to a range of 40 feet. Total weight: 1.2 lbs. BLU/3/B and BLU-36/B are similar.

**SUU-30B/B SUSPENDED UNDERWING UNIT**: A cylindrical sheet metal container filled with Sadeye 1-lb Fragmentation Bombs. Locked together in two halves, it splits open on release from its aircraft, and was known to the Vietnamese as the ''Guava'' because the bomblets falling from it resembled the seeds spilling from that fruit. Used in the CBU-24/29/49/52/58/70 series of cluster bomb munitions, its weight varies from 718 to 818 lbs. A somewhat smaller container is the SUU-14A/A, used in the Mk 5, Mk 15, Mk 21 and Mk 22 Sadeye dispensing systems. SUU-25/42/44 are flare dispensers. SUU-38/A and SUU-45//A are high-speed TFDM (Tactical Fighter Dispenser Munitons) dispensers.

**CBU-24/B 750-LB CLUSTER BOMB UNIT**: The SUU-30B/B dispenser with 665 BLU-26/B or BLU/36/B 1-lb Fragmentation Bombs, variously fused. The combination of three types of fuse in a single cluster bomb would create a mixture of airbursts, ground bursts and delayed-action bursts after the other Sadeye detonations had ceased and people had come out of protective cover believing they were safe. CBU-12/14/19/22/25/30/ 34/38/42/43/58/60/71/ are similar cluster bomb munitions of various sizes, CBU-43/B being a 1,000-lb unit and CBU-60/A weighing 750 lbs.

**BLU-66/B PINEAPPLE 1-LB FRAGMENTA-TION BOMB**: A cylindrical steel case with stabilizing fins and filled with cast TNT and 260 steel shards. It detonates on impact, and is an alternate to the Sadeye as a CBU filler. Total weight: 1.1 lbs.

**BLU-24/B ORANGE 1-LB FRAGMENTATION BOMB**: A round steel case with aerodynamic vanes which cause it to spin more than 2,000 rpm in descent, and filled with cast TNT in which up to 300 steel shards have been embedded. Equipped with a special jungle canopy penetration fuse, it detonates after passing through treetop cover, the effect of which slows its rate of spin to less than 2,000 rpm, activating the fuse. In this way, the bomb detonates just after it has cleared the canopy and before it reaches the ground, so that neither foliage nor ground dissipate its effects. Total weight: 1.2 lbs.

**SUU-7C/A SUSPENDED UNDERWING UNIT**: A dispenser with 19 compressed air ejection tubes for sustained release of Sadeye, Pineapple, Orange and other Fragmentation Bombs.

**CBU-46B/A 750-LB CLUSTER BOMB UNIT**: The SUU-7C/A dispenser with 640 of either the BLU-24/B Orange and BLU-66/B Pineapple 1-lb Fragmentation Bombs.

**MK 118 2-LB ANTITANK FRAGMENTATION BOMB**: A hardened heavy-density steel case filled with 1.1 lbs of Minol or H6 high explosive to produce fragments moving at speeds up to 4,000 feet per second, and of sufficient density to penetrate up to six inches of armour plate with a force exceeding that of a 105mm APDS round. Total weight: 1.93 lbs.

**MK 20 MOD O ROCKEYE 500-LB ANTITANK CLUSTER BOMB**: A sheet steel dispenser with 247 M118 Antitank Fragmentation Bombs. The Israelis used this bomb in Lebanon in March of 1978. Total weight: 476 lbs. The MK 20 MOD 2 is similar, but weighs 490 lbs.

**PLU-77/B APAM 1-LB FRAGMENTATION BOMB**: A dual-purpose anti-personnel and antitank bomb with a hardened steel case and a high explosive filler for high-velocity fragments. It is manufactured by Honeywell. Total weight: 1.02 lbs.

**CBU-59/B 750-LB APAM CLUSTER BOMB UNIT**: A steel sheet container with 717 PLU-77/B APAM 1-lb Fragmentation Bombs. Total weight: 766 lbs.

**SUU-54/B SUSPENDED UNDERWING UNIT**: A cylindrical sheet metal container for 1,500 Sadeye, APAM or other 1-lb Fragmentation Bombs. Total weight: 2,000 lbs.

# GUIDED BOMBS

Fitted with small cruciform vanes and planar control surfaces at their tails, to increase their glide range and stabilize their glide path, some of our standard demolition bombs, the MK 84 and M118, have been equipped with electro-optical and infrared seekers. Called HOBOS (Homing Bomb System) munitions, they are locked onto a target selected by the pilot, and thereafter guide themselves to it. This allows release of the bombs at much greater ranges from their targets, and also allows the aircraft to leave the target area more quickly. The guidance systems for EOGB (Electro-Optically Guided Bombs) and IRGB (Infra Red Guided Bombs) have been developed by Rockwell International.

Under the Air Force's Paveway air munitions improvement program, laser-seeking systems have also been developed, chiefly by Texas Instruments, for several standard demolition and fragmentation bombs. LGB (Laser Guided Bomb) seekers follow the path of a laser beam directed onto the target by a laser target designator operated by the launching aircraft, another aircraft or a ground unit. Under another program, the Navy developed a TVGB (Television Guided Bomb), the Walleye, in cooperation with Hughes Aircraft and the Martin Marietta Corporation. The Walleye is now in full production by Martin Marietta, and is scheduled for a number of improvements including the addition of an imaging infrared sensor head like that used on the AGM-56D Maverick, and the addition of larger planar wing surfaces for high-altitude launch and a longer glide range.

Known as "smart bombs," these weapons are not inexpensive, but neither do they miss their targets. By 1967 they had begun to enter service in Vietnam, where they were used with considerable success. Here are the major types now in production and service:

**WALLEYE I 1,100-LB TVGB**: A television guided bomb with an 850-lb high explosive warhead. No longer in production. Total weight: 1,100 lbs.

**WALLEYE II GW MK 4 MOD 4 2,000-LB TVGB**: A television guided bomb with a 1,000-lb high explosive warhead, based on the MK 84 2,000-lb bomb. USAF designation is GBU-15. Imaging infrared sensors, at a cost of $9,300 each, may be added to some units now in production. The airframe can also be adapted to the SUU-54/A container to dispense BLU-63 or BLU-86 Fragmentation Bombs. Israel has purchased 204.

**KMU-420/B 500-LB LGB**: The MK 20 MOD 2 Rockeye II antitank cluster munition with the addition of a laser guidance kit. Total weight: 650 lbs. Exported under FMS: 4,278.

**KMU-388/B**

**KMU-388/B: 500-LB LGB**: THE MK 82 Snakeye high-drag demolition bomb with the addition of a laser guidance kit.

**KMU-351A/B 2,000-LB LGB**: The MK 84 demolition bomb with the addition of a laser guidance kit. Total weight: 2,052 lbs.

**KMU/353A/B 2,000-LB EOGB/IRGB**: The MK 84 demolition bomb with the addition either of an electro-optical or an infrared guidance kit. Total weight: 2,247 lbs.

**KMU-342/B 750-LB LGB**: The M117 demolition bomb with the addition of a laser guidance kit. Total weight: 840 lbs.

**KMU-421/B PAVE STORM 2,000-LB LGB**: The SUU-54/B cluster bomb munition with the addition of a laser guidance kit. USAF designation is GBU-2. Total weight: 2,064 lbs.

**The Walleye I Mk 3 Television-guided 1,100- lb bomb mounted on a Navy A-7E aircraft.**

**KMU-370/B 3,000-LB LGB**: The M118E1 general purpose bomb with the addition of a laser guidance kit. Saudi Arabia has requested 1,000 of these. Total weight: 3,066 lbs.

**KMU-390/B 3,000-LB EOGB**: The M118E1 general purpose bomb with the addition of an electro-optical guidance kit. Total weight: 3,420 lbs.

# FUEL AIR MUNITIONS

Developed toward the end of the war in Vietnam, this new type of air munition uses highly volatile fuels, including ethylene oxide, propylene oxide, meththylacetlyene, propadiene, propane and butane, to produce an explosive rather than an incendiary effect. Released into the air, they form a highly combustible cloud that, on detonation, produces more than five times the energy of its equivalent weight in TNT. This is more than sufficient to detonate magnetic, electro-magnetic, hydraulic, seismic and infrared antitank and anti-personnel mines, whether of long impulse or double-impulse fusing. Fuel air munitions are also a formidable anti-personnel weapon, producing blast overpressures that cause lethal concussion. These are the major types in service or in development:

**CBU-55/B 500-LB FUEL AIR MUNITION**: Three 100-lb canisters, each with 72 lbs of fuel, which separate on release from the launching aircraft and disperse a cloud of fuel 56 feet across and 9 feet thick, that is detonated by delayed-action fuses 3 inches above the ground, producing a blast overpressure of 300 pounds per square inch, sufficient to incapacitate or kill men in bunkers, foxholes and tunnels. Total weight: 460 lbs.

**CBU-72/B 500-LB FUEL AIR MUNITION**: The CBU-55/B fitted with drogue parachutes to retard descent, for delivery by high-speed aircraft such as the A-4 Skyhawk and A-7 Corsair II.

**PAVE PAT II 2,500-LB FUEL AIR MUNITION**: A sheet steel container filled with 2,245 lbs of pressurized propane. The Pave Pat Blue 72 version is for delivery by the A-1 Skyraider, and the Pave Pat Blue 76 version is a reinforced container for delivery by high-speed aircraft such as the F-4 Phantom.

**MAD FAE (MASS AIR DELIVERY, FUEL AIR EXPLOSIVE)**: Twelve containers, each of 136 lbs of ethylene oxide or propylene oxide, attached on a line in single file to the freight hook of the CH-46, CH-53 or UH-1 helicopter, with stabilizing panels to keep the line from twisting, and released simultaneously or in sequence, dispersing a volatile cloud over an area of more than 1,000 feet in length. In development for the Marine Corps, and first tested at China Lake, California in 1960.

**FAESHED (FUEL AIR EXPLOSIVE, HELICOPTER DELIVERED)**: The CBU-44/B modified for use by the U.S. Army in mine clearance operations.

**SLUFAE (SURFACE LAUNCHED UNIT, FUEL AIR EXPLOSIVE)**: A mobile ground unit based on the chassis for the M-113A1 armoured personnel carrier, mounting a series of 30 launch tubes for the 5'' (121.8mm) Zuni rocket. Each rocket is equipped with the Pave Pat Blue 73 Fuel Air Munition warhead, and has a range of 750 yards (2,250 feet). Used for mine clearance, the system has a kill radius of 33 feet for pressure-fused mines and 112 feet for pull-fused trip-wired mines.

**BLU-82/B 15,000-LB GENERAL PURPOSE BOMB**: Also known as the Daisy Cutter or Big Blue 82, this is a cast steel case filled with 12,600 lbs of DBA-22M, an aqueous mixture of ammonium nitrate, aluminum powder and polystyrene soap as a binder. It produces an explosion of a size and intensity that observers have described as "the closest thing to a nuclear bomb," and is used not only for mine clearance but to create landing pads for helicopters and STOL aircraft. Producing blast overpressures in excess of 1,000 pounds per square inch, it literally shears off trees and other obstructions at ground level. The only way to understand the force of concussion it brings to bear on the human body is to picture a man being hit by a baseball bat at full length, and then to imagine him hit by that kind of force at every exposed portion of his body simultaneously.

# IN DEVELOPMENT

A number of highly advanced air munitions programs are in the early stages of development, including the following:

**WAAM (WIDE AREA ANTI-ARMOUR MUNITIONS)**: A program to develop a cluster munition with self-forging fragments. This weapon would release its fragments with an explosive force sufficient to melt them. Travelling through the air at high speeds, the fragments would reforge themselves into streamlined shapes that have demonstrated a capability far superior to ordinary fragments at penetrating armour.

**CYCLOPS**: A program to develop self-forging fragments of a pre-determined size, each one equipped with a small infrared or milimeter-wave sensor that remained unaffected by the explosion, and that would seek out large or warm targets. While more than one fragment might pick the same target, no fragment would be directed into empty space.

**TGSM (TERMINALLY-GUIDED SUB-MUNITIONS)**: A cluster munition bursting in air to release several small anti-tank bombs, each equipped with its own sensor to seek out a separate target, and retarded in its fall by a drogue parachute. TGSMs are planned to cover large concentrations of armoured vehicles, destroying several at once.

**WASP**: An Army program to develop a small missile about the size of the Rockwell International Hellfire. The missiles would be launched in salvos, and each one, equipped with its own infrared or milimeter-wave sensor, would acquire and lock onto a separate armoured vehicle after launch.

**ERAM (EXTENDED RANGE ANTITANK MINE)**: An airdropped antitank mine equipped with a seismic, acoustic, infrared or milimeter-wave sensor that would detect an approaching armoured vehicle and detonate when it was merely within lethal range, rather than requiring the vehicle to pass directly over it. The technology of electronic data processing has advanced to such a degree that it is now feasible to equip such a mine with a small, expendable signal processor pre-programmed with the characteristic milimeter-wave signatures of various armoured vehicles, adjusting it to detonate only in response to pre-selected signatures.

**HSF-I AND HSF-II**: A USAF program to develop two types of fuel air explosive munitions, one with a 500-lb warhead and one with a 2,000-lb warhead, to destroy light, high-value targets such as parked aircraft and radar and other electronic installations. Prime contractor is the Sandia Corporation.

**RBU-1/A PAVE ROCKET**: A USAF program to develop an unguided air-to-surface rocket with a warhead capable of penetrating concrete bunkers, aircraft shelters and heavy fortifications. Using the 2.75'' rocket airframe, and the LAU-61/A or LAU-69/A launching pod for 19 rockets, an aircraft would carry six of these pods in a low diving attack, and would thus be capable of delivering a total of 114 rockets with high-penetration warheads. The RBU-1/A Pave Rocket is now anticipated to cost $4,840 each.

**HSM (HARD STRUCTURE MUNITIONS)**: A top secret USAF progtion warheads. The RBU-1/A Pave Rocket is now anticipated to cost $4,840 each.

**HSM (HARD STRUCTURE MUNITIONS)**: A top secret USAF program to develop a weapon guided by laser, electro-optical or infrared seekers now standard in USAF inventory, with a low-cost warhead resistant to ricochet and capable of penetrating armour and concrete *before* releasing its main energy.

# GUIDED MISSILES

The guidance and propulsion systems of missiles make them far more expensive than surface-launched artillery projectiles or free-fall air munitions, but their advantages are several. Self-powered projectiles eliminate recoil forces and, in most cases, do not require gun tubes or other heavy launching equipment. Today's guided missiles also provide a means for the delivery of heavy explosive forces over much greater ranges than are accessible to the bomb or the howitzer shell, and with far greater accuracy.

A step in our improvement of free-fall air munitions which brought them closer in capability to the missile was the development of laser guidance and electro-optical guidance systems under the USN Walleye and USAF Paveway programs, somewhat extending their range and vastly improving the accuracy of glide bombs. A further step under the Paveway program was the development of SLAM (Semi-active Laser-guided Aerial Munition), a standard MK 81 250-lb bomb with a KMU-388A/B laser seeker and the addition of an M58A2 Falcon rocket motor, extending the bomb's guided range to about 6,000 yards. SLAM is really a form of guided missile.

While many of the guidance systems developed for the Paveway program were also employed to improve the accuracy of self-powered munitions, the technology of missiles, especially of inertial guidance systems for large unmanned rockets, and of powerful rocket propulsion systems, had in the meanwhile become highly sophisticated.

It is believed that rockets were first put to military use by the Chinese in 1232 A.D. Since that time, efforts to improve their range and accuracy have not ceased. By the early 1800s Sir William Congreve had de-

veloped a rocket with a reliable range of 3,000 yards which the British Army's Rocket Corps used with considerable effect against Napoleon at the Battle of Leipzig in October of 1813. However, these rockets could not be guided. Aimed at the enemy, they usually travelled the anticipated distance, but frequently veered off course.

Thereafter, the range of most tactical unguided rockets has not greatly increased, but their ballistic trajectory has become more and more reliable. Our now obsolete M-8 4.5″ aircraft rocket and its successor, the 5″ HVAR (High Velocity Aerial Rocket), precursor of the Zuni, had air-to-surface ranges of about 3,500 yards. The M-8 was also deployed as a barrage rocket from such surface launchers as the 24-tube Honeycomb and 60-tube Hornet's Nest, and used in great quantities by our Navy to support beachhead invasion forces during World War II and the Korean War. In this flat surface-to-surface trajectory it had a somewhat increased range of 4,000 yards. A spin-stabilized version, the M-16 4.5″ rocket, had a range of 5,250 yards. The 2.75″ FFAR (Folding Fin Aerial Rocket) currently in use has an air-to-surface range of 3,750 yards, but the release of a pod of these rockets places their shot group within an impact area of less than 100 square yards—a level of accuracy Sir William Congreve could not attain.

In the remaining decades of the 1900s, artillery projectiles outdistanced the unguided rocket, and have extended their range even further in this century. Today's XM-198 155mm howitzer has a range of over 21 miles. The RAP (Rocket Assisted Projectile) for the M-102 105mm howitzer increases its range by 2,750 yards. Accuracy, too, has improved. The Martin Marietta company has developed the Copperhead CLGP (Cannon-Launched Guided Projectile), a 155mm howitzer round guided by a laser target designator. It can hit a tank

at a range of over 14,000 yards.

However, as more powerful rocket motors were developed, very large warheads were soon being propelled to much greater distances than tube-launched artillery projectiles could ever be expected to travel. Today's LGM-52 Lance missile has a range of 68 miles, the MGM-29 Sergeant 85 miles, and the MGM-31 Pershing 460 miles.

These weapons, of course, are far more accurate than the V-2 rockets developed by the Germans in the closing years of World War II. Those rockets had a maximum range of 570 miles, but of the 1,027 V-2s fired, 79 failed to attain their trajectory, and of the remaining 948, only 518 fell within the London Civil Defense Region toward which they had all been aimed. Today's AGM-68A ALCM (Air-Launched Cruise Missile) has a range of 1,200 miles, and in precisely hitting its target it has a CEP (Circular Error Probability) of less than 10 yards.

In the era of the ICBM (Inter-Continental Ballistic Missile), much higher ranges have been achieved. Our LGM-30G Minuteman III ICBM has a range of 8,075 miles. But all of these large missiles, including the BSM (Battlefield Support Missile) types such as the Lance, Sergeant and Pershing, are ballistically aimed at a specific point on the Earth's surface, and thereafter inertially guided. While inertial guidance does not lack in sophistication, laboriously measuring every millimeter of distance travelled and precisely recording every sequential change in angle of bearing, it can still guide a missile only to one pre-selected point, or to alternate points for which it has been programmed prior to launch. If a target is moving, guidance is far more problematical, and requires even greater levels of technological sophistication.

A number of antitank missiles, such as the M-47 Dragon and the MGM-71 TOW, are wire-guided, receiving command signals through wires that unspool behind them as they close the distance to their targets, and they are optically aimed, sometimes with the assistance of television or infrared sights, which respectively magnify or brighten the image presented to the operator's eye. Alternatively, missiles are built without wire to respond to command signals by radio or telemetry data link.

In either case, however, such missiles cannot function without a human operator. Their speed of maneuverability is limited by the operator's reflexes, and their accuracy by what the operator can see. Therefore a number of guidance systems have been developed which automate the command function, giving the missile a much higher flexibility and speed of response, limited only by the thousandths of a second required by microcircuitry to process data and transmit electronic signals. The target is acquired, often by radar, and thereafter automatically illuminated, either by the same or a second radar, or by a laser beam, or by an infrared or electro-optical system that identifies a heat or visual image. A human operator need only note that a target has been acquired and command the weapon to launch, automatically locking its homing system to whatever signals are provided by the compatible target illumination system at hand.

Semi-active radar homing missiles are guided by the returning signals of a fire control radar operated at their source of launch. Laser-seeking missiles ride in on the beam of laser light illuminating a target. Electro-optical and imaging infrared missiles home on an image identified by a television, electro-optical or infrared sight.

While these systems greatly increase the speed and maneuverability of missiles, and no longer require target tracking by a human operator, they still require target illumination, and personnel must operate the illuminating equipment. In aerial combat, even the highly sophisticated AN/AWG-9 fire control radar of the F-14 Tomcat, or the AN/APG-63 radar of the F-15 Eagle, both of which have target detection ranges of over 100 miles, must be brought to within less than 10 miles of their targets, keeping their radar guidance cones no more than 65 degrees off boresight, in order successfully to guide their missiles home. Such a range exposes the pilots to identification and retaliatory fire by weapons equally sophisticated, and it has been determined that whenever such weapons are encountered, the pilots who have remained in the area in order to operate their guidance radars will not survive.

Personnel operating laser illuminators for missiles guided by these means must expose themselves at even closer ranges to the target, for in order to hold a laser illuminating beam on the target they must be able, with whatever telescopic or other means are available for magnifying the target image, visually to see it in the first place.

It has been recognized, therefore, that a self-guided missile is needed, with a much longer range, permitting launch from an aircraft or surface vehicle that does not then have to come within range of retaliatory fire in order to guide it. Consequently, an active terminal guidance radar has been developed for the AGM-54A Phoenix missile guidance head. Using semi-active radar homing during the first 90 miles of its flight to the target, which has been illuminated by the AN/AWG-9 fire control radar aboard its launching aircraft, the Phoenix locks onto the point from which these radar signals return, and over the final ten miles of its flight turns on its own radar to guide itself to that point. The only difficulty with this system is its cost. The 1978 Unit Procurement Cost of a Phoenix missile is $406,190.

Missiles with radar homing seekers have also been developed to respond not to returning signals from a command fire control radar, but to enemy radar emissions on a variety of identifiable frequency bandwidths previously programmed into the missile's signal processor. These are called anti-radiation missiles, and they are used for defense suppression to destroy the radars guiding enemy air defense systems. They include the AGM-45 Shrike, the AGM-88 Harm and the RIM-66D Standard ARM (Anti-Radiation Missile). The limitation on such a missile is that it cannot find its target if the radar emissions on which it homes are suddenly shut off.

An effective and less expensive self-guidance system is the infrared seeker. This homes a missile in on emissions of heat, and is especially effective in aerial combat where high levels of heat are emitted by powerful afterburning jet engines. French heat-seeking missiles were used to great

effect in the 1967 Arab-Israeli war, when Israeli aircraft undertook pre-emptive strikes on Arab airfields, timed so precisely that they were able to catch Egyptian fighters warming up on the tarmac, just after Israeli penetration of the defensive radar screen had alerted them but well before they were able to take off.

Infrared seekers, however, are affected by rain, haze and other weather conditions, and can detect heat only at ranges of less than 15 miles, bringing attacking forces into a compromising proximity. While radar, on the other hand, has a much longer acquisition range, it is also less accurate. Missiles with radar guidance are therefore equipped with proximity fuses and larger warheads whose explosive force will compensate for the distance they fail to close on the target prior to detonation.

Countermeasures are in development to challenge all of these seeking mechanisms. Command data links and radar guidance signals can be jammed. Ground forces can employ a simple and inexpensive technique to confuse infrared seekers and effectively blind laser and electro-optical systems, by producing a cloud of persistent smoke and gas to surround targets under attack. This muffles the radiation from heat emissions, requiring more sensitive infrared tracking than may be available to the attacking missile. In response, of course, more sensitive tracking will be developed. In response to jamming defenses, missiles are being provided with ECCM (Electronic Counter Counter Measures) circuitry, known to practitioners of the art as "redundant circuitry," which enables them to operate effectively by receiving and processing data on alternate frequencies not being jammed.

The major types of United States tactical missiles include AAMs (Air-to-Air Missiles), which are also known as AIMs (Air Intercept Missiles), ASMs (Air-to-Surface Missiles), which are also known as AGMs (Air-to-Ground Missiles), SSMs (Surface-to-Surface Missiles), which may be employed either by naval or ground forces, BSMs (Battlefield Support Missiles), ATGMs (Anti-Tank Guided Missiles), and SAMs (Surface-to-Air Missiles), among which are a type of light SAM known as MANPADS (Man Portable Air Defense Systems). A summary of all these types follows.

# AIM-4 FALCON
# AIM 26B/AIM 47A

This was the first guided air-to-air missile in the world. Some models are still in service. Development of the Falcon began in 1947, and the earliest AIM-4A, equipped with semi-active radar homing (SARH), entered service in 1954 as an anti-bomber weapon for the F-102A interceptors of our Aerospace Defense Command. The AIM-4C, an infrared homing (IRH) version, went into service in 1956, equipping our F-102As and F-101Bs. It is also produced under license in Sweden by SAAB/Scania as the RB28, and is used by that country to equip the J35-F Draken fighter and by Switzerland, as the HM58, to equip the Mirage IIIS. An improved IRH version, the AIM-4D, was developed in the 1960s with a speed of Mach 4 (2,640 mph) as an air intercept missile to combat fighters as well as bombers, and armed several United States aircraft as well as Canadian F-101Bs. Many AIM-4A and AIM-4C production missiles were subsequently rebuilt to AIM-4D standard.

With 30 lbs of added weight and a mile more range, the AIM-4E Super Falcon appeared in 1958, and was followed by the AIM-4F in 1960, the latter with improved ECCM circuitry.Both were SARH versions, but an IRH version of the Super Falcon, the AIM-4G, also appeared in 1960, and in that same year the heavier AIM-26 Falcon went into production. With SARH guidance and a longer range of 10 miles, the AIM-26 weighed 200 lbs. Those designated AIM-26A were equipped with nuclear warheads, and were similar in performance and weight to the McDonnell Douglas AIR-2A Genie missile, over 10,000 of which were produced with nuclear warheads between 1957 and 1962, equipping our F-101B and F-106 interceptors. 1,900 AIM-26As were produced.

Of the AIM-26B with a conventional high explosive warhead, only 800 were produced, entering service in 1963. These are the only Falcons remaining in United States service today. However, the AIM-26B is also produced under license in Sweden by SAAB/Scania. It is used in that country as the RB27, and in Switzerland as the HM55.

In 1969 development also began on the AIM-4H, a Falcon with an active optical seeker and a proximity fuse. The project was later suspended. The AIM-47A Falcon, weighing 800 lbs, was also placed in development as a long-range intercept missile with SARH guidance and IR terminal homing. Using the Hughes AN/ASG-18 fire control radar for target illumination, the AIM-47A was to have a speed of Mach 6 (3,960 mph) and a range of 100 miles, with either a nuclear or a high explosive warhead. This project, too, was suspended,

but much of the developmental technology was used in the production of the Hughes AIM-54A Phoenix long-range air-to-air missile, which is now operational.

**Type:** Short-range air-to-air missile, powered by solid propellant.

**Weight:** 120 lbs (AIM-4A/C/D), 150 lbs (AIM-4E/F/G), 200 lbs (AIM-26A/B), or 800 lbs (AIM-47A).

**Speed:** Mach 3 (AIM-4A/C/F), Mach 4 (AIM-4D/E/G/H), Mach 2 (AIM-26A/B), Mach 6 (AIM-47A).

**Range:** 6 miles (AIM-4A/C/D), 7 miles (AIM-4E/F/G), 10 miles (AIM-26A/B), 100 miles (AIM-47A).

**Guidance:** SARH (AIM-4A/E/F) and AIM-26A/B), IRH (AIM-4C/D/G), SARH/IRTH (AIM-47A).

**Manufacturer:** Hughes Aircraft Company, with licensed production by SAAB/Scania in Sweden. Production completed.

**Produced:** Over 59,800 of all types, including 4,000 AIM-4A designated GAR-1, 12,000 AIM-4A designated GAR-1D, 16,000 AIM-4C designated GAR-2, 9,500 AIM-4C designated GAR-2A, 4,000 SAAB/Scania AIM-4C (3,000 of which were designated RB28 and 1,000 HM58), 4,000 AIM-4D designated GAR-2B, 300 AIM-4E designated GAR-3, 3,400 AIM-4F designated GAR-3A, 2,700 AIM-4G designated GAR-4A, 1,900 AIM-26A, 800 AIM-26B designated GAR-11Ak 1,200 SAAB/Scania AIM-26B (800 of which were designated RB27 and 400 HM55), and several prototype AIM-4H and AIM-47A, the latter designated GAR-9.

**Exported under FMS:** 535.

**Exported under MAP:** 1,181.

**In US Service:** 600 AIM-26B in Aerospace Defense Command.

**In Service Abroad:** Canada (400 AIM-4D and 200 AIM-26B), Greece (360 AIM-4D), Sweden (3,000 AIM-4C designated RB28 and 800 AIM-26B designated RB27), Switzerland (1,000 AIM-4C designated HM58 and 400 AIM-26B designated HM55), Taiwan (320 AIM-4D), and Turkey (430 AIM-4D).

# AIM-9 SIDEWINDER

With less than 24 moving parts and fewer electronic components than the average radio, the short-range air-to-air Sidewinder missile has proved to be one of the most reliable weapons of its type. In combat in Vietnam the Navy's AIM-9H Sidewinder achieved a record of kills per engagement of 86 percent. In 1973, when 220 AIM-9D and 480 AIM-9G Sidewinders were rushed to Israel during the Yom Kippur War, she achieved with some of them a kill-per-

engagement record of 92 percent, even though these earlier models did not have the solid-state electronics of the Navy's AIM-9H. More than 110,000 Sidewinders of all types have been produced, and the missile, which operates with infrared homing, is in production today and continues in service with our Navy and Air Force as well as with 27 countries abroad.

Weighing 155 lbs and with a Rocketdyne motor which powered it to a speed of Mach 2.5 (1,650 mph), the first AIM-9B Sidewinder entered service with USAF and USN in 1956. With passive IRH guidance and proportional navigation, it had a range of 2.3 miles, a field of view of four degrees, and a target acquisition angle of 25 degrees, which allowed an aircraft to launch it to the same measure off boresight without hindering its track of the target. More than 80,000 AIM-9Bs were produced, half of them by Raytheon and half by the firm of Aeronutronic Ford.

Licensed production of the AIM-9B was undertaken in West Germany by Bodenseewerk Gerätetechnick, which produced 15,000 of this model for the Bundesluftwaffe and several NATO air forces, modifying them with the FWG Mod 2 infrared seeker head, which was equipped with a cooling device to sharpen its depth sensitivity, making it less responsive to sunlight, glare and heat emissions from sources other than the target itself. This model first came into service in 1969.

Meanwhile, an attempt had been made in 1965 to give the Sidewinder an all-weather capability, equipping it with a Motorola MK 12 Mod 3 semi-active radar homing head, and a new motor that increased its range to 11.5 miles. This introduced the AIM-9C, which is no longer in service, but its motor remained to power all subsequent Navy versions of the missile. Also for our Navy, and for the United Kingdom's Royal Navy, the AIM-9D appeared that same year, equipped with a Raytheon MK 18 Mod 1 IRH guidance head and a MK 25 Mod 5 motor. This was the version that was modified by the United States Army, after cancellation of the Mauler program, as the MIM-72 Chaparral low-level air defense missile.

Production for the Navy continued in 1970 with the AIM-9G and the AIM-9H, the latter with solid-state electronics. While the AIM-9H had a somewhat lower range, it was a more reliable and far more maneuverable weapon, with a rapid response to changes in target bearing. Cryogenic cooling kept its IRH seeker head sufficiently sensitive to variations in the range of targets emitting heat so that it was able to track these through haze and light cloud cover. This gave the AIM-9H a limited all-weather capability, without the use of radar.

In 1967 the Air Force had modified 5,000 of its AIM-9B missiles to AIM-9E standard, equipping them with a new IRH seeker head and somewhat extending their range. In 1975 these AIM-9Es were modified a second time to AIM-9J standard, equipped with solid-state electronics and with a thermo-electrically cooled seeker to give them an all-weather capability. In subsequent years, a total of 9,000 USAF AIM-9Bs were also converted to AIM-9J standard, similar in performance to the Navy's AIM-9H. The Unit Procurement Cost of an AIM-9H in 1975 was $19,375. Since the AIM-9B had cost $3,000 each in 1956 when it was originally procured, and since the cost to convert it to AIM-9J standard in 1975 was only $7,250 each, the Air Force appeared to have found a frugal means of acquiring a high-performance missile at roughly half the cost of its counterpart in the Navy inventory.

The only drawback was that the AIM-9J still used the motor of the AIM-9B, which had given the latter missile a range of only 2.3 miles in its 60 seconds of burn time. Later Sidewinders had attained ranges of over 11 miles with the equivalent burn time. To extend the range of the AIM-9J to 11 miles the Air Force modified its motor by sacrificing 20 seconds of burn time. It is a short-lived missile, best used only in frontal engagements. Fired at a departing supersonic aircraft, it may burn out its motor before it can reach the target.

The current production model of the Sidewinder is the AIM-9L, which first entered service with the Air Force and the Navy in 1977. Powered by a MK 36 Mod 6 motor, and with a WDU-17/B annular blast fragmentation warhead and a DSU-15/B active optical fuse, the AIM-9L is equipped with a TUM-72/B integral cooling system for its IRH seeker. More than 8,000 are planned for both services, to equip the F-4E, the F-14, the F-15 and AV-8A and the OV-10A. Some earlier Sidewinders were also mod-

ified as AGM-87A air-to-ground missiles, but further development work in this program was suspended. Large numbers of Sidewinders have been exported abroad, including quantities of several recent models to arm aircraft sold to Iran and Saudi Arabia.

---

**Type:** Short-range air-to-air missile, powered by solid propellant.

---

**Weight:** 155 lbs (AIM-9B) or 167 lbs (AIM-9B with FWG Mod 2), 164 lbs (AIM-9E), 171 lbs (AIM-9J), 195lbs (AIM-9C/D), 191 lbs (AIM-9G), 186 lbs (AIM-9H/L).

---

**Speed:** Mach 2.5 (1,650 mph).

---

**Range:** 2.3 miles (AIM-9B), 2.6 miles (AIM-9E), 11.1 miles (AIM-9J), 11.5 miles (AIM-9C/D/G/H/L).

---

**Guidance:** IRH (AIM-9B/D/E/G/H/J/L). SARH (AIM-9C).

---

**Manufacturer:** Raytheon (AIM-9B/G/H/L). Aeronutronic-Ford (AIM-9B/D/E/H/L). Licensed production of AIM-9B by Bodenseewerk Gerätetechnik. In production.

---

**Produced:** Over 110,000 to date, including 80,000 AIM-9B, 15,000 AIM-9B with FWG Mod 2, 1,000 AIM-9D, 2,120 AIM-9G, 7,720 AIM-9H, and 2,900 to date of 8,360 AIM-9L planned. 5,000 conversions of AIM-9B to AIM-9E, and 14,000 conversions of AIM-9B and AIM-9E to AIM-9L.

---

**Exported under FMS:** 14,233.

---

**Exported under MAP:** 14,008.

---

**In US Service:** 10,000 AIM-9J, 3,000 AIM-9H and 2,900 AIM-9L.

---

**In Service Abroad:** Argentina (800 AIM-9B), Australia (2,200 AIM-9B/D), Brazil (950 AIM-9B), Canada (3,750 AIM-9B/D), Chile (350 AIM-9C), Denmark (650 AIM-9B FWG Mod 2), Greece (1,350 AIM-9B FWG Mod 2), Iran (750 AIM-9B and 1,200 AIM-9D), Israel (150 AIM-9D, 300 AIM-9G and 1,500 AIM-9H), Japan (4,220 AIM-9D), Kuwait (300 AIM-9H), Malaysia (400 AIM-9B), Netherlands (1,500 AIM-9B FWG Mod 2), Norway (1,250 AIM-9B FWG Mod 2), Philippines (250 AIM-9B), Portugal (550 AIM-9B FWG Mod 2), Pakistan (450 AIM-9B), Saudi Arabia (400 AIM-9B), South Korea (750 AIM-9B), Spain (780 AIM-9B), Singapore (200 AIM-9B), Sweden (2,440 AIM-9B), Taiwan (3,800 AIM-9B), Tunisia (1,200 AIM-9B), Turkey (2,200 AIM-9B FWG Mod 2), United Kingdom (600 AIM-9D and 1,750 AIM-9H), and West Germany (7,500 AIM-9B FWG Mod 2).

---

**Price:** $41,238 @ (1979 Unit Procurement Cost for 3,150 AIM-9L to USN). $48,620 @ (1978 Unit Procurement Cost for 2,900 AIM-9L to USAF). $64,366 @ (1977 Unit Procurement Cost for 1,420 AIM-9H to USN). $19,375 @ (1975 Unit Procurement Cost for 800 AIM-9H to USN). $17,176 @ (1974 Unit Procurement Cost for 850 AIM-9H to USN).

---

**Conversion Cost:** $10,250 @ (1976 unit cost for 2,000 AIM-9B converted to AIM-9J for USAF, including unit conversion cost of $7,250).

---

**FMS Deliveries Pending:** Iran (2,262 AIM-9D and 288 AIM-9H), Saudi Arabia (850 AIM-9J).

---

**FMS Orders Pending:** Saudi Arabia (1,000 AIM-9J).

---

**Recent Transfers:** 3,462 AIM-9D to Iran in 1972 for $22,819 @. 750 AIM-9B to South Korea in 1973 for $27,733 @. 220 AIM-9D and 480 AIM-9G to Israel in 1973 for $24,893 @. 450 AIM-9B to Pakistan in 1974 for $31,555 @ 300 AIM-9H to Kuwait in 1975 for $35,700 @. 200 AIM-9B to Singapore in 1975 for $30,008 @. 850 AIM-9J to Saudi Arabia in 1975 for $32,666 @.

# AIM-7 SPARROW
# RIM-7H SEA SPARROW

A powerful and maneuverable medium-range air-to-air missile that has been used effectively as an ASM (Air-to-Surface Missile), and has also been adapted for use as a ship-launched SAM (Surface-to-Air Missile). Since it first entered service in 1958, over 40,000 of all types have been produced by Raytheon and General Dynamics in this country, Selenia in Italy, Mitsubishi in Japan, and Hawker Siddeley Dynamics in the United Kingdom. In one or more of its applications, the Sparrow is used today in our Air Force and Navy, and in 15 countries abroad.

Using Continuous-Wave SARH (Semi-Active Radar Homing) guidance, the AIM-7E is capable of determining the directional bearing of targets and distinguishing them from ground clutter, adjusting its flight either to climb or to dive by the use of movable wings. These features give it an operational capability in all conditions of weather and at all altitudes. Powered by a Rocketdyne MK 38 Mod 2 motor, it has a range of 28 miles in a head-on approach to its target, and a speed of Mach 3.5 (2,310 mph). This speed is not sufficient, however, to give it a range of more than 3 to 5 miles when approaching high-performance aircraft from the rear.

In 1974, under license from Raytheon, Hawker Siddeley Dynamics began production of the Skyflash missile based on the Sparrow, but incorporating the XJ-521 monopulse seeker developed by Marconi Space and Defense Systems, Ltd, improving the missile's target acquisition range, and an EMI Electronics active optical fusing system.

Similar improvements have been incorporated into the AIM-7F, the current production model of the Sparrow, which also has solid-state electronics and a Hercules MK 58 Mod 0 motor. General Dynamics has developed a dual-band, semi-active monopulse guidance system for the AIM-7F which substantially improves its "look-down" performance (the radar's ability to distinguish a target from ground clutter) and its resistance to ECM jamming. The missile's accuracy has been further improved by inclusion of a Von Karman radome with reduced error slopes and more stable wings with less flutter.

Solid-state electronics occupy less space in the AIM-7F, allowing more room for the warhead, which has been increased in size from 65 to 86 lbs, and which contains a continuous stainless steel rod that has been wrapped in a tight ring. On detonation, the warhead fragments this ring into more than 2,600 rods, each of which achieves a velocity of more than 1,700 feet per second. This ensures that an airburst over 400 yards from the target will still be lethal. Over 12,000 AIM-7F Sparrows are planned for production.

Basic air-to-air armament for the F-4 Phantom, the F-14 Tomcat and the F-15 Eagle, the Sparrow has been supplied in large quantities to many countries that have purchased or plan to purchase these aircraft. Two Sparrow missiles can also be carried on the licensed Aeritalia F-104S model of the Lockheed Starfighter.

Experimental Sparrows have been equipped with laser-homing heads under the USN Brazo and USAF Pave Arm programs. But the major adaptation of this air-to-air missile has been for the surface-to-air role in our Navy's BPDMS (Basic Point Defense Missile System) program. This produced the RIM-7H Sea Sparrow, an AIM-7D with folding wings, eight of which can be fitted into an ASROC launcher mounted on an automatic gun carriage for the deck of a surface ship. In conjunction with the Mk 115 fire control system and the Mk 51 radar director for target illumination, the RIM-7H provides basic ship defense against aircraft, missiles and small boats. BPDMS has been installed on all USN attack carriers, and is planned for installation on a total of 60 of our surface vessels.

In 1968 a NATO consortium was organized to produce missiles, lightweight launchers and fire control systems for the BPDMS, which had been adopted by the navies of Denmark, Norway, Belgium, the Netherlands and Italy—whose firm of Selenia produced the RIM-7H. A Canadian version of the BPDMS uses the AIM-7E2 without folding wings, and equips that country's DDH-280 destroyers. From the United States, 16 RIM-7H were supplied under MAP to Japan, 74 were sold to Spain and 108 to West Germany.

**Type:** Medium-range air-to-air or surface-to-air missile, with solid propellant.

**Weight:** 440 lbs (AIM-7C/D/E), 450 lbs (RIM-7H), or 500 lbs (AIM-7F).

**Speed:** Mach 3.5 (2,310 mph).

**Range:** 28 miles.

**Guidance:** Continuous-Wave SARH.

**Manufacturer:** Raytheon, and General Dynamics. Licensed production by Selenia in Italy, Mitsubishi in Japan, and Hawker-Siddeley in UK.

**Produced:** Over 40,000 of all types, including 34,000 AIM-7C/D/E, 600 Mitsubishi AIM-7E, 1,200 Selenia AIM-7E and 1,350 Hawker-Siddeley Skyflash, together with 1,320 to date of a total of 12,279 AIM-7F planned, 1,400 RIM-7H and 1,024 Selenia RIM-7H.

**Exported under MAP:** 2,182 AIM-7C/D/E and 16 RIM-7H.

**Exported under FMS:** 3,662 AIM-7D/E and 182 RIM-7H.

**In US Service:** 28,500 AIM-7D/E, 1,320 AIM-7F and 1,212 RIM-7H.

**AIM-7 in Service Abroad:** Greece (240 AIM-7C/E), Iran (2,616 AIM-7D/E), Israel (1,428 AIM-7D/E), Italy (1,000 Selenia AIM-7E), Japan (600 Mitsubishi AIM-7E), South Korea (460 AIM-7E), Turkey (240 AIM-7E2 and 200 Selenia AIM-7E), United Kingdom (1,350 Skyflash), West Germany 1,100 AIM-7D/E).

**RIM-7 in Service Abroad:** Belgium (128 Selenia RIM-7H), Canada (192 AIM-7E2), Denmark (160 Selenia RIM-7H), Italy (416 Selenia RIM-7H), Japan (16 RIM-7H), Netherlands (96 Selenia RIM-7H), Norway (224 Selenia RIM-7H), Spain (74 RIM-7H), West Germany (108 RIM-7H).

**Price:** $96,019 @ (1979 Unit Procurement Cost for 2,010 AIM-7F to USN). $103,072 @ (1978 Unit Procurement Cost for 1,725 AIM-7F to USAF/USN). $114,621 @ (1977 Unit Procurement Cost for 1,380 AIM-7F to USAF/USN). $148,061 @ (1976 Unit procurement Cost for 980 AIM-7E to USAF/USN).

**Recent Transfers:** 74 RIM-7H to Spain in 1974 for $121,000 @. 516 AIM-7E to Iran in 1975 for $199,541 @. 240 AIM-7E2 to Turkey in 1977 for $72,291 @.

# AIM-54A PHOENIX

This is probably the most sophisticated air-to-air missile in the world, and also the most expensive. Development of the Phoenix began in 1960 as an integral part of the Navy's F-111B tactical fighter program, which was subsequently cancelled. It was not until 1974 that the Phoenix first entered service, arming the Navy's Grumman F-14A Tomcat.

With a Rocketdyne MK 47 Mod 0 motor and a range of over 100 miles, the Phoenix incorporates SARH guidance, and after launch toward its target cruises for the first 90 miles of its flight. Within ten miles of the target, the missile activates its own terminal homing radar. The heart of the Phoenix system is the Hughes AN/AWG-9 fire control radar installed on the launching aircraft. It can guide six Phoenix missiles to their separate targets, while simultaneously tracking as many as 20 targets. A Control Data AN/5400-B computer codes the radar transmissions and interprets returning signals to guide each missile to its designated target. An infrared subsystem is also available, and can be used to guide the missiles at short range. Each Phoenix warhead is equipped with a Bendix infrared fuse and a Downey Mk 334 proximity fuse.

Tests with the Phoenix have been highly successful, including intercept of four out of six targets at a range of 50 miles, intercept of two targets in a high ECM environment while one of the targets employed active jamming, intercept of a target at a range of 126 miles, intercept of a maneuvering target, and intercept of a missile. Of 58 Phoenix missiles fired from the F-14, the Navy has achieved a kill-per-engagement record of 90 percent.

A total of 2,532 Phoenix missiles is planned to equip the Navy's F-14s, with an additional 484 to equip those F-14s purchased by Iran. Iran has to-date received 270 of the missiles, and the USN has in hand 1,722.

**Type:** Long-range air-to-air missile, with solid propellant.

**Weight:** 985 lbs.

**Speed:** Mach 3.8 (2,508 mph).

**Range:** Over 100 miles.

**Manufacturer:** Hughes Aircraft Company.

**Produced:** 2,206 of a total currently planned at 3,016.

**Exported under FMS:** 270.

**In US Service:** 1,722 in USN.

**In Service Abroad:** Iran (270).

**FMS Deliveries Pending:** Iran (280).

**Price:** $410,000 @ (1979 Unit Procurement Cost for 210 AIM-54A to USN). $406,190 @ (1978 Unit Procurement Cost for 210 AIM-54A to USN). $330,833 @ (1977 Unit Procurement Cost for 240 AIM-54A to USN). $363,823 @ (1976 Unit Procurement Cost for 340 AIM-54A to USN).

**Recent Transfers:** 484 AIM-54A to Iran in 1974 for $705,000 @.

# AGM-12 BULLPUP

An air-to-surface missile first developed in 1954 by the Navy. Commanded by radio signal to adhere to the pilot's line of sight to the target, the Bullpup attains speeds of Mach 1.8 (1,188 mph) and Mach 2 (1,320 mph). AGM-12B, which first entered service with the USN in 1959, was powered by a Thiokol LR-58RM4 liquid propellant, had a range of 7 miles and carried a 250-lb high explosive warhead. USAF adopted it in 1961, and in 1963 the Norwegian firm of Kongsberg Vaapenfabrikk undertook licensed production of this model for several NATO countries including Denmark, Greece, Norway, Turkey and the United Kingdom.

More than 8,000 were produced in Norway, in addition to 22,100 produced in this country by Martin Marietta and Maxson Electronics.

In 1964 an improved Bullpup missile, the AGM-12C, entered service with a larger 1,000-lb warhead and a range of 10 miles, powered by a Thiokol LR-62RM2 liquid propellant. Production, mostly by Maxson, continued through 1969. Martin Marietta developed two further versions of the Bullpup, the AGM-12D with a nuclear warhead and the AGM-12E, with an anti-personnel fragmentation warhead. After limited production of the AGM-12E for use in Vietnam, both projects were cancelled.

**Type:** Short-range air-to-surface missile, powered by liquid propellant.

**Weight:** 571 lbs (AGM-12B), or 1,785 lbs (AGM-12C).

**Speed:** Mach 1.8 (1,188 mph), or Mach 2 (1,320 mph).

**Guidance:** Radio command, visual sight.

**Range:** 7 miles (AGM-12B), or 10 miles (AGM-12C).

**Manufacturer:** Martin Marietta, and Maxson Electronics Corporation. Licensed production in Norway by Kongsberg Vaapenfabrikk. Production completed.

**Produced:** Over 35,000 of all types, including 30,100 AGM-12B (8,000 of which produced in Norway), 4,600 AGM-12C and 840 AGM-12E.

**Exported under FMS:** 2,516.

**Exported under MAP:** 3,768.

**In US Service:** Over 20,000 AGM-12B/C.

**In Service Abroad:** Argentina (880 AGM-12B), Australia (1,150 AGM-12B/C), Brazil (450 AGM-12B), Chile (620 AGM-12B), Denmark (560 AGM-12B), Greece (600 AGM-12B), New Zealand (400 AGM-12B/C), Norway (2,800 AGM-12B), Philippines (200 AGM-12B), South Korea (1,000 AGM-12B), Taiwan (850 AGM-12B), Turkey (940 AGM-12B), United Kingdom (3,100 AGM-12B), Venezuela (730 AGM-12B), Israel (416).

**Hughes AIM–54A Phoenix**

# AGM-65 MAVERICK

A highly accurate television-guided air-to-surface missile that has achieved a kill-per-engagement record of 92 percent in 178 test firings, and of which laser-guided and imaging infrared versions have also been developed. After seven years of development by Hughes Aircraft, the AGM-65A entered service in 1972 and was operational the following year. It operates with a small television homing system in its nose. The pilot of the launching aircraft focuses on the target with a cockpit television monitor, selects a missile, and locks the electro-optical tracker in the missile's nose to the same image on the monitor. This must be done before releasing the missile, but once it has been done the cockpit monitor need no longer be focused on the target. The missile will automatically home on its target, regardles of subsequent action by the aircraft, which is free to take evasive action and leave the target area. The Maverick was thus one of our first ''launch-and-leave'' or ''fire-and-forget'' missiles, a capability that has so far been developed only against stationary or slow-moving ground targets that are unable to move beyond a missile's limited field of view before being struck. In air-to-air or surface-to-air combat, missiles fired at rapidly moving aerial targets continue to require some form of guidance from their point of launch.

Yet the Maverick remains a formidable air-to-ground weapon, highly effective against field fortifications, tanks and other pinpoint targets. The AGM-65A was followed in 1976 by the AGM-65B Scene Magnification Maverick, with optics arranged for an enlarged view of the target, permitting earlier target acquisition and somewhat increasing the missile's range from 27 to 33 miles.

The AGM-65C, a laser-guided Maverick, was introduced in 1977. The first Maverick capable of operation by day or night, it is guided to its target by a laser designator in either the Westinghouse Pave Spike or the Ford Aerospace Pave Tack pod, or by a ground designator. This was followed by the AGM-65D, an imaging infrared version effective by day or night, in haze, smoke or cloud, and using the same Texas Instruments infrared seeker employed in the USAF GBU-15 and USN Walleye glide bombs. The AGM-65D has an extended range of 54 miles. Production of 15,000 AGM-65D Mavericks is planned.

**Type:** Medium-range air-to-surface missile, powered by Thiokol TX-481 solid propellant.

**Weight:** 460 lbs (AGM-65A/B/D/C), or 580 lbs (with Mk 19 250-lb fragmentation warhead).

**Speed:** Mach 1.2 (792 mph).

**Guidance:** TV (AGM-65A/B), Laser (AGM-65C) or IIH (AGM-65D).

**Range:** 27 miles (AGM-65A), 33 miles (AGM-65B/C), 54 miles (AGM-65D).

**Manufacturer:** Hughes Aircraft Company. In production and development.

**Produced:** Over 20,000, including 14,600 AGM-65A, 6,350 AGM-65B, 100 AGM-65C, and several prototypes of AGM-65D, of which 15,000 are planned. Production of AGM-65B continues, and procurement of additional AGM-65C in anticipated.

**Exported under FMS:** 5,950.

**In US Service:** Approximately 15,000 AGM-65A/B and 100 AGM-65C.

**In Service Abroad:** Iran (2,850 AGM-65A), Israel (600 AGM-65A), Saudi Arabia (650) AGM-65A), South Korea (200 AGM-65A), and Sweden (1,000 AGM-65A).

**Price:** $23,000 @ (1979 Unit Procurement Cost for 1,500 AGM-65B to USAF). $23,714 @ (1978 Unit Procurement Cost for 350 AGM-65B to USAF). $376,000 @ (1978 Unit Procurement Cost for 100 AGM-65C to USAF). $18,450 @ (1976 Unit Procurement Cost for 4,000 AGM-65A and 2,000 AGM-65B to USAF). $31,000 @ (1978 estimated of anticipated Unit Procurement Cost for 15,000 AGM-65D, in 1977 dollars).

**Recent Transfers:** 2,500 AGM-65A to Iran in 1973 for $25,600 @. 1,000 AGM-65A to Saudi Arabia in 1976 for $47,000 @. 1,000 AGM-65A to Sweden in 1976 for $21,700 @. 200 AGM-65A to South Korea in 1977 for $51,000 @.

**FMS Orders Pending:** Saudi Arabia requested 1,500 AGM-65A in 1976, and 650 were approved for sale in 1977. The Saudis have again requested the balance of 850. Additional requests, not yet approved, are pending from Brazil, Chile, Ethiopia, Malaysia, Taiwan, Tunisia and Venezuela.

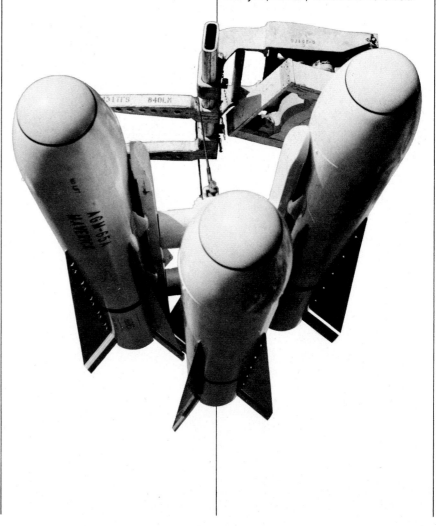

# AGM-53A CONDOR

A long-range supersonic air-to-surface missile developed for our Navy in 1966 as a standoff weapon against ships and other heavily-defended surface targets. Powered by a Rocketdyne solid propellant motor, and with a speed of Mach 2.9 (1,914 mph) and a range of over 70 miles, the Condor is launched toward its target, which has been acquired on a television display in the cockpit, guided by data link transmissions from a control pod attached to the aircraft and housing a navigational computer, and locked on the target by television alignment during the terminal phase of its flight. Its electro-optical seeker has an adjustable field of view, widened for improved target acquisition at long range and narrowed to eliminate background clutter as it homes on its target. Under development is a YAGM-53A1 Turbo Condor powered by a Garret AiResearch turbojet engine, with a range of 120 miles. The Navy has anticipated procurement of a total of 583 Condors and 65 pod control systems, to be operated by TRAM conversions of the Grumman A-6E Intruder aircraft. 305 of the missiles have been produced to date.

**Type:** Long-range air-to-surface missile, powered by solid propellant or turbojet.

**Weight:** 2,130 lbs with 630-lb warhead.

**Speed:** Mach 2.9 (1,914 mph).

**Guidance:** Data link and TV Homing.

**Range:** 70 miles (AGM-53A), or 120 miles (YAGM-53A1 Turbo Condor).

**Manufacturer:** Missile Systems Division, Rockwell International.

**Produced:** 305 of a total planned procurement of 583.

**In US Service:** 305.

**Price:** $292,500@ (1977 Unit Procurement Cost for 40 AGM-53A to USN). $447,551@ (1976 Unit Procurement Cost for 215 AGM-53A to USN).

# AGM-45A SHRIKE

Our first ARM (Anti-Radiation Missile), the Shrike was specifically developed in 1961 to counter the threat of Soviet surface-to-air missiles by destroying the radars that guided them. With a speed of Mach 2 and a range of from 19 to 25 miles, the Shrike uses passive radar homing with a seeker head adjusted to a specific frequency bandwidth known to be used by one of several hostile air defense radars. With a proximity-fused fragmentation warhead, it homes in on the radar emissions to which it has been attuned, and detonates at the radar site.

Developed by Texas Instruments and the Univac Division of Sperry Rand, and based in part on the AIM-7 Sparrow airframe, the first Shrike missiles entered service with carrier-based USN aircraft in 1964, and they were extensively used in Vietnam by the Navy and by Air Force F-105G Wild Weasel aircraft, specially equipped for the defense suppression role. Employed against early warning, ground control intercept and air defense radars, these missiles proved unreliable at first, but continued combat experience in Vietnam provided a convenient laboratory in which to work out their deficiencies. The frequency bandwidths of a variety of Soviet and other radars currently operational have now been identified with sufficient accuracy to have engendered 13 separate Shrike seeker heads, each of which is pretuned to a different bandwidth, the X and C bands, for example, being covered by the AGM-45A1, AGM-45A1A and AGM-45A2.

During the Middle-Eastern war in 1973, several hundred Shrikes were supplied to Israel with seeker heads pretuned at 2965-2990 MHz and 3025-3050 MHz, the bandwidths employed by Fanson A and B radars guiding SA-2 Guideline and SA-3 Goa surface-to-air missiles supplied by the Soviet Union to Egypt. Over 25,000 Shrike missiles have been produced.

**Type:** Medium-range anti-radiation missile, powered either by Rocketdyne Mk 39 Mod 7 or Aerojet Mk 53 solid propellant.

**Weight:** 400 lbs.

**Speed:** Mach 2 (1,320 mph).

**Range:** 19 to 25 miles.

**Guidance:** Passive radar homing, at preset frequency.

**Manufacturer:** Texas Instruments, and Univac.

**Produced:** Over 25,000.

**Exported under FMS:** 770.

**In US Service:** Approximately 21,260 with 13 separate types of seeker head.

**In Service Abroad:** Israel (490).

**Price:** $51,333@ (1979 Unit Procurement Cost for 600 AGM-45A to USN). $45,777@ (1978 Unit Procurement Cost for 900 AGM-45A to USAF/USN). $39,921@ (1977 Unit Procurement Cost for 1,275 AGM-45A to USAF/USN). $43,333@ (1976 Unit Procurement Cost for 1,350 AGM-45A to USAF/USN).

# AGM-78 STANDARD ARM/RGM-66D

First developed in 1966, this is an anti-radiation version of the Navy's RIM-66A Standard surface-to-surface missile, and can be used either as an air-to-surface weapon (AGM-78) or as a surface-to-surface ship-launched weapon (RGM-66D). The Navy is planning to equip 12 guided missile destroyers and 4 patrol boats with the RGM-66D. Both versions are used in conjunction with a TIAS (Target Identification and Acquisition System) using an IBM 4-Pi digital computer. The TIAS computes a full trajectory for the missile to its target, based on immediate analysis of the type and location of hostile radar emissions received before those emissions can be shut off. In combat in Vietnam, using the AGM-45A Shrike ARM, it was found that enemy radar operators would frequently shut off their radars so that the Shrike would not have time enough to home in on the source of emissions. The Standard ARM system is designed to counter this practice, an alternative means for which is the use of a missile travelling at much higher speed—now the subject of a separate program in development. The AGM-78B, using a seeker head developed by Maxson Electronics, went into service in 1968 with USN A-6A Intruder and USAF F-105F Wild Weasel aircraft. An improved AGM-78D with a seeker head developed by General Dynamics is planned for use by the Navy's EA-6B Prowler and E-2C Hawkeye aircraft.

**Type:** Short-range air-to-surface or surface-to-surface anti-radiation missile, powered by Aerojet Mk 27 Mod 4 solid propellant.

**Weight:** 1,400 lbs.

**Speed:** Mach 2 (1,320 mph).

**Range:** 15.5 miles.

**Guidance:** Passive broad-band radar homing, in conjunction with TIAS.

**Manufacturer:** General Dynamics, and Maxson Electronics.

**Produced:** 616 AGM-78A/B/C and 88 RGM-66D.

**In US Service:** Approximately 450 of all types. To be used on USAF F-4G Wild Weasel II.

**Price:** $127,600@ (1973 Unit Procurement Cost of 212 AGM-78C to USAF).

# AGM-84A HARPOON RGM-84A

A costly but devastating long-range anti-ship missile with highly sophisticated guidance, now in service with our Navy and in nine other countries, and shortly to join the inventories of another two. The Harpoon can be launched from aircraft or submarines as well as surface vessels, and carries a 500-lb high explosive warhead. Powered by a Teledyne CAE J402-CA-400 turbojet cruise motor, it has an all-weather capability and a range of 90 miles. Compatible with our Navy's AS-ROC, Tartar, Terrier and Mk 26 missile launchers, it can also be carried by the P-3 Orion, S-3 Viking, A-7 Corsair II or A-6 Intruder aircraft. Launched into an initial high arc, the Harpoon drops back to a low, flat trajectory, inertially guided toward the target, and kept at a height of only several feet above the surface of the sea by a radar altimeter. It uses active radar homing during its terminal phase of flight, gaining altitude to present a more difficult target for ship-based air defense weapons, and dropping down on its target at a steep angle.

The Harpoon has undergone a variety of successful test launches from surface vessels, submarine torpedo tubes, aircraft and a hydrofoil patrol boat, against both fixed and moving targets. In June of 1974 an air-to-surface version, the AGM-84A, was launched from a P-3A Orion patrol aircraft and sank a destroyer. Several nations have ordered substantial quantities of the Harpoon, including Iran, which purchased 222, to arm its P-3F Orion patrol aircraft and its Spruance class destroyers now under construction in the United States, and Saudi Arabia, which purchased 117 to arm 24 patrol vessels that are also under construction in this country.

**Type:** Long-range surface-to-surface, air-to-surface and subsurface-to-surface missile, powered by turbojet engine.

**Weight:** 1,100 lbs (AGM-84A), or 1,400 lbs (RGM-84A).

**Speed:** Mach .94 (620 mph).

**Range:** 90 miles.

**Guidance:** Inertial guidance and active radar terminal homing.

**Manufacturer:** McDonnell Douglas, with Texas Instruments.

**Produced:** Over 2,000 to date.

**Exported under FMS:** 1,011.

**In US Service:** 1,091 AGM-84A and RGM-84A, out of a planned procurement of 2,922.

**In Service Abroad:** Denmark (20), Iran (222), Israel (100), Netherlands (12), Saudi Arabia (117), South Korea (120), Turkey (40), United Kingdom (300), and West Germany (80).

**Price:** $537,500@ (1979 Unit Procurement Cost for 240 AGM-84A to USN). $485,079@ (1978 Unit Procurement Cost for 315 AGM-84A to USN). $589,795@ (1977 Unit Procurement Cost for 245 RGM-84A to USN). $734,199@ (1976 Unit Procurement Cost for 231 RGM-84A to USN). $534,700@ (1975 Unit Procurement Cost for 150 AGM-84A to USN).

**FMS Deliveries Pending:** Australia (56), Japan (38), United Kingdom (118).

**FMS Orders Pending:** Denmark may order another 280 missiles.

**Recent Transfers:** 222 AGM-84A to Iran in 1973 for $630,000@ 20 RGM-84A to Denmark in 1974 for $500,000@. 100 RGM-84A to Israel in 1975 for $135,000@. 12 RGM-84A to the Netherlands in 1975 for $333,000@. 120 RGM-84A to South Korea in 1975 for $675,000@. 33 AGM-84A to Turkey in 1977 for $105,000@. 300 RGM-84A to the United Kingdom in 1977 for $589,000@.

# RIM-8 TALOS

A long-range ship-based surface-to-air missile capable also of surface-to-surface applications and equipped either with a nuclear or a proximity-fused high explosive warhead, though today only the latter type is used. Powered by a Bendix liquid fueled ramjet sustainer and an Allegheny Ballistics tandem solid propellant booster, the Talos can be employed either as a single or dual-stage missile, selectable from the ship's magazine by an automatic loader, depending on the range to the target. It has a speed of Mach 2.5 (1,650 mph) and a maximum range of 75 miles. With a controlled radar beam-riding guidance system, it employs semi-active radar homing in its terminal stage of flight.

Development of the Talos began as long ago as 1944 under Project Bumblebee, carried out by the Applied Physics Laboratory of Johns Hopkins University. It was not until 1959, however, that the first Talos launcher was installed on the cruiser CLG-3 USS Galveston. In 1968, the light cruiser CGN-9 USS Long Beach successfully destroyed two MiG-21 aircraft in the Tonkin Gulf off Vietnam using Talos missiles at ranges of over 60 miles. The Talos is now being replaced by the RIM-67A ER (Extended Range) version of the General Dynamics Standard missile, but will remain in limited use in our Navy through the 1980s. A RIM-8H anti-radiation version is also in service.

**Type:** Long-range surface-to-air or surface-to-surface missile, powered by single or dual-stage liquid and solid propellants.

**Weight:** 7,000 lbs.

**SPEED:** Mach 2.5 (1,650 mph).

**Range:** 75 miles.

**Guidance:** Controlled radar beam-riding and terminal SARH.

**Manufacturer:** The Bendix Corporation.

**Produced:** Over 2,800.

**In US Service:** On USN heavy cruisers CG-10 USS Albany, CG-11 USS Chicago, and CG-12 USS Columbus, and guided missile cruisers CLG-3 USS Galveston, CG-4 USS Little Rock, CG-5 USS Oklahoma City, and CGN-9 USS Long Beach.

# RIM-2 TERRIER

A ship-based surface-to-air missile that has been in service with our Navy since 1956, and is now being gradually replaced either by the BPDMS (Basic Point Defense Missile System) using the RIM-7 Sea Sparrow, or by the RIM-67A ER (Extended Range) version of the Standard missile. It employs radar beam-riding guidance and terminal semi-active radar homing, has a maximum speed of Mach 2.1 (1,386 mph), a range of 22 miles, and a ceiling of 65,000 feet.

A further outgrowth of Johns Hopkins University's Project Bumblebee, begun in 1944, the Terrier was the subject of an initial development contract placed in 1949 with the Consolidated Vultee Company, which later became Convair and is now General Dynamics. It was the first in a family of ship-based missiles produced by General Dynamics that have undergone successive modifications and improvements over the past thirty years, including conversion to solid-state electronics and, at the beginning of their evolution, the development and incorporation of rocket motors with much higher thrust to achieve the speeds required to intercept the new types of supersonic aircraft that had begun to appear for the first time in the 1950s. The General Dynamics Standard missile is the most recent in this series.

Terriers first came into service aboard the cruisers CA-69 USS Boston and CA-70 USS Canberra, and were followed by Terrier installations on all USN attack carriers, some of which have subsequently reequipped with the BPDMS. A RIM-2D was developed with a nuclear warhead, and an improved RIM-2F with a proximity-fused high explosive warhead was operational in 1963. The Terrier also equips one Dutch and three Italian cruisers.

**Type:** Long-range surface-to-air missile, powered by two-stage solid propellant.

**Weight:** 3,000 lbs.

**Speed:** Mach 2.1 (1,386 mph).

**Range:** 22 miles.

**Ceiling:** 65,000 feet.

**Guidance:** Controlled radar beam-riding and terminal SARH.

**Manufacturer:** General Dynamics.

**Produced:** Over 3,000.

**Exported under FMS:** 194.

**Exported under MAP:** 114.

**In US Service:** On USN carriers CV-63 USS Kitty Hawk, CV-64 USS Constellation, and CF-66 USS America, and on cruisers CA-69 USS Boston, CA-70 USS Canberra, CG-6 USS Providence, CG-16 USS Leahy, CG-26 USS Belknap, CGN-9 USS Long Beach, CGN-25 USS Bainbridge, and CGN-35 USS Truxton.

**In Service Abroad:** Italy (cruisers Andrea Doria, Caio Duilio and Vittorio Veneto), and Peru (former Dutch cruiser De Zeven Provincien, which may be reequipped with Soviet SA-3 if the U.S. insists on removing its Terriers).

# RIM-24 TARTAR

A ship-based short-range surface-to-air missile similar in configuration to the final stage of the RIM-2 Terrier without its first stage booster. Using an Aerojet one-stage dual-thrust solid propellant, it achieves a speed of Mach 2.8 (1,848 mph), and has a maximum range of 10 miles. Guided by semi-active radar homing, and with a proximity-fused

**McDonnell Douglas AGM–84A Harpoon**

high explosive warhead, it became operational in 1961 as primary air defense armament for all USN destroyers and destroyer escorts, and secondary armament for USN cruisers. Now being replaced by the RIM-66A MR (Medium Range) Standard missile, it remains in service with 29 of our destroyers, 6 frigates and 3 cruisers, and is in service abroad in five countries.

**Type:** Short-range surface-to-air missile, powered by solid propellant.

**Weight:** 1,300 lbs.

**Speed:** Mach 2.8 (1,848 mph).

**Range:** 10 miles.

**Guidance:** SARH.

**Manufacturer:** General Dynamics.

**Produced:** Over 6,500.

**Exported under FMS:** 647.

**Exported under MAP:** 100.

**In US Service:** On 23 destroyers of DDG-2 USS Charles F. Adams class, 4 destroyers of DDG-31 USS Decatur class, 2 destroyers of DDG-35 USS Mitscher class, 6 frigates of FFG-1 USS Brooke class, and on cruisers CG-10 USS Albany, CGN-36 USS California and CGN-38 USS Virginia.

**In Service Abroad:** Australia (3 destroyers), France (4 Surcouf class destroyers), Italy (destroyers Impavido and Intrepido), Japan (1 destroyer), and West Germany (3 destroyers).

# RIM-66A
# RIM-67A STANDARD

These are the current USN surface-to-air missiles, the RIM-66A MR (Medium Range) replacing the Tartar and the RIM-67A ER (Extended Range) replacing the Terrier. Until the operational deployment in 1975 of the RGM-84A Harpoon, the Standard missiles also served as surface-to-surface weapons. Developed in 1964, they first entered service in 1971, the RIM-66A equipping the destroyer DDG-14 USS Buchanan. Guided by semi-active radar homing, the RIM-66A has a maximum range of 15 miles and the RIM-67A 35 miles, while both the MR and ER versions have a maximum ceiling of 65,000 feet. Anti-radiation versions of both missiles have been developed. By 1971, more than 70 surface vessels of the USN had been equipped with the Standard ME and ER.

Improvements in the Standard missile propulsion system, conversion to solid-state electronics, an all-electric control system, and a new guidance system employing command data link for mid-course corrections and terminal active radar homing, developed MR and ER versions with much greater accuracy and substantially longer ranges, respectively, of 30 and 60 miles.

These versions of the Standard missile have been designated SM-2, while all earlier versions are now designated SM-1. The RIM-66C and RIM-67C Standard SM-2 missiles will be used in the Navy's highly sophisticated and extravagantly expensive new AEGIS air defense system, which employs the Westinghouse AN/SPY-1 multifunction phased array radar, capable of simultaneous tracking and surveillance of multiple targets, a dual-purpose launcher that can interchangeably select, load and fire ASROC, Harpoon, SM-2 MR and SM-2 ER missiles, an AN/UYK-7 digital computer and the Mk 12 weapon direction system, Mk 99 fire control system, and Mk 130 command and control system. A new destroyer equipped with the AEGIS system was estimated to cost $858.5 million in 1977, and is currently estimated to cost $930 million.

**Type:** Ship-launched medium-range (RIM-66) or long-range (RIM-67) missile, powered, respectively, by a one stage or two-stage dual-thrust solid propellant.

**Weight:** 1,300 lbs (RIM-66 MR), or 3,000 lbs (RIM-67 ER).

**Speed:** Mach 2.8 (1,848 mph).

**Range:** 15 miles (RIM-66A SM-1 MR), 30 miles (RIM-66C SM-2 MR), 35 miles (RIM-67A SM-1 ER), or 60 miles (RIM-67C SM-2 ER).

**Guidance:** SARH (SM-1) or command data link and TARH (SM-2).

**Manufacturer:** General Dynamics.

**Produced:** Over 2,700 RIM-66A/B/C, RIM-67A/B/C, RTM-66D and RGM-66D/E (E version for ASROC launchers).

**Exported under FMS:** 301, with 989 on order.

**In US Service:** 2,435 of all types on more than 70 USN surface vessels.

**In Service Abroad:** Italy (2 destroyers and 3 cruisers) and West Germany (7 destroyers).

**Price:** $1.292 million@ (1979 Unit Procurement Cost for 40 SM-2 ER to USN). $1.192 million@ (1978 Unit Procurement Cost for 40 SM-2 ER to USN). $1.272 million@ (1977 Unit Procurement Cost for 36 SM-1 ER to USN). $2.431 million@ (1976 Unit Procurement Cost for 22 SM-1 ER to USN). $139,700@ (1974 Unit Procurement Cost for 22 SM-1 ER to USN). $192,083@ (1979 Unit Procurement Cost for 480 SM-2 MR to USN). $212,798@ (1978 Unit Procurement Cost for 480 SM-2 MR to USN). $148,600@ (1977 Unit Procurement Cost for 500 SM-1 MR to USN). $140,400@ (1976 Unit Procurement Cost for 250 SM-1 MR to USN). $106,500 (1974 Unit Procurement Cost for 444 SM-1 MR to USN).

**FMS Deliveries Pending:** *Australia, Israel, Japan, the Netherlands, and South Korea.*

# RUR-5A ASROC

The primary ship-launched anti-submarine weapon system in our Navy, ASROC (Anti-Submarine Rocket) is a rocket motor attached to the General Electric Mk 44 high-speed 1,000-lb acoustic-homing torpedo, the Aerojet-General Mk 46 Mod 0 570-lb acoustic-homing torpedo, the Honeywell Mk 46 Mod 1 torpedo or the Mk 57 or Mk 101 nuclear depth charge. It can be launched either from the Mk 46 8-round ASROC launcher or from the Mk 10 twin Terrier launcher, and it has a range of from 1 to 6 miles. After a submarine has been detected by ship sonar, its range, speed and directional bearing are computed and the ASROC launcher is aimed in the direction of the target. In unguided flight after launch, the weapon follows a ballistic trajectory until the rocket motor is shut off and jettisoned at a preset range. Torpedoes are dropped into the water by parachute, and activate their homing systems upon immersion, while depth charges detonate at preselected depths. First developed in 1956, ASROC went into operational service in 1961, and today equips 31 cruisers, 133 destroyers and 78 frigates of the United States Navy fleet, as well as the surface vessels of six other nations. An ASROC motor is being developed with an extended range of 12 miles.

**Type:** Ship-launched rocket system for surface-to-subsurface delivery, powered by solid propellant.

**Weight:** 640 lbs. Total weight with Mk 44 torpedo: 1,640 lbs. With Mk 46: 1,210 lbs.

**Speed:** Mach .85 (561 mph).

**Range:** 1 to 6 miles.

**Guidance:** Ballistically aimed for unguided flight.

**Manufacturer:** Honeywell, Inc.

**Produced:** Over 20,000 units.

**Exported under FMS:** 480.

**Exported under MAP:** 302.

**In US Service:** Over 3,000 on 242 USN surface vessels.

**In Service Abroad:** Canada (7 destroyers), Italy (1 cruiser), Japan (8 destroyers), Spain (2 destroyers), Turkey (2 destroyers), and West Germany (3 destroyers).

# MGM-29A SERGEANT

A surface-to-surface battlefield support missile first developed in 1955 to replace the Army's Corporal as a heavy field artillery tactical weapon assigned to fire support at the corps level. Inertially guided, maneuvering with hinged tail surfaces and jet-deflection vanes, the Sergeant is powered by a Thiokol M-100 single-stage solid propellant motor, and has a range of from 25 to 85 miles. It can carry either a nuclear or a high explosive warhead. Since production of the Sergeant ended, improvements in the guidance and propulsion systems, and the incorporation of a new digital computer, have greatly simplified operational procedures for handling the weapon, and have reduced the reaction time of firing units. The system is now fully mobile and air-transportable, and a crew of six can emplace and fire one of the missiles in less than ten minutes. A Sergeant battalion is composed of three batteries, each with a single launcher, and three battalions with a total of nine launchers are usually assigned to a field army. In support of a multidivision front, their conventional firepower is awesome. The detonation of a high explosive Sergeant warhead is sufficient to collapse a single-span steel bridge, or directed against concentrations of troops create lethal shrapnel over an area of almost one square mile.

**Type:** Surface-to-surface battlefield support missile, powered by solid propellant.

**Weight:** 10,000 lbs.

**Speed:** 690 mph.

**Range:** 25 to 85 miles.

**Guidance:** Inertial.

**Manufacturer:** Univac Division of Sperry Rand.

**Produced:** Over 700.

**Exported under FMS:** 195.

**Exported under MAP:** 19

**In US Service:** Approximately 500.

**In Service Abroad:** West Germany (214).

# MGR-1 HONEST JOHN/M-50

A surface-to-surface battlefield support missile first developed in 1950. The MGR-1A was operational by 1953 and an improved version, the MGR-1B, was introduced in 1960 and later redesignated M-50. It remains in service with the United States Army and in eleven countries abroad, though it is undergoing gradual replacement by the MGM-52 Lance. Each Honest John is individually launched by its own truck transporter. Powered by a Hercules M-31A1 solid propellant motor, the missile is unguided and ballistically aimed at its target, with a maximum range of 25 miles. It can be fitted either with a 1,500-lb high explosive warhead or a nuclear warhead with a yield of 100 kilotons. In 1957 a smaller 380mm missile weighing 780 lbs was developed and introduced into service the following year as the MGR-3A Littlejohn, and later redesignated M-15. The Littlejohn could be towed by a 3/4 ton truck or jeep on the M-34 launcher, and had a range of 10 miles.

**Type:** Surface-to-surface battlefield support missile, powered by solid propellant.

**Weight:** 4,700 lbs (Honest John), or 780 lbs (Littlejohn).

**Speed:** Mach 1.5 (900 mph).

**Range:** From 5 to 25 miles (Honest John), or from 2 to 10 miles (Littlejohn).

**Guidance:** Ballistically aimed.

**Manufacturer:** Douglas Aircraft and Emerson Electric Company.

**Produced:** Over 14,000 of MGR-1A and MGR-1B, and 3,600 MGR-3A.

**Exported under FMS:** 204 MGR-1A/B.

**Exported under MAP:** 300 MGR-1A/B.

**In US Service:** Approximately 120 MGR-1B, redesignated M-50, in U.S. Army.

**In Service Abroad:** Belgium (24), Denmark (12), France (72), Greece (24), Italy (24), Japan (96), Netherlands (24), South Korea (12), Turkey (36), United Kingdom (48), and West Germany (132).

**Recent Transfers:** In 1977 Turkey purchased 36 new cluster fragmentation warheads for its Honest John missiles for $4,027@.

# MGM-52 LANCE

A mobile and highly accurate surface-to-surface battlefield support missile developed in 1962 as a replacement for both the Sergeant and Honest John systems. With a range of from 3 to 75 miles and a speed of Mach 3 (1,980 mph), the Lance uses simplified inertial guidance with mid-course corrections supplied by command data link from a master ground control DME (Distance Measuring Equipment) station, which makes constant precision measurements of the missile's path. The high speed of the Lance, with a maximum flight time of 200 seconds, is achieved through the use of a storable liquid propellant, the first ever used for a missile by the United States Army, a pre-packed Rocketdyne dual-thrust system in two hermetically sealed cylindrical tanks, one containing UDMH (Unsymmetrical Dimethyl Hydrazine) fuel and the other IRFNA (Inhibited Red Fuming Nitric Acid) as an oxidizer. Two types of warhead are used, the 450-lb M-234 nuclear warhead with a yield of 10 kilotons, or a Honeywell 1,000-lb XM-251 cluster fragmentation warhead packed with 836 BLU-63 bomblets whose lethal fragments saturate an area over 900 yards in diameter. The XM-251 warhead equips Lance missiles in service in Israel and the Netherlands, and is now being supplied to units of the United States Army.

**LTV Aerospace Corporation's
MGM–52 Lance on M-752 vehicle**

Lance can be carried either on the M-752 vehicle, a fully-tracked carrier with a top speed of 40 mph, produced by the FMC Corporation, or by a lightweight wheeled launcher made by the Canadian firm of Orenda and designed compactly so that it may be carried by helicopter. One loaded launcher and two spare missiles on a second vehicle normally comprise a battery, two or three of which may be assigned to each Lance battalion. The Israeli Army has organized a Lance brigade with two battalions, each with nine M-752 launch or support vehicles, and is now forming a third battalion. Eight Lance battalions of the United States Army are now deployed in West Germany. The United Kingdom is forming its Lance battalions into regiments, and has now fully equipped its 50th Regiment of Royal Artillery with the Lance.

**Type:** Surface-to-surface battlefield support missile, powered by liquid propellant.

**Weight:** 3,424 lbs with XM-251 warhead, or 2,901 lbs with M-234 warhead.

**Speed:** Mach 3 (1,980 mph).

**Range:** 3 to 75 miles.

**Guidance:** Simplified inertial, with command data link from DME.

**Manufacturer:** LTV Aerospace Corporation. In production.

**Produced:** Over 2,200 to date.

**Exported under FMS:** 773.

**In US Service:** 1,454 in U.S. Army.

**In Service Abroad:** Belgium (60), Israel (330), Italy (60), Netherlands (60), United Kingdom (200), and West Germany (175).

**Price:** $357.222@ (1979 Unit Procurement Cost for 180 MGM-52 to U.S. Army). $413,888@ (1978 Unit Procurement Cost for 180 MGM-52 to U.S. Army). $206,944@ (1977 Unit Procurement Cost for 360 MGM-52 to U.S. Army). $335,600@ (1975 Unit Procurement Cost for 194 MGM-52 to U.S. Army). $222,200@ (1974 Unit Procurement Cost for 360 MGM-52 to U.S. Army). $258,300@ (1973 Unit Procurement Cost for 360 MGM-52 to U.S. Army).

**FMS Deliveries Pending:** Israel (109).

**Recent Transfers:** 200 MGM-52 and 36 M-752 to United Kingdom in 1974 for $128 million. 175 MGM-52 and 24 M-752 to West Germany in 1974 for $100 million. 60 MGM-52 and 9 M-752 to the Netherlands in 1975 for $35 million. 60 MGM-52 and 9 M-752 to Italy in 1975 for $36 million.

# M-47 DRAGON

Originally known as MAW (Medium Antitank assault Weapon), the Dragon is an infantry weapon system originally intended as a replacement for the 90mm recoilless rifle, and light enough to be carried and fired by one man. The missile itself, weighing 27 lbs and powered by 30 pairs of small side-thrusting rocket motors with a solid propellant, mounts a high-energy shaped charge warhead. Direct hits will penetrate medium and heavy armour plate. Developed in 1964, the Dragon first entered service with United States forces in 1973. Over 100,000 of these missiles have already been produced, and large numbers equip seven foreign armies thus far.

Carried in a sealed fiberglass transport and storage container that is also its own launch tube, the Dragon is guided by wire. From a sitting position, the operator stands the front end of the launch tube on a folding bipod rest with the back end over his shoulder, and attaches a tracking unit that contains a telescopic sight, sensor and electronic controls. Having acquired a target and launched the missile, he need only keep the target in the crosshairs of the sight. The tracker senses the position of the missile in relation to the target position established through the sight, and through a wire that unreels from the missile automatically transmits signals to maintain or correct its flight. The missile steers in response to these commands by adjusting the propulsive force of one or more pairs of its side-thrusting rocket motors.

While the Dragon is a highly effective weapon, a recent Army TRADOC (Training and Doctrine Command) report found that 47 percent of the trained Dragon crewmen could

not distinguish between Soviet and United States tanks, and that Dragon training simulators were of doubtful value in familiarizing these men with the missile's operational characteristics.

**Type:** Man-portable antitank missile, powered by solid propellant motors.

**Weight:** 27 lbs.

**Speed:** 560 mph.

**Range:** 3,280 feet.

**Guidance:** Wire-guided command to line of sight.

**Manufacturer:** McDonnell Douglas, and Raytheon.

**Produced:** Over 103,720 to date.

**Exported under FMS:** 37,960.

**Exported under MAP:** 1,440.

**In US Service:** 87,298 M-47 missiles and 7,750 tracking units in U.S. Army and USMC.

**In Service Abroad:** Denmark (3,000 M-47 and 450 Trackers), Iran (10,000 M-47 and 1,500 Trackers), Israel (4,000 M-47 and 600 Trackers), Jordan (2,500 M-47 and 380 Trackers), Netherlands (2,300 M-47 and 350 Trackers), Saudi Arabia (4,000 M-47 and 600 Trackers), and Switzerland (13,600 M-47 and 2,000 Trackers).

**Price:** $4,358@ (1978 Unit Procurement Cost for 20,671 M-47). $5,317@ (1977 Unit Procurement Cost for 16,080 M-57). $4,468@ (1976 Unit Procurement Cost for 34,443 M-47). $6,400@ (1976 Unit Procurement Cost for 15,154 M-47). $8,700@ (1974 Unit Procurement Cost for 7,000 M-47). $12,300@ (1973 Unit Procurement Cost for 3,950 M-47).

**Recent Transfers:** 10,000 M-47 and 1,500 Trackers to Iran in 1976 for $146.8 million. 4,000 M-47 and 600 Trackers to Saudi Arabia in 1976 for $26.1 million. 2,300 M-47 and 350 Trackers to the Netherlands in 1977 for $37.1 million. 3,800 M-47 and 400 Trackers to Morocco in 1977 for $57 million, delivery in 1979.

**McDonnell Douglas Raytheon
47 Dragon in firing position**

# MGM-71 TOW

A heavy antitank assault missile that is one of the most effective weapons of its kind. Developed as a replacement for the 106mm recoilless rifle, it first entered service in 1970, and was used to great effect in Vietnam, as well as on the Sinai front during the Middle-Eastern war of 1973. Today it is the subject of several programs to improve our antitank defense capabilities, including air-to-surface applications as standard armament for the Army's AH-1Q and AH-1S Cobra attack helicopters, the Marine Corp's AH-1T Cobra, and the new Hughes AH-64 attack helicopter. It is stocked in very large numbers in our own military services, and in those of 23 countries abroad. Over 217,000 of these missiles have been produced to date.

TOW (Tube-launched, Optically-tracked, Wire-guided) is powered by a Hercules K-41 solid propellant, and originally had a maximum range of 3,283 yards, but an improved version now in service has an extended range of 4,687 yards. Its warhead, a high-explosive armour-piercing shaped charge, produces heat of an intensity and directional force sufficient to melt and penetrate all known thicknesses of armour, leaving gaps, for example, of as much as two feet in diameter in the hull fronts and turret plating of a Soviet T-62 tank. The explosive blast will cut through three feet of concrete, or sever double foot-thick fortification logs.

Weighing just over 43 lbs, the TOW is fired from a fiberglass launch tube with an advanced optical sight equipped with a sensor and linked to an electronic guidance computer. Through its sight the magnification is such that the image of a tank at 1,000 yards will entirely fill the scope of the glass. Keeping the cross-hairs of his sight squarely on the target, the gunner fires, and the sensor tracks a light source in the departing missile in order to measure the angle between its direction of flight and the gunner's line of sight. Displacements in angle are automati-

**Hughes MGM-71 TOW**

cally transformed by the computer into steering commands, which are transmitted through two wires that uncoil as the missile flies. Promptly responding to these commands, the missile steers itself aerodynamically, twisting to adjust the angle of one of its rudders or wings to the air flow.

The TOW missile is powered by two rocket motors, one which burns out by the time it has left the launch tube, and another which doesn't ignite until it has travelled a safe distance away from the point of launch. Thus no protection is needed against hot exhaust gases. The second flight motor quickly accelerates the missile to its peak speed of 368 mph and then burns out. This procedure makes it impossible for an enemy to trace a visible smoke trail back to the missile's true point of origin.

The TOW launcher and guidance system weigh 158 lbs, and can be carried in pieces, assembled, loaded and fired in three minutes from a ground tripod mount by a crew of four infantrymen. Alternatively, the launcher can be mounted on the M-113A1 armoured personnel carrier, the M-151A2 jeep, the M-274 Mechanical Mule, or the XR-311 high-mobility reconnaissance vehicle with provision for a load of ten missiles. As helicopter armament, six TOW missiles can be carried by the UH-1B, eight by the AH-1 Cobra, or a maximum of sixteen by the Hughes AH-64. Emerson Electric has also received a contract from the Army to develop an ITV (Improved Tow Vehicle) based on the M-113, and with a hydraulically extendable arm, articulated on five axes, which supports a platform with two TOW launch tubes and aiming equipment. The ITV will be able to acquire targets and launch missiles from protected positions without exposing its crew to enemy fire. The Army plans procurement of 1,976 ITVs.

**Type:** Surface-to-surface or air-to-surface antitank assault missile, powered by solid propellant.

**Weight:** 43.2 lbs.

**Speed:** 368 mph.

**Range:** 4,687 yards (14,061 feet).

**Guidance:** Wire-guided command to line of sight.

**Manufacturer:** Hughes Aircraft Corporation, and Emerson Electric.

**Produced:** Over 217,000 TOW missiles, 16,200 launchers, and 10,200 helicopter launchers.

**Exported under FMS:** 48,480 TOW missiles and 2,068 launchers.

**Exported under MAP:** 5,620 TOW missiles and 391 launchers.

**In US Service:** Over 168,900 TOW missiles, 13,880 launchers and 7,728 helicopter launchers in U.S. Army and USMC.

**TOW Missiles in Service Abroad:** Canada (2,250), Denmark (712), Greece (1,431), Iran (6,700), Israel (5,000), Italy (5,000), Jordan (940), Kuwait (1,800), Lebanon (1,050), Luxembourg (178), Morocco (907), Netherlands (2,350), Norway (1,610), Oman (890), Pakistan (672), Saudi Arabia (1,000), Spain (3,000), South Korea (4,900), Sweden (6,700), Turkey (1,500), Vietnam (1,200), West Germany (4,000), and Yugoslavia (1,200).

**TOW Launchers in Service Abroad:** Canada (150), Denmark (46), Greece (88), Iran (300), Israel (200), Italy (130), Jordan (58), Kuwait (32), Lebanon (18), Luxembourg (2), Morocco (78), Netherlands (146), Norway (100), Oman (10), Pakistan (44), Saudi Arabia (62), Spain (113), South Korea (260), Sweden (340), Turkey (94), Vietnam (75),

West Germany (177), and Yugoslavia (40).

**Price of Missile:** $6,787@ (1978 Unit Procurement Cost for 14,866 MGM 71). $8,014@ (1977 Unit Procurement Cost for 13,051 MGM-71). $5,626@ (1976 Unit Procurement Cost for 26,926 MGM-71). $4,400@ (1975 Unit Procurement Cost for 30,179 MGM-71). $6,300@ (1974 Unit Procurement Cost for 23,425 MGM-71). $3,500@ (1973 Unit Procurement Cost for 12,000 MGM-71).

**Price of Launcher:** $36,400@ (1978 Manufacturer's Price for Standard Launcher). $42,040@ (1978 Manufacturer's Price for Helicopter Launcher).

**FMS Deliveries Pending:** Iran (8,300 TOW missiles and 150 launchers).

**FMS Orders Pending:** Saudi Arabia (800 TOW missiles requested).

**Recent Transfers:** 5,000 TOW and 130 launchers to Italy in 1972 for $51.2 million. 6,700 TOW and 340 launchers to Sweden in 1973 for $44.9 million. 2,250 TOW and 150 launchers to Canada in 1973 for $30 million. 1,000 TOW and 65 launchers to Israel in 1974 for $46 million. 1,050 TOW and 18 launchers to Lebanon in 1974 for $10 million. 1,610 TOW and 100 launchers to Norway in 1974 for $21.7 million. 4,000 TOW and 177 launchers to West Germany in 1976 for $30.2 million. 15,000 TOW and 550 launchers to Iran in 1976 for $103.9 million.

# MGM-51 SHILLELAGH

A cannon-launched antitank missile with an Octol shaped charge, powered by an Amoco single-stage solid propellant and fired from the 152mm gun and launcher mounted on the M-551 Sheridan reconnaissance tank and the M-60A2 main battle tank. Developed in 1959 and operational in 1967, the Shillelagh is fired with minimal recoil. After it leaves the gun barrel its rocket motor ignites, quickly accelerating it to its top speed of 3,854 feet per second. With a maximum burn time of 1.18 seconds and a total flight time of 4.43 seconds, the missile has a range of up to 5,686 yards (17,060 feet). It is guided by data link command from an infrared tracker which maintains the target in line of sight, and is 90 percent accurate to 3,750 yards. Under 1,250 yards, however, while it is still accelerating to peak speed, it is not accurate at all, and cannot even be steered by the tracker, for it dips below the line of sight until it has reached that range. Since the only other major antitank weapon for the 152mm gun is the M409 HEAT (High Explosive Anti-Tank) projectile, which as a maximum range of only 1,000 yards, tanks equipped with the Shillelagh gun and launcher system are unable to engage targets at all at ranges between 1,000 and 1,250 yards. 36,000 Shillelagh missiles have been produced for the United States Army by Aeronutronic Ford at an approximate cost of $13,890 per round. An additional $12 million development contract has also been awarded to that firm for improvements to the Shillelagh system, which may involve the addition of a booster motor to keep the missile within line of sight at all times, or a new propellant system to ensure a more stable trajectory while it attains its extraordinary speed. Weight of the missile is 59 lbs. None have yet been transferred abroad.

**MGM-51 Shillelagh**

# MIM-72C CHAPARRAL

A low level air defense missile utilizing the AIM-9D infrared homing Sidewinder, with a Mk 36 solid propellant motor, the AN/DAW-1 infrared guidance seeker, an M-250 blast fragmentation warhead developed at the Picatinny Arsenal, and the M-817 proximity fuse developed by Harry Diamond Laboratories. Developed in 1965, the first version of the Chaparral, MIM-72A, had a surface-to-air range of less than 3 miles, and could engage only departing aircraft. The improved MIM-72C can engage aircraft at any angle and attitude, and is effective at somewhat longer ranges with a ceiling of 20,000 feet. The Chaparral system mounts four missiles in ready status on monorail launchers carried on the M-730 tracked vehicle with a crew of five. The launchers have 360 degrees of radius, and the M-730 carries 12 reload missiles. In each of our Army's air defense battalions, two batteries of Chaparral launchers are organized together with two batteries of M-167 self-propelled Vulcan 20mm antiaircraft guns. Chaparral batteries equip units of our Seventh Army in West Germany, have been supplied to Israel, and have been ordered by Tunisia.

**Type:** Surface-to-air close range missile, powered by solid propellant.

**Weight:** 185 lbs.

**Speed:** Mach 2.5 (1,650 mph).

**Range:** 3 to 5 miles. Ceiling: 20,000 feet.

**Guidance:** Optically aimed, IRH.

**Manufacturer:** Aeronutronic Ford.

**Produced:** 6,000 MIM-72A and 3,082 MIM-72C to date.

**Exported under FMS:** 232, with 524 on order.

**In US Service:** Approximately 4,000.

**In Service Abroad:** Israel (190 MIM-72C and 16 M-730 launch vehicles).

**Price:** $35,294@ (1978 Unit Procurement Cost for 850 MIM-72C to U.S. Army). $29,550@ (1977 Unit Procurement Cost for 2,000 MIM-72C to U.S. Army).

**FMS Deliveries Pending:** Israel (440 MIM-72C), Tunisia (84 MIM-72C and 4 M-730).

**FMS Orders Pending:** Jordan, Morocco, Saudi Arabia, Turkey.

# MIM-23 HAWK

The most sophisticated, maneuverable and reliable surface-to-air missile in the world, with a kill-per-engagement record of 96 percent obtained in combat in the Middle East and Southeast Asia and in tests conducted since it first entered service in 1960, the HAWK (Homing All-the-Way Killer) today equips United States Army and Marine Corps air defense battalions stationed in Europe, Korea, Okinawa and Panama, and 334 batteries of its standard or improved version are now deployed by 22 countries abroad.

Guided by semi-active CW (continuous wave) radar, and with a proximity-fused blast fragmentation warhead, HAWK is powered by an Aerojet M22E8 two-stage solid propellant motor that gives it a speed of Mach 2.5 (1,650 mph) and a range of 22 miles. It can engage aircraft at all combat altitudes and at any speed. A formidable array of support equipment, including three kinds of acquisition radar and a separate tracking and fire control radar, target displays, highly advanced data processing and command and control systems, and complex ECCM circuitry to resist known types of aircraft self-protection jammers, instantaneously separates moving targets from the heavy clutter of fixed objects on the ground, computes their range, speed and bearing, and enables the HAWK to engage them in dense ECM environments at altitudes of no more than 100 feet off the ground.

In response to "pop up" targets which suddenly appear at close range, a HAWK battery has a reaction time limited only by human reflex, and can track and engage multiple maneuvering targets simultaneously.

In 1964 development began on an improved HAWK missile with solid-state-electronics, a larger warhead and a more powerful propellant. The improved HAWK came into service in 1972, organized into Triad batteries, each with 9 three-round firing units as opposed to 6 in former standard batteries. The firing units may either be towed or mounted on a self-propelled tracked vehicle which tows other battery equipment. This equipment is not inexpensive. The 1978 Unit Procurement Cost for one Triad battery set of equipment is $5.883 million. The 1978 cost for one MIM-23 HAWK missile is $113,416.

In 1959 a NATO consortium was formed for licensed coproduction of the HAWK missile by Selenia in Italy and two other firms, to provide a new primary air defense system for Belgium, Denmark, France, Italy, the Netherlands and West Germany. The improved HAWK is also produced under license by Mitsubishi in Japan. In 1977 Sweden spent $22 million to modify its HAWK missiles to improved standard.

Large purchases of the improved HAWK system have also been made by several Arab

## HAWK Battery Equipment

**AN/MPQ-50** Pulse Acquisition Radar (Volume Search) [1]

**AN/MPQ-48** Continuous Wave Acquisition Radar (Low Altitude Search) [2] [3 in Triad Btty]

**AN/MPQ-51** Range Only Radar (J-Band to Defeat ECM) [1]

**AN/MSQ-95** Information Coordination Central [1]

**AN/TSW-8** Battery Control Central [1]

**AN/MSW-11** Platoon Command Post [1] [2 in Triad Btty]

**AN/GSA-132** Launcher Section Controls [2] [3 in Triad Btty]

**AN/MPQ-46** High Power Illuminator (Target Guidance) [2] [3 in Triad Btty]

**MIM-23B** HAWK Missile [18] [27 in Triad Btty]

**AN/M-192** Launcher [6] [9 in Triad Btty]

countries, including Iran, which purchased 1,800 missiles in 1976 for $600 million, contracting at the same time for the creation of HAWK automated fire distribution and depot maintenance systems for $400 million, and a HAWK training program for $183.7 million. Iran today deploys 37 HAWK Triad batteries in conjunction with her Seek Century air defense network. Saudi Arabia, which purchased 10 batteries in 1974, purchased another 6 fully mobile batteries on tracked vehicles in 1976, in a $1.4 billion commercial sale negotiated directly with Raytheon. At the same time, the Saudis financed a Jordanian purchase of 14 batteries. These, too, were intended as mobile batteries on self-propelled mounts, and were to cost $792 million, but when Congress objected to deployment of the HAWK in that configuration by Jordan, towed equipment was purchased instead for a reduced price of $540 million.

**Type:** Mobile surface-to-air missile, powered by solid propellant.

**Weight:** 1,294 lbs.

**Range:** 22 miles.

**Guidance:** Semi-active CW radar homing.

**Manufacturer:** Raytheon, with coproduction by Selenia in Italy and Mitsubishi in Japan.

**Produced:** Over 38,300 of all types, including more than 11,300 MIM-23B Improved HAWK.

**Exported under FMS:** 3,334.

**Exported under MAP:** 1,820.

**In US Service:** 22,135 Standard and 5,000 Improved HAWK in 900 United States Army and 105 USMC Triad batteries.

**HAWK Missiles in Service Abroad:** Belgium (648), Brazil (244), Denmark (364), France (244), Greece (324), Iran (1,800), Israel (625), Italy (324), Japan (1,058), Jordan (532), Kuwait (360), Morocco (1,498), Netherlands (244), Philippines (244), Saudi Arabia (780), South Korea (244), Spain (244), Sweden (122), Taiwan (122), Thailand (244), West Germany (972), and United Kingdom (788).

**Battery Sets of HAWK Equipment:** Belgium (24), Brazil (9), Denmark (12), France (9), Greece (12), Iran (37), Israel (15), Italy (12), Japan (28), Jordan (14), Kuwait (14), Morocco (37), Netherlands (9), Philippines (3), Saudi Arabia (16), South Korea (9), Spain (6), Sweden (3), Taiwan (3), Thailand (6), West Germany (36), United Kingdom (20).

**Price:** $118,914@ (1979 Unit Procurement Cost for 608 MIM-23B). $113,416@ (1978 Unit Procurement Cost for 559 MIM-23B). $116,349@ (1977 Unit Procurement Cost for 536 MIM-23B). $130,454@ (1976 Unit Procurement Cost for 660 MIM-23B).

**Price of Battery Equipment:** $5.883 million (1978 Unit Procurement Cost for six Triad battery sets, each including 24 major equipment items).

**Recent Transfers:** 10 Batteries to Saudi Arabia in 1974 for $270 million. 3 Batteries to Taiwan in 1975 for $90 million. 14 Batteries to Kuwait in 1975 for $85 million. 37 Batteries to Morocco in 1975 for $224 million, ($148 million paid under MAP). 6 Batteries to Spain in 1976 for $106.3 million. 14 Batteries to Jordan in 1976 for $540 million, (paid by Saudi Arabia). 6 Mobile Triad Batteries to Saudi Arabia in 1976 for $1.4 billion.

# MIM-14B NIKE HERCULES
# MIM-3 NIKE AJAX

A series of strategic long-range surface-to-air missiles which provided primary air defense in the continental United States, integrated with our SAGE air defense system, from the introduction of the Nike Ajax in 1953, through its replacement in 1958 by the more powerful Nike Hercules, until 1974 when all but four training batteries in Florida were disbanded. Substantial numbers were transferred to NATO and other countries where they continue to serve, though some are being replaced by the HAWK and other systems. The Nike Hercules, with a conventional high explosive warhead, is still under licensed production by Mitsubishi in Japan.

**Type:** Surface-to-air missile, powered by two-stage solid propellant, with either a nuclear or conventional high explosive warhead.

**Weight:** 10,400 lbs (MIM-14B), 2,445 lbs (MIM-3).

**Speed:** Mach 3.65 (MIM-14B), or 2,409 mph. (Mach 2.25 (Mim-3), or 1,485 mph.

**Range:** 86 miles (MIM-14B), 25 miles (MIM-3).

**Guidance:** Radar acquisition and tracking, command data link guidance.

**Manufacturer:** Western Electric Company, and Mitsubishi in Japan. Original development by Douglas Aircraft.

**Produced:** 40,000 of all types, including 15,000 MIM-3 and 25,000 MIM-14A/B/C.

**Exported under FMS:** 1,764.

**Exported under MAP:** 2,050.

**MIM-14B Nike Hercules**

**In Service Abroad:** Belgium (56 MIM-14B), Denmark (128 MIM-14B), Greece (64 MIM-14B), Italy (384 MIM-14B), Japan (320 MIM-14C), Netherlands (128 MIM-14B), Norway (128 MIM-14B), South Korea (62 MIM-14B), Spain (64 MIM-14B), Taiwan (96 MIM-14B), Turkey (80 MIM-3 and 192 MIM-14B), West Germany (864 MIM-14B).

**Price:** $3 million@ (1976 Unit Procurement Cost for 36 MIM-14C to Japanese Air Self Defense Force).

**FIM-43A Redeye**

# FIM-43A REDEYE

An optically-aimed, infrared homing shoulder-fired MANPADS (Man-Portable Air Defense System) based on the 2.75″ rocket frame. Developed in 1959 and operational by 1964, the Redeye weighs 29 lbs, has a range of 3 miles and a ceiling of 8,000 feet, and is powered by a two-stage propellant motor to a maximum speed of Mach 1.6 (1,056 mph). When a grip buzzer indicates the missile is ready to fire, it is launched and a booster motor carries it twenty feet in the air, protecting its operator from blast, before the sustainer motor takes over. It has a contact-fused high explosive warhead. Six two-man Redeye teams are attached to every infantry, artillery and armoured battalion in our Seventh Army in Europe, and the missile is also used in seven countries abroad.

**Manufacturer:** General Dynamics.

**Produced:** Over 90,000 to date.

**Exported under FMS:** 4,744.

**In US Service:** Over 80,000 in United States Army and USMC.

**In Service Abroad:** Australia (1,000), Denmark (200), Greece (500), Israel (1,200), Jordan (300), Sweden (440), and West Germany (1,000).

**Price:** $16,600@ (1974 Unit FMS Cost for 300 FIM-43A to Jordan, purchased by Saudi Arabia).

# FIM-92A STINGER

Shoulder-fired, like the Redeye, from its own sealed, disposable transport container and launch tube, the Stinger incorporates a similar dual-stage solid propellant motor, the booster launching the missile to a safe distance from the gunner prior to ignition of the main motor. But the propellant has been considerably improved, and the missile reaches a peak speed of Mach 2.2 (1,452 mph), enabling it to engage high-speed maneuvering targets at any angle, up to a maximum range of 3.5 miles (over 6,000 yards). Using proportional navigation and passive infrared homing, the Stinger is also highly resistant to ECM jamming. In 1973, a Stinger intercepted and destroyed a supersonic target drone in a test at White Sands, New Mexico. The missile weighs 34.5 lbs, and is scheduled to replace the Redeye in the U.S. Army and USMC as our primary infantry MANPADS.

In cooperation with Aeronutronic Ford, a Stinger Alternate has also been developed with a laser designator built into its optical tracking sight. The missile homes on the reflected laser light from the tracking unit, which must simply be kept on the target. A helicopter drone was destroyed by a Stinger Alternate in a test at White Sands in August of 1976.

**Manufacturer:** General Dynamics. In production. Stinger Alternate is still in development by General Dynamics and Aeronutronic Ford.

**Produced:** 258 production FIM-92A Stinger missiles, and 16 prototype Stinger Alternates.

**Price:** $45,705@ (1979 Unit Procurement Cost for 2,678 FIM-92A). $143,798@ (1978 Unit Procurement Cost for 258 FIM-92A. 890 were originally to be procured in 1978 for $97,865@, but funding was cut).

**FIM-92A Stinger**

# IN DEVELOPMENT

Several missile programs are now in engineering development or initial production stages in this country, but have not yet become operational with active service units. They include the following:

**Roland II:** Winner in 1975 of the U.S. Army's SHORADS (Short Range Air Defense System) competition, this missile was developed in 1965 by the French firm of Aerospatiale and the West German firm of Messerschmitt-Bölkow-Blohm, which formed the Euromissile consortium to produce it. It is one of the few weapon systems of foreign design to be selected by our military services. Weighing 140 lbs, the Roland II missile has a range of 5 miles and a speed of Mach 1.6 (1,056 mph), and carries a proximity-fused high explosive warhead. Using the chassis of the M-109 tracked vehicle with a revolving turret mount, the Roland II system will carry two missiles on twin turret launch tubes together with eight reload missiles, optical aiming and infrared tracking sights for clear weather use, and Doppler search and tracking radars for all-weather operations. The Army plans procurement of 40 launch vehicles and 1,000 missiles.

In the $256 million coproduction agreement with Euromissile, Hughes Aircraft is the prime contractor with Boeing Aerospace, and these two firms will produce under license or subcontract $108 million worth of Roland II components. Initial procurement begins in 1979, when $200.1 million worth of equipment will be delivered, including 314 missiles at $465,296 each. 145 Roland I and 75 Roland II have been sold to France, mounted on the AMX-30 chassis. 40 Roland II vehicles and 900 missiles have been sold to Norway for $100 million, and 140 Roland II have been sold to West Germany, mounted on the Marder tracked vehicle, for $189 million.

**SAM-D Patriot:** Now in a $425 million engineering development program, this long-range high-altitude surface-to-air missile is planned as a replacement in the 1980s for both the Nike Hercules and HAWK systems. An outgrowth of the FABMS (Field Army Ballistic Missile Defense System) and AADS (Army Air Defense System) programs, the Patriot is guided by a multifunction phased array radar that performs at once the volume search, low altitude search, separation of moving targets from background clutter, target tracking, missile guidance and countermeasures that previous systems accomplished with several separate radar units.

Automatically controlled by digital computer, the radar scans electronically rather than by the mechanical rotation characteristic of dish or mesh antennas.

Powered by a single solid TX-486 propellant motor, and guided to midcourse by command data link with terminal semi-active radar homing, the Patriot will carry either a nuclear or high explosive warhead, and in tests has already demonstrated its capabilities for fast response against saturation attacks in a dense ECM environment, and its high rate of accuracy and lethality against targets at all altitudes and in any kind of weather. Weighing 2,200 lbs and with a speed of Mach 3.9 (2,574 mph), the Patriot will be organized into air defense battalions, each with four Mobile Tactical Fire Platoons (MTFP). Each MTFP will have its own fire control vehicle with phased array radar, a radar and weapons control vehicle with tactical displays and digital computer, and 5 tracked launching vehicles, each with six SAM-D Patriot missiles.

The phased array radars for the Patriot system are anticipated to cost $2.8 million each for 125 units, the weapons control vehicles $887,000 each for the same number of units, the tracked launching vehicles $250,000 each for 625, and the missiles themselves $90,000 each for 6,250. The Army plans a total of 30 operational battalions in a program that will cost $1.175 billion for procurement alone, and $4.5 billion with research and development added. Raytheon is the prime contractor, with Martin Marietta. Procurement begins with $67.3 million in 1979.

**AGM-88A HARM:** A 660-lb air-to-surface anti-radiation missile developed in 1971 by Texas Instruments. Used in conjunction with the AN/APR-38 radar warning receiver developed by Loral, the Itek AN/ALR-46 radar warning receiver and the Dalmo-Victor DSA-20N signal analyser, the HARM missile uses passive broadband RF radiation homing, has a range of 10 miles and a speed of Mach 4 (2,640 mph). Operated from the Navy's A-7E or the USAF F-4E Wild Weasel II that is now replacing the F-105G, the HARM will use its high speed to defeat hostile air defense radars by homing in on their loca-

tions before they even have time to shut off. Cost per missile is estimated at $85,000 each. $43.4 million will be spent in 1979 for research and development.

**AGM-83A Bulldog:** A laser-guided version of the AGM-12 Bullpup air-to-ground missile, incorporating a Texas Instruments AN/DSM-125 guidance control group and a Mk 19 Mod 0 high explosive warhead, and powered either by a Thiokol LR-58RM4 liquid propellant or a Mk 8 Mod 2 solid propellant motor. Successful launching tests were carried out in 1973, and the USN ordered 500 units, but production was cancelled in favor of the AGM-65D laser-guided version of the Maverick. Due to its low cost, however, the program may be revived. Weight of the Bulldog is 600 lbs, and its range is 7.5 miles.

**HELLFIRE:** Developed by Hughes Aircraft and Rockwell International, the HELLFIRE (Heliborne, Laser-guided, Fire-and-forget) has been designed specifically for the Hughes AH-64 Advanced Attack Helicopter as an air-to-surface antitank missile to replace the TOW. Its semi-active laser-homing guidance allows its launching aircraft to leave the target area while another aircraft or a ground unit illuminates the target with a laser designator. Highly successful tests were conducted in 1974, using one laser designator and two HELLFIRE missiles fired 8 seconds apart at two target tanks. The designator illuminated the first target and remained on it until the first missile impacted, then switched to the second tank and was immediately tracked by the second missile, which also scored a direct hit. Two designators were then used with a single missile, one guiding the missile and the other inactive. The guiding designator was turned off and the other turned on. The missile immediately locked onto the new laser beam, and was successfully guided home to its target. $65.1 million will be spent in 1979 for continuing HELLFIRE development.

**AIM-95 Agile:** A program to develop a new short-range air-to-air missile using infrared guidance and thrust vector control. Weighing under 300 lbs, the missile was estimated to cost $50,000 each. The program was cancelled in 1978.

**ZAGM-64A Hornet:** A program to develop a new ATGAR (Anti-Tank Guided Rocket) with either electro-optical or laser-guidance. The program was cancelled in 1968, but Hornet prototypes were extensively used in research and development for the HELLFIRE and other programs.

**Roland II**

# TANKS AND ARMOURED VEHICLES

Essentially an assault weapon, designed to carry a gun of heavy caliber into areas of the battlefield under hostile fire, and bringing along with it the men required to operate it while affording them some measure of armoured protection, the tank is most effective when concentrated in mass, and when used in combination with units of infantry, artillery and close air support that provide additional forms of protection as well as attack capabilities that tanks themselves cannot offer. These requirements have often been ignored throughout history, and tanks have consequently been misused. Sent alone into battle, a column of tanks will blast its way through front-line defenses and suddenly find itself cut off from infantry support in rear areas, where individual units then become highly vulnerable to attack from hostile infantry. Used as subsidiary fire support for infantry operations, as the British used the Matilda and other tanks in North Africa in World War II, small groups of tanks are easily overcome by massed armoured assaults. Used as barrage artillery, tanks are the original form of self-propelled gun, but lack the range and heavy firepower of large cailber howitzers and siege guns.

Today, tanks are threatened by a growing proliferation of air-to-surface and surface-to-surface antitank missiles with sophisticated guidance systems and a high degree of accuracy, as well as by larger caliber high-velocity guns using projectiles with shaped charges, discarding sabots and other techniques for concentrating explosive or kinetic forces to penetrate armour. Communications between armoured units have also grown more problematical, due to the growth of sophisticated jamming techniques in our age of electronic warfare. It is likely that armoured units of the future will return, as the Israelis have already learned to do, to more reliable visual communications sys-

tems using the pennants, flags, flares and smoke grenade signals of World War II, which are unaffected by electromagnetic interference.

Simultaneously, a continuing battle for tank supremacy calls for the development of more powerful guns, sloped armour to maximize the possibilities of ricochet from hostile shot, heavier armour to provide more protection against more powerful guns, a tank chassis with a lower profile to offer a minimal target, and of course greater speed and maneuverability. These needs conflict. The heavier the gun, the greater its recoil, and the larger the chassis required to withstand it, increasing the size of the tank profile and reducing the vehicle's speed. The heavier the armour protection, again the greater the weight of the tank and the slower its speed.

But the tank endures, growing lower and flatter and heavier to fit more powerful guns, but with more powerful engines, more durable tracks and more reliable suspension systems to support these greater weights and simultaneously increase speed, with smoke dispensing systems to interfere with the laser and infrared guidance mechanisms of the new precision munitions, with ballistic computers, laser rangefinders, infrared trackers and highly advanced thermosights for night fighting, and with a series of ever more sophisticated antitank munitions whose projectiles stand a better chance of defeating the heavier armour of its opponents. It appears that the tank will continue for some time to be the decisive factor in land warfare. Along with it, a new series of armoured personnel carriers has also been developed, with greater armoured protection and more powerful armament, and capable of speeds sufficient to carry it into battle alongside the new breed of tank, providing the complement of infantry now better recognized as an essential support of tank operations. United States tanks and armoured fighting vehicles now in service or soon to enter service, follow in this section.

## M-551 SHERIDAN

An armoured reconnaissance tank developed in 1959 as a replacement for the M-41 light tank and the M-56 Scorpion self-propelled 90mm gun, the Sheridan today equips the tank battalions of the 82nd Airborne Division and 101st Air Assault Division, as well as the armoured cavalry squadrons of United States mechanized and armoured divisions and armoured cavalry regiments. Fully amphibious, it has a steel turret and a hull of welded aluminum armour for air transportability. Unfortunately, the heavy machine gun fire to which it was subjected in Vietnam cut through this armour with ease. Heavier armour was applied to many of these vehicles, which consequently lost their airdrop capability.

Armed with the 152mm gun and launcher, firing conventional HEAT (High Explosive Anti-Tank) rounds and the Shillelagh missile, the Sheridan is too light a vehicle to withstand the gun's recoil. The firing of a conventional round will shake its laser rangefinder, a precision instrument developed by Hughes, out of alignment almost every time, and will destroy its Shillelagh guidance mechanism 33 percent of the time. The Sheridan also has a tank engagement blind spot at ranges between 1,000 and 1,250 yards, more fully discussed in the entry on the MGM-51 Shillelagh missile. The Sheridan became operational in 1966, and 1,700 were produced by the Allison Division of General Motors Corporation.

**Weight:** 34,898 lbs fully loaded (17.4 tons).

**Speed:** 29.8 mph maximum road speed.

**Range:** 372 miles.

**Armament:** 1 x 152mm gun/launcher with 9 MGM-51 Shillelagh and 20 M-409 HEAT or other conventional rounds, 1 x coaxial 7.62mm MG with 3,000 rounds, 1 x M-2 .50 Cal HMG with 1,000 rounds, 8 x Smoke Grenade Launcher.

**Crew:** Four.

**In US Service:** 1,610 M-551 in U.S. Army, many stationed with Seventh Army in Europe.

**In Service Abroad:** Vietnam (70 left abandoned by U.S. Forces).

# M-60 MAIN BATTLE TANK

A direct descendant of the Patton series of M-47 and M-48 tanks, but unlike its predecessor armed with the heavier M-68 105mm gun based on the British L7A1, the M-60 has the firepower and armour of tanks of a heavier class, and was the first of our tanks to be designated the U.S. Army's MBT (Main Battle Tank). Developed in 1956 and first operational in 1960, the M-60 continues in full production today, and is expected to remain in service throughout the 1980s, making up 70 percent of our front-line tank force even after the introduction of the new XM-1 Abrams.

1,514 of our M-60A1 tanks are undergoing conversion to an improved M-60A3 standard with the addition of a Hughes laser rangefinder with a range of 6,250 yards, a solid-state M21 ballistics computer, passive and thermal night vision equipment, a top-loading air filtration system for chemical, bacteriological and radiation protection, more durable tracks, a tube-over-bar suspension system to improve cross-country mobility, and increased engine power of 900 hp coupled to a hydrostatic transmission. This program has almost been completed, and additional M-60A1s may then be converted to the same standard.

A variant of the M-60 was the M-60A2, the first battalion of which, comprising 54 front-line and 5 reserve tanks, became operational at Fort Hood, Texas in 1974. The M-60A2 mounts a 152mm gun/launcher similar to that used by the M-551 Sheridan, and fires either the MGM-51 Shillelagh missile or one

of four types of conventional 152mm ammunition. Additional variants using the M-60 chassis are the M-60 AVLB (Armoured Vehicle Launched Bridge), which can lay a 31,000-lb aluminum alloy bridge over a 72 foot span in three minutes, and the M-728 CEV (Combat Engineer Vehicle), which has been fitted with a 165mm demolition gun, a hull-mounted A-frame for tank recovery, a two-speed winch and a hydraulically-operated bulldozer blade. All of the M-60 vehicles have been produced by the Chrysler Corporation's Detroit Tank Arsenal.

**Loaded Weight:** 53 tons (M-60A1/A3), 57.2 tons (M-60A2), 57.4 tons (M-728).

**Speed:** 30.1 mph maximum road speed.

**Range:** 310 miles.

**Crew:** 4.

**M-60A1/A3 Armament:** 1 x M-68 105mm gun with 63 rounds of M-494E3 APERS-T, M-392A2 APDS-T, M-456 HEAT-T, M-393 HEP-T, M-416 WP-T, or M-393A1 TP-T. 1 x M-73 7.62mm MG with 5,950 rounds, and 1 x M-85 .50 Cal HMG with 900 rounds. XM-735 APFSDS 105mm round now being introduced.

**M-60A2 Armament:** 1 x M-162 152mm gun/launcher with 13 MGM-51 Shillelagh missile and 33 rounds of M-625 Canister, M-657E2 HE-T, M-409E5 HEAT, or M-411E3 TP-T. 1 x M-73 7.62mm MG with 5,560 rounds and 1 x M-85 .50Cal HMG with 1,080 rounds.

**M-728 Armament:** 1 x M-135 165mm gun with 30 rounds of M-123A1 HEP. 1 x M-73 7.62mm MG with 2,000 rounds and 1 x M-85 .50 Cal HMG with 600 rounds.

**M-60A1/A3 Organization:** Armoured Battalion: 34 tanks, in two companies of 17 tanks each. Mechanized Battalion: 24 tanks, in one

company of 17 tanks and one Recon Platoon of 7 tanks. Armoured Cavalry Regiment: 54 tanks, in three companies of 17 tanks each and 1 Recon Platoon of 3 tanks. Armoured Division: 320 tanks, in six armoured and five mechanized battalions. Mechanized Division: 270 tanks in six mechanized and five armoured battalions.

**Produced:** 10,316 of all types to date, including 9,390 M-60 and M-60A1 (1,514 of which converted to M-60A3), 200 M-60A1 produced by Oto-Melara in Italy, 14 prototype and 526 production M-60A2, 80 M-60 AVLB, and 106 M-728 CEV.

**Exported under FMS:** 2,380 M-60 and M-60A1 and 20 M-60 AVLB.

**Exported under MAP:** 82.

**In US Service:** 5,140 M-60 and M-60A1, 540 M-60A2, 1,514 M-60A3, 101 M-728 CEV and 60 M-60 AVLB in U.S. Army, and 274 M-60A1 in USMC.

**In Service Abroad:** Austria (120), Ethiopia (36), Iran (460), Israel (810), Italy (300), Jordan (150), Pakistan (200), Saudi Arabia (250), Somalia (36), South Korea (60), Singapore (60), Spain (20 M-60 AVLB), Turkey (120), Yugoslavia (60), North Vietnam (160 left abandoned by U.S. forces).

**Price:** $624,687@ (1978 Unit Procurement Cost for 960 M-60A1). $522,006@ (1977 Unit Procurement Cost for 927 M-60A1). $636,861@ (1976 Total Unit Cost for 1,128 M-60A3, including unit procurement of M-60A1 at $526,861 each, and cost of conversion to M-60A3 standard at $110,000 each). $458,000@ (1974 Unit Procurement Cost for 526 M-60A2). $680,000@ (1978 Unit Procurement Cost for 5 M-728 CEV).

**FMS Deliveries Pending:** Israel (450).

# M-48 PATTON II

Forbear of the M-60, in service in seventeen countries including our own, and the subject of several major improvement and modification programs since it first entered service in 1953, the M-48 will remain a front-line battle tank throughout the 1980s in most of the countries in which it serves. Though almost 6,000 have been transferred abroad, the M-48 remains much in demand, and while its original unit procurement cost was approximately $145,000, a rebuilt M-48 today will sell for as much as $500,000 on the open market.

The M-48 has seen combat in Korea, Vietnam, the Sinai, Syria, Lebanon and on the India-Pakistan frontier. In time for this last conflict, 100 M-48s were transferred in 1965 from Iran, which had originally received them from Turkey. Israel has 650 M-48s, and has requested another 125. Her combat experience with them in three Middle-Eastern wars led to the development of a new turret cupola that affords superior protection to the M-48 tank commander. In a program to convert 1,209 of our M-48A3 tanks to M-48A5 standard for transfer to units of the Army National Guard and Army Reserve, the United States has purchased 600 of these cupolas from Israel for $10,000 each, and is expected soon to order the final 699.

Between 1951 and 1959, over 8,500 M-48 tanks were produced in various versions by the Fisher Body Division of General Motors, Alco Products, the Chrysler Corporation and the Ford Motor Company. Various improvements on the M-48 and M-48A1 include the M-48A2, with improved fire control and fuel-injection systems and additional fuel tanks increasing its range to 248 miles, the M-48A3 with infrared driving lights and an infrared Xenon searchlight, and the M-48A5, which substitutes a 105mm gun for the 90mm gun of its predecessors. Of its 1,400 M-48A2 and M-48A3 tanks, West Germany

has converted 350 to M-48A5 standard with the 105mm gun. Saudi Arabia has financed the construction of a tank workshop in Jordan, where that country's 160 M-48A2 and M-48A3 tanks will also be fitted with the 105mm gun. Israel has already fitted a gun of that caliber on most of its M-48s.

Major variants of the M-48 are the M-48 AVLB (Armoured Vehicle Launched Bridge), the M-67A1 and M-67A2 flamethrower tanks, mounting an M7A1-6 flame gun with a range of from 125 to 310 yards, and the M-103, a heavy fire support tank weighing 62 tons and using the M-48 chassis with a larger turret mounting a 120mm gun.

**Weight:** 51.9 tons (M-48A1/2/3), 52 tons (M-48A5), 54 tons (M-67A2), 62 tons (M-103).

**Speed:** 29.9 mph.

**Range:** 134 miles (M-48A1), 248 miles (M-48A2/M-67A2), 287 miles (M-48A3), 299 miles (M-48A5), 75 miles (M-103).

**Crew:** 4 (3 on M-67A2, 5 on M-103).

**Armament:** 1 x 90mm gun with 60 rounds (M-48 and M-48A1), 64 rounds (M-48A2) or 62 rounds (M-48A3). 1 x 105mm gun with 57 rds (M-48A5). 1 x 120mm gun with 34 rds (M-103).

**Secondary Armament:** 1 x .30 Cal M1919A4E1 coaxial MG with 5,900 rounds (M-48/48A1/A2), or 1 x M-73 7.62mm coaxial MG with 6,000 rounds (M-48A3), 6,950 rounds (M-48A5) or 3,500 rounds (M-67/67A1), and 1 x Browning M-2 .50 Cal HMG with 180 rounds (M48), 500 rounds (M-48A1), 1,365 rounds (M-48A2), 630 rounds (M-48A3), 900 rounds (M-48A5) or 600 rounds (M-67/67A1). (M-103 has 8,000 rounds 7.62mm and .50 Cal).

**Produced:** Over 8,800 of all types, including 8,573 M-48, M-48A1/2/3 (of which 2,319 conversions to M-48A5, 1,209 by U.S.A.,

600 by Israel, 350 by West Germany and 160 by Jordan, and 74 conversions to M-67), and 300 M-103. Over 6,000 M-48 produced by Chrysler Corporation, and 900 by Ford Motor Company.

**Exported under FMS:** 1,119.

**Exported under MAP:** 4,725.

**In US Service:** 1,011 M-48A1/2/3 and 1,209 M-48A5 in United States Army, Army Reserve or Army National Guard, and 430 M-48A3, 74 M-67A2 and 300 M-103 in USMC.

**In Service Abroad:** Bolivia (120), Chile (270, including 40 M-48A5), Denmark (40), Greece (500 M-48A2), Iran (240), Israel (650, including 600 M-48A5), Jordan (160 M-48A5), Morocco (107, including 54 M-48A5), Norway (140), Pakistan (100), South Korea (640), Spain (266, all undergoing conversion from M-48A2 to M-48A3), Taiwan (380), Thailand (50), Turkey (160), Vietnam (940, including 340 abandoned by U.S. forces), and West Germany (1,400, including some AVLB and 350 M-48A5).

**Price:** $145,000@ (1959 Unit Procurement Cost for 412 M-48A3). $270,000@ (1976 Unit FMS Price for 30 M-48A1 to Taiwan). $310.752@ (1978 Total Unit Cost for 1,209 M-48A5, including original unit procurement of M-48A3 at $145,000@ and cost of conversion to M-48A5 at $195,757@).

**FMS Deliveries Pending:** Israel (125).

**Available for Sale:** Independent brokers are now offering on the open market ten reconditioned M-48A3 modified to M-48A5 standard with a 105mm high velocity gun, a 12-cylinder AVDS 17902A 750-hp engine, coaxial 7.62mm MG and a .50 Cal HMG, an M-60 night vision system, M-32 infrared periscope, a Starlight Scope and a laser rangefinder. Price: $500,000@.

# M-47 PATTON I

Predecessor of the M-48, and standard equipment today in the armies of 21 countries, the M-47 is a descendant of the M-26 Pershing. Developed during the Korean War, it first entered service in 1951. With a 90mm gun, a crew of five and a loaded weight of 50 tons, the M-47 has a top speed of 37 mph and a range of 80 miles. Built by the American Locomotive Company and the Detroit Tank Arsenal of the Chrysler Corporation, the M-47 was supplied by the thousands to NATO and SEATO countries after the end of the Korean War, and has been the subject of a number of modifications abroad, including a bridge-laying tank built by the Italian firm of Astra in Piacenza, an armoured recovery vehicle for the South Korean Army, fitted with an A-frame and winch, and two versions with the heavier 105mm gun produced expressly for export, one by the Italian firm of Oto

**M-48 Patton II**

Melara in La Spezia and the other by DTAT in France, using the gun developed for the AMX-30. 110 of the Spanish Army's 400 M-47s are being rebuilt to M-47S standard by Chrysler España, with the installation of a Continental AVDS 1790A2 750-hp diesel engine and the substitution of a German Rheinmetall MG-42 machine gun for the original Browning Turret-mounted coaxial weapon. None remain in United States service.

**Armament:** 1 x 90mm gun with 71 rounds, 2 x M-1919A4E1 .30 Cal MG, in in bow and one coaxially mounted with main armament, and 1 x M-2 .50 Cal HMG, with 4,125 rds of .30 Cal and 440 rds of .50 Cal.

**Produced:** Over 9,100, including 3,440 by Chrysler and 5,136 by American Locomotive.

**Exported under FMS:** 6.

**Exported under MAP:** 8,570.

**In Service Abroad:** Austria (320), Belgium (124), Bolivia (40), Brazil (680), Denmark (100), Greece (300), Iran (160), Israel (200), Italy (800), Japan (20), Jordan (140), Pakistan (200), Portugal (1000), Saudi Arabia (75), South Africa (104), South Korea (920), Spain (400), Taiwan (1,620), Turkey (1,340), Thailand (470), Yugoslavia (300), and Vietnam (140).

# M-41 WALKER BULLDOG

Developed in 1949, and now replaced in United States service by the M-551 Sheridan, this light reconnaissance tank was named after U.S. Army General W. W. Walker, who was killed in Korea in 1951. With a 76mm gun and 65 rounds, 2 machine guns and a crew of four, it weighs just over 25 tons fully loaded, has a maximum speed of 44 mph, and a range of 100 miles. It is still in service in 26 countries today.

**Produced:** Over 5,500 of all types, by the Cadillac Car Division of General Motors.

**In Service Abroad:** Argentina (60), Austria (120), Belgium (62), Bolivia (36), Brazil (250), Chile (60), Denmark (48), Ecuador (25), Ethiopia (50), Greece (250, including 150 ex-West German M-41), Iran (100), Italy (200), Japan (150), Lebanon (18), New Zealand (10), Pakistan (50), Portugal (230), Philippines (90), Saudi Arabia (60), South Africa (96), Spain (160), Taiwan (700), Thailand (175), Tunisia (20), Turkey (200), and Vietnam (260).

# M-24 CHAFFEE

A light tank with a 75mm gun first produced in 1944 and still used today in 19 countries. Weighing 20.3 tons, it is equipped with 3 machine guns, has a crew of five, a maxi-

mum speed of 34 mph and a range of 107 miles. For less than 1 million Crowns each, the Norwegian Army has converted its 72 M-24s to NM-16s, equipped with a laser telemeter, two 12.7mm machine guns and a 90mm low-pressure gun.

**Produced:** 4,070, by the Cadillac Car Division of General Motors, and Massey-Harris.

**In Service Abroad:** Austria (54), Cambodia (36), Ethiopia (34), Greece (200), Iran (180), Iraq (78), Japan (46), Laos (4), Norway (72 NM-16), Pakistan (100), Portugal (60), Philippines (22), Saudi Arabia (52), Spain (78), Taiwan (120), Thailand (20), Turkey (64), Uruguay (17), and Vietnam (32).

# M-26 PERSHING

A medium tank with a 90mm gun, 2,494 of which were built by Chrysler's Detroit Tank Arsenal beginning in 1945. 1,610 were supplied to the United Kingdom, and 884 to the United States Army, which used them extensively in Korea. The Pershing design led directly to the development of the M-47 Patton I. 28 Pershings remain in service in Greece, and 36 in Turkey.

# M-3A1 STUART/M-5A1

A light tank with a 37mm gun, which was produced in World War II and first saw action at Sidi Rezeg, Libya, in 1941. With a crew of four and a fully loaded weight of 14.2 tons, it had a maximum speed of 34 mph and a range of 74 miles. An improved version, the M-5A1, had a sloped glacis plate, and a gun stabilized in elevation for accurate fire while moving. Weighing 17.2 tons, it had a range of 100 miles. The first M-5A1 entered active service at Casablanca in 1942, was used by the Marine Corps in the Pacific, and as a reconnaissance tank by Allied forces in Italy and France. After 37 years, it is still in service in 16 countries.

**Produced:** Over 18,000, by the American Car and Foundry Company, the Cadillac Car Division of General Motors, and Massey-Harris.

**In Service Abroad:** Bolivia (90), Brazil (200), Chile (80), Colombia (56), Dominican Republic (30), Ecuador (16), Guatemala (25), Haiti (12), Honduras (22), Indonesia (108), Mexico (200), Paraguay (6), South Korea (80), Taiwan (40), Uruguay (18), and Venezuela (12).

# M-4 SHERMAN

One of the most important tanks of World War II, the Sherman is still in service in 25 countries. Prior to its production, the major United States heavy tank had been the M-2A1 Grant, known to the British as the Lee, which had a riveted body construction and mounted

a 75mm gun in its hull. Chrysler produced a total of 3,350 Grants by the end of 1942. The Sherman was the first of our tanks with a fully-welded body and a rotating turret to give its 75mm gun a traverse of 360 degrees. Over 48,000 were produced by nine manufacturers with a variety of armament and special modifications including bridgelaying equipment, bulldozer blades and flail equipment for mine clearance. Two armoured recovery vehicles based on the Sherman chassis, the M-32 and the M-74, are still in use today. The British substituted a high-velocity 76.2mm gun on their Sherman tank and named it the *Firefly*. Many of these are also in use. The Israelis have modified their Shermans with 105mm guns, and call them *Ben Gurions*. These have seen heavy service in three Middle Eastern wars.

**Weight:** 35 tons (M-4), 30 tons (M-32), 46.8 tons (M-74).

**Crew:** 5 (M-4), or 4 (M-32 and M-74).

**Speed:** 29 mph (M-4), 26 mph (M-32), or 21 mph (M-74).

**Range:** 102 miles.

**Armament:** 1 x 75mm gun with 97 rds, or 1 x 76mm gun with 71 rds, or 1 x 76.2mm gun (Firefly) with 68 rds. 1 x .30 Cal MG with 6,250 rds and 1 x .50Cal HMG with 600 rds. M-34: 1 x 81mm mortar and 2 x MG. M-74: 1 x 3.5" rocket launcher and 2 x MG.

**Produced:** Over 48,000 of all types, by Baldwin Locomotive Works, Chrysler Corporation's Detroit Tank Arsenal, Pressed Steel Car Company, Pullman Standard Car, Lima Locomotive Works, Pacific Car and Foundry Company, Fisher Tank Division of General Motors, Federal Machine and Welding Company, Food Machinery Corporation, and American Locomotive Company.

**In Service Abroad:** Argentina (120 Firefly), Belgium (24), Brazil (140), Chile (76), Colombia (12), India (150), Iran (66), Israel (200 Ben Gurion), Japan (52), Lebanon (6 Firefly), Mexico (90), Nicaragua (14), Pakistan (30), Paraguay (9), Peru (60), Portugal (31), Philippines (50), South Korea (210), Spain (83), Turkey (70), Uganda (12 ex-Israeli), Yugoslavia (630 Firefly).

**M-32 and M-74 in Service Abroad:** Austria (16 M-32), Belgium (5 M-74), Brazil (10 M-32 and M-74), Greece (20 M-32 and 10 M-74), Guatemala (10 M-32 and M-74), Israel (6 M-32), Japan (12 M-32), Spain (6 M-74), Turkey (10 M-74), Yugoslavia (18 M-32 and 3 M-74).

**Price:** $215,000@ (1978 unit open market price for second-hand M-4 with reconditioned engine).

# XM-1 ABRAMS

Winner in 1976 of the U.S. Army's competition for a new MBT (Main Battle Tank), the XM-1 is expected to enter service in 1980. Chrysler Corporation delivered its first 11 pilot XM-1s to the Anniston, Alabama arsenal for trials in February of 1978. Far more powerful and sophisticated than any tank before it, the Abrams is expected to defeat improvements in Soviet armour and armament through the 1980s. Weighing 59 tons with a crew of four, and mounting the M-68 105mm gun with 55 rounds, the Abrams will be fitted with an Avco-Lycoming AGT 1500HP-C turbine engine, far more reliable, quieter and producing less smoke than previous diesel engines, and giving the vehicle a road speed of 44mph, a cross-country speed of 34 mph, and a range of 300 miles. Three machine guns will be carried, along with smoke dispensing systems, a digital ballistics computer, a laser rangefinder and an automatic gun stabilization system.

Among the additional highly advanced systems to be fitted in the Abrams is a Hughes thermosight that is capable, at ranges of up to 2,000 yards, of producing a clear target image in complete darkness, through smoke, fog or rain, by electro-optical reenforcement of the thermic radiation produced by the target itself. Each thermosight in the initial production run will cost $450,000. The Abrams will also be one of the first tanks to be fitted with the new Chobham armour recently developed by two British engineers, and so expensive that the British Army has not yet ordered it for its own tanks, although it is being fitted to the 2,000 British Chieftain tanks now in production for Iran, and is also expected to be used on the new Israeli Chariot, a heavy tank now in development with the assistance of $107 million in United States military aid.

Exploiting the principles of spaced armour, Chobham armour is believed to comprise several layers of nylon micromesh bonded on either side by a plate of titanium alloy. The nylon micromesh, similar to that used in body armour and flak jackets, has the effect of laterally dispersing much of the energy inflicted by high-velocity antitank projectiles, so that fragments that have penetrated the outer plate have too little remaining energy to penetrate the second.

The first 2,000 XM-1s are expected to mount the M-68 105mm gun, for which two new high-velocity projectiles have been developed. One, the XM-774, has a depleted uranium core of high density, and the other, the XM-735 APFSDS (Armour Piercing Fin-Stabilized Discarding Sabot), has a tungsten alloy core, and develops a muzzle velocity of 5,875 fps, sufficient to penetrate 15 inches of armour. In a memorandum of understanding signed in January of 1978 between the United States and West Germany, the United States agreed to equip the remaining Abrams tanks with a Rheinmetall 120mm gun whose bore, unlike that of the rifled barrel of the British 120mm Chieftain gun, is smooth. This reduces the projectile spin, achieving a higher velocity. An Abrams equipped with the Rheinmetall gun will carry a maximum of 48 rounds of 120mm ammunition, using a combustible cartridge.

While the Rheinmetall gun will add $16,000 to the cost of each XM-1 tank, its future adoption has been anticipated for other tanks, helping to achieve NATO standardization in the 1980s. In addition, the agreement with West Germany calls for adoption of the XM-1 turbine engine and fire control system in the new German Leopard II tanks of the Bundeswehr. The fire control systems now in production cost $165,000 each.

Originally estimated in 1972 to cost $550,000 each, and in 1976 at $754,000 each, the XM-1 has grown more and more expensive. In 1977 the Army set a requirement for 3,312 XM-1s, and by that time they were estimated to cost $1.42 million each. By March of 1978 the requirement had more than doubled to 7,058 tanks, at a newly estimated cost of $1.473 million each. This raises the total procurement cost in the Abrams program to $10.4 billion.

**Manufacturer:** Chrysler Corporation.

**Price:** $1.473 million@ (1978 estimate of Unit Procurement Cost for 7,058 XM-1 to U.S. Army, with deliveries over next 9 years).

**XM-1 Abrams**

# M-113A1 ARMOURED PERSONNEL CARRIER

A fully-tracked armoured personnel carrier with a hull of welded aluminum, first produced in 1959 by FMC (Food Machinery Corporation) and in service with the United States Army and Marine Corps by 1964. Weighing 12.2 tons, with a maximum speed of 42 mph and a range of 300 miles, the M-113A1 carries 13 combat troops, and normally mounts a Browning M-2 .50 Cal machine gun on the commander's cupola with 2,000 rounds of ammunition. It is one of the most popular armoured fighting vehicles in the world, and serves in several versions and with a variety of modifications in the armies of 41 nations abroad. More than 70,000 have been produced, including over 9,700 by the Italian firm of Oto Melara under license from FMC.

Combat experience in Vietnam led to the development of the more heavily armed ACAV (Armoured Cavalry) M-113A1 with the M-2 .50 Cal machine gun fully enclosed by armour shielding, and with the addition of two M-60 7.62mm machine guns, also provided with shields. Welded racks on the outer hull allowed for storage of additional equipment and ammunition, so that a single one of these vehicles could bring into battle 3,570 rounds of .50 Cal ammunition, 8,400 rounds of 7.62mm machine gun ammunition, 5,050 rounds of 7.62mm rifle ammunition for squad weapons, 144 40mm grenades, four M-118E1 Claymore mines, ten M-21 antitank mines, three M-47 Dragon antitank missiles, six M-72A1 LAW (Light Antitank Weapon) launchers, and 12 lbs of TNT.

There has been a proliferation of specialized vehicles based on the M-113A1 hull and chassis, including the M-106A1 4.2″ (107mm) mortar carrier with a crew of six and 88 rounds of 4.2″ ammunition, the M-125A1 81mm mortar carrier with a crew of six and 114 rounds of 81mm ammunition, the M-577A1 APC (Armoured Command Post) with control and communications equipment, the M-132A1 flamethrower mounting the M10-8 flame gun with a range of 180 yards, the M-806E1 ARV (Armoured Recovery Vehicle) with a hydraulically-driven winch and crane, the M-579 fitter's vehicle with a crane for heavy parts installations, the M-548 six-ton cargo carrier, the M-730 Chaparral missile carrier, the M-741 chassis for the M-163 Vulcan weapon carrier with a turret-mounted M-61A1 20mm Vulcan gun, the M-727 HAWK missile carrier, the M-667 chassis for the Lance missile system, including the M-752 Lance launching vehicle and the M-688 Lance missile loader and transporter, and additional M-113A1s fitted with bulldozer blades or bridgelaying equipment, or mounting a TOW missile launcher or a 106mm recoilless rifle.

Modifications of these basic vehicles include British Aircraft Corporation's use of the M-548 cargo carrier as the chassis to mount 200 of its Rapier antiaircraft missile launchers. The finished units will be sold to Iran for $1.89 million each. Australia has fitted 63 of her M-113A1s with the Alvis turret for the British Scorpion tank, mounting a 76mm gun. The West German firm of Rheinstahl has equipped 500 of the Bundeswehr's M-113A1s with a Tampella 120mm mortar. The Swiss Army has fitted many of its M-113A1s with a Hägglunds turret mounting a 20mm gun, and a similar version is being offered for export by Oto Melara of La Spezia who, in addition to mounting a cupola with a 20mm cannon, have redesigned the hull with heavier armour and firing ports, calling their creation the Camillino. The British, who have replaced their large number of M-113A1s with the FV432 and other vehicles of indigenous manufacture, now offer it for export with a Fox turret mounting a 30mm Rarden cannon.

For all of its versatility and popularity, the M-113A1 offers insufficient protection against mortar fragments and heavy machine gun fire, which pierce its aluminum armoured hull too easily. Combat losses have been high, including more than 1,000 vehicles in Southeast Asia and more than 300 operated by the Israelis in the Middle East. For this reason, FMC has developed a laminate armour to fit over the hulls of new vehicles now in production or development.

**Weight:** 12.2 tons (M-113A1), 13.2 tons (M-106A1), 12.4 tons (M-125A1), 12.6 tons (M-577A1), 14.1 tons (M-548A1).

**Speed:** 42 mph (38 mph for M-548).

**Range:** 300 miles.

**Produced:** Over 70,000, including more than 60,800 by FMC and 9,700 by Oto Melara in Italy.

**Exported under MAP:** 4,225.

**Exported under FMS:** 17,903.

**In US Service:** Over 16,000 M-113A1, 1,014 M-577A1, 201 M-132A1, 785 M-106A1 and M-125A1, and over 2,000 M-163, M-730, M-572, M-727 and M-548 in U.S. Army, 13,372 of all types in U.S. Army Reserve and National Guard, and 3,400 M-113A1, M-577A1, M-106A1, M-125A1 and M-727 in USMC.

**In Service Abroad:** Argentina (250), Australia (1,753), Bolivia (18), Brazil (500), Cambodia (160), Chile (300), Canada (1,820), Denmark (650), Ecuador (20), Ethiopia (50), Guatemala (32), Greece (300), Haiti (12), Iran (1,683), Israel (2,341), Italy (3,600), Lebanon (80), Libya (170), Jordan (320), Kenya (38), Laos (20), Morocco (334), Netherlands (200), New Zealand (66), Norway (120), Pakistan (350), Peru (150 ex-Argentina), Philippines (420), Saudi Arabia (1,312), Somalia (80), South Africa (414), South Korea (2,400), Spain (400), Switzerland (1,250), Taiwan (1,155), Thailand (200), Turkey (500), Uruguay (15), Venezuela (810), Vietnam (1,780, including over 750 abandoned by U.S. forces), West Germany (3,350), and Zaire (20).

**Oto Melara Production:** Australia (340), Canada (300), Denmark (225), Greece (300), Iran (358), Italy (3,600), Libya (170), Norway (120), Somalia (80), South Africa (414), Switzerland (710), Turkey (500), and West Germany (2,218). (NB: these figures are *included* in totals above.)

**M-125A1 in Service:** Australia, Spain.

**M-106A1 in Service:** Italy, Netherlands, Switzerland, West Germany.

**M-577A1 in Service:** Australia, Canada, Israel, Italy, Netherlands, Norway, South Korea, Spain, Iran.

**Price:** $75,833@ (1978 Unit Procurement Cost for 960 M-113A1 to U.S. Army). $73,250@ (1977 Unit Procurement Cost for 1,200 M-113A1 to U.S. Army). $65,361@ (1976 Unit Procurement Cost for 1,175 M-113A1 to U.S. Army). $95,929@ (1978 Unit Procurement Cost for 565 M-577A1 to U.S. Army). $97,400@ (1977 Unit Procurement Cost for 115 M-125A1 to U.S. Army).

**M-113A1 Armoured Personnel Carrier**

# M-59 ARMOURED PERSONNEL CARRIER

Predecessor of the M-113A1, this fully-tracked vehicle was produced by FMC between 1954 and 1959. Weighing 21.2 tons, it carried a crew of two and ten combat troops, mounted an M-2 .50 Cal machine gun, had a maximum speed of 32 mph and a range of 100 miles. Some were equipped with 106mm recoilless rifles and others, designated M-84 carried a 4.2″ (107mm) mortar with 88 rounds of ammunition. Over 4,000 were produced, and none remain in service in the United States.

**In Service Abroad:** Brazil (500), Ethiopia (120), Greece (200), Lebanon (16), Turkey (1,550), and Vietnam (866).

# M-75 ARMOURED PERSONNEL CARRIER

Predecessor fo the M-59, and designed by the International Harvester Company, this tracked vehicle weighed 20.7 tons, carried a crew of two and ten combat troops, mounted an M-2 .50 Cal machine gun with 1,800 rounds of ammunition, had a maximum speed of 32 mph and a range of 115 miles. A total of 1,729 M-75s were built by International Harvester and FMC between 1951 and 1954.

**In Service Abroad:** Belgium (1,300).

# M-114 COMMAND AND RECONNAISSANCE CARRIER

A tracked vehicle with a hull of welded aluminum armour, weighing only 7.6 tons but mounting an M-139 Hispano-Suiza 20mm cannon with 100 rounds of HEIT (High Explosive Incendiary Tracer) or APIT (Armour-Piercing Incendiary Tracer) ammunition, an M-2 .50 Cal machine gun with 1,000 rounds, and an M-60 7.62mm machine gun with 3,000 rounds. It carries a crew of three or four, has a maximum speed of 36 mph and a range of 298 miles. 3,710 M-114 and M-114A1 vehicles were produced by the Cadillac Car Division of General Motors, first entering service in 1962. Withdrawn from combat in Vietnam due to poor cross-country mobility, they all remain in service in the U.S. Army. They are expected, however, to be phased out by 1980, and will then become available for transfer abroad.

# LYNX COMMAND AND RECONNAISSANCE CARRIER

Based on the design of the M-113 chassis but weighing only 9.6 tons, this tracked vehicle was developed by FMC especially for export. With a crew of three, a maximum speed of 43 mph and a range of 324 miles, it is amphibious and can be airdropped. Normal armament includes an M-2 .50 Cal machine gun with 1,155 rounds, an M-60 7.62mm

machine gun with 2,000 rounds, and three smoke grenade launchers. Those vehicles supplied to the Netherlands, however, have also been fitted with a turret mounting an Oerlikon KBA 25mm cannon with 80 rounds of APDS-T and 120 rounds of HEI-T ammunition.

**In Service Abroad:** Canada (174), and the Netherlands (250).

# ARMOURED INFANTRY FIGHTING VEHICLE

Developed in 1967 by FMC as a private venture, and incorporating many improvements learned from combat experience in Vietnam, the AIFV weighs 14.8 tons, and carries a crew of three and seven combat troops at a maximum speed of 38 mph for a range of 304 miles. With a welded aluminum hull, it has steel laminate armour plating bolted to the hull front, sides and rear for added protection against heavy caliber projectiles and high-velocity fragments. A power-operated weapon station mounts either a 20mm gun with 600 rounds or a 25mm gun with 415 rounds, together with a coaxial 7.62mm machine gun. Alternatively, an M-26 weapon station can be mounted with a .50 Cal machine gun. The vehicle is equipped with five infantry firing ports, an M-34 day sight and an M-36 night sight. In addition to the basic vehicle, FMC is offering versions equipped as command posts, mortar prime

**Armoured Infantry Fighting Vehicle**

movers, cargo carriers, ambulances, recovery vehicles, or TOW launching vehicles. To date, 850 AIFVs have been purchased by the Netherlands, equipped with an Oerlikon KBA 25mm cannon with 165 rounds and a Belgian MAG 7.62mm machine gun with 230 rounds, for $270,588 each.

**In Service Abroad:** Netherlands (850).

# XM-723 MECHANIZED INFANTRY COMBAT VEHICLE

Developed by FMC in 1972 as a replacement for the U.S. Army's standard M-113A1 armoured personnel carrier, the MICV affords the mechanized infantry squad much heavier armoured protection and more powerful armament. Based on the earlier FMC design for the AIFV family of vehicles, one of which is now used in the Netherlands, the MICV employs the same steel laminate armour plating bolted to its aluminum hull, with the spaces between filled with foam to give added protection against HEAT (High Explosive Anti-Tank) rounds. It weighs considerably more, however, at 21.5 tons, and it has a higher road speed of 44 mph. Fully amphibious, with a range of 300 miles, the MICV has five infantry firing ports and will carry a crew of two and nine combat troops. Early MICVs will be equipped with a power-operated weapon station mounting the M-139 Hispano-Suiza 20mm gun with 600 rounds, together with a coaxial M-60 7.62mm machine gun with 3,400 rounds. Vehicles delivered after 1980 will replace the 20mm gun with a 25mm cannon now in develop-

ment under the Bushmaster program. It is a vehicle with a very high performance, and the Army has judged it suitable to accompany the new XM-1 Abrams tank into battle. 3,162 XM-723 MICVs have been ordered. The initial 107 vehicles may cost as much as $600,000 each, but the average unit cost over the full program is expected to drop to $347,800 each in 1977 dollars.

# M-2A1 ARMOURED HALF-TRACK/M-16

The famous armoured personnel carrier used by United States and Allied troops in World War II, exported under MAP in enormous quantities after the war, and still used today in 30 countries. Under various designations, including M-2, M-2A1, M-3, M-3A1, M-5, M-5A1, M-7A1 and M-9A1, these vehicles normally carried one .50 Cal machine gun with 700 rounds, one .30 Cal machine gun with 7,750 round and 10 combat troops, had a top speed of 40 mph and a range of 173 miles. Weighing 9.7 tons, and too lightly armoured to provide protection against fire from heavy machine guns or light cannon, it was frequently fitted with extra frontal armour plate, which dangerously overloaded the chassis, reducing speed and range. A number of conversions appeared as weapons carriers, including the M-14, M-16 and M-27 vehicles weighing 10.8 tons, carrying a crew of five and an M-55 multiple quad

anti-aircraft mount with four .50 Cal machine guns and 5,000 rounds of ammunition, the M-15 vehicle with a 37mm antitank gun and 200 rounds and one .50 Cal machine gun with 1,200 rounds, and the M-21 81mm mortar carrier with 97 rounds. Some halftracks were also mounted with 75mm pack howitzers, 105mm howitzers and other weapons. The Israelis have equipped some of their numerous halftracks with 106mm recoilless rifles, twin 20mm antiaircraft guns, or 120mm Soltam mortars with a maximum range of 8,000 yards and storage for 30 rounds. From an original U.S. Army requirement in February of 1942 for 334,054 vehicles, 42,607 halftracks of all types were produced from 1941 through the end of production in 1944 by the Autocar Company, the White Motor Company, the Diamond T Motor Company, and International Harvester.

**In Service Abroad:** Argentina (150), Bolivia (65), Brazil (120), Cambodia (50), Chile (10), Dominican Republic (35), Ecuador (15), Greece (150), Guatemala (10), Haiti (30), Honduras (22), Indonesia (112), Israel (1,280), Madagascar (38), Malaysia (40), Malagasy Republic (14), Mexico (315), Morocco (40), Paraguay (24), Portugal (40), Peru (50), South Africa (50), Spain (80), Taiwan (150), Thailand (90), Uruguay (10), Venezuela (80), Vietnam (165), Yugoslavia (300), Zaire (40).

**Special Vehicles in Service:** Argentina (12 M-16), Brazil (20 M-21), Greece (22 M-16), Mexico (4 M-16), Portugal (40 M-16), Spain (80 M-16), Thailand (30 M-16), Yugoslavia (60 M-16 and 20 M-15). (NB: these figures are *included* among those for the M-2 above.)

**XM-723 Mechanized Infantry Combat Vehicle**

## M-3A1 WHITE SCOUT CAR

Also developed during World War II, and manufactured by the White Motor Company, this four-wheeled armoured car was similar in appearance but with a shorter body than the White half-tracked vehicle. Weighing 6.5 tons, it carried a .50 Cal and a .30 Cal machine gun, had a top speed of 55 mph and a range of 254 miles. Several thousand were produced, and they are still used in 21 countries.

**In Service Abroad:** Argentina (30), Bolivia (40), Brazil (25), Cambodia (16), Chile (20), Congo Republic (60), Colombia (42), Cuba (80), Dominican Republic (36), Greece (50), Laos (55), Liberia (22), Italy (112), Mexico (50), Nicaragua (28), Peru (9), Philippines (54), South Africa (350), Taiwan (30), Turkey (42), and Yugoslavia (70).

## M-8 GREYHOUND/M-20

A six-wheeled armoured car developed by the Ford Motor Company in 1942, and still used today in 30 countries abroad. Weighing 8.6 tons, it has a speed of 55 mph and a range of 347 miles. The M-8 mounts a 37mm gun with 80 rounds, a coaxial .30 Cal machine gun with 1,500 rounds, and a .50 Cal antiaircraft machine gun with 400 rounds, while the M-20 mounts only a single .50 Cal machine gun with 1,000 rounds. 8,523 M-8s and 3,791 M-20s were produced by Ford from 1942 until the end of World War II, when they were supplied in large numbers abroad.

**M-8 In Service Abroad:** Benin (5), Brazil (16), Cambodia (12), Cameroun (6), Colombia (8), Congo Republic (18), Dahomey (5), Ethiopia (23), Greece (20), Guatemala (14), Iran (32), Laos (20), Malagasy Republic (6), Mexico (38), Morocco (50), Niger (2), Norway (24), Peru (33), Saudi Arabia (55), Senegal (8), South Korea (45), Taiwan (40), Thailand (16), Togo (5), Tunisia (20), Turkey (48), Upper Volta (3), Venezuela )15), Vietnam (45), and Yugoslavia (30).

**M-20 In Service Abroad:** Brazil (4), Colombia (24), Greece (40), Iran (48), Niger (8), and South Korea (61). (NB: these figures are *in addition* to M-8s operated by these countries.)

## T-17E1 STAGHOUND/T-17E2

A four-wheeled armoured car first produced in 1941 by the Chevrolet Division of General Motors. Weighing 15.3 tons, it had a crew of five, a speed of 56 mph, and an exceptional range of 449 miles. 3,633 of all types were produced, most of them armed with a 37mm gun with 103 rounds and a coaxial .30 Cal machine gun with 5,250 rounds. 789 of them, however, were armed with twin .50 Cal machine guns. During World War II they were supplied in large numbers to the United Kingdom, and after the war the British re-transferred many to Saudi Arabia, Rhodesia and South Africa, where they are still in service.

**In Service Abroad:** Cuba (60), Honduras (5), Lebanon (12), Rhodesia (162), Saudi Arabia (94), and South Africa (448).

## V-150 COMMANDO/V-200

A series of four-wheeled armoured cars developed in 1963 as a private venture by the Cadillac Gage Company, and now used as a scout, reconnaissance or internal security vehicle in 21 countries abroad as well as by the United States Army, which has designated it the M-706. With an all-welded hull and firing ports for a crew of up to 12 combat troops, the V-150 is fully amphibious, has a maximum speed of 56 mph and a road range of 500 miles or a cross-country range of 400 miles. Weighing 10.5 tons fully loaded, it carries 12 smoke grenade launchers and can be equipped with a variety of armament, including one .50 Cal and one 7.62mm machine gun, an 81mm mortar with 80 rounds and a 7.62mm machine gun with 2,000 rounds, an Oerlikon 20mm cannon with 400 rounds and two 7.62mm machine guns (one of them coaxial with the main gun) with 3,000 rounds, a 76mm gun, a 90mm Mecar gun with twin 7.62mm machine guns, or a TOW launcher.

**V-150 Commando with Oerlikon 20mm Gun**

The heavier V-200 is also being offered with many of these alternate combinations of armament, and the earlier V-100, first produced in 1964, has sometimes been fitted with an M-134 six-barreled 7.62mm Minigun. Over 5,000 of all types have been produced to date, including more than 1,000 manufactured in Portugal as the Bravia Cgaimite, from plans which Cadillac Gage claims were stolen. Over 3,000 Cadillac Gage vehicles have been sold abroad under commercial license.

**Weight:** 8.1 tons (V-100), 10.5 tons (V-150), 14 tons (V-200).

**Speed:** 62 mph (V-100), 56 mph (V-150), 60 mph (V-200).

**Range:** 500 miles (V-100/V-150), 372 miles (V-200).

**Produced:** Over 5,000 to date, including 1,000 allegedly without license in Portugal.

**In US Service:** 260 V-100 and V-150, designated M-706, in U.S. Army.

**V-100 in Service Abroad:** Bolivia (10), Laos (29).

**V-150 in Service Abroad:** Ethiopia (12), Haiti (6), Indonesia (60), Jamaica (5), Malaysia (211), Lebanon (36), Oman (20), Portugal (120 Bravia Cgaimite), Peru (44), Philippines (20), Saudi Arabia (180), Somalia (42), South Africa (100 Bravia Cgaimite), South Vietnam (400), Sudan (45), Thailand (20), and Turkey (34).

**V-200 in Service Abroad:** Angola (12 Bravia Cgaimite), Portugal (360 Bravia Cgaimite), Singapore (250), and South Africa (220 Bravia Cgaimite).

**Price:** $125,100@ (1978 open market price for V-150 equipped with twin 7.62mm MG).

# COMMANDO SCOUT

A high-speed four-wheeled vehicle with a very low profile (only 6 feet and 7 inches high) and specially-hardened armour plate, recently developed by Cadillac Gage to compete for the U.S. Army's new ARSV (Armoured Reconnaissance Scout Vehicle). The Commando Scout has a top speed of 60 mph and a range of 500 miles. Carrying a crew of two or three, and weighing only 6.75 tons, it can be armed with twin .30 Cal or 7.62mm machine guns, a combination of one .50 Cal and one 7.62mm machine gun, a Mk 19 40mm automatic grenade launcher, a powered turret mounting either a 20mm or 30mm cannon, a 106mm recoilless rifle or a TOW launcher. Several prototypes have been built.

**Commando Scout**

235

## XR-311 HIGH MOBILITY WHEELED VEHICLE

Developed in 1969 as a private venture by FMC, and also entered in the U.S. Army ARSV competition, this four-wheeled vehicle is built around a tubular steel frame but has armoured protection only for its radiator and fuel tank. However, it has a top speed of 80 mph, a range of 300 miles, can climb a 60 percent grade without losing speed, and fords 30 inches of water. It has been considered a likely replacement for the Jeep. It can be armed with a ring-mounted .50 Cal machine gun, a pintle-mounted 7.62mm machine gun, a 106mm recoilless rifle with six rounds, or a TOW launcher with storage for ten rounds. It is thus far in service only with the Israeli Army, but is available for production.

---

**In Service Abroad:** Israel (260).

**Price:** $56,000@ (1978 open market price).

**XR-311 with TOW Launcher**

## LVT-4 AMPHIBIOUS ASSAULT VEHICLE

One in a series of amphibious vehicles produced for the USMC during World War II and popularly known as the *Alligator*, the LVT-4 weighs 18.1 tons, carries 30 combat troops, mounts two M-2 Browning .50 Cal heavy machine guns with 5,000 rounds and three M1919A4 .30 Cal machine guns, one in a ball mount, with 4,000 rounds, and in water has a maximum speed of 7 mph and a range of 99 miles, while on land its speed is 15 mph and its range 149 miles. Variants of the LVT *Alligator* include the LVT(A)1, mounting a turret identical to that on the M-3 Stuart tank with a 37mm gun, and the LVT(A)5 with the turret used on the M-8 self-propelled howitzer, mounting a 75mm weapon. From 1941 through the end of World War II a total of 18,620 *Alligators* were produced under the designations LVT-1/2/3/4 and LVT(A)1/5 by Donald Roebling, the Graham-Paige Motor Company, Ingersoll Steel, the Disc Division of Borg Warner, FMC and the St. Louis Car Company. Replaced in the USMC by the LVTP-7, they are still in service in three countries abroad.

---

**In Service Abroad:** Italy (240), Taiwan (386), and Thailand (190).

## LVTP-7 AMPHIBIOUS ASSAULT VEHICLE

A fully amphibious tracked vehicle with a welded aluminum armour hull developed in 1965 by FMC as a replacement for the Marine Corp's previous generation of landing assault vehicles. The LVTP-7 first entered service with the USMC in 1971. It weighs 26 tons, carries a crew of three and 25 combat troops, mounts one M-85 .50 Cal heavy machine gun with 1,000 rounds, has a remarkable speed on land of 40 mph and a range of 300 miles, and has a top speed in water of 8.4 mph which it achieves with a waterjet propulsion system. It is equipped with infrared driving lights and an M-24 infrared sight. Variants include the LVTR-7 recovery vehicle, the LVTC-7 command and communications vehicle, and the LVTE-7 engineer vehicle equipped with a bulldozer blade for mine clearance. For the LVTP-7 General Electric has developed the Mk 29 power-operated weapon station with a 20mm cannon and 140 rounds. A total of 1,579 LVTP-7 and related vehicles have been produced to date, including 17 prototypes and 942 vehicles for the USMC.

---

**In Service Abroad:** Argentina (20), Italy (360), Spain (200), Thailand (40).

**Price:** $129,000@ (1972 Unit Procurement Cost for 942 LVTP-7 to USMC).

# M-88 ARMOURED RECOVERY VEHICLE

Based on the M-48 tank chassis, this vehicle is used to recover disabled tanks and other heavy equipment from the battlefield. Weighing 60 tons, it has a crew of four, mounts an M-2 .50 Cal machine gun with 1,500 rounds, has a maximum speed of 30 mph and a range of 224 miles. The M-88 was first developed in 1954 and became operational in 1961. It is equipped with a hydraulically-operated bulldozer blade and an A-frame boom with a lift capacity of 6.7 tons without use of the blade and 28 tons with the blade entrenched. Over 1,000 M-88s were built by Bowen-McLaughlin-York from 1961 through 1964, and today they serve in the United States Army and Marine Corps, and in six foreign countries. The M-88A1, an improved model, continues in production.

**Produced:** Over 1,400 to date, including 1,000 M-88 and over 340 M-88A1.

**In US Service:** Approximately 900 M-88 and M-88A1 in U.S. Army, 60 in USMC and 100 in Army Reserve and Army National Guard.

**In Service Abroad:** Austria (26), Greece (40), Israel (34), Norway (12), Pakistan (8), and West Germany (64).

**Price:** $595,348@ (1978 Unit Procurement Cost for 43 M-88A1 to U.S. Army). $568,085@ (1977 Unit Procurement Cost for 141 M-88A1 to U.S. Army). $484,076@ (1976 Unit Procurement Cost for 157 M-88A1 to U.S. Army).

# M-578 ARMOURED RECOVERY VEHICLE

A light armoured recovery vehicle with a crane boom and a crew of three, and weighing 27 tons. It mounts a .50 Cal machine gun with 500 rounds, has a maximum speed of 37 mph and a range of 450 miles. First developed by FMC, based on the chassis for the M-107 and M-110 self-propelled guns, it is manufactured by Bowen-McLaughlin-York and the Pacific Car and Foundry Company. The crane boom is mounted in a turret, and has a lift capacity of 15 tons. Over 1,000 have been produced to date. Used primarily as a tank recovery vehicle in seven foreign countries, it is used in United States forces mostly as an air-transportable wrecker assigned to armoured cavalry squadrons and self-propelled artillery battalions for the recovery of light vehicles weighing up to 30 tons.

**In US Service:** Over 600 in the U.S. Army, Army National Guard and Army Reserve, and USMC.

**In Service Abroad:** Brazil (25), Canada (40), Denmark (58), Netherlands (44), Pakistan (25), Spain (34), and the United Kingdom (70).

**Price:** $308,333@ (1978 Unit Procurement Cost for 60 M-578 to U.S. Army). $185,221@ (1978 Unit Procurement Cost for 203 M-578 to U.S. Army).

LVTP-7

# ARTILLERY

Substantial advances have been made in the last few decades to improve the accuracy and lethality of artillery fire, and to increase the mobility of artillery units. Lighter and tougher alloys have been adopted for the manufacture of towed artillery pieces, reducing their weight and increasing their mobility. Changes in the chemical composition of propellant charges have increased the velocity of projectiles, and hence their range, while simultaneously reducing barrel wear, thus increasing the life of a barrel. Caseless ammunition has further reduced barrel wear. New methods to reduce the forces of recoil have been employed, reducing fatigue to all parts of a weapon at the same time as they increase its rate of fire.

Laser systems have brought about pinpoint accuracy in the measurement of range. Laser, electro-optical and radar target acquisition and designation systems have eliminated error in the precise location of targets, almost ensuring that the first round fired will hit its target. This has substantially increased the efficiency of operations, though the cost remains high due to the staggering cost of the new technology employed. The use of electronic data processing in fire control systems has enabled guns to be trained by computer in elevation, depression and azimuth, further increasing accuracy and impressively reducing the time between target acquisition and first round.

A greater proportion of major caliber weapons is now self-propelled, increasing mobility and reducing the threat posed by counter-battery fire. A field artillery unit today may halt, deploy, receive its coordinates, train its guns on a designated target, open fire and complete its fire support mission and move on in a matter of minutes, before the position from which it fired can be located.

These are the criteria that have guided the development of self-propelled and towed artillery pieces and antitank and antiaircraft guns produced in the United States, many of them in World War II and still in service in surprising numbers throughout the world, others brand new. The major types are summarized in this section.

## M-109 SELF-PROPELLED HOWITZER/M-109A1

Developed in 1952 by the Cadillac Car Division of General Motors, and in production since 1952 by the Allison Division of GMC, this fully-tracked vehicle has an aluminum hull, weighs 25.9 tons, and has a maximum speed of 35 mph and a range of 220 miles. Its gun, mounted in a turret with 360 degrees of traverse, has a range of 18,250 yards (10.3 miles). A longer-barreled version weighing 26.5 tons has a range of 22,500 yards (12.7 miles) firing the new M-119 charge, and it is designated M-109A1. The M-109A1 is also produced under license in Italy, mounting an FH-70 gun, by the firm of Oto Melara in La Spezia. Over 4,000 of all types have been produced to date, and are in service in 28 countries.

**In US Service:** 2,100 in United States Army.

**In Service Abroad:** Argentina (6), Austria (12), Australia (38), Belgium (41), Cambodia (30), Canada (50), Denmark (27), Ecuador (6), Ethiopia (4), Greece (36), Iran (390), Israel (120), Italy (108), Jordan (16), Libya (24), Morocco (36), Netherlands (32), Norway (20), Pakistan (6), Peru (48), South Africa (52), Spain (36), Switzerland (150), Turkey (72), United Kingdom (60), Vietnam (10), and West Germany (587).

**US Organization:** Six per battery, 18 per battalion, 54 per division.

**Price:** $475,200@ (1978 Unit Procurement Cost for 250 M-109A1 to U.S. Army). $454,368@ (1977 Unit Procurement Cost for 103 M-109A1 to U.S. Army).

**Recent Transfers:** 390 M-109 to Iran in 1973 for $310,000@, 120 Oto-Melara M-109A1 to Switzerland, designated M-109U, for $1.066 million @, 36 M-109 to Morocco in 1975 for $560,000 @.

## M-108 SELF-PROPELLED 105MM HOWITZER

Produced between 1962 and 1963 by General Motors, the M-108 has a hull and chassis similar to the M-109 with the same speed and range. Weighing 32.5 tons, it mounts an M-103 105mm gun with storage for 87 rounds (as opposed to only 28 rounds of 155mm ammunition in the M-109), and with a range of 15,000 yards (8.5 miles). Over 1,000 have been produced, and serve in 11 countries.

**In US Service:** 200 M-108 in U.S. Army and 250 in Army Reserve and Army National Guard.

**In Service Abroad:** Belgium (95), Brazil (24), Israel (130), Spain (50), Sweden (28), Switzerland (44), Taiwan (225), Tunisia (10), Turkey (40), and Yugoslavia (60).

## M-107 SELF-PROPELLED 175MM GUN

Developed in 1957, using a standard chassis developed by the Pacific Car and Foundry Company, the M-107 began production in 1962 by Pacific Car and Foundry, FMC and Bowen-McLaughlin-York. It mounts the M-113 175mm gun developed by the Watervliet Arsenal, with a maximum range of 40,750 yards (23.1 miles) firing the M-437A2 high explosive projectile. The complete vehicle weighs 31 tons, has a

**M-109 Self-Propelled Howitzer**

maximum speed of 34 mph and a range of 450 miles. Over 1,200 have been produced, and serve today in eleven countries.

**In US Service:** 300 in U.S. Army and 400 in USMC.

**In Service Abroad:** Greece (14), Iran (8), Israel (60), Italy (36), Netherlands (24), Spain (22), Turkey (22), United Kingdom (38), Vietnam (175, including 80 abandoned by U.S. forces), and West Germany (150).

**Price:** $166,000@ (1978 open market price for reconditioned second-hand M-107).

**Recent Transfers:** 8 M-107 to Iran in 1976 for $1.64 million@ .

# M-110 SELF-PROPELLED 203MM HOWITZER/ M-110A2

On a chassis identical to that of the M-107, and with the same performance, the M-110 mounts an M-2A1E1 203mm howitzer with a maximum range of 21,000 yards (11.9 miles) firing either a nuclear or a conventional HE round. An improved version, the M-110A2, is scheduled to replace both the M-110 and M-107 in United States forces, and mounts an XM-201 203mm cannon with a much longer barrel and capable of a range of 38,900 yards (22.1 miles). The use of a RAP (Rocket Assisted Projectile) incorporating a solid-propellant motor with 2.5 seconds of burn time will further increase the range of this weapon to 44,000 yards (25 miles). RAPs for heavy caliber weapons are now in development. Over 750 M-110 and M-110A2 vehicles have been produced to date by Pacific Car and Foundry, FMC and Bowen-McLaughlin-York. They are in service in eleven countries.

**In US Service:** 450 M-110 and M-110A2 in U.S. Army.

**In Service Abroad:** Belgium (11), Greece (10), Iran (37), Israel (48), Netherlands (12), South Korea (16), Spain (18), Turkey (18), United Kingdom (12), and West Germany (80).

**Price:** $522,966@ (1978 Unit Procurement Cost for 209 M-110A2 to U.S. Army).

**Recent Transfers:** 37 M-110 to Iran in 1975 for $440,000@ .

# M-55 SELF-PROPELLED 203MM HOWITZER

Developed in 1958 by the Pacific Car and Foundry Company, this vehicle is still in service in three foreign countries, though its companion vehicle, the M-53 155mm howitzer, is no longer in service anywhere.

**In Service Abroad:** Austria (40), Belgium (6), Italy (13).

# M-44 SELF-PROPELLED 155MM HOWITZER

Developed in 1947, 608 of these vehicles were produced by Massey Harris, with production ending in 1952. 300 continue in the U.S. Army reserve, and the remainder have been transferred abroad.

**In Service Abroad:** Belgium (26), Greece (20), Israel (12), Italy (24), Japan (10), Jordan (20), Spain (34), Turkey (12), and Portugal (100 ex-West German).

## M-52 SELF-PROPELLED 105MM HOWITZER

684 of these vehicles were built at the Detroit Tank Arsenal in 1950. 400 remain in service with the U.S. Army reserve.

**In Service Abroad:** Austria (200), Belgium (30), Greece (48), Japan (30), and Jordan (35).

## M-7 SELF-PROPELLED 105MM HOWITZER

Using the chassis of he M-3 Stuart tank, a total of 4,267 of these vehicles were built between 1942 and 1945 by the American Locomotive Company, the Pressed Steel Company and the Federal Machine and Welding Company. Large numbers were supplied to the United Kingdom, and they first saw action in North Africa with the British Eighth Army, which gave them the nickname of *Priest*. An additional 2,150 of the vehicles were produced by the Montreal Locomotive Works in Canada, and called the *Sexton*. One or the other type still serves today in twelve countries.

**In Service Abroad:** Argentina (20), Belgium (36), Brazil (52), India (42 Sexton), Israel (120), Italy (70), Jordan (45 Sexton), Pakistan (12), Portugal (26 Sexton), South Africa (214 Sexton), Turkey (103), and Yugoslavia (84).

## M-56 SCORPION

A lightweight air-transportable self-propelled antitank weapon with a 90mm gun, first developed in 1950 by the Cadillac Car Division of GMC. It has been replaced in United States service by the M-551 Sheridan tank, but it remains in service abroad.

**In Service Abroad:** Belgium (133), Chile (6), Morocco (50), Spain (16).

## M-18 HELLCAT SELF-PROPELLED GUN

Developed in 1944, this vehicle mounts a 76mm antitank gun and carries 45 rounds. 2,507 Hellcats were produced by the Buick Motor Division of GMC. They remain in service in five countries overseas.

**In Service Abroad:** Greece (22), South Korea (85), Taiwan (200), Venezuela (20), and Yugoslavia (33).

## M-10 SELF-PROPELLED 76MM ANTITANK GUN

Produced by the Grand Blanc Tank Arsenal during World War II, the M-10 has been retired from service in all but two countries. The British reequipped their M-10 vehicles with a more powerful 17-pounder antitank gun, and called it the *Achilles*.

**In Service Abroad:** Denmark (41) Achilles), South Korea (60).

## M-36 SELF-PROPELLED 90MM ANTITANK GUN

Built, as was the M-10, on the chassis of the M-4 Sherman tank, the M-36 mounted a more powerful 90mm weapon. Several hundred were produced by the Grand Blanc Tank Arsenal, American Locomotive, Massey Harris, and the Montreal Locomotive Works.

**In Service Abroad:** Pakistan (8), South Korea (110), Turkey (16), and Yugoslavia (10).

## M-42 DUSTER SELF-PROPELLED 40MM ANTI-AIRCRAFT GUN

Mounting two 40mm cannon firing at a rate of 240 rpm to a maximum range of 5,875 yards (3.3 miles), and carrying 480 rounds of 40mm ammunition, 3,700 of these vehicles were built between 1952 and 1957 by the Cadillac Motor Car Division of GMC. In a turret with 360 degrees of traverse, this weapon is effective against ground as well as air targets. 1,200 remain in the U.S. Army Reserve and the Army National Guard.

**In Service Abroad:** Austria (60), Italy (124), Japan (64), Jordan (200), Lebanon (32), Vietnam (58), West Germany (360), and Yugoslavia (0).

## M-50 ONTOS SELF-PROPELLED TANK DESTROYER

Developed in 1952 under a U.S. Army contract for a lightweight tank destroyer, this vehicle weighs 8.5 tons and is fitted with six M-40A1 106mm recoilless rifles, two of which can be dismounted and fired from the ground. 240 vehicles were produced, and in 1966 entered service not with the Army but with the USMC. None remain in service in the United States.

**In Service Abroad:** Guatemala (4), Lebanon (6), Morocco (24), Venezuela (14), Vietnam (10).

**Scorpion 90mm Self-Propelled Gun**

# M-163 VULCAN AIR DEFENSE SYSTEM

Using the M-741 chassis derived from the M-113 armoured personnel carrier, the M-163 mounts an AVADS (Autotrack Vulcan Air Defense System) turret with a General Electric M-168 six-barreled Vulcan 20mm cannon and 1,900 rounds, firing at selectable rates of from 1,000 to 3,000 rpm, an M-134 telescope, an AN/TVS-2B night vision sight, an M-61 gyro lead-computing gunsight and an AN/VPS-2 range-only radar with a range search time of one second and a target detection probability of 100 percent at 3,000 yards. The M-168 gun, a modified version of the M-61A1 Vulcan gun, has an effective range of 5,625 yards. With General Electric as the prime contractor, the M-163 was developed in 1966 and entered service in 1968. More than 3,800 have been produced to date, 2,200 of which have been assigned to the U.S. Army's new composite air defense battalions, comprised of two batteries each of the M-730 Chaparral low level air defense missile carrier and two of either the M-163 self-propelled Vulcan air defense system or its M-167 towed equivalent.

**In Service Abroad:** Israel (40), Jordan (100), Morocco (80).

**Recent Transfers:** 100 M-163 to Jordan in 1974 for $870,000@, financed by Saudi Arabia. 80 M-163 to Morocco in 1975 for $900,000@.

# M-167 VULCAN AIR DEFENSE SYSTEM

The M-168 six-barreled 20mm Vulcan gun on a wheeled chassis weighing only 1.75 tons, sufficiently light to be transported by helicopter. With 500 ready rounds of 20mm ammunition, it can be towed by a variety of vehicles. It has been in production since 1967, and is anticipated for use by a number of NATO nations. Of the 1,800 produced to date, 1,200 are in service in the U.S. Army's composite air defense battalions.

**In Service Abroad:** Belgium (24), Israel (40), Saudi Arabia (48).

**Recent Transfers:** 48 M-167 to Saudi Arabia in 1975 for $258,333@.

# M-55 .50 CALIBER QUAD ANTI-AIRCRAFT GUN

Four .50 Cal machine guns with a rate of fire of 450 to 555 rpm for each gun, mounted with four ammunition chests, each holding 200 rounds, on a towed trailer, in trucks, on jeeps or on halftracks. Developed in World War II, the M-55 and its predecessor, the M-45 Maxson mount, were produced in great numbers and supplied to our allies all over the world. It is still in service today in ten countries.

**In Service Abroad:** Belgium (56), Italy (109), Japan (280), Jordan (36), Netherlands (90), Pakistan (45), Portugal (18), Spain (132), Sweden (54), and Turkey (160).

# M-1 40MM ANTIAIRCRAFT GUN

A towed light antiaircraft gun developed in 1941 from the Swedish 40mm Bofors gun. It remains in service in 23 countries, having been transferred abroad in great quantities under Lend-Lease during World War II. The M-2 and M-2A1, similar versions produced for United States forces, are no longer in service.

**In Service Abroad:** Argentina (24), Australia (100), Brazil (30), Canada (80), Ecuador (10), Greece (55), India (28), Indonesia (40), Iran (20), Israel (50), Italy (80), Japan (100), Malaysia (35), Norway (120), Pakistan (60), Portugal (30), Spain (80), Taiwan (115), Thailand (40), Turkey (60), Vietnam (100), West Germany (310), and Yugoslavia (60).

**M-163 Self-propelled Vulcan Air Defense System**

# M-51 SKYSWEEPER 75MM ANTI-AIRCRAFT GUN

Developed during World War II, the Sky-sweeper gun has a rate of fire of 45 rpm and a range of 11,250 yards. Inadequate against modern supersonic aircraft, it is retained in service in three countries as an effective fire support weapon for ground forces, in which role it has an increased horizontal range of 16,250 yards.

**In Service Abroad:** Greece (52), Japan (20), Turkey (110).

# M-117 90MM ANTIAIRCRAFT GUN/M-118

A series of towed 90mm guns developed during World War II as primary air defense weapons for United States forces. Large numbers were transferred abroad after the end of the war, and a substantial number remain in service in eleven countries.

**In Service Abroad:** Argentina (12), Brazil (40), Greece (61), Japan (120), Pakistan (15), South Africa (32), Spain (40), Sweden (30), Switzerland (60), Taiwan (24), and Turkey (116).

# M-115 203MM HOWITZER

First developed by the Hughes Tool Company in World War II, this gun remains in service in sixteen countries, including the United States. Weighing 15.9 tons, it is towed by the M-6 artillery tractor or a heavy truck. With a crew of 14 and an emplace-ment time of 20 minutes, it can fire up to 30 rounds per hour to a maximum range of 21,000 yards (11.9 miles). A small number of these guns were mounted on self-propelled tracked chassis and designated M-53, but none of this type remains in ser-vice.

**M-115 203mm Howitzer**

**In US Service:** 200 M-115 in U.S. Army.

**In Service Abroad:** Belgium (15), Denmark (12), Greece (20), India (10), Iran (14), Italy (36), Japan (40), Jordan (4), Nether-lands (16), South Korea (48), Spain (24), Taiwan (10), Turkey (30), United Kingdom (32), and West Germany (60).

# M-1A1 LONG TOM 155MM HOWITZER

A long-barreled 155mm gun developed in 1938 from a French design, and produced throughout World War II, using the same chassis as that for the M-115 203mm how-itzer. Weighing 15.2 tons, the Long Tom can be towed by the M-4 artillery tractor or a heavy truck. It has a crew of 14, and can fire one round per minute to a maximum range of 29,375 yards (16.6 miles). 120 are kept in the U.S. Army reserve.

**In Service Abroad:** Argentina (6), Austria (10), Belgium (4), Brazil (6), Cambodia (12), Denmark (24), Ethiopia (2), Greece (18), Iran (12), Israel (24), Italy (16), Japan (20), Jordan (20), Laos (2), Libya (4), Netherlands (12), Peru (4), Portugal (6), South Korea (24), Spain (16), Taiwan (20), Turkey (18), Vietnam (20), West Germany (8), Yugoslavia (10).

# M-114 155MM HOWITZER/M-114A1

Still a primary artillery weapon in 35 coun-tries, the M-114 was first developed in 1932. Over 6,000 were produced by the Rock Island Arsenal. With a hydropneu-matic variable recoil and a manually-operated breechblock, the M-114 weighs 6.3 tons, and can be airlifted by a CH-47 Chinook helicopter, or towed by a 5 ton truck. With a crew of 11 and an emplace-ment time of 5 minutes, it can fire 16 rounds in 10 minutes, or 8 rounds in the first 4 minutes, to a maximum range of 20,750 yards (11.78 miles).

**In US Service:** 1,200 M-114A1 in U.S. Army, and 600 in USMC.

**In Service Abroad:** Argentina (90), Austria (30), Belgium (56), Brazil (20), Denmark (96), Ethiopia (12), Greece (200), Iran (102), Israel (250), Italy (180), Japan (240), Jordan (10), Kuwait (20), Lebanon (20), Netherlands (100), Norway (30),

Pakistan (40), Peru (30), Philippines (5), Portugal (80), Saudi Arabia (240), Singa-pore (16), South Africa (40), South Korea (400), Spain (100), Sweden (100), Switzer-land (62), Taiwan (300), Thailand (12), Tunisia (10), Turkey (330), Vietnam (300, 250 of which abandoned by U.S. forces), West Germany (600), Yugoslavia (48).

# M-123A1 155MM AUXILIARY PROPELLED HOWITZER

The M-114A1 155mm howitzer with an aux-iliary 4 cylinder hydraulic power unit pro-duced by Continental Motors Corporation, and capable of driving the entire assembly at a speed of 4.3 mph to a maximum range of 25 miles. The entire unit weighs 6.99 tons with its engine and drive wheels. To date, none have been transferred abroad.

# M-101A1 105MM HOWITZER

First developed in 1928, the M-101A1 was used in every major campaign of World War II and serves today in 68 countries. 10,202 had been built by the Rock Island Arsenal when production ended in 1953. Weighing 2.48 tons, it can be lifted by helicopter, towed by a light truck or jeep, and if neces-sary manhandled into position. With a crew of 8 and an emplacement time of 3 minutes, it utilizes hydropneumatic recoil and can fire up to 100 rounds per hour to a maximum range of 13,750 yards (7.8 miles).

**In US Service:** 1,000 M-101A1 in U.S. Army and 400 in USMC.

**In Service Abroad:** Argentina (200), Austria (100), Australia (154), Bangla Desh (12), Belgium (29), Benin (3), Bolivia (25), Brazil (134), Burma (80), Cambodia (100), Cam-eroun (6), Canada (50), Chile (210), Col-ombia (48), Denmark (144), Dominican Re-public (20), Ecuador (18), El Salvador (30), Finland (28), France (100), Ghana (14), Greece (466), Guatemala (32), Guinea (5), Haiti (19), Honduras (12), India (90), In-donesia (15), Iran (130), Israel (180), Italy (100), Ivory Coast (4), Japan (280), Jordan (30), Laos (65), Liberia (20), Libya (75), Malaysia (60), Mexico (120), Morocco (160), Nepal (8), Netherlands (100), New Zealand (20), Nicaragua (6), Nigeria (32), Norway (80), Pakistan (125), Paraguay (48), Peru (92), Philippines (60), Portugal (72), Rhodesia (55), Saudi Arabia (110), South Korea (1,000), Spain (180), Sudan (20), Sweden (180), Switzerland (100), Taiwan (125), Thailand (130), Turkey (115), United Kingdom (112), Uruguay (24), Ven-ezuela (138), Vietnam (1,200, including 1,000 abandoned by U.S. forces), West Germany (280), and Yugoslavia (105).

# M-102
## 105MM HOWITZER

A lightweight howitzer with an aluminum box trail carriage which first entered service in 1966. Weighing only 1.65 tons, it is easily towed by jeeps or light trucks and can be airlifted. With a crew of 8 and an emplacement time of 4 minutes, it is equipped with a variable recoil mechanism and can sustain a rate of fire of three rounds per mintue to a maximum range of 16,000 yards (9 miles). Over 1,200 have been produced by the Rock Island Arsenal.

**In US Service:** Approximately 1,000 in U.S. Army and USMC.

**In Service Abroad:** Cambodia (30), Vietnam (115).

# M-101 105MM
## AUXILIARY PROPELLED HOWITZER

The M-101 105mm howitzer with an auxiliary propulsion system and sets of major and minor wheels developed by Lockheed Aircraft Service Company. Weighing 3.24 tons, the entire assembly can travel under its own power at up to 15 mph to a maximum range of 25 miles. It is anticipated for use in difficult terrain or under conditions of heavy combat in which it might be deprived of its towing vehicle. In such an event, it would still be able to remove itself for short distances from areas under hostile fire. The program is in development.

# XM-204
## 105MM HOWITZER

Developed in 1968 by the Rock Island Arsenal, the XM-204 will replace the M-101A1 and M-102 howitzers as the standard artillery fire support weapon for light divisions and brigades in the U.S. Army and USMC. It utilizes the new principle of FOOBS (Fire Out of Battery System), a soft recoil cycle in which the barrel, held by lanyards to the rearmost position on the gun carriage, is equipped with a velocity sensor which automatically releases the lanyards just before the gun is fired, so that the barrel is moving forward at the moment the charge is ignited, counteracting and reducing the forces of recoil by as much as 75 percent. This gives the weapon increased stability, a more rapid

emplacement time and a higher rate of fire. Weighing 2.23 tons, the XM-204 can be easily airlifted and towed. Its projectiles, using the new XM-200 charge, will have a maximum range of 18,750 yards (10.6 miles). The first six prototype weapons will be delivered in 1979 at a cost of $1.337 million each, but the average unit cost, under conditions of full production, is expected to stabilize at approximately $347,000 each in 1977 dollars.

# XM-198
## 155MM HOWITZER

Developed in 1968 by the Rock Island Arsenal, the XM-198 will replace the M-114A1 as the standard fire support weapon in the artillery battalions of infantry and airmobile divisions and in the general support battalions at corps level. Equipped with a muzzle brake and pneumatic equilibration, it employs hydropneumatic recoil and is capable of firing a variety of projectiles, including those with conventional high explosive or nuclear warheads, a new breed of RAP (Rocket Assisted Projectile) with an increased range, and the precision laser-guided Copperhead CLGP (Cannon-Launched Guided Projectile) developed by Martin Marietta. Weighing 7.5 tons, it can be towed and airlifted, and fires standard ammunition to a range of 37,500 yards (21.3 miles). The XM-198 has just entered service in the United States within the last few years, and while no formal requests have yet been received for the weapon abroad, a number of countries, including Australia, have expressed interest both in this gun and the XM-204.

**In US Service:** Over 200 in U.S. Army.

**Price:** $305,405@ (1978 Unit Procurement Cost for 148 XM-198 to U.S. Army). $333,333@ (1977 Unit Procurement Cost for 51 XM-198 to U.S. Army).

# IN DEVELOPMENT
Several new projects are worthy of note:

**XM-70:** The Pacific Car and Foundry Company has developed a rapid-fire artillery piece which is the first major caliber weapon of its kind. Built largely of aluminum and powered by recoil energy, it is reported to be capable of single-shot, semi-automatic or full automatic fire, and using a special loading system and magazine holding thirty-two 105mm howitzer rounds, has a maximum rate of fire of sixty rounds per minute. The gun can be quickly emplaced, and has a traverse of 360 degrees.

**GLAAD:** Under the U.S. Army's program for an improved GLAAD (Gun, Low Altitude, Air Defense) to replace the AVADS (Autotrack Vulcan Air Defense System), and in conjunction with the Bushmaster program to develop a new 25mm cannon, Aeronutronic Ford may undertake licensed production in the United States of the Oerlikon 25mm KBA gun to meet Bushmaster specifications, and mount two of these with advanced fire control and optical sighting systems in a full-traverse turret atop Pacific Car and Foundry Company's XM-701 chassis, a losing contender in the MICV (Mechanized Infantry Combat Vehicle) competition. Each GLAAD vehicle, fully-equipped, is expected to cost $504,000 in 1977 dollars.

**Gepard:** As a possible air defense weapon, the U.S. Army has been testing the new West German *Gepard* Flakpanzer I built on a Krauss-Maffei chassis with two turret-mounted Oerlikon/Contraves 35mm KDA cannon firing at a cyclical rate of 550 rpm. Equipped with its own target acquisition and fire control radars, the *Gepard* carries 640 rounds of 35mm antiaircraft and 40 rounds of antitank ammunition, and its guns have a maximum elevation of 85 degrees. Thus far, Krauss-Maffei have received orders for 55 of the *Gepard* for Belgium, 155 for the Netherlands, and 420 for the Bundeswehr.

**Kraus-Maffei Gepard Flakpanzer I**

# TANK AND ARTILLERY AMMUNITION

In the past ten years, at more than twenty arsenals and ammunition plants across the country, the United States has produced not millions but billions of rounds of ammunition of every standard caliber in current service. Tons of ammunition are stockpiled at military camps, air bases and naval depots throughout the continental United States, and tons more are stored in West Germany, the United Kingdom, Spain, Korea, Okinawa, the Philippines, Diego Garcia and almost every other major military base we operate abroad. Tons are shipped, year after year, to every nation friendly with the United States. When we evacuated our forces from Vietnam we left behind more than 130,000 tons of ammunition, including 2 million 105mm projectiles, 1.3 million 90mm projectiles, 60 million rounds of 7.62mm and 35 million rounds of 5.56mm rifle ammunition, and 18 million rounds of 7.62mm and 495,000 rounds of .50 Cal machine gun ammunition.

At the Picatinny Arsenal, home of the Army Armament Research and Development Command, research has been expanded only in the last few years to develop more sensitive fuzing systems and more versatile multioption fuzes, more powerful explosives, both to increase the forces of blast from detonation of a warhead and to increase the propellant force behind a projectile, extending its range, increasing its penetrating power and stabilizing its trajectory, more streamlined ballistic shapes for projectile casings and warheads, thereby again increasing velocity and range, and antipersonnel fragmentation warheads far more lethal than any of the devices that have existed before. Development continues on the highly successful Beehive program begun in the early 1960s and tested in Vietnam, to improve a series of 90mm and 105mm APERS (Antipersonnel) rounds such as the M-494 and XM-546 105mm projectiles, each of which can be filled with as many as 5,000 flechettes, slender, pointed aluminum needles two or three inches long that have been found to shred the flesh of their victims, sometimes pinning them to the walls of wooden buildings or to trees.

Much attention has been given to the development of antitank rounds to penetrate the increasingly heavier armour of modern tanks at engagement ranges that are in-creasingly longer. It was long ago recognized that the higher the velocity of a projectile, the greater its probability of penetrating a given thickness of armour plate by sheer kinetic energy, and that the heavier the caliber of a weapon, the greater the propellant charge it could accomodate, increasing propellant force and the velocity of the projectile. Larger guns were therefore sought. The problem was that the larger the caliber of the weapon, the larger the projectile too. It was soon found that guns of too great a size fired projectiles whose weight slowed them down too much over the ranges normal for tank engagements, so that by the time they arrived on target they had lost the kinetic energy required to penetrate armour. This led to the development by the Germans in World War II of the APDS (Armour Piercing Discarding Sabot) round, which used a large caliber cartridge case with high propellant force and a projectile of compatible diameter, most of which fragmented the moment it cleared the gun barrel, leaving only a dense inner core whose weight and minimal aerodynamic drag were insufficient to reduce its very high velocity. This projectile proved to retain enormous kinetic energy on impact, penetrating substantial thicknesses of armour.

Increasing the length of the gun barrel was also found somewhat to increase the muzzle velocity of most projectiles fired from it, and rifling the barrel to give the projectile spin proved to stabilize its trajectory, increasing accuracy of fire. Unfortunately, spin simultaneously reduced forward velocity. Many military services therefore preferred to retain an unrifled smooth-bored barrel for maximum velocity, and hoped that its shot would be sufficiently accurate over the ranges at which they had to fight. The ranges for engagement, however, have been increasing. The French have consequently developed a gun with a rifled barrel for maximum accuracy, firing a projectile with small fins for stabilizing its spin, so that it would not lose quite so much velocity. On this principle, the Picatinny Arsenal has recently developed the XM-735E2 APFSDS (Armour-Piercing Fin-Stabilized Discarding Sabot) round for the M-68 105mm gun used on the M-60 series of tanks and the M-48A5. A higher kinetic energy round than those previously in service, it develops a muzzle velocity of 5,875 fps, sufficient to penetrate 15 inches of armour at a range of over 2,000 yards.

The M-392A2 APDS-T round now in service with the M-68 105mm tank gun weighs 41 lbs and has a muzzle velocity of 5,467 fps. After the sabot, an outer casing of light metal alloy, fragments and is discarded, there remains in the air a tungsten carbide core weighing about 10 lbs. As a result of aerodynamic drag while moving through its trajectory, as well as a loss of kinetic energy due to spin and yaw, the impact velocity of the projectile is considerably reduced. After a flight of 1,800 yards, for example, it is moving at approximately 4,800 fps. This, however, is more than sufficient to ensure penetration of the projectile core through 100mm of armoured plate. As it breaks through the plate the core fragments, usually into an average of more than 100 particles weighing over an ounce each, and another 600 particles weighing only a fraction of an ounce. Penetration of the plate has slowed these fragments, but they are at this point still moving at a velocity of from 2,800 to 3,100 fps according to size.

Little has been understood, or at any rate described, about precisely what results from the release of such a quantity of particles of dense metal moving at such speed within the narrow confines of a tank's fighting compartment, or about what happens to human beings exposed to them.

This much is clear: particles moving in the open air, on the explosion, for example, of a mortar shell or fragmentation grenade, will travel in a single direction until obstructed or spent. Within a tank turret, each particle will ricochet against the steel inner walls of the space, taking a new direction after each contact with those surfaces, and losing some momentum after each such contact, as well as after passing through any obstructions in its path, until spent. Fragments of an ounce or more, at these speeds, will ricochet and pass through human flesh several dozen times, and through bone rather less often, before losing sufficient momentum to come to rest. Smaller fragments will do somewhat less harm and spend more quickly. But all of the fragments of an APDS core, upwards of 700 separate particles, are in the air at once, moving at extremely high speeds and changing directions continuously within the first few fractions of a second after impact, each one of them passing through human bodies scores of times, at all points of the body and from all directions, and all of them simultaneously.

It is simple to understand from this that human survival in such a situation is nearly impossible, and that later identification of the personnel involved is often equally impossible.

The M-456A1 HEAT (High Explosive Anti-Tank) round in use with the M-68 105mm gun weighs 48 lbs and has a muzzle velocity of only 4,398 fps. But it works on a different principle, using a charge of explosive shaped within the warhead into an inverse cone that has been found, on detonation, to concentrate all the forces of the explosion at a single point at the base of the cone directly in front of the warhead, making up in the convergence of explosive energy for what it lacks in kinetic force. HEAT rounds are therefore commonly used with recoilless rifles and man-portable rocket launchers whose propellant charges achieve comparatively low muzzle velocities for their projectiles.

When the probe of the HEAT projectile makes contact with the outer surface of the target a fuse generates an electric current that explodes the base detonator, igniting the explosive charge. The resulting release of heat and pressure from the shaped internal cone produces a narrow, high-velocity jet stream that burns through armoured plate much like an acetylene torch—except that the process is instantaneous. Molten metal and fragments from the armour itself then spray inside the tank. The effects are not always devastating because of the limited debris produced, so new charges have been developed which splinter off large fragments able to ignite everything they strike that is inflammable.

The M-393 HEP-T (High Explosive Plastic-Tracer) round, also in use with the M-68 105mm gun, works on yet another principle. Weighing 52 lbs and with a muzzle velocity of 4,208 fps, the M-393 has a warhead filled with plastic explosive. When the projectile strikes its target the filler spreads out to form a blob which is detonated by a base fuse. A dent the size of a dinner plate is left on the outside of the armour plate, but inside a shock wave is produced, causing a phenomenon metallurgists call "spalling." Chunks of metal from the inside of the armour plate chip away to fly off within the compartment, moving at speeds equivalent to APDS fragments. The results are much the same.

Successful at any angle of impact, HEP rounds can also extensively damage running gear and equipment externally mounted on tanks, and they are a useful form of ammunition against field fortifications and thin-skinned vehicles. A major drawback to their use, however, is that HEP projectiles must hit exposed armour plating for full effect. Exterior stowage racks or protective screens can absorb their shock without harm to the occupants of the vehicle—a protective principle that led to the development of spaced armour. HEP ammunition has also been criticized for its lower velocity and reduced accuracy, and it is therefore generally ranked behind the APDS and HEAT rounds for tank engagements.

HEAT rounds can also be fired from howitzers. The XM-622 HEAT round for the

**Left to right:** M-84A1 Smoke Round for 105mm Howitzer, M-40 AP Round for 105mm Gun, M-490E1 TP-T Round for 105mm Gun, M-246 HE Round for 105mm Gun, M0307E2 AP Projectile for 155mm Howitzer, M-175 HE Projectile for 155mm Howitzer.

105mm howitzer, for example, can penetrate 102mm of armour plate at a range of over 1,800 yards. The M-327 HEP-T round has also been developed for the 105mm howitzer. Generally, however, howitzers and field artillery guns use a wide variety of high explosive rounds for the demolition of specific targets, or fragmentation rounds in barrage fire against enemy personnel. These projectiles are fired to much greater ranges, but at far lower muzzle velocities. The M-107 HE round used by the M-109 self-propelled 155mm howitzer weighs 96 lbs and can be fired to a range of 18,375 yards (10.4 miles), but it leaves the gun tube at a muzzle velocity of only 2,103 fps. The M-437A2 HE round fired by the M-107 self-propelled 175mm gun weighs 147 lbs (including 31 lbs of Composition B explosive filler), and can be fired to a range of 40,000 yards (22.7 miles). Its muzzle velocity is 3,440 fps.

The destructive power of high explosive artillery projectiles is proportional to their weight and caliber. The explosive force of our largest caliber HE projectile, for example the M-423 HE round fired by the M-110A2 8″ (203mm) howitzer, is approximately equal to that of a 250-lb Mk 81 Snakeye demolition bomb. On impact it will form a crater 25 feet in diameter and 10 feet deep, displacing over 5,000 cubic feet of earth, penetrating up to three feet of concrete or 5 inches of steel, and sending lethal shrapnel

to a radius of 300 feet. A 90mm Beehive APERS round packs approximately the same number of antipersonnel flechettes (3,000) as the WDU-4A/A warhead of the 2.75″ aerial rocket.

In comparison with the weapons that fire them, the many types of ammunition in service or in production today are cheap. The average 105mm HE howitzer round cost $120 in 1977. That year we sold 28,000 rounds of 105mm howitzer ammunition to Pakistan for $385 each. The previous year we sold 40,000 rounds of 155mm ammunition to Israel for $522 each, approximately the price for which the same or improved projectiles may still be purchased today.

The business of making munitions appears to be fraught with danger. In January of 1978, in an explositon that could be heard 20 miles away, 5,000 lbs of nitroglycerine blew up in a building operated by Hercules, Inc. at the Radford Army ammunition plant in Virginia, levelling the building, killing two workers and injuring six more. In May of 1974 a stock of TNT blew up at the same plant in a much larger explosion that injured 100 workers and incurred $10 million in damages.

During the late 1950s a large number of 155mm howitzer shells were filled with nerve gas. When the existence of these shells became a political issue a decade lat-

er, the Army announced that it would deactivate them all in a neutralization program to be carried out at the Rocky Mountain Arsenal near Denver. It is difficult to determine whether the program was completed, for some of those responsible for its execution have proven unreliable. In January of 1978 it was discovered that the Toole Army Depot had found 24 of its nerve gas shells missing two years earlier, and instead of searching for them or notifying higher authority, had taken the liberty of painting 24 dummy shells to resemble the missing ones, so that their inventory would appear complete. The current depot commander now claims that there was an error in the original inventory records, and that the missing 24 shells never existed. Instead of painting 24 dummy shells, of course, those in charge two years ago might have chosen the option of saying the same thing.

**Left to right:** XM-735 APFSDS Round for M-68 105mm Tank Gun, M-456A1E2 HEAT Round for M-68 105mm Tank Gun, M-393 HEP-T Round for M-68 105mm Tank Gun, M-392A2 APDS-T Round for M-68 105mm Tank Gun, M-313 WP Smoke Round for 90mm Gun.

# IN DEVELOPMENT

Under a yearly $5 million research and development program, the Picatinny Arsenal is studying the use of sulphur-polynitrides, long chains of sulphur and nitrogen atoms that form highly explosive compounds whose properties change drastically under changing conditions of temperature and pressure. Inert when stored in pressurized magazines, they would become highly volatile whenever they were needed, merely on exposure to normal environmental conditions. Some sulphur-polynitrides will be able to act as their own detonators.

Caseless ammunition, which not only reduces the wear on gun barrels but also eliminates a significant portion of the weight of ammunition, increasing firepower by enabling storage of a greater number of rounds in a given space, has been taken a step further. Scientists at the Army's arsenals are developing a mixture of chemical fuel and air that would be sprayed into the chamber behind a projectile just before firing. By adjusting the composition of the propellant mixture, diluting or intensifying its proportion of chemical fuel, and so reducing or increasing its explosive force, a gunner would be able with great precision to control the range of the projectiles being fired. A machine gun embodying this principle is now under evaluation.

**XM-712 Laser-Guided Copperhead CLGP for 155mm Gun.**

Under the direction of the Rock Island Arsenal, Martin Marietta has developed the Copperhead CLGP (Cannon-Launched Guided Projectile) which can be fired either from the M-109 self-propelled 155mm howitzer gun or the XM-198 155mm towed howitzer. Homing on reflected light from a laser target designator, the Copperhead gives each gun in an artillery battery the capability to engage and destroy a moving tank with one round from a range of up to 19 miles. A forward air controller or observer must, of course, be in visual line of sight with the target, illuminating it with a laser designator. The first Copperhead round, the XM-712 antitank round, has been tested at the White Sands Missile Range, where it achieved 8 hits out of 9 firings. Each XM-712 155mm Copperhead round is anticipated to cost $5,000.

**Left to right:** M-103 APDS Round for 76mm Gun, M-319E1 HEAT Round for 76mm Gun, M-31A1 AP-T Round for 90mm Gun, M-336 APERS Canister Round for 90mm Gun, M-82 APC-T Round for 90mm Gun, M-142 HEP-T Round for 90mm Gun, M-77 AP-T Projectile for 90mm Gun.

# INFANTRY WEAPONS

Over the years, the weapons that infantry carry into battle have not appreciably changed in their basic design, though numerous modifications have been made to improve their performance. These have mostly involved the use of lighter and tougher alloys in their construction, to make them more portable and give them longer life, improved ammunition feed and chambering systems for automatic weapons to reduce the frequency with which recoil mechanisms and bolt assemblies jam or break down, as well as to increase the rate of fire, and improved ammunition to increase the range and accuracy of solid projectiles and the lethality of explosive projectiles.

Along with these steady improvements has come a revolution in sighting, rangefinding and target designation systems, including the entry into service of the AN/PVS-2 night vision device, better known as the Starlight Scope, which presents a clear image, magnified four times, at up to 400 yards by intensifying ambient starlight, the AN/GVS-3 laser range finder, the Hughes GLLD (Ground Laser Locator Designator) to guide laser-seeking munitions, the handheld AN/APQ-1 LWLD (Light Weight Laser Designator), and such artillery locating systems for the direction of counter-battery fire as the AN/TPQ-37 Artillery Locating Radar System and the AN/MPQ-4A Mortar Locating Radar System. All of these devices, of course, increase severalfold the efficiency and combat potential of small infantry units.

Following are the major types of recoilless rifles, rocket launchers, mortars, machine guns, squad automatic weapons, rifles, pistols, grenades and mines of American manufacture now in production or in service.

## RECOILLESS RIFLES

Developed in the late 1940s, these highly portable weapons provided heavy firepower previously unavailable to infantry units, and have since their introduction been much in demand throughout the world, chiefly for use in the antitank role. The recoilless rifle makes use of a simple principle of counter-thrust based on the third law of dynamics. While conventional artillery balances the forward thrust of a projectile from the gun tube with a large recoiling mass, usually weighing several tons, the recoilless rifle eliminates this mass by creating a backward thrust of gas escaping at high velocity through holes in the cartridge case and nozzles in the breech block. This places no stress on the mount or the ground. Unfortunately, the flashback of smoke and gas is easily seen and is also dangerous, preventing use of such weapons in confined spaces. Additionally, the barrels wear quickly, but their relatively low cost ensures their continuing use. The United States has designed and produced several types.

**M-40A1 106mm Recoilless Rifle Mounted on Jeep**

**M-40A1 106mm Recoilless Rifle:** The most popular of our recoilless weapons, and the heaviest in caliber, the M-40A1 first entered service in 1953, and has been produced in the tens of thousands by several firms, among them Babcock and Wilcox Tubular Products. It is also produced under license in Spain. Weighing 286 lbs, it fires a HEAT round at a muzzle velocity of 1,886 fps to a range of 3,400 yards, or a HEP-T round at a muzzle velocity of 1,867 fps to a range of 8,500 yards. It can be mounted on a ground tripod, or on trucks, jeeps or other vehicles. In service in the United States Army and USMC.

**In Service Abroad:** Austria, Australia, Brazil, Cambodia, Cameroun, Canada, Chile, Denmark, France, Greece, India, Indonesia, Iran, Israel, Italy, Japan, Jordan, Lebanon, Liberia, Luxembourg, Netherlands, New Zealand, Norway, Pakistan, Philippines, Singapore, South Korea, Spain, Taiwan, Thailand, Turkey, United Kingdom, Venezuela, Vietnam, West Germany.

**Price:** $47,000@ (1978 Unit Procurement Cost to U.S. Army). $21,150@ (1977 price for M-40A1 made under license in Israel). $32,500@ (1978 open market price, new). $16,420@ (1976 open market price, second-hand).

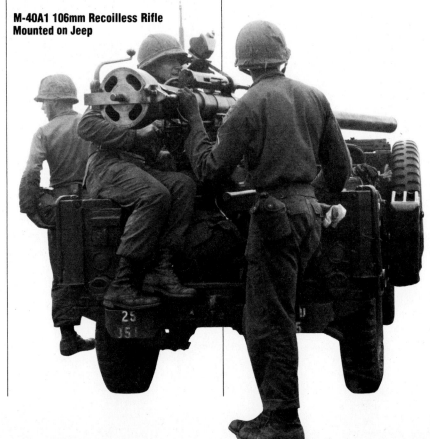

**M-27A1 105mm Recoilless Rifle/M-57A1:** Weighing considerably more than the M-40A1 at 363 lbs, these weapons have a maximum effective range of 1,250 yards with HEAT and HEP rounds, and are no longer in service in the United States.

**In Service Abroad:** France, Israel, Japan, Morocco, Yugoslavia.

**M-67 90mm Recoilless Rifle:** Replaced in the United States by the M-47 Dragon antitank missile, the M-67 is served by a crew of two, weighs 35 lbs and fires a HEAT round to a range of 560 yards.

**In Service Abroad:** Argentina, Belgium, Japan, Taiwan, Vietnam. Produced under license in Belgium.

**M-20 75mm Recoilless Rifle:** Weighing 147 lbs on an M-74 tripod mount, this weapon first entered service in 1945, and was produced by the Miller Printing Machinery Company. Licensed copies are in production in Argentina, and an unlicensed copy is made in mainland China. It can fire a HEAT round to 4,000 yards and a HEP-T round to 8,200 yards.

**In Service Abroad:** Argentina, Austria, Bangla Desh, Brazil, Denmark, France, Greece, Iran, Italy, Japan, Morocco, Netherlands, North Yemen, Norway, Pakistan, People's Republic of China, Philippines, Saudi Arabia, South Korea, Taiwan, Thailand, Turkey, Vietnam, Yugoslavia, and Zaire.

**M-18A1 57mm Recoilless Rifle:** Weighing 46 lbs with its mount, the M-18 first entered production in 1945. It can fire a HEAT round to a maximum range of 2,250 yards and HE or WP round to 5,000 yards. It remains in service with U.S. Army National Guard and Reserve units, and a perfect copy is made in mainland China.

**In Service Abroad:** Austria, Bolivia, Brazil, Chile, Cuba, Cyprus, France, Greece, Honduras, India, Iran, Italy, Japan, Laos, Norway, People's Republic of China, South Korea, Taiwan, Thailand, Turkey, Vietnam, Yugoslavia and Zaire.

# ROCKET LAUNCHERS

Precursor of the recoilless rifle and similar to that type of weapon in its operational principles, the rocket launcher is substantially smaller and lighter, portable by one man, and fires its projectiles at lower muzzle velocities and to a much reduced effective range. The original M-9A1 2.36″ rocket launcher, better known as the Bazooka, was developed and use in World War II, but is no longer in service today.

**M-20A1 3.5″ Rocket Launcher:** Introduced in 1950 and heavily used in the Korean War, the M-20 replaced the M-9A1 Bazooka and remains in service today with U.S. Army National Guard and Reserve units. Copies are made in mainland China and under license in Spain. Weighing 8.9 lbs, it fires a rocket projectile with a shaped-charge warhead at a muzzle velocity of 551 fps to a maximum effective range of 140 yards. Copies are made in mainland China.

**In Service Abroad:** Argentina, Chile, Denmark, France, Greece, Guatemala, India, Indonesia, Iran, Italy, Japan, Malawi, Malaysia, Liberia, Norway, Pakistan, Panama, People's Republic of China, Portugal, South Korea, Spain, Taiwan, Turkey and Vietnam.

**M-72A1 66mm LAW/M-72A2:** Developed and produced in the early 1970s as a replacement for the M-20A1 rocket launcher, the LAW (Light Antitank Weapon) comprises a waterproof, fiberglass tube which stores, carries and launches its own projectile, after which it is discarded. The entire system weighs only 2.2 lbs and the projectile, of smaller caliber than that of the 88.9mm M-20A1, has more than twice the effective range of the latter weapon, penetrating 70mm of armour plate at distances up to 375 yards. In front-line service with the United States Army and Marine Corps, it is produced under license by Raufoss in Norway to equip NATO forces.

**In Service Abroad:** Austria, Australia, Belgium, Canada, Denmark, Greece, Iran, Israel, Italy, Japan, Netherlands, New Zealand, Norway, Saudi Arabia, South Korea, Spain, Taiwan, Turkey, Vietnam and West Germany.

**Price:** $135@ (1978 open market price). $100@ (1975 Unit Procurement Cost for 6,707 M-72A1 to U.S. Army).

**M-20 3.5″ Rocket Launcher**

**M-72A1 LAW and Projectile**

# MORTARS

Standard equipment in almost every army in the world, the mortar provides immediate fire support for infantry operations in areas inaccessible to artillery units or at close range over territory rapidly changing hands. Mortars are produced in many countries, but those of American manufacture are much in demand, and serve today in at least 40 nations abroad.

**M-2 4.2″ Mortar:** Weighing 332 lbs, this weapon can fire high explosive 4.2″ (107mm) projectiles at a maximum rate of 20 rpm and a sustained rate of 5 rpm to ranges from 645 to 5,027 yards. No longer in service in the United States, it is produced under license in Spain.

**In Service Abroad:** Belgium, Canada, Ethiopia, Greece, India, Israel, Italy, Japan, Jordan, Liberia, Norway, Paraguay, Philippines, South Korea, Spain, Turkey and Vietnam.

**Price:** $5,700@ (1978 open market price). $834@ (1946 Unit Procurement Cost to U.S. Army).

**M-30 4.2″ Mortar:** The heavy mortar currently in service with United States forces. It began to replace the M-2 in 1951, and is mounted today in the M-106A1 weapons carrier based on the M-113A1 chassis. Weighing 667 lbs with baseplate and mount, it can fire at a maximum rate of 20 rpm or a sustained rate of 5 rpm, and will launch high explosive projectiles at a muzzle velocity of 366 fps to a maximum range of 5,931 yards.

**In Service Abroad:** Austria, Belgium, Canada, Ethiopia, Greece, India, Israel, Italy, Japan, Jordan, Liberia, Norway, Oman, Paraguay, Philippines, South Korea, Spain, Turkey, Vietnam and Zaire.

**M-1 81mm Mortar:** Weighing 136.6 lbs, this weapon was developed during World War II and mounted in the M-4 and M-21 halftrack weapons carriers. It can fire at a maximum rate of 30 rpm or a sustained rate of 18 rpm, launching the M-43A1 HE projectile at a muzzle velocity of 791 fps to a maximum range of 3,770 yards, or the M-57A1 WP (White Phosphorous) projectile at a muzzle velocity of 652 fps to a maximum range of 3,210 yards. Licensed copies are produced in Belgium, Spain and Yugoslavia.

**In Service Abroad:** Austria, Australia, Belgium, Brazil, Cambodia, Cuba, Chile, Greece, Guatamala, Haiti, Iran, Italy, Japan, Liberia, Luxembourg, Morocco, Netherlands, New Zealand, Niger, Philippines, South Korea, Taiwan, Thailand, Trinidad, and Vietnam.

**M-29E1 81mm Mortar:** Weighing only 107 lbs, this weapon has replaced the M-1 mortar in United States service, and is mounted in the M-125A1 weapons carrier based on the M-113A1 chassis. With rates of fire identical to those achieved by the M-1, it launches its projectiles considerably further, throwing the same M-43A1 HE round used with the M-1 to a maximum range of 4,187 yards. Its destructive blast is equal to that of a 2.75″ rocket.

**In Service Abroad:** Austria, Belgium, Brazil, Cambodia, Cuba, Denmark, Greece, India, Indonesia, Israel, Italy, Japan, Liberia, Luxembourg, Netherlands, North Yemen, Norway, Pakistan, Philippines, South Korea, Spain, Switzerland, Taiwan, Thailand, Turkey, Vietnam and Yugoslavia.

**Price:** $4,200@ (1978 open market price, new). $3,180@ (1978 open market price, second-hand). 1978 open market price for M-43A1 or M-374 HE Round: $25.27@.

**M-19 60mm Mortar**

**M-2 60mm Mortar:** While the larger 81mm and 4.2" (107mm) mortars are normally assigned to the heavy weapons companies of infantry battalions and regiments, the lighter 60mm types are carried in the weapons platoons of each infantry company. The M-2 weighs only 42 lbs, and can fire a variety of HE, WP, Smoke and Illuminating rounds with an average muzzle velocity of 518 fps to a maximum range of 1,990 yards. It can achieve a maximum rate of fire of 35 rpm or a sustained rate of 18 rpm. Copies are made in mainland China and Yugoslavia.

**In Service Abroad:** Denmark, Greece, Guatemala, Haiti, India, Indonesia, Morocco, Panama, People's Republic of China, South Korea, Taiwan, Vietnam and Yugoslavia.

**M-19 60mm Mortar:** Weighing 45.2 lbs, the M-19 can attain rates of fire equal to those of the M-2 it replaces, but its range has been improved. It will launch the 3-lb

M-49A2 HE projectile to a maximum range of 2,237 yards. A licensed copy is produced in Canada.

**In Service Abroad:** Belgium, Canada, Chile, Iran, Japan, Vietnam.

**Price:** $3,500@ (1978 open market price, new). $2,485@ (1978 open market price, second-hand). 1978 open market price for M-49A2 HE Round: $17.29@.

**XM-224 60mm LWCM:** Developed in the early 1970s to replace both the M-19 60mm mortar and the M-29E1 81mm mortar, the LWCM (Light Weight Company Mortar) will launch an improved 60mm projectile whose explosive force and lethality are equivalent to the effects of a larger 81mm round and whose range is over 4,000 yards, a mile further than the projectiles from previous mortars of this caliber. The XM-224 is now entering service with U.S. Army airborne and airmobile units, as well as with the

Marine Corps. Weighing 44.9 lbs, it is used in conjunction with the XM-64 sight and the AN/GVS-5 laser rangefinder, which is accurate to within 12 yards in measuring distances up to 12,500 yards (7.1 miles). Several of the new ammunition types in service with the LWCM, such as the XM-720 HE projectile, have been fitted with a new XM-734 multioption fuze developed by Harry Diamond Laboratories of Adelphi, Maryland. Replacing seven previous types of fuze, the XM-734 may be set for proximity, near-surface, instantaneous contact or delayed detonation merely by rotation of the fuze head. The XM-224 has not yet been transferred abroad, though many requests have been received. It is anticipated that these will be honored after the delivery of sufficient numbers to our own armed services.

**Price:** $14,210@ (1978 Unit Procurement Cost for 190 XM-224 to U.S. Army).

**4.2" (107mm) Mortar Projectile, Center, Flanked on the Left by 60mm Mortar Projectiles, and on the Right by 81mm Mortar Projectiles**

# MACHINE GUNS

Large numbers of American machine guns fill the arsenals of several major military powers, and those of older vintage that are no longer produced still find a brisk trade on the open market, even though there has been a steady growth of competition from the armouries of Belgium, Czechoslovakia, France, Israel, Italy, the Soviet Union, Sweden, Switzerland, the United Kingdom and West Germany. In one case the United States has itself purchased a foreign machine gun, the MAG-58, a 7.62mm gas-operated air-cooled weapon produced by the Belgian firm of Fabrique Nationale. This gun will replace the M-219 as our standard armour machine gun to be mounted coaxially with the main armament on tanks. We plan a total procurement of 14,000 MAG-58s. While these originally were estimated to cost $1,517 each, we purchased the first 7,200 of them in 1977 for $2,097 each, and the next 2,800 in 1978 for $2,250 each. It is believed that we probably would not have purchased them at all, had we not promised to offer Belgium some compensation for its purchase of our F-16 fighter aircraft.

**M-2HB Browning .50 Caliber Machine Gun:** First developed in 1918, the Browning M-2 is still used by our own miltiary services, and in 29 countries abroad. The M-2HB (Heavy Barreled) version is an air-cooled gun weighing 84 lbs, firing .50 Cal projectiles at selectable rates of 450 or 550 rpm with a muzzle velocity of 2,930 fps to a maximum range of 1,250 yards. Of the several standard types of ammunition it fires, the M-8 .50 Cal API (Armour Piercing, Incendiary) round can penetrate an inch of armour plate at 1,000 yards. The M-2HB can be mounted on ground tripod assemblies or vehicle pintle mounts.

**In Service Abroad:** Argentina, Austria, Australia, Belgium, Brazil, Canada, Chile, Denmark, Ethiopia, France, Haiti, Iran, Israel, Italy, Japan, Jordan, Lebanon, Liberia, Morocco, Netherlands, Norway, Pakistan, South Korea, Spain, Taiwan, Thailand, Turkey, United Kingdom and Vietnam.

**Price:** $1,560@ (1978 open market price, second-hand). 1978 open market price for M-8 API .50 Cal round: $1@ or $720@ for linked belt of 110 rounds. $770@ (1978 Unit Procurement Cost for 18,822 M-2 to U.S. Army).

**M-1917A1 Browning .30 Caliber Machine Gun:** The development of this venerable weapon began in 1910, and by the time production was completed 56,608 had been built. In World War I it entered service in time only to equip one unit of the 79th Division in September of 1918, but it was heavily used throughout World War II and still serves today, after 60 years, in 21 countries. Weighing 41 lbs with its water coolant, the M-1917A1 fires at a cyclic rate of 450 to 600 rpm or an automatic rate of 250 rpm. With a muzzle velocity of 2,800 fps, it will fire the M-1 .30 Cal ball ammunition to a maximum range of 5,500 yards. The M-1917A1 was produced by Colt's Patent Firearms Manufacturing Company and Remington Arms.

**In Service Abroad:** Argentina, Bolivia, Brazil, Colombia, Congo Republic, Dahomey, Ecuador, Ethiopia, Indonesia, Malawi, Nigeria, Pakistan, Paraguay, Peru, Philippines, Portugal, Rhodesia, Singapore, South Africa, Sudan and Uganda.

**Browning M-1917A1 .30 Caliber Machine Gun**

**M-1919A4 Browning .30 Caliber Machine Gun:** With a perforated steel barrel casing, this is an air-cooled version of the earlier Browning M-1917A1, and was heavily used throughout World War II as coaxial armament in tanks and by infantry units on the M-2 ground tripod mount. It still serves in 22 countries. Weighing 31 lbs, it fires at a cyclic rate of 400 to 500 rpm or an automatic rate of 120 rpm with a muzzle velocity of 2,800 fps. Using a variety of .30 Cal ammunition types, it has a maximum effective range of 1,100 yards.

**In Service Abroad:** Belgium, Canada, Denmark, Dominican Republic, Greece, Guatemala, Haiti, Iran, Israel, Italy, Lebanon, Liberia, Mexico, Pakistan, Panama, South Korea, Spain, Taiwan, Turkey, United Kingdom and Vietnam.

**Price:** $579@ (1978 open market price, second-hand). 1978 open market price for M-2 .30 Cal ball ammunition: )126 per thousand.

**Maremont M-60 General Purpose Machine Gun**

**M-60 7.62mm General Purpose Machine Gun:** Introduced in 1960 as the standard machine gun for all United States military services, the M-60 has replaced previous .30 Cal light and heavy machine guns used by infantry, armoured and mechanized units, the BAR (Browning Automatic Rifle) as an infantry squad weapon, the M-3A1 .45 Cal Grease Gun and M-1928A1 Thompson .45 Cal submachine gun as an assault weapon, and the M-73 as a fixed armour machine gun. Several versions are produced, including the standard M-60 with either a tripod or bipod mount for infantry use, the M-60C aircraft machine gun for remote firing on outboard stations of helicopters, the M-60D for pintle-mounted applications in helicopters, on armoured vehicles, or on riverine warfare craft, and the M-60E2 fixed armour machine gun for internal installation on tanks.

An air-cooled, belt-fed gas-operated automatic weapon, the M-60 is fired from an open bolt position, at a cyclic rate of 550 rpm or an automatic rate of 200 rpm. It fires standard NATO 7.62mm ammunition to a maximum range of 4,600 yards. Its effective range, tripod mounted, is 2,250 yards, and with a bipod mount this drops to 1,000 yards. Weighing only 23.1 lbs, it was often carried as a squad automatic weapon in Vietnam, fired from the hip. The gun creates minimal flash and smoke, but the barrel heats quickly and takes time to change. Over 190,000 have been produced, primarily by the Maremount Corporation, with additional units supplied by the Bridge Tool & Die Manufacturing Company and the Inland Manufacturing Division of GMC.

**In US Service:** U.S. Army, USAF, USN and USMC.

**In Service Abroad:** Australia, Cambodia, Laos, South Korea, Taiwan, Thailand and Vietnam.

**Price:** $922@ (1977 Unit Procurement Cost for 413 M-60E2 to USMC). $2,000@ (1978 open market price for M-60 new). $1,500@ (1978 open market price for M-60, second-hand). 1978 open market price for standard NATO 7.62mm ball ammunition: $135 per thousand.

**In Development:** The Maremont Corporation is now offering on the market its 7.62mm Universal Machine Gun, lighter in weight at 15 lbs than the M-60 before it, with a higher rate of fire of 650 rpm and effective ranges equivalent to those of the M-60. To compete in the U.S. Army's SAW (Squad Automatic Weapon) program, Maremont entered this weapon as the XM-233, rechambered for a new 6mm ammunition round required by SAW specifications, and fitted with a magazine clip containing 200 rounds. XM-234 and XM-235 prototypes were also developed, respectively, by Aeronutronic Ford and Rodman Laboratories. The Army, however, opted for SAW standardization with the 5.56mm ammunition already in production for the M-16 rifle, and it was found that neither the Maremont nor the Aeronutronic Ford entries could be further modified to accomodate this caliber.

General Electric, who produce the M-73 and M-219 .30 Cal tank machine guns as well as the heavier M-85 .50 Cal tank machine gun, have proposed use of their XM-214 six-barreled 5.57mm Minigun as an infantry weapon on the M-122 tripod mount. The entire system, called the GE SixPack, weighs 85 lbs with 1,000 rounds of ammunition, and can be quickly broken down into two loads for carrying. The XM-214 fires at selectable rates of from 400 to 4,000 rpm at a muzzle velocity of 3,250 fps, and its 5.56mm projectiles have a maximum effective range of 2,000 yards.

**Maremont Universal Machine Gun on M-122 Tripod Mount**

# SUBMACHINE GUNS

For use as infantry assault weapons, submachine guns were produced by the hundreds of thousands in this country during World War II. Normally not capable of sustained fire, they nonetheless brought withering amounts of firepower to individual combat situations. Because weapons of this kind produce substantial recoil, they cannot be relied upon for accurately aimed fire.

**M-1928A1 Thompson .45 Caliber Submachine Gun:** Developed during World War I, the Thompson submachine gun entered service with our military forces in the early 1920s, and gained notoriety at that time for its proliferation among elements of organized crime in this country. It was a Thompson that performed the infamous Valentine's Day Massacre in Chicago in 1929. Weighing 11.9 lbs with a loaded box magazine and 20 rounds, or as much as 19 lbs with a drum magazine containing 100 rounds, the weapons fires single shots at 40 rpm or multiple bursts at a cyclic rate of 700 rpm and an automatic rate of 120 rpm. Its .45 Caliber projectiles have a muzzle velocity of 1,057 fps and a maximum effective range of 250 yards. Over 1,400,000 of these weapons were produced by the Auto Ordnance Corporation and Savage Arms, and copies have been made in Egypt, mainland China and Vietnam. They are still in official service or in use in at least 17 countries.

**In Service Abroad:** Cambodia, Egypt, Greece, Guatemala, Haiti, Ireland, Israel, Lebanon, Mexico, Panama, People's Republic of China, Philippines, Rhodesia, Taiwan, Turkey, Venezuela and Yugoslavia.

**M-3A1 .45 Caliber Submachine Gun:** With a minimum pf parts, most of them made from metal stampings, this weapon proved simpler to produce in mass than the Thompson submachine gun, and was therefore adopted in 1942 by the U.S. Army, where it became known as the *Grease Gun.* Over 600,000 M-3 and 50,000 M-3A1 submachine guns were produced by the Guide Lamp Division of GMC and the Ithaca Gun Company. 1,000 M-3A1s were supplied to the OSS (Office of Strategic Services), which also took delivery of 25,000 M-3s specially chambered for the 9mm ammuni-

tion used by the Germans in World War II and available throughout Europe during the period in which the OSS operated there. With a detachable box magazine holding 30 rounds, the M-3A1 weighs 10.3 lbs. Operated by blowback, it fires at a cyclic rate of 450 rpm and has an effective range of 250 yards. Copies have been produced in Argentina and mainland China, and the weapon is popular with insurgent forces throughout the world.

**In Service Abroad:** Argentina, Belgium, Bolivia, Ecuador, Guatemala, Iran, Japan, People's Republic of China, Philippines, South Korea, Taiwan, Turkey, Uruguay and Vietnam.

**Ingram M-10 9mm Submachine Gun/M-11:** A sturdy, lightweight weapon with a high cyclic rate of fire developed in 1969 by George Ingram of Sionics and produced by the Military Armament Corporation, whose MAC suppressor can be fitted to external threads on the M-10 or M-11 barrels. Complete with this silencer, which keeps the speed of the bullet above sonic levels, and with a box magazine holding 32 rounds of 9mm ammunition, the M-10 weighs 8.8 lbs. It can fire single shots at 40 rpm, or multiple bursts at a cyclic rate of 1,090 rpm and an automatic rate of 96 rpm. Its effective range is 125 yards.

**In Service Abroad:** Chile, Colombia, Dominical Republic, Jordan, Morocco, Rhodesia, Saudi Arabia, United Kingdom and Yugoslavia.

**Price:** $120 @ (1978 open market price, new).

**Ingram M-10 Submachine Gun**

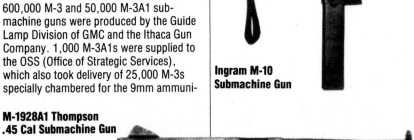

**M-1928A1 Thompson .45 Cal Submachine Gun**

**MAC 9mm Assault Submachine Gun:** This is the Ingram M-10 submachine gun chambered for 9mm ammunition and with the addition of a longer carbine barrel and either a folding metal or fixed wooden stock. With the latter it weighs 9.4 lbs loaded. These modifications increase stability and accuracy of fire. Its performance characteristics are otherwise identical to those of the .45 Cal weapon.

**Atchisson M-1957 9mm Submachine Gun:** An unusually lightweight blowback weapon with a steel wire stock similar to that of the M-3A1 Grease Gun, and using its own magazine for a trigger grip. With a full magazine holding 32 rounds the weapon weighs 4.6 lbs. It has an effective range of 250 yards. Designed by Maxwell Atchisson, the M-1957 is sold by Defense Systems International of Powder Springs, Georgia, which happens also to be the home of Military Armament Corporation, makers of the Ingram submachine guns. Both the Ingram and Atchisson weapons are popular with clandestine contract agents, mercenaries and elite special service units in the United States, Southeast Asia and Africa.

**Foote MP-970 9mm Submachine Gun:** A compact, blowback weapon utilizing a fixed firing pin and bolt, and manufactured with a minimum of parts. It has a cyclic rate of fire of 650 rpm, and an effective range of 250 yards. With its box magazine holding 32 rounds of 9mm ammunition, it weighs 6.8 lbs.

# RIFLES AND ASSAULT GUNS

The basic infantry weapon, whose development in the United States has been affected chiefly by the 1953 decision among NATO nations to standardize infantry weapons to fire 7.62mm ammunition, with a higher muzzle velocity and a lower effective range.

**M-1903 Springfield .30 Caliber Rifle:** Standard equipment in the U.S. Army throughout World War I, this bolt-action rifle remains in limited service in at least 22 countries. Weighing 8.7 lbs, it accepts a top-loaded cartridge clip with five rounds of .30-06 Cal ammunition, firing at a muzzle velocity of 3,806 fps to a maximum effective range of 750 yards.

**In Service Abroad:** Bolivia, Brazil, Colombia, Costa Rica, Dominican Republic, Ecuador, Guatemala, Haiti, Honduras, India, Liberia, Mexico, Morocco, Nigeria, Paraguay, Philippines, Tunisia, Turkey, Uganda, Uruguay, Venezuela, Yugoslavia.

**M-1 Garand .30 Caliber Rifle:** A gas-operated semi-automatic weapon in service with the U.S. army from 1932 through 1954.

Weighing 9.4 lbs, it can be loaded only with an eight-round clip, and fires standard .30-06 Cal ammunition at a muzzle velocity of 3,243 fps to an effective range of 750 yards. Over 5,500,000 M-1s were produced in this country, together with several thousand more manufactured under license in Italy. Substantial numbers still serve in 28 countries abroad, as well as with units of our Army National Guard. For the Danish Army, the Italian firm of Beretta has rechambered the M-1 to accept 7.62mm ammunition, and this version, as well as the original M-1, is still available in quantity on the open market. In testimony in March of 1978 before the House Armed Services Investigations Sub-committee, an official of the National Board for the Promotion of Rifle Practice, a U.S. government agency, disclosed that the Pentagon was considering a sale of 700,000 surplus M-1 rifles to private gun clubs and their members throughout the United States.

**In Service Abroad:** Austria, Brazil, Chile, Costa Rica, Denmark, Ethiopia, Greece, Guatemala, Haiti, Honduras, Indonesia, Iran, Italy, Japan, Jordan, Mexico, Norway, Pakistan, Cyprus, Liberia, Panama, Philippines, South Africa, South Korea, Taiwan, Thailand, Tunisia, Turkey and Vietnam.

**Price:** $250@ (1980 open market price, new). $112.50@ (1980 surplus price from DOD, new). $31@ (1946 Unit Procurement Cost to U.S. Army).

**M-14 7.62mm (.308 Cal) Rifle:** The first United States Army rifle capable of fully automatic fire, the M-14 was similar in many respects to the M-1 Garand but could accept a larger magazine holding 20 rounds. It was also the first United States rifle to be chambered for the new standard NATO 7.62mm ammunition. Weighing 14.5 lbs, it can fire single shots at a rate of 40 rpm or multiple

bursts at a cyclic rate of 700 to 750 rpm or an automatic rate of 60 rpm. Its muzzle velocity is 3,198 fps, and its effective range is 875 yards. A total of 1,500,000 were produced, and the weapon is still in licensed production in Taiwan. The M-14 serves today in many units of our Army National Guard, as well as in ten nations abroad.

**In Service Abroad:** Australia, Indonesia, Laos, Malaysia, New Zealand. Philippines, Singapore, South Korea, Taiwan and Thailand.

**Price:** $135@ (1978 open market price, new).

**M-16A1 5.56mm (.223 Cal) Rifle:** The first U.S. Army rifle to fire the smaller 5.56mm high-velocity ammunition, the M-16A1 was selected to provide the infantryman with a weapon capable of higher rates of fire than its predecessors, and with greater "stopping power." The advantages of the new ammunition seemed obvious at the time it was chosen. The 5.56mm cartridge was smaller and lighter than the 7.62mm round, and did the job, it was held, just as well. A cartridge clip of 20 rounds weighed 11 ounces, as compared with a clip of 10 rounds of 7.62mm ammunition weighing 24 ounces. More could be carried and more could be fired. As for its stopping power, the 5.56mm bullet performed with devastating effect at close range. Like the rifle projectiles developed earlier, which spin in flight to keep their noses pointed forward, the 5.56mm projectile does the same, but when it enters the human body it tumbles end over end, often creating gaping wounds.

The difficulty with this, however, is that this design feature also rapidly reduces forward velocity, so that at ranges beyond 500 yards it has no stopping power at all. Earlier rifles were effective at greater distances, and could also be more accurately aimed.

The M-16A1, with a bolt closure plunger added, was purchased by the Army after the Air Force had already purchased the M-16, based on the Armalite AR-15 designed by Eugene Stoner. Weighing 8.4 lbs with a magazine holding 30 rounds, it can fire single shots at a rate of 45 to 65 rpm, or multiple bursts at a cyclic rate of 650 to 850 rpm and an automatic rate of 150 to 200 rpm, with a muzzle velocity of 3,712 fps. It first entered service in 1963, and to date over 4,500,000 have been produced, including 3,500,000 in the United States by the Firearms Division of Colt Industries, Harrington and Richardson and the Hydramatic Division of GMC, 510,000 under license in Korea, and several hundred thousand each under license in the Philippines and Singapore. Thailand may also undertake licensed production of this weapon, along with production of the M-14, the Stoner 63, and the M-2HB and M-60E2 machine guns, and with the assistance of the Winchester Division of Olin Corporation, has planned construction of a factory capable of producing one million tons of ammunition.

Australia and New Zealand have purchased large stocks of the M-16, which they regard superior in jungle warfare to other weapons because of its light weight. Some of these M-16s may have come directly from Hanoi, which was left with a stock of 791,000 M-16s when United States forces evacuated Southeast Asia. Several thousand of these weapons have already been purchased by Saudi Arabia, and another 1,000 were sent to Montevideo, where they were reconditioned and sold to the Tupamaros in Uruguay. A further large stock of abandoned M-16s and M-60E2 machine guns was reportedly sold by Hanoi to the American firm of Interarms,

**M-1 30.06 Cal Rifle**

**M-14 7.62mm Rifle**

but in September of 1975, when these weapons were en route, a U.S. Navy vessel stopped the freighter carrying them while it was still in Asian waters, boarded her and confiscated the cargo.

The M-16A1 remains in production, and is in service today in the United States and 17 foreign countries.

**In Service Abroad:** Argentina, Australia, Israel, Italy, Jordan, Lebanon, Malaysia, New Zealand, Panama, Saudi Arabia, South Korea, Taiwan, Thailand, United Kingdom, Uruguay, Vietnam.

**Price:** $207.25@ (1977 Unit Procurement Cost for 2,895 M-16A1 to U.S. Army). $275@ (1978 open market price, new). $225@ (1978 open market price, second-hand).

**XM-177E2 Colt 5.56mm Commando:** Produced in small numbers for use by United States Special Forces units in Southeast Asia, this is a version of the M-16A1 with a shorter barrel for simpler handling in jungle warfare. The shorter barrel reduces the weapon's weight to 7.1 lbs, but it also reduces the muzzle velocity to 3,456 fps and the effective range to 250 yards. In United States service only.

**M-21 7.62mm Sniper Rifle:** This is the M-14 rifle fitted with a Redfield range-finding telescope capable of variable magnifications of three or nine power, or an AN/PVS-3 electro-optical night sight which amplifies existing ambient light, and with a sound suppressor that does not reduce the velocity of departing projectiles. In United States service only.

**Armalite AR-18 5.56mm Rifle:** Developed as an inexpensive version of the M-16A1, the AR-18 can be mass-produced entirely from metal stampings and plastic parts. Licensed production is now being arranged in Japan and with the Sterling Armament Company in the United Kingdom. Weighing 7.8 lbs with a magazine holding 20 rounds, the AR-18 fires single shots at a rate of 40 rpm or multiple bursts at a cyclic rate of 750 to 800 rpm and an automatic rate of 80 rpm. With a muzzle velocity of 3,712 fps, it has an effective range of 500 yards. Also available from Armalite are the AR-180, equipped for semi-automatic fire only, the AR-18S, a shorter-barreled submachine gun version, and the AR-18 equipped with a three power scope. None of these weapons has yet been adopted by United States services.

**In Service Abroad:** Japan, United Kingdom

**Price:** $294@ (1978 open market price, new). $237@ (1978 open market price, second-hand).

**AR-10 7.62mm (.223 Cal) Assault Rifle:** Originally designed to fire .30 Caliber ammunition, the AR-10 was rechambered for standard 7.62mm NATO ammunition just as the U.S. Army opted for the smaller 5.56mm round. Consequently, the weapon was not adopted by United States services. From prototypes developed in 1954, several thousand AR-10s were produced under license in 1959 and 1960 by Hembrug Artillerie Inrichtingen in the Netherlands, and subsequently found their way to various countries. With a magazine holding 20 rounds, the weapon weighs 10.6 lbs, fires single shots at a rate of 40 rpm or multiple bursts at a cyclic rate of

700 rpm and an automatic rate of 80 rpm. Its muzzle velocity is 3,168 fps and it has an effective range of 625 yards.

**In Service Abroad:** Burma, Italy, Netherlands, Nicaragua, Portugal, and Sudan.

**Price:** $160@ (1978 open market price, new).

**M-1A1 .30 Caliber Carbine/M-2:** Designed in 1940 to provide a lightweight weapon with high firepower for service, command and other rear echelon units of field armies, the M-1A1 and M-2 carbines are still used by our Army National Guard and Reserve, as well as by at least 23 foreign countries. Weighing 6.1 lbs, the M-1A1 accepts a magazine clip with 15 or 30 rounds, fires single shots at a rate of 40 rpm and multiple bursts at a cyclic rate of 750 rpm and an automatic rate of 75 rpm, has a muzzle velocity of 2,276 fps and an effective range of 375 yards.

Over 6,000,000 M-1, M-1A1 and M-2 carbines were produced by the Winchester Division of Olin Corporation, and large numbers of them were reportedly included in the clandestine shipment by Winchester of 3,200 weapons and 20 million rounds of ammunition to South Africa between 1971 and 1975 through dealers in Austria, Greece, Spain and Mozambique. Charged in March of 1978 with deliberate falsification of State Department certificates of end use in connection with export licenses for these arms, and of violation of the 1963 United Nations embargo on arms shipments to South Africa and violation, in turn, of United States foreign policy, Olin pleaded *nolo contendere*, and was placed on probation under the condition that

**M-16A1 5.56mm Rifle**

**M-1918 Browning Automatic Rifle**

it pay a total of $510,000 to charity programs as reparation for the illegal sales. The M-2 carbine is also produced under license in Italy.

**In Service Abroad:** Austria, Belgium, Cambodia, Chile, Dominican Republic, Ethiopia, Greece, Guatemala, Honduras, Italy, Japan, Laos, Liberia, Mexico, Norway, Philippines, Rhodesia, South Korea, Spain, Taiwan, Thailand, Tunisia and Vietnam. Possibly also in South Africa.

**Price:** $218.75@ (1978 open market price, new). $118.95@ (1978 open market price for commercially-manufactured copy, new).

**Ruger Mini-14 5.56mm Rifle:** A lightweight semi-automatic rifle based on the gas-operated principle of the M-1 Garand, but using the new 5.56mm ammunition. Not used in the United States, but becoming popular abroad. Weighing 6.8 lbs with a clip of 20 rounds, it fires at a semi-automatic rate of 40 rpm, with a muzzle velocity of 3,768 fps to a maximum effective range of 375 yards.

**In Service Abroad:** Argentina, Chile, Israel, Jordan, Saudi Arabia, Venezuela.

**Price:** $200@ (1978 open market price, new). 1978 open market price for 5.56mm ball ammunition: $135 per thousand.

**M-1918A2 .30 Caliber Browning Automatic Rifle:** Used by the United States Army as a squad automatic weapon from 1918 until 1961, when it was replaced by the M-60 machine gun, the BAR was heavily used throughout World War II and the Korean War, was produced under license in Poland and Sweden, and by Fabrique Nationale in Belgium, and serves today in at least 12 countries abroad. Weighing 19.4 lbs with a magazine holding 20 rounds, it fires at a cyclic rate of 550 rpm and an automatic rate of 350 rpm, with a muzzle velocity of 3,225 fps to an effective range of 750 yards. Over 52,000 were produced by the Firearms Division of Colt Industries, the Winchester Division of Olin Corporation, the New England Small Arms Corporation, Marlin-Rockwell, the Royal McBee Typewriter Corporation, and IBM.

**In Service Abroad:** Belgium, Costa Rica, Greece, Guatemala, Indonesia, Mexico, Norway, Liberia, Pakistan, Philippines, Sweden and Vietnam.

**Price:** $319.50@ (1978 open market price, second-hand).

**XM-22 Stoner 63 5.56mm Assault Rifle:** Originally designed by Cadillac Gage in 1962 to fire the standard NATO 7.62mm ammunition, this weapon was rechambered for the 5.56mm round when that was adopted by the U.S. Army. The Stoner 63 can easily be adapted for use as an assault rifle, sub-machine gun, belt-fed or magazine-fed light machine gun or heavy machine gun with only slight modifications, while using a common receiver, rotating bolt, piston, firing mechanism, return spring and trigger assembly. The XM-207 light machine gun version was very popular with U.S. Marine Corps and Navy SEAL teams in Southeast Asia, and its light weight, high rate of fire and reliability have made it much in demand among clandestine contract agents and mercenaries throughout the world. It has not, however, been selected by any official military service, and only small numbers have been produced in this country and under license by Hertgenbosch in the Netherlands. The XM-22 weighs 6.6 lbs with a full magazine holding 30 rounds, fires single shots at a rate of 30 rpm or multiple bursts at a cyclic rate of 600 rpm and an automatic rate of 90 rpm, has a muzzle velocity of 3,750 fps and an effective range of 500 yards.

**Price:** $375@ (1978 open market price, new).

**XM-19 5.56mm Serial Flechette Rifle/XM-70:** Developed in 1973 from the U.S. Army's SPIW (Special Purpose Individual Weapon) program, which had begun in 1954 as Project Salvo, the XM-19 and the improved XM-70 which followed it fire semi-automatic or three-round serial bursts of XM-645 ammunition. The XM-645 contains a small flechette dart and a plastic sabot, which is stripped mechanically from the dart as it leaves the gun muzzle, thereby achieving a very high muzzle velocity of 4,650 fps for the flechette. Weighing 8.5 lbs with a magazine holding 50 rounds of XM-645 ammunition, the XM-70 has an effective range of 500 yards. The project is still in development.

There is some question as to whether the flechette, fired individually, can inflict an incapacitating wound at ranges useful for infantry operations. The three-round serial burst is meant to compensate for this. There is no question at all, however, that 40 or 50 flechettes packed into a single 12-gauge shotgun shell and fired at once will literally tear their victim to shreds at close range. Private arms makers have discovered this, and now produce such ammunition for standard 12-gauge shotguns, one of the most popular of which, for this purpose, is the Mossberg 12-gauge assault rifle, priced in 1978 at $95.00 new.

**M-1911A1 .45 Cal Automatic**

# REVOLVERS AND SELF-LOADING AUTOMATIC PISTOLS

More than forty types of automatic pistol and revolver have been made in the United States, in such numbers that each of their manufacturers, whose records are rarely complete, can only guess at their own individual output. A very conservative estimate of the total of these types of weapon produced in America since 1910 is over 140,000,000. With the exception of the M-1911A1 Colt .45 Caliber automatic, and the Smith & Wesson Model 15 .38 Caliber Combat Masterpiece revolver, few of these weapons have been adopted for official military service abroad, though almost every type remains in private use in abundant quantity throughout the world. Only the major types follow.

**M-1911A1 Colt .45 Caliber Automatic:** A short recoil self-loading pistol with a detachable box magazine holding seven rounds. Weighing 2.9 lbs loaded, it fires .45 Cal ball and other types of ammunition at a rate of 35 rpm, with a muzzle velocity of 830 fps to a maximum effective range of 50 yards. It remains in service with the United States Army after 67 years, and is also in service in 14 countries abroad. Several million have been produced by the Firearms Division of Colt Industries, the Ithaca Gun Company, Remington Rand, the Springfield Armoury, and the Union Switch and Signal Company. It has been licensed for production abroad in Argentina and Norway, and unlicensed copies have been produced in six other nations.

**In Service Abroad:** Austria, Dominican Republic, Guatemala, Haiti, Indonesia, Japan, Liberia, Mexico, Panama, Philippines, South Korea, Taiwan, Turkey and Vietnam.

**Price:** $140@ (1978 open market price, new). 1978 open market price for .45 Cal ball ammunition: $91 per thousand.

**Smith & Wesson Model 15 .38 Caliber Combat Masterpiece:** A favorite with the United States Marine Corps during the Korean War, this revolver holds six rounds of .38 Cal ammunition and weighs 1.8 lbs.

**In Service Abroad:** Dominican Republic, Haiti, Liberia and Panama.

**Price:** $135@ (1978 open market price, new).

**Colt .357 Magnum Trooper Mk III:** Weighing 2.4 lbs, this heavy-duty revolver fires 6 rounds to a maximum effective range of 60 yards.

**Price:** $188@ (1978 open market price, new).

**Colt 9mm Commander:** Introduced in 1971, and patterned after the Colt Government Model .45 Cal automatic, this weapon weighs 1.6 lbs with a detachable box magazine holding 6 rounds of 9mm Parabellum ammunition, has a maximum rate of fire of 35 rpm and an effective range of 60 yards. In service in Lebanon. Also available chambered for .38 Cal ammunition.

**Price:** $179.50@ (1978 open market price, new).

**Smith & Wesson Model 39 9mm Automatic/Model 59:** Weighing 1.6 lbs, Model 39 carries 8 rounds of 9mm ammunition, while Model 59 carries 14 rounds and weighs 1.8 lbs.

**Price:** $125@ (Model 39) or $150@ (Model 59) (1978 open market prices, new).

# GRENADES AND MINES

Infantry have thrown fragmentation devices at one another since the Middle Ages, and ever since the mechanisms were developed to detonate explosives by pressure or other means, they have planted mines in the ground as well. Refinements in the chemistry of high explosives have produced devices that detonate today with far more violent force than ever before, and advances in metallurgy have produced alloys more suitable to the casings of mines and grenades, bursting under greater pressure, producing a greater number of fragments moving at higher velocities, so that the lethal ranges of such weapons have greatly increased. The sizes and weights of grenades thrown by hand very quickly stabilized at between 1 and 1.5 lbs, and consequently the lengths to which they could be thrown at about 40 yards, when it was discovered that those too large could not be thrown a safe distance away and those too small failed to incapacitate their victims. The introduction of the rifle grenade during World War II increased the range of these projectiles to roughly 250 yards. In the 1960s the advent of the grenade launcher and its range of new 40mm high explosive projectiles further increased the individual infantryman's capacity to inflict fragmentation wounds upon his enemy at distances beyond the reach of the rifle grenade and up to the minimum range of the mortar. When automatic grenade launchers with high rates of fire followed in the 1970s, the combat potential of small infantry units was accordingly further increased.

**M-79 40mm Grenade Launcher:** Developed by the Springfield Armoury, the M-79 first entered U.S. Army service in 1965. A break-open single-shot weapon with an aluminum tube, it weighs 6.45 lbs when loaded with its six-ounce 40mm round, and fires with a muzzle velocity of 250 fps, sufficient at point blank range to shear a man's

head off even when the grenade does not arm. Its maximum range is 430 yards, and it is highly accurate to a range of 180 yards. A stock of 10,000 of these weapons, together with 175,000 40mm grenades, was abandoned when United States forces evacuated Vietnam.

**In Service Abroad:** Australia, Israel, New Zealand, Vietnam.

**M-203 40mm Grenade Launcher:** A lightweight, single-shot launcher that first entered U.S. Army service in 1970 to replace the M-79. Weighing only 3 lbs, it is fitted to the M-16A1 rifle, breech-loaded and manually opearted by pump action. Its maximum range is 500 yards. Colt Industries are the prime contractor.

**In Service Abroad:** Australia, New Zealand, United Kingdom and Vietnam.

**Price:** $231.88@ (1978 Unit Procurement Cost for 1,725 M-203 to U.S. Army).

**XM-174 40mm Grenade Launcher:** Developed in 1960 and introduced in 1968, the XM-174 is capable either of automatic or semi-automatic fire at a cyclic rate of 300 rpm, and is belt-fed or operated with a magazine holding twelve 40mm grenade rounds. Weighing 17 lbs, it can be mounted on a ground tripod or a vehicle pintle mount, has a muzzle velocity of 250 fps, and a maximum range of 500 yards. The XM-174E3 version has been developed to fire the new XRM-79 RAP (Rocket Assisted Projectile) version of the 40mm grenade, to a maximum range of 1,250 yards. In United States service only.

The M-129 40mm grenade launcher, developed for use in helicopter armament systems, and with a cyclic rate of fire of 230 to 450 rpm, has also been adapted for use by ground forces on a tripod mount, and is often operated from a pintle mount on riverine warfare craft or armoured vehicles. Its effective range is 1,875 yards. Maremont Corporation is the prime contractor.

**M-57 Fragmentation Hand Grenade:** One of the standard hand grenades in current U.S. service, the M-57 has a body of thin sheet steel with a notched fragmentation coil, and is filled with 5.5 ozs of Composition B and tetryl pellets and an M-217 electrical impact fuze with a one-second dealy. Weighing one lb, it sends lethal fragments to a radius of 18 yards. The M-26A2 is similar, and both types are packed 30 to a box.

**in Service Abroad:** Australia, Canada, Chile, Guatemala, Israel, Japan, Liberia, New Zealand, Pakistan, South Korea, Taiwan and Vietnam.

**Price:** $4.64@ (1978 open market price). $127.50@ (1978 open market price for box of 30 M-26A2 or M-57).

**M-61 Fragmentation Hand Grenade:** A sheet steel case with an inner steel fragmentation liner, filled with 5.5 ozs of Composition B explosive and tetryl pellets, and an M-204A1 four to five-second delay-detonating fuze. Weighing one lb, and similar in shape to the M-57 and M-26A2 impact hand grenades, it has been in service since the Korean War. It creates lethal fragments to a radius of 18 yards. The M-26A1 grenade is similar, but has three tenths of an ounce more explosive filler. Both types are packed 30 to a box.

**In Service Abroad:** Japan, New Zealand, Vietnam.

**M-67 Fragmentation Hand Grenade:** A somewhat lighter grenade at 14 ozs, and with a more spherical shape, the M-67 has a sheet steel case with an inner steel fragmentation liner and is filled with 6.5 ozs of Composition B explosive and an M-213 four to five-second delay-detonating fuze. It creates lethal fragments to a radius of 20 yards. The M-33 is similar in shape and weight, and both types are packed 30 to a box.

**In Service Abroad:** Canada, New Zealand and Vietnam.

**M-68 Fragmentation Hand Grenade:** Identical in composition, shape, weight and per-

**M-79 Grenade Launcher and 40mm Grenades**

formance to the M-67 and M-33 delay-detonating hand grenades, the M-68 is fitted with an M-217 electrical impact fuze with a one-second delay. Should the grenade fail to explode, an added safety feature inactivates the power supply to the fuze after 30 seconds, so the grenade may be discarded. The M-69 is similar, and both types create lethal fragmentation to a radius of 20 yards. They are available packed 30 to a box.

**M-34 Hand or Rifle Incendiary Fragmentation Grenade:** Weighing one lb 8 ozs, and filled with 15 ozs of WP (White Phosphorous), the M-34 has a case of rolled steel that has been serrated for fragmentation, and is fitted with an M-206A2 four to five-second delay-detonating fuze. On explosion, the M-34 sends lethal fragments to a radius of 31 yards and WP fragments to a radius of 40 yards. These burn at a heat of 280.5 degrees Centigrade for about 60 seconds. Packed 16 to a box.

**In Service Abroad:** Japan, South Korea, Vietnam.

**Price:** $6.55@ (1978 open market price).

**Mk 2 Fragmentation Hand Grenade:** The famous "Pineapple" grenade of World War II, the Mk 2 weighs one lb 5 ozs, and its heavy cast iron case, serrated for fragmentation, is filled with 2 ozs of flaked or granular TNT and an M-204A1 four to five-second delay-detonating fuze. It creates lethal fragments to a radius of 12 yards. In the United States, it is in service today only with our Navy. Packed 25 to a box.

**In Service Abroad:** Netherlands and Vietnam.

**Price:** $3.57@ (1978 open market price).

**M-67 Fragmentation Hand Grenade**    **Mk 2 Fragmentation Hand Grenade**

**M-19 Antitank Mine**

**Mk3A2 Offensive Hand Grenade:** With a cylindrical body of asphalt-impregnated pressed fibre, the Mk 3A2 weighs 15.6 ozs and is filled with 8 ozs of flaked TNT and an M-206A2 four to five-second delay-detonating fuse. It is meant to incapacitate by concussion, at which it is quite effective, but obviously its pressed fibre body does not create lethal fragments. In a curious perversion of nomenclature, it has therefore been termed an "offensive" grenade, to be used only by assault troops, while our steel fragmentation grenades are regarded as "defensive" weapons. This would suggest that we believe it is only proper to kill and maim when we have not taken the offensive, but are under assault ourselves. In fact, of course, our fragmentation grenades are used in every combat situation, and the choice of type is guided by the available supplies at hand and the impulse of the individual soldier.

**AN/M-8 Smoke Grenade:** A cylindrical sheet metal container weighing one lb 8 ozs and filled with 19 ozs of HC smoke mixture and an M-201A one-second delay-igniting fuze. It burns for up to two and a half minutes. Placed 16 to a box.

**ABC/M-25A1 Gas Grenade:** Two plastic hemispheres together weighing 7.5 ozs and filled with 3.2 ozs of CN1 tear gas mixture, fitted with the Olin 2926A one to three-second delay detonating fuze. Packed 50 to a box.

**In Service Abroad:** Japan, Norway.

**Ring Aerofoil Grenade:** Now in development, the RAG grew from a United States Army requirement based on experience in the jungles of Southeast Asia, for a shoulder-fired grenade with a flat trajectory to reduce interference from tree canopy and dense foliage. An increase in the velocity of the projectile would, of course, flatten its trajectory for a longer distance, but would also create recoil forces too great for a shoulder-fired weapon. It was recognized that the projectile itself would have to contribute some form of aerodynamic lift to the solution of the problem. A ring shape was chosen, with a high ratio of lift to drag, incorporating a pre-fragmented outer surface with an inner explosive filling producing a high ratio of charge to mass. The current RAG is 2.5 inches in diameter, weighs 3.2 ozs, and is fired at a muzzle velocity of 450 fps. In 2.4 seconds of flight time is will travel 375 yards with a drop of only 4 feet, producing fragments with an initial velocity of 2,600 fps. Its maximum range, far more than that of any previous grenade launcher, is 2,550 yards, with a drop of 84 feet.

**M-16A1 Anti-Personnel Mine:** A manually laid cast iron and steel case weighing 7.93

lbs and filled with 1.1 lbs of TNT. Activated by trip-wire or pressure of more than 8 lbs, it is spring-released to a height of three feet in the air, at which point it bursts to produce lethal fragmentation to a minimum radius of 33 yards and wounding fragments for up to 225 yards.

**Price:** $95@ (1978 open market price).

**M-18A1 Claymore Anti-Personnel Mine:** Developed by the Picatinny Arsenal, the Claymore Mine is an RFD (Remote Firing Device) that was heavily used in Southeast Asia, and successfully copied by the Viet Cong. Weighing 3.2 lbs, it consists of a rectangular case of polystyrene and fiberglass curved outwards to cover a forward front of 60 degrees, with a charge of 1.5 lbs of Composition C-4 explosive behind a plastic filler in which 700 steel shards have been embedded. Set on six-inch folding metal legs to face the enemy, the Claymore can be detonated by trip-wire or remote control. When exploded, the charge sends the steel shards forward in an arc of 60 degrees that is lethal to 80 yards. The case has been vertically shaped with a slight concavity to channel dispersion of the shards into a single plane from one to five feet above the ground. The Claymore is in service with the U.S. Army and USMC, and is produced by Standard Kollsman Industries and other firms.

**In Service Abroad:** Israel, United Kingdom, Vietnam and West Germany.

**Price:** $119@ (1978 open market price).

**M-7A2 Anti-Personnel and Anti-Tank Mine:** A manually-laid rectangular steel box weighing 4.8 lbs and filled with 3.5 lbs of tetrytol with an M-603 pressure-activated fuze, which responds to pressure of more than 130 lbs. Its blast is equivalent to the force of a high-explosive round from a 105mm howitzer. Being of metal construction, however, it is subject to electro-magnetic detection.

**M-19 Antitank Mine:** A plastic container weighing 27.9 lbs filled with 20.9 lbs of high explosives and a pressure-activated fuze. Undetectable by electro-magnetic means, it creates a blast equivalent to the force of a high-explosive round from an 8'' (203mm) howitzer.

**Astrolite:** A liquid mine now in development, Astrolite is a form of fuel air munition which remains in a combustible state for as long as 96 hours before evaporation has rendered it inert. Manually poured over the ground, or sprayed from vehicles or aircraft, it soaks into the topsoil, and has no detectable odor. It is exploded by remote control, creating over the area treated a blast pressure of up to 1,000 psi, sufficient to kill personnel, blow the wheels and tracks off vehicles and stun or kill the personnel within them. Prime contractor is the Explosives Corporation of America.

# NAVAL VESSELS

Of the three major branches of United States military service, our Navy is the only one that contains integral elements of the other two, including both air and ground forces, under its own command. This organization evolved in World War II, in response to the need for a unified structure of command under which assault landing forces with air support could be launched from ships to reconquer the Western Pacific. Today, the immense cost of maintaining a force so flexible that it can carry out air strikes and amphibious assaults while simultaneously defending our sea lanes, has brought the future role of the Navy under close scrutiny, and it is likely that one or more of these capabilities will be reduced in favor of another deemed more important by current planners. A greater number of more highly specialized ships may be less expensive to produce than fewer multipurpose ships equipped to deal with every contingency for which our Navy has tried to prepare itself. It is likely that sea-based air power will be reduced somewhat in favor of land-based air—though by no means will it be eliminated, for we can never be certain that an overseas land base on which we may depend will remain accessible to United States forces. It is likely that the size of our amphibious forces will be reduced, though we are bound to keep a significant number of specialized ships for this purpose available to carry out limited intervention. This series of tactical and strategic questions, together with an examination of the complex organization of our Navy, its equipment and capabilities, properly deserves a book of its own. There is only sufficient space here to summarize the major types of United States naval vessels in service abroad today or planned for future transfer.

## AIRCRAFT CARRIERS

Those carriers stricken from the Naval Vessel Register have generally been scrapped, and have not been made available for transfer abroad. Six such vessels, including CVS-9 *USS Essex*, CVS-14 *USS Ticonderoga* and CVS-18 *USS Wasp*, were stricken as recently as 1973, though one of them, CVS-10 *USS Yorktown*, has become a memorial at Patriot's Point, South Carolina. However, in 1972 we did transfer the light carrier CVL-28 *USS Cabot* to Spain under FMS, and in 1973 a former *Cleveland* class cruiser, originally commissioned in 1942

and rebuilt as a light carrier, was also transferred to Spain and renamed PH-01 *Dedalo*. The *Dedalo* operates the Spanish Navy's small force of AV-8A Harrier VSTOL aircraft. The light carriers *Langley* and *Belleau Wood*, transferred to France on loan under MAP in 1951 and 1953 respectively, were returned to the United States in 1960 and 1963, and were subsequently scrapped. Another vessel, built under MAP for loan to the United Kingdom in 1942, was transferred to France in 1945 and then returned to the United States in 1966 and scrapped.

## CRUISERS

Two former *St. Louis* class cruisers were transferred to Brazil in 1951 and renamed *Barroso* and *Tamandare*. In the same year, we sold two former *Brooklyn* class cruisers, CL-46 *USS Phoenix* and CL-47 *USS Boise*, to Argentina for $7,800,000. Each displacing 13,645 tons and armed with fifteen 6'' guns, eight 5'' guns and two twin 40mm antiaircraft guns, these vessels have a maximum speed of 32.5 knots and a range of 7,600 miles. They have been renamed *General Belgrano* and *Nueve de Julio*. Two cruisers in the same class were also sold that year to Chile. One, the *O'Higgins,* ran aground in 1974, sustaining too much damage to return to sea. The other, the former CL-43 *USS Nashville*, renamed the *Prat*, remains on active duty. The *Nashville* was sold for $37,000,000.

*USS Allen M. Sumner*

# DESTROYERS

Since 1951, we have sold 195 destroyers under FMS and given away another 105 under MAP. Most of these remain in service abroad today. Here are the major types:

**Allen M. Sumner Class:** Displacing 3,320 tons fully loaded, and with six 5'' guns, four 3'' twin antiaircraft guns, depth charges and two Mk 32 triple torpedo launchers, these vessels have a maximum speed of 34 knots. Of the 58 originally built between 1944 and 1946 by the Bath Iron Works, 24 underwent FRAM II (Fleet Rehabilitation and Modernization) conversions, removing the 3'' guns but installing more modern radar equipment. None remain in active service with our Navy, but 25 are now in service abroad, including the most recent transfer in 1973 of DD-97 and DD-98 to South Korea, where they are now named the *Dae Gu* and *In Cheon* respectively.

**In Service Abroad:** Argentina (2), Brazil (1), Chile (2), Colombia (2), Greece (2), Iran (2), Italy (1), Spain (1), Taiwan (8), Turkey (1), South Korea (2), and Venezuela (1).

**Charles F. Adams Class:** Displacing 4,500 tons fully loaded, these vessels mount two 5'' guns, one or two twin Tartar surface-to-air missile launchers, one eight-tube ASROC launcher and two Mk 32 triple torpedo launchers each, and have a top speed of 35 knots. Built by the Bath Iron Works of Bath, Maine, the Todd Shipyards Corporation of Seattle, Defoe Shipbuilding of Bay City, Michigan, and the Puget Sound Bridge and Dry Dock Company, 23 of these destroyers are now in service in the USN, and six have been transferred abroad. These are DD-25 *Perth*, DD-26 *Hobart* and DD-27 *Brisbane* in Australia, and DDG-28 *Lutjens*, DDG-29 *Molders* and DDG-30 *Rommel* in West Germany.

**In Service Abroad:** Australia (3), and West Germany (3).

**Forrest Sherman Class:** Displacing 4,000 tons, and with a maximum speed of 33 knots, this class of destroyer mounts one, two or three 5'' guns, two or four 3'' antiaircraft guns, one Tartar surface-to-air missile launcher, one eight-tube ASROC launcher and two Mk 32 triple torpedo launchers. Of the 26 vessels originally built between 1953 and 1959 by the Bath Iron works and Bethlehem Steel Corporation's Quincy yards, 9 are now in service with the USN and 3 have been transferred abroad, including DD-960 and DD-961 to Japan, and DD-962 to Pakistan.

**In Service Abroad:** Japan (2), and Pakistan (1).

**Gearing Class:** 99 of these vessels were built between 1944 and 1949 by the Bath Iron Works, Bethlehem and Consolidated Steel Corporations, and many have undergone FRAM I and FRAM II conversions. Displacing 3,500 tons fully loaded, and with a maximum speed of 34 knots, they mount four 5'' guns and two Mk 32 triple torpedo launchers. While FRAM I conversions mount an eight-tube ASROC launcher, FRAM II vessels carry a Mk 15 Hedgehog launcher and an ASW helicopter. 48 *Gearing* class destroyers are in service in the USN today. South Korea received two in 1972, and has named them DD-95 *Chung Buk* and DD-96 *Jeong Buk*. In 1977, two more were transferred to that country, DD-818 *USS New*, which is now DD-99 *Taejion*, and DD-849 *USS Richard E. Kraus*, which is now DD-100.

**In Service Abroad:** Argentina (1), Brazil (2), Greece (4), Spain (5), Taiwan (6), Turkey (5) and South Korea (4).

**Fletcher Class:** More than 100 of this class of destroyer were built between 1942 and 1943, and while none remain today in service with the USN, over 70 serve abroad in 16 countries. Displacing 3,050 tons with a top speed of 35 knots, this destroyer mounts either four or five 5'' guns together with six 3'' or six twin 40mm antiaircraft guns, a depth charge rack, and two five-tube 21'' torpedo launchers. In 1974 Saudi Arabia purchased 26 of them for $19.23 million each.

**In Service Abroad:** Argentina (5), Brazil (6), Chile (2), Colombia (1), Greece (6), Italy (2), Japan (2), Mexico (2), Peru (2), Saudi Arabia (6), Spain (5), South Korea (3), Taiwan (4), Portugal (2), Turkey (6), Venezuela (1) and West Germany (4).

**Price:** $19.23 million@ (1974 unit FMS price to Saudia Arabia for 6).

**Spruance Class:** A sophisticated new class of destroyer, 30 of which are now being built by the Ingalls Shipbuilding Division of Litton Systems, Inc., to replace some of the World War II destroyers still in service with the USN. Displacing 7,800 tons, they will be equipped with two Mk 45 5'' gun mounts, a Mk 26 twin BPDMS (Basic Point Defense Missile System) launcher for ASROC, Sea Sparrow, Harpoon or Standard missiles, two Mk 32 triple torpedo launchers, an eight-tube ASROC launcher, one SH-3 Sea King or two SH-2D LAMPS helicopters, two Vulcan Phalanx CIWS (Close In Weapon System) mounts for missile defense, an AN/SPS-40A air search system, AN/SQS-35 and AN/SQS-53 ECM systems, and a Mk 86 fire control system. Despite their size, they will have a maximum speed of more than 30 knots. To date, 20 *Spruance* class destroyers have been laid down, 14 launched and 9 commissioned, and while each vessel had originally been estimated to cost $81 million, that cost has now risen to $134 million.

Iran, in 1973, agreed to purchase two modified *Spruance* class destroyers for $116 million each, and increased its order the following year to six. But the FMS price, in response to increasing domestic costs, rose to $238 million in 1975 and $333 million in 1976. The Iranian government reacted by cutting its order to four vessels, which will now cost $366.6 million each. The first of these, when it is delivered in 1981, will be named the *Khouroosh*. Litton still hopes to restore the two vessels declined to the Iranian order.

**In US Service:** Of a total of 30 planned, 9 now in service in USN, some undergoing sea trials.

**Price:** $134 million@ (1978 estimate of unit procurement cost for 30 *Spruance* class destroyers to USN, in 1977 dollars). $116 million@ (1973 unit FMS price for two *spruance* class destroyers to Iran). $238 million@ (1975 unit FMS price for six *Spruance* class destroyers to Iran). $366.6 million@ (1978 unit FMS price for four *Spruance* class destroyers to Iran).

**USS Fletcher**

# MINESWEEPERS

Also much in demand abroad, and transferred in great numbers. Following are the major types:

**Agile Class:** Displacing 750 tons, with a maximum speed of 15.5 knots, these vessels mount one twin 40mm antiaircraft gun and either two .50 Cal or two 20mm guns. 48 remain in United States service.

**In Service Abroad:** Belgium (7), France (14), Italy (4), Netherlands (6), Portugal (4), Spain (4), and Uruguay (1).

**Auk Class:** Displacing 1,250 tons, with a top speed of 18 knots, these vessels mount one 3'' gun and either two single or four twin 40mm guns. 40 serve in the USN today.

**In Service Abroad:** Mexico (18), Norway (4), Peru (2), Philippines (2), South Korea (3), Taiwan (3), and Uruguay (1).

**Admirable Class:** Displacing 4,300 tons and with a top speed of 15 knots, these ships mount one 3'' gun and four twin 40mm guns. None remain in U.S. service.

**In Service Abroad:** Mexico (17).

**Redwing Class:** Displacing 412 tons, these vessels mount one 20mm gun. Seven are in USN service.

**In Service Abroad:** Saudi Arabia (4), Spain (2), and South Korea (2).

**Bluebird Class:** Thirteen remain in service with the USN, but over 170 have been transferred to 19 countries abroad.

**In Service Abroad:** Belgium (0), Denmark (8), France (27), Greece (10), Indonesia (6), Iran (4), Italy (18), Japan (4), Netherlands (14), Norway (10), Pakistan (8), Philippines (2), Portugal (8), Spain (12), South Korea (6), Taiwan (14), Thailand (4), Turkey (12) and Vietnam (2).

# ASSAULT SHIPS

Intended to carry troops, equipment and armoured vehicles ashore in amphibious landing operations, and to keep them supplied while they carry out their mission, a large number of these craft were produced in the United States during and after World War II. They have been transferred abroad in substantial quantities, though we keep a large force of our own for amphibious operations, including seven *Iwo Jima* class aircraft carriers, a new class of five general purpose amphibious assault ships, each displacing 39,500 tons, and the first of which, produced by Ingalls, is the LHA-1 *Tarawa*, twenty LSD (Landing Ship, Dock) and 41 LST (Landing Ship, Tank) vessels, and an assortment of specialized cargo and command ships. The new *Tarawa* class of LHA will carry 30 helicopters, and will each cost approximately $230 million.

**Casa Grande Class:** Displacing 9,375 tons with a maximum speed of 15.4 knots, these vessels mount two quad 40mm guns and can carry 200 fully equipped combat troops to shore. Some remain in USN service.

**In Service Abroad:** United Kingdom (4).

**Cabildo Class:** Similar to the Casa Grande vessels, but mounting two quad 40mm guns and two twin 40mm guns. Three remain in USN service.

**In Service Abroad:** Greece (1), Spain (1).

**County Class LST:** Displacing 4,080 tons and mounting two twin 40mm guns and two single 40mm guns, these ships have a maximum speed of 11.6 knots, and can carry ashore either 634 fully equipped combat troops or ten main battle tanks. Several types remain in United States service.

**In Service Abroad:** Brazil (1), Greece (5), Indonesia (8), Italy (2), Japan (3), Malaysia (1), Mexico (1), Philippines (6), Spain (4), South Korea (8), Singapore (1), Taiwan (21), Thailand (4), Turkey (2), Venezuela (1) and Vietnam (6).

**LSM Assault Ship:** Displacing 1,000 tons and with a top speed of 12 knots, these smaller vessels can carry up to 200 combat troops and mount two twin 40mm guns.

**In Service Abroad:** Dominican Republic (1), Greece (6), Japan (1), Philippines (3), Taiwan (4), Thailand (3), and West Germany (2).

# FRIGATES AND DESTROYER ESCORTS

Smaller than destroyers, and normally assigned to convoy and amphibious landing escort duties, these vessels have also been heavily transferred abroad, where most are still known as destroyer escorts, though our Navy has reclassified them as frigates.

**Bostwick Class:** Displacing 1,900 tons, and with a top speed of 21 knots, these vessels mount three 3'' guns and two twin 40mm antiaircraft guns, together with Hedgehog launchers and depth charges.

**In Service Abroad:** Brazil (5), France (1), Greece (4), Italy (1), Japan (2), Peru (3), Philippines (1), South Korea (2), Taiwan (4), Tailand (1), and Uruguay (2).

**Dealey and Courtney Class:** Displacing 1,914 tons with a top speed of 25 knots, these escort ships were produced between 1952 and 1958. The *Dealey* Class types have four 3'' guns while the *Courtney* Class have two. All are equipped with Mk 32 triple torpedo launchers.

**In Service Abroad:** Colombia (1), Indonesia (4), Portugal (1), and Uruguay (1). (NB: the Indonesian vessels are of a similar *Claud Jones* class).

**Rudderow Class:** Displacing 2,230 tons with a top speed of 24 knots, *Rudderow* class ships mount two 5'' guns, four or eight twin 40mm antiaircraft guns, a Mk 15 Hedgehog launcher and often a depth charge rack as well.

**In Service Abroad:** Taiwan (1), South Korea (1).

**Brooke and Garcia Class:** Sixteen of these vessels, together with two ships of a similar *Bronstein* class, are now in service in the USN, and seven have been transferred abroad. Displacing 3,425 tons, and with a maximum speed of 27 knots, they mount either one or two 5'' guns, an eight-tube ASROC launcher, two Mk 32 triple torpedo launchers and often carry an ASW helicopter. *Brooke* class ships are also fitted with one twin Tartar surface-to-air missile launcher, and carry two Mk 25 fixed stern torpedo tubes.

**In Service Abroad:** Portugal (2), Spain (5). (NB: the Spanish vessels are of *Brooke* class).

**Oliver Hazard Perry Class:** Displacing 3,605 tons, and with a maximum speed of 28 knots, this new class of frigate, nine of which are expected to be in service with the USN by 1981, are intended not to replace but to complement the existing force of frigates, emphasizing both AAW (Antiair Warfare) and ASW (Anti Submarine Warfare) capabilities. They will be equipped with one compact 76mm gun mount produced by Oto Melara of La Spezia, one 20mm Vulcan Phalanx CIWS mount, one Mk 13 single launcher for Standard or Harpoon missiles, two Mk 32 triple torpedo launchers, and two SH-2 LAMPS helicopters each.

The Navy has planned on procurement of a total of 38 of these frigates, which were estimated in 1972 to cost $60 million each. Procurement of eight in 1977, however, cost $147.4 million each. A further eleven had been planned for procurement in 1978 at $145.5 million each, but two were cut from the budget, raising the unit cost in 1978 to $146.5 million each. For a unit FMS price of $160.5 million each, Australia ordered two of these vessels in 1976, for delivery in 1981. They will be named the *Adelaide* and the *Canberra*. Prime contractors for production of the *Oliver Hazard Perry* class frigates are Bath Iron Works and Todd Shipyards.

**Price:** $147.4 million @ (1977 Unit Procurement Cost for eight FFG-7 to USN). $146.5 million@ (1978 Unit Procurement Cost for nine FFG-7 to USN). $160.5 million@ (1976 unit FMS price for two FFG-7 to Australia).

# PATROL AND RIVERINE WARFARE CRAFT

A variety of small patrol craft and specially equipped vessels, heavily armoured, for riverine warfare and close combat have been built in surprising numbers in the United States, from the Higgins boats and PT boats of World War II to the heavily armed Swift boats used in Southeast Asia.

**Asheville Class Patrol Combatant:** Displacing 245 tons with a top speed of 40 knots, this vessel mounts one 3″ gun, one 40mm gun and four .50 Cal machine guns. Sixteen are in service in the USN.

**In Service Abroad:** Greece (2), South Korea (2), Vietnam (2).

**PC Patrol Craft:** Displacing 450 tons and with a speed of 19 knots, these vessels mount one 3″ gun, one 40mm gun and four 20mm guns, as well as depth charges.

**In Service Abroad:** Cambodia (2), Indonesia (4), Philippines (4), South Korea (3), Venezuela (10), and Vietnam (1).

**PCE Patrol Vessel:** Displacing 903 tons with a top speed of 15 knots, this vessel mounts one 3″ gun and six 20mm guns.

**In Service Abroad:** Cuba (2), Ecuador (2), Philippines (5), South Korea (8), Taiwan (1) and Vietnam (3).

**PBR Mk I, Mk II and Mk III:** From 61 to 65 feet long, these vessels have a top speed of 25 knots and can be mounted with one or two .50 Cal machine guns or 20mm cannon, as well as pintle-mounted M-129 grenade launchers. In 1976 Iran ordered 19 of the Mk III version for $505,260 each, and may order another 21. In 1977 Sri Lanka ordered five of the same type, and Syria has asked for sixteen.

**In Service Abroad:** Cambodia (65 Mk I and Mk II), Iran (19 Mk III), Philippines (40 Mk III), Vietnam (200 Mk I and Mk II).

**Price:** $505,260@ (1976 unit FMS price for 19 PBR Mk III to Iran).

**Strike Assault Patrol Boat**

**Honeywell Mk 46 Mod 1 Acoustic-Homing Torpedo**

**PCF Swift Boat:** Manufactured by Sewart Seacraft of New Orleans, these boats are 50 feet long and have top speeds of 25 to 30 mph, mounting twin .50 Cal machine guns in a forward tub above the cabin, and an unusual combination of a .50 Cal machine gun and an 81mm mortar mounted on a rear deck pedestal. Belt-fed pintle-mounted M-129 grenade launchers would often be fitted on the decks as well, and when these boats were operated in the Mekong Delta in Southeast Asia, the crew often carried M-60 machine guns as additional armament.

**In Service Abroad:** Cambodia (14), Thailand (7), Vietnam (82).

# SUBMARINES

Of our vast fleet of submarines, only the diesel-powered varieties have been made available abroad. But as we embark on additional programs of submarine procurement, including 26 new nuclear-powered attack submarines of the SSN-688 Los Angeles class, three of which were purchased in 1977 for $319.5 million each, and one of which was procured in 1978 for $278.5 million, more of our older nuclear-powered submarines may be withdrawn from active service, and become available for transfer. Our very first nuclear-powered submarine, the SSN-571 Nautilus, commissioned in 1954, was in fact just retired in 1978.

**Balao Class:** Displacing 1,829 tons surfaced and 2,424 submerged, these boats have a speed of 10 knots under water, are equipped with six bow and four stern torpedo tubes and carry a complement of 24 torpedoes. The SS-307 Tilefish in this class, transferred to Venezuela in 1960 and renamed S-11 Carite, was retired in 1977.

**In Service Abroad:** Chile (1), Greece (1), Italy (3), Spain (1), and Turkey (8).

**Tang Class:** Displacing 2,100 tons surfaced and 2,700 submerged, Tang class boats have a maximum speed of 18 knots under water. They are fitted with six bow and two stern torpedo tubes. In 1975, Iran purchased three of these boats, including the SS-565 Tang itself, for $17.833 million each.

**In Service Abroad:** Italy (2), Iran (3).

**Price:** $17.833 million@ (1975 unit FMS price for three SS-565 to Iran).

**Guppy Class Patrol Submarines:** A series of patrol submarines manufactured between 1943 and 1951, and reconditioned or modernized between 1948 and 1962, displacing 1,870 to 1,975 tons surfaced and a maximum of 2,540 tons submerged, with a top speed of 15 knots under water. All are equipped with six bow and four stern torpedo tubes, and the Guppy IA class are capable of minelaying as well.

**Guppy IA In Service Abroad:** Argentina (1), Greece (1), and Turkey (1).

**Guppy II In Service Abroad:** Argentina (1), Brazil (5), Greece (1), Peru (1), Venezuela (2).

**Guppy IIA In Service Abroad:** Greece (1), Spain (2), and Turkey (5).

**Guppy III In Service Abroad:** Brazil (2), Greece (1), and Italy (2).

**Torpedoes:** Several types are currently in service, including the Mk 48, the Mk 46, and Captor, an ASW (Anti Submarine Warfare) mine with an encapsulated Mk 46 torpedo for submerged targets. Northrop have developed the Mk 37 wire-guided torpedo, fired from submarines against submarines, but equally effective against surface targets, and powered by an internal combustion engine.

**Mk 48 in Service Abroad:** Australia.

**Mk 46 In Service Abroad:** Canada, France, Greece, Iran, Italy, Netherlands, Norway, Turkey, United Kingdom and West Germany.

**Price of Mk 46:** $169,082@ (1975 unit FMS price for 414 Mk 46 to Iran).

**Price of Mk 48:** $541,666@ (1978 Unit Procurement Cost for 300 Mk 48 to USN).

**Price of Captor:** $154,000@ (1978 Unit Procurement Cost for 550 Captor to USN).

# OUR NUCLEAR ARSENAL

While each year enormous sums are spent in the United States on the development and procurement of conventional weapon systems, even greater amounts are spent on the development of new strategic weapon systems, or on the expansion and improvement of existing ones. A total of $40 billion alone has been planned for the development of the new M-X mobile ICBM system, and $158.2 million of that amount will come from the Fiscal Year 1979 U.S. Defense Department budget. Following is a summary of the major weapon systems in America's strategic and tactical nuclear arsenal, together with the major improvement and development programs now in progress for strategic systems.

**Boeing B-52 Stratofortress.** Still the backbone of our Strategic Air Command, this eight-engine bomber was originally designed to carry four thermonuclear gravity bombs in internal weapons bays. From an operational strength of 640 aircraft in 1962, 349 B-52s now remain with SAC, having undergone a variety of improvements and modifications at a cost of more than $1.1 billion.

80 B-52Ds remain operational, organized into 5 bomber squadrons. Structural modifications, principally to the wings of the B-52D, have cost $2.6 million per aircraft. Of 296 operational B-52Gs and B-52Hs, 151 B-52Gs, and 90 B-52Hs are organized into 17 bomber squadrons. Cartridge starters have been added to the Pratt & Whitney J57 turbojet engines on the B-52G, and Pratt & Whitney TF33 turbofan engines have replaced the J57 on the B-52H, at a cost of $35 million. An electro-optical viewing system has been installed on all the B-52Gs and B-52Hs, at a cost of $1 million per aircraft. Phase 6 ECM (Electronic Countermeasures) suites have been added to all B-52Gs and B-52Hs, including ITT's ALQ-117 deception jammer, which counteracts Soviet pulse radars, at a total cost of $296 million. Finally, all B-52Gs and B-52Hs have been fitted with SRAM (Short-Range Attack Missile) launchers and their associated equipment, at a cost, excluding the missiles themselves, of $359 million.

The B-52D can carry four nuclear gravity bombs, either the B-28 or the B-61—the latter being the newest operational SAC hydrogen bomb, available in a variety of yields. The B-52G and B-52H can carry the above load, in addition to either six SRAM missiles or two AGM-28B Hound Dog missiles mounted on underwing pylons. Alternatively, they can replace nuclear gravity bombs in the weapons bays with additional SRAM launchers, for a maximum load of 20 SRAM missiles. The B-52 has a top speed of 546 mph (Mach 0.85) and a range of 10,000 miles.

**General Dynamics FB-111A.** 76 of these aircraft have been built, and 68 are deployed in 4 bomber squadrons to make up the present balance of the SAC bomber force. With a ceiling of 60,000 feet and a range of 4,000 miles, the twin turbofan engined bomber can reach speeds up to Mach 2.5. Since January of 1976, these aircraft have been modified to accept up to six SRAM missiles. Alternatively, they can carry six B-61 nuclear gravity bombs. Their highly sophisticated avionics system utilizes 14 onboard computers, and by the end of this year they will have completed modification to the ALQ-137 automatic ECM system, affording exceptional protection against Soviet radar and missile defenses.

**Rockwell International B-1.** Powered by four General Electric F-100 turbofan engines, with a wingspan of 137 feet and a length of 143 feet (about two-thirds the size of the B-52), this aircraft incorporates the most sophisticated advances science has achieved in avionics and countermeasures capabilities, including the APQ-144 forward-looking radar, and ECM equipment that reduces its infra-red "signature" and radar cross-section to improve penetration of enemy defenses. It is designed to fly under Soviet radar at treetop levels, travelling at speeds of up to Mach 1.6, and it has a range of 6,100 miles. It is also capable of carrying up to 32 SRAM missiles, 24 in the weapons bays and 8 on the wing pylons. The USAF had proposed it as a replacement for the B-52, and planned to build a force of 244 B-1s. Three prototypes were built and a fourth was under construction when the program was cancelled in 1977, in favor of development of the ALCM cruise missile. Each of the three completed aircraft cost $93.8 million. They will be used as research and development testbeds for other programs.

**AGM-28 Hound Dog.** Developed by Rockwell International, and supplied to 29 SAC wings in August 1963, several hundred of these missiles remain operational. Two can be carried on each B-52G or B-52H. With a thermonuclear warhead, the missile travels at a speed of Mach 2, and has a range of over 600 miles.

**AGM 69A SRAM.** Built by Boeing Aerospace Company, the SRAM, or short-range attack missile, has a speed of Mach 3 and a range of from 25 to 100 miles. 1500 of the missiles have been produced, and by August 1975 they were delivered to the 18 SAC bases scheduled to receive them, equipping 17 B-52 and 2 FB-111A bomber wings. The cost of the SRAM program was $1.567 billion, or $391,000 per missile—*excluding* the warhead. The Mark 12A reentry vehicle, a three-warhead MIRV (Multiple Independently Targetable Reentry Vehicle) with a yield of 200 kilotons for each warhead, costs $610,000. Therefore, the complete cost of one armed SRAM missile is $1.001 million.

**AGM-68A Air-Launched Cruise Missle (ALCM).** This is the USAF's cruise missile, developed by Boeing Aerospace Company. The B-52 could carry up to 12 of these, and the B-1 as many as 24. Powered by an air-breathing turbofan engine, and navigating by a combination of inertial guidance and pre-programmed terrain contour mapping, it is continuously corrected in its course by satellite data links, and can deliver a 170 kiloton warhead over a range of 1,200 miles to within 10 yards of its target. The USAF has ordered 2000 ALCMs. After development costs of $1.5 billion, the total program has run to $4 billion. Thus, the cost of each ALCM, including development, is $625,000. Subsequent production runs should reduce the unit ALCM cost to about $500,000.

**BGM-109 Tomahawk (SLCM).** This is the USN's submarine-launched cruise missile, developed by the Convair Division of General Dynamics. There is both a strategic version with a nuclear warhead yielding 200 kilotons, and a tactical version with a conventional high-explosive warhead. The guidance is equally as sophisticated as the USAF's ALCM, utilizing inertial and TERCOM (Terrain Contour Mapping) systems. The range of the tactical missile is 250 miles, while the strategic version, flying at subsonic speeds and very low in altitude, reaches over 2,000 miles. The unit cost of the strategic Tomahawk is $792,000.

**Titan II Intercontinental Ballistic Missile (LGM-250).** Developed by the Martin Marietta Corporation, the Titan II became operational in 1963. 54 of them remain operational today, in six squadrons under SAC command. Armed with the General Electric Mark 6 warhead, with a yield of 10 megatons, they have a range of 7,250 miles, and a three-target selection capability.

**Minuteman II Intercontinental Ballistic Missile (LGM-30F).** Developed by Boeing Aerospace Company, 450 of these missiles today equip SAC wings in Montana, Missouri and Utah. Armed with the Avco Mark 11B single warhead, yielding 2 megatons, they have an eight-target selection capability and a range of over 7,000 miles.

**Minuteman III Intercontinental Ballistic Missile (LGM-30G).** An improvement on the Minuteman II, this missile employs the Mark 12 MIRV reentry vehicle, with three warheads, each of which yields 170 kilotons. 550 Minuteman IIIs currently comprise our strongest ICBM force, and are positioned at SAC bases in North and South Dakota and Wyoming. Minuteman III has a range of 8,075 miles, and travels at 15,000 mph, taking approximately 30 minutes to reach its target. Each Minuteman III costs $4.58 million. In 1977, the Senate passed an appropriations bill that included $274.5 million for the purchase of 60 more Minuteman III missiles. This will raise our ICBM strength from its current total of 1,054 missiles to 1,114.

**Retrofitting of Mark 12A Warhead in Minuteman III.** Among the programs to improve existing Minuteman III capabilities, aside from hardening of silos, is the retrofitting of the improved Mark 12A MIRV reentry vehicle, with three separate warheads yielding 335 kilotons each. At a cost of $610,000 each, the retrofitting of 550 missiles will cost a total of $335 million.

**SSBN Polaris Submarine.** The United States currently deploys 10 of these nuclear-powered long-range patrol submarines, 5 in the Ethan Allen class, and 5 in the George Washington class. 380 feet long and weighing 7,000 tons, the boats have a range of 4,500 miles and 70 patrol days, and each has sixteen launching tubes and carries 16 missiles aboard. The missile itself, the *UGM-27C Polaris A-3,* has a range of 2,880 miles and delivers three MIRV warheads, each with a yield of 200 kilotons. The Polaris fleet, therefore, disposes 160 SLBMs, (submarine-launched ballistic missiles), or 480 warheads. Each submarine with its complement of SBLMs costs $50 million.

**SSBN Poseidon Submarine.** The USN deploys 31 Poseidon submarines, 19 in the Lafayette class and 12 in the Benjamin Franklin class. The Poseidon SSBN is somewhat larger than the Polaris, weighing 8,500 tons, and is longer by 55 feet, but it has the same range of 4500 miles and 70 patrol days. The missile system, however, is far more sophisticated. The *UGM-73A Poseidon C-3 SLBM* has a MIRV delivery capability of from 10 to 14 warheads, each yielding 50 kilotons. 32 feet long, and weighing 34 tons, the missile has a range of 2,880 miles, and takes 15 to 20 minutes to reach its target. With sixteen missiles aboard each SSBN, the 31 boats of the Poseidon fleet carry 496 missiles, with anywhere from 4,960 to 6,944 warheads. Each Poseidon SSBN with its complement of SLBNs cost $110 million.

Together, the Polaris and Poseidon fleets, operating from bases in Holy Loch, Scotland, Rota, Spain, and Guam, carry 720 SLBMs with from 5,632 to 7,616 warheads.

**SSBN Trident Submarine.** The USN plans to build 10 General Dynamics Trident SSBNs, and eventually to build another 20. The first is under construction now, and is due for completion in 1979. After that, construction is planned for 2 to 3 boats per year. $18 billion has been estimated for cost to completion of the program for the first 10 Trident SSBNs, or $1.8 billion per boat.

The Trident SSBN will be 535 feet long and weigh 18,000 tons. It will hold not 16 but 24 missile launchers, and each missile, with a MIRV reentry vehicle, will deliver 17 warheads. The yield of each warhead has not been disclosed. This means, however, that each Trident SSBN will dispose 408 warheads, adding another 4,080 warheads to our SLBN arsenal. The first 96 Trident I missiles, designated *UGM-96A Trident C-4,* with a range of 4,600 miles, have been ordered, at a cost of $15.6 million each. The Trident II missile will have a range of 6,000

miles, and may incorporate the new Mark 500 Evader, which is a MARV or maneuvering reentry vehicle, to counteract advanced Soviet anti-ballistic missile defenses.

**Retrofitting of Trident I missile to 10 Poseidon SSBNs.** A program is under way to retrofit 16 Trident I missiles, developed by Lockheed Missile and Space Company, into each of 10 Poseidon SSBNs, at a cost of $2.7 billion, or $16.88 million for each missile and launch tube.

**ABM (anti-ballistic missile) System.** We have dismantled our Safeguard ABM complex at Grand Forks, North Dakota. The total cost of the program for the 100 Spartan and Sprint missiles at this site was $5.4 billion, including construction and launching equipment. We have also deactivated the Nike-Hercules SAM (surface-to-air) system in the continental United States. Nike-Hercules SAMs remain operational, however, at all overseas sites. The United States Army has just placed its Nike-Hercules batteries in South Korea under the control of the Korean government forces. Involved are 144 nuclear weapons in the 5 kiloton range. Additional Nike-Hercules batteries are under the control of West German, Taiwanese and Japanese forces, and the Nike-Hercules system is still under manufacture by Mitsubishi Heavy Industries, Ltd., under license from Western Electric Company.

**Tactical Nuclear Forces.** In addition to those nuclear weapons we define as strategic, the United States has an additional 22,000 weapons classed as tactical because of their shorter range—even though a number of them are more powerful than the strategic weapons. About half of these tactical nuclear weapons are kept in domestic arsenals, and the rest are deployed around the world with American air, ground and naval carrier forces, or with the forces of NATO and SEATO countries.

There are a total of 7,000 nuclear weapons in Europe, 1,700 in Asia, 1,500 with the United States Pacific Fleet, and 1,000 with the Atlantic Fleet. Each aircraft carrier stores about 100 nuclear weapons in the form of nuclear air-to-surface bombs, including the B-28, B-43, B-57, B-61 and B-72, which have yields from 5 kilotons to as much as 1 megaton. This same inventory of bombs is stored at forward American air bases within easy reach of the Soviet Union and China. Our forward-based aircraft include 72 F-111Es in England, 224 F-4Cs and F-4Ds in England, Spain and Germany, 72

F-4Ds in Korea, 36 F-4Ds in Taiwan, 72 A-7s and 24 A-6s aboard two carriers in the Mediterranean, and 108 A-7s and 36 A-6s aboard three carriers in the Western Pacific. This is a total of 664 tactical aircraft capable of reaching targets within the Soviet Union and China. Their combat radiuses vary between 400 and 1,110 miles.

In addition to nuclear surface-to-air bombs, the *GW Walleye Mark I*, a self-homing television-guided air-to-surface missile developed by the Naval Weapons Center, Martin Marietta and Hughes Aircraft, has been delivered in small quantities to forward-based aircraft in Europe and Asia, and to carriers in both the Atlantic and Pacific fleets. The Walleye is the first "smart bomb." It has a range of 35 miles, a warhead yield of from 5 to 10 kilotons, and doesn't miss its target. It can be carried by the F-4, F-111, A-4, A-6 and A-7 aircraft. Some Walleyes with high-explosive warheads have been sold to Israel.

Standard equipment with United States and NATO ground forces in Europe are the Lance, Pershing, Honest John and Sergeant surface-to-surface battlefield support missile systems. Nuclear warheads for all of these systems are stocked in forward bases. The Honest John, with a range of 25 miles and a warhead yield of 100 kilotons, and the Sergeant, with a range of 85 miles and a similar kiloton yield, are now being phased out of service and replaced by the Lance, which has a range of 70 miles and a warhead of 50 kilotons. The Pershing, with a warhead yield of 400 kilotons and a range of 450 miles, is capable of reaching targets in the Soviet Union from its positions in Germany. Nuclear ordnance has also been stored in Europe and in Asia for the 155mm and 203mm howitzer, which is standard equipment in battalion and division artillery units of the United States, West German and Korean armies. With a 1 kiloton yield, these shells have a range of about 10 miles.

The USN's Atlantic and Pacific fleets, totalling 284 ships and submarines, carry an additional variety of tactical nuclear naval weapons, aside from those delivered by carrier-based attack aircraft. Standard USN equipment is the TALOS surface-to-air missile, with a warhead yield of 5 kilotons and a range of 70 miles and a warhead yield of 1 kiloton. These weapons are regarded as defense against air attack. Naval ASW (anti-submarine warfare) aircraft, such as the P-3, the S-3 and a variety of helicopters, also carry the Mark 57 and Mark 101 nuclear depth bombs, with yields of from 5 to 10 kilotons.

Completing America's nuclear arsenal at sea are the ASROC and SUBROC missiles used, respectively, by cruisers and destroyers to hunt submarines, and by submarines to hunt other submarines. Both have warhead yields of 1 kiloton, but the ASROC has a range of 6 miles while the SUBROC, a very sophisticated weapon fired below the surface of the sea and travelling in the air before it reenters the water, has a range of 30 miles.

All of these tactical weapons are regarded to have no effect on the strategic balance between the United States and the Soviet Union, though it is easy to see how they could affect that balance, and difficult to believe that contingency plans have not been drawn to employ them to maximum effect as a fourth strategic force. Certainly, we have no difficulty in acknowledging how the Soviets might use *their* tactical weapons. Defense Secretary Donald Rumsfeld, in presenting his budget to Congress in 1976, noted that the Soviet Navy possessed a variety of short-range cruise missiles. He said, "If the Soviets were to divert their sea-based cruise missiles from the anti-shipping missions to which we believe they are currently assigned and extend their range, they could attack large portions of the U.S. population and industry." The Soviets must be aware that we are equally capable of doing precisely the same thing.

**The MX Missile.** Martin Marietta is the prime contractor for this system, now in full-scale development. Each MX missile would be allocated a separate track of its own, 20 miles long and covering an area the size of Manhattan, on which it would periodically move from one to another of 23 shelters, while transporter vehicles with dummy missiles would move between these shelters rather more frequently. It is held that hostile forces, each of whose attacking missiles would have to strike within 1,500 feet of the real MX with a warhead of at least one megaton to destroy it, could not determine its true location with sufficient accuracy to carry out a first strike. Thus, for the full force of 200 MX missiles proposed, a system of 4,600 shelters is planned, connected by over 10,000 miles of track occupying an area of more than 7,000 square miles in eight counties of Utah and Nevada. It is the largest contruction project ever undertaken by the United States, surpassing even the Panama Canal, and is currently estimated to cost between $34 billion and $59 billion.

Initially presented as a defensive system, the MX has now been acknowledged as a counter-force weapon, whose accuracy will enable the United States to carry out its own first strike against Soviet missile forces. With a range of more than 9,000 statute miles, the MX will be equipped with an inertial guidance system built by Rockwell International, and armed not with

10 warheads as Congress has been told, but either with 15 Mk 12A MIRV warheads, each with a yield of 335 kilotons, or with 20 Mk 500 MIRV warheads whose terminal guidance will bring them to within 400 feet of their target centers.

In its defensive mode, it is doubtful whether the MX system will even succeed in hiding the real missile on each loop of track, since magnetic and thermal instruments on satellites could locate it with relative ease, and since tilt meters planted in the earth can detect it by its weight as it moves between shelters. These liabilities could only be overcome by elaborate deceptions and point security measures costing millions of dollars more.

Congress has approved an expenditure of $1.6 billion in 1981 to develop the MX "with all reasonable speed," though it has required the Pentagon to submit a report on the feasibility of basing the MX in more states than those already chosen, where strong environmental objections have been raised.

An alternate SUM (Shallow Underwater Mobile) system for the MX has been proposed that would eliminate environmental risks, cost only half as much as the land-based MX system, and be fully operational three years earlier than the scheduled land-based MX deployment of 1986. SUM would comprise a fleet of 50 diesel-electric submarines, each armed with two to four MX missiles and operating in United States coastal waters, where their mobility would keep them as safely immune from first strike as our deep water Polaris and Poseidon fleets already are and our Trident fleet will soon be.

**Ground-Launched Cruise Missile (GLCM).** The land-based version of the BGM-109 Tomahawk, with an extended range of 2,500 miles that will enable it to reach Moscow and other Soviet cities from the NATO countries in which it will be deployed. The United Kingdom will be allotted 160 GLCMs and 40 launchers, West Germany 96 GLCMs and 24 launchers, Italy 112 GLCMs and 28 launchers, and Belgium and the Netherlands each 48 GLCMs and 12 launchers. In 1980, $188 million was spent in procurement toward the total GLCM program cost of $2.1 billion. In 1981 we will procure 11 GLCMs for $7.990 million@.

**Pershing II.** With a range of 1,200 miles, this missile will also be able to strike Moscow from West Germany. While initially opposed by NATO nations as strongly as was the GLCM, 108 Pershing II missiles and launchers are now scheduled for deployment in West Europe within the next five years. $146 million will be spent for Pershing II procurement in 1981. The estimated total program cost is $1.7 billion.

**Neutron Bomb.** Designed with a small warhead that can be fired by the Lance missile or the M-109 155mm and M-110 203mm artillery systems, this weapon has a kiloton yield, which is only a fraction of that of the Hiroshima bomb. Its minimal explosive force ensures that buildings and other capital assets more than a mile from its impact center will remain undamaged by heat and blast, and only lightly contaminated, while its intense radiation will expose troop concentrations at which it has been aimed to lethal levels of radiation poisoning. Since death by radiation is painful and slow, our announcement in April of 1978 that we had attained this capability was met with worldwide criticism, including initial West German hesitation to approve its deployment. This resulted in President Carter's decision to postpone the bomb's production, and was quickly followed by a well-organized campaign of media leaks from those who wanted to proceed with it, suggesting he had made a dangerous error without ever showing why. Components of the bomb, in any case, have been produced and are ready for assembly. France has meanwhile announced that it will test and produce its own. Because this "enhanced radiation" weapon was devised in part to counter the Soviet superiority in numbers of tanks, new Soviet tanks are understood to be equipped with a thick inner lead shielding to protect crews against it, somewhat reducing the speed of these vehicles.

# REGISTRY OF MAJOR AMERICAN ARMS TRANSFERS SINCE 1978

Following are those agreements reached in the past three years and valued at more than $1 million each for the transfer of military equipment or services from this country to governments or organizations abroad. Due to limitations of space, it has not been possible to incorporate this information in the individual entries for each weapon system. Consequently, for the current total of any country's inventory of a given weapon, what is listed here should be added to what already appears in the entry for that weapon.

While almost all the following agreements have taken place since the first edition of this book went to press, a few earlier transfers have come to light since that time. They are included here, with the dates of their delivery, to ensure that the book's record of all transfers is as complete as possible.

## ALGERIA

3 x Beech King Air transport aircraft for $810,000@ in 1978.

6 x Beech T-34C Turbo Mentor training aircraft for $583,000@, and 2 x Beech Sierra 200 aircraft for $612,000@ in August of 1979.

## ANGOLA

2 x Swift 58' boat, 12 X M-113A1 armoured personnel carrier, 20 x M-151A1 Jeep, 180 x military truck, 14 x M-40AI 106mm recoilless rifle with 3,774 rounds of ammunition, 470 x M-20A1 3.5" rocket launcher with 2,629 3.5" rockets, 56 x M-30 4.2" mortar, 133 x M-29E1 81mm mortar, 1,318 x XM-224 60mm mortar, 67,486 rounds of mortar ammunition, 64 x M-2HB .50 Cal machine gun, 584 x M-60C 7.62mm machine gun, 2,054 x .30 Cal machine gun, 10 x Browning automatic rifle, 10,210 x light antitank weapon (LAW), 1,030 x M-79 grenade launcher with 272,710 40mm grenades, 41,015 x M-1A1. 30 Cal carbine, 5,379 x M-3A1 .45 Cal submachine gun, 876 x M-10 9mm submachine gun, 7,771 x M-14 7.62mm rifle, 9,487 x M-16A1 5.56mm rifle, 1,350 x M-1911A1 .45 Cal automatic pistol, 500 x 9mm automatic pistol, 97,470 x M-67 hand grenade, 948 military radios and over 28 million rounds of small arms ammunition covertly supplied by the CIA to Jonas Savimbi's UNITA and Holden Roberto's FNLA forces in July and August of 1975.

## ARGENTINA

1 x Boeing 707-320B transport aircraft in 1976.

6 x Swearingen Merlin IIIA and IVA transport aircraft for $2.084 million@ in 1978.

2 x Beech Super King Air transport aircraft for $980,000@ in 1978.

6 x Grumman S-2E Tracker antisubmarine warfare aircraft for $9.6 million@ in 1978.

2 x Lockheed SP-2H Neptune maritime patrol aircraft for $11.3 million@ in 1978.

2 x Rockwell Sabreliner transport aircraft for $1.4 million@ in 1978.

2 x Fletcher class destroyer for $22.314 million@ in 1978.

8 x Bell 212 helicopter for $1.4 million@ in 1978.

16 x Beech T-34C Turbo Mentor training aircraft for $593,750@ in 1978.

6 x Boeing CH-47 Chinook transport helicopter for $6.32 million@ in 1978. Only 3 were delivered by 1979. Further deliveries were halted to demonstrate our government's concern over Argentina's human rights violations. Deliveries of other equipment, however, continued.

2 x Bell UH-1H utility helicopter for $744,000@ in 1979.

2 x Lockheed KC-130 tanker aircraft for $14.7 million@ in 1978.

6 x Beech King Air transport aircraft for $803,000@ in 1979.

## AUSTRALIA

100 x RGM-84A Harpoon antiship missile for $485,079@ in March of 1978.

1 x FFG-7 Oliver Hazard Perry class guided missile frigate for $183.5 million in 1978.

10 x Mk 48 Torpedo with support for $1.45 million@ in 1978.

$50 million in support equipment for two FFG-7 Oliver Hazard Perry class frigates in 1978.

1 x Ford Aerospace AN/FSS-78 60' diameter satellite communications antenna dish terminal for $4.375 million in February of 1979.

1 x FFG-7 Oliver Hazard Perry class guided missile frigate for $208 million in July of 1980 (Australia has now purchased a total of four frigates in this class).

(Note: Letters of offer have been tendered by the United States for 75 x F-15, F-16, F-18A or A-18 aircraft. Australia will shortly pick that number of one of these aircraft—most likely the F-18A Hornet—as its new air defense interceptor. An initial procurement of 25 aircraft is planned, with the total of 75 to be in service by 1983.)

## AUSTRIA

1 x AN/GPN-22 fixed base approach radar system for $2.8 million in June of 1978.

12 x AB-212 helicopter for $1.083 million@ in 1978.

50 x M-60A3 main battle tank for $1.14 million@ in 1979.

24 x AB-212 helicopter for $1.083 million@ in 1979. All have been delivered.

(Note: an order from this country for 24 x F-5E Tiger II fighter aircraft has long been expected, but it now appears that the Mirage 50 will be chosen instead. In February of 1981 the Reagan administration offered a third choice: 24 x F-16 fighter aircraft for $20.833 million@.)

# BANGLADESH

6 x Bell 212 helicopter for $1.333 million@ in 1978.

# BARBADOS

1 x former US Navy tank landing ship (LST) for $490,000 in 1976.

# BELGIUM

60 x Loral Rapport ECM (Electronic Counter Measures) system sets for $333,300@ in August of 1978. These will be installed on Belgium's Mirage V aircraft.

14 x F-16 air combat fighter for $7.088 million@ in September of 1978, bringing Belgium's total procurement of this aircraft type to 130. By 1980, 30 F-16s had been delivered to the Belgian Air Force.

6 x Triad battery sets of MIM-23 Improved HAWK air defense missile equipment for $23.6 million@ in March of 1979.

# BOLIVIA

1 x former US Navy transport ship in 1976.

8 x Cessna A-37B Dragonfly counterinsurgency aircraft for $630,000@ in 1978.

21 x PBR Mk I small patrol boat for $388,000@ in 1978.

6 x Curtiss C-46 Commando transport aircraft, 2 x Douglas C-47 transport aircraft, and 10 x North American T-6 Texan training aircraft from Taiwan for $6 million in 1979.

(Note: Bolivia operates 2 Gates Learjet 25B transport aircraft not previously recorded.)

# BRAZIL

2 x Boeing 727-300L in 1976.

2 x Lockheed KC-130 tanker aircraft for $13.7 million@ in 1978.

# BURMA

980 x M-79 grenade launcher for $256@, with 120,000 40mm grenade at $6.04@ in 1979.

(Note: Burma continues to operate its nine Kaman HH-43B Huskie helicopters, but its eight C-47 transport aircraft are no longer in service.)

# CANADA

1,728 x MGM-71A TOW antitank missile for $7,523@ in 1978.

123,388 rounds 81mm mortar ammunition for $11 million in 1978.

Data processing equipment for two regional operations control centers for $95 million in September of 1978.

24 x LRPA (Long Range Patrol Aircraft) flight stations for $187,500@ in 1978. These will be installed on the Canadian CP-140 Aurora version of the Lockheed P-3C Orion antisubmarine warfare aircraft. Delivery began in May of 1980.

1 x Tactical display system for Canada's fleet of CP-140 Aurora aircraft, for $4.6 million in 1978.

18 x Communications equipment sets for CP-140 Aurora aircraft, for $566,666@ in March of 1979.

$28.6 million in spares for the CF-101B Voodoo, the CF-5A and the CF-104G Starfighter, in July of 1979.

137 x CF-18 Hornet fighter interceptor aircraft for $18.248 million@ in April of 1980, with an offset guarantee of $2 billion in Canadian production contracts from McDonnell Douglas, the aircraft's manufacturer. Delivery will begin in 1982 and end in 1989.

# CHAD

5 x Cessna-Reims F-337 Milirole counterinsurgency aircraft for $720,000@ in 1979.

# CHILE

14,600 rounds 106mm recoilless rifle HEAT and APERS ammunition for $325@ delivered in 1978, despite a Congressional embargo against arms to the Pinochet regime imposed in June of 1976. This ammunition was originally ordered in 1974 to accompany 760 M-40A1 106mm recoilless rifles delivered before the embargo. The Defense Department claimed the ammunition was exempt from embargo because it had been ordered prior to its imposition and was therefore ''in the pipeline.'' In fact, the contract for its manufacture was not awarded until September of 1977.

2 x Beech King Air transport aircraft for $803,000@ in 1978.

18 x Cessna R172 Hawk training aircraft for $61,100@, delivered in 1979.

6 x T-38A Talon training aircraft for $5.238 million@ in 1978.

3 x C-47 transport aircraft for $344,000@ in 1978.

(Note: Chile operates 4 Lockheed L-188 Electra and 4 Swearingen Merlin III transport aircraft not previously recorded.)

# COLOMBIA

6 x Cessna A-37B Dragonfly counterinsurgency aircraft for $650,000@ in 1979.

25 x M-113A1 armoured personnel carrier for $75,833@ in 1979.

3 x Lockheed C-130H transport aircraft for $10.2 million@ in 1979.

# DENMARK

62 x MGM-71A TOW antitank missile launcher for $61,000@ and 840 x MGM-71A TOW antitank missile for $3,085@ in May of 1980.

15 x RGM-84A Harpoon antiship missile for $693,000@ in July of 1980.

# DOMINICAN REPUBLIC

1 x former US Navy AOG tanker ship in 1978.

1 x Bell UH-1H utility helicopter for $575,000 in 1978. In connection with this sale, Textron, Inc. of Providence, Rhode Island was accused in May of 1977 of having paid a bribe of $31,670 to General Rene Beauchamp, former Dominican secretary of defense. Textron pleaded guilty not to the bribe itself, but to having failed to file a report, as required by law, that it was transporting more than $5,000 in US currency out of the country. The company was fined $131,670 for currency violation in July of 1979.

8 x Cessna T-41 Mescalero light reconnaissance aircraft for $524,000@ in 1978.

# ECUADOR

12 x M-102 105mm towed howitzer for $132,000@ in 1978.

3 x Vulcan/Chaparral composite air defense battalion equipment sets, including 18 x M-730 Chaparral tracked launch vehicle, 288 x M-72C Chaparral antiaircraft missile, 44 x M-163

Vulcan self-propelled antiaircraft gun and 28 x M-167 Vulcan towed antiaircraft gun, for $220 million in 1979.

(Note: Ecuador operates 4 Lockheed L-188 Electra transport aircraft not previously recorded.)

# EGYPT

14 x Lockheed C-130H transport aircraft for $9.96 million@, together with $44.9 million in support equipment, in 1978. All have been delivered, bringing Egypt's total of that aircraft type to 19. Eleven more may be ordered soon.

12 x Teledyne-Ryan reconnaissance drone remotely piloted vehicle (RPV) for $2.39 million@ in 1978, with $37.8 million in support equipment.

2 x airborne reconnaissance and ground processing systems for $28.2 million in 1978.

42 x F-5E and 8 x F-5F Tiger II fighter aircraft for $11.6 million@ 2,000 x AIM-9J Sidewinder air intercept missile for $35,000@, and $80 million in support equipment in February of 1978, as part of a series of sales linked together by the Carter administration in order to facilitate the sale of advanced aircraft to Saudi Arabia. Saudi Arabia was to pay for these aircraft for Egypt, but withdrew from its commitment in response to President Sadat's peace initiatives. Delivery has consequently been postponed, and 20 of the aircraft originally produced for Egypt have meanwhile been sold to Morocco.

35 x F-4E Phantom II fighter-bomber aircraft for $17.14 million@ in June of 1979. These were purchased with Foreign Military Sales credits extended as part of the initial $2 billion in military aid allotted to Egypt under the Middle Eastern Peace Treaty. All the aircraft have been delivered.

12 x Mobile Triad battery sets of MIM-23B Improved HAWK air defense missile equipment for $50.9 million@, 40 x F-16 air combat fighter for $23.575 million@, 500 x AGM-65A Maverick air-to-ground missile for $66,000@, 70 x AIM-7E Sparrow medium-range air intercept missile for $156,000@, 100 x AIM-9E Sidewinder short-range air intercept missile for $32,400@, 250 x AIM-9P Sidewinder missile for $35,400@, 300 x M-60A3 main battle tank for $1.16 million@, 43 x M-88A1 armoured recovery vehicle for $736,000@, and 800 x M-113A2 armoured personnel carrier for $136,700@ in March of 1979. Deliveries will extend through 1988. Valued at more than $2 billion, this equipment will be paid by Foreign Military Sales credits and

grant aid allotted under the Middle Eastern Peace Treaty, including future annual commitments of more than $900 million per year through 1985. These funds will also pay for 12 Sea Spectre naval patrol boats, four destroyers and one submarine. One HAWK battery and 50 M-113A2 vehicles were delivered in February of 1980. Two further transfers of this equipment, including a $37 million shipment of 43 x M-88A1 armoured recovery vehicles, with spares, and a $28 million shipment of 73 x Hughes TOW ground launchers with missiles, were submitted to Congress for approval in January of 1981.

550 x M-113A2 armoured personnel carrier equipped with the Emerson M-109 ITV (Improved TOW Vehicle) antitank missile launcher for $165,600@, including support equipment, in July of 1980. At a total cost of $82.2 million, these are being transferred as part of the Middle Eastern Peace Treaty allotment of grant aid under the Military Assistance Program (MAP). They will raise Egypt's total inventory of the M-113A2 to 1,350 vehicles. Under a separate contract for $150 million, the 800 vehicles ordered in March of 1979 will also be fitted with the Emerson M-109 ITV.

(Note: Egypt also operates one Boeing 707-320 and one 737-200 not previously recorded.)

# EL SALVADOR

After the death of three American nuns and a lay missionary in El Salvador in December of 1980, the delivery of $10 million in military equipment, including $5 million in "non-lethal" items, was halted. The Carter administration resumed shipments the following month, after having received "assurances" that the Salvadoran government troops had not been involved in this incident, though in fact they were. The equipment included 10 UH-IH armed troop transport helicopters on lease, M-16 5.56mm rifles, M-60 7.62mm machine guns, 81mm mortars, M-79 grenade launchers, hand grenades and 57mm recoilless rifle ammunition. In February of 1981 the Reagan administration increased military aid to El Salvador by $25 million and sent 54 military advisors to that country. It sought $65 million in military aid in 1982. The new administration claims that "Soviet-bloc" countries have promised to supply Salvadoran insurgents with 800 tons of military equipment. According to the State Department's report "Communist Interference in El Salvador," said to be based on documents captured from the guerillas, but first published in the United States rather than by the government that allegedly captured them, Vietnam has promised to supply the guerillas with 60 tons of abandoned American arms, including 1,620 M-16 5.56mm rifles, 36 M-60 7.62mm machine guns, 12 81mm mortars, 4,000 rounds of 81mm mortar ammunition and 1.5 million rounds of 5.56mm ammuni-

tion. The report further claims that about 200 tons of arms and equipment have been delivered thus far to the insurgents through Cuba and Nicaragua.

# ETHIOPIA

33 x M-113A1 armoured personnel carrier for $75,833@ and 12 x M-109A1 155mm self-propelled howitzer for $475,000@ in 1976.

# FRANCE

60 x General Electric/SNECMA CFM56 jet engine for $1 million@ as power plant replacements for France's twelve KC-135F tanker aircraft, in March of 1979.

(Note: France is considering the purchase of 4 x Grumman E-2C Hawkeye early warning aircraft and 40 x Beech King Air or Cessna 425 aircraft.)

# GABON

1 x Grumman Gulfstream II transport aircraft for $7.1 million in 1976.

6 x V-150 Commando armoured car for $135,000@ in 1979.

1 x C-130H transport aircraft for $9.96 million in 1979.

# GREECE

11 x M-88A1 armoured recovery vehicle for $736,300@ in 1978.

11 x M-109A1 155mm self-propelled howitzer for $475,000@ and 144 x M-102 105mm towed howitzer for $133,100@ in 1978.

100 x AIM-7E Sparrow air intercept missile for $128,000@ in 1978.

5 x Cessna T-37 training aircraft for $423,000@ in 1978.

300 x AIM-9J Sidwinder air intercept missile for $35,700@ in 1978.

1 x Gearing class destroyer for $26.330 million in 1978.

2 x PBR Mk III naval patrol boat for $757,800@ in 1978.

10 x Boeing Ch-47 Chinook helicopter for $15.72 million@ in 1978. Delivery was completed in 1980.

6 x LTV TA-7H Corsair II training aircraft for $4.33 million@ in May of 1978. Delivery was completed in 1980.

600 x M-48A3 tank conversion kit for $233,166@ in June of 1979.

18 x F-4E Phantom II fighter-bomber aircraft for $17.14 million@ in 1979.

37 x M-730 Chaparral air defense system tracked launch vehicle for $937,783@, and 600 x MIM-72C Improved Chaparral air defense missile for $130,000@ in April of 1980.

32 x RGM-84A Harpoon antiship missile for $775,000@ in April of 1980.

(Note: Greece has also expressed its interest in the purchase of 100 F-16 fighter aircraft.)

# GUATEMALA
5 x Cessna A-37B Dragonfly counterinsurgency aircraft for $630,000@ in 1978.

10 x M-42 Duster self-propelled twin 40mm antiaircraft gun for $110,000@ in 1978.

2 x PBR Mk I naval patrol boat for $460,000@ in 1978.

10,000 x M-16A1 5.56mm rifle for $210@ in 1979.

$3.1 million in jeeps and trucks in June of 1981.

# GUYANA
2 x former US Navy tank landing ship (LST) for $620,000@ in 1979.

# HONDURAS
3 x Bell UH-1H utility helicopter for $590,000@ in 1978.

1 x former US Navy tank landing ship (LST) for $542,000 in 1978.

2 x PBR Mk I naval patrol boat for $388,000@ in 1978.

8 x T-28D Trojan and Fennec light strike aircraft from Morocco for $446,000@ in August of 1978. Funding problems have held up delivery.

# INDONESIA
12 x F-5E and 4 x F-5F Tiger II fighter aircraft for $7.812 million@ in June of 1978. All have been delivered.

12 x Rockwell T-2C Buckeye training aircraft for $6.550 million@ in 1978.

31 x Beech Musketeer light reconnaissance aircraft for $110,000@ in 1978.

3 x Forrest Sherman class destroyer for $31.110 million@ in 1978.

3 x PBR Mk I naval patrol boat for $466,000@ in 1978.

16 x T-34C Turbo Mentor training aircraft for $625,000@ in 1978.

16 x Bell 205A helicopter for $718,750@ in 1978.

3 x Lockheed L-100-30 Super Hercules transport aircraft for $13.3 million@ in August of 1979.

14 x A-4E and 2 x TA-4H Skyhawk fighter-bomber aircraft for $1.612 million@ in October of 1979. These were purchased from Israel.

16 x A-4E Skyhawk fighter-bomber aircraft for $1.687 million@ in February of 1981. These were purchased from surplus U.S. Navy stocks.

# IRAN
250 x M-113A1 armoured personnel carrier for $81,102@ in 1976. Delivered.

304 x M-577 armoured communications and command vehicle for $131,000@ in 1976. Delivered.

80 x Westinghouse AN/ALQ-119 Tactical Jamming System ECM pod for $393,750@ in 1977. Delivered.

$183.7 million for Improved HAWK air defense missile training in 1977. Program discontinued in 1978.

$50 million in Improved HAWK air defense missile components in 1977. Delivered.

$28.7 million to train 200 F-14 crew members in 1977. Training completed.

$56 million for helicopter logistics support equipment in 1977. Delivered.

$150 million to expand production facilities for the Bell 214 helicopter in 1977. Contract cancelled.

288 x Bell 214 helicopter for $2.601 million@ in 1977. 67 had been delivered when the contract was cancelled in 1978. The balance represented a loss to Textron of $575 million.

$167 million to establish a helicopter training center in 1977. Cancelled.

$139 million for a helicopter logistics depot system in 1977. Cancelled.

$250 million for a series of helicopter area support centers in 1977. Cancelled.

5 x RF-4E Phantom II reconnaissance aircraft for $13.64 million@ in 1977. Cancelled.

11 x RF-4E Phantom II reconnaissance aircraft for $15.454 million@ in 1978. Cancelled.

(Note: Iran already has 16 of these aircraft in service.)

172 x Dalmo-Victor AN/ALR-62 passive ECM radar warning receivers for retrofit on Iranian F-4E aircraft at $325,580@ in May of 1978. Equipment delivered, but retrofit completed for only 26 aircraft.

$15 million for a fighter aircraft training system in 1978. Cancelled.

$86.7 million for an aviation training center to be operated by the US Army in 1978. Cancelled.

$46 million in support equipment for the AIM-54A Phoenix missile system asociated with the F-14A Tomcat fighter interceptor, in April of 1978. Cancelled.

$78 million in engineering changes for the F-14A fighter interceptor and its missile systems, in May of 1978. Cancelled.

$68 million in support equipment for the AIM-54A Phoenix missile, in June of 1979. Cancelled.

$38 million in spares and support equipment for 65 Iranian Army AH-I Cobra helicopters equipped with the TOW missile, in August of 1978. Cancelled.

$130 million in support equipment for Iranian Navy RH-53D, SH-3D and AB-212 helicopters, in May of 1978. Cancelled.

$200 million in helicopter logistics support equipment in August of 1978. Cancelled.

$125 million in supply and support equipment for Iranian F-5E, F-4E and C-130 aircraft, in May of 1978. This contract was not cancelled by the Khomeini government, and the United States is continuing to deliver the equipment.

$33 million for contract training personnel associated with the Improved HAWK air defense missile training program, in May of 1978. Cancelled.

$250 million for construction and supply of a depot for maintenance and repair of HAWK, Rapier and Oerlikon weapon systems, in 1978. Not cancelled. The United States is subcontracting work to foreign companies, and construction may continue.

84 x M-110A1 203mm self-propelled howitzer for $375,000@ and 214 x M-109A1B 155mm self-propelled howitzer for $753,500@ in August of 1978. Cancelled.

100 x M-548 tracked cargo carriers with machine guns for $110,000@ in August of 1978. Cancelled.

31 x F-4G Phantom II Wild Weasel defense suppression aircraft for $11.290 million@ in September of 1978. Cancelled.

1,000 x AGM-45A Shrike anti-radar defense suppression missiles to arm the RF-4G, for $105,000@ in September of 1978. Cancelled.

186 x AIM-9H Sidewinder air intercept missiles for $75,268@ in August of 1978. Cancelled.

2 x AFT ocean tugboats for $19.5 million@ in August of 1978. Cancelled.

4 x Spruance class destroyer for $382.5 million@ in 1978. Six had originally been ordered by the Shah in 1973 for $116 million@, but the order was cut to four vessels when the price rose to $333 million@ in 1976. The Khomeini regime cancelled the remaining four, two of which have since been purchased for the US Navy.

6 x Boeing KC-135 tanker aircraft for $18.221 million@ in 1978. Cancelled.

3 x Lockheed P-3C Orion antisubmarine warfare patrol aircraft for $24.686 million@ in 1978. Cancelled. (Note: Iran already has six of these aircraft in service.)

7 x Boeing E-3A AWACS command and surveillance aircraft for $102.671 million@, together with a contribution of $510.3 million to AWACS research and development costs, in 1978. Cancelled. The aircraft planned for Iran will be delivered instead to NATO in partial fulfillment of an order for 18.

12 x armament suite to equip frigates on order for the Iranian Navy, and under construction in Dutch and West German shipyards, for $29.166 million@, in August of 1978. Cancelled.

160 x F-16 air combat fighter for $14.844 million@, including a contribution to F-16 research and development costs, in 1978. Cancelled. After the Shah's request for 250 x F-18L Hornet fighter aircraft was refused, a letter of offer was drawn for 300 F-16 aircraft, and the Shah probably would have accepted it had he remained in power. 55 of the F-16s in production for the original Iranian order will now be delivered to Israel as part of that country's allotment of military aid under the terms of the Middle Eastern Peace Treaty. Another 75 F-16s, purchased by Israel in the Carter administration's series of linked aircraft sales to the Middle East in February of 1978, will also be drawn from the Iranian production run.

(Note: the total value of the foregoing contracts cancelled by the Khomeini regime is $8.703 billion.)

# IRAQ

6 x Lockheed JetStar transport aircraft for $42.188 million@ in 1979.

3 x Boeing 727 and 2 x Boeing 747 transport aircraft for $200 million in August of 1980.

8 x General Electric gas turbine engine for $1.4 million@ in August of 1980. These will be used to power four Lupo class frigates for the Iraqi Navy now under construction in Italy. The license for this sale was originally suspended in February of 1980, after complaints in Congress over Iraqi support of acts of international terrorism. Six months later, however, the licenses for the engines, as well as for the Boeing aircraft, were approved. A Commerce Department spokesman pointed out that the United States now does more than $1 billion annually in trade with Iraq, including imports of $600 million per year in Iraqi oil.

# ISRAEL

125 x M-60A1 main battle tank for $624,687@ in 1978.

16 x M-728 combat engineer vehicle with 165mm demolition gun for $756,250@, together with $2.4 million in support equipment, in 1978.

144 x MGM-71A TOW antitank missile launcher for $61,000@, with $800,000 in support equipment, in 1978.

700 x M-113A1 armoured personnel carrier for $107,857@, together with $16.9 million in support equipment, in 1978.

40,000 rounds 155mm high explosive (HE) artillery projectile for $522@ in 1978.

316,300 rounds 81mm mortar ammunition at $26@ and 20,980 rounds 60mm mortar ammunition at $18@ in 1978.

60 x MIM-23B Improved HAWK air defense missile for $132,000@ and 2 x radar test site for HAWK air defense missile system for $540,000@ in 1978.

15 x F-15 Eagle fighter interceptor aircraft for $28.733 million@ in February of 1978, as part of the Carter administration's series of linked aircraft sales to the Middle East.

75 x F-16 air combat fighter for $15.453 million@ in February of 1978, as part of the series of linked aircraft sales to the Middle East.

2 x Flagstaff Mk 2 PHM hydrofoil naval patrol combatant craft for $42.988 million@ in 1978, with an option on 14 more vessels.

18 x AH-1J Cobra attack helicopter for $3.555 million@ in 1978.

30 x Hughes 500MD Defender attack helicopter for $766,670@ in 1978.

$3.6 million in support equipment for the F100 engine installed in the F-15 Eagle fighter interceptor, in August of 1978.

200 x AGM-45A Shrike anti-radar defense suppression missile for $95,000@ in August of 1978.

170 x AIM-7F Sparrow air intercept missile for $141,176@ in August of 1978.

48,000 rounds 175mm high explosive (HE) artillery projectile for $291@ in August of 1978.

4 x Teledyne-Ryan 124/l Firebee reconnaissance drone remotely piloted vehicle (RPV) for $2.39 million@, together with $796,000 in support equipment, in 1978. One of these was shot down by a Syrian SAM-6 missile over Lebanon's Bekaa Valley on May 14, 1981.

100 x GBU-15(V)4/B Walleye II television guided glide bomb kit, less warhead, for $188,680@, and 200 FMU-124A/B fuze for $5,660@ in August of 1978.

200 x Walleye I Mod 22 extended range data link guided glide bomb for $182,000@ in August of 1978.

25 x F-15 Eagle fighter interceptor aircraft for $28.733 million@ in November of 1978. Together with the 25 F-15s now in service and 15 ordered in February of 1978, this will bring Israel's total of this aircraft type to 65.

200 x M-60A3 main battle tank for $1.16 million@, 800 x M-113A2 armoured personnel carrier for $136,700@, 200 x M-109A2 155mm self-propelled howitzer for $753,500@, 200 x M-107 175mm self-propelled gun for $578,000@, 600 x AGM-65A Maverick air-to-ground missile for $48,666@, 600 x AIM-9J Sidewinder air intercept missile for $66,666@, and 55 x F-16 air combat fighter for $23.575 million@ in March of 1979. Valued at $1.849 billion, this equipment will be paid by Foreign Military Sales credits and grant aid allotted under the Middle Eastern Peace Treaty, including future annual commitments of more than $1.8 billion per year through 1985. The 55 F-16s are in addition to 67 F-16A and 8 F-16B aircraft ordered in February of 1978, and will bring Israel's total of this aircraft type to 130. Due to the cancellation of an Iranian order for F-16s, initial delivery of this aircraft to Israel has been advanced from 1983 to 1980, and delivery of the first 75 should be completed by 1982.

$43.8 million for 175mm and 155mm artillery ammunition and thermal night sights in June of 1979.

250 x MIM-72C Improved Chaparral antiaircraft missile for $130,000@ in April of 1980.

100 x GBU-15(V)4/B Walleye II television guided glide bomb with warhead, for $351,000@ in April of 1980.

14 x Mk 15/2 Vulcan Phalanx CIWS (Close In Weapons System) 20mm multibarreled naval antiaircraft gun for $4.635 million@ in August of 1980.

$940 million for construction of two airbases in the Negev, together with $40 million in management and support services, awarded to United States construction corporations in May of 1979 by the US Army Corps of Engineers. The funds will be supplied as part of the Middle Eastern Peace Treaty allotment of grant aid under the Military Assistance Program (MAP).

(Note: Israel has 50,000 rounds of a special 175mm artillery projectile with extended range, not previously recorded. Under a secret Pentagon contract, these shells were ballistically improved by the Space Research Corporation, and delivered in 1974. From positions on the Golan Heights, they can strike Damascus.)

# ITALY
6 x DE1164 Sonar system for installation on Italian Navy warships for $3 million@ in December of 1978.

$4.2 million in GTE communications transmission equipment for the Italian Ministry of Defense in April of 1979.

35 x General Dynamics RIM-66B Standard SM-I (MR) Medium Range air defense missile for $428,500@, with support, in January of 1981.

# JAMAICA
1 x Beech Duke transport aircraft for $790,000 in 1978.

3 x Bell 212 helicopter for $1.333 million@ in 1978.

3 x PBR Mk I naval patrol boat for $390,000@ in 1978.

# JAPAN
24 x RGM-84A Harpoon antiship missile for $637,500@, including support equipment, in August of 1978.

4 x Grumman E-2C Hawkeye early warning aircraft for $42.5 million@ in August of 1978.

8 x F-15CJ and F-15DJ Eagle fighter interceptor aircraft for $18 million@ in September of 1978, with partial production and assembly in Japan by Mitsubishi. Japan had originally planned on 123 of these aircraft, but procurement for only 100 has been approved. Delivery of these should be completed by 1987.

$4.5 million for a Rockwell communications interface system between E-2C Hawkeye aircraft and Japan's Base Air Defense Ground Environment (BADGE) system, in February of 1979.

13 x Beech Super King Air 200T maritime patrol aircraft for $2 million@, including special electronics, in July of 1979.

13 x AN/APS-128 radar for Super King Air 200T aircraft, at $146,153@, in July of 1979.

6 x Mk 15/2 Vulcan Phalanx CIWS (Close In Weapons System) 20mm multibarreled naval antiaircraft gun for $4.433 million@ in May of 1980.

24 x RGM-84A Harpoon antiship missile for $800,000@, with support equipment, in May of 1980.

(Note: 2 of Japan's E-2C Hawkeye aircraft will be delivered in 1982, and 2 in 1983. An order is shortly expected for four additional E-2Cs at $40 million@, for delivery in 1984 and 1985. Japan has also expressed interest in the purchase of 56 AH-1S Cobra attack helicopters.)

# JORDAN
24 x M-110A1 203mm self-propelled howitzer for $425,000@, with $2.4 million in support equipment, in 1978.

200 x M-48A5 medium tank for $510,000@ in 1978.

420 x M-113A1 armoured personnel carrier for $81,000@ in 1978.

36 x M-109A1 155mm self-propelled howitzer for $475,000@ in 1978.

36 x MGM-71A TOW antitank missile launcher at $66,400@ and 760 x MGM-71A TOW antitank missile for $6,787@ in 1978.

1,200 x AIM-9J Sidewinder air intercept missile for $35,200@ in 1978.

4 x Sikorsky S-76 transport helicopter for $1.133 million@ in 1979.

10 x AH-1J Cobra attack helicopter for $1.91 million@ in 1979.

4 x F-5E Tiger II fighter aircraft for $7.812 million@ in May of 1979.

100 x M-113A1 armoured personnel carrier equipped with Emerson M-109 ITV TOW anti-

tank missile launcher for $140,000@ in May of 1979.

18 x M-109A2 155mm self-propelled howitzer for $794,444@ in May of 1979.

6 x F-5F Tiger II fighter training aircraft for $5.3 million@ in November of 1979.

2 x Sikorsky S-76 transport helicopter for $1.282 million@ in 1979.

14 x M-60A3 main battle tank for $1.428 million@ in April of 1980.

100 x M-60A3 main battle tank for $1.466 million@ in June of 1980.

24 x AH-1S Cobra attack helicopter for $4.75 million@ and TOW missiles and support equipment, in a sale valued at a total of $156 million, in January of 1981.

# KENYA
17 x Hughes 500MD QAS (Quiet Advanced Scout) helicopter for $822,000@, 15 x Hughes 500MD attack helicopter equipped with TOW antitank missile launchers for $966,000@, and 2,100 x MGM-71A TOW antitank missile for $7,292@ in March of 1979.

# KUWAIT
30 x AH-1J Cobra attack helicopter for $1.933 million@ in July of 1978.

175 x M-113A1 armoured personnel carrier for $107,857@ in May of 1979.

47 x MGM-71A TOW antitank missile launcher for $66,000@ and 930 x MGM-71A TOW antitank missile for $7,309@ in August of 1979.

4 x Triad battery of MIM-23B Improved HAWK air defense missile equipment for $22.9 million@ and 32 x MIM-23B Improved HAWK missile for $132,000@ in September of 1979.

(Note: Kuwait operates two DC-9 transport aircraft not previously recorded.)

# LEBANON
100 x M-35 military cargo truck for $103,000@ in 1978.

4 x Agusta-Bell AB212 helicopter for $1.666 million@ in 1978.

47 x M-113A1 armoured personnel carrier for $107,857@ in 1979.

100 x M-2HB .50 Cal machine gun for $1,560@ in 1979.

15 x M-113A1 armoured personnel carrier for $107,857@, 4 x M-102 105mm towed howitzer for $132,000@, and 20,000 rounds 105mm HE and APERS ammunition for $403@, part of a series of shipments valued at more than $100 million in a program to rebuild the Lebanese Army, seized by the Libyan government at Benghazi in September of 1979.

70 x M-113A2 armoured personnel carriers for $135,000@ and 4 x M-577A2 armoured command and communications vehicle for $312,500@ in April of 1980.

1 x Rockwell Shrike Commander transport aircraft for $890,000 in May of 1980.

(Note: Lebanon is also where former CIA employee Frank E. Terpil and his partner George Gregory Korkola are said to have fled in September of 1980 to escape trial in New York State Supreme Court under an indictment of conspiracy to sell 10,000 British Sten submachine guns and 10 million rounds of ammunition through their New Jersey firm of Amstech International to two undercover detectives, posing as Latin American terrorists, for $3.3 million. Both were found guilty in May of 1980. According to Assistant District Attorney Matthew Crosson, Mr. Terpil, after his discharge from the CIA, trained Libyan terrorists in the use of binary liquid explosives, and also gave assistance to former Ugandan president Idi Amin. With another associate, former CIA employee Edwin P. Wilson, Mr. Terpil has set up a plant to manufacture assassination weapons in Libya, illegally shipped arms and explosives to Libya from the United States, recruited several other former CIA employees and several former Green Berets to train Libyan terrorists, and helped plan political assassinations in Europe and the Middle East. These activities on the part of so many American citizens make it difficult for the Reagan administration to claim that the Soviet Union must take sole responsibility for the support of acts of international terrorism.)

# LIBERIA
2 x Cessna Model 172 Skyhawk training aircraft for $61,100@ in 1979.

1 x Cessna Model 185 Skywagon light utility aircraft for $57,000 in 1979.

1 x Cessna Model 207 Stationair utility aircraft for $90,000 in 1979.

2 x Douglas C-47 transport aircraft for $516,000@ in 1979.

# LIBYA
400 x Oshkosh heavy truck for $175,000@ in 1979, not delivered. The license for this sale was revoked by the State Department.

1 x Agusta-Bell AB212 helicopter produced under license in Italy for $2.102 million in 1979.

2 x Lockheed JetStar transport aircraft for $16.448 million@ in 1979. The license for this sale was revoked by the State Department.

8 x Lockheed C-130H Hercules transport aircraft for $6.25 million@ in 1970, still awaiting delivery at Marietta, Georgia. A total of 16 of these aircraft was ordered, and the full $100 million paid, but only 8 C-130E were delivered before 1976, when the State Department imposed a ban on further deliveries in response to Libyan support of terrorist activities. The Libyan government has made numerous attempts, some legal, some allegedly not, to obtain the final 8 C-130H aircraft, including an offer of $1 million per aircraft for help in gaining their release, attempts at a complex bribery scheme allegedly masterminded by fugitive financier Robert L. Vesco, and alleged attempts to involve President Carter's brother Billy to intercede on their behalf.

12 x Lockheed L-100-30, the civilian version of the C-130 Hercules, for $10 million@, 2 x Boeing 727 transport aircraft for $15 million@, and 3 x Boeing 747 aircraft for $21.670 million@, ordered in 1979 but refused by the State Department. The total value of this order is $215 million.

20 x Agusta-Boeing Vertol EMB/CH-47C Chinook helicopter produced under license in Italy for $8.222 million@ in 1979, and now being delivered.

(Note: Libya has 3,000 Startron night surveillance scopes not previously recorded. These were sold by the Smith & Wesson Division of the Bangor Punta Corporation for $2,600@ in March of 1974. The license for the sale was revoked after an embargo had been imposed against arms to Libya, but the Startrons were later delivered anyway. The US Attorney in Boston has asked permission to seek criminal indictments against Smith & Wesson. Instead, Joseph Tafe of the Justice Department's Internal Security Division is negotiating a $120,000 civil settlement with the firm.)

# MALAGASY
1 x Piper Aztec light transport aircraft for $110,000 in 1978.

4 x Cessna-Reims Model 172 Skyhawk training aircraft for $72,000@ in 1979.

# MALAYSIA
5 x Bell 212 helicopter for $1.333 million@ in 1978.

12 x Cessna model 402B training aircraft for $194,000@ in 1978.

8 x Sikorsky SH-3 helicopter for $1.614 million@ in 1979.

32 x V-150 Commando armoured car for $132,500@ in 1979.

4 x F-5E/F Tiger II fighter aircraft for $6.25 million@ in August of 1979. These will in part replace two F-5Es lost by Malaysia's No. 12 Squadron in training accidents.

88 x A-4C and A-4L Skyhawk fighter-bomber aircraft for $261,360@ from surplus US Navy stocks in August of 1979. All had been delivered by April of 1980.

(Note: Malaysia operates 2 former US Navy landing ship tank (LST) vessels not previously recorded.)

# MEXICO
8 x Grumman HU-16A Albatross maritime patrol aircraft, refurbished from US Navy stocks, for $2.4 million@ in 1978.

18 x North American T-28D Trojan light strike aircraft for $403,666@ in 1978. This brings the total of Mexico's inventory of this aircraft type to 50.

2 x Piper Aztec light transport aircraft for $108,000@ in 1978.

1 x Gates Learjet 24D for $1.895 million in 1978.

10 x F-5E and 2 x F-5F fighter aircraft for $9.583 million@ in February of 1981.

# MOROCCO
6 x C-130H Hercules transport aircraft for $13.7 million@ in 1979, bringing Morocco's total of this aircraft type to 12.

180 x AIM-9J Sidewinder air intercept missile for $35,700@ in 1979.

190 x M-48A3 medium tank for $450,000@ in 1979.

42 x M-730 Chaparral tracked launch vehicle for $488,000@ and 504 x MIM-72A Chaparral antiaircraft missile for $38,500@ in 1979.

10 x M-113A1 armoured personnel carrier for $112,000@ in 1979.

125 x M-47 Dragon antitank missile for $11,500@ in 1979.

5 x Agusta-Bell AB212 helicopter for $2.102 million@, 8 x Agusta-Bell AB206 Jet Ranger II helicopter for $612,000@, and 6 x Agusta-Boeing Vertol EMB/CH-47C Chinook transport helicopter for $8.222 million@ in 1979. All have been delivered.

5 x Beech King Air transport aircraft for $810,000@ in 1979.

$200 million for a Westinghouse early warning air defense communications and target acquisition system in March of 1979. The system has been operational since October of 1980.

20 x F-5E and F-5F Tiger II fighter aircraft for $8.5 million@ in January of 1980. These were diverted from a production run originally intended for delivery to Egypt, until Saudi Arabia withdrew its offer to pay for them. The Saudis are paying, however, for the first 8 of the same aircraft now being delivered to Morocco. The 20 new F-5Es will bring Morocco's acquisition of this aircraft type to a total of 42, though its inventory will number only 37, as Polisario Front forces in the Western Sahara have shot down 5.

6 x Rockwell OV-10A Bronco reconnaissance and counterinsurgency aircraft for $3.333 million@ and 24 x Hughes 500MD attack helicopters with spares and support equipment for $1.875 million@ in May of 1980. 12 of the Hughes 500MD aircraft will be equipped to fire the TOW antitank missile. Morocco had originally requested 24 of the OV-10 Bronco aircraft, and 24 AH-1J Cobra attack helicopters. The Carter administration refused these after objections in Congress that they would be used by King Hassan in his attempt to conquer the Western Sahara, an area rich in uranium that is now the scene of an attempt by 75,000 people of the Polisario Front to achieve a status of self-determination. They are entitled to it, according to the Organization of African

Unity, the International Court of Justice, and United Nations General Assembly Resolution 1514(XV). But after some Polisario attacks had crossed the same Moroccan borders Moroccan forces had earlier crossed to get to the Western Sahara, the Carter administration approved the current sales on the grounds that Morocco had a legitimate claim for self defense. Delivery of the new equipment will be completed by 1981.

108 x M-60A3 main battle tank for $1.516 million@ in February of 1981.

# NATO
18 x E-3A AWACS battlefield command and surveillance aircraft for $104.6 million@ in 1979. Deliveries began in 1980.

$89 million in support equipment for the Nike-Hercules air defense system, in 1979.

$11.3 million for the NICS/TARE computer telegraph relay system, in 1979.

$80 million for modifications to the NATO satellite communications ground station terminal network, in 1979.

$11 million for 23 x HF-80 Scope Signal Phase II transportable radio communications systems and 5 x HF-80 fixed-station systems, with antenna sub-systems, in October of 1979.

# NETHERLANDS
2,840 x M-47 Dragon antitank missile for $11,500@ and 350 x M-47 Dragon antitank missile tracker for $12,751@ in 1979.

13 x P-3C Orion antisubmarine warfare and patrol aircraft for $23.538 million@ in April of 1979. Deliveries will begin in 1981, replacing the current force of Lockheed SP-2H Neptune aircraft.

25 x M-163 Vulcan SHORADS self-propelled 20mm multibarreled antiaircraft gun system for $906,000@ in 1979.

173 x M-113A2 armoured personnel carrier equipped with the Emerson M-109 ITV TOW antitank missile launcher for $140,000@ in April of 1979.

12 x Mk 48 Torpedo for $1.333 million@ including spares and support equipment in June of 1979.

8 x AN/TPQ-36 Mortar Locating Radar for $2.625 million@ in October of 1979.

12 x Collins AN/USC-35 Link II digital data communications systems with terminal sets for $416,666@ in October of 1979. These will be delivered by June of 1981.

30 x F-16 air combat fighter for $7.199 million@ in July of 1980. These will bring the total inventory of this aircraft type in the Netherlands to 132, and an order for 81 additional F-16s is expected shortly.

(Note: the Netherlands Army is also considering the purchase of 450 XM-I main battle tanks.)

# NICARAGUA
3 x Cessna A-37B Dragonfly counterinsurgency aircraft for $610,000@ in 1978.

18 x V-150 Commando armoured car for $131,000@ in 1978.

5,000 x M-16 5.56mm rifle for $212@ in 1978.

General Modesto Rojas-Berrios and Colonel Sidney Muller-Schroeder of the Nicaraguan Air Force were arrested in January of 1981 for attempting to smuggle two UH-1B helicopters out of the United States without proper export licenses.

# NIGER
1 x Rockwell Aero Commander transport aircraft for $844,000 in 1978.

2 x C-130H Hercules transport aircraft for $10 million@ in 1979.

# NIGERIA
7 x Boeing Model 161 CH-47C Chinook transport helicopter for $7.666 million@ in 1978.

# NORTH YEMEN
4 x M-109A1 155mm self-propelled howitzer for $475,000@ in 1978.

16 x M-163 Vulcan self-propelled 20mm multibarreled antiaircraft gun for $960,000@ in 1978.

12 x F-5E Tiger II fighter aircraft for $25 million@ with support equipment, 2 x C-130H transport aircraft for $13.7 million@, 64 x M60A3 main battle tank for $1.187 million@ with support equipment, 100 x M-113A1 armoured personnel carrier for $112,000@, 12 x M-113A2 armoured personnel carrier equipped with the Emerson M-109 ITV TOW anti-

tank missile launcher for $142,000@, 72 x M-167 Vulcan towed 20mm antiaircraft guns for $288,333@, 1,800 x M-47 Dragon antitank missile for $11,500@, 220 x M-47 Dragon antitank missile tracker for $12,571@, 4 x M-114A1 155mm towed howitzer for $202,000@, and 200 x M-79 40mm grenade launcher for $288@ in February of 1979. Valued at $540 million, together with ammunition and support material, this equipment was paid for by Saudi Arabia, which also supplied 50 of the M-113A1 vehicles from its own stock. Deliveries began in March of 1979, and were completed by the end of that year.

# OMAN

4 x Bell 214A helicopter for $1.708 million@ in 1978.

5 x Agusta-Bell AB205A helicopter for $798,800@ in 1978.

# PAKISTAN

$52.7 million in military radio communications equipment in 1978.

25,000 rounds 105mm HE and APERS artillery ammunition for $388@, together with $1.1 million in support equipment, in 1978.

30 x M-113A1 armoured personnel carrier for $107,000@ in 1978.

100 x Mk 46 Mod O Torpedo for $202,000@ in 1978.

48 x ASROC antisubmarine missile equipped with Mk 46 Mod 2 torpedo payload for $197,916@ in 1978.

1,200 x MGM-71A TOW antitank missile for $6,488@ and 60 x MGM-71A TOW antitank missile launcher for $42,040@ in 1978.

200 x AN/GRC-171 UHF air-to-ground radio communications receivers for $9,000@ in December of 1978.

40 x Mk 46 Mod 2 air-launched torpedo for $237,500@ in December of 1978.

8 x T-37 training aircraft for $464,000@ in March of 1980.

15 or more F-16 air combat fighter aircraft for $14.5 million@ in June of 1981, as part of a $3 billion program of military and economic aid over the next five years. Military aid to Pakistan had been suspended previously in 1965, after this nation's war with India, and

again in 1979, when Pakistan refused our request to abandon its nuclear program, but the recent sale of $8 billion in Soviet arms to India, the presumed threat posed by the Soviet presence in Afghanistan, and our desire to use Karachi as a naval base have offset our former reluctance to resume such assistance.

# PANAMA

4 x Bell UH-1N helicopter for $1.383 million@ in 1978.

(Note: Panama operates 1 Lockheed L-188 Electra transport aircraft not previously recorded.)

# PARAGUAY

6 x Cessna A-37B Dragonfly counterinsurgency aircraft for $630,000@ in 1978.

# PERU

9 x Grumman S-2E Tracker antisubmarine warfare and maritime patrol aircraft for $9.612 million@ in 1978.

1 x Fletcher class destroyer for $22.780 million in 1978.

6 x T-34C Turbo Mentor training aircraft for $593,750@ in 1979.

1 x Piper Aztec light transport aircraft for $110,000 in 1979.

2 x Gates Learjet 25D transport aircraft for $1.991 million@ in 1979.

# PEOPLE'S REPUBLIC OF CHINA

In June of 1981, Secretary of State Alexander Haig announced that the United States government had decided in principle to sell arms to China as part of a growing cooperation between the two nations. The initiative toward this decision was actually taken nine months earlier, when the Carter administration sent a team of defense specialists to the People's Republic to analyse its defense needs. A sale of up to 200 F-16 fighter aircraft is expected to be announced before the end of this year. Henry Kissinger suggested this sale as long ago as 1976. Sales of antitank, antiship and antiaircraft missiles, and of antisubmarine warfare equipment and diesel marine engines are expected too. Meanwhile, American arms manufacturers have not been prevented from making private agreements prior to Washington's announcement of official cooperation. The Bell Division of Textron, for example, is now concluding arrangements to construct a helicopter production plant in Harbin province.

# PHILIPPINES

12 x Boeing ACH-47A gunship helicopter for $7.880 million@ in 1978.

5 x Bell UH-1H utility helicopter for $575,500@ in 1978.

33 x M-113A1 armoured personnel carrier for $102,000@ in 1978.

44 x M-113A1 armoured personnel carrier for $112,880@ in 1978. A licensed commercial sale through the State Department's Office of Munitions Control.

97 x M-102 105mm towed howitzer for $136,500@ in 1978.

100,000 x M-14 7.62mm rifle for $141@ in 1978.

22 x Former US Navy landing ship tank (LST) for $670,000@ in 1978.

6 x PBR Mk III naval patrol boat for $588,000@ in 1978.

6 x Forward Air Control ground communications system for $6.666 million@ in 1979.

# PORTUGAL

4 x C-130H Hercules transport aircraft for $5 million@ in 1978, bringing Portugal's complement of this aircraft type to 5.

66 x M-113A1 armoured personnel carrier for $102,000@ in 1978.

16 x MGM-71A TOW antitank missile launcher for $42,040@ and 320 x MGM-71A TOW antitank missile for $6,488@ in 1978.

# QATAR

6 x Triad battery sets of MIM-23B Improved HAWK air defense missile equipment for $22.9 million@ and 162 x MIM-23B Improved HAWK missile for $132,000@ in September of 1979.

# SAUDI ARABIA

6 x Kawasaki-Boeing Vertol KV-107 II Chinook helicopter for $16.666 million@ including support equipment in 1978.

2,400 x M-113A1 armoured personnel carrier for $102,000@ in 1978.

150 x V-150 Commando armoured car for $135,000@ in 1978.

24 x PBR Mk III naval patrol boat for $610,000@ in 1978.

8 x Asheville class patrol combatant for $13.9 million@ in 1978.

1 x Boeing 747 transport aircraft for $21.188 million in 1978.

3,400 x FIM-43A Redeye MANPADS (Man-Portable Air Defense System) missile for $18,962@ in 1978.

4 x Tacoma class PCG naval patrol combatant for $13.125 million@ in 1978.

9 x PPG 180' Peterson boat for $540,000@ in 1978.

$420.2 million for naval port facilities construction in 1978.

45 x F-15 and 15 x TF-15 Eagle fighter interceptor aircraft for $41.081 million@, 600 x AIM-9B short range air intercept missile for $29,350@, 170 x AIM-7E medium range air intercept missile for $103,072@, and support equipment in February of 1978. This was an unpopular sale which the Carter administration linked to the sales of other aircraft in the Middle East in order to ensure its passage through Congress. The price for the aircraft includes a contribution to F-15 research and development costs, a factor which made the sale desirable in the administration's view.

$52.6 million for the design and manufacture of uniforms for the Saudi Air Force in 1978.

$174 million for the construction of a military administration school in Riyadh, in 1978.

$496 million for the construction of a field artillery center and school in 1978.

$605 million for support activities by the US Army Corps of Engineers on behalf of the Saudi Ordnance Corps Program, in 1978.

$40 million for parts and support equipment for the Saudi Naval Supply Center at Jubail and the supply depot at Jidda, in 1978.

$150 million in technical training for Saudi Naval Forces in 1978.

76 x M-163 Vulcan self-propelled 20mm multi-barreled antiaircraft gun for $986,842@ in 1978.

15 x M-728 combat engineer vehicle equipped with 165mm demolition gun for $1.134 million@ including support equipment, in 1978. In one report to Congress, these were referred to as "bulldozers."

$460 million for construction of the Ministry of Defense and Aviation Headquarters at Riyadh, in 1978.

$35 million for the installation of one 35 Megawatt power station in a military cantonment, in 1978.

$1.64 billion for continued training and support through 1981 on behalf of the Saudi Peace Hawk air defense system, in August of 1978.

$272 million for construction on behalf of the Saudi Naval expansion program at Jubail in September of 1978.

$800 million for planning and operation of Saudi Naval Forces bases and other facilities, in September of 1978.

$220 million for training and support equipment for the Saudi Arabian National Guard in September of 1978.

94 x V-150 Commando armoured car fitted with a 90mm Mecar gun for $168,085@ in October of 1978.

86 x M-60A1 tank chassis for $704,651@ in October of 1978. These will be fitted with twin turret-mounted Oerlikon/Contraves 35mm KDA cannon for air defense.

5 x Mk 15/2 Vulcan Phalanx CIWS (Close In Weapons System) 20mm multibarreled naval antiaircraft gun for $2.96 million@ in 1979.

100 x RGM-84A Harpoon antiship missile for $807,000@ in 1979.

24 x Northrop Chukar II target drone for $644,303@ in 1979.

$671.2 million for training of Saudi Naval Forces in the operation and maintenance of bases and ships, in May of 1979.

$850.7 million for training and support equipment for the Saudi Air Force, in May of 1979.

32 x M-60A1 main battle tank for $1.450 million@, 127 x M-109A1 155mm self-propelled howitzer for $794,444@, 76 x M-163 Vulcan self-propelled 20mm multibarreled anti-aircraft gun for $1.014 million@, and 2 x M-108 105mm self-propelled howitzer for $568,666@ in July of 1979, in a program to create a light armoured brigade and equip four battalions of the Saudi National Guard. As this goes to press in the spring of 1981, 88 of the M-109A1 and 56 of the M-163 vehicles have been delivered.

172 x M-47 Dragon antitank missile tracker for $12,860@ and 4,292 x M-47 Dragon antitank missile for $9,806@ in September of 1979.

$12 million for software programming on behalf of an automatic command, control and communications center for the Saudi Ministry of Defense in September of 1979.

32 x M-60A1 main battle tank for $1.450 million@ in October of 1979.

1,650 x AGM-65A Maverick air-to-ground missile for $48,666@ and 850 x AIM-9P Sidewinder air intercept missile for $32,560@ in September of 1979. The Saudis had originally requested 2,500 Maverick and 2,000 Sidewinder missiles in 1975, and Henry Kissinger had recommended these amounts be approved. Though Congress reduced the quantities at the time of this sale, Saudi Arabia was later to receive more than these amounts in subsequent sales.

1,000 x CBU-58 APAM cluster bomb dispenser munition for $11,472@ and 518 x CBU-71 cluster bomb dispenser munition for $14,961@ in October of 1979.

916 x AGM-65A Maverick air-to-ground missile for $48,666@, 660 x AIM-9P Sidewinder air intercept missile for $32,560@, and 3,435 x GBU-12 laser-guided bomb for $18,949@ in December of 1979.

$77.5 million for 140,000 rounds of 105mm HE and APDS tank ammunition, 155mm HE and APERS howitzer ammunition and 81mm mortar ammunition in April of 1980.

$72.2 million for training and maintenance support of Saudi Naval Forces bases in May of 1980.

$4 million for additional equipment associated with Saudi Air Force multi-environmental training program, in May of 1980.

$1.5 billion for the construction of shelters for Saudi Air Force F-15 Eagle fighter interceptor aircraft, in May of 1980.

$900 million in construction, training and service contracts for the support and maintenance of 114 F-5 and 60 F-15 fighter aircraft, in January of 1981.

$846 million for the Army Corps of Engineers to build "facilities essential to support of the Royal Saudi Navy," including construction of deep water ports on the Red Sea and Persian Gulf, and expansion of facilities at Jubail, Jidda, Dammam and Riyadh.

$200 million for the sale of repair parts, spares and other equipment for the Royal Saudi Navy supply depots at Jubail and Jidda.

(Note: Saudi Arabia will take delivery of its force of 60 F-15 Eagle aircraft between 1981 and 1983. In June of 1980, in anticipation of their arrival, the Saudis requested FAST Pack conformal fuel pallets to extend their range, KC-135 tanker aircraft to refuel them in flight, E-3A AWACS or E-2C Hawkeye command and surveillance aircraft to direct and control them, AIM-9L Sidewinder air intercept missiles to better arm them for air combat, and multiple ejection racks to equip them for ground attack with munitions already ordered.

Congress had meant to deny these aircraft a ground attack role when it approved their sale in 1978. The Carter administration gave assurances that it would not sell such equipment to the Saudis. Saudi Arabia could be told its new request will be honored provided it commits itself to support of Egypt's pact with Israel, thus fulfilling its implicit obligation to promote stability in the Middle East—the purpose for which such equipment is presumably intended. Saudi Arabia has done just the reverse, withdrawing its financial commitments to Egypt. It is likely the new request will be approved without such stipulations. The administration announced it had been ''forced to reconsider'' its 1978 assurances, in light of events in Iran and Afghanistan that had ''altered the regional security atmosphere.'' The Reagan administration initially approved the sale of the FAST Pack fuel pallets and AIM-9L missiles, in order to test the political response in this country and abroad. Apparently satisfied, it subsequently announced its intention to sell the Saudis five E-3C Sentry AWACS aircraft for $131 million@, together with $2 billion in contracts for training, spares, communications equipment and maintenance facilities for these aircraft. Because of the increased threat this added equipment presents for Israel, Saudi Arabia is now almost bound to be drawn into any new outbreak of Arab-Israeli hostilities. In order to protect itself, Israel may now be expected to launch a preemptive strike against Saudi air fields to eliminate this threat. Israel would feel compelled to do this, even had the Saudis not repeated their call this year for a new jihad.)

# SIERRA LEONE
1 x Hughes 300 helicopter for $784,000 in 1978.

# SINGAPORE
294 x M-113A1 armoured personnel carrier for $82,506@ in 1978.

6 x former US Navy landing ship tank (LST) craft for $342,000@ in 1978.

20 x former US Army UH-1B utility helicopter for $95,000@ in 1979.

17 x Bell UH-1H Iroquois troop transport helicopter for $575,000@ in 1979.

$22.8 million in parts and support equipment for A-4 Skyhawk, F-5E Tiger II and C-130 Hercules aircraft in 1980.

# SOUTH AFRICA
200 x AIM-9B Sidewinder air intercept missile, in 1976. Since these were shipped in violation of an arms embargo, every effort was made to conceal the shipment. The price is therefore unknown.

45,836 rounds of G-5 155mm howitzer ammunition, ballistically improved by the Space Research Corporation to extend their range by 20 percent, together with two radar vans and one G-5 155mm howitzer assembly. Ostensibly destined for the firm's test ranges in Antigua and Barbados, this equipment was illegally shipped to Cape Town and Durban between March of 1977 and March of 1978. Price unknown. John Stockwell, former CIA Angola Task Force Chief, says the CIA agreed to help South Africa locate 155mm shells during the Angolan campaign in 1975. The governments of Antigua and Barbados have since closed down Space Research Corporation's offices on their islands.

16 x Cessna 185 Skywagon utility aircraft for $500,000@ in 1978.

2 x Helio 295 Super Courier light transport aircraft for $163,000@ in 1978.

15 x Lockheed L-100-30 and 1 x Lockheed L-100-20 transport aircraft, civilian versions of the C-130 Hercules, for $9.987 million@ in 1978. These aircraft were commercially licensed, and were not considered a violation of the embargo ostensibly in force against arms to South Africa, because the US government does not consider them to have military application. All of the L-100 aircraft have been fitted with paratroop doors.

(Note: South Africa also operates 7 Swearingen Merlin IVA transport aircraft not previously recorded. Unconfirmed transfers of additional aircraft include the Cessna 310, Cessna 320 Skylight, Beech A36 Bonanza, Beech Baron 55 and 58, and the Rockwell Turbo Commander. A variety of illegal sales of small arms, often marked ''sporting goods,'' have also occurred. Both the Winchester Division of Olin Corporation and the Colt Firearms Division of Colt Industries were found to have made such sales in 1978 and 1979. Instead of investigating corporate officers and seeking criminal indictments against them, fines are imposed and civil settlements are usually negotiated between the Justice Department and Washington law firms whose partners often previously served

in that agency. Subordinate employees fare less well. Colt's Walter Plowman is serving a year in jail for having falsified State Department end-use certificates, though his superiors were neither charged nor even investigated. The most recent seizure of arms bound for South Africa in violation of our arms embargo occurred in May of 1981, when Customs agents at Houston Intercontinental Airport held a Boeing 707 owned by the Austrian private charter firm of Montana Austria, which was scheduled to depart for Johannesburg, and confiscated its cargo of 1,146 M-16 5.56mm rifles, 89 9mm automatic pistols, 111 M-1911A1 .45 Cal automatic pistols, 100 grenade launchers and 15,000 M-16 rifle ammunition magazines, which had been delivered by truck from Colt Industries in Connecticut, and were valued at a total of $1.2 million. The aircraft's crew and two British businessmen, John Parks and Peter T. Towers, were taken into custody and charged with violating the Federal neutrality law by conspiring to export arms with a falsified State Department license, whose end-use certificate indicated the shipment was bound for the Sudan. At the request of Servotech, a company registered in Khartoum and Lichtenstein that had chartered the aircraft, Montana Austria had applied for and received United States authorization to change the aircraft's destination to South Africa, upon assurances from Servotech's Hamburg agent that its cargo comprised ''harmless steel fabricates'' rather than weapons.

# SOUTH KOREA
6 x C-130H Hercules transport aircraft for $8.783 million@, together with $23.5 million in support equipment, in 1978.

18 x F-4E Phantom II fighter-bomber aircraft for $7.472 million@, together with $29.8 million in support equipment, in 1978.

14 x F-5E Tiger II fighter aircraft for $4.321 million@, together with $8.7 million in support equipment, in 1978.

48 x UH-1H Iroquois troop transport helicopter for $764,000@, together with $3.8 million in support equipment, in 1978.

30 x UH-1B utility helicopter for $590,000@, in 1978.

14 x Cessna 0-1 Bird Dog light reconnaissance aircraft, valued at $204,000@, transferred as grant aid under the Military Assistance Plan (MAP) in 1978.

6 x Boeing CH-47C Chinook transport helicopter for $6.683 million@ in 1978.

15 x M-88A1 armoured recovery vehicle for $693,333@, together with $2.4 million in support equipment, in 1978.

421 x M-48A5 main battle tank for $510,000@, together with $14.4 million in support equipment, in 1978.

2 x Allen M. Sumner class destroyer for $28.928 million@ in 1978.

3 x Asheville class patrol combatant for $13.660 million@ in 1978.

208 x General Dynamics RIM-66A Standard air defense missile for $1.192 million@ in 1978.

341 x AIM-7F Sparrow air intercept missile for $99,413@, together with $23 million in support equipment, in 1978.

37 x M-109A2 155mm self-propelled howitzer for $648,648@ in 1979.

44 x Hughes 500MD attack helicopter equipped with stabilized TOW antitank missile sight and TOW launchers for $766,670@ in 1979. An additional 66 of these aircraft will be produced from sub-assemblies in South Korea by the Hanjin Corporation.

1,100 x MGM-71A TOW antitank missile for $7,272@ in 1979.

$59 million for spares and support equipment for South Korea's F-4, F-5, A-37, T-37, T-33 and C-123 aircraft, in 1979.

1,108 x MGM-71A TOW antitank missile for $8,122@ in 1979.

22 x AN/TPQ-36 mortar locator radar set for $2.5 million@ in 1979.

$60 million for spares and support equipment for F-4, F-5, A-37 and C-123 aircraft in 1979.

10 x MGM-71A TOW antitank missile launcher for $61,000@, and 1,800 x MGM-71A TOW antitank missile for $7,272@ in 1980.

4 x AN/TSQ-73 Missile Minder fire control system for $7.25 million@ in April of 1980.

3 x Triad battery of MIM-23B Improved HAWK air defense missile equipment for $22.9 million@ in May of 1981.

(Note: South Korea has requested 80 x F-16 air combat fighter aircraft for $7.760 million@, excluding the costs of support equipment. In March of 1981, we agreed to supply 36 of these aircraft at that price. An additional 48 F-16s will shortly be deployed to Kunsan Air Base in two US Air Forcce squadrons.)

# SPAIN

6 x SH-3D antisubmarine warfare helicopter for $5.483 million@, together with $6.2 million in support equipment, in 1978.

64 x RIM-7F Seasparrow naval air defense missile for $140,625@ in 1978.

17 x Hughes 300C helicopter for $784,000@ in 1978.

12 x Agusta-Bell AB212 helicopter for $2.102 million@ in 1978.

18 x M-109A1 155mm self-propelled howitzer for $633,333@ in 1978.

2 x Lockheed C-130H Hercules transport aircraft for $9 million@ in 1979.

4 x RF-4C Phantom reconnaissance fighter aircraft for $2.75 million@ in 1979.

40 x RGM-84A Harpoon antiship missile for $725,000@ in 1979.

2 x Northrop MGM-74C Chukar II target drone for $600,000@ in 1979.

102 x M-113A1 armoured personnel carrier for $107,857@, 18 x M-125A1 armoured 81mm mortar carrier for $115,560@, and 4 x M-577A1 armoured command and communications vehicle for $131,000@ in May of 1979.

30 x Avionics system for Spanish Air Force C-101 aircraft for $33,333@ in May of 1979.

30 x AN/ARN-118(V) airborne TACAN tactical navigation system for Spanish C-101 aircraft for $40,000@ in May of 1979.

1,100 x MGM-71A TOW antitank missile for $7,272@ in June of 1979.

3 x Mk 13 Mod 4 naval guided missile launching system, to be mounted on Spanish surface combatants, for $13.666 million@ in June of 1979.

108 x AIM-7F Sparrow air intercept missile for $111,000@, including 8 practice rounds, in August of 1979.

77 x M-113A1 armoured personnel carrier for $107,857@, 33 x M-125A1 armoured 81mm mortar carrier for $115,560@, 11 x M-577A1 armoured command and communications vehicle for $131,000@, and 8 x M-548 armoured cargo carrier for $110,000@ in September of 1979.

$1 million for AN/WSC-3 Whiskey 3 shipboard UHF radio communications terminals in May of 1980.

(Note: Spain may soon order 3 x Lockheed P-3C Orion antisubmarine warfare and maritime patrol aircraft.)

# SUDAN

10 x F-5E and 2 x F-5F Tiger II fighter aircraft for $11.666 million@ including support equipment, 2 x Lockheed C-130H Hercules transport aircraft for $13.7 million@, 50 x M-60A1 main battle tank for $1.450 million@, and 100 x M-113AI armoured personnel carrier for $107,857@ in February of 1979. Paid by Saudi Arabia.

6 x AN/TPS-43E air defense radar and communications system for $11.83 million@ in September of 1979.

# SWEDEN

12 x RGM-84A Harpoon antiship missile launching system for $1.791 million@ and 100 x RGM-84A Harpoon antiship missile for $725,000@ in 1978.

340 x MGM-71A TOW antitank missile launcher for $17,058@ and 6,700 x MGM-71A TOW antitank missile for $6,701@ in 1978.

2 x Lockheed C-130H Hercules transport aircraft for $9 million@ in August of 1979.

3,600 x MGM-71A TOW antitank missile for $7,523@ in April of 1980.

(Note: Sweden's Ministry of Defense is considering the purchase of 100 x F-16 air combat fighter aircraft.)

# SWITZERLAND

8 x M-47 Dragon antitank missile tracker for $12,860@ and 15,544 x M-47 Dragon antitank missile for $4,800@ in 1978.

207 x M-109A2 155mm self-propelled howitzer for $794,444@, with $21.6 million in support equipment, and 225 x M-113A2 armoured personnel carrier equipped with Emerson M-109 ITV TOW antitank missile launcher for $140,000@, with $12 million in support equipment, in January of 1979.

50 x F-5E Tiger II fighter aircraft for $8.240 million@, together with $32.4 million in support equipment, in June of 1979.

6,200 x M-47 Dragon antitank missile for $3,586@ in May of 1980.

# SYRIA

18 x Agusta-Bell AB212 helicopter, produced under license in Italy, for $2.333 million@ in 1978.

279

# TAIWAN

$35 million in spares and support equipment for F-86, F-100, F-104, F-5, T-33, C-119, C-47 and C-54 aircraft in 1978.

52 x MIM-23B Improved HAWK air defense missile for $134,615@ in 1978.

30 x Northrop T-38A Talon training aircraft for $5.545 million@ in 1978.

100 x M-48A1 medium tank for $393,000@, with $8.1 million in support equipment, in 1978.

2 x Tacoma class gunboat for $16.242 million@ in 1978.

15 x PSMM Mk 5 naval patrol boat for $933,333@ in 1978.

44 x RGM-84A Harpoon antiship missile for $685,000@ in 1978.

3 x RIM-72C Sea Chaparral shipboard air defense missile launch system for $900,000@ in 1978.

150 x Mk 46 Mod 2 torpedo for $181,333@ in 1978. Delivery by 1982.

100 x M-109A2 155mm self-propelled howitzer for $750,000@ in 1978. Delivery by 1982.

25 x M-110A1 203mm self-propelled howitzer for $740,000@ in 1978. Delivery by 1983.

600 x AIM-9L Sidewinder air intercept missile for $26,333@ in 1979. Delivery by May of 1981.

28 x ASROC antisubmarine missile for $210,710@ in 1979. Delivery by 1982.

500 x AGM-65C Maverick air-to-ground missile for $50,000@, 29 x LLDS (Laser Locator Designator System) target illuminators for the AGM-65C Maverick missile for $710,000@, and 100 x single Maverick underwing launch rail for $1,050@ in October of 1979. Delivered.

48 x F-5E Tiger II fighter aircraft, to be produced in Taiwan, with United States coproduction support of $4.062 million per aircraft, committed in October of 1979. Production scheduled for completion by November of 1982.

12 x Hughes 500MD helicopter equipped for antisubmarine warfare for $1.066 million@ in October of 1979. Delivery completed.

2 x Beech Super King Air transport aircraft for $845,000@ in December of 1979.

14 x Mk 75 76mm naval gun and mount for $5.178 million@ in April of 1980.

49 x MGM-71A TOW antitank missile launcher for $65,600@ and 1,053 x MGM-71A TOW antitank missile for $8,786@ in April of 1980.

5 x Triad battery sets of MIM-23B Improved HAWK air defense missile system equipment for $25 million@ and 280 x MIM-23B Improved HAWK air defense missile for $150,360@ in April of 1980.

284 x RIM-72C Sea Chaparral shipboard air defense missile for $123,239@ including support equipment in April of 1980.

25 x M-109A2 155mm self-propelled howitzer for $720,000@ in July of 1980.

$264.7 million in spares and support equipment for F-100, RF-100, F-104, F-5, T-33 and C-119 aircraft in July of 1980.

(Note: In 1978 Taiwan requested 60 x F-4E Phantom II fighter-bomber aircraft. A far more maneuverable and lethal weapon system than any aircraft in that country's inventory, the F-4E would have brought about a significant increase in Taiwan's military power. In a gesture to Peking, we refused to sell them. Instead, we offered to arrange the sale of 60 x Israeli Kfir fighter-bomber aircraft, over whose transfer we retained approval because they are fitted with the General Electric J79 jet engine. In a gesture to the Arabs, Taiwan refused to purchase them. This dilemma may be solved by the new FX (Fighter/Export), whose development President Carter approved in reversal of his policy that the United States would not again produce weapons solely for export. The FX requirement will be met either by the General Dynamics F-16/79, a version of the F-16 that substitutes for its F100 engine the less powerful J79 engine, or the Northrop F-5G, a version of the F-5E that replaces its two J85 engines with a single F404, improving the aircraft's thrust-to-weight ratio to yield 60 percent more thrust. The F-16/79 is anticipated to cost $9 million per unit, while the F-5G will cost $6 million.
(Note: Taiwan has also requested the Grumman E-2C Hawkeye early warning aircraft, but approval of this transfer is still pending.)

# THAILAND

6 x Rockwell OV-10C Bronco counterinsurgency aircraft for $2.133 million@, together with $600,000 in support equipment, in 1978.

13 x Bell UH-1H Iroquois troop transport helicopter for $730,770@, together with $1 million in support equipment, in 1978.

3 x Swearingen Merlin IVA transport aircraft for $1.750 million@ in 1978. One of Thailand's Merlin III aircraft, delivered earlier, was lost in a crash.

180 x AIM-9B Sidewinder air intercept missile for $35,560@ in 1978.

170 x M-29EI 81mm mortar for $4,200@ and 90,000 rounds M-374 81mm HE mortar ammunition for $24@ in 1978.

1,110 x M-203 40mm grenade launcher for $304@ and 165,000 rounds 40mm grenade for $6.04@ in 1978.

7,000 x M-16A1 5.56mm rifle for $236@ in 1978. This was a commercial sale, licensed by the State Department's Office of Munitions Control.

94 x V-150 Commando armoured car for $139,360@ in 1978.

4 x F-5E Tiger II fighter aircraft for $3.750 million@ in 1978.

4 x Boeing CH-47 Chinook transport helicopter for $6.683 million@ in 1978.

24 x PBR Mk I naval patrol boat for $494,900@ in 1978.

$34 million in 105mm HE and APERS ammunition, 90mm tank ammunition, and 81mm and 60mm mortar ammunition in 1978.

18 x F-5E and F-5F Tiger II fighter aircraft for $5.544 million@ in March of 1979. Six of these aircraft were immediately airlifted to Thailand by a US Air Force C-5A Galaxy in May of 1979.

34 x T-33 training aircraft for $302,941@ in March of 1979.

3 x Lockheed C-130H Hercules transport aircraft for $13.3 million@ including support equipment, in May of 1979.

40 x AN/TRN-26 transportable TACAN tactical navigation system for $36,333@ in July of 1979.

40,000 x 2.75'' FFAR (Folding Fin Aerial Rocket) for $275@ in 1979.

15 x M-48A2 medium tank for $393,000@, 31 x M-113A1 armoured personnel carrier for $102,660@, 6 x MGM-71A TOW antitank missile launcher for $61,000@, 80 x MGM-71A TOW antitank missile for $7,272@, 300 x M-47 Dragon antitank missile for $4,799@, and 244 x M-60C 7.62mm machine gun for $1,644@ in November of 1979.

24 x M-163A1 Vulcan self-propelled 20mm multibarreled antiaircraft gun for $966,670@ including spares, support equipment and ammunition in April of 1980.

35 x M-48A5 Patton II main battle tank for $895,000@, 18 x M-102 105mm towed howitzer for $136,000@, 38 x M-40A1 106mm recoilless rifle for $61,840@, 11,000 rounds 105mm tank and artillery ammunition for $503@ and 5,250 rounds 106mm recoilless rifle ammunition for $343@, in July of 1980.

# TUNISIA

10 x F-5E and 2 x F-5F Tiger II fighter aircraft for $4.466 million@ in 1978.

380 x AIM-9L Sidewinder air intercept missile for $32,226@ in 1978.

26 x M-163 Vulcan self-propelled 20mm multi-barreled antiaircraft gun for $819,230@ including spares, support equipment and ammunition in 1978.

4 x Bell UH-1H Iroquois transport helicopter for $728,800@ in 1978.

4 x PBR Mk I naval patrol boat for $488,666@ in 1978.

60 x M-113A2 armoured personnel carrier equipped with the Emerson M-109 ITV TOW antitank missile launcher for $165,600@, 12 x M-577A1 armoured command and communications vehicle for $131,000@, 1,200 x MGM-71A TOW antitank missile for $8,122@ and $1.9 million in support equipment in 1979.

18 x Agusta-Bell AB205 helicopter for $1.325 million@ in October of 1979.

# TURKEY

32 x F-4E and 8 x RF-4E Phantom II fighter-bomber aircraft for $2.342 million@ in 1978. These were purchased with Foreign Military Sales credits extended as part of a $400 million program of grant aid arranged before Congress voted an end to the Turkish arms embargo.

350 x AGM-65A Maverick air-to-ground missile for $48,666@ in 1978.

240 x AIM-7E Sparrow medium range air intercept missile for $72,080@ in 1978.

3 x Gearing class destroyer for $32.448 million@ and 1 x former US Navy salvage ship for $21.088 million in 1978. This transfer still has not been approved by Congress, some of whose members feel it should be held pending Turkey's release of American citizens detained on charges of drug smuggling.

30 x Northrop T-38A Talon training aircraft for $10.5 million@ in July of 1979.

258 x AIM-7F Sparrow medium range air intercept missile for $92,000@ in July of 1979.

400 x AIM-9L Sidewinder short range air intercept missile for $36,555@ in July of 1979.

$111 million in spares, training, ammunition and support equipment for Turkish F-4E Phantom fighter-bomber aircraft in August of 1979.

$30 million for the lease of equipment by the firm of MKEK to rehabilitate Turkish M-48 medium tanks and equip them with the 105mm tank gun.

(Note: Turkey may receive 40 x F-16 air combat fighter aircraft, pending approval by Congress.)

# UGANDA

1 x Grumman Gulfstream II transport aircraft for $7.202 million in 1977.

# UNION OF SOVIET SOCIALIST REPUBLICS

The sale of one Control Data Cyber-32 computer was blocked in October of 1979, on the ostensible grounds that it might have been put to military use. The Defense Department now concedes that such equipment has no military application, and that the sale was really blocked as a political response to the discovery of a Soviet "combat brigade" in Cuba. Though it has since been established that the Soviet troops in Cuba have no combat role, and that we have known of their presence for the past 17 years, the computer still has not been released.

# UNITED KINGDOM

500 x Mk 46 Mod 2 torpedo for $144,000@ in 1978.

284 x RGM-84A Harpoon antiship missile for $602,820@ in 1978.

30 x Boeing Ch-47C Chinook troop transport helicopter for $15.72 million@ including support equipment, in 1978. All have been delivered.

100 x Westinghouse AN/ALQ-119 aircraft Tactical Jamming System (TJS) electronic counter measures pod for $391,000@ in 1978.

8,000 x MGM-71B Improved TOW antitank missile for $11,875@ in 1978.

$56.4 million for 6 x LORAN receiver and 12 x navigational computer for British Polaris submarines in 1978.

$14 million for electronic warfare equipment for British Nimrod aircraft in August of 1978.

$44 million for fuselage extension on British C-130 transport aircraft in November of 1978.

18 x M-109A2 155mm self-propelled howitzer for $762,000@ and 3 x M-578 armoured recovery vehicle for $1.094 million@ in February of 1979.

1 x Boeing Jetfoil PGM hydrofoil naval patrol combatant for $6 million in March of 1979.

$23 million for Loral electronic support measures systems for British Nimrod early warning aircraft in March of 1979.

62 x Litton LTN-2M Omega navigation and communications system, for British VC-10 and Nimrod aircraft, for $11,000@ in March of 1979.

$8 million for Loral EW-1017 electronic support measures systems for British Nimrod aircraft in October of 1979.

50 x Sperry GM9 compass and RL8F compass repeater systems for $32,500@ in October of 1979. These will be installed on British Westland helicopters.

200 x Westinghouse AN/ALQ-131 aircraft Tactical Jamming System (TJS) electronic counter measures pod for $687,500@ in November of 1979.

51 x M-109A2 155mm self-propelled howitzer for $629,411@ in April of 1980.

100 x Trident I SLBM (Submarine-Launched Ballistic Missile) for $25 million@, including a contribution of 5 percent of the Trident I research and development costs, in July of 1980. This is likely to be followed by an agreement for Britain's purchase of nuclear materials to manufacture 800 to 1,000 of its own nuclear warheads for these missiles. It will mark the first time the United States has ever made such materials available for transfer abroad, and will require some changes in existing law, which currently forbids such transfers.

(Note: the United Kingdom may soon purchase a quantity of the Mk 48 acoustic homing torpedo. The RAF may also purchase 14 x Beech Super King Air 200 aircraft.)

# URUGUAY

1 x Fletcher class destroyer for $24.199 million in 1978.

1 x Cessna 310L light transportation aircraft for $210,000 in 1979.

(Note: Uruguay continues to operate 10 Beech AT-11 aircraft.)

# VENEZUELA

16 to 24 x F-16 air combat fighter aircraft for $14.5 million@ in June of 1981. This is the first time since 1968 that the United States has sold advanced combat aircraft to a Latin American nation, even though State Department officials acknowledge that Venezuela "has no serious security problem." The sale is expected substantially to destabilize the regional arms balance, and may trigger a new arms race in the Western Hemisphere. While it will recycle some Venezuelan petrodollars, it is believed that the sale was effected primarily to pave the way for a sale of the same aircraft to Pakistan, announced ten days after this one, on the ground that a precedent had already been set for the supply of such highly sophisticated weaponry to a nation with a security problem less serious than the one we claim Pakistan has.

# WEST GERMANY

3 x Mk 86 naval gun fire control systems for $4.3 million@, together with $6.2 million in support equipment, in 1978.

$26.4 million in Pershing I missile components in 1978.

$25 million for modernization of three West German destroyers, in 1978.

15,000 x MGM-71A TOW antitank missile for $5,266@ in 1978.

9,000 x Active Optical Target Detector for the AIM-9L Sidewinder air intercept missile, for $9,333@ in 1978.

96 x RIM-7F Sea Sparrow shipboard air defense missile for $73,958@ in 1978.

142 x RGM-84A Harpoon antiship missile for $602,820@ in 1978. 10 practice missiles included.

$3 million for helicopter gyroscopes in May of 1978.

6 x AN/UYK-4 data display consoles for West German F-122 Frigates, for $1.5 million@ in September of 1978.

4 x AN/TPS-43E air defense radar and communications system for $8.75 million@ in 1978.

92 x AN/AAD-5 FLIR (Forward Looking Infra Red) aircraft reconnaissance system for $290,220@ in 1978.

$25 million for electronic support measures sytems in January of 1979.

$20 million for Itek Vector V radar warning receivers for West German Tornado aircraft in March of 1979.

$12 million for E-Systems inertial navigation systems for West German Atlantic class patrol combatants in March of 1979.

$150 million for the computerized Hughes GEADGE (German Air Defense Ground Environment) early warning radar and communications system in Bavaria, to replace the 412L radar network installed in the 1960s. The agreement was approved in May of 1979.

5 x E-Systems Radar and Electronic Warfare system for $9.998 million@, in a program to modernize the West German Atlantic 1150 class naval patrol combatants, in July of 1980.

(Note: In October of 1979, the Bundesluftwaffe suffered its 185th F-104G Starfighter crash.)

# YUGOSLAVIA

13 x Bell 205 Jet Ranger III and Long Ranger II helicopter for $798,850@ in July of 1979.

# ZAIRE

15 x Cessna Model 150 light reconnaissance aircraft for $244,000@ in 1978.

20 x Cessna-Reims Model 337 Milirole counter-insurgency aircraft for $682,333@ in 1978.

# ZAMBIA

16 x Agusta-Bell AB-47B light observation helicopter for $455,500@ in 1978.

# ZIMBABWE

22 x Cessna-Reims Model F337 Milirole counterinsurgency aircraft, which the Rhodesian Air Force called the "Lynx," for approximately $700,000@ in 1977 and 1978.

17 x SIAI-Marchetti SM-260 Warrior light strike aircraft, in January of 1977. Because these aircraft are fitted with an American Lycoming engine, their transfer was in violation of an embargo against arms to Rhodesia. The price of this sale is unknown. Produced in Italy, the aircraft were flown from that country to Gooselies, Belgium, in care of the firm of Spare Parts Europe. From Gooselies they were taken to Antwerp, disassembled and placed aboard the Portuguese freighter *Melange*, which took them to Durban, South Africa, where they were reassembled and flown to Salisbury.

11 x Agusta-Bell AB205A Iroquois troop transport helicopter, originally produced under license in Italy and sold to Israel in 1968. In August of 1977 these aircraft left Haifa, bound for Jamson Aviation in Singapore on the German freighter *Hartford Express*. At Majorca the ship was given new papers to sail for Durban. The state Department at first claimed no knowledge of this sale, which was probably valued at close to $7 million. Months later the Commerce Department announced it had licensed the sale, and that the transfer was not in violation of the prevailing embargo because the aircraft had been "demilitarized." In Rhodesia they were armed with 7.62mm machine guns and 20mm cannon to serve as gunships.

(Note: there have been many reports of the transfer of 4 x Rockwell OV-10F Bronco counterinsurgency aircraft to Rhodesia in 1978. The new government of Zimbabwe, which would have no reason to hide their presence, has not yet indicated whether they are there. These aircraft are normally valued at approximately $2.5 million@.)

# CURRENT UNIT PROCUREMENT PRICES

Following are the prices recently paid or now being paid by the United States military services for items of major defense equipment, together with the quantities purchased. The Reagan administration's key procurement plans for 1982 are included.

## COMBAT AIRCRAFT

Fairchild Republic A-10A Thunderbolt II and N/AW (Night/Adverse Weather) A-10 close air support aircraft: $5.620 million@ for 144 in 1979. $6.213 million@ for 144 in 1980. $9.966 million@ for 60 in 1981. $11.083 million@ for 60 in 1982. Of 733 aircraft planned for procurement, approximately 320 are now in service.

General Dynamics F-16 air combat fighter: $9.482 million@ for 145 in 1979. $9.465 million@ for 175 in 1980. $14.088 million@ for 120 in 1981. $17.608 million@ for 120 in 1982. Total procurement of 1,388 aircraft is planned.

Grumman A-6E Intruder attack bomber: $13.861 million@ for 12 in 1979. $14.178 million@ for 4 in 1980. $19.186 million@ for 2 in 1981. $24.583 million@ for 12 in 1982.

Grumman EA-6B Prowler electronic counter measures aircraft: $28.933 million@ for 6 in 1979. $29.833 million@ for 6 in 1980. $42.366 million@ for 3 in 1981. $45.333 million@ for 6 in 1982. Total procurement of 77 aircraft is planned.

Grumman F-14A Tomcat fighter interceptor: $23.569 million@ for 36 in 1979. $25.496 million@ for 30 in 1980. $34.187 million@ for 24 in 1981. $39.2 million@ for 30 in 1982. Of 390 aircraft planned for procurement, approximately 350 are now in service.

McDonnell-Douglas F-15 Eagle fighter interceptor: $17.785 million@ for 78 in 1979. $17.545 million@ for 60 in 1980. $25.023 million@ for 42 in 1981. $33.047 million@ for 42 in 1982. Of 729 aircraft planned for procurement, approximately 600 are now in service.

McDonnell-Douglas/Northrop F-18A Hornet fighter interceptor and A-18A attack bomber: $44.408 million@ for 15 in 1980. $35.516 million@ for 60 in 1981. $42.619 million@ for 63 in 1982. With allowances for inflation, the unit cost of this aircraft is expected to average $21.060 million after the planned procurement of 1,377 aircraft is completed.

Vought A-7E Corsair II attack bomber: $9.187 million@ for 12 in 1979. $9.134 million for one aircraft in 1981. $8.812 million@ for 16 twin-seat A-7D for the Air National Guard in 1979. $10.038 million@ for 12 twin-seat A-7K in 1979. Air Force and Navy procurement of this aircraft was completed in 1979, but Congress has kept the production line open.

McDonnell-Douglas AV-8B VSTOL attack bomber: on completion of procurement of 336 aircraft, an average cost of $10.119 million@ is currently projected.

## COMBAT SUPPORT AND SPECIAL MISSION AIRCRAFT

Boeing E-3A AWACS (Airborne Warning and Control System) surveillance and battlefield command aircraft: $81.700 million@ for 3 in 1979. $108.933 million@ for 3 in 1980. $123.646 million@ for 2 in 1981. $164.5 million@ for 2 in 1982.

Grumman E-2C Hawkeye surveillance and command aircraft: $34.850 million@ for 6 in 1979. $33.016 million@ for 6 in 1980. $38.566 million@ for 6 in 1981. $42 million@ for 6 in 1982.

Lockheed EC-130Q TACAMO radio relay communications aircraft: $31.688 million for one aircraft in 1979. $32.033 million@ for 3 in 1980. $38.25 million@ for 2 aircraft in 1981. Total procurement of 18 aircraft is planned by 1983.

(Note: The EC-130Q is used to support communications for the strategic missile submarine fleet. Now stationed at Guam, the TACAMO squadron will shortly be relocated on the West Coast to support the new Trident program.)

Lockheed P-3C Orion antisubmarine warfare and maritime patrol aircraft: $26.833 million@ for 12 in 1979. $27.499 million@ for 12 in 1980. $28.862 million@ for 8 in 1981. $41.25 million@ for 12 in 1982.

Lockheed TR-1 tactical reconnaissance aircraft: $22.100 million@ for 2 in 1980. $25.975 million@ for 4 in 1981. $23.666 million@ for 6 in 1982. Total procurement of 25 aircraft is planned.

(Note: based on the U-2R strategic reconnaissance aircraft, the TR-1 is equipped with the UPD-X standoff SLAR (Side Looking Airborne Radar) to provide imagery of very high resolution and several miles of depth on the NATO battlefield.)

McDonnell-Douglas KC-10A Extender ATCA (Advanced Tanker/Cargo Aircraft): $71.750 million@ for 2 in 1979. $47.525 million@ for 4 in 1980. $49.166 million@ for 6 in 1981. $60.25 million@ for 8 in 1982. Total procurement of 26 aircraft is planned.

# AIRCRAFT MODIFICATION PROGRAMS

Beech RC-12A Huron guardrail modifications for the US Army: $6.150 million@ for 8 in 1981.

Boeing B-52G/H Stratofortress long-range strategic bomber avionics modernization program: $11.858 million@ for 5 in 1979. $11.792 million@ for 29 in 1980. $3.740 million@ for 64 in 1981. $3.413 million@ for 61 in 1982.

Boeing B-52G Stratofortress modifications to carry the ALCM (Air-Launched Cruise Missile): $10.269 million@ for 3 aircraft in 1979.

$4.188 million@ for 19 in 1980. $2.875 million@ for 40 in 1981. $2.972 million@ for 40 in 1982.

(Note: the first B-52G squadron equipped with the ALCM will be operational at Griffiss AFB, New York in 1982. Further squadrons will be operational in 1983 at Wurtsmith AFB, Michigan and Grand Forks AFB, North Dakota, and in 1984 at Ellsworth AFB, South Dakota. Each base will deploy 300 ALCMs.)

Boeing KC-135 Stratotanker aircraft reengining program: $44.500 million for one aircraft in 1981.

Boeing RC-135A conversion to KC-135C standard: $4 million for one aircraft in 1979.

Civil Reserve Air Fleet modifications program: $5.788 million@ for 5 in 1979. $8.183 million@ for 9 in 1980. $11.271 million@ for 7 in 1981. $17.56 million@ for 3 in 1982.

Grumman/General Dynamics EF-111A electronic counter measures aircraft conversion program: $30.260 million@ for 5 aircraft in 1979. $55 million for one aircraft in 1980. $19.875 million@ for 12 in 1981. $19.683 million@ for 12 in 1982. A total of 42 F-111A aircraft is planned for conversion to EF-111A standard.

Lockheed C-5A Galaxy wing modifications: $17.080 million@ for 5 aircraft in 1980. $13.891 million@ for 12 in 1981. $10.694 million@ for 18 in 1982. This program is intended to increase the service life of the aircraft from 7,100 to 30,000 hours.

Lockheed C-141A Starlifter fuselage stretch and aerial refueling modification to C-141B standard: $738,823@ for 85 aircraft in 1979. $625,806@ for 124 in 1980. $752,900@ for 34 in 1981. A total of 271 C-141A aircraft will be so modified.

Lockheed P-3C Orion Update prototype development: $7 million for one aircraft in 1979.

# TRANSPORT, TRAINING AND UTILITY AIRCRAFT

Beech T-34C Turbo Mentor training aircraft: $830,000@ for 34 in 1978. $700,000@ for 60 in 1981. $833,333@ for 60 in 1982.

Beech T-44A Advanced Multi-Engine Trainer: $770,000@ for 23 in 1978.

Beech UC-12B Huron utility aircraft: $980,000@ for 20 in 1978. $1.214 million@ for 22 in 1979. $1.238 million@ for 22 in 1980.

Grumman VC-4 Gulfstream II transport aircraft: $6 million for one aircraft in 1980.

Lockheed C-130H Hercules transport aircraft: $8.560 million@ for 8 in 1979.

McDonnell-Douglas C-9B Skytrain II transport aircraft: $12.8 million for one aircraft in 1979.

# HELICOPTERS

Bell AH-1S Cobra attack helicopter: $1.798 million@ for 66 in 1979. $2.000 million@ for 15 in 1980.

Bell AH-1G Cobra attack helicopter conversion to AH-1S standard: $853,012@ for 83 aircraft in 1978. $1.348 million@ for 137 in 1979. $1.603 million@ for 160 in 1980. $1.715 million@ for 64 in 1981.

Bell AH-1T Sea Cobra attack helicopter for the Marine Corps: $1.565 million@ for 23 in 1978. $3.650 million@ for 8 in 1979.

Bell UH-1H Iroquois troop transport helicopter: $242,857@ for 49 in 1979.

Boeing Vertol CH-47 Chinook transport helicopter modernization to CH-47D standard: $16.266 million@ for 9 aircraft for 1981. $13 million@ for 10 in 1982.

Hughes Advanced Attack Helicopter: $39.071 million@ for 14 in 1982.

Sikorsky UH-60A Blackhawk troop transport helicopter: $2.786 million@ for 129 in 1979. $2.452 million@ for 145 in 1980. $6.387 million@ for 80 in 1981. $6.781 million@ for 96 in 1982.

Sikorsky SH-60B Seahawk LAMPS (Light Amphibious Multi-Purpose System) MK III helicopter: $3.750 million@ for 200 in 1979. $40.2 million@ for 25 in 1981. $47.888 million@ for 18 in 1982.

Sikorsky CH-53E Super Stallion heavy lift helicopter: $12.014 million@ for 14 in 1979. $10.431 million@ for 15 in 1980. $12.378 million@ for 14 in 1981. $21.454 million@ for 11 in 1982.

Kaman SH-2F Seasprite LAMPS MK I helicopter: $13.222 million@ for 18 in 1982.

# MISSILES

Boeing AGM-68A ALCM (Air-Launched Cruise Missile) with nuclear warhead: $3.780 million@ for 24 in 1979. $1.621 million@ for 225 in 1980. $1.132 million@ for 480 in 1981. $1.353 million@ for 440 in 1982.

Ford Aerospace MIM-72C Improved Chaparral air defense missile: $38,275@ for 870 in 1978. $41,294@ for 850 in 1979. $42,500@ for 80 in 1981.

General Dynamics/Convair BGM-109 Tomahawk GLCM (Ground-Launched Cruise Missile) with nuclear warhead: $7.990 million@ for 11 in 1981. $6.142 million@ for 88 in 1982. Range of the GLCM is 2,500 miles.

General Dynamics/Convair AGM-109 Tomahawk ALCM (Air-Launched Cruise Missile) with nuclear warhead: $3.545 million@ for 20 in 1981. $1.034 million@ for 54 in 1982.

General Dynamics AGM-45A Shrike antiradar missile: $51,333@ for 600 in 1979.

General Dynamics RIM-66B Standard SM-1 (MR) medium range air defense missile: $194,666@ for 480 in 1979. $219,000@ for 480 in 1980. $306,538@ for 260 in 1981. $281,833@ for 600 in 1982.

General Dynamics RIM-66C Standard SM-2 (MR) improved supersonic medium range air defense missile: $640,000@ for 30 in 1980. $562,857@ for 70 in 1981. $526,666@ for 120 in 1982.

General Dynamics RIM-67B Standard SM-2 (ER) improved extended range air defense missile: $1.289 million@ for 40 in 1979. $890,000@ for 55 in 1980. $513,818@ for 275 in 1981. $583,533@ for 375 in 1982.

General Dynamics FIM-92A Stinger MANPADS (Man-Portable Air defense System) short range missile: $45,710@ for 2,678 in 1979. $34,212@ for 2,654 in 1980. $52,320@ for 1,703 in 1981. $95,911@ for 2,544 in 1982.

General Support Rocket System (GSRS) un-guided 8.9" battlefield support barrage missile: $35,090@ for 1,764 in 1980. $50,427@ for 2,340 in 1981. $73,717@ for 2,496 in 1982. This is also known as the Multiple Launch Rocket System (MLRS).

Hughes AIM-54A Phoenix and AIM-54C improved Phoenix long range air intercept missile: $439,047@ for 210 AIM-54A in 1979. $610,000@ for 180 AIM-54A in 1980. $1.840 million@ for 60 AIM-54C in 1980. $1.918 million@ for 60 AIM-54C in 1981. $2.241 million@ for 72 AIM-54C in 1982.

Hughes AGM-65D Maverick imaging infrared guided air-to-ground missile: $408,000@ for 490 in 1982.

Hughes/Boeing Roland SHORADS (Short Range Air Defense System) missile: $724,146@ for 410 in 1980. $670,166@ for 600 in 1981. $709,433@ for 795 in 1982.

Hughes MGM-71A TOW (Tube-launched, Optically-tracked, Wire-guided) antitank missile: $4,496@ for 10,920 in 1979. $4,581@ for 16,805 in 1980. $6,700@ for 12,000 improved TOW in 1981. $8,258@ for 12,000 improved TOW in 1982.

(Note: the improved TOW missile has a more powerful warhead and a guidance system more resistant to electronic counter measures. The improvements will be retrofitted on all TOW missiles procured earlier.)

Lockheed UGM-96A Trident I (C-4) SLBM (Submarine-Launched Ballistic Missile) with nuclear MIRV (Multiple Independently-Targetable Reentry Vehicle) warheads: $10.348 million@ for 86 in 1979. $9.300 million@ for 82 in 1980. $11.951 million@ for 72 in 1981. $12.969 million@ for 72 in 1982.

Martin Marietta Pershing 1A battlefield support missile with nuclear warhead: $3.116 million@ for 6 in 1979. $1.682 million@ for 39 in 1980. $2.277 million@ for 31 in 1981. Pershing II: $5.048 million@ for 39 in 1982.

McDonnell-Douglas AGM-84A Harpoon antiship missile: $540,000@ for 240 in 1979. $590,000@ for 240 in 1980. $724,580@ for 240 in 1981. $1.005 million@ for 340 in 1982.

Raytheon/Ford AIM-9L Sidewinder short range air intercept missile: $38,560@ for 2,500 to USAF and $50,923@ for 650 to USN in 1979. $42,390@ for 2,050 to USAF and $73,125@ for 320 to USN in 1980.

Raytheon/Ford AIM-9M Sidewinder short range air intercept missile with all-weather capability: $175,384@ for 260 to USAF and $181,818@ for 220 to USN in 1981. $78,333@ for 1,800 to USAF and $56,043@ for 910 to USN in 1982.

Raytheon/Ford AIM-7F Sparrow medium range air intercept missile: $81,866@ for 1,500 to USAF and $128,292@ for 410 to USN in 1979. $94,393@ for 1,320 to USAF and $274,166@ for 240 to USN in 1980.

Raytheon/Ford AIM-7M Sparrow III medium range air intercept missile: $130,219@ for 910 to USAF and $165,584@ for 770 to USN in 1981. $136,267@ for 1,060 to USAF and $145,193@ for 905 to USN in 1982. This may be changed to a combined 1982 purchase of 1,670 missiles for both services at $146,706@.

Raytheon MIM-23B Improved HAWK (Homing All-the-Way Killer) air defense missile: $121,381@ for 608 in 1979. $185,279@ for 197 in 1980. $207,142@ for 14 in 1981. $209,090@ for 440 in 1982.

Raytheon XMIM-104 Patriot air defense missile: $2.843 million@ for 155 in 1980. $2.653 million@ for 184 in 1981. $2.752 million@ for 364 in 1982.

(Note: a Patriot air defense battalion will deploy 192 missiles organized into 6 fire units with 32 missiles each. The 1980 procurement cost of one fire unit, including the command vehicle, phased-array acquisition and target illumination radar, power supply trailer and missile launch truck is $82.1 million. The cost of a full battalion with its complement of missiles therefore exceeded $500 million in that procurement year.)

Raytheon/Kollsman M-47 Dragon man-portable antitank missile: $4,058@ for 20,671 in 1978. $4,300@ for 2,000 in 1981.

Texas Instruments AGM-88A HARM (High-Speed Anti-Radiation Missile): $1.685 million@ for 80 in 1980. $1.255 million@ for 80 in 1981. $992,537@ for 134 to USN and $683,823@ for 136 to USAF in 1982.

Vought MGM-52C Lance battlefield support missile: $202,777@ for 360 missiles with conventional high explosive warheads in 1979. $204,126@ for 315 missiles with nuclear warheads in 1980.

Hellfire antitank missile: $146,046@ for 1,075 in 1982.

# TANKS AND ARMOURED VEHICLES

Chrysler XM-1 Abrams main battle tank: $3.390 million@ for 110 in 1979. $1.839 million@ for 352 in 1980. $1.814 million@ for 569 in 1981. $1.834 million@ for 569 in 1982. Total procurement of 7,058 vehicles is planned. Production will reach the rate of 90 per month by 1985, with emergency funds available to increase production to 150 per month.

Chrysler M-60A3 main battle tank: $832,880@ for 438 in 1979. $863,750@ for 251 in 1980.

M-60A1 tank conversion to M-60A3 standard: $348,421@ for 380 vehicles in 1979. $235,807@ for 687 in 1980. $366,216@ for 148 in 1981. $392,134@ for 445 in 1982.

Chrysler M-728 CEV (Combat Engineer Vehicle) with 165mm demolition gun: $919,640@ for 56 in 1980.

FMC Corporation XM-2 IFV (Infantry Fighting Vehicle) and XM-3 CFV (Cavalry Fighting Vehicle): $2.254 million@ for 100 in 1980. $1.161 million@ for 400 in 1981. $1.493 million@ for 464 in 1982. (Note: XM-2 IFV and XM-3 CFV are new designations for the former XM-723 Mechanized Infantry Combat Vehicle or MICV. Equipped with the Bushmaster automatic dual-feed 25mm cannon and a TOW antitank missile launcher, the two new vehicles differ only in role, the IFV carrying an infantry rifle section of nine men, while the CFV carries a crew of five and several thousand extra rounds of 25mm ammunition.)

FMC Corporation M-113A1 and M-113A2 armoured personnel carrier: $80,910@ for 550 M-113A1 in 1979. $86,914@ for 512 M-113A2 in 1979. $102,295@ for 1,002 in 1982.

(Note: the M-113A2 is equipped with a diesel engine and improved suspension and cooling systems.)

FMC Corporation M-113A2 with the Emerson M-109 ITV (Improved TOW Launcher): $111,904@ for 42 in 1981. $122,857@ for 35 in 1982.

M-113A1 conversion to M-113A2 standard: $35,545@ for 1,100 vehicles in 1979. $24,041@ for 1,460 in 1980. $24,648@ for 1,282 in 1981. $12,558@ for 2,333 in 1982.

FMC Corporation M-125A1 armoured 81mm mortar carrier: $103,850@ for 52 in 1980.

FMC Corporation M-548 armoured cargo carrier: $97,930@ for 193 in 1979. $95,460@ for 441 in 1980.

Bowen-McLaughlin-York M-88A1 ARV (Armoured Recovery Vehicle): $660,260@ for 78 in 1979. $691,040@ for 67 in 1980.

# ARTILLERY, GUN SYSTEMS, AND ASSOCIATED EQUIPMENT

M-109A2 self-propelled 155mm howitzer: $392,800@ for 250 in 1979. $475,000@ for 136 in 1980. $555,555@ for 36 in 1981.

M-198 155mm towed howitzer: $268,983@ for 187 in 1979. $265,019@ for 263 in 1980. $311,805@ for 144 in 1981. $338,383@ for 99 in 1982.

M-39 carriage for towed 155mm howitzer: $82,233@ for 197 in 1979.

Royal Ordnance Factories XM-252 81mm mortar: $13,460@ for 780 in 1980.

M-224 60mm LWCM (Light Weight Company Mortar): $6,770@ for 2,098 in 1979.

Ford/General Dynamics DIVAD (Division Air defense) gun system: $15.258 million@ for 12 in 1981. $8.24 million@ for 50 in 1982. (Note: to complement and eventually replace the M-167 20mm Vulcan and M-163 self-propelled 20mm AVADS or Autotrack Vulcan Air Defense System, the DIVAD mounts twin 40mm Bofors or twin 35mm Oerlikon cannon with General Dynamics radar fire control on an M-48A5 tank chassis.)

Hughes M-242 Bushmaster 25mm automatic dual-feed cannon: $57,096@ for 310 in 1980. This is the cannon that equips the IFV and CFV. It fires single rounds or multiple bursts at selectable rates of 100 or 200 rounds per minute.

FMC Corporation Bushmaster VRFWS (Vehicle Rapid Fire Weapon System): $119,350@ for 310 in 1980. This is the Bushmaster 25mm cannon fitted in the IFV/CFV turret.

Emerson M-109 ITV (Improved TOW Launcher) antitank missile launch system: $63,636@ for 1,100 in 1980.

Helicopter Lightweight Launcher for the 2.75" FFAR (Folding Fin Aerial Rocket): $130,000@ for 50 in 1980.

M-2 .50 Caliber heavy machine gun: $8,627@ for 1,570 in 1979.

M-240 (Fabrique Nationale MAG 58) 7.62mm armor machine gun: $12,000@ for 625 in 1979. $3,905@ for 2,970 in 1980.

XM-231 5.56mm FPW (Firing Port Weapon): $1,260@ for 3,168 in 1980.

MHU-141/M munitions trailer: $6,975@ for 2,007 in 1979.

M-915 truck: $50,000@ for 5,000 vehicles in 1980.

# AMMUNITION

GAU-8/A 30mm API (Armor Piercing Incendiary) high-density ammunition for the GAU-8/A Avenger multibarelled cannon: $13.14@ for 25,100,000 rounds in 1980 from Aerojet and Honeywell. The GAU-8/A cannon is mounted in the Fairchild Republic A-10A Thunderbolt II close air support aircraft as an antitank weapon system.

CBE (Combined Effects Bomblet): $420@ for 25,000 in 1980.

XM-712 Copperhead 155mm laser-guided CLGP (Cannon-Launched Guided Projectile): $31,571@ for 2,100 in 1980. $28,139@ for 4,300 in 1981.

155mm Conventional Munition: $437@ for 519,000 to USAR in 1981. $392@ for 14,000 to USMC in 1981.

M-483 155mm Improved Conventional Munition: $3,005@ for 37,000 to USAR in 1981. $850@ for 2,000 to USMC in 1981. This artillery projectile delivers RAMM (Remote Anti-Armour Munition) or ADAM (Area-Denial Artillery Munition) scatterable mines.

155mm RAP (Rocket Assisted Projectile) with extended range: $588@ for 18,000 in 1981.

155mm Propelling Charge: $133@ for 1,154,000 to USAR in 1981. $60@ for 217,000 to USMC in 1981.

203mm Propelling Charge: $264@ for 51,000 to USAR in 1981. $125@ for 8,000 to USMC in 1981.

203mm RAP (Rocket Assisted Projectile): $1,508@ for 12,000 in 1981.

# NAVAL VESSELS

SSBN Trident class nuclear-powered ballistic missile submarine: $866.750 million@ for 2 in 1979. $1.121 billion for one boat in 1980. $1.329 billion for one in 1982.

SSN-688 Los Angeles class nuclear-powered attack submarine: $287.3 million for one boat in 1978. $363.1 million for one in 1979. $461.5 million for one in 1980. $714.5 million@ for 2 in 1982. At the end of World War

II, conventionally-powered submarines cost approximately $3.9 million@.

DD-963 Spruance class destroyer: $543 million for one ship in 1979. The estimated cost for this class of 30 destroyers was $134.2 million@ in 1978. World War II destroyers cost approximately $5 million@.

DDG-47 Aegis class guided missile destroyer: $930 million for one ship in 1979. $820.2 million for one in 1980. $1 billion for one in 1982. This is a more expensive destroyer due to its highly sophisticated air defense system.

FFG-7 Oliver Hazard Perry class guided missile frigate: $214.4 million@ for 3 in 1979. $277.3 million@ for 4 in 1981. $368 million@ for 3 in 1982.

FFG-47 Knox class guided missile frigate: $187.46 million@ for 9 in 1979. $200.7 million@ for 6 in 1980.

CVV Vinson class aircraft carrier: $1.617 billion for one in 1980.

CVN Nimitz class aircraft carrier: $2.2 billion for one from Tenneco, for delivery in 1987.

LHA-1 Tarawa class amphibious assault ship: $311.7 million for one in 1979. The estimated cost for this class of five ships was $230 million@ in 1978.

LACV-30 (Lighter than Air-Cushion Vehicle): $5.250 million@ for 4 in 1979.

T-AGOS ocean surveillance ship: $35.448 million@ for 2 in 1979. $30.789 million@ for 5 in 1980.

T-AKX maritime pre-positioning ship: $103.544 million@ for 2 in 1981. $257.54 million for one in 1982.

Coast Guard cutter: $27.5 million@ for 4 in 1980.

$473 million in 1981 and 1982 to reactivate CV ORISKANY aircraft carrier.

$300 million in 1981 to reactivate BB NEW JERSEY battleship, replacing its aft 16" gun turret with the Tomahawk Cruise Missile launcher.

$600 million in 1982 and 1983 to reactivate BB IOWA battleship, replacing its aft 16" gun turret with the Tomahawk Cruise Missile launcher.

(Note: The NEW JERSEY and IOWA will each carry 320 Tomahawk Cruise Missiles.)

# NAVAL WEAPON SYSTEMS

FMC Corporation Mk 75 76mm Gun Mount: $2.93 million@ for 3 in 1978. $3.2 million for one in 1979. $3.43 million@ for 3 in 1980.

General Dynamics Mk 15/2 Vulcan Phalanx CIWS (Close In Weapon System) 20mm multi-barreled naval antiaircraft gun: $2.68 million@ for 27 in 1979. $1.88 million@ for 61 in 1980.

Mk 46 Torpedo: $124,910@ for 570 in 1979. $108,510@ for 576 in 1980.

Mk 48 Acoustic Homing Torpedo: $538,330@ for 300 in 1978. $871,650@ for 127 in 1979.

Mk 60 CAPTOR antisubmarine mine with encapsulated torpedo: $184,070@ for 390 in 1978. $237,310@ for 260 in 1980.

# ENGINES

Avco AGT 1500 gas turbine engine for the XM-1 tank: $284,090@ for 352 in 1980.

General Electric T700-GE-700 turboshaft engine for the UH-60A Blackhawk helicopter: $250,000@ for 170 in 1979.

Vought MGM-52C Lance missile Engine: $36,745@ for 381 in 1979.

# FIRE DIRECTION AND TARGET DESIGNATION EQUIPMENT

Hughes AN/ASB-19(V) Angle Rate Bombing System: $705,410@ for 37 in 1979.

Westinghouse/Ford PAVE TACK aircraft target designation system: $1.66 million@ for 149 in 1980. This sytem combines the Westinghouse Neodymium YAG laser designator, aimed by the pilot's television camera sight, with a rangefinder and a FLIR (Forward Looking Infra Red) sensor for adverse weather and night operations. It is used by F-4E and RF-4C and F-111 aircraft.

Westinghouse PAVE SPIKE target designation system, without the Ford Aerospace FLIR sensor: $1.334 million@ for 221 in 1979. This is used by F-4D and F-4E aircraft.

GLLD (Ground Laser Locator Designator) target designation system: $203,846@ for 130 in 1980. $154,042@ for 235 in 1981. $172,340@ for 235 in 1982.

TACFIRE computer-assisted artillery fire allocation and direction system: $2.767 million@ for 31 in 1979. $2.204 million@ for 43 in 1980. $4.139 million@ for 23 in 1981.

FAMAC field artillery target acquisition system: $1 million@ for 5 in 1979.

Hughes AN/TPQ-36 mortar locator radar: $666,670@ for 106 in 1979. $1.210 million@ for 60 in 1980.

Hughes AN/TPQ-37 artillery locator radar: $2.574 million@ for 35 in 1979. $2.250 million@ for 56 in 1980. $2.686 million@ for 72 in 1981.

FIREFINDER divisional mortar and artillery locating radar system: $3.518 million@ for 22 in 1980. This system comprises three AN/TPQ-36 and two AN/TPQ-37 radars.

# SIGHTING AND SURVEILLANCE EQUIPMENT

LAAT (Laser-Augmented Airborne TOW) helicopter-mounted antitank missile sight: $295,450@ for 44 in 1980.

Bell and Howell ANVOS (Aviator's Night Vision Imaging System): $47,222@ for 36 in 1980.

Baird AN/VVS-2(V)1 night vision viewer for the XM-1 tank driver: $6,850@ for 292 in 1980.

AN/PUS-4 and AN/TVS-5 individual and crew night sights: $959@ for 4,900 in 1979.

Helmet-mounted sight: $16,228@ for 228 in 1980.

Man-Portable Night Sight: $74,698@ for 83 in 1980.

ITT 25mm Image Intensifier: $2,677@ for 3,735 in 1980.

Motorola AN/APS-94F SLAR (Side Looking Airborne Radar) for Mohawk and other reconnaissance aircraft: $377,780@ for 45 in 1980.

EODSS (Electro-Optical Deep Space Surveillance) system: $6.6 million@ for 5 in 1980.

# NAVAL ELECTRONICS EQUIPMENT

Hughes AN/UYA-4 data display console for FFG-7 Oliver Hazard Perry class frigate: $2 million@ for 8 in 1980.

Sperry Combat System Integration Unit for FFG-7 frigate: $1.447 million@ for 17 in 1980.

AN/USC-35(V) Link 11 communications system for DDG-2 destroyer: $300,000@ for 5 in 1979.

AN/SQQ-23 PAIR Sonar: $3.550 million@ for 2 in 1979. $3.677 million@ for 10 in 1980.

AN/SYR-1 communications tracking system for SM-2 ER Standard missile: $1.683 million@ for 6 in 1980.

AN/SPS-40 shipboard long-range air surveillance radar: $390,909@ for 11 in 1980.

# NAVIGATION AND AVIONICS EQUIPMENT

NAVSTAR Global Positioning System satellite: $20 million@ for 4 in 1980.

F-15 Eagle fighter interceptor avionics set: $48,453@ for 97 in 1979.

Honeywell inertial navigation system for the B-52D strategic bomber: $173,770@ for 61 in 1979.

E-3A AWACS surveillance and command aircraft navigation system: $1.13 million@ for 3 in 1979.

Mobile TACAN tactical navigation system for the RF-4E reconnaissance aircraft: $266,000@ for 9 in 1980.

AN/TRN-41 air-droppable TACAN set: $37,500@ for 40 in 1979.

AN/ARN-118(V) TACAN for the US Coast Guard: $10,060@ for 328 in 1980.

AN/GYQ-21(V) minicomputer for the US Air Force: $696,551@ for 29 in 1979.

AN/GPN-22 precision approach radar: $888,888@ for 18 in 1979.

AN/TPN precision landing radar: $1.38 million@ for 4 in 1980.

AN/UPM-145 radar test set: $7,389@ for 812 in 1980.

Bendix modified colour weather radar for SH-60A helicopter: $27,780@ for 90 in 1980.

Transportable weather satellite receiver terminal: $1.18 million@ for 4 in 1980.

# COMMUNICATIONS EQUIPMENT

TRW FLTSATCOM (Fleet Communications Satellite) satellite: $26.5 million@ for the 4th and 5th satellites in 1979.

UHF receiver for FLTSATCOM satellite: $3.6 million for one in 1979.

RCA AN/TSC-100 transportable satellite ground station: $2.75 million@ for 4 in 1980.

E-3A AWACS surveillance and command aircraft UHF radio: $666,600@ for 3 in 1980.

AN/MSQ-103 special purpose receiver for the EC-130Q TACAMO aircraft: $508,110@ for 37 in 1980.

MD-522/GRC radio teletypewriter: $1,908@ for 786 in 1980.

Hughes ROCC (Regional Operations Control Center) for the Joint Surveillance System: $79.289 million for one in 1979. The completed JSS system will comprise seven ROCC centers with 175 associated sensor sites.

AEWS (Arctic Early Warning System) operation and support: $273 million in 1979.

# ELECTRONIC WARFARE EQUIPMENT

AN/APR-31(V)1 signal detection set: $1,666@ for 1,500 in 1979.

General Dynamics AN/MST-T1 MUTES (Multiple Threat Emitter System): $5.926 million for one in 1979.

Litton AN/ALR-59 ESM (Electronic Support Measures) system upgrade for the E-2C Hawkeye surveillance and command aircraft: $1 million@ for 5 in 1980.

AN/GLQ-3 communications jammer: $212,000@ for 50 in 1980.

GTE AN/MLQ-34 TACJAM mobile tactical jamming system: $4 million@ for 6 in 1979.

AN/ALQ-144(V) infrared heat emission jammer for helicopter installation: $26,000@ for 450 in 1979.

XM-130 chaff dispenser: $7,500@ for 320 in 1979.

AN/LTQ-17A electronic counter measures system: $128,000@ for 25 in 1979.

AN/ALQ-99 electronic counter measures system for the F-111 fighter-bomber aircraft: $1.916 million@ for 6 in 1980.

Northrop AN/ALQ-135(V) electronic counter measures system: $376,500@ for 111 in 1979.

Westinghouse AN/ALQ-119 TJS (Tactical Jamming System) aircraft pod: $477,600@ for 220 in 1979.

Westinghouse AN/ALQ-131 TJS (Tactical Jamming System) aircraft pod: $684,492@ for 128 in 1980.

AN/ALR-67 Compass Go signal processor: $33,000@ for 244 in 1979. When paired with the AN/ALQ-119 or AN/ALQ-131, the Compass Go processor creates the Compass Tie system. The US Navy pairs these tactical jamming systems with the AN/ALR-46.

AN/ALQ-155 electronic counter measures system for the B-52 strategic bomber: $900,000@ for 31 in 1980.

# TRAINING EQUIPMENT

E-3A AWACS surveillance and command aircraft flight and systems simulator: $13.2 million for one in 1979.

NEWTS (Naval Electronic Warfare Training Center): $11.8 million in 1979.

Goodyear F-15 Eagle fighter interceptor aircraft flight simulator: $6.866 million@ for 3 in 1980.

MIM-23 HAWK air defense missile systems simulator: $1.6 million for one in 1979.

LGM-30G Minuteman III intercontinental ballistic missile crew procedures trainer: $700,000@ for 2 in 1979.

Northrop MGM-74C Chukar II aircraft target drone: $48,026@ for 152 in 1979.

# MAJOR DEFENSE CONTRACTORS

The most recent official compilation of major defense contractors in the United States was issued by the Pentagon in 1976, based on reconfirmed figures for contract awards given in Fiscal Year 1975. Here are the top 100, in their order of rank, with the total sums awarded to each in that year.

1 Lockheed Aircraft Corporation ($2,080,303,000)

2 Boeing Company ($1,560,827,000)

3 United Technologies Corporation ($1,407,447,000)

4 McDonnell Douglas Corporation ($1,397,939,000)

5 Grumman Corporation ($1,343,535,000)

6 General Dynamics Corporation ($1,288,756,000)

7 General Electric Company ($1,264,180)

8 Litton Industries, Inc. ($1,038,050,000)

9 Hughes Aircraft Company ($1,026,021,000)

10 Rockwell International Corporation ($732,306,000)

11 Raytheon Company ($680,566,000)

12 Northrop Corporation ($620,324,000)

13 Textron, Inc. ($545,904,000)

14 American Telephone and Telegraph Company ($510,076,000)

15 Sperry Rand Corporation ($437,103,000)

16 General Motors Corporation ($390,386,000)

17 LTV Corporation ($366,208,000)

18 International Business Machines Company ($360,086,000)

19 EXXON Corporation ($330,329,000)

20 Martin Marietta Corporation ($320,272,000)

21 Westinghouse Electric Corporation ($314,515,000)

22 Standard Oil Company of California ($301,386,000)

23 Honeywell, Inc. ($291,465,000)

24 TRW, inc. ($286,177,000)

25 RCA Corporation ($286,107,000)

26 Chrysler Corporation ($282,555,000)

27 Ford Motor Company ($259,671,000)

28 Tenneco, Inc. ($241,732,000)

29 Teledyne, Inc. ($236,143,000)

30 International Telephone and Telegraph Corporation ($233,397,000)

31 Texaco, Inc. ($226,501,000)

32 Singer Company ($213,902,000)

33 Mobil Oil Corporation ($204,030,000)

34 Fairchild Industries, inc. ($191,711,000)

35 Amerada Hess Corporation ($190,541,000)

36 Bendix Corporation ($180,529,000)

37 General Tire and Rubber Company ($168,963,000)

38 General Telephone and Electronics Corporation ($165,240,000)

39 R. J. Reynolds Industries, Inc. ($153,954,000)

40 FMC Corporation ($144,693,000)

41 Hercules, Inc. ($144,349,000)

42 Texas Instruments, Inc. ($144,075,000)

43 Santa Fe Engineers, Inc. ($143,944,000)

44 Harris Corporation ($141,670,000)

45 Sanders Associates, Inc. ($141,142,00)

46 Goodyear Tire and Rubber Company ($135,003,000)

47 Titan Group, Inc. ($126,030,000)

48 Control Data Corporation ($115,178,000)

49 American Motors Corporation ($114,478,000)

50 Standard Oil of Indiana ($112,284,000)

51 Guam Oil and Refining Company, Inc. ($109,796,000)

52 Norris Industries ($106,866,000)

53 Gould, Inc. ($100,552,000)

54 Thiokol Corporation ($100,464,000)

55 E Systems, Inc. ($100,125,000)

56 Massachusetts Institute of Technology ($97,863,000)

57 Dupont E. I. de Nemours and Company ($97,368,000)

58 Pan American World Airways, Inc. ($95,664,000)

59 Ogden Corporation ($93,487,000)

60 AVCO Corporation ($93,192,000)

61 Harsco Corporation ($91,541,000)

62 Johns Hopkins University ($91,138,000)

63 Signal Companies, Inc. ($90,037,000)

64 Pacific Resources, Inc. ($89,635,000)

65 North American Philips Corporation ($86,251,000)

66 Motorola, Inc. ($85,791,000)

67 Charles Stark Draper Laboratories, Inc. ($84,837,000)

68 Automation Industries, Inc. ($80,874,000)

69 Kidde Walter and Company, Inc. ($80,795,000)

70 Vinnell Corporation ($80,098,000)

71 Gulf Oil Corporation ($78,531,000)

72 Aerospace Corporation ($78,181,000)

73 Atlantic Richfield Company ($72,852,000)

74 Emerson Electric Company ($71,971,000)

75 Towne Realty Woerfel Corporation ($71,230,000)

76 Chamberlain Manufacturing Corporation ($70,420,000)

77 Algernon Blair, Inc. ($69,576,000)

78 Sverdrup and Parcel and Associates, Inc. ($68,940,000)

79 Day and Zimmerman, Inc. ($67,067,000)

80 Eastman Kodak Company ($62,886,000)

81 Loral Corporation ($61,286,000)

82 Lear Siegler, Inc. ($56,348,000)

83 Shell Oil Company ($52,915,000)

84 System Development Corporation ($52,316,000)

85 Burroughs Corporation ($50,325,000)

86 Mitre Corporation ($49,613,000)

87 Coastal States Gas Corporation ($49,149,000)

88 Cutler-Hammer, Inc. ($49,020,000)

89 National Presto Industries, Inc. ($48,607,000)

90 ATO, Inc. ($48,503,000)

91 Caterpillar Tractor Company ($47,605,000)

92 Continental Oil Company ($47,495,000)

93 Computer Sciences Corporation ($47,442,000)

94 Uniroyal, Inc. ($46,889,000)

95 General Foods Corporation ($46,324,000)

96 Clabir Corporation ($45,795,000)

97 Xerox Corporation ($45,005,000)

98 Procter and Gamble, Inc. ($44,687,000)

99 Tesoro Petroleum Corporation ($44,545,000)

100 Ashland Oil, Inc. ($44,354,000)

This amounts to a total of $27,138,033,-000 in FY 1975. Defense Department procurement in that year, however, totalled $39,500,615,000, the balance of $12,362,582,000 being made up by contract awards in smaller amounts to a much larger number of companies.

# BIBLIOGRAPHY

Akerman, Nordal, ON THE DOCTRINE OF LIMITED WAR, Lund, Sweden, Berlingska Boktryckeriet, 1972.

Aldridge, Robert C., THE COUNTERFORCE DOCTRINE: *A Guide to U.S. Nuclear Weapons and Strategic Doctrine*, Amsterdam and Washington, D.C., Transnational Institute, 1978.

Alperovitz, Gar, ATOMIC DIPLOMACY: *Hiroshima and Potsdam*, New York, Simon and Schuster, 1965.

Apt, Clark C., SERIOUS GAMES, New York, The Viking Press, 1970.

Archer, Dennis H.R., editor, JANE'S INFANTRY WEAPONS annual editions from 1976 through 1980, London, Macdonald & Jane's, 1975 through 1979.

Armbrister, Trevor, A MATTER OF ACCOUNTABILITY: *The True Story of the Pueblo Affair*, New York, Coward-McCann, Inc., 1970.

Art, Robert J., THE TFX DECISION: *McNamara and the Military*, Boston, Little Brown, 1968.

Barnaby, Frank, Ronald Huisken and the Stockholm International Peace Research Institute, ARMS UNCONTROLLED, Cambridge, Harvard University Press, 1975.

Barnet, Richard J., A TIME TO STOP, Washington, D.C., World Peacemakers, 1978.

Barnet, Richard J., and Ronald E. Muller, GLOBAL REACH: *The Power of the Multinational Corporations*, New York, Simon and Schuster, 1974.

Barnet, Richard J., INTERVENTION AND REVOLUTION: *The United States in the Third World*, New York and Cleveland, World Publishing Company, 1968.

Barnet, Richard J. and N. Gordon Crosby, MOVING TOWARDS TRUE SECURITY, Washington, D.C., World Peacemakers, 1979.

Barnet, Richard J., NO ROOM IN THE LIFEBOATS, Washington, D.C., World Peacemakers, 1978.

Barnet, Richard J., OUR CHOICE IS LIFE: *A Policy in Search of a President and a Strategy of Survival*, Washington, D.C., World Peacemakers, 1980.

Barnet, Richard J., THE WAY WE WANT TO END THE ARMS RACE, Woodmont, Connecticut, Promoting Enduring Peace, 1980.

Barnet, Richard J., REAL SECURITY: *Restoring American Power in a Dangerous Decade*, New York, Simon and Schuster, 1981.

Bidwell, Shelford, editor, BRASSEY'S ARTILLERY OF THE WORLD, New York, Bonanza Books, 1979.

Bidwell, Shelford, general editor, WORLD WAR 3: *A Military Projection Founded on Today's Facts*, Englewood Cliffs, Prentice-Hall, 1978.

Bonds, Ray, editor, THE U.S. WAR MACHINE, New York, Crown, 1978.

Bosch, Juan, PENTAGONISM: *A Substitute for Imperialism*, New York, Grove Press, 1968.

Boston Study Group, THE PRICE OF DEFENSE: *A New Strategy for Military Spending*, New York, Times Books, 1979.

Boulton, David, THE GREASE MACHINE: *The Inside Story of Lockheed's Dollar Diplomacy*, New York, Harper & Row, 1978.

Boyd, Alexander, THE SOVIET AIR FORCE SINCE 1918, New York, Stein & Day, 1977.

Brewer, Major Jerry D., SOUTH AFRICA'S CLOSE AIR SUPPORT CAPABILITIES IN COUNTERINSURGENCY, Fort Leavenworth, Army Command and General Staff College, 1978.

Bueschel, Richard M., COMMUNIST CHINESE AIR POWER, New York, Frederick A. Praeger, 1968.

Burbank, Spider, FOREIGN MILITARY TRANSFERS: *Credit Arrangements and Sales to the Third World*, Washington, D.C., Military Audit Project, 1978.

Burleson, Clyde W., THE JENNIFER PROJECT, Englewood Cliffs, Prentice-Hall, Inc., 1977.

Burns, Thomas S., THE SECRET WAR FOR THE OCEAN DEPTHS, New York, Rawson Associates, 1978.

Calder, Nigel, NUCLEAR NIGHTMARES: *An Investigation Into Possible Wars*, New York, The Viking Press, 1980.

Calder, Nigel, editor, UNLESS PEACE COMES: *A Scientific Forecast of New Weapons*, New York, The Viking Press, 1968.

Caldicott, Helen, NUCLEAR MADNESS, New York, Bantam Books, 1980.

Caldicott, Helen, RUSSIA, SALT II AND THE ARMS RACE, Woodmont, Connecticut, Promoting Enduring Peace, 1980.

Calti, Pierangelo, MODERN ARMOUR: *A Comprehensive Guide*, Parma, Italy, Delta Editrice, 1978.

Canan, James W., THE SUPERWARRIORS: *The Fantastic World of Pentagon Superweapons*, New York, Weybright & Talley, 1975.

Chant, Christopher, editor, HOW WEAPONS WORK, Chicago, Henry Regnery, 1976.

Chayes, Abram and Jerome B. Wiesner, editors, ABM: *An Evaluation of the Decision to Deploy an Antiballistic Missile System*, New York, Harper & Row, 1969.

Childers, Barry, NUCLEAR ARMS AND NUCLEAR POWER: *The Connections*, Woodmont, Connecticut, Promoting Enduring Peace, 1980.

Chinnock, Frank W., NAGASAKI, New York and Cleveland, World Publishing Company, 1969.

Chomsky, Noam, AMERICAN POWER AND THE NEW MANDARINS, New York, Pantheon Books, 1967.

Chomsky, Noam, FOR REASONS OF STATE, New York, Pantheon Books, 1970.

Cincinnatus, SELF-DESTRUCTION: *The Disintegration and Decay of the United States Army During the Vietnam Era*, New York, W.W. Norton, 1981.

Clark, Mike, IN THE U.S.S.R. AFTER AFGHANSITAN, New York, Riverside Church Disarmament Program, 1980.

Clark, Ronald W., EINSTEIN: *The Life and Times*, New York and Cleveland, World Publishing Company, 1971.

Clarke, Robin, THE SILENT WEAPONS: *The Realities of Chemical and Biological Warfare*, New York, David McKay Company, Inc., 1968.

Cline, Ray S., WORLD POWER TRENDS AND U.S. FOREIGN POLICY FOR THE 1980s, Boulder, Westview Press, 1980.

Close, General Robert, EUROPE WITHOUT DEFENSE?, Elmsford, New York, Pergamon Press, 1979.

Coalition for a New Foreign and Military Policy, BUILDING NATIONAL SECURITY, Washington, D.C., 1980.

Coalition for a New Foreign and Military Policy, GUNS VS. BUTTER: *Setting Priorities in the 80s*, Washington, D.C., 1981.

Coffin, Tristram, THE PASSION OF THE HAWKS: *Militarism in Modern America*, New York, The Macmillan Company, 1964.

Coffin, William Sloane, THE CHALLENGE OF DISARMAMENT, New York, Riverside Church Disarmament Program, 1978.

Coffin, William Sloane, Richard J. Barnet et al., REVERSE THE ARMS RACE, New York, Riverside Church Disarmament Program, 1978.

Collins, John M., AMERICAN AND SOVIET MILITARY TRENDS SINCE THE CUBAN MISSILE CRISIS, Washington, D.C., Center for Strategic and International Studies, Georgetown University, 1978.

Collins, John M., and Anthony H. Cordesman, IMBALANCE OF POWER: *Shifting U.S.-Soviet Military Strengths*, San Rafael, Presidio Press, 1978.

Collins, John M., U.S.-SOVIET MILITARY BALANCE: *Concepts and Capabilities*, 1960-1980, Washington, D.C., Aviation Week & Space Technology, 1981.

Committee on Foreign Relations, United States Senate, IMPLICATIONS OF PRESIDENT CARTER'S CONVENTIONAL ARMS TRANSFER POLICY, Washington, D.C., U.S. Goverment Printing Office, 1977.

Committee on Foreign Relations, United States Senate, MIDDLE EAST ARMS SALES PROPOSALS, *Hearings, May 1978*, Washington, D.C., U.S. Government Printing Office, 1978.

Cook, Chris, and John Stevenson, THE ATLAS OF MODERN WARFARE, New York, G.P. Putnam's Sons, 1978.

Cooper, Bryan, and John Batchelor, FIGHTER, New York, Ballantine Books, 1973.

Cormack, A.J.R., editor, SMALL ARMS IN PROFILE, Garden City/New York, Doubleday & Company, 1973.

Corwin, Norman, OVERKILL AND MEGALOVE, Cleveland and New York, World Publishing Company, 1963.

Cosby, N. Gordon, and Mark Gerzon, A VISION OF PEACE: *Redeeming the American Dream*, Washington, D.C., World Peacemakers, 1981.

Crowe, Kenneth, AMERICA FOR SALE, Garden City/New York, Doubleday & Company, 1978.

Cullin, William H., HOW TO CONDUCT FOREIGN MILITARY SALES, Washington, D.C., American Defense Preparedness Association, 1977.

Dagget, Stephen, WHAT YOU NEED TO KNOW ABOUT THE NEW GENERATION OF NUCLEAR WEAPONS, Washington, D.C., Institute for Policy Studies, 1980.

Daniels, Marta, and Everett Mendelsohn, NEW U.S. MISSILES IN EUROPE: *Challenge to Arms Control and Disarmament*, Voluntown, Connecticut, American Friends Service Committee, 1980.

DeGrasse, Robert, Jr., SHIFTING MX EXPENDITURES TO ENERGY EFFICIENCY: *Memo on the National Security Implications of Alternative Energy Development*, New York, Council on Economic Priorities, 1980.

Department of Defense, ANNUAL REPORT, Fiscal Years 1970 through 1981, Washington, D.C., U.S. Government Printing Office, 1969 through 1980.

Department of Defense, FOREIGN MILITARY SALES AND MILITARY ASSISTANCE FACTS, Washington, D.C, Defense Security Assistance Agency, 1977 through 1980.

Department of Defense, IMPACT OF ARMS TRANSFER RESTRAINT ON OUR MILITARY POSTURE, Washington, D.C., Office of the Secretary of Defense, 1977.

Department of Defense, PROGRAM ACQUISITIONS COSTS BY WEAPON SYSTEM, with amendments, Fiscal Years 1974 through 1981, Washington, D.C., Defense Printing Service, 1973 through 1980.

Department of Defense, PROGRAM OF RESEARCH, DEVELOPMENT, TEST AND EVALUATION, Fiscal Years 1974 through 1981, Washington, D.C., U.S. Government Printing Office, 1973 through 1980.

Department of Defense, SELECTED ACQUISITIONS REPORT, Fiscal Years 1970 through 1980, Washington, D.C., Defense Printing Service, 1970 through 1980.

Department of the Army, HANDBOOK ON SOVIET GROUND FORCES, FM 30-40, Washington, D.C., U.S. Government Printing Office, 1975.

Department of the Treasury, STUDY OF THE EFFECTS OF ECONOMIC RESTRAINT IN ARMS TRANSFERS, Washington, D.C., Office of the Secretary of the Treasury, 1977.

Detzer, David, THE BRINK: *Cuban Missile Crisis*, 1962, New York, Thomas Y. Crowell, 1979.

DiCerto, J.J., MISSILE BENEATH THE SEA: *The Story of Polaris*, New York, St. Martin's Press, 1967.

Dickson, Paul, THE ELECTRONIC BATTLEFIELD, Bloomington and London, Indiana University Press, 1976.

Director of Central Intelligence, SOVIET CIVIL DEFENSE, Washington, D.C., U.S. Government Printing Office, 1978.

Divine, Robert A., editor, THE CUBAN MISSILE CRISIS, Chicago, Quadrangle Books, 1971.

Donovan, Colonel James A., MILITARISM, U.S.A., New York, Charles Scribner's Sons, 1970.

Duncan, Donald, THE NEW LEGIONS, New York, Random House, 1967.

Dupuy, Colonel R. Ernest, THE COMPACT HISTORY OF THE UNITED STATES ARMY, Second Revised Edition, New York, Hawthorn Books, 1973.

Ellis, John, THE SOCIAL HISTORY OF THE MACHINE GUN, New York, Pantheon Books, 1975.

Engler, Robert, and Barry Commoner, OIL, ENERGY, AND ARMS, New York, Riverside Church Disarmament Program, 1980.

Eustace, Harry F., editor, THE INTERNATIONAL COUNTERMEASURES HANDBOOK, First through Fifth Editions, 1976 through 1980, Palo Alto, EW Communications, 1975 through 1979.

Fallows, James, NATIONAL DEFENSE, New York, Random House, 1981.

Ferry, W.H., BY WHAT RIGHT?, Woodmont, Connecticut, Promoting Enduring Peace, 1980.

Ferry, W.H. HOPE IN THE AMERICAN CRISIS, Washington, D.C., World Peacemakers, 1980.

Fleminster, Carl, and Pat Wagner, POVERTY AND THE PENTAGON, New York, Riverside Church Disarmament Program, 1980.

Forsberg, Randall, DISARMAMENT AND INTERNATIONAL SECURITY, Woodmont, Connecticut, Promoting Enduring Peace, 1980.

Foss, Christopher F., ARMOURED FIGHTING VEHICLES OF THE WORLD, New York, Charles Scribner's Sons, 1971 and 1977.

Foss, Christopher F., ARTILLERY OF THE WORLD, London, Ian Allan, 1976.

Foss, Christopher F., and T.J. Gander, INFANTRY WEAPONS OF THE WORLD, New York, Charles Scribner's Sons, 1977.

Foss, Christopher F., JANE'S WORLD ARMOURED FIGHTING VEHICLES, London, Macdonald & Jane's, 1976.

Fromm, Erich, THE ANATOMY OF HUMAN DESTRUCTIVENESS, New York, Holt, Rinehart and Winston, 1973.

Fromm, Erich, MAY MAN PREVAIL?, Garden City/New York, Doubleday & Company, 1961.

Frank, Jerome D., SANITY AND SURVIVAL: *Psychological Aspects of War and Peace*, New York, Random House, 1967.

Gabriel, Richard A., and Paul L. Savage, CRISIS IN COMMAND: *Mismanagement in the Army*, New York, Hill and Wang, 1978.

Galbraith, John Kenneth, THE NEW INDUSTRIAL STATE, Boston, Houghton Mifflin Company, 1967.

Garwin, Richard L., et al., NUCLEAR WEAPONS AND WORLD POLITICS, New York, McGraw-Hill, 1977.

Gervasi, Sean, THE UNITED STATES AND THE ARMS EMBARGO AGAINST SOUTH AFRICA, Binghampton, Fernand Braudel Center for the Study of Economics, Historical Systems and Civilizations, 1978.

Giffin, Sidney F., THE CRISIS GAME, Garden City/New York, Doubleday & Company, 1965.

Glasstone, Samuel, editor, THE EFFECTS OF NUCLEAR WEAPONS, prepared by the Defense Atomic Support Agency for the U.S. Atomic Energy Commission, Washington, D.C., U.S. Government Printing Office, 1962.

Gold, David, Christopher Paine and the Council on Economic Priorities, THE PROPOSED MX WEAPON SYSTEM, Testimony before the Subcommittee on the DOD, Committee on Appropriations, House of Representatives, July 1, 1980, New York, Council on Economic Priorities, 1980.

Goulding, Phil G., CONFIRM OR DENY: *Informing the People on National Security*, New York, Harper & Row, 1970.

Graham, Lieutenant General Daniel O., SHALL AMERICA BE DEFENDED? *Salt II and Beyond*, New Rochelle, Arlington House, 1979.

Graham, Lieutenant General Daniel O., U.S. INTELLIGENCE AT THE CROSSROADS, Washington, D.C., United States Strategic Institute, 1976.

Grand Pre, Donn R., CONFESSIONS OF AN ARMS PEDDLER, Lincoln, Virginia, Chosen Books, 1979.

Green, William , and Gordon Swanborough, THE OBSERVER'S BASIC MILITARY AIRCRAFT DIRECTORY, New York, Frederick Warne, 1974.

Green, William, THE OBSERVER'S BOOK OF AIRCRAFT, New York, Charles Scribner's Sons, 1979.

Grimmett, Richard, UNITED STATES ARMS TRANSFERS, Washington, D.C., Congressional Research Service, 1979.

Gunston, Bill, THE ILLUSTRATED ENCYCLO-PEDIA OF THE WORLD'S MODERN MILITARY AIRCRAFT, New York, Crescent Books, 1977.

Hackett, General Sir John, et al., THE THIRD WORLD WAR: *August 1985*, New York, The Macmillan Company, 1978.

Harvey, Frank, AIR WAR VIETNAM, New York, Bantam Books, 1967.

Heaps, Leo, OPERATION MORNING LIGHT: *Terror in Our Skies, The True Story of Cosmos 954*, New York and London, Paddington Press, 1978.

Heise, Juergen Arthur, MINIMUM DISCLOS-URE: *How the Pentagon Manipulates the News*, New York, W.W. Norton, 1979.

Herbert, Lieutenant Colonel Anthony B., and James T. Wooten, SOLDIER, New York, Holt, Rinehart and Winston, 1973.

Hersh, Seymour M., CHEMICAL AND BIO-LOGICAL WARFARE: *America's Hidden Arsenal*, Indianapolis and New York, The Bobbs-Merrill Company, 1968.

Herzog, Arthur, THE WAR-PEACE ESTABLISH-MENT, New York, Harper & Row, 1963.

Hezlet, Vice Admiral Sir Arthur, ELECTRONICS AND SEA POWER, New York, Stein & Day, 1975.

Hochman, Sandra, and Sybil Wong, SATEL-LITE SPIES, Indianapolis and New York, the Bobbs-Merrill Company, 1970.

Hoffmann, Stanley, PRIMACY OR WORLD ORDER: *American Foreign Policy Since the Cold War*, New York, McGraw-Hill, 1978.

Hogg, Ian, and John Batchelor, ARTILLERY, New York, Charles Scribner's Sons, 1972.

Holland, Max, THE MYTH OF ARMS RE-STRAINT, Washington, D.C., Center for International Policy, 1979.

Howard, Michael, editor, RESTRAINTS ON WAR, New York, Oxford University Press, 1979.

Hook, Sidney, THE FAIL-SAFE FALLACY, New York, Stein & Day, 1963.

Huntington, Samuel P., THE SOLDIER AND THE STATE, Cambridge, Harvard University Press, 1957.

Hurley, Colonel Alfred F., and Major Robert C. Ehrhart, AIR POWER AND WARFARE: *Proceedings of the Eighth Military History Symposium, USAF Academy, 1978*, Washington, D.C., U.S. Government Printing Office, 1979.

International Institute for Strategic Studies, THE MILITARY BALANCE, annual editions from 1975 through 1981, London, IISS, 1975 through 1981.

International Institute for Strategic Studies, STRATEGIC SURVEY, annual editions from 1978 through 1981, London, IISS, 1978 through 1981.

Ireland, Bernard, WARSHIPS OF THE WORLD, London, Ian Allan, 1976.

Johansen, Robert, THE NATIONAL INTEREST AND THE HUMAN INTEREST: *An Analysis of U.S. Foreign Policy*, Princeton, Princeton University Press, 1979.

Johnson, Brian, THE SECRET WAR, London, British Broadcasting Corporation, 1978.

Johnson, David T., IS THE U.S.S.R. NOSING AHEAD IN THE ARMS RACE?, Woodmont, Connecticut, Promoting Enduring Peace, 1980.

Jones, R.V., THE WIZARD WAR: *British Scientific Intelligence, 1939-1945*, New York, Coward McCann & Geoghegan, 1978.

Jungk, Dr. Robert, BRIGHTER THAN 1000 SUNS, London, Victor Gollancz and Rupert Hart-Davis, 1958.

Kahn, Herman, ON THERMONUCLEAR WAR Princeton, Princeton University Press, 1961.

Kahn, Herman, THINKING ABOUT THE UN-THINKABLE, New York, Horizon Press, 1962.

Kanegis, Arthur L., NUCLEAR WAR PREVEN-TION KIT, Washington, D.C., Center for Defense Information, 1980.

Kaufman, Richard F., THE WAR PROFITEERS Indianapolis and New York, the Bobbs-Merrill Company, 1970.

Kecskemeti, Paul, and The Rand Corporation, STRATEGIC SURRENDER, Stanford, Stanford University Press, 1958.

Keliher, John G., THE NEGOTIATIONS FOR MUTUAL AND BALANCED FORCE REDUC-TIONS: *The Search for Arms Control in Central Europe*, New York, Pergamon Press, 1980.

Kincade, William H., and Jeffrey D. Porro, NEGOTIATING SECURITY: *An Arms Control Reader*, New York and Washington, D.C., Carnegie Endowment for International Peace, 1979.

Kistiakowsky, George, THE ARMS RACE: *Is Paranoia Necessary for Security?*, revised edition, Washington, D.C., World Peace-makers, 1981.

Klare, Michael T., and Nancy Stein, EXPORT-ING THE TOOLS OF REPRESSION, Washington, D.C., Center for National Security Studies, 1976.

Klare, Michael T., HARD AND SOFT WEAP-ONS, New York, Riverside Church Disarmament Program, 1981.

Klare, Michael T., WAR WITHOUT END: *American Planning for the Next Vietnams*, New York, Vintage Books, 1972.

Kolko, Joyce, AMERICA AND THE CRISIS OF WORLD CAPITALISM, Boston, Beacon Press, 1974.

Korb, Lawrence J., THE FALL AND RISE OF THE PENTAGON: *American Defense Policies in the 1970s*, Westport, Greenwood Press, 1979.

Kuniholm, Bruce R., THE ORIGINS OF THE COLD WAR IN THE NEAR EAST: *Great Power Conflict and Diplomacy in Iran, Turkey and Greece*, Princeton, Princeton University Press, 1980.

Lapp, Ralph E., KILL AND OVERKILL: *The Strategy of Annihilation*, New York, Basic Books, 1962.

Lapp, Ralph E., THE WEAPONS CULTURE, New York, W.W. Norton, 1968.

Lall, B.G., PROSPERITY WITHOUT GUNS, New York, Institute for World Order, 1977.

Langford, David, WAR IN 2080: *The Future of Military Technology*, London, Westbridge Books, 1979.

LaRocque, Admiral Gene R., THE REAL THREAT OF NUCLEAR WAR, Woodmont, Connecticut, Promoting Enduring Peace, 1979.

LaRocque, Admiral Gene R., SALT FOR SECURITY, New York, Riverside Church Disarmament Program, 1979.

Lee, William T., THE ESTIMATION OF SOVIET DEFENSE EXPENDITURES, 1955-1975, New York, Praeger, 1977.

Lee, William T., SOVIET DEFENSE EXPENDI-TURES IN AN ERA OF SALT, Washington, D.C., United States Strategic Institute, 1979.

Lens, Sidney, DOOMSDAY MINUS ONE, New York, War Resisters League, 1977.

Lewin, Leonard C., REPORT FROM IRON MOUNTAIN ON THE POSSIBILITY AND DESIR-ABILITY OF PEACE, New York, The Dial Press, 1967.

Libby, Leona Marshall, THE URANIUM PEO-PLE, New York, Crane, Russak and Charles Scribner's Sons, 1979.

Lifton, Robert Jay, DEATH IN LIFE: *Survivors of Hiroshima*, New York, Random House, 1967.

Lifton, Robert Jay, THE BROKEN CONNECTION, New York, Simon and Schuster, 1979.

Lydenberg, Steven, WEAPONS FOR THE WORLD: *The U.S. Corporate Role In International Arms Transfers*, New York and San Francisco, Council on Economic Priorities, 1977 and 1978.

Mandelbaum, Michael, THE NUCLEAR QUESTION: *The United States and Nuclear Weapons*, New York, Cambridge University Press, 1979.

Manno, Catherine, DISARMAMENT FOR A SMALL PLANET: *Messages from the United Nations*, Philadelphia, Women's International League for Peace and Freedom, 1976.

Manno, Catherine, WHO'S AFRAID OF DISARMAMENT?, Philadelphia, Women's International League for Peace and Freedom, 1979.

Marriot, John, and the Royal United Services Institute for Defence Studies, INTERNATIONAL WEAPONS DEVELOPMENT, Third Edition, London, Brassey's Publishers, 1979.

Maynard, Crosby, editor, FLIGHT PLAN FOR TOMORROW: *The Douglas Story*, Santa Monica, Douglas Aircraft, 1966.

McCloskey, Paul N., Jr., TRUTH AND UNTRUTH: *Political Deceit in America*, New York, Simon and Schuster, 1972.

Melman, Seymour, OUR DEPLETED SOCIETY, New York, Holt, Rinehart and Winston, 1965.

Melman, Seymour, THE PERMANENT WAR ECONOMY, New York, Simon and Schuster, 1974.

Melman, Seymor, INFLATION AND THE MILITARY BUDGET, New York, Riverside Church Disarmament Program, 1978.

Melman, Seymour, INFLATION AND UNEMPLOYMENT: *Products of a War Economy*, Washington, D.C, SANE, 1979.

Melman, Seymour, Mark Hipp et al., PENTAGON THRIVES ON URBAN DECAY, New York Riverside Church Disarmament Program, 1979.

Meselson, Matthew, editor, CHEMICAL WEAPONS AND CHEMICAL ARMS CONTROL, New York and Washington, D.C., Carnegie Endowment for International Peace, 1978.

Metzger, H. Peter, THE ATOMIC ESTABLISHMENT, New York, Simon and Schuster, 1972.

Millis, Walter, editor, AMERICAN MILITARY THOUGHT, Indianapolis and New York, The Bobbs-Merrill Company, 1966.

Millis, Walter, THE MARTIAL SPIRIT, Boston, Houghton Mifflin Company, 1931.

Millis, Walter, and James Real, THE ABOLITION OF WAR, Santa Barbara, The Fund for the Republic, 1963.

Millis, Walter, AN END TO ARMS, New York, Atheneum, 1965.

Ministry of Information and Broadcasting, Government of India, NUCLEAR EXPLOSIONS AND THEIR EFFECTS, New Delhi, 1958.

Morganstern, Oskar, THE QUESTION OF NATIONAL DEFENSE, New York, Vintage Books, 1961.

Moore, Captain John E., editor, JANE'S FIGHTING SHIPS, annual editions from 1976 through 1980, London, Macdonald & Jane's, 1975 through 1979.

Morison, Samuel L., and John S. Rowe, THE SHIPS AND AIRCRAFT OF THE U.S. FLEET, Tenth Edition, Annapolis, Naval Institute Press, 1965.

Morris, Eric, TANKS, London, October Books, 1975.

Moskin, J. Robert, THE U.S. MARINE CORPS STORY, New York, McGraw-Hill, 1977.

Moulton, Major General J.J., editor, BRASSEY'S ANNUAL: *The Armed Forces Yearbook*, annual editions from 1970 through 1980, London, William Clowes and Sons, 1970 through 1980.

Munson, Kenneth, THE POCKET ENCYLCOPEDIA OF WORLD AIRCRAFT IN COLOR: BOMBERS, New York, The Macmillan Company, 1966.

Munson, Kenneth, THE POCKET ENCYLCOPEDIA OF WORLD AIRCRAFT IN COLOR: FIGHTERS, New York, The Macmillan Company, 1966.

Murphy, Harry J., Office of Security, Central Intelligence Agency, SOURCES OF INFORMATION FOR FEDERAL INVESTIGATORS, New York, Warner Books, 1976.

Medvedev, Zhores A., NUCLEAR DISASTER IN THE URALS, New York, W.W. Norton, 1979.

Nathan, Otto, and Heinz Worden, editors, EINSTEIN ON PEACE, New York, Simon and Schuster, 1960.

National Action Research on the Military-Industrial Complex, ATOMS FOR PEACE—ATOMS FOR WAR, Philadelphia, American Friends Service Committee, 1979.

National Action Research on the Military-Industrial Complex, MX MISSILE CONTRACTORS, Philadelphia, American Friends Service Committee, 1980.

National Action Research on the Military-Industrial Complex, NUCLEAR WEAPONS STORAGE AND DEPLOYMENT SITES, Philadelphia, American Friends Service Committee, 1980.

National Security Council, REPORT TO CONGRESS ON ARMS TRANSFER POLICY, Washington, D.C., NSC/PRM-12, 1977.

New Directions, THE TRUTH ABOUT ARMS CONTROL Washington, D.C., 1980.

Newman, James R., THE RULE OF FOLLY, New York, Simon and Schuster, 1962.

Neuman, Stephanie G., and Robert E. Harkavy, editors, ARMS TRANSFERS IN THE MODERN WORLD, New York, Praeger, 1979.

Novick, Sheldon, THE CARELESS ATOM, Boston, Houghton Mifflin, 1969.

Office of the Assistant Chief of Staff for Intelligence, Department of the Army, UNDERSTANDING SOVIET MILITARY DEVELOPMENTS, Washington, D.C., U.S. Government Printing Office, 1977.

Office of the Chief of Naval Operations, Department of the Navy, UNDERSTANDING SOVIET NAVAL DEVELOPMENTS, Revised Edition, Washington, D.C., U.S. Government Printing Office, 1978.

Office of Technology Assessment, United States Congress, THE EFFECTS OF NUCLEAR WAR, Montclair, Allanheld and Osmun, 1980.

Ogorkiewicz, Richard M., ARMOURED FORCES, London, Lionel Leventhal, 1970.

Ogorkiewicz, Richard M., DESIGN AND DEVELOPMENT OF FIGHTING VEHICLES, Garden City/New York, Doubleday & Company, 1968.

O'Neill, William L., COMING APART, Chicago, Quadrangle Books, 1971.

O'Rourke, G.G., THE F-4 PHANTOM II, New York, Arco Publishing, 1969.

Okun, Bob, WAKING AMERICA UP TO THE NUCLEAR NIGHTMARE Woodmont, Connecticut, Promoting Enduring Peace, 1980.

Owen, J.I.H., editor, BRASSEY'S NATO INFANTRY WEAPONS, London, Brassey's Publishers, 1976.

Panofsky, W.K.H., ARMS CONTROL AND SALT II, Seattle, University of Washington Press, 1979.

Perlmutter, Amos, and Valerie Plave Bennett, editors, THE POLITICAL INFLUENCE OF THE MILITARY, New Haven, Yale University Press, 1980.

Peters, Charles, HOW WASHINGTON REALLY WORKS, Reading, Addison-Wesley, 1980.

Pierre, Andrew J., editor, ARMS TRANSFERS AND AMERICAN FOREIGN POLICY, New York, New York University Press, 1979.

Pike, Charles A., LASERS AND MASERS, Indianapolis, Howard W. Sams, 1968.

Plate, Thomas Gordon, UNDERSTANDING DOOMSDAY: *A Guide to the Arms Race for Hawks, Doves and People*, New York, Simon and Schuster, 1971.

Pocock, Chris and Colin Smith, THE USAF TODAY, London, West London Aviation Group, 1975.

Pretty, R.T., editor, JANE'S WEAPON SYSTEMS, annual editions from 1976 through 1980, London, Macdonald & Jane's, 1975 through 1979.

Proxmire, Senator William, THE FLEECING OF AMERICA, Boston, Houghton Mifflin, 1980.

Proxmire, Senator William, UNCLE SAM: *The Last of the Bigtime Spenders*, New York, Simon and Schuster, 1972.

Price, Alfred, INSTRUMENTS OF DARKNESS: *The History of Electronic Warfare*, New York Charles Scribner's Sons, 1980.

Quick, John, editor, DICTIONARY OF WEAPONS AND MILITARY TERMS, New York, McGraw-Hill, 1973.

Ravenal, Earl C., et al., TOWARD WORLD SECURITY: *A Program for Disarmament*, Washington, D.C., Institute for Policy Studies, 1978.

Raymond, Jack, POWER AT THE PENTAGON, New York, Harper & Row, 1964.

Real, James, and Harrison Brown, COMMUNITY OF FEAR, Santa Barbara, The Fund for the Republic, 1960.

Rogers, Barbara, and Zdenek Cervenka, THE NUCLEAR AXIS, London, Julian Friedmann Books, 1978.

Rossiter, Clinton, CONSERVATISM IN AMERICA, Second Edition Revised, New York, Alfred A. Knopf, 1962.

Rowan, Roy, THE FOUR DAYS OF MAYAGUEZ, New York, W.W. Norton, 1975.

Rudoy, Dean William, ARMED AND ALONE: *The American Security Dilemma*, New York, George Braziller, 1972.

Russell, Bertrand, COMMON SENSE AND NUCLEAR WARFARE, New York, Simon and Schuster, 1959.

Sabrosky, Alan Ned, DEFENSE MANPOWER POLICY: *A Critical Reappraisal*, Philadelphia, Foreign Policy Research Institute, 1978.

Said, Edward S., THE QUESTION OF PALESTINE, New York, Times Books, 1979.

Sampson, Anthony, THE ARMS BAZAAR: *From Lebanon to Lockheed*, New York, The Viking Press, 1977.

Schell, Jonathan, THE TIME OF ILLUSION, New York, Alfred A. Knopf, 1976.

Schemmer, Benjamin F., THE RAID, New York, Harper & Row, 1976.

Schlesinger, Robert J., PRINCIPLES OF ELECTRONIC WARFARE, Los Altos, Peninsula Publishing, 1979.

Scott, Harriet Fast and William F., THE ARMED FORCES OF THE USSR, Boulder, Westview Press, 1979.

Secretary of Defense, REPORT TO CONGRESS, Fiscal Years 1972 through 1981, Washington, D.C., U.S. Government Printing Office, 1971 through 1980.

Von Senger und Etterlin, Dr. F.M., THE WORLD'S ARMOURED FIGHTING VEHICLES, Garden City/New York, Doubleday & Company, 1962.

Sharp, Jane M.O., editor, OPPORTUNITIES FOR DISARMAMENT: *The United Nations Special Session on Disarmament*, New York and Washington, D.C., Carnegie Endowment for International Peace, 1978.

Sharp, Admiral Ulysses Grant, STRATEGY FOR DEFEAT: *Vietnam in Retrospect*, San Rafael, Presidio Press, 1978.

Shea, Ed, editor, AERIAL RECONNAISSANCE SYSTEMS: *Pods/Aircraft*, Palos Verdes Estates, Society of Photo-Optical Instrumentation Engineers, 1976.

Sheehan, Neil, THE ARNHEITER AFFAIR, New York, Random House, 1971.

Simmons, Brigadier General Edwin H., THE UNITED STATES MARINES: *The First Two Hundred Years*, 1775-1975, New York, The Viking Press, 1976.

Sivard, Ruth Leger, WORLD MILITARY AND SOCIAL EXPENDITURES, Leesburg, Virginia, World Priorities, 1980.

Smith, H.B. and Joseph E., SMALL ARMS OF THE WORLD, Harrisburg, Stackpole Books, 1962.

Smith, Peter, and the Council on Economic Priorities, EFFICIENCY IN DEATH: *The Manufacturers of Anti-Personnel Weapons*, New York, Harper & Row Perennial Library, 1970.

Smyth, Henry D., ATOMIC ENERGY FOR MILITARY PURPOSES, Princeton, Princeton University Press, 1945.

Stephenson, Hugh, THE COMING CLASH: *The Impact of Multinational Corporations on Nation States*, New York, Saturday Review Press, 1973.

Stockholm International Peace Research Institute, THE ARMS TRADE WITH THE THIRD WORLD, Revised and Abridged Edition, New York, Holmes & Meier Publishers, 1975.

Stockholm International Peace Research Institute, WORLD ARMAMENTS AND DISARMAMENT YEARBOOK, annual editions from 1974 through 1980, Stockholm, Almqvist & Wiksell, 1974 through 1980.

Stockholm International Peace Research Institute, NUCLEAR ENERGY AND NUCLEAR WEAPONS PROLIFERATION, New York, Crane, Russak, 1979.

Stockholm International Peace Research Institute, TACTICAL NUCLEAR WEAPONS: European Perspectives, London, Taylor & Francis, 1978.

Stockwell, John, IN SEARCH OF ENEMIES: *A CIA Story*, New York, W.W. Norton, 1978.

Stonier, Tom, NUCLEAR DISASTER, New York and Cleveland, The World Publishing Company, 1964.

Szulc, Tad, THE BOMBS OF PALOMARES, New York, The Viking Press, 1967.

Szulc, Tad, THE ILLUSION OF PEACE: *Foreign Policy in the Nixon Years*, New York, The Viking Press, 1978.

Talbott, Strobe, ENDGAME: *The Inside Story of SALT II*, New York, Harper & Row, 1979.

Taylor, John W.R., AIRCRAFT OF THE WORLD, New York, International Publications Service, 1978.

Taylor, John W.R. and Michael J., ENCYCLOPEDIA OF AIRCRAFT, New York, G.P. Putnam's Sons, 1978.

Taylor, John W.R., editor, JANE'S ALL THE WORLD'S AIRCRAFT, annual editions from 1974 through 1980, London, Macdonald & Jane's, 1973 through 1979.

Taylor, John W.R., MILITARY AIRCRAFT OF THE WORLD, New York, Charles Scribner's Sons, 1980.

Taylor, John W.R. and Gordon Swanborough, MILITARY AIRCARFT OF THE WORLD, London, Ian Allan, 1975.

Taylor, John W.R. and David Mondey, SPIES IN THE SKY, London, Ian Allan, 1972.

Taylor Michael J.H. and John W.R., HELICOPTERS OF THE WORLD, London, Ian Allan, 1976.

Taylor, Michael J.H. and John W.R., MISSILES OF THE WORLD, London, Ian Allan, 1976.

Thayer, George, THE WAR BUSINESS: *The International Trade in Armaments*, New York, Simon and Schuster, 1969.

Thurow, Lester C., THE ZERO-SUM SOCIETY: *Distribution and the Possibilities for Economic Change*, New York, Basic Books, 1980.

Timbergen, Jan, coordinator, RESHAPING THE INTERNATIONAL ORDER: *A Report to the Club of Rome*, New York, E.P. Dutton & Company, 1976.

Tompkins, John S., THE WEAPONS OF WORLD WAR III: *The Long Road Back from the Bomb*, Garden City/New York, Doubleday & Company, 1966.

United States Arms Control and Disarmament Agency, WORLD MILITARY EXPENDITURES AND ARMS TRANSFERS, 1966-1976 and 1968-1977, Washington, D.C., U.S. Government Printing Office, 1977 and 1979.

United States Arms Control and Disarmament Agency, ARMS CONTROL AND DISARMAMENT AGREEMENTS, *Publication 105, August 1980*, Washington, D.C., U.S. Government Printing Office, 1980.

United States Air Force, AIRWAR VIETNAM, Indianapolis and New York, The Bobbs-Merrill Company, 1978.

United States Defense Intelligence Agency, HANDBOOK ON THE CHINESE ARMED FORCES, DDL-2680-32-76, Washington, D.C., Defense Intelligence Agency, 1976.

United Nations, General Assembly, Thirty-Fifth Session, GENERAL AND COMPLETE DISARMAMENT: *Comprehensive Study on Nuclear Weapons*, Report of the Secretary General A/35/392, September 12, 1980, New York, United Nations, 1980.

University of Michigan, Institute of Science and Technology, ELECTRONIC COUNTERMEASURES, Washington, D.C., U.S. Army Signal Corps DA-36-039 SC-71204, 1971, and Los Altos, Peninsula Publishing, 1978.

Van Cleave, William R., and S.T. Cohen, TACTICAL NUCLEAR WEAPONS: *An Examination of the Issues*, New York, Crane, Russak, 1978.

Van Cleave, William R., and W. Scott Thompson, editors, STRATEGIC OPTIONS FOR THE EARLY EIGHTIES: *What Can Be Done?*, New York, National Strategy Information Center, 1979.

Varner, Roy, and Wayne Collier, A MATTER OF RISK, New York, Random House, 1978.

Wagner, Ray, AMERICAN COMBAT PLANES, revised and enlarged edition, Garden City/New York, Doubleday & Company, 1968.

War Resisters League, NUCLEAR AMERICA MAP, New York, War Resisters League, 1979.

Weigley, Russell F., HISTORY OF THE UNITED STATES ARMY, New York The Macmillan Company, 1967.

Western Massachusetts Association of Concerned African Scholars, U.S. MILITARY INVOLVEMENT IN SOUTHERN AFRICA, Boston, South End Press, 1978.

Winpisinger, William W., PLANNED ECONOMIC CONVERSION: *Getting Off the Hook of Defense Dependency*, Woodmont, Connecticut, Promoting Enduring Peace, 1979.

Wheeler, Barry C., AIR FORCES OF THE WORLD, New York, Charles Scribner's Sons, 1979.

Wise, David, and Thomas B. Ross, THE U-2 AFFAIR, New York, Random House, 1962.

Wolfe, Alan, TILT TOWARDS WAR, New York, Riverside Church Disarmament Program, 1980.

York, Herbert, RACE TO OBLIVION: *A Participant's View of the Arms Race*, New York, Simon and Schuster, 1970.

Zumwalt, Admiral Elmo R., Jr., ON WATCH, New York, Quadrangle, 1976.

## Periodicals

Adelphi Papers
Addifa' Wal-Amn
Africa Report
Air Force Magazine
Air International
Air Progress
Armed Forces Journal International
Armées d'Aujourd'hui
Armies & Weapons
Armor
Army Administrator
Army Journal, The
Army Magazine
Army Research and Development
ASMZ
Australia Bulletin
Australian Daily News
Aviation & Marine International
Aviation Week & Space Technology
Battle
Biweekly Scientific and Technical Intelligence Summary
Bulletin de Cavalerie
Bulletin of the Atomic Scientists
Bundeswehr, Die
Bundeswehr Aktuell
Business Week
Columbia Journalism Review
Combat
Comander's Digest
CounterSpy
Covert Action Information Bulletin
Defense Electronics
Defense & Foreign Affairs
Defense Magazine
Defense Monitor, The
Defense Transportation Journal
DMS Intelligence
Electronic Warfare
Events
Field Artillery Journal
First Principles
Flugwehr und Technik
Forces Armées Francaises
Foreign Affairs
Foreign Policy
Fortune
German Tribune, The

Infantry
Interavia Data
International Defense Review
International Security
Japan Report
Jeaune Afrique
Journal of Commerce
Kampftruppen
Marine Corps Gazette, The
Marine Rundschau
Middle East Journal, The
Militartechnik
Military Affairs
Military Aviation Review
Military Engineer, The
Military Journal, The
Military Review
Mother Jones
Nation, The
National Defense
NATO's Fifteen Nations
Nephadsereg
New Republic, The
New York Times, The
News of Norway
Newsweek
Norsk MIlitaert Tidsskrift
OMZ (Osterreichische Militararische Zeitschrift)
Pakistan Affairs
Political Science Quarterly
Proceedings of the United States Naval Institute
Progressive, The
Scientific American
Soldat und Technik
Soldier of Fortune
Soldier: The British Army Magazine
Spiegel, Der
Strategic Review
Surface Warfare
Swedish Information Service
Swedish International Press
TAM
Time Magazine
Truppendienst
Truppenpraxis
U.S. News & World Report
Wall Street Journal, The
Washington Monthly
Washington Post, The
Wehr und Wirtschaft
Wehrforschung
Wehrkunde
Wehrtechnik

# ACKNOWLEDGEMENTS

The author wishes to express his gratitude to the following for their invaluable help in the preparation of this book:

Mr. Moses Acosta, Mr. Gordon Adams of the Council on Economic Priorities, Mr. Bob Adelman, Mr. Roy C. Ballard of ITT Gilfillan's Defense Space Group, Mr. Richard Barnet of the Institute for Policy Studies, Lieutenant Colonel Peter J. Barrett, AUS, Mr. Gordon Le Bert of the McDonnell Douglas Corporation, Mr. Fred J. Bettinger of General Dynamics, Mr. Don Biggs, Mr. Peter Bloch, Mr. A.P. Blouin of Century Arms, Inc., Major Michael Burch, USAF, Mr. Richard Burt, Mr. C.F. Bushey of the Aircraft Equipment Division of General Electric, Mr. Robert A. Carlisle, Department of the Navy, Mr. Kent Carroll, Captain Glenn Childs, USAF, Mr. Charles Cobb, Ms. Leslie Cockburn, Mr. Tom Coggleman of the Trident Conversion Program, Ms. Wendy Cooper, Mr. Peter S. Copeland, U.S. Army ARRADCOM, Mr. John A. Cox of Pratt & Whitney Aircraft Group, United Technologies, Ms. Ann Crittenden, Mr. Samuel Cummings, Mr. Bart Cusick III of the Electronics and Space Division of Emerson Electric, Ms. Adalyn Davis of the United States Arms Control and Disarmament Agency, Specialist Joel T. Day, AUS, Captain R.P. Ducharme, USAF, Mr. Steve Emerson of the Senate Foreign Relations Committee, Mr. J.V. Esry of Motorola, Inc., Mr. David Evans of the Department of Defense, Dr. Richard Falk, Mr. Don Flamm of Ford Aerospace and Communications Corporation, Mr. C.W. Folley of the Maremont Corporation, Major John E. Ford III, USAF, Ms. Randall Forsberg of the Institute for Defense and Disarmament Studies, Mr. Rick Foley of the General Accounting Office, Mr. Julian Friedmann, Mr. Andrew Frohlich of Teledyne Systems Company, Lieutenant General Howard M. Fish, USAF, Mr. Stephen Galat, General James M. Gavin, AUS, Ret., Mr. Sean D.

Gervasi, Mr. Harold Gettings of Martin Marietta Aerospace, Mr. N. Kent Goldsmith of Alkan, Inc., Mr. Edward J. Gray of Cessna Aircraft Company, Mr. Richard Grimmett of the Congressional Research Service, Ms. Nancy Gross, Mr. John J. Hadder, U.S. Army ARRADCOM, Ms. Helena Hansen, Mr. Eric Hausmann, Ms. Virginia Heiserman of the Institute for World Order, Mr. Seymour Hersh, Ms. Nancy Lee Hindman of the Department of State, Sergeant Robert Hoffman, USMC, Mr. Pierson J. Holcombe of the Norden Division of United Technologies, Mr. Rice Hopkins, Mr. Robert Hotz, Mr. W.J. Hutchins, Mr. David Isby, Mr. Thomas S. Jambriska of Cadillac Gage Company, Mr. Charles B. Johnson of Systron Donner, Inc., Mr. Tom Kegelmyn of the Community for Nonviolent Action, Mr. David Kennerly, Mr. Michael Klare of the Institute for Policy Studies, Mr. Martin Klemow of Commodore Aviation, Inc., Mr. Gary Korkala of XID X-Ray Industrial Distributors, Mr. Lewis Lapham, Admiral Gene R. LaRocque of the Center for Defense Information, Mr. Daniel J. Luchsinger of General Dynamics, Mr. James A. Lundberg, Mr. Robert Manoff, Mr. C.P. Marselis, Mr. Brian Masterson of Grumman Aerospace Corporation, Mr. R.M. Maze of Litton Systems of Canada, Inc., Major Thomas Maypole, USAF, Mr. John J. McCardle of the Detroit Diesel Allison Division of General Motors Corporation, Mr. William K. McCoy of the Norden Division of United Technologies, Mr. Bob McLennan, assistant curator of the Ammunition Museum, Picatinny Arsenal, Ms. Claudia Menza, Dr. Emmanuel Meyers, U.S. Army ARRADCOM, Mr. David W. Menard, Mr. Gerald Milstead, Department of Defense, Mr. Lawrence J. Montgomery of John Roberts, Ltd., Mr. Richard Morris of the Defense Security Assistance Agency, Mr. Colin Murray, Mr. David P. Murphy, Mr. John H. Newland of Boeing Commercial Airplane Company, Ms. Jeanne Noble of Honeywell, Inc., Mr. Arthur

J. Oberg of FMC Corporation, Mr. John O'Grady of the Center for Defense Information, Mr. Robert L. Parrish of the Hughes Helicopter Division of Summa Corporation, Mr. L.G. Phillips of EMI Pantak, Ltd., Mr. Charles Poisall, U.S. Army ARRADCOM, Ms. Olga T. Puspoki of Westinghouse Electric Corporation, Mr. James W. Ragsdale of Lockheed Aircraft Corporation, Ms. Dina Rasor of the Project on Military Procurement, Mr. Theron Rinehart of Fairchild Republic Company, Mr. Clarence A. Robinson, Mr. William N. Robinson of the Department of State, Mr. R. Ray Roby of RPB Industries, Inc., Ms. Rosemary Rogers of Kaman Aerospace Corporation, Mr. Edward A. Romanowski of the Boeing Vertol Company, Mr. Barney Rossett, Ms. Emma Rothschild, Mr. Anthony Sampson, Ms. Jo Ann Schachman of International Technical Products Corporation, Lieutenant JG T.J. Scott, USN, Mr. John E. Severance of the Raytheon Company, Mr. Neil Shakery, Mr. James T. Shaver, Mr. William H. Schmidt of Lockheed Aircraft Corporation, Mr. R.L. Shirley of the Ordnance Engineering Division of FMC Corporation, Colonel Peter Sloan, USAF, Mr. Edward B. Smith of BEI Electronics, Inc., Major Raymond G. Smith, AUS, Mr. Bill Spuckes, U.S. Army ARRADCOM, Mr. John Stockwell, Mr. Keith D. Suter, Mr. Sandy Tolan, Mr. J.N. Torchetti of Pratt & Whitney Aircraft of Canada, Ltd., Dr. Kosta Tsipis of Massachusetts Institute of Technology, Mr. R.R. Turner of Litton Systems, Inc., Mr. Bernard Weinraub, Mr. Roy E. Wendell of Fairchild Republic Company, Mr. William Wertenbaker, Ms. Marion Wheeler, Ms. Lee Wiggins, Mr. L.E. Whittaker of the Pacific Car and Foundry Company, Mr. P.O. Wiley of ArmaLite, Inc., Major Ralph R. Williams, USAF, Mr. W.B. Wilson, Jr., of Sundstrand Aviation Mechanical, Mr. Joel T. Wit of the Congressional Research Service, Mr. Giovanni Woods, Jr., and Mr. Sidney Wray.

# PHOTO CREDITS